NOSTRADAMUS
COUNTDOWN TO APOCALYPSE

NOSTRADAMUS
COUNTDOWN TO APOCALYPSE
and
INTO THE TWENTY-FIRST CENTURY

Jean-Charles de Fontbrune

Translated by Alexis Lykiard
Preface by Liz Greene

CRESSET BOOKS

To my father,
Max de Fontbrune

Nostradamus: Countdown to Apocalypse
© Editions du Rocher 1980
Illustrations © Editions du Rocher 1980
Translation © Hutchinson & Co (Publishers) Ltd. 1983
Preface © Liz Greene 1983

Nostradamus 2: Into the Twenty-First Century

© Editions du Rocher 1982
Translation © Hutchinson & Co (Publishers) Ltd. 1984

The right of Jean-Charles de Fontbrune to be identified as
Author of this work has been asserted by Jean-Charles de
Fontbrune in accordance with the Copyright, Designs and
Patents Act, 1988

Nostradamus first published in 1983 by Hutchinson & Co
(Publishers) Ltd
Nostradamus 2 first published in 1984 by Hutchinson & Co
(Publishers) Ltd

This new edition first published by Cresset 1992

ISBN 0 09 177111 0

CONTENTS

COUNTDOWN TO APOCALYPSE

INTO THE TWENTY-FIRST CENTURY

PREFACE

The prophecies of Nostradamus are as indestructible as the Revelation of St John, and equally obscure. Nowhere is man's fascination with the irrational as evident as in the matter of prophecy; and no prophet since biblical times has enjoyed as long a life in the popular imagination as Michel de Nostredame, the sixteenth-century Provençal physician turned seer. Since the Centuries of Nostradamus were first published at Lyon in 1555 they have not been out of print, nor has there been any dearth of interpretations in the intervening four centuries. It would seem that decoding the bizarre outpourings of prophets is as irresistible as decoding the unfathomable language of dreams.

The quality of interpretations of the Centuries has varied, and Nostradamus has been described as everything from a Rosicrucian initiate intimate with the secrets of God to a drunkard whose badly rhymed quatrains are a dubious alternative to the proverbial pink elephant. Yet however accurate and astute some of these interpretative efforts have undoubtedly been, there is something stubbornly elusive about Nostradamus' verses which, once again, suggests a similarity to the elusive dream-language that so fascinated Freud and Jung.

Jean de Fontbrune is alone among interpreters of Nostradamus in being wise enough to concede that he does not know it all, even though he has every right to be boastful because of the enormous labour involved in his impeccable historical research. It is possibly because of his humility that his work is unusually sane – too sane, perhaps, for the reader who expects wild, esoteric revelations. M. de Fontbrune is wise, too, in his use of documented history to validate the meanings he attaches to Nostradamus' verses. It is easy to forget that Nostradamus was very much a man of his time, and used the peculiar images and associations of Renaissance symbolism to describe events and persons within his own national and spiritual sphere. He is speaking not in the language of the twentieth century, but in that of the sixteenth, and M. de Fontbrune is the only interpreter I have read who seems to remember this.

The most unusual aspect of M. de Fontbrune's work, however, lies in its chronological approach. Nostradamus himself admitted that he had scrambled his quatrains, and this has made a dog's breakfast of most efforts to interpret them. The prophet leaps about from one time frame to another with no apparent order or continuity. Rather than simply plodding through the verses hoping for inspiration, which is the usual way interpreters have approached them, M. de Fontbrune has followed the unfolding of history through time, beginning with the events occurring around the publication of the Centuries and connecting them with the verses which seem to describe them. He then moves slowly forward through history, gathering verses as he goes.

The effect is magical: Nostradamus no longer sounds like a lunatic, but rather like a careful chronicler of the awesome unfolding of man's fate through world events. The patterns of history are suddenly apparent, and the prophet becomes disturbingly credible. It is only when M. de Fontbrune arrives at the present that he must, obviously, dispense with historical validation of his interpretations, and leave us to believe or disbelieve in the future that is presented. It remains for the reader to decide whether he or she can accept this grim vision. Perhaps it also remains for readers to decide whether there is anything they might do to contribute to or alter that vision.

The questions which the Centuries raise are profound ones, and even if only two or three of Nostradamus' peeps into the future were accurate we would still be confronted by them. The primary question is, of course, whether it is possible to predict the future. If it is, then what does this say about our treasured belief in free will, and in the possibility of a better world built upon conscious efforts toward understanding and good will? Some of Nostradamus' prophecies are so specific that they are impossible to contradict; it is hard to explain away how he managed to see that England's Parliament would behead its king a century after the prophet's own death. So, then, some of history at least *is* predictable. That is a frightening thought, and it is no wonder that so many people use scepticism as a shield to protect themselves from such a revelation.

Perhaps we ought to consider the perspective of Nostradamus himself, because he was after all working with beliefs and techniques which were perfectly appropriate in the context of the world view of his time. He was not unique in his utilization of astrology, magic and prophecy; he was simply better at it than his contemporaries. Prophecy was completely acceptable in the sixteenth century because the universe was viewed as a living organism, governed in its orderly development by the cyclical and inexorable patterns of the planets moving through the zodiac. And the patterns of astrology, as any sixteenth-century magus would have said, were considered the visible signatures of God's inscrutable will and purpose. Fate, which only the philosopher considers now in this age of mechanistic cause-and-effect, was not an issue in Nostradamus' time. Since Oliver Cromwell told his Protectorate Parliament in London that they should not speak of fate because it was too pagan a word, we have tended to obey; nowadays fate is not only pagan, it is unscientific. But in the sixteenth century everyone spoke of fate, because fate and divine providence were the same thing, and the cosmos was organized and run by its celestial governors in accordance with divine intent. Man, as a small part of this larger living body, was inevitably fated by those governors as part of the natural order. And history, the moving tapestry of millions of tiny decisions made by millions of tiny lives, was seen as no less a part of the pattern.

The judicial astrology of which Nostradamus speaks in his Letter to his son César was, for him, a method of ascertaining the timing of important world events. This was regarded not as a supernatural feat, but as an acceptable practice based on learning. Every king, cardinal and prince had an astrologer without whom he would not have dreamed of starting a war, passing an edict, or making a journey. The great conjunctions of the major planets known in the sixteenth century – Mars, Jupiter and Saturn – were always believed to herald certain types of upheavals and changes in the world and among its spiritual and temporal rulers. If Jupiter and Saturn conjoined – as they did when Anwar Sadat of Egypt was assassinated and attempts were made on the lives of President Ronald Reagan and Pope John Paul II – then, for the sixteenth-century astrologer, a king or head of state would die. If Mars and Saturn conjoined – as they did when Argentina invaded the British sovereign territory of the Falkland Islands – then, for the sixteenth-century astrologer, war loomed on the horizon.

We do not view history in this way today, and so the question of prophesying the events of history is a disturbing one. Now we look at linear developments, social and economic pressures, movements of wealth, the operations of the CIA and the KGB, population explosions, chance. That there might be some correlation between the movements of the heavens and the movements of society is an idea which, since the so-called Age of Enlightenment, until the most recent researches, has been considered appropriate fodder for hysterical old ladies. But what if the mind of the sixteenth century, educated in the subtler language of the irrational world, was aware of something we have since forgotten?

Nostradamus also used magic in his prognostications. Like all intelligent heretics, he would never have called it by its name for fear of the Inquisition and the stake. A little research into the prophet's life, his habits, his friends and his library reveals his involvement in ritual magic. This too now seems to us absurd, or, at the other end of the spectrum,

supernatural and therefore frightening. The practice of mouthing incan-
tations, drawing pentagrams on the floor of one's study à la Dennis
Wheatley, and sliding into a trance in which the processes of history are
revealed through strange shapes and visions, would today earn the prac-
titioner an entry ticket to institutions like Bellevue or the Maudsley clinic
rather than a claim to undying fame and the favour of kings. But all
these lost disciplines of the Renaissance – astrology, magic, prophetic
trance – are not so strange if we view them as psychological processes.
We are forced to keep an open mind because we know so little about the
real nature of the psyche and its mysterious depths. Instead of that
annoying word 'trance' we have a modern term, *abaissement du niveau
mental*, coined in the early days of psychology to describe the lowering
of the threshold of consciousness that occurs naturally in sleep and
fantasy, and unnaturally in delirium, drugged states and psychosis. For
Nostradamus this meant opening himself to visions from God about the
future. For the modern explorer of the human psyche it means opening
oneself to the archetypal images in the depths of the unconscious. Of
those depths we know perilously little, save that, in the light of research
by such modern giants as Jung, the unconscious can indeed be prophetic,
not only in personal terms but in universal ones as well. The encroaching
shadow of war is cast in the dreams of a nation long before its soldiers
are on the march.

Those deep and unknown layers of the psyche are common to us all,
and have spawned the world's great religious symbols and myths over
the ages. Men have always used ritual and incantation to reach the
depths, whether in a fashion acceptable to orthodox religion or in more
heretical pursuits. The prophet is perfectly valid in psychological terms.
He is a man or woman who, through innate temperament and/or training,
finds a way, accidentally or deliberately, to penetrate those deeper layers
of the mind where time and space cease to be relevant, and where
potentialities for future and past merge. In other words, the prophet
touches the place where patterns are made, and those patterns, although
not yet concrete, are eventually forced into outer manifestation by the
blindness and unconsciousness of men.

In Nostradamus' time much was known of the more obscure approaches to this inner realm, although his sixteenth-century language
does present complexities now. We are only beginning to rediscover this
realm through the fields of depth psychology and parapsychology. The
question is really no longer whether prophetic vision might be true, but
on what level we are to interpret it. M. de Fontbrune understands
Nostradamus' theme of the Great King as a future restoration of the
French monarchy, which will reconstruct and lead a ravaged but united
Europe. I would not quarrel with that; it is perfectly possible, even

probable, in the light of trends which are observable now. But whether this *must* be, or *might* be, is a tricky question. To Nostradamus a king meant only one thing: the physical king of a physical country. We, however, are somewhat more sophisticated now. There are not many kings left these days, and though they rule they do not govern as they once did. Now we have presidents and prime ministers, juntas and governing committees. More fancifully, perhaps, there are also inner rulers: dominant ideas, governing our morals and values, little petty tyrants of our minds and souls, benign spiritual leaders that we call our good will or our higher principles. What if an inner king, rather than an outer one, retrieved his lost throne at the end of the millennium? What if the great war that Nostradamus foresees were a psychological battle-field, rather than a physical one? Like an image from a dream, the Great King ruling by right of heaven is open to many levels of interpretation, and they may all occur at once. The French monarchy may indeed be restored; but if there is a possibility of an inner restoration of some long-lost spiritual value, therein lies our possibility of free will in the midst of fate. If one took a dream about the Great King to a Freudian analyst, he might speak of the father problem and its resolution, and he would be perfectly right in his interpretation. If one took that dream to a Jungian analyst, he might speak of the inner King, the symbol of the Self, the Great Man within each individual who represents the essence of one's individual life meaning. And he, too, would be perfectly right.

M. de Fontbrune is concerned that we will make Nostradamus' proph-ecies come true because of our inability to deal with our own natures: our greed, aggression, blindness, intolerance. Perhaps the patterns of history of which Nostradamus speaks are the inevitable confrontations at which we are given the opportunity to handle these ancient issues in new ways; and our capacity to deal with them depends upon how aware we are that war can be an inner thing, and that an enemy can lie within one's own soul – that the old king ripe for dethronement may be an internal and highly individual matter. Perhaps we make prophecy real in concrete life because it is real in the dream world, and in our ignorance of the dream world we force it to enact itself outwardly as fate because it has nowhere else to go.

For many readers a perusal of M. de Fontbrune's marvellous study of the prophecies of Nostradamus may be a sobering and even a frightening experience. Perhaps it is not a bad thing if this is so. I do not believe that either Nostradamus or Jean de Fontbrune intended the reader's response to be one of helpless fatalism. The end of the world might be the end of *a* world, and as such this might be a *world view* rather than a concrete landscape. Any analyst worth his salt will inquire, when brought a dream in which various characters enact their dramas great and small, what that dream has to do with the dreamer. I am inclined to feel that Nostradamus' prophetic vision has very much to do with the individual who explores it. Society is after all made up of individuals, and wars and plagues and the vicissitudes of kings and popes are also inner experiences encountered in the bedroom and over the breakfast table as much as they are great events enacted on the world stage. Jung once wrote that if there is something wrong with society, then there is something wrong with the individual. Prophecy is about fate, but fate is not always so solid and concrete as we imagine it to be. The panorama of struggle and battle and catastrophe and redemption which Nostradamus unrolls before us may, in the end, be the inner responsibility of each one of us.

Liz Greene, 1983

TRANSLATOR'S NOTE

As Jean Charles de Fontbrune himself observes, it should be pointed out that this edition, although of considerable length, does not include *all* the Centuries, presages and sixains of Nostradamus. He hopes to complete this huge task with a second volume in due course. In fact there is currently no complete edition in English of Nostradamus, and most previous versions have been prone to wild error and dubiously Procrustean interpretation. What this edition does provide, unlike others erroneously claiming to be complete – and here it is both unique and impressive – is comprehensive, wide-ranging, impartial annotation drawn from an enormous variety of sources. It represents the fruits of almost fifty years of research by the de Fontbrunes, father and son, and their dedication, scholarship and finally even the services of a computer have shed considerable light on many of the intentional and unintentional obscurities of the prophecies.

By its very nature this is a compilation to be sampled and argued over, rather than a consecutive or 'easy' read; it will, I am sure, continue to exert considerable fascination. Like myself, readers, however sceptical initially, may well find themselves becoming uneasily convinced by a disturbing percentage of these predictions.

They may find, too, that Nostradamus' Letter to his son César, included here for the first time in an English-language edition, often remains obscure, odd or ambiguously phrased, important though it is. By the time he wrote it Nostradamus must have been more than a little apprehensive about the Inquisition; nor did he wish his son to decipher and disseminate his visions too readily or prematurely. One feels also that the seer wanted to impose a sort of extra, unofficial education upon the youth, for human beings possess a compulsive urge to explore and solve mysteries, and where the works of Nostradamus are concerned this twin process requires, as de Fontbrune notes, a considerable fund of learning, often specialized, and acquired slowly and with patience. 'Please do not understand me too quickly,' André Gide once wrote. One incomplete edition of the Centuries now available (and Nostradamus has never been out of print in some form or other since his own time), which includes what seem to be wilfully inaccurate interpretations by contrast with de Fontbrune's sober and painstaking approach, merely states that the Letter to César has been omitted 'because of length and obscurity'! Readers must judge for themselves.

It should be stressed that the latter part of this edition deals with predictions for the future and such prophecies obviously cannot be precisely dated, verified by events or checked as yet, since they remain in the realm of speculation. De Fontbrune's interpretations of the prophecies, as a whole, have not been 'tidied up' or made to read more smoothly by this translator, but are set down as literally as possible. Readers should bear in mind that this is rhyming sixteenth-century French with a Provençal accent, employed by a polymath author virtually thinking in Latin and Greek and deliberately juggling with anagrams and all the other linguistic and riddling devices de Fontbrune describes more fully in his own preface. Inevitably the result is compression and obscurity: imagine, for instance, trying to send future generations a coded rhymed telegram in a mixture of high-flown yet colloquial language and in which, say, the destruction of London might be foretold in terms of 'The Great Wen lanced' or 'The Smoke dispersed', and then contemplate a hapless commentator's difficulty four hundred years later when attempting to break this sort of condensed, archaic, gnomic quatrain.

When the author wishes to emphasize a parallel between Nostradamus' work and the historical verification, he will sometimes repeat the word or phrase in brackets or place it in italics (for example, *sous la ramée*, CIV,Q62 where both these devices have been employed, or *naked* in CIII,Q30, which has simply been italicized). Similarly, if a quatrain strongly implies a crucial link, for instance '*le grand*' in CXII,Q36, de Fontbrune will sometimes include in his interpretative passage the 'missing' word – in this case 'armies', but place it in brackets. Other points regarded as particularly significant by de Fontbrune have been italicized in the histories following quatrains.

There are further complications. Imagine too Nostradamus' sixteenth-century frame of reference, and recall how he 'sees' and describes the furniture van into which Mussolini's body was flung. A metal box upon wheels – that certainly makes sense. And how, accordingly, would *you* yourself predict events revealed to you – very visually, sometimes specifically, but bewilderingly too – situated in the twenty-fifth century, without any real knowledge of how technology, politics or human biology had by then developed? Nostradamus' panoramic or cosmic viewpoint, almost from aloft like Hardy's in *The Dynasts*, represents a curious perspective of history, time and space, and whether or not readers agree with the interpretations offered here, they will find much to interest them.

Alexis Lykiard, 1983

I
ON METHOD

'The wise man will rule over planetary influences, which do not necessarily bring their properties to bear upon terrestrial bodies; but he only influences the latter, because it is possible to protect oneself through prudence and discretion.'

Ptolemy

Of all the famous men of the sixteenth century, Michel de Nostredame, known as Nostradamus, has probably prompted the most controversy. A considerable body of criticism and study has accumulated, especially in the twentieth century which is the main subject of his prophetic vision. All this interest suggests a work of unusual and considerable fascination. Excluding apocrypha and keeping to the 1568 edition, the *oeuvre* of Nostradamus consists of:

1. *The letter to his son César.* This text is really in the nature of a foreword to his future translator and is of prime importance in understanding his writings.

2. *Twelve books or 'Centuries'* containing a total of 965 quatrains, subdivided as follows:

Centuries I, II, III, IV, V, VI, IX, X, each of one hundred quatrains.
Century VII, of forty-six quatrains.
Century VIII, of one hundred quatrains, together with an additional eight quatrains.
Century IX, of two quatrains.
Century XII, of eleven quatrains.

3. *One quatrain in Latin*, at the end of Century VI and before Century VII, constituting a supplementary foreword.

4. *Portents (présages)* totalling 141.

5. *Sixains*: fifty-eight in all.

6. *The letter to Henri, Second King of France*: prose text at the end of Century VII, which constitutes a sort of synopsis of Nostradamus' vision.

In deciphering any of Nostradamus' writing, complete accuracy is essential – readers will be aware of how a subtle shift of emphasis can alter the whole meaning of a phrase. This letter just mentioned is introduced by a dedicatory greeting reproduced as follows in all the early editions of Nostradamus' work until that of Chevillot at Troyes in 1611:

'To the Invincible, Almighty and Christian Henri, the second King of France, Michel Nostradamus, his very humble and obedient servant and subject sends victory and happiness.'

In many editions after 1611, the following modification appears:

'To the Invincible, Almighty and Christian Henri II, King of France, Michel Nostradamus . . .'

The transformation of '*Henri Roy de France second*' to '*Henri II Roy de France*' changes both the sense of the letter and the identity of the addressee. If indeed it refers to Henri II, the description of him as invincible and all-powerful hardly applies since his reign was so brief and, moreover, he died somewhat ingloriously in a jousting accident on 11 July 1559. In the earlier editions, however, the word '*second*' is placed not directly after the name Henri, but where it refers specifically to 'King'. If we look at the word's Latin origin, *secundus* means favoured, propitious or fortunate. Now the letter refers not to Henri II but to a future king of France who will accede at a particularly crucial time in that country's history. Certain authors have assumed accordingly that Henri IV was intended. This hypothesis cannot be supported, since in several quatrains Nostradamus specifically states that he is referring to a king whose christian name is Henri, but associates the name with the number V: this letter must therefore be addressed to a person of exceptional qualities who has not yet played his role in history.

The verses of Nostradamus – 4772 lines – are in old French, a language still very close to its Latin and Greek roots. This explains the problems encountered by commentators lacking the literary background, first in translating the work into contemporary French and then in reconstituting the vast jigsaw puzzle of the quatrains. Consequently, innumerable linguistic errors appear in many editions, which has given rise to the opinion that Nostradamus' writings are obscure or incomprehensible, and to the frequently levelled criticism that virtually any meaning can be attributed to them.

Various attempts were made at expounding Nostradamus' Centuries before the twentieth century, but these were few compared to the many important studies published since 1938, the year in which my father, Dr

Max de Fontbrune, published the first complete critique of the *Works*. The first attempt to expound the work of Nostradamus dates back to 1594, and was made by a friend of Nostradamus, Jean Aimé de Chavigny.[1] Then came Guynaud[2] in 1693, and Bareste[3] in 1840, the latter inspired by his two predecessors. There followed Le Pelletier[4] in 1867, who in his turn drew upon these three earlier commentators, then the Abbé Torné-Chavigny[5] in 1870, who made use of all the forerunners. In 1929 P. V. Piobb,[6] taking no notice of Nostradamus' cautions, claimed to have found the key to the problem in occultism.

However all these writers translated only a few of the quatrains. Even the most important, Le Pelletier, only translated 194 out of 965 quatrains, four out of 141 portents and five out of fifty-eight sixains – a far from complete study. Perhaps Nostradamus' ultimate 'message' was intended for the twentieth century and the texts relating to earlier periods of history simply bear witness to the value and accuracy of his prophecy.

In 1934 my father was sent a 1605 edition; he slowly began translating Nostradamus' quatrains, and published the first major commentary in 1938. Apart from describing Nostradamus' prediction of the German army's advance through Belgium to invade France, he wrote of Germany's loss of the war and Hitler's wretched end. These grim prophecies resulted in his being hounded by the Gestapo and having his book confiscated and withdrawn from every bookshop in France; the type itself was broken up and melted down. The following article is from the *Journal Sud-Ouest* in September 1944:

LAVAL BANNED THE PROPHECIES OF NOSTRADAMUS
because they referred to an old man 'mocked by everyone' and
'a general who returned in triumph'.

Some time ago Pierre Laval personally intervened to withdraw from sale and ban Dr de Fontbrune's edition of *The Prophecies of Nostradamus*. Who could have expected this to have been a wise move?

Dr de Fontbrune lives quietly at Sarlat. This learned man, who has provided the best translation of the sayings of the great sage, now has something of a reputation as a soothsayer. In any case, during the war, with incredible generosity

[1] *La Première Face du Janus français extraite et colligée des centuries de Michel Nostradamus*, les héritiers de Pierre Roussin, Lyon, 1594.
[2] *Concordance des prophéties depuis Henri II jusqu'à Louis Le Grand*, Jacques Morel, Paris, 1693.
[3] Edition of *Centuries*, Maillet, Paris, 1840.
[4] *Les Oracles de Nostradamus, astrologue, médecin et conseiller ordinaire des rois Henry II, François II et Charles IX*. 2 vols, self-published by Le Pelletier (also printer and typographer), Paris, 1867.
[5] Several works published at the author's expense between 1860 and 1878.
[6] *Le Secret de Nostradamus*, Adyar, Paris, 1929.

he has actively resisted in his capacity as a doctor, saving many of our young compatriots.

In his Nostradamus book, Dr de Fontbrune predicted the war in North Africa; the future victors' invasion of Italy; aerial combat on the grand scale, followed by fighting on French soil (specifically at Poitiers and Belfort). Finally, too, France's misfortune 'under an old man who will subsequently be despised', and according to the ancient text, 'mocked by everyone'; and the glorious rescue by a general 'temporarily absent and who shall return in triumph'.

This last remark caused the book to be banned: its concluding chapter forecasts the defeat and partition of Germany. Not bad going, we must admit. Dr de Fontbrune and his friend Nostradamus have been avenged . . . and so have we!

Here is the censorship order, dated 13 November 1940, banning my father's book:

> From M. Nismes, Principal Censor, Cahors, to the Managers,
> Coueslant Press, Cahors.

This is to confirm that subsequent to a decision by the Vice-President of the Council, the work printed by your firm and entitled *The Prophecies of Master Michel Nostradamus* by Dr de Fontbrune, published by Michelet of Sarlat, has now had its permit revoked. Accordingly it is illegal to offer the work for sale and, should you yourselves be its distributors to local bookshops, you are requested to take the appropriate measures to call back all copies to your premises, such copies in due course to be forfeit whether on your premises or those of the publishers at Sarlat. The question of first, limited editions or reprints is irrelevant, given that in all versions of this work Dr de Fontbrune's commentary risks provoking severe reaction from the occupying authorities.

Born in 1935, I can almost say I was born and bred into Nostradamus studies, living with my father as I did until his death at Montpellier in 1959. So it is not surprising that after military service I took up my father's work in 1963. I found that there were a good many errors and obscurities in it. Starting from the nonetheless extraordinarily coherent vision he had of the work, I began a detailed analysis of the text. This involved my restoring to the past certain prophecies thought by my father to relate to the future, but I also translated and interpreted various texts never previously translated nor understood by any earlier commentator.

Since 1938 numerous books about Nostradamus have appeared, many inspired by my father's, but also some cases of blatant plagiarism. For instance, a 'reputable' astrologer, Maurice Privat, published a work on Nostradamus in 1938. Its title alone is nothing if not schematic: *1940,*

Year of French Greatness[1]. This was at a time when my father's book was warning that the Second World War would prove catastrophic for France – warnings based, of course, on centuries-old predictions.

Some authors did give my father his due:

Before the Second World War, Dr de Fontbrune published a profound study of the Prophecies.[2]

Dr de Fontbrune's interpretation seems the most generally accepted since Bareste in 1840 began the first attempts at decoding.[3]

In memory of Dr de Fontbrune, through whose work I came to know Nostradamus.[4]

Without a doubt, one of the most serious works is Dr de Fontbrune's.[5]

In a letter to my father, after meeting him in the Dordogne in 1953, Henry Miller wrote:

'Once again I must stress your gift for making everything clear in a very few words. It's a rare gift, believe me. One senses your unswerving integrity – which makes all you say seem lucid. You see, without your wanting to do so, you have become a sort of 'confessor' for me. What I could never tell a priest I can tell you quite freely. I like men who have won through to their own vision of the world and the life everlasting. The more I think about your creative work of interpretation, the more I admire you. The way in which you have gone into the prophecy always astounds me, despite the fact that it was the only, the inevitable way of undertaking this. It takes inspiration to make such a discovery.

Labor omnia vincit improbus [Persistent toil conquers everything] wrote Virgil in his *Georgics*. This is why I am now making public the fruits of a total of forty-four years' research by father and son. Readers will find here all those texts which history has already proved correct: they are presented as a virtually irrefutable demonstration of Nostradamus' authentic powers as a prophet, although he himself never claimed to be one.

To understand the hermetic nature of the work, one must read the Letter to César, included here in its entirety. The prefatory admonitions Nostradamus addressed to his future translators are essential in deciphering his message. In this way magic and occultism can be dismissed.

[1] Editions Médicis, Paris, 1938.
[2] Michel Touchard, *Nostradamus*, Grasset, 1972.
[3] Eric Muraise, *Saint-Rémy de Provence et les Secrets de Nostradamus*, Julliard, 1969.
[4] Jean Monterey, *Nostradamus, prophète du XXe Siècle*, la Nef de Paris, 1961.
[5] Camille Rouvier, *Nostradamus*, la Savoisienne, Marseille, 1964.

Preface by
M. Nostradamus to his Prophecies
Greetings and Happiness to César Nostradamus my son

Your late arrival, César Nostredame, my son, has made me spend much
time in constant nightly reflection so that I could communicate with you
by letter and leave you this reminder, after my death, for the benefit of
all men, of what the divine spirit has vouchsafed me to know by means
of astronomy. And since it was the Almighty's will that you were not
born here in this region [Provence] and I do not want to talk of years to
come but of the months during which you will struggle to grasp and
understand the work I shall be compelled to leave you after my death:
assuming that it will not be possible for me to leave you such [clearer]
writing as may be destroyed through the injustice of the age [1555]. The
key to the hidden prediction which you will inherit will be locked inside
my heart. Also bear in mind that the events here described have not yet
come to pass, and that all is ruled and governed by the power of Almighty
God, inspiring us not by bacchic frenzy nor by enchantments but by
astronomical assurances: predictions have been made through the inspiration of divine will alone and the spirit of prophecy in particular. On
numerous occasions and over a long period of time I have predicted
specific events far in advance, attributing all to the workings of divine
power and inspiration, together with other fortunate or unfortunate
happenings, foreseen in their full unexpectedness, which have already
come to pass in various regions of the earth. Yet I have wished to remain
silent and abandon my work because of the injustice not only of the
present time [the Inquisition] but also for most of the future. I will not
commit it to writing, since governments, sects and countries will undergo
such sweeping changes, diametrically opposed to what now obtains, that
were I to relate events to come, those in power now – monarchs, leaders
of sects and religions – would find these so different from their own
imaginings that they would be led to condemn what later centuries will
learn how to see and understand. Bear in mind also Our Saviour's words:
*Nolite sanctum dare canibus, nec mittatis margaritas ante porcos ne conculcent
pedibus et conversi dirumpant vos* [Do not give anything holy to the dogs,
nor throw pearls in front of the pigs lest they trample them with their
feet and turn on you and tear you apart]. For this reason I withdrew my
pen from the paper, because I wished to amplify my statement touching
the Vulgar Advent (1), by means of ambiguous and enigmatic comments
about future causes, even those closest to us and those I have perceived,
so that some human change which may come to pass shall not unduly
scandalize delicate sensibilities. The whole work is thus written in a

nebulous rather than plainly prophetic form. So much so that, *Abscondisti haec a sapientibus et prudentibus, id est potentibus et regibus et eunuculeasti ea exiguis et tenuibus* [You have hidden these things from the wise and the circumspect, that is from the mighty and the rulers, and you have purified those things for the small and the poor], and through Almighty God's will, revealed unto those prophets with the power to perceive what is distant and thereby to foretell things to come. For nothing can be accomplished without this faculty, whose power and goodness work so strongly in those to whom it is given that, while they contemplate within themselves, these powers are subject to other influences arising from the force of good. This warmth and strength of prophecy invests us with its influence as the sun's rays affect both animate and inanimate entities. We human beings cannot through our natural consciousness and intelligence know anything of God the Creator's hidden secrets, *Quia non est nostrum noscere tempora nec momenta* [For it is not for us to know the times or the instants], etc. So much so that persons of future times may be seen in present ones, because God Almighty has wished to reveal them by means of images, together with various secrets of the future vouchsafed to orthodox astrology, as was the case in the past, so that a measure of power and divination passed through them, the flame of the spirit inspiring them to pronounce upon inspiration both human and divine. God may bring into being divine works, which are absolute; there is another level, that of angelic works; and a third way, that of the evildoers. But my son, I address you here a little too obscurely. As regards the occult prophecies one is vouchsafed through the subtle spirit of fire, which the understanding sometimes stirs through contemplation of the distant stars as if in vigil, likewise by means of pronouncements, one finds oneself surprised at producing writings without fear of being stricken for such impudent loquacity. The reason is that all this proceeds from the divine power of Almighty God from whom all bounty proceeds. And so once again, my son, if I have eschewed the word prophet, I do not wish to attribute to myself such a lofty title at the present time, for whoever *Propheta dicitur hodie, olim vocabatur videns*; since a prophet, my son, is properly speaking one who sees distant things through a natural knowledge of all creatures. And it can happen that the prophet bringing about the perfect light of prophecy may make manifest things both human and divine, because this cannot be done otherwise, given that the effects of predicting the future extend far off into time. God's mysteries are incomprehensible and the power to influence events is bound up with the great expanse of natural knowledge, having its nearest most immediate origin in free will and describing future events which cannot be understood simply through being revealed. Neither can they be grasped through men's interpretations nor through another mode of cognizance or occult power under the firmament, neither in the present nor in the total eternity to come. But bringing about such an indivisible eternity through Herculean efforts (2), things are revealed by the planetary movements. I am not saying, my son – mark me well, here – that knowledge of such things cannot be implanted in your deficient mind, or that events in the distant future may not be within the understanding of any reasoning being. Nevertheless, if these things current or distant are brought to the awareness of this reasoning and intelligent being they will be neither too obscure nor too clearly revealed. Perfect knowledge of such things cannot be acquired without divine inspiration, given that all prophetic inspiration derives its initial origin from God Almighty, then from chance and nature. Since all these portents are produced impartially, prophecy comes to pass partly as predicted. For understanding created by the intellect cannot be acquired by means of the occult, only by the aid of the zodiac, bringing forth that small flame by whose light part of the future may be discerned. Also, my son, I beseech you not to exercise your mind upon such reveries and vanities as drain the body and incur the soul's perdition, and which trouble our feeble frames. Above all avoid the vanity of that most execrable magic formerly reproved by the Holy Scriptures – only excepting the use of official astrology. For by the latter, with the help of inspiration and divine revelation, and continual calculations, I have set down my prophecies in writing. Fearing lest this occult philosophy be condemned, I did not therefore wish to make known its dire import; also fearful that several books which had lain hidden for long centuries might be discovered, and of what might become of them, after reading them I presented them to Vulcan [i.e. burned them]. And while he devoured them, the flame licking the air gave out such an unexpected light, clearer than that of an ordinary flame and resembling fire from some flashing cataclysm, and suddenly illumined the house as if it were caught in a furnace. Which is why I reduced them to ashes then, so that none might be tempted to use occult labours in searching for the perfect transmutation, whether lunar or solar, of incorruptible metals (3). But as to that discernment which can be achieved by the aid of planetary scrutiny, I should like to tell you this. Eschewing any fantastic imaginings, you may through good judgement have insight into the future if you keep to the specific names of places that accord with planetary configurations, and with inspiration places and aspects yield up hidden properties, namely that power in whose presence the three times [past, present, and future] are understood as Eternity whose unfolding contains them all: *quia omnia sunt nuda et aperta*, etc. That is why, my son, you can easily, despite your young brain, understand that events can be foretold naturally by the heavenly bodies and by the spirit of prophecy: I do not wish to ascribe to myself the title and role of prophet, but emphasize inspiration revealed to a mortal man whose perception is no further from heaven than the feet are from the earth. *Possum non errare, falli, decipi*: although I may be as great a sinner as anyone else upon this earth and subject to all human afflictions. But after being surprised sometimes by day while in a trance, and having long fallen into the habit of agreeable nocturnal studies, I have composed books of prophecies, each containing one hundred astronomical quatrains, which I wanted to condense somewhat obscurely. The work comprises prophecies from today to the year 3797. This may perturb some, when they see such a long timespan, and this will occur and be understood in all the fullness of the Republic (4); these things will be universally understood upon earth, my son. If you live the normal lifetime of man you will know upon your own soil, under your native sky, how future events are to turn out. For only Eternal God knows the eternity of His light which proceeds from Him, and I speak frankly to those to whom His immeasurable, immense and incomprehensible greatness has been disposed to grant revelations through long, melancholy inspiration, that with the aid of this hidden element manifested by God, there are two principal factors which make up the prophet's intelligence. The first is when the supernatural light fills and illuminates the person who predicts by astral science, while the second allows him to prophesy through inspired revelation, which is only a part of the divine eternity, whereby the prophet comes to assess what his divinatory power has given him through the grace of God and by a natural gift, namely, that what is foretold is true and ethereal in origin (5). And such a light and small flame is of great efficacy and scope, and nothing less than the clarity of nature itself. The light of human nature makes the philosophers so sure of themselves that with the principles of the first cause they reach the loftiest doctrines and the deepest abysses. But my son, lest I venture too far for your future perception, be aware that men of letters shall make grand and usually boastful claims about the way I interpreted the world, before the worldwide conflagration which is to bring so many catastrophes and such revolutions that scarcely any lands will not be covered by water (6), and this will last until all has perished save history and geography themselves. This is why, before and after these revolutions in various countries, the rains will be so diminished and such abundance of fire and fiery missiles shall fall from the heavens that nothing shall escape the holocaust. And this will occur before the last conflagration [1999]. For before war ends the [twentieth] century and in its final stages [1975–99] it will hold the century under its sway. Some countries will be in the grip of revolution (7) for several years, and others ruined for a still longer period. And now that we are in a republican era, with Almighty God's aid, and before completing its full cycle, the monarchy will return, then the Golden Age (8). For according to the celestial signs, the Golden Age shall return, and after all calculations, with the world near to an all-encompassing revolution – from the time of writing 177 years 3 months 11 days (9) – plague, long famine and wars, and still more floods from now until the stated time. Before and after these, humanity shall several times be so severely diminished that scarcely anyone shall be found who wishes to take over the fields, which shall become free where they had previously been tied. This will be after the visible judgement of heaven, before we reach the millennium which shall complete all. In the firmament of the eighth sphere, a dimension whereon Almighty God will complete the revolution, and where the constellations will resume their motion which will render the earth stable and firm, but only if *non inclinabitur in saeculum saeculi* [He will remain unchanged for ever] – until His will be done. This is in spite of all the ambiguous opinions surpassing all natural reason, expressed by Mahomet; which is why God the Creator, through the ministry of his fiery agents with their flames, will come to propose to our perceptions as well as our eyes the reasons for future predictions. Signs of events to come must be manifested to whomever prophesies. For prophecy which stems from exterior illumination is a part of that light and seeks to ally with it and bring it into being so that the part which seems to possess the faculty of understanding is not subject to a sickness of the mind. Reason is only too evident. Everything is predicted by divine afflatus (10) and thanks to an angelic spirit inspiring the one prophesying, consecrating his predictions through divine unction. It also divests him of all fantasies by means of various nocturnal apparitions, while with daily certainty he prophesies through the science of astronomy, with the aid of sacred prophecy, his only consideration being his courage in freedom. So come, my son, strive to understand what I have found out through my calculations which accord with revealed inspiration, because now the sword of death approaches us, with pestilence and war more horrible than there has ever been – because of three men's work – and with famine. And this sword shall smite the earth and return to it often, for the stars confirm this upheaval and it is also written: *Visitabo in virga ferrea iniquitates eorum, et in verberibus percutiam eos* [I shall punish their injustices with iron rods, and shall strike them with blows]. For God's mercy will be poured forth only for a certain time, my son, until the majority of my prophecies are fulfilled and this fulfilment is complete. Then several times in the course of the doleful tempests the Lord shall say: *Conteram ergo et confringam et non miserebor* [Therefore I shall crush and destroy and show no mercy]; and many other circumstances shall result from floods and continual rain (11) of which I have written more fully in my other prophecies, composed at some length, not in a chronological sequence, *in soluta oratione* [in prose], limiting the places and times and exact dates so that future generations will see, while experiencing these inevitable events, how I have listed others in clearer language, so that despite their obscurities these things shall be understood: *Sed quando submovenda erit ignorantia*, the matter will be clearer still. So in conclusion, my son, take this gift from your father M. Nostradamus, who hopes you will understand each prophecy in every quatrain herein. May Immortal God grant you a long life of good and prosperous happiness.

Salon, 1 March 1555

Notes

1. *le commun advènement*, the Vulgar Advent, or the accession of the people to power, is generally taken by commentators to refer first to republicanism (via the French Revolution), then to its development towards and change into communism. (*Tr.*)

2. Nostradamus here compares his work, the twelve Centuries, to the Twelve Labours of Hercules, in order to stress their difficulty and importance.

3. Moon and Sun are constant symbols in Nostradamus of the republic and the monarchy respectively, hence the alchemic imagery also has a political aspect here.

4. Reference to *toute la concavité de la lune*. Cf. note 3 above.

5. Ether: originally personified as a deity of the upper atmosphere, and later confused with Zeus. (DL 7V).

6. Water and flooding are often taken as a symbol of revolution in Nostradamus.

7. The French text refers to Aquarius, i.e. the water-bearer. Cf. note 6 above.

8. Golden Age: rule of Saturn, the happy, peaceful time, to commemorate which the Romans celebrated with Saturnalia.

9. 1555 + 177 = 1732, the exact date when Rousseau arrived in Paris, Nostradamus considered Rousseau the father of revolutionary and atheistic ideas.

10. Breath or inspiration, oracular possession.

11. Upheavals and revolution. Cf. notes 6 and 7 above.

The specifically 'scientific' side of Nostradamus' personality is in no way vitiated by his recourse to hermeticism so as not to be witch-hunted: when his fellow citizens of Salon burned him in effigy outside his house he went to the French court to seek protection from Queen Catherine de Médecis. She not only granted protection but visited him at Salon, which soon stopped the gossip in that small town.

Nostradamus also found out how the plague was transmitted, and discovered a form of asepsis four centuries before Pasteur. Indeed, sixteenth-century chronicles which describe the methods used by Nostradamus to control the plague epidemics at Aix-en-Provence, Marseille and Lyon make one realize that this Provençal doctor took quite sophisticated antiseptic precautions, though he had to invent a special powder to conceal his true scientific discovery, for had the extent of his knowledge been made known, he would have been burned at the stake for sorcery. At this time the Church still considered that sickness and plague were God's way of punishing man for his sins. The Inquisition's reign of terror was being enforced and Galileo, born in 1564, two years before the death of Nostradamus, would himself fall foul of this anti-scientific consensus for stating that the earth revolved.

It is thus all the more understandable that Nostradamus deliberately shrouded his prophecies in linguistic and even astrological mists, for had he openly expressed his vision of the future it would certainly not have survived. The religious authorities would very likely have destroyed it. My father's own misfortunes with his book in 1940 illustrate what can happen when a prophet's 'message' is expressed absolutely directly.

The prophecies of Nostradamus, then, were written in the sixteenth century in order to depict the twentieth, to which two-thirds of the work is devoted, for their author seemed to know that his text would be expounded and understood only in the century which was the focus of his vision. As for the fulfilment of his prophecy, writers have discovered or invented this either by resorting to astrological calculations, more or less arithmetical 'keys', or the Cabbala and so on. Actually the prophecies end with the seventh millennium, which according to biblical chronology is the conclusion of the Piscean Age, approximately 2000 AD. Here again, Nostradamus cunningly concealed this fact: the calculation can only be arrived at using the biblical reckoning he gives in the letter to 'Henry Roy de France Second', as follows:

From Adam, the first man, to Noah	1242 years
Noah to Abraham	1080 years
From Abraham to Moses	515 years
Moses to David	570 years
David to Jesus Christ	1350 years

i.e. from Adam to Christ, a total of 4757 years.

In the letter to César, Nostradamus mentions prophecies from the year of writing until 3797. From the time of writing (the letter is dated 1555) until 3797 there is a difference of 2242 years. If one adds this length of time to the biblical chronology above the result is 6999, or in Christian (taking into account Christ's thirty-three years) chronology 1999, the date clearly given by Nostradamus as the starting point of the Wars of the Anti-Christ:

L'an mil neuf cent nonante neuf sept mois
Du ciel viendra un grand Roy d'effrayeur
Ressusciter le grand Roy d'Angoulmois,[1]
Avant après Mars regner par bonheur.

CX,Q72

Interpretation

In July, the seventh month of 1999, a great and terrifying leader will come by air, reviving or recalling the great conqueror of Angoulême. Before and after, war will reign happily.

Nostradamus gives only a few specific dates. Other than 1999, he mentions in the letter to '*Henry Roy de France Second*' that the monarchy 'will last until the year 1792 which will be considered the start of a new age'. The way in which he wrote down his visions suggests that these two specific dates are more important if taken as points of departure and arrival rather than in isolation. 1792 (the year of the proclamation of the French Republic) represents the beginning of the end of the Christian Era (Piscean Age) and 1999 its actual end, which thus begins the Age of Aquarius with the pains of apocalyptic childbirth necessary in order for man to stop concentrating his efforts upon more and more horrifying means of destruction. This is the reason why Nostradamus completes his quatrain with this surprising line, 'Before and after Mars [War] will reign *happily*' [*par bonheur* = happily, or, as luck would have it].

A prophecy that comes true becomes history. For example, Nostradamus writes of Napoleon I:

> De la cité marine et tributaire,
> La teste raze prendra la Satrapie:[2]
> Chassez sordide qui puis sera contraire,
> Par quatorze ans tiendra la tyranie.

> CVII,QI3

Interpretation

From the port under foreign domination the shaven-headed man will take power. He will drive out the squalid revolutionaries, the wind of history having changed, and will rule tyrannically for fourteen years.

---

[1] Angoulême was conquered by the Visigoths, then threatened by the Mongolian race of Huns led by Attila, 'the scourge of God'. Note the neat analogy in the fact that the Huns first occupied Pannonia so as to ravage France and Italy.

[2] Satraps were governors of provinces under Persian rule, filling the dual roles of administrators and tax collectors.

History

From Alexandria, which had become a French dependency, Bonaparte organized Egypt into a sort of prefecture, then embarked for France, whose political situation was giving him cause for anxiety.[1] He helped to overthrow the Directorate and in the coup of 18 Brumaire assumed power, which was absolute until the Allies entered Paris on 31 March 1814, i.e. after fourteen years, four months and eleven days of his rule.

I have chosen this particular quatrain because like many others its message covers a span of time. The first part of the quatrain was accomplished on 18 Brumaire 1799, becoming history while the second part remained prophecy until 31 March 1814.

This 'stroll' across time and space which is the prophet's habit defies all rational chronological classification. Should a quatrain referring to the retreat from Moscow (CII,Q99) be placed before or after the one just quoted? The retreat occurred after the 1799 coup but preceded Napoleon's Fontainebleau abdication on 6 April 1814. Nostradamus' prophecy constitutes a vision of history which has nothing in common with the version taught in schools.

This quatrain leads me to formulate a useful principle for anyone interested in prophecies like those of Nostradamus and hence obliged to abandon preconceived ideas. Events in particular, and history in general, never unfold according to man's Cartesian pattern. I need only instance the eminent French economists of the 'Club of Rome' who in 1972 boldly forecast that France would be the third major world power by 1980. In September 1973 the Arab–Israeli war precipitated the world economic crisis and shook the West, reducing our economic pundits' fine promises to nothing.

To illustrate history's caprice let us return to Napoleonic times, to 2 December 1805, the date of Austerlitz, when the Emperor had the world at his feet. Imagine that a prophet were to announce Napoleon's ignominious end as a prisoner of the English on an island in the mid-Atlantic. He would have risked imprisonment, execution or internment in a psychiatric hospital. My father was ridiculed in much the same way in 1946 and later when he maintained that General de Gaulle – who had just withdrawn from the political arena for what might be termed a 'period in the wilderness' – would return to power in a coup d'état. Friends who had once mocked wrote politely to him after 13 May 1958, astonished by an event which twelve years earlier they had all thought impossible.

History, and events that lie ahead, almost always completely contradict

[1] LCH3

in both matter and manner the times which we are living through. This
is why so few can aspire to the perception the prophet has tried to
transmit to posterity. The obstacle to understanding the spirit of prophecy lies basically in the antagonism between vision and rationalism.
Adherents of the latter cannot abandon their system of logic to enter into
any other form of reasoning. The essential requirement for getting to
grips with prophecy is a very open mind.

Continuing my father's work, I spent five years making an exhaustive
study of Nostradamus' vocabulary. This enabled me to explicate the
prophet's language, except for a few minor details, and to correct errors
of translation made by the Centuries' innumerable previous commentators. Many errors perpetrated by Le Pelletier were repeated verbatim by
other authors.

Take, for example, the most famous quatrain predicting the death of
Henri II while jousting:

> Le Lyon jeune le vieux surmontera,
> En champ bellique par singulier duelle,
> Dans cage d'or les yeux lui crèvera
> Deux classes une, puis mourir mort cruelle.

CI,Q35

Interpretation

The young lion shall overcome the old in a tourney (single combat).
Inside a golden cage his eyes will be put out in one of the two contests,
then he shall die grievously.

Montgoméry, captain of the Scottish Guard, whose arms were
'or, with lion of Scotland passant, gules' jousted with Henri II. Montgoméry's lance splintered and penetrated the visor of the King's gilded
helmet.

In this quatrain Le Pelletier and his followers derive *classes* from the
Greek word χλασις (breakage or lopping of a branch) and translate:
'Here is the first of the two breakages.' What they fail to note is that Le
Pelletier himself translates the word *classes* correctly in CII,Q99. It comes
from the Latin and means 'fleet' or 'armed combat', and is always used
in this way by Nostradamus. Le Pelletier, not understanding that the
king was fatally injured in one of the two jousts he fought, conveniently
dropped the *s* from *classis* so that the Greek word might be interpreted
instead. Similar philological errors occur elsewhere. This begins to explain how one can ascribe virtually anything to Nostradamus, and why
I have here tried to demonstrate that in fact the prophet wrote precisely.

Mistakes are inevitable if one assumes that the text is ambiguous where it is, in fact, specific.

Readers will find that, in order to follow the text as faithfully as possible and extract its full meaning, when translating the quatrain I have decided that the only possible 'key' is a linguistic one. The result was a Sherlock Holmesian investigation that left no detail unconsidered. It seemed clear to me that Nostradamus, playing with anagrams, puns and etymology, put the Latin language through an alchemic transmutation, 'gallicizing' it to conceal his prophetic message and bringing to his intellectual riddling an immense fund of classical learning which has discouraged many interpreters.

One of the first books to be written about Nostradamus' texts after Jean Aimé de Chavigné and Guynaud was the Curé de Louvicamp's *Key to Nostradamus or Introduction to the True Meaning of the Prophecies of this Celebrated Author* (Pierre Giffart, Paris, 1710). This writer is only rarely mentioned, although he was the first to understand Nostradamus' method of setting down his prophecies. (Le Pelletier was, however, deeply indebted to him.) 'I wish to state in conclusion,' writes de Louvicamp,

. . . that when France's oracle made his Gallic prophecies, he hardly ever departed from the Latins' usage, often writing Latin under the pretext of writing French, and not only etymologically, i.e. when he describes a Prince *Flagrand d'ardent libide* as if thinking *flagrans ardenti libidine*, rather than writing *burning with the horrid fire of lust*. Often he even employed a Latinate French, drawing attention and alluding to the Latin phraseology in word order and placement – what we call syntax . . . The Latin poets often had recourse to metaplasm – the changing or transformation of words – by adding, dropping, changing or transposing letters and syllables to and from words so as to scan or embellish their verses. In the same way Nostradamus too sometimes metamorphosed or altered ordinary words in his verses, not just for the sake of keeping the rhythm and scansion but at the same time to divert unlettered persons from the real meaning of his prophecies. In this book examples may be found of aphesis, syncope, apocope, prothesis, epenthesis, antithesis, metathesis, anastrophe, etc, as in the Latin authors, with the exception of paragoge – the addition of a letter or syllable to the end of a word.

It will probably be helpful to readers to define these grammatical terms:

1. *Aphesis.* The omission of a letter or syllable at the beginning of a word: *bondance* for *abondance* (abundance); *verse* for *renverse* (reverse); *tendant* for *attendant* (waiting).

2. *Syncope.* Letter or syllable dropped from the middle of a word: *donra* for *donnera* (will give); *emprise* for *entreprise* (enterprise).

3. *Apocope*. Letter or syllable dropped from the ending of a word (i.e. *profond' colon'* for *profonde colonne*).

4. *Prothesis, epenthesis and paragoge*. Instead of dropping a letter or syllable, one is added to the beginning, middle or end of a word. Virgil took this to apply also to metathesis and even apocope, e.g. *Tymbre* for *Tiberis* (the Tiber). Nostradamus sometimes imitates him in this, using *Tymbre* for *Tibre* (Fr.).

Elsewhere, as he indicated in the Letter to his son César, Nostradamus 'condenses' his prophecies, either to obscure his text or to preserve the required number of feet in each line, since he wrote his Centuries in decasyllabic verse.

A modern translation can therefore only be achieved by attentive and close study of the words, phrases and constructions employed by Nostradamus.

Among his Latinisms he frequently uses the ablative absolute, that bane of schoolboys. He often omits prepositions, as if French were similar to Latin in possessing genitive, ablative and dative cases. This means that one must reassess a word in its context before discovering what its precise case is. Thus '*la voye auxelle*' (CVIII,Q27) is the equivalent of the Latin '*medium auxillio*' (the means by whose aid . . .). It is clear that though Nostradamus was writing in sixteenth-century French he was thinking in Latin, which accounts for the apparent obtuseness of most scholars in the face of such daunting difficulties.

To complicate matters still further and lead the 'common herd' astray, he gallicized Greek words too. This suggests that he wanted to prevent *all* commentators who were not classicists from understanding his prophecies. For example, he invented words like *oruche* and *genest*. The first derives from ὀρυχη, an excavation pit, while the second comes from γενέσθαι, aorist infinitive of the verb γιγνομαι, meaning 'to be born'. No reader without a knowledge of Greek, since the words *oruche* and *genest* will not be found in any French dictionary, nor even a Latin one, could make sense of the quatrains where these coinages appear.

The text I use here is that of the second edition of 1605 (Benoit Rigaud, Lyon), acquired by my father in 1934. This is a complete copy of the 1568 edition, considered the most reliable and containing the fewest misprints. Comparing it with more modern editions, it is evident at first glance that errors proliferate in the later works. Take the fourth line of CVIII,Q61:

Portant au coq don du TAG armifère

Many editions after Chevillot's (Troyes, 1610) give: 'TAO armifère', which enables wilfully esoteric commentators to introduce Taoism to the texts of Nostradamus! I deemed it important to assure readers that I have taken enormous pains to ensure the authenticity of my decodings.

I hoped, for the first time ever, to match history itself against the writings of Nostradamus. The most frequent criticism levelled at previous commentators is that they used Nostradamus' work to put across their personal ideologies. My approach on the other hand involved various history books by very different authors with completely opposed philosophical, political or religious viewpoints. I even drew for my documentation from school textbooks. Readers will realize from this that the prophecy of Nostradamus is history in its purest state, beyond the narrow vision of the historians themselves. They may be surprised, too, at some of the value judgements made by Nostradamus, e.g. 'the miserable, unfortunate Republic' (CI,Q61) or that Napoleon Bonaparte 'will be found to be less prince than butcher' (CI,Q60).

I had to consult numerous history books, too, because none was complete enough to contain Nostradamus' vision. This is why against one quatrain may be set extracts from several different works. It has often amused me to juxtapose and reunite in this way, say, two historians as different as Victor Duruy, a Republican and anti-clerical atheist, and the conservative Pierre Gaxotte, and thus observe that history transcends people's confined, partisan, ephemeral and above all presumptuous conceptions. This is especially true of the twentieth century in which Manicheanism has penetrated all realms of thought, setting son against father, country against country, one political party against another, and finally, worst of all, has created peoples or races internally divided by liberation movements of one kind or another, thus realizing this prophecy of Christ's:

And ye shall hear of wars and rumours of wars; see that ye be not troubled: for all these things must come to pass, but the end is not yet. For nation shall rise against nation, and kingdom against kingdom; and there shall be famines, and pestilences, and earthquakes, in divers places. All these are the beginning of sorrows.

Matthew 24, 6–8, Authorized Version.

As regards the choice of definition, and from which dictionary, in every instance that choice was influenced by the meaning of the line, itself set in the context of its whole quatrain. Indeed, if I found myself faced with particular words which, in their current meaning or in their original or specialized sense, rendered the text incomprehensible, I then felt it essential to examine the etymological aspects or the text's symbolic meaning. Take '*Par cinq cens un trahyr sera titré*' (CIX,Q34). Given that the verb *trahir* (betray) is here used as a noun, since it is preceded by the indefinite article, one cannot use *titrer* in its contemporary sense of 'to give a title to'; and 'a betrayal shall be given a title' is meaningless. But a dictionary eventually reveals that this verb can also mean 'to scheme' or 'to intrigue', so the text swiftly becomes very specific: a treacherous act will be plotted by five hundred persons. This is a good example of the linguistic traps Nostradamus set for his future translators.

My father fell into some of them, setting too much store by his own researches and not enough on the verbal mannerisms and gallicisms liberally employed by Nostradamus. My father's book *What Nostradamus Really Said* (Stock, 1976) includes only sixty-three quatrains covering the period 1555 to 1945; this seems to me very few, given the importance of the work and the profuse details lavished upon certain events. So I had to re-examine the whole work from A to Z, to advance step by step, doggedly reconstituting the puzzle by eliminating along the way various quatrains either without prophetic purpose or ambiguous, and which Nostradamus inserted to mislead commentators still further.

Matching up Nostradamus' work with historical events required considerable research. As he wrote in the Letter to César, Nostradamus did indeed supply a translator with very precise geographical guidelines. When the small town of Varennes is mentioned (CIX,Q20) it is easy to see the significance of the quatrain, for the capture there of Louis XVI is well known, which is why we find this quatrain, give or take an occasional error, commented upon in all the post-1792 books. However when a quatrain mentions Vitry-le-François, the commentator will be unable to see its significance unless he knows or finds out that in this town Kellermann reassembled the French army to surrender after the Battle of Valmy. Take another example: Nostradamus mentions the small Italian town of Buffalora (CVIII,Q12). Comparatively few people know that the Napoleonic General MacMahon's army was encamped there before launching the Italian campaign which led to the victories of Magenta and Solferino.

Nostradamus would conceal the names of towns destined to become famous or important by using instead those of small, neighbouring villages. Thus Aquinas, Italy will stand for nearby Naples; the village of Apameste indicates Calabria, of which it is a part; while Rimini or Prato indicate Mussolini's birthplace, equidistant as it is from these two towns. To necessitate still more research, Nostradamus vulgarized town names, disguising them by means of popular names or nicknames, transcribed of course, without capital letters. Hence Apameste in Calabria becomes *apamé*, its last syllable disappearing through apocope (CIX,Q95). But the most striking illustration of this method is the word *herbipolique* which

Nostradamus fabricated partly from Herbipolis, the Latin name for the town of Würzburg in Germany (CX,Q13).

Finally, Nostradamus gallicized foreign names while respecting the rules of phonetics or of letters which correspond in both languages. Thus the East German town of Ballenstedt becomes Ballènes, gallicized and by apocope; the town of Lunegiane, Lunage, through a combination of apocope and anagram, and Llanes, a small port in Asturia, Spain, becomes by gallicization Laigne.

Various typographical errors, mercifully rare, further complicate the decoding process. Some mistakes are simple to correct, i.e. 'Madric' for 'Madrid', but others are more difficult and can only be spotted if set against other quatrains referring to the same persons or events. Thus CVI,Q49 contains the word 'Mammer' which needs to be compared to 'Mammel' (CX,Q44), both words for the River Niemen, which until 1772, the year Poland was partitioned, ran through the centre of that country. In addition to all this, sixteenth-century printing commonly substituted 'y' for 'i', 'u' for 'v' as in Latin script, and 'z' for 's' and vice versa. Sometimes too the letter 'h' might be added to or removed from a word, as in Hébreux/Ebreu (for Hebrew).

For general poetic reasons, and metrical requirements in particular, Nostradamus was obliged to shorten words by using grammatical devices – as in '*d'mour*' for '*Dumouriez*' (CX,Q46), modified by both syncope and apocope. Like Latin authors Nostradamus frequently omits the auxiliaries 'be' and 'have', which must be read in to restore the modern construction. Parodying Tacitus, he leaves out nouns like 'person' or active verbs like 'go', 'return', 'attack', etc., omissions the context alone clarifies. All this will give the reader some idea of the immense effort required to decipher quatrains which the prophet has almost completely codified by using Latin constructions, etymology, figures of speech and rhetoric, obscure topography, and anagrams, the latter sometimes in combination with the rhetorical figures.

Many have speculated about the following passage from the Letter to his son César: 'Fearing lest various books which have been hidden for centuries be discovered, and dreading what might happen to them, I presented them to Vulcan.' This has been taken to mean that Nostradamus had a secret library upon which he drew for his prophecies, taking all the credit without acknowledging his debt to the occultists, magi, astrologers or cabbalists who preceded him. My own studies lead me to a far less esoteric or mysterious conclusion, which will doubtless disappoint enthusiasts of the occult.

Indeed, as I went into the linguistic and historical aspects of Nostradamus' text, I became more and more convinced of one thing. We know that the sixteenth-century classical scholars were immensely learned, especially in languages and ancient history. The longer my researches progressed, the less likely it seemed that a single mind could contain such a store of knowledge. I could imagine Nostradamus in his study consulting many erudite literary, historical and geographical works to codify the vision which had just been vouchsafed him. I became even more convinced of this when I was confronted with the huge mass of documentation and cross-reference which I myself needed, first to understand the meaning of the quatrains, then to collate them with the historical events they were describing.

The books used by Nostradamus must have been the key to the Centuries; since he knew what would happen to his message if it were understood immediately, he destroyed these books, simultaneously hurling into the fire both the code and the key to the treasure chest his work represents. To break into this coffer, one must first assemble a very comprehensive toolkit drawn from a variety of different disciplines.

All fanciful notions and personal theories had to be dispensed with, along with imagination, 'that mistress of error and falsehood, all the more of a cheat because she is not so always', as Pascal wrote in his *Pensées*. Nostradamus offered the same advice, but it was hardly ever followed. To César he wrote: '. . . eschewing any fantastic imaginings, you may through good judgement have insight into the future if you keep to the specific place-names. . . .' This constitutes a true appeal to reason and objectivity.

In this book I have given exhaustive references for everything – quotations, definitions, extracts from history books – so that readers can check, verify or expand whatever historical point is being made by a quatrain or sixain. I have also repeated various definitions of recurrent words so that readers may gradually memorize some of them and so facilitate their reading, for I am well aware that such a work cannot be read like a novel.

Both with quatrains already authenticated by history and with those which will be verified by future events, I have abstained from speculating, offering opinions or otherwise commenting. I wanted my attitude towards the work of Nostradamus to differ from that of previous 'interpreters' and to respect the caveat he left César: 'But, my son, lest I venture too far for your future perception, be aware that men of letters shall make such grand, unusually boastful claims about the way in which I interpreted the world. . . .' Nostradamus unequivocally, not prophetically, stated that numerous books about his prophecies would ultimately turn out to be no more than 'grand, unusually boastful claims', proof of which is provided by the lengthy bibliography at the end of this book. So I trust readers will excuse my lack of theorizing, for I feel that far too much of this sort of thing has already harmed Nostradamus' work and detracted from its seriousness.

The commentators' numerous, often glaring, errors have been the result of scanty research and a lack of attention to minutiae, but above all to excess – whether of subjectivity or of political, philosophical or religious commitment.

While decoding quatrains particularly specific about place-names, I realized that commentators had systematically ignored many of them in order to preserve only the ones which accorded with, or showed off, their peculiar convictions: historical events had been twisted or even invented at will so as to fit in with their theories. I also discovered that quite a few of these books contained definitions of words or translations from Latin not to be found in any dictionary, which leads one to conclude that the so-called definitions had been created by translators bent on bestowing particular meanings upon one word or another. Then again, Nostradamus writes in his letter to César that he has set down his quatrains in no special order, so I often wonder how some interpreters, obviously thinking they were on the right track, have written books describing a grid system or some concealed numerical pattern – but which, on reading and examining their results, has still led them to a dead end.

As for astrology, why is it no professional astrologer ever manages to predict an important historical event? If the position of the stars in the sky determined the history of mankind, all such events would have been programmed long ago, day by day, month upon month, year after year. Hence we should have known by the position of the stars on 1 September 1939 that the Second World War would begin, or that on 13 May 1958 Algeria would experience a convulsion which would lead to independence. One understands Nostradamus' stern warning: 'Let all astrologers, fools and barbarians keep away from my work.' Astrology would thus remove from man his free will and make him a robot programmed for an endless succession of catastrophes. The prophet only sees in advance the behaviour of men writing their history themselves, with their own wills, decisions, and above all their complete, heavy and inalienable responsibilities.

What was the purpose of Nostradamus' prophecy? What were the areas, countries and historical changes into which Nostradamus 'received' detailed insights? This is probably the most vexed question as far as interpreters are concerned. British and American writers in particular have tried to find in the Centuries as many events as possible concerning the USA. It must be remembered that Nostradamus was French and a devout Catholic. The Church to which he belonged and refers in his work is his only allegiance and his message accordingly centres upon France, the history of the Catholic Church, and that of the papacy itself as the backbone of Western Christian civilization. And when we know that the end of Western civilization coincides with the end of the Roman Catholic Church and the destruction of Rome, we can understand why the countries Nostradamus refers to most are, in order of frequency, France, Italy and Spain, the three upholders of Catholicism.

This also explains why many writers, fired by a violently emotional agnosticism and unable to rise above such bias, could not acknowledge the profundity of Nostradamus' message. Perhaps too this is the reason for the consistent and recurrent blindness of American leaders to the dangers threatening Catholic Europe – with the exception, perhaps, of John F. Kennedy, the first Catholic President of the USA. Concerned as he was by the destruction of the Church, Nostradamus looked closely at the period from 1792, the year of the beginning of the end of Western civilization, until 1999, its actual end.

One can appreciate too why he devoted a great many quatrains to Napoleon I, judging him sternly for his struggle against the Catholic Church. The anti-clericalism of the eighteenth-century philosophers was put into practice by the revolutionaries and pursued by the child of the Revolution, Napoleon himself. It also explains why Napoleon III and Garibaldi, whose common battle with the papacy ended the pope's temporal power, are given considerable attention. For Nostradamus the history of Christian civilization is closely linked with that of the people of Israel, for Christianity began in Palestine. Thus everything that concerns the Moslem world, especially during the second half of the twentieth century, so interested Nostradamus that he devoted many texts to it. He refers to the Moslem world with a multiplicity of names and adjectives: Barbarians (because of the Barbary Coast), Arabs, Crescent, Ishmaelites, Moors, Lunars, Persians, Tunis, Algeria, Byzantium, Turkey, Morocco, Fez, Mahomet, Hannibal and Punic (because of the Carthaginians' hatred of Rome), Syria, Judea, Palestine, Hebron, Soliman and Mesopotamia (Iraq). These words appear in no fewer than 110 quatrains. Nostradamus simultaneously foresaw the defeat of the expansionist Ottoman Empire at Lepanto in 1571 and the revival of Moslem power in the second half of the twentieth century.

If Nostradamus included a significant number of particularly precise quatrains such as those mentioning Varennes (CIX,Q20), Buffalora (CVIII,Q12) and Magnavacca (CIX,Q3), it was so that on the day these texts were at last understood the value of his work would be acknowledged. This he also predicted in his Letter to César:

. . . and the reasons shall be universally understood throughout the earth. . . .
For God's mercy will only be poured forth for a certain time, my son, until the
majority of my prophecies are fulfilled and this fulfilment be complete . . .
despite their obscurities, these things shall be understood, but when ignorance
has been dispersed, the meaning will be clearer still.

Aix-en-Provence
June 1980

Abbreviations

AE	*ALPHA Encyclopédie*, 17 vols.
AVL	*Atlas Vidal-Lablache*.
AU	*Atlas Universalis*.
CUCD	*Chronologie Universelle*, Ch. Dreyss, Hachette, 1873.
DAFL	*Dictionnaire d'Ancien Français Larousse*.
DDP	*Dictionnaire des Papes*, Hans Kuhner, Buchet-Chastel, 1958.
DENF	*Dictionnaire étymologique des noms de famille*, Albert Dauzat, Librairie Larousse, 1951.
DGF	*Dictionnaire Grec-Français*, A. Chassang.
DH3	*Documents d'Histoire*, 3, Cours Chaulanges.
DH4	*Documents d'Histoire*, 4, Cours Chaulanges.
DHB	*Dictionnaire d'Histoire*, N. M. Bouillet, Hachette, 1880.
DHCD	*Dictionnaire d'Histoire*, Ch. Dezobry, 2 vols.
DL	*Dictionnaire Littré*, 4 vols.
DLLB	*Dictionnaire Latin*, Le Bègue.
DL7V	*Dictionnaire Larousse*, 7 vol.
DP	*Dictionnaire de la Provence et du Comté Venaissin*, Jean Mossy, Marseille, 1785.
DSGM	*Dictionnaire de la Seconde Guerre mondiale*, Jean Dumont, Historama, 1971.
DSH	*Dossiers secrets de l'Histoire*, A. Decaux, Librairie académique Perrin, 1966.
EU	*Encyclopaedia Universalis*, 20 vols.
GP & MR	*Garibaldi*, Paolo et Monika Romani, Les géants de l'Histoire, Fayolle, 1978.
HAB	*Hitler*, Alan Bullock, Marabout University, 1963.
HC4	*Histoire classe de 4ᵉ*, Fernand Nathan.
HDA	*Histoire de l'Allemagne*, André Maurois, Hachette, 1965.
HDCAE	'Histoire de Chypre', Achille Emilianides, *Que sais-je?* no. 1009.
HDGM	'Histoire de la Grèce moderne', Nicolas Svoronos. *Que sais-je?* no. 578.
HDMJG	'Histoire de Malte', Jacques Grodechot, *Que sais-je?* no. 509.
HDVFT	'Histoire de Venise', Freddy Thiriet, *Que sais-je?* no. 522.

HEFDP	*Histoire d'Espagne*, Fernando Diaz Plaja, France-Loisirs.
HFA	*Histoire de France*, Anquetil, Paris. 1829
HFACAD	*Histoire de France et des Français*, André Castelot et Alain Decaux, 13 vols, Plon et Librairie académique Perrin, 1972.
HFAM	*Histoire de France*, Albert Malet.
HFJB	*Histoire de France*, Jacques Bainville.
HFPG	*Histoire des Français*, Pierre Gaxotte.
HFVD	*Histoire de France*, Victor Duruy.
HRU	*Histoire du Royaume-Uni*, Coll. Armand Colin, 1967.
HISR	*Histoire de l'Italie, du Risorgimento à nos jours*, Sergio Romano, Coll. Point, Le Seuil, 1977.
HLFRA	*Histoire de la Libération de la France*, R. Aron, Fayard.
HSF	*Histoire de la Société Française*, L. Alphan et R. Doucet.
LCH3 et 4	*La Classe d'Histoire*, 3, 4.
LCI	*La campagne d'Italie*, Maréchal Juin, Ed. Guy Victor, 1962.
LDG	*La Dernière Guerre*, Éd. Alphée, Monaco.
LDR	*Le Dossier Romanov*, Anthony Summers, Tom Mangold, Albin Michel, 1980.
LFL XIV	*La France de Louis XIV*, Culture, Art, Loisirs.
LGESGM	*Les Grandes Enigmes de la Seconde Guerre mondiale*, Ed. St-Clair, Paris.
LGR	*Les Guerres de Religion*, Pierre Miquel, Fayard, 1980.
LGT	*La Grande Terreur*, Robert Conquest. Stock, 1970.
LMC	*Le Monde Contemporain*, Hatier.
LMSH	*Le Mémorial de Saint-Hélène*, Las Cases.
LRFPG	*La Révolution française*, Pierre Gaxotte, Fayard.
LSEOA	*Le Second Empire*, Octave Aubry, Fayard.
LTR	*Le Temps des Révolutions*, Louis Girard.
LXIVJR	*Louis XIV*, Jacques Roujon, Ed. du Livre Moderne, 1943.
MAB	*Mussolini, le Fascisme*, A. Brissaud, Cercle Européen du Livre, Robert Langeac, 1976.
MCH	*Mussolini*, Christopher Hibbert, R. Laffont, 1963.
MGR	*Mythologie grecque et romaine*, Classiques Garnier.
NEE	*Napoléon et l'Empire*, Hachette, 1968.
NELGI	*Napoléon et la Garde Impériale*, Commandant Henry Lachouque, Ed. Bloud et Gay.
NLM	*Napoléon*, Louis Madelin, Hachette.
PCHF	*Précis chronologique d'Histoire de France*, G. Dujarric, Albin Michel, 1977.
PGB	*Pétain*, Georges Blond, Presses de la Cité, 1966.
VCAHU	*Vingt-cinq ans d'Histoire Universelle*, Michel Mourre, Ed. Universitaires, 1971.

2
NOSTRADAMUS AS HISTORIAN

THE PREFATORY QUATRAINS

Estant assis de nuict secret[1] estude,
Seul, reposé sur la selle[2] d'aerain?
Flambe[3] exiguë sortant de sollitude,
Fait prospérer[4] qui n'est à croire vain.

CI,QI

Interpretation

At night, studying alone in a secluded place, and rested on a bronze chair, a small flame comes out of the solitude and brings things to pass [predictions] which should not be thought vain.

History

Some commentators have gone to great lengths to present Nostradamus as an 'initiate', working with some occultist group or sect. He denied this vehemently in his very first quatrain of the first century, twice repeating in two verses that he was inspired and worked alone in his study at Salon.

The bronze seat has been the subject of many rather fantastic and esoteric interpretations. Without falling over backwards to prove anything, it seems more obvious [knowing Nostradamus' preoccupation with obscure imagery. Tr.] to find parallels in Christian symbolism and opt for 'mortification of the flesh'. By sitting on a hard seat and working by night Nostradamus could both fight off drowsiness and keep the spirit pure and receptive. The little flame resembles the one which descended on the Apostles' heads at Pentecost, symbolizing the Holy Spirit and thus divine inspiration.

[1] Latin *secretum*: secluded spot, retreat. DLLB.
[2] Latin *sella*: seat, chair. DLLB.
[3] Old French *flamme*. DAFL.
[4] Latin *prospero*: I make succeed, favour. DLLB.

La verge[1] en mains mise au milieu de Branches,[2]
De l'onde[3] il moulle[4] et le limbe[5] et le pied,
Un peur[6] et voix fremissent par les manches,[7]
Splendeur divine le divin près s'assied.

CI,Q2

Interpretation

The magic wand [or his doctor's symbol, the caduceus of Mercury], placed in the hands of him who has the gift of prophecy. With a wave [of words] he shapes the fringes and feet [of his verses]; which makes the weak tremble with fear for divine splendour, divinity itself, sits beside him.

This quatrain too has prompted magical or hermetic interpretation, even though it follows on from the first quatrain in explaining the whys and wherefores of the ensuing prophecies. So that the reader does not dwell under any scurrilous misapprehensions as to his inspiration, Nostradamus (as in the preceding quatrain) twice repeats the most important word – divine – thus reaffirming what he wrote on the subject in his Letter to César.

[1] Latin *virga*: thin branch, magic wand, but also caduceus. DLLB.
[2] Branchus, priest of Apollo, who received from the latter the gift of prophecy. DLLB.
[3] Latin *unda*: water movement, wave. DLLB.
[4] Latin *mollire*: *modeler* or *modles* (old French) = to mould, model. DLLB.
[5] Latin *limbus*: fringe, border, edging. DLLB.
[6] Latin *pavor* (noun, m.): fear, fright. DLLB.
[7] Old French: weak, feeble-minded.

Legis Cautio Contra Ineptos Criticos[1]
(Precautionary Words against Foolish Critics)

Qui legent hosce versus nature censunto:
Prophanum vulgus et inscium ne attrectato:
Omnesque Astrologi, Blenni, Barbari procul sunto,
Qui aliter faxit, is, rite sacer esto.

Interpretation

Let those who read these verses judge them naturally:
Let the vulgar and stupid rabble not approach them:
And let all Astrologers, fools and barbarians keep away;
May whoever does otherwise be justly accursed.

Here we have a series of emphatic warnings, especially those concerning astrologers – classed here with fools and barbarians. It might be considered at variance with what Nostradamus wrote in his Letter to César when he said he had practised official astrology, but there is nothing contradictory here, for astrology in the sixteenth century was simply the study of the stars, and hence a synonym for astronomy. In the twentieth century, however, these two words define very different disciplines: it is thus clear that Nostradamus was addressing modern astrologers. This can be exemplified by citing a book written in 1938 by an 'eminent' astrologer applying his knowledge to Nostradamus: Maurice Privat's *1940 World Predictions, Year of French Glory*, which appeared some months after my father's book predicting the war with Germany.

---

[1] The only quatrain in Latin. Unnumbered, it is placed between CVI,Q100 and CVII,Q1, i.e. exactly in the middle of the twelve Centuries.

The Duke of Alba's Revolt Against
Pope Paul IV, 1557.
The War between
the Dukes of Alba and Guise, 1557

Le grand Duc d'Albe se viendra rebeller,[1]
A ses grandes pères fera le tradiment:[2]
Le grand de Guise le viendra debeller,[3]
Captif mené et dressé monnument.[4]

CVII,Q29

Interpretation

The great Duke of Alba will rebel and betray the fathers [of the Church] and will end the war with a victory over the Duke of Guise, prisoners being taken. He will be remembered.

History

'Paul IV intercepted letters from the Spanish minister to his court which informed the Duke of Alba of armed retainers kept by certain Roman noblemen, together with details of their possible disaffection or rebellion, in order that they might be taken over by him. Learning this, the Pope not only ruined some and excommunicated others but even had one of the Spanish envoys arrested. The Duke asked in vain for his release and suggested peace negotiations: the Pope was deaf to all such propositions. The Duke then ordered his troops to invade Church territory and seize a number of towns in the name of the Holy See and the future Pope. The Pope was already in dire need of French aid. The French Council's decision soon restored all his pride and he issued a fiery pronouncement that declared King Philip of Spain to be a rebel against his sovereign, and, this being so, he was relieved of his kingdom of Naples. Philip took every step to precipitate war with France. The exchange of prisoners, which had prompted the truce, was daily postponed. The Duke of Guise, at the head of an army, rapidly crossed the mountains and, hurrying towards Naples, got as far as Milan. The Vice-Regent, the Duke of Alba, did not have enough troops to match such a powerful army and was at first in difficulties. The Duke of Guise made no progress; the land army weakened itself by marches and counter-marches in order to tempt Alba to battle. The latter had grasped that he only had to remain on the defensive in order to wear down an enemy attempting an invasion. He could not be drawn from his tactics, and all the *honours* [*dressé monument*] of the campaign were his.'5

---

[1] Latin *rebello*: I revolt, rise up, begin fighting again. DLLB.
[2] Latin *trado*: I betray. DLLB.
[3] Latin *debello*: I end the war through a victory. DLLB.
[4] Latin *monumentum*: anything that recalls a memory. DLLB.
[5] HFA.

The Death of Henri II, 10 July 1559

Le Lyon jeune le vieux surmontera,
En champ bellique[1] par singulier duelle,
Dans cage d'or les yeux lui crèvera,
deux classes[2] une puis mourir mort cruelle.

CI,Q35

Interpretation

The young lion will triumph over the old, jousting in the lists. His eyes inside his golden helmet will be put out, in one of the two combats; then he will die a cruel death.

History

'The third tourney is due to begin. The king is mounted on a steed belonging to Emmanuel-Philibert. Delighted by this spirited horse, he tells his brother-in-law so, but the latter asks him, on the Queen's behalf, "to toil no more", since it is already "late, and the weather exceeding hot". In fact it is just twelve noon, but Henri replies that he is *champion*, and because of this, as is the custom, he must joust thrice. His opponent is already in the saddle. It is Gabriel de Lorges, Comte de Montgoméry, Captain of the Scottish Guard. "Trumpets and bugles sound deafening fanfares." Then the two men take up positions and charge. The shock is fearful and both lances shatter, but neither combatant falls to the ground. The King could now stop, but wishes to tilt again [*deux classes une*]. "Sire," begs Vieilleville, "I swear by Almighty God that for more than three nights running I have dreamed that some misfortune will befall you today and that the end of June would be fatal for you. Make of this what you please." Montgoméry also argues for stopping the tournament, but the King wishes to continue. The champion and the challenger rush towards each other. Again the collision is frightful and both lances break, and riders and steeds have difficulty recovering their balance. Reaching the end of the lists, the two combatants execute a half-turn. Henri II takes a new lance but Montgoméry forgets to throw down the stump he still holds. Contrary to convention – no one knows why – the trumpets are silent. The mailclad horsemen set off again at full gallop and there is a deafening noise of clanging, clattering steel and hooves pounding the raked sand of the track. The spectators gasp, seeing that the Captain of the Scottish Guard has not flung aside his broken weapon but is still levelling it. The two men clash yet again and

Montgoméry's fragment of lance slips off the King's cuirass, lifting *the visor of the helmet* and piercing the King's head. The King is borne to Tournelles. His wound is appalling: the lance has entered his right *eye* and emerged through the ear. While the King lay in *agony* [*mort cruelle*], Diane remained cloistered at home. On the morning of 10 July, the King died.'[3]

[1] *champ bellique*: the lists, palisade enclosing the area marked out for the jousting. DAFL.
[2] Latin *classis*: army, fleet, combat; *classe depugnare*: to surrender a battle. DLLB.
[3] HFACAD.

The Conspiracy of Amboise, March 1560

Un coronel[1] machine[2] ambition[3]
Se saisira de la plus grande armée:
Contre son prince feinte invention
Et descouvert sera sous la ramée.[4]

CIV,Q62

Interpretation

Intrigues with a view to seizing the crown result in the seizure of the main armed forces of the country. A trick will be contrived against the King, which will be discovered under the branches.

History

'The Protestants *plotted to abduct* the King from the castle of Amboise to remove him from the influence of the Guises. An obscure person called La Renaudie was the nominal arch-conspirator, but its real, secret organizer was the Prince of Condé. But the Conspiracy of Amboise was discovered: *surprised in the neighbouring forests* [*sous la ramée*], the plotters were drowned, decapitated, and hanged from the castle battlements.'[5]

'Once the first angry realization was over, it was hoped to lend an air of justice to the previous executions by legally sentencing some of the chief conspirators. One of the leading lights was Castelnau who had surrendered to Jacques de Savoie, the Duke of Nemours, whose superior forces had surrounded him in the castle of Noizai, *the army depot* of the plotters, and had parleyed with him. Nemours swore to give him safe conduct, and Castelnau followed him, but no sooner was he at Amboise than he was put in chains.'[6]

[1] Latin *coronalis*: of the crown. DLLB.
[2] Latin *machina*: (figurative) artifice, intrigue, ruse. DLLB.
[3] Latin *ambitio*: cabal, intrigues. DLLB.
[4] Latin *rami*: branches. DAFL.
[5] HFAM.
[6] HFA.

The Guise War, 1560. The Condé War, 1562

Guerres, débats,[1] à Blois guerre et tumulte,
Divers aguets,[2] adveux inopinables:[3]
Entrer dedans Chasteau Trompette,[4] insulte,[5]
Chasteau du Ha,[6] qui en seront coupables.

CXII,Q52

Interpretation

There will be wars and debates [parliaments] at Blois, as well as up-heavals, ambushes and incredible confessions. The *Chasteau Trompette* [Trumpet Castle] will be attacked by those seeking entry, but the guilty ones will be imprisoned.

History

'To obtain Calvin's absolution, it was necessary to rally the royal princes. They were wary of taking sides, but clandestinely supported the opposition who thus appeared to be *conspirators*. Condé, who had least to lose, was boldest. Bourbon made no move. At last a gentleman in reduced circumstances, La Renaudie, was found to head a strong *conspiracy* that intended to accuse the Guises of peculation and lèse-majesté! Condé agreed to head the whole affair. When La Renaudie sent messengers into the provinces urging the King's supporters to rise and put a stop to the evil politicking of the Guises, thousands of men went on the march. In February 1560, an *immense tumult* occurred at the mouth of the Loire. The court, then at *Blois*, thought it safest to take refuge immediately in the castle of Amboise.

Condé, however, was recruiting troops. The coast was clear: Bourbon was Catherine's hostage. In the provinces the Huguenots mobilized and the uprising was general. But Condé hesitated at Paris. He was caught unawares by Guise, who had left the castle of Fontainebleau and led the King and Queen back to Paris. Condé believed that they were prisoners and said so. Yet Catherine continued to issue declarations favouring the Guises and denouncing the Huguenot plotters. The Guises must have let her do so: she assumed leadership of their party. From Meaux, Condé took Orleans, which he "liberated" with a handful of mounted troops. The whole of the Loire Valley fell into his hands. Towns surrendered to him, enthusiastically organizing reformed *assemblies* [*débats*], which were particularly well attended at Tours, *Blois* and Angers. This was a sort of revenge for the failed *tumult* or civil commotion. Since early April men had taken up arms throughout the provinces as if a fuse had been lit. In 1562 Duras failed to seize *Château Trompette*, on Condé's orders. Montluc had driven him out of the town. After this intervention the magistrates or "aldermen" *promised* "to spare neither their possessions nor their lives in the King's service and that of the righteous, ancient, Catholic and Roman religion". The persecution had disposed of the most prominent Calvinists. The rest lay low or returned to Catholicism."[7]

[1] The Parliament of Blois, 1576, was a triumph for the League. Its members asserted the state's rights to administer matters of public welfare and voted to continue *the struggle* against the Protestants. The second Parliament of Blois, 1588, was just as successful for the League's members, who were by then even more *violent* then in 1576. DL7V.

[2] Ambush.

[3] Latin *inopinabilis*: inconceivable, incredible, DLLB.

[4] Famous fortress in Bordeaux, beside the Garonne, demolished in 1785. DL7V.

[5] Latin *insulto*: I attack, defy. DLLB.

[6] Ha = Ham: chief town of the canton of the Somme, another famous fortress, built in 1470, and which served as *state prison*. DHB. Example of apocope.

[7] LGR.

The King of Navarre, Antoine of Bourbon, Surrenders to the Triumvirate, 1561. His Death at the Siege of Rouen, 1562

Le grand Antoine[1] du nom de faict sordide,
De Phtyriase[2] à son dernier rongé:
Un qui de plomb[3] voudra estre cupide.
Passant le port d'esleu sera plongé.

                                          CIV,Q88

Interpretation

Great Antoine of the name [Bourbon] will give in/surrender to a sordid
act. On his last [day] he will be gnawed by vermin, because he will be
one who is greedy for lead; in the port he will be casually plunged [into
the grave] by those who have chosen him.

History

'To keep the King of Navarre on the side of the Triumvirate, the King
of Spain, by way of indemnity for the part of Navarre he still retained,
promised him the Kingdom of *Sardinia*. The most enticing and flattering
descriptions of this island's fertility, *seaports* and towns were circulated.
The weak *Antoine* was led to think that this was the only way to wrest
from Spain lands equivalent to those which Spain was keeping and that
if he sided with the Protestants he would never become rich. These
considerations made up his mind for him: he openly allied with the
Guises, coming out clearly in favour of the Catholics. He also broke with
the Calvinists.

The siege of Rouen[4] is remembered for the death of the King of
Navarre. He was wounded during it, and the surgeons were not at first
unduly concerned, but in a few days his wound took him to his grave.
He *sank into* it, along with the seductive promises that the King of Spain
had given him – the possession of Sardinia, and the thought of the
pleasant life he had counted upon leading on that island.'[5]

[1] Antoine of Bourbon, King of Navarre, Duke of Vendôme, b. 1518, became King of
Navarre through his marriage to Jeanne d'Albret. Heading the Catholic army, he had to
fight his own brother, Condé, who led the Protestants. Born a Protestant, he incurred their
hatred by abandoning them, and was scarcely mourned even by the Catholics. DHB.

[2] Pediculosis, lice. DL7V.

[3] Sardinia: rich in minerals, mines sunk by the Romans yielded *lead*, silver, zinc and
iron. DL7V.

[4] Rouen: *port* on the Seine, 120 km from the sea.

[5] HFA.

The Death of Nostradamus, 2 July 1566

De retour d'Ambassade, don de Roy mis au lieu
Plus n'en fera: sera allé à Dieu
Parans plus proches, amis, frères du sang,
Trouvé tout mort près du lict et du banc.

Presage 141

Interpretation

Having returned from a visit and placed the gift given him by the King in safe keeping, he will do no more, being dead. With his family, kin and friends nearby, he will be found dead near his bed and by the bench.

History

This famous quatrain foretelling his own death is quoted by most commentators. In 1564 Nostradamus visited Charles IX, who gave him 300 gold crowns. His friends and family found him dead beside the bed, near the bench on which he usually sat. His work was done.

The quatrain is the last in Nostradamus' work, since it is followed by the 58 sixains which conclude it. In his letter to his son, on page xxiv of this book, Nostradamus was already talking of his own death.

The Siege of Malta by the Turks, 1565.
Maltese Participation in the Battle of Lepanto, 1571.
The Christian Fleet Reunited at Messina,
24 August 1571

> La pille faite à la coste marine,
> Incita[1] nova[2] et parens amenez:
> Plusieurs de Malte par le fait de Messine,
> Estoit serrez seront mel[3] guerdonnez.[4]

CIX,Q61

Interpretation

Pillage around the sea coasts, new raids and the abduction of families will cause several men of Malta to take part in the fighting at Messina. Those besieged will be rewarded with sweetness.

History

'In 1565, there could be no more doubt that old Suliman II was arming impressively at Constantinople. His objective remained a mystery, but *Malta* seemed most likely. At dawn on 18 May, lookouts spotted 38 Turkish galleys on the horizon. They were carrying an invasion force of more than 38,000 men and 50 cannon, under the command of Mustapha

Pasha. At last on 26 August the relief expedition left Syracuse. Without tempting providence further, the Turks re-embarked. On 12 September, the last Moslem vessels left Maltese waters. The great *siege* [*serrez*] was lifted. It had seemed that on Malta's fate hung that of the entire West. The victory at Malta marks the beginning of the decline of Turkish maritime power. This was not clear immediately, and during the succeeding years another Moslem offensive was still feared. But six years after the siege of Malta, the great victory of Lepanto, in the Gulf of Corinth, won by the Holy League assisted by four galleys of the *Maltese Order*, showed spectacularly that the Turks had lost control of the Mediterranean. There were 230 Turkish vessels captured or sunk; 30,000 killed or wounded; 3000 prisoners; 15,000 Christian slaves freed [*parens amenez*]. It was decided to build a new town surrounded by huge fortifications. All the Catholic sovereigns sent *gifts*, with the King of France subscribing the most – 140,000 livres [*mel guerdonnez*]).'[5]

'The Battle of Lepanto: the entire nobility of Italy and Spain flocked to the banner of Don John of Austria. The rendezvous was agreed – *Messina*. From Genoa 25 galleys raised anchor, commanded by the most illustrious nobles. Don John arrived at *Messina* on 24 August with 90 Spanish galleons and left on 16 September. He wrote to the King that he had decided to search for the Turkish fleet.'[6]

[1] Latin *incitus*: hurried, impetuous, violent. DLLB.
[2] Latin *novus*: new. DLLB.
[3] Latin *mel*: honey, sweet thing. DLLB.
[4] To recompense, reward. DAFL.
[5] HDMJG.
[6] 'Lepanto, a battle of the giants, to save the West.' André Thévenet in *Historama*.

The Capture and Sack of Cyprus by the Turks, 1571

Assault farouche en Cypre se prépare,
La larme à l'oeil,[1] de ta ruine proche:
Bysance classe, Morisque si grand tare;
Deux différents le grand vast par la roche.

CXII,Q36

Interpretation

A savage attack is being directed against Cyprus, which begins to bewail its impending fate – sacking by the Turkish fleet. Islam will wreak havoc and two different [armies] will lay waste these rocky places.

History

'The growing power of Turkey alarmed the Venetian Republic, which in order to keep its territories wanted to preserve the strictest neutrality. But it was impossible. In 1566 the Turks occupied the island of Chios; in 1567 they seized Naxos. Sultan Selim II grew more and more arrogant towards the Venetians, *no longer concealing his intention of occupying Cyprus*. In 1570 he sent an ambassador to Venice demanding the surrender of Cyprus for reasons of security and its nearness to Turkey. The Venetian Senate scornfully rejected this demand and instructed the ambassador that Venice intended keeping Cyprus at all costs. Hostilities commenced. The Sultan ordered Lala Mustafa, his army commander, to prepare *an expedition against Cyprus*. Several months later, on 1 July 1570, the *Turkish fleet* disembarked at the port of Larnaca and occupied it without resistance. But the Venetians concentrated their forces on defending Nicosia, the capital, and Famagusta, the main port.

Despite continuous attacks the Turks did not succeed in defeating the Venetians, so they proposed that their adversaries should voluntarily surrender the town: the defenders at once rejected this suggestion. The besiegers then renewed their attacks, reinforced by Piali Pasha's recently disembarked army. In early September the Venetians' position became more desperate, and Nicosia capitulated on the ninth. The crescent flag waved above the ramparts. For three days *there was total carnage, and all the Christians were massacred* and the Cathedral of St Sophia was turned into a mosque.

In April 1571 Mustafa, whose army had been reinforced by troops newly arrived from Syria and Asia Minor [*two different*], laid siege to the last Venetian fortress on Cyprus. In the besieged town Bragadino, its brave commander, and his 7000 defenders fought to the bitter end.

By early August they surrendered Famagusta honourably, on conditions that Mustafa had accepted. But Mustafa did not keep his promise: he arrested Bragadino, put him in irons, forced him to watch his companions being tortured, and finally flayed him alive.'[2]

---

[1] To have tears in one's eyes, be about to weep. DL7V.
[2] HDCAE.

The Battle of Lepanto, 7 October 1571

Le chef[1] de Perse remplira grands Olchades[2]
Classe trirème[3] contre gent mahométique
De Parthe et Mede,[4] et piller les Cyclades[5]
Repos longtemps au grand port Ionique.[6]

CIII,Q64

Interpretation

The Persian *Shah* will fill up great ships, whereupon a Roman fleet will
sail against the Moslems because of him who will resemble a Parthian or
Mede, in order to pillage the Cyclades; all this will ensure peace for a
long time in Ionia.

History

'In the Gulf of Lepanto in 1571 a great sea battle took place, when the
combined fleets of Venice, Spain and the Papacy, under Don John of
Austria, defeated the Turks, who lost 200 galleys and 30,000 men, and
because of this defeat had to *halt their invasion.*

Selim II, the Ottoman Sultan (1566–74), nicknamed the Drunkard,
succeeded his father Suliman II, captured Cyprus from the Venetians,
lost the Battle of Lepanto the same year and died of *dissipation.* He was
the first of a series of effeminate and ignoble sultans. . . .

The pride, cruelty and capriciousness of the Parthians were proverbial.
The King and nobility quickly adopted the ostentation, *vices and corruption*
of oriental monarchs. . . .

The weakness of the Medes' princes encouraged insurrections.'[7]

[1] *Shah*: Persian = king, sovereign. DL7V.
[2] Ὀλκας/αδος: transport vessel and by extension any ship.
[3] Trireme: three-decker rowed warship, adopted by the Greeks. The Romans adapted
this form of galley, giving it the name of *trireme.*
[4] Parthia, Medea and Persia were provinces of the Persian Empire which extended as
far west as Turkey.
[5] Aegean islands.
[6] Ionia: an area of Asia Minor comprising roughly the Aegean coastline between the
Gulf of Smyrna to the north and the Gulf of Mendelia to the south.
[7] DHCD.

Don John of Austria
Commands the Christian Fleet at Lepanto, 1571.
Rebellion in the Low Countries, 1578

Le grand Pilot sera par Roy mandé,
Laisser la classe pour plus haut lieu attaindre:
Sept ans après sera contrebandé,
Barbare armée viendra Venise craindre.

CVI,Q75

Interpretation

The great leader of the fleet will be named by the King. He will leave
to make for a more northerly place. Seven years later he will fight against
the rebels [*contre des bandes*]. The Moslem army will need to fear Venice.

History

'The Holy League, formed on Pope Pius V's initiative, with *Venice* and
Spain, avenged the disaster of Cyprus, which fell to the Turks on 1
August 1571. Don John of *Austria* and Sebastian Venier fully succeeded
in blocking the Turkish fleets from the western approaches and destroy-
ing the Turks at Lepanto (7 October 1571).'[1]
  '*Philip II*, son and successor of Charles V of Spain, in 1570 delegated
Don John of Austria, Charles V's natural son [*sera par Roy mandé*] to
suppress a revolt by the Moors in Granada. Chosen in 1571 by the
Christian princes to command *the fleet* [*le grand Pilot*] they were sending
against the Turks, he won the famous victory of Lepanto. In 1573 he
seized Tunis, but lost it again the following year. In 1576 he was sent by
Philip II to the rebellious Low Countries [*plus haut lieu*] and defeated
the rebels at Gembloux [January 1578].[2] He died of a malignant fever a
few months later near Namur.'[3]

[1] HDVFT.
[2] 1571–78 = 7 years.
[3] DHB.

The Massacre of St Bartholomew, 24 August 1572

La grand Cité qui n'a pain qu'à demy
Encore un coup la Sainct Barthelemy
Engravera au profond de son âme
Nismes, Rochelle, Genève et Montpellier
Castres, Lyon; Mars[1] entrant au Bélier,[2]
S'entrebatront le tout pour une dame.

Sixain 52

Interpretation

Paris, suffering from hardship, will at the second toll [of the bell] record St Bartholomew in her history. Nîmes, La Rochelle, Geneva, Montpellier, Castres and Lyon will be the scenes of battles because of a woman, war [of religion] breaking out [at the sound of] the bell.

History

'Civil War enriches only the foreigner. Charles IX and his mother, short of funds, had already enlisted the aid of the King of Spain and the Duke of Savoy.'[3]

'Reconciliation seemed to have been agreed between the two parties. Protestant gentlefolk came to court in great numbers. Charles IX appointed Admiral Coligny to his Council. This favour shown Coligny proved fatal to the Protestants. *Catherine de Médicis*, whose influence was waning, feared loss of power. She had just signed in 1570 an edict similar to the Edict of Amboise whereby the Protestants were granted *four places of safety* where they could establish garrisons. She agreed with Henri, Duke of Guise to get rid of Coligny by murdering him. She then plotted with Guise to arrange a general massacre of Protestant leaders.'[4]

'The bell tower of St-Germain l'Auxerrois was to give the signal, at 3 a.m. on 24 August. It was not necessary to wait that long. *At two o'clock* [*encore un coup*] *the bell* began ringing and soon afterwards the tocsin *sounded* in reply from every church.'[4]

'The example set by Paris was followed in *many towns*. The total number of victims was about 8000.'[5]

---

[1] God of war, symbol of strife and massacre.
[2] Small bell (because the ram, leader of the herd, carries around its neck the bell that *rallies* its members). DL7V.
[3] HFPG.
[4] HFAM.
[5] HFVD.

The Massacre of St Bartholomew's Day.
Coligny's Assassination, 24 August 1572.
The Defender of St Quentin, 1557

La grand Cité d'assaut prompt et repentin[1]
Surprins de nuict, gardes interrompus:[2]
Les excubies[3] et veilles Sainct Quintin
Trucidez[4] gardes et les portails rompus.

CIV,Q8

Interpretation

Paris will be surprised by night. There will be a rapid unexpected attack, the guards having been silenced and the city gates broken open.

History

'Two things make his [Coligny's] name famous forever: his first action – *the defence of St-Quentin*. . . .

St Bartholomew's Day: Paris was ready. The merchant provost, instructed by the Louvre, received the King's order *to close the gates*. The bell of St-Germain l'Auxerrois was to give the signal at three o'clock during the night of 24 August, St Bartholomew's Day. A German, Besme, was the first to enter the room [and] plunged his sword into Coligny's chest. . . .

Philibert-Emmanuel, Duke of Savoy, suddenly fell upon *St-Quentin*, where 7000 English joined up with him. Admiral Coligny resisted with 700 men. Philibert-Emmanuel attacked him and was utterly defeated . . . more than *10,000 dead or injured* [10 August 1557].'[5]

'Coligny dug in at St-Quentin, besieged by the Spaniards, and his brave defence gave the French time to take up arms.'[6]

[1] Latin *repentinus*: sudden, unexpected. DLLB.
[2] Latin *interrumpere*: intercept. DLLB.
[3] Latin *excubiae*: guards, factions.
[4] Latin *trucidare*: massacre, butcher.
[5] HFVD.
[6] DL7V.

Assassination of Admiral Coligny, 24 August 1572

Celui qu'en luitte et fer au fait bellique
Aura porté plus grand que lui le pris:
De nuict dans lict six lui feront la picque,
Nud sans harnois[1] subit sera surpris.

CIII,Q30

Interpretation

He who has fought in the war and has supported someone greater than himself shall be taken. By night six persons shall stab him in his bed, and he shall be taken by surprise, naked and unprotected.

History

'Gaspard de Châtillon, lord of Coligny, admiral of France, after distinguishing himself in *several campaigns* was in 1552 made colonel-general and admiral by Henri II. He played a part in winning the *Battle* of Renty, defending St-Quentin against the Spanish. After the Treaty of St-Germain in 1570 he reappeared at court and was welcomed and flattered like all those of his party. But the Massacre of St Bartholomew was being arranged and the Admiral was one of its first victims.'[2]

'The vindictive Guise scarcely waited for the signal to go to the Admiral's house. Three colonels from the French army, together with Petrucci, from Sienna and Besme, a German, charged up the staircase. Besme plunged his sword into the Admiral's body: scores of blows followed and the Admiral fell, drenched in his own blood. At the frightful cries and yells which broke out on all sides as soon as the bell tolled, the Calvinists rushed *half naked* from their houses, still half asleep and unarmed.'[3]

---

[1] Military term: armour worn by most military men from the fifteenth to the seventeenth centuries. It was still worn in Charles IX's day and even in Henri III's – the *Huguenots* had worn it at the Battle of Coutras.
[2] DHB.
[3] HFA.

The Struggle between Henri III
and the Duke of Alençon, 1574–75

Des sept rameaux à trois seront reduicts,
Les plus aisnez seront surprins par morts,
Fratricider les deux seront séduicts,
Les conjurez en dormant[1] seront morts.

                                        CVI,QII

Interpretation

There will be only three of the seven branches [offspring] left. The eldest
being dead, two [of the three] will engage in fratricidal combat; the
plotters will die, ineffectual or inactive.

History

Deaths of the four eldest children of Henri II: François II [d. 1560];
Elisabeth [d. 1568]; Claude [d. 1573]; Charles IX [d. 1574]. So there
remained in 1574 three children: Henri III, Marguerite [Queen Margot],
and the Duke of Alençon.

'Apart from the Catholic nobility and the fanatical Protestants, there
emerged a new party, that of the "Politicals". The King's brother, the
Duke of Alençon, was its leader. The new King was angered by his
brother's intrigues and *thought of killing him.* . . .
   At the critical moment, d'Alençon unmasked everything.'[2]
   'La Mole, d'Alençon's favourite, and the Piedmontese Count Cocon-
asso, another friend of the Duke's, were *condemned to death and executed*.'[3]

----

[1] *Latin*: (figurative) to be inactive, idle.
[2] HFVD.
[3] DL7V.

The Fifth War of Religion, 1574–76

Deux Royals frères si fort guerroyeront,
Qu'entre eux sera la guerre si mortelle,
Qu'un chacun places fortes occuperont,
De règne[1] et vie sera leur grand querelle.

                                        CIII,Q98

Interpretation

Two brothers of royal blood will wage war upon each other, with the result that both die. They are both in strong positions and will quarrel over power and life.

History

'The last son of Henri III, Henri Duke of Anjou, succeeded to the Crown. With such a king the kingdom soon lapsed into anarchy. The Huguenots began the *war* again from 1574; this time their allies were a group of titled Catholics, who supported religious tolerance, and were headed by the younger *brother* of Henry III, Alençon. This group was called "the politicals" or "the malcontents". With 30,000 men the Protestants and malcontents marched upon Paris and forced Henri III to sign the Edict of Beaulieu [1576].'[2]

'The Duke of Anjou, put in command of the Loire army, rested on his laurels after the capture of La Charité and Issoire. Henri III took advantage of these paltry successes to conclude the Peace of Bergerac, which allowed the Protestants eight *places of safety*.'[3]

[1] Latin *regnum*: monarchic government, absolute power. DLLB.
[2] HFAM.
[3] HFVD.

The Origins of the League.
The Assassination of the Duke of Guise –
23 December 1588

Paris conjure[1] un grand meurtre commettre
Blois le fera sortir en plein effect:
Ceux d'Orléans[2] voudront leur chef remettre,
Angiers, Troyes, Langres, leur feront grand forfait.

CIII,Q51

Interpretation

At Paris, a plot is hatched to commit a notorious murder which will take place at Blois; those who will hold Orleans [the Protestants] will want to restore their leader to the throne, [the Leaguers of] Angers, Troyes and Langres will make them pay dearly.

History

The League was a Catholic association formed in France by Henri, Duke
of Guise in 1568. Its aim was the defence of the Catholic religion against
the Huguenots. There had been founded, though, since the beginning
of the religious conflict, local unions of defence against the Reformation
[1563 at Toulouse, 1565 at *Angers*, 1567 at Dijon, 1568 at *Troyes*, etc].
From the start Henri III had proclaimed himself head of the League,
but it was the Duke of Guise, known as Scarface, who almost immediately took control, using it to aid his *schemes* for taking over the throne
himself, especially after the death of the heir presumptive, the Duke of
Anjou, who *promised this royal succession to the King of Navarre* [the future
Henri IV]. The Day of the Barricades failed to achieve a change of
dynasty. The coup failed because of a lack of determination by Guise;
but the King, chased from his capital, could only resort to *assassinating*
this formidable *troublemaker* and his cardinal brother [at the States General at Blois, 1588] as a remedy for the increasing unrest.

[1] To conspire, plot. DL7V.

[2] Henri I of Lorraine, Duke of Guise, Scarface, elder son of François de Guise, b.
1550, witnessed the murder of his father on the walls of *Orleans*, and from that moment
vowed vengeance and hatred against the Protestants. He it was who started the *Massacre
of St Bartholomew* by ordering the murder of the Admiral [1572].

Henri III and the Murder of Henri of Guise, 23 December 1588

> En l'an qu'un oeil[1] en France régnera,
> La Cour sera en un bien fascheux trouble,
> Le Grand de Bloys son amy tuera,
> Le regne mis en mal et doubte double.

CIII,Q55

Interpretation

In the year when power is shared in France the court will be in great
embarrassment and difficulty; the King will kill his friend at Blois, and
power will be disputed because of a double doubt.

History

'The *de facto* head of the League, Henri of Guise, set his *sights* higher.
For him the League was the stepping stone to the throne. But the King's

conduct spoiled his best efforts and satirical pamphlets exposed the corruption of that amoral and vicious court where murder and licence were the order of the day. The States General assembled in Blois on 6 December 1576 and showed Henri III the extent of the danger. Strangely in these appalling times some important legislative reforms were accomplished. The Statute of Blois [1579] laid down some liberal civil rights measures. . . .

The death of the Duke of Anjou, brother and heir to Henri III, had inflamed religious and political feeling yet again. Until then it was almost unimaginable that a Bourbon and apostate might become the heir of the Valois; but now this danger existed, since Henri III, the last surviving son of Henri II, *had no descendants.* . . .

Killing Guise did not kill off the League, however. Paris was momentarily stunned at the news of his death, then the city *erupted in anger.* The Sorbonne decreed that the French people were released from their oath of allegiance to Henri III. It was difficult to shake *the loyalty of Parliament to the monarch, though, and so there was a purge.* . . .

Henri III was no better off as a result of the violence at *Blois*, but he had saved the fortune of the King of Navarre, to whom he now had to resort. Before the final tragedy the Béarnais [Henry IV's nickname] had been in *dire straits.*'[2]

[1] Power, as in 'keeping an eye on' or 'under his master's eye'.
[2] HFVD.

The Assassination of Henri III, 2 August 1589, and of the Guises, 23 and 24 December 1588

> Les sept enfants[1] en hostage laissez
> Le tiers[2] viendra son enfant trucider,
> Deux par son fils seront d'estoc[3] percez,
> Gennes, Florence viendra enconder.[4]
>
> CIV,Q60

Interpretation

The seven children left as hostages [by Henri II], someone from the Third Order will come and kill his child [Henri III]. Two [persons] will be pierced by swordthrusts by his son [Henri II's, i.e. Henri III], the towns near Genoa and Florence will no longer be preserved.

History

'When Mary Stuart appeared at the ceremony of her husband Francis II's coronation wearing the jewels taken from Diane, it was a sign that for a long time the real sovereign had been Catherine de Médicis.'[5]

'The morning before, a young friar from the *Dominican* monastery, Jacques Clément, left Paris and made for St-Cloud. Led to the King, the assassin pulled a knife from his sleeve and thrust it into his abdomen.'[5]

'Henri III's first actions showed what might be expected of him. At Turin he repaid the hospitality of the Duke of Savoy with prodigal generosity, returning to him the towns of *Pignerol and Savigliano* [near Genoa] and *Perugia* [near Florence].'[5]

'Henri distributed their daggers. One of the forty-five seized Guise's shoulder and sank his *poniard* into his breast. Then all the daggers were immediately drawn. The Cardinal cried out on hearing the noise, "They're killing my brother." Marshal d'Aumont had him taken away and the next morning he was killed with blows from a *halberd*.'[5]

---

[1] By his marriage with Catherine de Médicis, Henri II had ten children, including two stillborn and a boy who died soon after birth. The others were: Francis II, future husband of Mary Queen of Scots, b. 1544; Elizabeth, wife of Philip II, b. 1545; Claude, Duchess of Lorraine, b. 1547; Charles IX, b. 1549; Alexandre, to become Henri III, b. 1551; Marguerite, Queen Margot, wife of Henri IV, b. 1553; Hercule-François, Duke of Alençon, b. 1555. EU.

[2] Third Order: name given to secular clergy, even married men, attached to certain religious orders (Franciscan, Augustinians and *Dominicans*). They were also called *Tertiaries*. DHCD.

[3] *Estoc*: long, thin sword. DAFL.

[4] Latin *inconditus*: not held together, not preserved. DLLB.

[5] EU.

Henri IV, King from 1589.
Absolution from Pope Clement VIII, 1595

Le grand Lorrain fera place à Vendosme,[1]
Le haut mis bas et le bas mis en haut,
Le fils d'Hamon[2] sera esleu dans Rome
Et les deux grands seront mis en défaut.

CX,Q18

Interpretation

Charles of Lorraine will give way to [Henri IV] Duke of Vendôme. The one who was high will be put low, he who was low will be king. The son of the Huguenot will be elected in Rome and the two great ones [of royal blood] will not reign.

History

'Charles of *Lorraine*, Duke of Guise, was arrested after his father's murder, though aged only seventeen, and held prisoner at Tours. He managed to escape in 1591 and at first took arms against Henri IV, but soon afterwards made his *submission* and was given the governorship of Provence.'[3]

'Clement VIII swiftly dispatched a cardinal to persuade King Philip of Spain not to baulk at reconciliation with the King [Henri IV]. The Holy Father declared the matter important enough to warrant more serious discussion than most, and that the best way to do this would be to hear the views of each cardinal in secret. Thus the Pope controlled the *votes*. During these deliberations, public prayers were said in *Rome* on the Pope's orders. The King's request for absolution and its conditions were read out, with du Perron and d'Ossat, his proxies, promising to observe them. According to the prescribed formula they then abjured errors contrary to the Catholic Faith.'[4]

'Mayenne, Henri IV's cousin, attended the absolution ceremony to make his submission. His nephew, the Duke of Guise, did better still: he wrested back Provence and Marseille from the Duke of Savoy, Philip II's troops and the traitors.'[5]

---

[1] Duchy established in 1515 by François I for Charles of Bourbon, Henri IV's grandfather. He bestowed the title of Duke of Vendôme on one of his sons by Gabrielle d'Estrées. DHB.

[2] Amon, King of Judah, son of Manasseh, imitated the blasphemies of his father and was *assassinated* by his own servants. DL7V.

[3] DHB.

[4] HFA.

[5] HFVD.

The Siege of Paris by Henri IV, 1589–94.
His Coronation at Chartres, 27 February 1594,
and Entry into Paris, 22 March 1594

Du bourg Lareyne parviendront droit à Chartres
Et feront près du pont Anthoni[1] pause:
Sept pour la paix cauteleux[2] comme martres[3]
Feront entrée d'armée à Paris clause.[4]

CIX,Q86

Interpretation

From Bourg-la-Reine [Henri IV and his group] will go straight to
Chartres and take a rest near Anthony [at Etampes], then thanks to seven
[persons] ready to become martyrs, and who will conspire together to
restore peace, they will enter Paris, which had been closed.

History

'On 1 November 1589, Henri IV was at *Montrouge*. He risked an attack
on the left bank. The gate of St-Germain resisted. The King did not
press the action. Then once again he abandoned the siege, this time
marching on the south. The capture of *Etampes* allowed him to surround
the capital completely. The King himself had occupied the Beauce region: the Parisians would no longer have any corn. . . .

In 1593 Henri IV, from the hill of *Montmartre*, could look out over
Paris at the privileged subjects of his kingdom who, impatient to regain
their comforts, had already surrendered the town to him. . . .

Orleans and Bourges threw in their lot with him and the towns of
Picardy were ready to do so. In order to hasten this Henri IV knew he
had to appeal to the imagination, to appear as the rightful king decked
out in coronation robes and regalia. Rheims was in the hands of the
Guises, so it was at Chartres, where his family had a chapel, that the
coronation would take place. The ancient ritual began on 27 February
1594. The unusual circumstances of the ceremony did him no harm:
henceforth the King of Navarre was the true King of France. The
Spanish could no longer oppose him. Paris had to surrender. On 22
March 1594, less than a month after his coronation, the king *entered
Paris*. By *conspiracy* the town was his. The conspirators were *Charles de
Cossé, Comte de Brissac*, the governor, *Jean L'Huillier*, merchant-prov-
ost, *Martin Langlois*, advocate to Parliament, and its first President, *Le
Maistre*. The *Duchess of Neumours*, mother of Neumours of Lyon and

Mayenne, was apprised of it also. "It seems clear," said Cazaux, "that *Mayenne* consented to the handover of the capital." During the night of the twenty-first to the twenty-second Brissac and L'Huillier themselves went to the Porte Neuve to get the soldiers to unblock it: it was *closed* up by means of steep ramps. The Porte St-Denis was also cleared. A detachment of a thousand men, led by *St-Luc* [*seven*] immediately entered.[5]

[1] Bourg-la-Reine and Anthony are situated roughly on a line between Montrouge and Etampes.
[2] *Cauteler*: to scheme, hatch a plot. DAFL.
[3] Popular form of *martyrem*. Persists in *Montmartre* – hill of the martyrs. DAFL.
[4] Latin *clausum*: past participle of *claudo*, I close. DLLB.
[5] LGR.

Henri IV's Power Contested.
His Official Recognition by Henri III, 1 August 1589.
Cambrai Captured by Henri III, 1581,
and Lost by Henri IV, 1595

L'ombre[1] du règne de Navarre non vray,
Fera la vie de fort illégitime,
La veu promis incertain de Cambrai,
Roy Orléans[2] donra mur[3] légitime.

CX,Q45

Interpretation

The illusory reign of [Henri] Navarre will be deceptive and render this strong man's activities illegitimate. What had been promised for Cambrai will be seen to be uncertain. [Henri III] Duke of Orleans will legitimize it by his support.

History

'It was thought at first that Henri III's injury was not fatal; but soon he was seized by a severe fever which heralded his demise. Henri of *Navarre* came to see him. "My brother," said the King, "you see how your enemies and mine have treated me: you may be sure you will never be king if you do not become a Catholic." Then, turning to those with him, he said: "I beseech you as my friends and order you as your king to recognise my brother here as King, after my death; swear the oath of allegiance to him in my presence" [*donra mur legitime*]. All swore.

"You are the King of the *strong*," one of the Catholic nobles had said to Henri. Despite these loyal words, many Catholics defaulted; to keep the rest loyal, Henri solemnly undertook [in an assembly of the principal nobles] to uphold the Catholic faith. At Paris, everyone agreed on religion but not on personalities."[4]

'Cateau-Cambrésis: in 1559 a treaty was signed between Henri II, King of France, and Philip II, King of Spain, by which France regained St-Quentin and Ham, while her possession of Calais and the three bishoprics of Metz, Toul and Verdun were also guaranteed. In 1581 the French took *Cambrésis* [the Cambrai region]. The Spaniards recaptured it from them around 1595. Regained in 1677, it became French once and for all in 1678 by the Treaty of Nijmegen."[5]

---

[1] Latin *umbra*: shadow, simulacrum, appearance. DLLB.
[2] Henri III was Duke of *Orleans* (1560), then Duke of Anjou (1566), before succeeding his brother Charles IX (d. 1574). EU.
[3] Symbolic: defence, support.
[4] HFVD.
[5] DHB.

The Conversion of Henri IV, 23 July 1593. The Battle of Ivry, 14 March 1590. The Occupation of Savoy 1596. The Attempted Assassination of Henri IV by Châtel, 1595

Trop tard tous deux les fleurs[1] seront perdues
Contre la loi serpent[2] ne voudra faire,
Des ligueurs forcés par gallots[3] confondus[4]
Savone, Albingue,[5] par monech[6] grand martyre.

CVI,Q62

Interpretation

Being too late, they will both lose the monarchy; the Protestant will not want to act against the [Catholic] law; the forces of the Leaguers will be routed by cavalry; the Duke of Savoy, after the monk [Leaguer] will be made a martyr.

History

Henri III and Henri IV, the two last French kings bearing this Christian name, were both assassinated.

'Although it cost the son of Jeanne d'Albret dear to break with the Huguenots who had carried him on their shoulders across the River Loire, he took his counsellors' advice and on 23 July 1593, after a debate lasting several hours with the Catholic divines reassembled at Nantes, he declared himself converted. 'I swear,' he said, 'before Almighty God, *to live and die in the Catholic religion*; and to protect and defend it before and against all, *renouncing all heresies contrary to the said faith.*'

The King [Henri IV] besieged Dreux. To save the town, Mayenne joined battle on the plain of Saint-André, near Ivry, on 14 March 1590. *The Leaguers* had 15,000–16,000 men, 4000 of them *cavalry*, so that their van resembled a thick forest of lances; the Royalists were 8000 infantry and 3000 *horse* in strength. *Every company* charged at once, the King attacking the French lancers and the Walloons. After two hours, the Leaguers' whole army *was in flight.*

Spain might possibly have been implicated in an assassination attempt against the King. Jean Châtel[7] stabbed at his throat. Henri, bending to embrace a nobleman, avoided this blow and was struck only upon the lip. Châtel had studied under the *Jesuits*, and in the League these *priests* had shown themselves to be most zealous supporters of the Spanish claims. *One of them was executed after Châtel.*

'Mayenne perhaps saved the royal army before Amiens. His nephew the Duke of Guise did better still, for he recaptured Provence and Marseille from the *Duke of Savoy*,[8] thus extending the frontiers towards Savona and Albenga.'

---

[1] The three *fleurs de lis*, symbol of the French monarchy.

[2] The Protestants were accused by the Catholics of diabolism.

[3] Alternative orthography of '*galops*' (gallop).

[4] Latin *confundere*: to throw into disorder, overwhelm. DLLB.

[5] The states of Savoy then comprised Bresse and Bugey, Lake Geneva and the surrounding area, Nice and *various Piedmontese territories* whose capital was Turin. In the sixteenth century the House of Savoy suffered simultaneously from the Reformation, which took over its Swiss possessions, and from *French designs upon Italy*. It lost Bresse and Bugey, ceded to Henry IV in 1601, and saw its territory frequently reoccupied by French armies using *Piedmont* as a defensive fortress. DHCD.

[6] Latin *monachus*: monk, *priest*, hermit. DLLB.

[7] Jean Châtel: 'The *Jesuits*, accused of having incited him to this crime, were driven out of the kingdom. The famous Jean Boucher wrote an apologia for Jean Châtel and the Leaguers incorporated this assassin into their *martyrology*.' DHCD.

[8] HFVD.

The Persecution of Astronomers in the Sixteenth and Seventeenth Centuries: Copernicus and Galileo

> Des plus lettrez dessus les faits celestes,
> Seront par princes ignorans reprouvez[1]
> Punis d'Edit, chassez, comme scelestes,[2]
> Et mis à mort la où seront trouvez.

> CIV,Q18

Interpretation

Some of the most learned men in astronomy will be condemned by ignorant rulers, punished by edicts, hounded like criminals and put to death wherever found.

[1] Latin *reprobo*: I reprove, condemn. DLLB.
[2] Latin *scelestus*: criminal (French = *scélérat. Tr.*). DLLB.

> Croistra le nombre si grand des Astronomes
> Chassez, bannis et livres censurez:
> L'an mil six cens et sept par sacre glomes[1]
> Que nul aux sacres ne seront assurés.

> CVIII,Q71

Interpretation

The number of astronomers will so increase that they will be hounded, banished and have their books banned, in 1607, by bulls, so that they will not be safe from the Holy [Office].

History

Astronomers revere Galileo for the two following reasons: first, as forerunner and *martyr* in the fight by the spirit of Science against the forces of obscurantism which at that time were strongly entrenched in the Catholic Church; secondly, for introducing, in 1610, the telescope for astronomical observation. Though Galileo confined himself to insisting (with many reservations) upon the resemblances between the Earth and the Moon in their relationship to the Sun . . . it was the affirmation of the homogeneity of the planets and stars, including the Earth, which played a part in the *condemnation* of Giordano Bruno to the stake in 1604.

At the end of 1615 Galileo went back to Rome to try to contest a disturbing decision, and once there, openly spoke in favour of arguments which his observations supported, but in spite of his talent he did not convince enough people. On 3 March 1616 the *work* of Copernicus was *placed on the Index. Condemned* by the *Holy Office* [Inquisition] on 22 June 1633, Galileo remained under house arrest until his death.

[1] Latin *glomus*, from *globus*: globe, ball, sphere. DLLB. Since the late Byzantine Empire important acts of civil administration were authenticated by means of a seal attached to parchment. This round seal was called a *bulla* (bull); thereafter, acts thus sealed were habitually referred to as bulls. DL7V.

From the Peace of Cateau-Cambrésis, 1559, to the Peace of Vervins, 1598. The Executions During the Papacy of Clement VIII

Lors que celuy qu'à nul ne donne lieu,
Abandonner viendra lieu prins non prins:
Feu Nef par saignes,[1] Regiment[2] à Charlieu,[3]
Seront Guines,[4] Calais, Oye[5] reprins.

CIX,Q29

Interpretation

When he [Philip II of Spain] to whom no one wishes to yield any territory, abandons a territory captured and recaptured, the Church will use fire to shed blood, the Charolais will be occupied and Guines, Calais and Oye will be taken back [from the Spanish].

History

'The Peace of Cateau-Cambrésis: Henri II was obliged to restore *Calais, Guines* and the county of *Oye.* Henri II, in exchange for the places Philip II had seized in Picardy, returned Luxembourg and the *Charolais.*'[6]

'Henri IV ended the religious war through the Edict of Nantes, 13 April 1598. This was the definitive breach with the Middle Ages. Nineteen days later the King's deputies signed a peace treaty with Spain at Vervins. Philip II had been defeated by England, the Dutch, and by the man he called the Prince of Béarn [Henri]; after so much striving he saw his ambitions disappointed everywhere [*nul lieu*] and his kingdoms, like himself, ruined. He wished at least to die in peace. The Treaty of

Vervins established between the two states the borders marked out forty years *earlier* by the Treaty of Cateau-Cambrésis. *Spain and France both seemed to have reverted to the same position [prins, non prins].*[7]

'The Treaty of Vervins: Spain returned Calais, Ardres, la Capelle, Doullens and the Catelet, i.e. all the Vermandois plus part of Picardy. France gave up Cambrai and the *Charolais*.'[8]

'Two tragedies still of interest today occurred in the papacy of Clement VIII: the execution of the famous heretic Giordano Bruno, and that of the patricide Beatrice Cenci. In both cases the Pope had been prevailed upon to take sides.'[9]

'Giordano Bruno was arrested at Venice by the Inquisition, taken to Rome and *burned alive*, as a heretic and violator of his vows, in 1600. Francesco Cenci had four sons and one daughter: he maltreated them or viciously used them for his illicit pleasures. Revolted by such horrors his daughter, together with two of her brothers and Lucrezia her mother, assassinated Cenci. Accused of patricide, all four died on the scaffold by order of Clement VIII.'[10]

[1] From *saignier*: to stain or cover with blood. DAFL.
[2] Latin *regimentum*: act of ruling. DLLB.
[3] Town in the Charolais, 45 km south of Charolles. DHB.
[4] Chief town of the canton of the port of Calais. DHB.
[5] Pays d'Oye: small area of ancient France (Lower Picardy), part of the *recaptured land*. Today part of the *département* of the Port of Calais. DHB.
[6] HFA.
[7] HFAM.
[8] DL7V and DHB.
[9] DDP.
[10] DHB.

Biron's Treason with Spain, 1599, and His Execution, 1602

Quand de Robin[1] la traistreuse entreprise
Mettra Seigneurs et en peine[2] un grand Prince,
Sceu par La Fin, Chef on lui trenchera:
La plume au vent,[3] amye dans Espagne,
Poste attrapé estant dans la campagne
Et l'escrivain dans l'eau se jettera.[4]

Sixain 6

Interpretation

When Biron's treacherous plan embarrasses the nobility and a great prince, he will be discovered by La Fin and his head will be cut off, because of his deviation and his friendship with Spain; letters being seized in the countryside, he who wrote them will, avoiding one evil, fall into a worse.

History

'Charles de Gontaut, Duke Biron, was celebrated for Henri IV's friend-ship and notorious for his own *treason*. Henri had saved his life in battle at Fontaine-Française in 1595. Despite such beneficence, Biron, *led astray* by pride, ambition and greed, *conspired* against his King, nego-tiated with *Spain* and Savoy and agreed to take arms against his own country. *The plot* was revealed by *La Fin* who had been its instigator. Biron wanted to *deny everything* [*se jetter à l'eau*] but he was convicted by his *written words*. Henri IV tried in vain on several occasions to obtain his confession and repentance, so as to pardon him. He was *beheaded* in 1602.'[5]

'The degree of complicity of the Count of Auvergne and the Duke of Bouillon with Biron is not exactly known. Possibly the two *nobles* were not the only ones involved in this affair.'[6]

[1] Anagram of Biron.
[2] Difficulty, embarrassment, trouble. DL7V.
[3] *Mettre la plume au vent*: to be carried along, drift, with the wind. DL7V.
[4] *Se jeter, se mettre dans l'eau*: out of the frying pan into the fire; avoiding a lesser evil and falling into a greater one.
[5] DHB.
[6] HFA.

Henri IV, 1589. The Edict of Nantes, 1598. Brittany, 1610

Le successeur vengera son beau-frère,
Occuper règne sous[1] ombre de vengeance:
Occis ostacle son sang mort vitupère,[2]
Longtemps Bretagne tiendra avec la France.

CX,Q26

Interpretation

The successor will avenge his brother-in-law and hold power without the least thought of vengeance. He who was the obstacle [to power] having been killed, a bad omen for his blood, Brittany will be united with France for a long time.

History

Henri IV, Henri III's brother-in-law, succeeded him; Henri IV had represented an obstacle to the reconciliation between Catholics and Protestants.

'*The Assassination of Henri III* by Jacques Clément was the culmination of a plan drawn up by Mayenne. Henri of Navarre went to see the dying King. "Brother," said the King, "you see how your enemies and mine have used me; rest assured that you will never be King if you do not turn Catholic.". . .

The victory of Ivry won, Henri remembered he was King. "*Quarter for the French!*" he cried. . . .

Mercoeur, Prince of Lorraine, who had *turned Brittany into a sort of dominion*, had been bargaining for four years for its surrender. Seeing the royal army on its way against him, he deemed it sensible to make peace before it reached his territory. He offered his daughter in marriage, *with her inheritance*, to César de Vendôme, son of the King and Gabrielle d'Estrées. Mercoeur abdicated in favour of his son-in-law; he was the last of the great Leaguer rulers. The civil war had ended. . . .

Shortly afterwards Henri ended *the religious war* through the Edict of Nantes, 13 April 1598. . . .

Henri embraced Mayenne and made him walk briskly through the gardens. Mayenne, who was grossly overweight, sweated and puffed. Henri finally stopped and offered him his hand. "That is the only harm that you will ever come to through me." Indeed, it was the only *revenge* he took upon the head of the League.'[3]

---

[1] *sous* for *sans*; probable printing error. '*Sans l'ombre de*' was a current phrase.
[2] Latin *Cur omen mihi vituperat?* (Why is it a bad omen for me?): Plautus. DLLB. Note the Latin construction of line 3.
[3] HFVD.

The Siege of La Rochelle, 1625–28.
The Prince of Rohan at the Blavet, Royan and La Rochelle

Le Prince hors de son terroir Celtique,
Sera trahy, deceu[1] par interprete:[2]
Roüan,[3] Rochelle par ceux de l'Armorique
Au port de blave deceus par moyne et prestre.

CVI,Q60

Interpretation

The Prince [of Rohan] will leave France after being tricked and betrayed by a negotiator [Walter Montague]. Royan and La Rochelle will be attacked by Breton troops [the Duke of Vendôme's]. After the Blavet expedition they will be outwitted by one of the clergy.

History

'At *La Rochelle*, power politics were making the people uneasy. Opposite the town walls the king had built Fort Louis. The Duke of Guise had based the royal fleet on the island of Ré: thus the area's pirates were under surveillance. Although at peace, the people of La Rochelle were subjected to the threat of pirates. They summoned Rohan and Soubise. To relieve the town, Soubise planned an exceptionally bold expedition: with several lightly armed ships, crammed with secretly recruited soldiers from Poitiers, he took the island of Ré in a surprise attack in January 1625. At the mouth of the River *Blavet* [au port de Blave] he captured seven great ships of the royal fleet. He eluded the forces of the Duke of Vendôme, Governor of *Brittany* [ceux de l'Armorique] and seized the isle of Oléron. Richelieu was angry at not being able to mobilize and retaliate: his own troops were in Italy fighting the Spanish. Soubise's vessels attacked *Royan*, and advanced into the Gironde, threatening Bordeaux. . . .

On the Isle of Ré, the resisting royal forces came up against English invasion troops. At last the citizens of La Rochelle themselves declared war, after two months of hesitation. Richelieu at once blockaded all the land approaches. The fleet was entrusted to a churchman [*moine et prêtre*], Sourdis, Bishop of Maillezais, an extraordinarily resourceful leader. Thanks to his efforts, a convoy of thirty-five vessels landed on the island on 16 October. From October 1627 to January 1628 an army of stonemasons worked on the sea wall. Buckingham, who was preparing an expedition, was assassinated at the beginning of September. The

English fleet still took to sea, however, commanded by Lindsey. On 18 September this fleet, together with Soubise's 5000 troops, was opposite the town of St Martin-de-Ré. Facing fusillades and cannonades from the harbour batteries, they did not risk a landing. An ambassador [*interprète*], Walter Montague, was sent to propose peace on the English behalf, and the fleet put out to sea again. La Rochelle capitulated on condition that its inhabitants would retain freedom of both life and religion. [It had been for some years a Huguenot bastion. *Tr.*] Most of the survivors had to go into exile, and the town walls and defences were razed.'[4]

'Henri, Duke of Rohan, *prince* of Leon, b. 1579 a Protestant, became leader of the French Calvinists after Henri IV's death and waged three wars against the government of Louis XIII (1620–22, 1625–26 and 1627–29). The last of these was disastrous for him, since La Rochelle, which he was defending, was taken by Richelieu and he was *compelled to leave France* [*hors de son terroir Celtique*].'[5]

[1] *Decevoir*: to trick. DAFL.
[2] Latin *interpres pacis*: peace negotiator. DLLB.
[3] Note *ü* for *y*.
[4] LGR.
[5] DHB.

The Revolt of Gaston of Orleans and the Duke of Montmorency against Richelieu, 1632. The Siege of Beaucaire and its Defence by Monsieur, the King's Brother

> Le petit coing,[1] Provinces mutinées,
> Par forts Chasteaux se verront dominées,
> Encore un coup par la gent militaire,
> Dans bref seront fortement assiegez,
> Mais ils seront d'un tres-grand soulagez,
> Qui aura fait entrée dans Beaucaire.

Sixain 43

Interpretation

A small area of Provence will revolt, but will be defeated by powerful fortresses and then by the strength of the army. The sieges will be short and they will be raised by a very powerful person who will enter Beaucaire.

History

'Gaston, Duke of Orleans, halted in the Duchy of Montpensier, counting on considerable support from those wishing to join his ranks, but no one came forward. This delay gave the royal troops a chance to close on him; Gaston feared being surrounded and, despite the Duke of Montmorency's remonstrances, rushed into Languedoc. Two armies, commanded by Marshals de la Force and Schomberg, advanced into the *province* as soon as the court was sure of the Governor's defection, and waited for him there. The support of the provincial assembly, which the latter was relying upon, was not forthcoming since the government had arrested suspect members, while the rest were under such close surveillance that they could not help him. The Spanish, despite their promises, failed to send men or money. During his trial of Monsieur's[2] troops, the attack on the *Castle of Beaucaire*, he was forced to give up *the siege* and realized that he could rely neither on the bravery of his soldiers nor on the skill of their commanders. *The King's forces*, on the other hand, flourished: wherever they advanced, anyone found bearing arms paid for his *rebellion* with his head – a frightening omen for Montmorency. His position became critical. Although greatly liked by his administration he could not rely on any *town*, because they were all *held in check* [dominated or bested] by the King's forces who filled *the province*.'[3]

[1] Small area of some particular place. DL7V.

[2] *Monsieur*: title given to the French king's eldest brother, Orleans, i.e. exalted or very great person. (Tr.)

[3] HFA.

The Siege of La Rochelle, 1627.
The Execution of the Duke of Montmorency, 1632.
Occupation of Lorraine, 1634. War against
the House of Austria, 1636

Le Lys Dauffois[1] portera[2] dans Nansi
Jusques en Flandre Electeur de l'Empire,[3]
Neufve obturée[4] au grand Montmorency,[5]
Hors lieux[6] prouvez[7] délivre[8] a clere[9] peine.

CIX,QI8

Interpretation

The Dauphin [become] king will carry [the war] into Lorraine, as far as Flanders and Germany. The great [Admiral] Montmorency, having been before the new closure [the sea-wall fortification of La Rochelle], will be elsewhere [Castelnaudary] found guilty and delivered over to an exemplary fate.

History

'The Duke of *Lorraine* paid for the war. Louis XIII avoided Bar-le-Duc and his *military occupation of the duchy* [1634] meant that for many years it remained in French hands.

The many treaties signed by Richelieu pointed towards the imminent *extension of the war*. Richelieu *carried on* the war along all our frontiers: to the *Low Countries*, to share them with Holland; along the Rhine to protect Champagne and *Lorraine*; into *Germany* to ally with the Swedes and destroy Austrian omnipotence.'[10]

'Henri de Montmorency, made Admiral by Louis XIII in 1612, in 1625 conquered the isles of Ré and Oléron. When *La Rochelle* was attacked by Richelieu, he offered his services for a huge sum. Alienated from the court because he had been refused the title of constable, he rebelled, with the King's brother, Gaston of Orleans. He was defeated by Schomberg at Castelnaudary, *captured*, judged and beheaded at Toulouse.'[11]

'This *terrible example* [made of Montmorency] was worth ten years of peace to Richelieu.'[12]

'On the land side, Richelieu surrounded the town with a 12-kilometre entrenchment. In order to *close the harbour* and prevent any English assistance from entering by sea, he organized in *six months* the building of a stone dyke or wall, 1500 metres long and 8 metres tall.'[12]

---

[1] French Dauphins: Louis XII ascended to the throne without having been Dauphin. He had two sons, both of whom died young and bore the title. Then the title passed to François I's son. Henri II and François II succeeded, but Henri IV was not Dauphin. Louis XIII was of his line. DL7V.

[2] *Porter*: to introduce, carry war into a country. DL7V.

[3] Elector of the German Empire. Title of prince or bishop having a vote in the election of the Emperor of Germany. DL7V.

[4] Latin *obturo*: I close up, stop up. DLLB.

[5] Henri, 2nd Duke of Montmorency, b. Chantilly 1595, d. Toulouse, September 1632.

[6] Plural = precise spot where event occurs. DL7V.

[7] *Prouver*: to be found guilty, convicted, DAFL.

[8] *Délivrer, livrer*: to put something into someone else's hands, make over. DL7V.

[9] Latin *clarus, clara exempla*: famous examples. DLLB.

10 HFVD.
11 DHCD.
12 HFAM.

Louis XIII's Army Besieges Barcelona, 1640. The Occupation of the Duchy of Montferrat by Louis XIII's Forces, 1640. The Title of 'King of France and Navarre'

De Catones[1] trouvez en Barcelonne,
Mys descouvers lieu terrouers[2] et ruyne:
Le grand qui tient ne tient voudra Pamplonne,[3]
Par l'abbage de Montferrat[4] bruyne.

CVIII,Q26

Interpretation

Licentious men, to be found at Barcelona, shall be exposed and the place will be stricken with fear and sacked. The King will not occupy Navarre but will want the title of 'King of Navarre', and will occupy the Duchy of Montferrat that autumn.

History

'The Marquis of Léganez had besieged *Casal*, which a French garrison still *held*. Count Harcourt, with forces only half as strong, marched to relieve the place. The Marquis, instead of going to meet him, lost his numerical advantage and let himself be attacked in his positions. His lines were breached in three places. The Spaniards lost most of their artillery and a quarter of their troops and were obliged to raise the siege.

The huge funds required to maintain such an expensive war meant that there were rebellions in Spain as well as in France. The Duke of Olivares had a plan to make Catalonia contribute to the common defence: the Catalans thought this a violation of their privileges. Their discontent increased when they were compelled to do forced labour for the Castilian army sent to defend Roussillon, and they also particularly objected to the excesses committed by the undisciplined army. Some soldiers among the more unruly elements, those *abandoned to licence* [Catones], were *recognized* [discovered] in *Barcelona* one day by a mob of peasants and became targets for their wrath and indignation. There were further

disturbances because the peasants disagreed with the Governor's resistance: the latter's murder brought about the *revolt* [*ruyne*] centred on this
town which then solicited the aid of the French. Substantial aid was sent
to Catalonia as a result of the Catalan decision to renounce their original
plan for a republic and to cede to Louis XIII, which revived their
courage. In alliance with the French, they defied the Spanish beneath
the cannons of Mont-Joui, the citadel of *Barcelona*.'[5]

[1] Latin *Cato, Catonis*: Cato. DLLB. In the sixteenth century 'cato' had become a
mocking term for those outwardly serious or soft-spoken, who were in fact unruly and
vicious. Amyot. DL.

[2] Latin *terreo*: I frighten, shock. DLLB.

[3] Capital of Navarre. Henri III of Bourbon, son of Anthony, King of Navarre, ascended
the throne in 1589 as 'Henri IV', and his successors added the title 'King of Navarre' to
that of King of France. DHB.

[4] Ancient duchy in Italy, bordered in the north and west by Piedmont, to the south by
the Republic of Genoa and east by the Milanese; its capital was *Casal*. DHB.

[5] HFA.

The Thirty Years' War. The French Fleet Sunk off Corsica, 1646. The Fronde Wars

Classe Gauloise n'approche de Corseigne,
Moins de Sardaigne tu t'en repentiras:
Trestous mourrez frustrez de l'aide grogne,[1]
Sang nagera, captif ne me croiras.

CIII,Q87

Interpretation

French fleet, do not approach Corsica or Sardinia, or you will regret it:
you will all die, deprived of help because of the Fronde, the sea will
become bloodstained, and the prisoner will not believe me.

History

'In 1646, Italy was the main theatre of war. Mazarin and de Lionne
considered making Prince Thomas of *Savoy-Carignan* King of Naples.
Pope Innocent X declared himself hostile to this plan. A *French fleet*
assembled at Toulon and was placed under the command of the Duke
of Brezé, Admiral of France. It sailed rapidly towards the Tuscan
coastline and disembarked French and Piedmontese troops who besieged

Orbetello (which faces Corsica and Sardinia). The siege dragged on. Prince Thomas showed little enthusiasm and the Duke of Brezé was *killed* in a naval engagement with the Spanish which he himself had blithely instigated. His death flung the French fleet and army into disarray. The effects of this unfortunate enterprise were far-reaching: in Paris the Prince of Condé seized the opportunity of demanding that the new admiral should be the Duke d'Enghien who had married the Duke of Brezé's sister.[2] Mazarin refused and the Condés immediately allied with Gaston of Orleans.'[3]

'Condé surrounded himself with all *the malcontents* and prepared for war: his party, like the war, was called the Fronde. Mazarin decided to have Condé arrested [*captif*], along with his brother-in-law the Duke of Longueville [18 January 1650]. Master of Paris, Condé instigated a reign of terror, arranging for the *massacre* of Mazarin's supporters.'[4]

---

[1] Discontent, manifested by grumbling [*grogne*]. DL7V.
[2] Hence the link Nostradamus establishes between Brezé and the Prince's group, the Fronde.
[3] Louis XIV. JR.
[4] DL7V.

The Age of Louis XIV

De brique en marbre seront les murs réduicts,
Sept et cinquante années pacifiques,
Joye aux humains, renoué l'aqueduict,
Santé, grands fruits, joye et temps melifique.[1]

CX,Q89

Interpretation

Brick walls shall be rebuilt in marble, fifty-seven years of peace, joy to men, the aqueduct renewed, health, great results, time of joy and gentleness.

History

'Versailles is a compendium of architecture. At least three Versailles exist. The "House of Cards" Louis XIII had had constructed, beginning in 1631, is the earliest. Today this forms the main *"marble forecourt"*.

When Louis XIV decided to take the place on, in 1661, he limited himself to *beautifying* it . . . a terrace with *marble* flagstones and a fountain. . . .

On 24 November 1658, faced with Spanish indecision over the marriage of the Infanta to Louis XIV, Mazarin, at Lyon, feigned wedding negotiations involving Marguerite of Savoy. Immediately Philip IV, fearing that the *peace* might thus be lost, sent a secret messenger to Lyon, offering both *the peace and the marriage*, and this offer was at once accepted by Louis. On 7 November 1659 France and Spain signed the Treaty of the Pyrenees.'[2]

There are almost fifty-seven years between 1659 and 1715, the date of Louis XIV's death.

'If Louis XIV did not found the state, he left it far stronger still. *For fifty years* the Parliament had neither revoked any edicts nor challenged the ministers and the royal power. There was no more than a single ruling authority in France. Contemporaries were well aware that the strength of the *French nation*, which had enabled her to resist European attacks, stemmed from this. Versailles symbolized a civilization which *for many years was* European civilization, so that France was in the forefront, her political prestige helping to spread her language and art.'[3]

[1] From *miel* (honey). Nostradamus' symbol for sweetness and gentleness.
[2] LFLXIV.
[3] HFJB.

The Execution of Charles I of England, 1649.
The French Occupation of Belgium, 1658–1714.
England's Problems

Gand et Bruceles marcheront contre Anvers,
Senat[1] de Londres mettront à mort leur Roy:
Le sel et vin luy seront à l'envers,
Pour eux avoir le règne en désarroy.

CIX,Q49

Interpretation

[The French] after Ghent and Brussels, will march against Anvers. The English Parliament will put its king to death. England will experience economic reverses for having overturned authority.

History

'In August 1658 Turenne seized Gravelines, which was still part of France. Then he took Oudenarde and Ypres. He threatened *Ghent* and *Brussels*. Flanders was almost completely conquered. The English had designs on capturing Calais and Philip IV of Spain hoped that there would be discord between Cromwell and Mazarin. But Cromwell died and England suffered a fresh period of *difficulties*.

In February 1677 Louis XIV planned an impressive campaign so that he could negotiate from a position of strength. Heading an army of 120,000 he forged on towards Lorraine, which deceived the enemy; then he doubled back towards Flanders and on reaching *Ghent*, besieged the town, which surrendered after five days. The fortress fell three days after that. It was now *Anvers* which was threatened.

On 22 March 1701 England and Holland sent their list of conditions to the French ambassador at the Hague. They demanded the French evacuation of *Belgium*; a promise that no Spanish possession would be ceded to France; the occupation of ten frontier towns by the Dutch and of Ostend and Nieuport by the English. Louis XIV responded by proposing simply to confirm the Peace of Ryswick – which did not preclude his fortifying *Anvers* and the main Belgian towns under French occupation.'[2]

'The Revolution which began in 1642 ended on 30 January 1649 with the execution of Charles I and an Act by which the proclamation of his heir was forbidden. A week later the House of Lords was abolished, as was royalty itself [*règne en désarroy*]. On Cromwell's death his son Richard succeeded him, but proved unable to maintain a balance between a politicized Army and a Parliament whose members wanted the respect that came with legality. A new Parliament, formed in January 1659, had to be dissolved that April, and Richard resigned. In the grip of *anarchy*, England then went through several months of extreme uncertainty.'[3]

[1] Latin *senatus*: assembly, council. DLLB.
[2] HFACAD.
[3] HRU.

The Glorious Revolution, 1688.
The Conspiracy against James II. The Landing of William of Orange, 7 November 1688.
The Bill of Rights.
William and Mary, 1689

Trente de Londres secret conjureront,
Contre leur Roy, sur le pont[1] l'entreprise:
Luy fatalites la mort desgouteront
Un Roy esleu blonde, natif, de Frize.[2]

CIV,Q89

Interpretation

Thirty people in London will plot against their king; the enterprise will take place by sea. The fatalities of death [his father's] will disgust him, then a king, a native of Friesland, will be chosen with a blonde woman. [Mary].

History

'When he ascended to the throne in 1685 James II knew the dangers threatening him, and that his religion would cause as much hostility as his political views. This hostility reached a peak on 20 June 1688 when a Roman Catholic heir was born, Prince James Edward. This event (the King was then fifty-five) put paid to all hopes of a Protestant successor. Ten days after the birth Arthur Herbert, former Vice-Admiral, brought William of Orange [*native of Friesland*] an appeal for assistance signed by various [*trente de Londres*] great noblemen. William, the son-in-law of James II by his marriage to Mary, *had been having discussions for several months with opponents of the English King*, and was therefore invited to lead the second English revolution. The 1688 Revolution was remarkably short. On 7 November 1688 William landed at Torbay. On 25 December James II, persuaded to flee, landed on French soil. On 23 February 1689 the royal succession was settled. The blundering James II had been unable to make the necessary concessions rapidly, so that the question of who should be king had not been posed by William himself, whose personal popularity remained doubtful. *The memory of his father's execution* greatly influenced the King's attitude and made him too eager to concede defeat. On 13 February 1689 Parliament adopted a law setting out the rights and liberties of every citizen and determining *the succession to the Crown* [*Roy esleu*], known as the Bill of Rights. This law legitimized

William and Mary as joint monarchs, established their succession and excluded Catholics from the throne in future. On 23 February the two new sovereigns were proclaimed, since they adhered to this Bill.'[3]

---

[1] Greek πόντος: the sea. DGF.
[2] One of the provinces of the Kingdom of Holland. DHB.
[3] HRU.

Villars and the War of the League of Augsburg. The Liberation of Provence, 1707, after its Occupation by the Duke of Savoy. Villars and the Camisard Rebellion, 1702–5

La mer Tyrrhene, l'Occean par la garde,
Du grand Neptune[1] et ses tridens soldats:
Provence seure par la main du grand Tende,[2]
Plus Mars Narbon l'héroiq de Vilars.

Presage 2

Interpretation

The Tyrrhenian Sea and the Ocean will be guarded by England and her sailors, Provence will be delivered from the Duke of Savoy, [the great one from Tende], and the heroic Duke of Villars will put an end to the war in Languedoc.

History

'The greatest calamity was *at sea*. The King [of France] had still not given up hope of restoring James to the throne. A landing force of 20,000 men was to have been supported by a fleet totalling 65 vessels, when all the squadrons had joined up. One contingent was *in the Mediterranean*; winds and storms prevented its arriving on time. The success tasted by *Villars* meant that the original plan was expanded. He was deprived of several detachments which were then redirected to *Provence*, recently invaded by the *Duke of Savoy*. Despite prudence the invasion of *Provence* did not proceed as planned. *An English fleet* supported the land army and was given the task of transporting the heavy artillery which could not have been carried over the mountain route. The enemy pushed forward without difficulty deep into Provence and neared Toulon by the end of July 1707. The Allies [the English and the Duke of Savoy] were luckier at Naples [Tyrrhenian Sea], which they captured from Philip II of Spain. This expedition was *the salvation of Provence*, which might have succumbed had all the armies separately employed been reunited against it. The Elector of Bavaria, who could not play second fiddle to his nephew the Prince, was sent to the Rhine against Prince Eugène; Villars was destined for Dauphiné and *Provence*, still menaced by the Duke of Savoy [*the great one from Tende*].'[3]

'The Camisard Rebellion was one of the repercussions of the Revocation of the Edict of Nantes. For two years Louis XIV had been obliged to dispatch armies totalling 20,000 men against the rebels. Various marshals of France had led his forces: first de Broglie, then de Montrevel, and finally Villars, who showed himself to be both soldier [*Mars*] and diplomat. Assisted by Nicolas Lamoignon de Basville, Intendant of *Languedoc*, Villars negotiated with Cavalier, whom he persuaded to support the rebel cause no longer. Deprived of their main leader, the rebels were soon defeated.'[4]

[1] God of the Sea (DL7V). For Nostradamus, a symbol of English naval might.
[2] Name of a county belonging to the Lascaris of Ventimiglia, and which finally by marriage passed to the House of Savoy. DHB.
[3] HFA.
[4] DL7V.

The Regency, 1715

Coeur, vigueur, gloire, le règne changera,
De tous points, contre ayant son adversaire!
Lors France enfance par mort subjuguera,
Le Grand Régent sera lors plus contraire.

CIII,QI5

Interpretation

In spite of courage, strength, glory, power will change hands, having its adversary opposed in all areas: the childhood [of the King] will then put France under a deadly yoke, the Great Regent will be even more harmful to the country.

History

'The throne of France reverted to Louis XV who was the Duke of Burgundy's son and hence great-grandson of Louis XIV, but this prince was still only *five years old*. Louis XIV had set out in his will the Council of Regency which was to govern until Louis XV's majority. But Louis XIV's nephew, Philippe, Duke of Orleans intervened. He had Parliament rescind Louis XIV's will and confer the Regency upon him unconditionally. He is generally only referred to in French history by the title of *Regent*, and the period for which he governed is simply called the Regency.

The Duke of Orleans was highly intelligent and renowned for his gallantry, but his fickleness, love of pleasure and lack of moral fibre led to *great misfortunes* for France.'[1]

[1] PCHF.

The Marseille Plague, 1720

La grande peste de cité maritime
Ne cessera que mort ne soit vengée;
Du juste sang par pris damné sans crime,[1]
De la grand dame par feinte n'outragée.

CII,Q53

Interpretation

The great plague of Marseille will cease only when death is avenged, the blood of the just shed by the damned without being accused for fear that the monarchy might be outraged by this crime.

History

'The nationwide *mourning* after the *death* of the Dauphin began again in early 1712, in even sadder manner. People mourned the Duke of Burgundy, who had assumed the title of Dauphin, his wife the Princess of Savoy, and finally the Duke of Brittany, the eldest of their two surviving children. All three deaths occurred within a month of each other. *Such a heavy loss* in the royal family was *thought to be unnatural*; and the public thoughtlessly accused the Duke of Orleans, who had adopted a scornful attitude towards all virtue and was quite shamelessly immoral. Thus he prompted the mingled suspicion, grief and hatred of all.

In 1720 Marseille was in the grip of a frightful plague due to the negligence of its health officers in the quarantine station. Their carelessness at the end of May led to the premature clearance of a vessel from Syria infected with the plague. At the end of September a north wind began to clear the putrid effluvia hovering over the town, which had stricken almost half the population of 100,000. The main ravages of the plague ended about this time but the last traces only disappeared a year after the original epidemic.'[2]

[1] Latin *crimen*: accusation.
[2] HFA.

The Republic of Letters, 1720.
The Eighteenth-century Philosophers

Lors que Venus[1] du Sol sera couvert
Soubs l'esplendeur sera forme occulte:
Mercure[2] au feu les aura descouvert,
Par bruit bellique sera mis à l'insulte.[3]

CIV,Q28

Interpretation

When venomous words are under the monarchy's shelter, under its splendour the real idea will hide, the flame of eloquence will bring it to light, [the monarchy] will be attacked with warlike noise.

History

'In theory, men of letters are *under the surveillance* of authority, guardian of religion, morals and the social order. In reality, they do, *say* and publish what they please. In general, the eighteenth-century French literature of importance and influence was anti-Christian. It was a *militant*, ambitious and *aggressive* literature. Writers became philosophers. Writing stopped being a lofty diversion in which the spirit freely wandered, and sought instead to establish a mastery of ideas over and against the *Church, authority* and tradition.

For thirty years Voltaire, ever bolder, more powerful and more *outrageous*, would exert upon the thought of a whole age a dictatorship almost without precedent.

In 1720 the republic of letters was a dream; half a century later, it was a reality.'[4]

[1] Venom: in Latin, *venus, veneris*: sexual desire personified by Venus, goddess of love. DL7V.

2 Son of Jupiter, the gods' messenger, himself god of eloquence. DL7V.
3 Latin *insulto*: I taunt. DLLB.
4 HFPG.

Eighteenth-century Literature Paves the Way for the French Revolution, the Cause of the Great Wars of the Nineteenth and Twentieth Centuries

> La grande perte, las que feront les lettres,
> Avant le cicle de Latona[1] parfait,
> Feu grand déluge plus par ignares sceptres
> Que de long siècle ne se verra refait.
>
> CI,Q62

Interpretation

Literature will make great subversive inroads before the Republic has completed its cycle, then incompetent powers will cause great wars which will be prolonged throughout the nineteenth and twentieth centuries.

History

'The philosophers and economists had an enormous influence, not simply on the uncultured and largely uneducated masses, but on literature too, especially amongst the bourgeoisie. In order to spread new ideas, and since large political newspapers did not yet exist, they used the theatre, books and anonymous pamphlets, with such success that closures and confiscations ordered by Parliament or the police were not effective. At the same time the publication of the Encyclopaedia powerfully assisted the propaganda of the philosophers and economists. Its publication was completed in 1772 and it consisted of twenty-eight volumes. It was an unwieldy but forceful war machine, destined to *shake the foundations* [*grande perte*] of the *ancien régime* and to disseminate, together with atheism, all the key ideas of the new philosophy.

From France the new ideas infiltrated the whole of Europe.'[2]

'War against Europe: since 1792 victory had produced its own problems. Was France to negotiate or *carry on waging war*? To revolutionize the conquered territories or to leave the old order intact? To make protectorates or annex them? The pacifism of 1789, the Girondin cosmopolitanism, plans for universal revolution, the old dream of natural frontiers, the fear of engaging in *an endless war* – everything was in a state of flux. The radical solution was not slow to present itself. Humanitarian in principle, the Revolution very soon became *bellicose. The Revolution was swept into continental war*; its *heir*, the Emperor Napoleon, was finally destroyed by it and *France paid for the struggle, to her cost.*'[3]

[1] Apollo's mother. Allusion to the First Republic, which would spawn Napoleon, the New Apollo. Cf. CI,Q76.
[2] HFAM.
[3] HFPG.

France on the Eve of the Revolution, 1789.
The Execution of Louis XVI and Marie-Antoinette

Le trop bon temps, trop de bonté royale
Faicts et déffaicts prompt, subit, négligence,
Léger croira faux d'espouse loyale.
Luy mis à mort par sa bénévolence.[1]

                                        CX,Q43

Interpretation

The age being too good, the king also too good, will be annihilated promptly and suddenly through negligence. The king's wife will be wrongly supposed to be licentious and she will be put to death because of his genial nature.

History

'France at the end of the eighteenth century was the largest European state and *one of the richest* and most advanced. A general unrest, however, pervaded the whole country.'[2]

'Times were too good.

Poverty can cause riots. It never creates revolutions. These have deeper-rooted causes, and in 1789 the French were not badly off. On the contrary, documents show that *individual wealth had considerably increased* over the previous half-century and that most classes of society except the rural nobility were distinctly more affluent.'[3]

'Also, for centuries kings had been in the habit of borrowing; but part of the revenue was swallowed up by interest due [*par negligence.*]'[2]

'Queen Marie-Antoinette made herself unpopular by her trifling [*Léger*].'[4]

'Louis XVI, *full of good will*, had even appointed ministers capable of bringing about reforms: first Turgot, then Necker [*par sa bénévolence!*].'[2]

[1] Latin *benevolentia*: good will, kindness. DLLB.
[2] LCH3.
[3] LRFPG.
[4] *futilité* (Fr.). See also note 1.

Promissory Notes and State Bankruptcy, 1789–96. The Persecution and Execution of Men of Letters. The Emigrés

Ceux qui estoient en regne pour scavoir,
Au Royal change[1] deviendront appovris:
Uns exilez sans appuy, or n'avoir,
Lettrez et lettres ne seront a grand pris.

CVI,Q8

Interpretation

Those who were in power because of their learning [the nobility] will be impoverished by promissory notes. Some will be exiled without aid or fortune. Literary men and their works will be in low repute.

History

'Promissory notes were paper money whose value was redeemable against so-called "national" assets [royal change]. The promissory note played a part in the dawn of the 1789 Revolution. The issues continued without reserve or limit. Depreciation would be rapid, almost instantaneous. The fall was halted by converting 558 million francs in cash into bills payable to bearer, by the suppression of cash discounts and the redemption of shares by promissory notes, and by a compulsory wealth tax of 1000 million francs as decreed by the Convention.

The Laws of 29 Messidor, 5 Thermidor Year IV and 16 Pluviose Year V abolished dealings between holders of promissory notes and the mandated territories. *The state* [*ceux qui estoient en règne*], after having declared itself *bankrupt* [*approvris*] organized a sort of receivership with individual holders of notes. The *paper money* experiment [royal change] was over. As a business scheme it had proved disastrous, ruining thousands of families.'

'*French emigration* began after 14 July 1789 and did not end until 1825, with the special Emigration Law. The week following the Storming of the Bastille saw the exodus of princes of royal descent (Count of Artois, Dukes of Angoulême and Berry, Prince de Broglie, Vandreuil, Lambesc-Conti) [*ceux qui etaient en règne*]. The Convention later sentenced the émigrés to perpetual banishment [23 October 1792].'[2]

'Madame Roland, Lavoisier the great chemist, Malesherbes, and a thousand others were executed.'[3]

'André Chénier, disgusted by revolutionary excesses, dared to criticize the Revolution openly in the *Letters* he had published in the *Journal de Paris*. Charged before the Revolutionary Tribunal, he was sentenced to death in 1794.'[4]

---

[1] *Lettre de change*: ancient term for paper money, *bonds or credits* issued by the state and repayable to the holder on demand. DL7V.
[2] DL7V.
[3] HVD.
[4] DHB.

The Storming of the Bastille, 14 July 1789.
War, 20 April 1792

Avant conflit le grand mur tombera,
Le Grand à mort, mort trop subite et plainte.
Nef imparfait[1] la plus part nagera,[2]
Auprès du fleuve de sang la terre teinte.

CII,Q57

Interpretation

Before the war the great wall will fall, the King will be executed, his death too sudden and lamented. Most [of the guards] will swim in blood; near the Seine the soil shall be bloodstained.

History

'Marat wrote in *The People's Friend* (14 April 1791): "When an extraordinary conjunction of circumstances caused the poorly defended Bastille *walls to fall*, the Parisians appeared before the fortress: curiosity alone brought them there." . . .

De Launay, Governor of the Bastille, and the *entire garrison* with the exception of the King's lieutenant du Puget, were *massacred* by the mob, as well as the invalids Ferrand and Bécarel.'[3]

'Since *June 1791* there had been talk of *war*. The spirit of aggression was also prevalent abroad. It took the advent of the Emperor Leopold's son, Francis II, to spark off this *war*. The King, for once in agreement with his ministers and the majority of the Legislative Assembly, *declared war* in response to Francis' demand that France should return Avignon to the Pope [20 April 1792]. . . .

The execution of Louis XVI prompted Royalist indignation and the *horrified censure* of foreign monarchs [*mort trop subite et plainte*] who now considered alliance against a Republican, aggressive France which had just declared war upon England (1 February 1793).'[4]

[1] i.e. unfinished, incomplete. DL7V.
[2] Different phrasing: to swim in blood, i.e. be covered in it. DL7V.
[3] DL7V.
[4] LCH3.

The End of the Monarchy, 1792. Letter to Henry Roy de France Second

> . . . Et durera ceste cy jusqu'à l'an mil sept cens
> nonante deux que l'on cuidra estre une rénovation
> de siècle . . .

Interpretation

And the latter [the monarchy] will last until the year 1792 which will be thought to be a renewal of the century.

History

The year 1792, not 1789, was specified by Nostradamus. The end of the *ancien régime* actually dates from 21 September 1792, the date when Year 1 of the Republic began.

Nostradamus makes a statement which might seem surprising when he mentions 'a renewal of the century'. In fact he knew that the monarchy would last thirteen centuries from the coronation of Clovis at Rheims in

496 to 1792, but he also knew that not one of the five subsequent republics would endure for a single century:

1st Republic, September 1792 to December 1799: 7 years, 3 months.
2nd Republic, February 1848 to December 1851: 3 years, 7 months.
3rd Republic, September 1870 to June 1940: 69 years, 9 months.
4th Republic, October 1946 to September 1958: 11 years, 11 months.
5th Republic, from September 1958.
Hence the phrase 'renewal of centuries'.

The End of the Ancien Régime, 1792

Le teste bleue[1] fera la teste blanche,[2]
Autant de mal que France a faict leur bien,
Mort à l'Anthene,[3] grand pendu sus la branche,[4]
Quand pris des siens le roi dira combien.

CII,Q2

Interpretation

Republican power will do as much harm to monarchical power as the monarchy has done [good] to France. Death to the fleur-de-lis, the King will hesitate greatly when he can say how many of his party have been arrested.

History

'If Napoleon did not save the Republic, he saved whatever could be salvaged from the Revolution: its mystique, personalities, foreign policy, cosmopolitanism and social organization. Until then France could only conceive of the return to order in the form of *restoration of the monarchy*. In ten years the Revolution had confounded all expectations and disappointed all hopes. A stable and ordered government had been expected; solvency, wise laws, peace abroad and tranquillity at home. But *there had been anarchy, war, terror, bankruptcy, famine and failure*. The idealists of 1789 had wanted to regenerate mankind and reconstruct the world. To escape the Bourbons, they had been reduced to taking up the sword. . . .

Louis XVI and Marie-Antoinette had at first shown some spirit. They ended up panic-stricken. At the last minute the King still *hesitated*.

In ten days everything was ready: the lists of *proscriptions* were printed and the cut-throats chosen and enrolled. At Carmes, at the Abbey, the

Salpêtrière, the Châtelet, Bicêtre. In four days there were more than
1100 murders. Among the dead were the *former minister* Montmorin, the
Archbishop of Arles, the bishops of Saintes and Beauvais, and the *Swiss*
who had escaped the events of 10 August.'[5]

'The revolutionary Commune sentenced the royal family to internment
in the Temple Prison, and *arrested numerous persons on suspicion.*'[6]

[1] A name that the inhabitants of the Vendée gave the *Republican* soldiers because of
the colour of their uniform. DL7V.
[2] White, under the *ancien régime*, always represented the nation and French *royalty.*
DL7V. Cf. CX,Q20: the white stone.
[3] Greek ἀνθίνος: flower. DGF. NB capital A.
[4] Cf. CX,Q20.
[5] LRFPG.
[6] LCH3.

The Seven Years of the First Republic, 21 September 1792 to 15 December 1799

La Dame seule[1] au règne[2] demeurée,
L'unic[3] éteint premier au lict d'honneur,
Sept ans sera de douleur explorée,
Plus longue vie au règne par grand heur.

CVI,Q63

Interpretation

The Republic having attained power, the King dead in the front rank of
honours, it shall be known in sorrow for seven years, but will not have
longer to rule happily.

History

'The Convention reassembled on 20 September 1792 and abolished royalty. Next day it decreed that official Acts would thereafter be dated
from Year I of the Republic.

By applying severe penalties, most often the death sentence, the gov-
ernment became known as the Terror. The law concerning suspects (17
September 1793) silenced all possible forms of opposition. At Paris, the
Tribunal sent accused persons to the guillotine after *summary trials*
(Marie-Antoinette, the Girondins, etc.). Robespierre obtained the death

sentence upon the followers of Hébert in March, then on Danton's supporters in April 1794.

After this sort of apotheosis, Robespierre took one of his most merciless measures: the Law of Prairial (10 June 1794) which gave any accused person practically no chance of escaping the scaffold. During this *Great Terror* more than one thousand executions took place in forty-five days in Paris.

On 20 May 1795 an *impoverished, wretched rabble* aroused the Parisians with cries of "Bread and the 1793 Constitution!" The Thermidorians called out the troops against the rioters. From street brawls the Royalists progressed to organize massacres in the provinces. The *White Terror* claimed numerous victims in the south-east. The Chouans [or Royalists, *Tr.*] supported an English landing at Quiberon Bay which was soon foiled by General Hoche's troops. On 5 October 1795 the Royalists tried to instigate an insurrection in Paris. The Convention entrusted their defence forces to a young general named Bonaparte, who shot down the rebels.

On the steps of the Church of St-Roch the Directorate came up against the same enemies: the Royalists and the Jacobins. So it practised pendulum politics, swinging sometimes against the right (the execution in spring 1796 of the Chouan leaders Stofflet and Charette), sometimes against the left (destroying the Conspiracy of Equals instigated by Gracchus Babeuf).'[4]

During 1792–99 France suffered an unparalleled series of disturbances and massacres, unrivalled even by the darkest days of the Inquisition! [*Sept ans sera de douleur explorée.*]

'The businessmen and the contented, reassured bourgeoisie favoured Bonaparte, who had raised their spirits. He authorized the return of the émigrés to France and gained the support of many of them by giving them government posts. He offered the Chouans an amnesty.'

'The Constitution of Year VIII (15 December 1799) gave executive power to three Consuls elected for ten years, but the first Consul, Bonaparte, *had sole power of decision*; increasingly he initiated laws.'[4] The First Republic thus lasted seven years and almost two months' [*plus longue vie au règne par grand heur*].

---

[1] Marianne, the woman without a husband, was the symbol of the French Republic.
[2] Latin *regnum*: reign, power. DLLB.
[3] The king was unique in the exercise of monarchical power.
[4] LCH3.

The Tuileries, 20 June 1792 and 10 August 1792

Le part[1] soluz[2] Mary sera mittré[3]
Retour conflict passera sur le thuille[4]
Par cinq cens un trahyr[5] sera tiltré,[6]
Narbon et Saulce par contaux[7] avons d'huille.[8]

CIX,Q34

Interpretation

Having made up his mind alone the King shall wear the Phrygian cap, after his return [from Varennes] conflict will continue into the Tuileries, treason will be plotted by 500 persons. No force, because of the Count of Narbonne and Sauce.

History

'The population of Paris, warned by the clubs, rose against the King. On 20 June a crowd of armed demonstrators invaded the *Tuileries*, surrounded the King by a window and demanded the *withdrawal of the veto*; the King had to don *the red cap*, but would *not relent*. On 10 August, Federates from Marseille and people from the Paris suburbs invaded the Tuileries and massacred the Swiss Guard.'[9]

'*Narbonne*: in 1791, after promotion to brigadier on his return to Paris, he became War Minister. Soon *suspected* however, by both the revolutionaries and the court, he resigned from office on 10 March 1792 and went back to the northern army. When he returned to Paris, three days before 10 August, *he tried to save the monarchy*.'[10]

'At last on 30 June the Marseille group arrived. There were 500 of them.'[11]

'When the coach arrived, it was suddenly surrounded by armed National Guardsmen commanded by the *procureur* of the commune, *Sauce*. Growing ever more embarrassed, Sauce had time to send word to Paris. Twenty hours later, in Sauce's bedroom, through power of attorney a warrant for Louis XVI's arrest was handed to the King, who cried out, "There is no longer a King in France!" '[12]

---

[1] Masculine noun: decision (DAFL); determination, resolution (DL7V). 'During the Revolution the Suspensive Veto was retained by the King.' DL7V.

[2] Latin *solus*: alone, solitary. DLLB.

[3] Mitre: 'For Latin and Greek authors this term signified headgear worn by men and women of India and Phrygia.' DL7V.

[4] Tuilerie: place where tiles (*tuiles*) are made.
[5] Verb used as noun.
[6] *Titrer*: (symbolic) to scheme or intrigue. DL7V.
[7] *Comtal, comtaux*: belonging to a count or counts. DL7V.
[8] Popular usage: strength. DL7V.
[9] LCH3.
[10] DL7V.
[11] A. Thiers, *History of the French Revolution*.
[12] LRFPG.

The Year 1792: Revolts in the Provinces, the Royal Family in the Temple

Deux estendars[1] du costé de l'Auvergne,
Senestre[2] pris, pour un temps prison regne,
Et une Dame enfans voudra mener,
Au[3] Censuart[4] mais descouvert l'affaire,
Danger de mort murmure[5] sur la terre,
Germain,[6] Bastille[7] frère et soeur prisonnier.

Sixain 9

Interpretation

When there are revolts in the Auvergne area, the left having taken power, imprisonment will prevail for some time and the Queen will wish to take her children away, but Sauce will unveil the affair; popular discontent will constitute mortal danger; brother and sister of the same parents will be imprisoned in a castle flanked by turrets [the Temple].

History

'In February 1792 not a day passed without news of some alarming insurrection. There were pillage and massacres in the Yonne and Nièvre where the troublemakers this time were the inhabitants of the *Morvan*. In March and April 1792 the Cantal department was troubled by a peasant revolt which terrorized a score of communes: castles were burnt, properties were forcibly requisitioned, and the authorities were powerless or acquiescent.'[8]

'Amid the agitation after 10 August the civil powers, Assembly and Executive Council, had to come to terms with the Revolutionary authority, *the Paris Commune* [*senestre*], which exercised virtual dictatorship. Despite the Assembly's decree that Louis XVI and the *royal family* should be interned in the Luxembourg Palace, the Commune had them *imprisoned* in the *tower* of the Temple. Soon thousands of "suspects" were *incarcerated*."[9]

For the flight to Varennes and the part played by Sauce, see CIX,Q34.

[1] To raise the *standard* or banner of revolt; to revolt. DL7V.
[2] Latin *sinister*: left.
[3] For the Latin preposition, *a* or *ab* = by.
[4] Anagram of Sauce. The letters N, R and T added by epenthesis and paragoge.
[5] Act of complaining; complaints of discontented persons; murmurs of dissatisfaction from the people. DL7V.
[6] Issue of the same father and the same mother; brother and sister german. DL7V.
[7] Castle flanked by turrets, and by extension any prison. DL7V.
[8] LRFPG.
[9] HFAM.

The Battle of Valmy, 20 September 1792.
The Triumvirate, 1790. Robespierre and Mirabeau.
Mirabeau at the Pantheon

Au costé gauche[1] à l'endroit de Vitri,
Seront guettez les trois rouges de France:
Tous assoumez rouge,[2] noir[3] non meurdry:[4]
Par les Bretons remis en asseurance.

CIX,Q58

Interpretation

Because of the left [there will be a battle] near Vitry. The three reds of France will be spied upon and killed by the red, the aristocrat [Mirabeau] will not be killed and will be placed in safety by the Jacobins.

History

'On 17 September 1792 Kellermann climbed up from Vitry-le-François towards the north-east. All the Allies and all the French troops then faced each other. On 20 September the Battle of Valmy was won. . . .

On the *left* were many lawyers like Tronchet or Le Chapelier, who founded the *Breton* club which would become the Jacobin Club. Very soon the left split into sects and coteries. The most famous was the *Triumvirate* of Adrien du Port, Charles de Lameth and Barnave. They opposed La Fayette and Mirabeau. The important figure was Barnave.

When Mirabeau grew closer to the court party, Barnave violently opposed him. In 1791 he defended the Jacobin Club against the Monarchists' Club. After Varennes, Mirabeau became reconciled with the King and turned into a supporter of constitutional monarchy. He was to be arrested, condemned and executed.'[5]

'The decree of martial law followed: if any riotous assembly became threatening the alarm cannon would be fired, and *a red flag* would be hung from a window of the Hôtel de Ville as a signal for the populace to disperse. The decree was backed by Mirabeau and attacked by Robespierre,[6] whose *demagogy*, already demonstrated more than once, began to be even more marked.

The discussions and decisions of the *Jacobins* were growing increasingly extreme and heated. Almost all of one whole session was devoted to the fate of the church of St Genevieve, which had not yet been consecrated by the Catholics. It was solemnly decreed that it would be known as the *Panthéon*. *Count* Mirabeau was the *first* to receive funeral honours there.'[7]

---

[1] Political ref. In assembly, benches would be placed to the right or left of the President; the members who occupied such benches. DL7V.

[2] Latin *rubeus*. Name for the most extreme Republicans. DL7V.

[3] *Noirs*: name given to the deputies of the Constituent Assembly who sat to the right of the room. The name of 'Blacks' was given to the aristocrats as much by analogy as because most of them wore ecclesiastical garb. DL7V.

[4] *Meurtrir*: i.e. kill, cause to perish by murder. DL7V.

[5] HFACAD.

[6] Cf. CVIII,Q19 and CVIII,Q80. Robespierre = *la pierre rouge*, the red stone.

[7] HFA.

The Trial of Louis XVI, 17 January 1793.
The Affair of the Iron Cabinet

Lettres trouvées de la Royne les coffres,[1]
Point de subscrit[2] sans aucun nom d'autheur:
Par le police seront cachez les offres,[3]
Qu'on ne sçaura qui sera l'amateur.

CVIII,Q23

Interpretation

The letters found in the Queen's cupboards will be discovered, without signature or author's name. The police will conceal the payment offers [contract of defence] so well that the beneficiary [of the funds] will not be known.

History

'A letter from Laporte was said to be in Louis's own hand and dated, but he maintained he recognized neither the letter nor its date. Two others from the same source, both annotated in the hand of Louis, 3 March and 3 April 1791. He denied all knowledge of them. An unsigned paper, containing a "defence contract": before questioning Louis about this, the President asked the following: "Did you cause to be built in one wall of the Tuileries Castle *a cabinet* with an iron door, and keep papers therein?" Louis: "I know nothing about that, nor about the *unsigned* paper." '[4]

'I observed that even with the official seals affixed to the papers of every accused person, no inventory had ever been made in the presence of the accused of the individual papers thus bound together. I should add that nothing would be easier for hostile or malicious persons than to slide under the seals papers which might compromise an accused person and to *remove those which might justify him*. Louis's domicile was invaded and his *cabinets* forced open. During the confusion pieces of paper could have been *lost* or *stolen*, especially the ones which might have explained those used against him. Septeuil, in a public statement, explained away such a speculation by maintaining that not only did it concern himself alone, but that a special register was kept for Louis' *accounts, about which no one has given us any information*, and that it listed the particulars of such funds.'[5]

'In his cross-examination Louis XVI tried nonetheless to deny all knowledge of the notorious *cabinet* and the *papers* inside it. Besides, the most important documents would have been taken away in a large satchel and entrusted to *Marie-Antoinette*'s lady-in-waiting, Madame Campan.'[6]

---

[1] The importance of chests or coffers declined in the mid-sixteenth century with the increased use of cupboards and cabinets. DL7V.

[2] Latin *subscriptio*: signature at the foot of a document. DLLB.

[3] Contract statement akin to an IOU setting out terms of obligation in order to prevent or halt a court action. DL7V.

[4] Cross-examination of Louis XVI. HFA.

[5] Defence of Louis by Citizen de Sèze. HFA.

[6] DL7V.

The Flight to Varennes, 20 June 1792.
The Vote to Pass the Death Sentence on the King.
War, 1 February 1793

De nuict viendra par la forêt de Reines,[1]
Deux pars voltorte[2] Herne[3] la pierre blanche[4]
Le moine[5] noir[6] en gris dedans Varennes
Esleu cap[7] cause tempeste, feu, sang, tranche.

CIX,Q20

Interpretation

He will arrive by night through the forest of Rheims, tortured by two parties in his willingness to be a devout monarch, the noble monk in grey, at Varennes. The head of Capet put to the vote will cause storm, war, blood, guillotine.

History

'In France, an absolute king reigned [who governed *alone*] by *divine right* [*hernute*]. The King had been too weak to impose *his will* [*voltorte*]. Louis XVI in spite of his *private virtues* [*hernute*] had not the qualities of a sovereign.'[8]

'Louis XVI was deeply *pious. Troubled by his conscience*, he then decided to escape.'[9]

'The King was *guillotined* on 21 January 1793. This execution prompted Royalist indignation and the horrified censure of foreign monarchs who now considered alliance against the Republic. France had just declared war upon England [1 February 1793].'[10]

'By 683 *Votes*, Louis *Capet* was found guilty of conspiring against the security of the state.'[11]

---

[1] All old editions give 'Reines'. It can therefore be taken either as a typographical error or as a modification by Nostradamus to preserve the rhyme. The Forest of Rheims is near Varennes and was crossed by the royal coach.

[2] Composite word from two Latin words: *voluntas*, will, and *tortus*, twisted. Early commentators translated it as *short cut* or *diversion*, and later ones (Hutin, Guerin, Monterey, Colin de Larmor etc.) followed this reading. But Propertius uses the phrase *torta via*, i.e. *labyrinthine detours*. Editions after 1610 have *vaultorte* for *voltorte*.

[3] *Herne*: abbreviation of *Hernute*, a Christian sect distinguished for its purity of morals. DL7V.

[4] 'The white rock or stone' was a symbol of the establishment. White was the Royalist colour, the Rock was the Church (cf. Christ's words to St Peter). Cf. also CII,Q2.

[5] Greek μόνος: only, unique, single. DGF. Cf. CVI,63: '*L'unic*'. Also reiterates the idea of king-as-monk.

⁶ *Noir*: see CIX,Q58, note 3.
⁷ Cap. Abbreviated pun whereby Nostradamus suggests both Latin *caput*: head and a shortened form of *Capet*.
⁸ LCH3.
⁹ HFAM.
¹⁰ HFDG.

The Execution of Louis XVI, 21 January 1793

> Par grand discord la trombe[1] tremblera
> Accord rompu dressant la tête du Ciel
> Bouche sanglante dans le sang nagera
> Au sol la face oincte de laict et de miel.

CI,Q57

Interpretation

Amid great discord the hunting horn shall sound, the agreement having been broken, [the executioner] lifting up the head [of the King] to heaven, the bloody mouth swimming in blood, his face anointed with milk and honey shall be on the ground.

History

'The King had been imprisoned from 10 August 1792 (the taking of the Tuileries and the massacre of the Swiss Guard). The Montagnards demanded his trial, but the Girondins wanted to prevent it' [*Amid great discord*].

'Execution of Louis XVI: the executioner *displayed the King's head* to the people' [*Holding aloft the head*].[2] The King's head, which had been crowned at Rheims in 1774, fell to the ground, into the basket below the guillotine.

[1] Kind of trumpet, esp. hunting horn.
[2] LCH3.

The Execution of Louis XVI. His Succession

Devant le peuple sang sera respandu,
Que du haut ciel ne viendra eslonger;[1]
Mais d'un long temps ne sera entendu,
L'esprit d'un seul le viendra témoigner.

CIV,Q49

Interpretation

Blood will be shed before the people and he will not be far from heaven. For a long time he will no more be understood, until the spirit of one who comes one day to bear witness.

History

'The King slowly descended from the tumbril, let his hands be tied, climbed the steps, and at the top of the platform cried out: "People! I die innocent!"

In his will, dated 25 December 1792, after forgiving his enemies and urging his son to set aside all hatred and resentment, he ended by declaring to God, as he was ready *to appear before Him*, that he was not guilty of any of the crimes of which he was accused.'[2]

'Abbé Edgeworth calmed the King's brief resistance with the now legendary words: "Son of St Louis, *climb up to heaven!*" '[3]

The last two lines of the quatrain suggest that Louis XVII would not die in the Temple and that one of his descendants would one day come to bear witness.

[1] Cf. CI,Q57: *'dressant la tête au Ciel.'*
[2] DHCD.
[3] HFAM.

The Execution of Louis XVI.
The Terror, 21 January 1793

Le juste à tort à mort l'on viendra mettre
Publiquement et du milieu estaint.[1]
Si grande peste[2] en ce lieu viendra naistre
Que les jugeans fouyr seront contraints.

CIX,QII

Interpretation

It will be wrong to put the just man to death, executed amid the people.
It will bring upon this spot [Paris] such a great calamity [the Terror]
that those who did not vote [for the King's death] will be compelled to
flee.

History

'Louis is not an accused man, you are not *judges*. You do not have to
pronounce sentence for or against a man, but to take a measure of public
safety. Victory and the people have decided that he alone was the rebel.
Louis cannot therefore be *judged*, he is already condemned.'[3]

'The Montagnards took power and had to deal with the Vendée
uprising backed by the Girondins against the dictatorship in Paris. They
constituted a revolutionary government. This was the Reign of Terror.
On 9 Thermidor (27 July 1794) Robespierre was accused. He *fled*, was
recaptured and executed without trial.'[4]

'Robespierre was lying at my feet and I was told that Henriot *was
escaping* by a concealed staircase. I still had a loaded pistol and ran after
him. I hit a *fugitive* on that staircase – it was Couthon who was *running
away*.'[5]

---

[1] Latin *exstinguo*: I put to death, execute. DLLB.
[2] Latin *pestis*: misfortune, plague, disaster, calamity. DLLB. Cf. CVI,Q63: '*Sept ans sera
de douleur explorée*'.
[3] Robespierre's speech to the Convention (3 December 1792).
[4] DHC.
[5] Report by the gendarme sent to arrest Robespierre, who had just been outlawed by
the Convention.

Marie-Antoinette and the
Duchess of Angoulême at the Temple, 1793

La Royne Ergaste[1] voyant sa fille blesme[2]
Par un regret dans l'estomach[3] enclos:
Crys lamentables seront lors d'Angoulesme,
Et au germain mariage forclos.[4]

CX,QI7

Interpretation

The Queen detained like a slave, seeing her daughter waste away will regret within her womb that she had children, swayed by the lamentations of the Duchess of Angoulême, married to her first cousin in an unacceptable union.

History

'Marie-Antoinette, imprisoned in the Temple until 1 August 1793, endured every outrage and agony, whether as queen, wife or *mother*, and her captivity was a true martyrdom.

The Duchess of Angoulême, daughter of Louis XVI and Marie-Antoinette, entered the Temple to share her family's captivity. She married her cousin the Duke of Angoulême, son of the Count of Artois (the future Charles X), third brother of Louis XVI.'[5]

[1] Latin *ergastulus*: slave, prisoner. DLLB.
[2] *Blesmer*: to waste away. DAFL.
[3] Womb. DL7V.
[4] Legal term: inadmissible. DAFL.
[5] DHCD.

The Survival of the Bourbons after Thirty Generations

Peuple assemblé voir nouveau expectacle
Princes et Roys par plusieurs assistans,
Pilliers faillir, murs, mais comme miracle
Le Roy sauvé et trente des instans.[1]

CVI,Q51

Interpretation

The people will assemble for a spectacle hitherto unseen [a king's execution in a public place], together with several princes and leaders of royal blood; the pillars and walls [of the Bastille] will be broken down but miraculously the blood royal will be preserved after thirty successors.

History

After the demolition of the Bastille, the public execution of Louis XVI took place. A prince of the royal blood, Philippe Egalité, had voted for his death.

There were indeed thirty generations of French monarchs between Robert the Strong, father of King Odo, and Louis XVII.

Most historians now accept the hypothesis that the Dauphin did escape from the Temple Prison.

[1] Latin *insto*: I follow, succeed. DLLB.

Louis XVII's Escape from the Temple Prison

Sans pied ne main[1] dent aiguë et forte
Par globe[2] au fort du port[3] et l'aisne nay,[4]
Près du portail desloyal se transporte,
Silène[5] luit, petit grand emmené.

CII,Q58

Interpretation

Without trial and without force he who has a sarcastic and eloquent tongue will be carried to power by the masses, and the eldest having died soon after birth, one will be transported disloyally to the main gate [of the Temple]. The Republic rules, the little [young] great one [by birth] is led away.

History

'Robespierre's name was picked from the *electoral urn* in the open polls in Paris for the elections to the Convention. During Louis XVI's trial he played the most *hateful* role until the fatal climax on 21 January 1793. On 31 May the Girondins were defeated, in which he was instrumental. From then on his power was immense. He entered the Committee of Public Safety and imposed a yoke of force and terror, pitilessly sacrificing men's lives to his political machinations. Arrested in the great chamber of the Hôtel de Ville on 10 Thermidor, he perished on the scaffold.'[6]

'The Temple was actually a palace. Its layout was quite similar to that of the Hôtel Soubise, with a long courtyard surrounded by arcades

ending in a semi-circle at the *gate*. The procession bringing the prisoners
was considerably delayed.'[7]

[1] Latin *manus*: hand, strength. DLLB.
[2] Latin *globus*: group of men, crowd, mob. DLLB.
[3] Action of bearing away or carrying. DL7V.
[4] Louis XVII, b. 1785, first had the title of Duke of Normandy, and became Dauphin
on the death of his elder brother Louis-Joseph (4 June 1789).
[5] Phrygian god. (DL7V). The Phrygian cap or bonnet was adopted as a symbol of the
Republic.
[6] DHCD.
[7] *Louis XVII and the Temple Enigma*, G. Lenôtre, Flammarion, 1920.

Louis XVII Escapes from the Temple Thanks to the Simons

> Sur le palais[1] au rocher[2] des fenestres
> Seront ravis les deux petits royaux,
> Passer aurelle[3] Luthèce, Denis Cloistres[4]
> Nonnain,[5] mollods[6] avaller verts noyaux.

CIX,Q24

Interpretation

In the palace with the steeply sloping windows the two royal children
will be taken away, they will traverse Paris like a breeze, escaping from
the Cloisters of St-Denis, thanks to a monk,[7] the wicked wretched ones
will devour green kernels.

History

'If Paris itself lived through that dark day of 21 January 1793 in a sort
of stupor, there *on the third floor* of the Temple Tower the Queen was
plunged into anguish and despair.'[8]

'Antoine Simon: keeper of Louis XVII in the Temple. A master
cobbler in Paris, he became member for his district and belonged to the
Jacobin Club.'[9]

'Another riddle adds to the mystery. Simon left the Temple on 19
January, grumbling loudly about Chaumette's and the Commune's ingratitude. The next morning he went to the poor lodgings of two old
ladies, recluses and former *nuns*, who sheltered a *priest* who like themselves had escaped the Terror. They were celebrating mass in their garret

and the sound of knocking on their door startled them greatly. Yet they opened it to a man they did not know. "Do not be afraid," he said. "I know you have a priest here, but I won't betray you. I am Simon." A number of the most fervent and sincere Republicans remained devoted to the old beliefs and respected past traditions. Until at least 1792 the great majority of the Convention, the *Jacobins* and the members of the Commune went to church services and performed their religious *devotions*. Surprising as it may seem, Simon was one of these. The representatives thus knew that Citizeness Simon (among others), who lived in a house close to the Temple, used this passage. What could the shoemaker's wife do?"[10]

[1] The Tower of the Temple, a square building with thick walls, flanked by turrets at its four corners. The Palais du Grand Prieuré was built in 1767. DL7V.

[2] Rock, i.e. great mass of hard stone, sloping or steep.

[3] *Aurelle*: from Latin *aura*, wind. Diminutive = breeze. DL7V.

[4] '. . . the Church of St-Denis had the privilege of being the Royal Sepulchre.' DL7V.

[5] Nun, or general term including priests. DL7V.

[6] Composite word, from *mol* (mal) = bad, evil and *lods* = miserable, wretched. DAFL.

[7] Jacobin: monk or nun of the Order of St Dominic; member of the Jacobin Club, founded in 1789. DL7V.

[8] *Louis XVII and the Temple Enigma*, G. Lenôtre, Flammarion, 1920.

[9] DL7V.

[10] *Louis XVII and the Temple Enigma*, G. Lenôtre, Flammarion, 1920.

The Execution of Marie-Antoinette, 16 October 1793. Madame Royale at the Temple

Un peu devant ou après très grand Dame[1]
Son âme au Ciel[2] et son corps sous la lame,
De plusieurs gens regrettée sera,
Tous ses parents seront en grand'tristesse:
Pleurs et soupirs d'une Dame[3] en jeunesse
Et a deux grands[4] le deuil délaissera.

Sixaine 55

Interpretation

Before [the people] shortly after [the execution of Louis XVI] the Queen will be guillotined and her soul will go to heaven. She will be mourned by many. Her relatives will lament: tears and sighs from her daughter. She will leave her two [brothers-in-law] in mourning.

History

'Marie-Antoinette, imprisoned in the Temple until 1 August 1793, endured every outrage and agony, whether as Queen, *wife* or *mother*, and her captivity was a true martyrdom. Tried before the Revolutionary Tribunal, she was *condemned to death*. She nevertheless possessed enough fine qualities to be *generally beloved* in more normal circumstances, when she could or would have been judged dispassionately. Led in a tumbril to her fate, she showed great courage and, like her husband, died *forgiving* her enemies.'[5]

[1] Superlative designating the Queen.

[2] Cf. CIV,Q49: '*Que du haut ciel ne viendra éloigner.*'

[3] The Duchess of Angoulême, daughter of Louis XVI and Marie-Antoinette, received at birth the title of *Madame* Royale. After 10 August 1792 she entered the Temple to share her family's imprisonment. DHCD.

[4] Louis, Dauphin of France, son of Louis XV and Marie-Leczinska, left three sons, *Louis XVI, Louis XVIII and Charles X*, and two daughters, Clotilde, Queen of Sardinia, and Elizabeth. DL7V.

[5] DHCD.

The Trial of Marie-Antoinette, 14 October 1793. Her Execution, 16 October 1793

La grande Royne quand se verra vaincue,
Fera excez de masculin courage:
Sur cheval, fleuve passera toute nuë,[1]
Suite par fer, a foy fera outrage.

CI,Q86

Interpretation

When the great Queen [Marie-Antoinette] sees herself lost, she will put on excessive manly courage. She will cross the river [Seine] drawn by a horse, ill-clad. Then she will die by the sword [guillotine], and it will outrage belief.

History

'Since August the clubs, the deputies of the main assemblies, and the popular societies had been demanding the Queen's trial, which opened on 14 October before the Revolutionary Tribunal presided over by Herman. Fouquier-Tinville was Public Prosecutor. She was asked the most insidious questions. The accusations concerning the monarchy by pamphleteers hostile to her were again dug up and used against her. Simple and dignified, the Queen replied that she had only obeyed her husband. In order to set the debate ablaze, Hébert made the most *outrageous* accusations against her. The grief-stricken woman managed to answer these calumnies movingly. Despite the pleas of Tanson-Ducoudray and Chauveau-Lagarde, the Queen was condemned to death. On the morning of 16 October she climbed on to a wagon and sat with her back to the *horse: clad in a loose gown*, wearing a white bonnet, her hands tied behind her back, and her eyes half-closed, *erect and impassive [excès de masculin courage]*, this woman who had received such adulation heard the crowd hurling *insults* at her. Marie-Antoinette rapidly mounted the steps leading to the scaffold. A few moments later her *tortured* body [*suite par fer*] was on its way to rejoin the remains of Louis XVI, at the Madeleine Cemetery. . . .

On 14 October 1793 Marie-Antoinette appeared before the Revolutionary Tribunal, wearing a *shabby* black dress [*nue*] and a lawn bonnet trimmed with "widow's weeds".[2]

'I have just been condemned, not to a shameful death, which is only for criminals, but to rejoin your brother: innocent like himself, I hope to show *the same steadfastness as he* in his last moments' [*manly courage*].[3]

[1] By exaggeration, ill-clad. DL7V.
[2] HFACAD.
[3] Will of Marie-Antoinette, in the form of a letter to her sister-in-law Elizabeth. HFA.

The Alliance of Philippe of Orleans with the Revolution. His Death, 6 November 1793

Celui du sang resperse[1] le visage,
De la victime proche sacrifice,
Venant en Leo[2] augure[3] par présage,
Mis estre à mort lors pour la fiancée.

CII,Q98

Interpretation

He whose face is bespattered with the blood of the victim, his close [relative] sacrificed, the adoption of the Phrygian bonnet will be an evil omen for him and he will be put to death because of his alliance.

History

'Louis-Philippe of Orleans, called Philippe-Egalité, initially *allied* with Mirabeau and was one of the first to commit himself to the Third Estate. His followers were certainly privy to the events which led to the storming of the Bastille. He secretly supported the republicans of the Champ du Mars (July 1791) and became a member of the Jacobin Club. He developed *closer links* with the Cordeliers, the Jacobins and the Paris Commune. Overshadowed by the Montagnards, he sought favour with their leaders who, seeing that he intended to be impartial in Louis XVI's trial, forced him by various threats to vote with them. *He therefore voted for the King's death sentence without reprieve*, without appeal to the people, and *thereby became just as suspect*, especially at the first signs of Dumouriez's plan for re-establishing the 1791 constitution and restoring the throne for a prince of Orleans. He was arrested on 7 April 1793, taken back to Paris, adjudged a Girondin by the Revolutionary Tribunal, sentenced and *executed*.'[4]

[1] Latin *respergo*: I sprinkle water. DLLB.
[2] Latin *Leo*, priest of Mithras, worshipped by the Persians in the form of a lion. DLLB. Mithras is represented by a young man wearing the *Phrygian cap*. DHCD.
[3] Latin *auguro*: I predict. DLLB.
[4] DHCD.

The Execution of Philippe-Egalité, 6 November 1793

Le Grand Baillif[1] d'Orléans mis à mort,
Sera par un de sang vindicatif:
De mort merite ne mourra ne par fort,
Des pieds et mains mal le faisoit captif.

CIII,Q66

Interpretation

The great representative from Orleans will be put to death by order of a bloodthirsty and vengeful person, he will die a deserved death but only by force, evil binding his hands and feet.

History

'Defender of the rights of the Third Estate in the Assembly of Notables in 1787, and at the States-General in 1789, the people's protector. Declared enemy of the royal family, he was openly revolutionary. A member of the Convention, he sat on the extreme left. Although he had voted for the death of his kinsman, the King, and was always a Montagnard, he became suspect to his former friends. The same day he appeared before the Revolutionary Tribunal he died very bravely on the scaffold.'[2]

[1] Ancient form of *bailli*, bailiff-governor(s), later replaced by deputies. DAFL.
[2] DL7V.

The Committee of Twelve, May 1793. Their Arrest, 2 June 1793

Celuy qu'aura couvert de[1] la grand cappe,
Sera induict à quelques cas[2] patrer[3]:
Les Douze rouges viendront fouiller[4] la nappe,[5]
Soubz meurtre, meurtre se viendra perpetrer.

CIV,QII

Interpretation

He [Robespierre] who will have covered the great Capet [Louis XVI] with shame will be led to accomplish various falls: the twelve reds will come to look through the plans minutely, and under cover of murder he shall perpetrate their own murders.

History

'Invested with great powers and composed of deputies whose names would reassure all honest persons, the *Committee of Twelve* could frustrate all subversion against the Convention or any of its members. It might have spoiled all the *plans* of the Jacobins and the Montagnards. Thus the *Twelve* were destined to be targets for *assassins* the moment they began functioning as a group, and the struggle against them became a struggle to the *death*. Information indicated that a plot was being hatched against the lives of twenty-six deputies, which prompted them to issue a warrant for Hébert's arrest. The Committee considered him to be involved in the plot, and that for better or worse his writings were provoking the *murder* of the people's representatives. Couthon reported to the Tribunal and combined irony with arrogance: "Citizens," he said, "every member of the Convention must be reassured of their liberties," and he demanded that the Convention should decree the house arrests of the twenty-six along with the Committee of Twelve.'[6]

'The *coup* of 2 June provoked insurrection in several regions. The Convention resolved to pursue the struggle against its enemies to the bitter end. It entrusted power to the most intransigent Montagnards: Robespierre and his friends Couthon and St-Just. By the end of 1794, *2596 persons had been executed* in Paris.'[7]

[1] To cover with either shame or infamy, or glory. DL7V.
[2] Latin *casus*: fall, end, decline, death. DLLB.
[3] Latin *patro*: I do, execute, accomplish. DLLB.
[4] Figurative: to scrutinize, study attentively, examine the ills of society. DL7V.
[5] By analogy, a flat surface. DL7V.
[6] HFA.
[7] HFAM.

The Nantes Massacres, November 1793

Des principaux de cité rebellée
Qui tiendront fort pour liberté ravoir:
Destrencher[1] masles infelice[2] meslée
Cris, hurlemens à Nantes; piteux voir.

CV,Q33

Interpretation

Of the main rebels of the town, who will fight to the end to preserve their freedom, the men shall be guillotined, the unfortunates being mixed together, cries and shrieks at Nantes, all constituting a dreadful spectacle.

History

'At *Nantes* Carrier, a member of the Convention, ruled. He was present at Cholet, but fled from the battle, and thereafter, consumed by fear, had only one obsession: to *kill* in order not to be killed. This deep-seated mania, exacerbated by his drunkenness, degenerated into lunacy.

On the hulks at *Nantes* were a hundred elderly and ailing priests, whom it had not been possible to deport to Guyana. They were therefore taken from one prison to the next. On the night of 16 to 17 November, on the pretext of moving them once more to land, their captors made them climb aboard an old barge which had once plied the lower Loire and now, owing to the decline in trade, had fallen into disuse. *Tied up in pairs,* they showed no resistance, although at the outset their money and watches had been taken from them. Suddenly one of the prisoners noticed that the barge had been holed in several places below the water-line and that water was slowly seeping through these apertures. The priests fell to their knees and gave each other absolution. A quarter of an hour later the barge sank with all its passengers except four. Of these, three were recaptured and put to death. Only one, picked up by fisher-men, managed to hide, and the little that is known of the last moments of the victims derives from him.

On 5 December arrived fifty-eight more helpless priests. "Fling all those buggers in the water," Carrier ordered. On the night of the ninth they were drowned at Indret Point. The Proconsul immediately announced this new "shipwreck" to the Convention and ended his dis-patch with this cynical remark: "What a revolutionary torrent the Loire is!" *At least eleven other executions by drowning followed,* some by night, some by day, *which claimed 4800 victims.* To this must be added *guillo-tinings*: there were three travelling committees and the Paris tribunal eagerly fed on the rich pastures of Brittany. One historian assures us that in fact Carrier killed fewer people than the typhus and other epidemics which were rife in the prisons of Nantes, which must be some sort of consolation."[3]

---

[1] *Détrenchier* = to cut into pieces, slice. DAFL.
[2] Latin *infelix*: unhappy. DLLB.
[3] LRFPG.

The Abbé Vaugeois, President
of the Committee of Insurrection, August 1792.
The Capture of Chalonnes-sur-Loire by the Vendéans,
22 March 1793. Massacres of Priests on the Loire,
17 November and 5 December 1793

Au temple[1] hault de Bloys Sacre[2] Salonne
Nuict pont de Loyre, Prelat, Roy pernicant:[3]
Cuiseur victoire aux marests de la Lone,[4]
D'ou prélature de blancs[5] abormeant.[6]

                                        CIX,Q21

Interpretation

The important personage of the Church of Blois will be cursed at Chalonnes-sur-Loire. A priest will be found by night on the bridge of the Loire, the King having been made light [dethroned], the people of Olonne will win sharp victories in the marshes; the royalist priests having been bound.

History

'There was a concentration of Federates and a stir in the divisions. These were the two initial factors leading to the events of 10 August 1792. Everything was directed by a Committee of Insurrection presided over by the Abbé Vaugeois, Vicar-General of the *Bishopric of Blois*. It was Robespierre who drew up the Federates' petitions for the *dethronement of the King*.'[7]

'On 22 March 1793, the Vendéan army seized *Chalonnes*.'[8]

'There were a hundred or so elderly priests on the prison *hulks* [Fr: *ponton*] of Nantes. *On the night* of 16 November they were made to board an old barge. [*"Tied up in pairs"*, etc. (Cf. *CV,Q33*).]

Carrier was recalled in February 1794. His departure marked the end of the drownings, but General Turreau, Marceau's successor in the Vendée, carried on the terror in his own way. Almost all the leaders of the Vendée uprising had been killed. Charette and Stofflet, the two survivors, had no option but to take up arms again, one in the *Marais* [marshlands], the other in the *forest areas*. This was a new, appalling and futile war. At the start of 1794 the Revolution had completely triumphed over its internal enemies.'[9]

[1] Poetic: the Catholic Church.

[2] Latin *sacro*: I vow to gods of vengeance, curse. DLLB.

[3] Latin *pernix*: light. DLLB.

[4] Contraction of *Olonne*: area of La Vendée 5 km from Sables-d'Olonne; the Vendéans had a headquarters there in 1793. DL7V.

[5] During the *ancien régime* white was always taken to represent the nation and royalty. DL7V.

[6] From *ormeger*: to bind or tie up. DAFL.

[7] LRFPG.

[8] HFACAD.

[9] LRFPG.

Pitt the Younger against the French Revolution, 1793–96 British Aid to the Vendéans, 1795. The Return to Power of Pitt the Younger

Le jeune nay au regne Britannique,
Qu'aura le père mourant recommandé:
Iceluy mort LONOLE[1] donra topique[2]
Et à son fils le regne demandé.

CX,Q40

Interpretation

[Pitt] the Younger returned to power in England, and he will have received instructions from his dying father. After the latter's death, he will bring aid to the Vendéans [those of d'Olonne] and the son will be asked to take power again.

History

'From 1793 to 1802 the British war effort increased, urged on by Pitt *the Younger* until 1801. He had *inherited from his father* a definite distrust of France.'[3]

'In the western departments [of France] the Royalist party offered bold resistance, which was helped by intrigues in *England*. Charette and Larochejacquelin had reappeared at the head of the *Vendéans* [*ceux d'Olonne*]. After giving the British hope of a general uprising throughout the areas, if an invasion force of émigrés, arms and supplies could be landed, the Marquis de Puisaye allied with the Chouans and was confident of striking a deadly blow at the Republic. *The English minister*, disappointed by the coalition's lack of success against the French forces, espoused this cause fervently and undertook to supply *60,000 rifles*, as well as *complete equipment* [*topiques*] for an army of 40,000 men.'[4]

'To raise funds for the war Pitt had to subject England to a regime of emergency regulations, but managed to prevent neither French victories nor the ruin of British trade. He resigned in 1801. Addington, his successor, concluded the Peace of Amiens [1802]. War having begun again, *Pitt once more accepted office* [1804].'[5]

[1] Anagram of Ollone or Olonne: see CIX,Q21, note 4.
[2] Word for localized medications, acting on specific parts of the body.
[3] HRU.
[4] HFA.
[5] DL7V.

Robespierre, His Friends and Enemies

A[1] soustenir la Grand Cappe troublée
Pour l'esclaircir les rouges marcheront
De mort famille sera presque accablée,
Les rouges rouges le rouge assomeront.

CVIII,Q19

Interpretation

Without support the great Capet family will be disturbed. The reds will start decimating it. The royal family will be almost overwhelmed by death. The red extremists will kill the red [Robespierre] and other reds.

History

With the execution of Louis XVI, Marie-Antoinette, and Louis' sister Elizabeth, also the presumed death of Louis XVII in the Temple Prison, the Capet family was certainly 'thinned out' [éclaircie].

'As for Robespierre, his undoubted virtues were, in his colleagues' eyes, eclipsed by his pride, fanaticism and intransigence: he inspired fear. His *enemies* banded together in order *to get rid of him*.'[2]

'The followers of Robespierre who had been outlawed by the Convention were arrested. Robespierre's jaw was shattered by a pistol bullet. The same evening, on 10 Thermidor, he was *guillotined along with twenty-two of his supporters*; the next day and the day after that, it was the turn of *eighty-three more*. Thus the Great Terror ended with a new slaughter.'[3]

[1] Privative prefix = without.
[2] LCH3
[3] LTR.

Robespierre, the Bloodthirsty Red. The Fall of the Monarchy, 1792

Celuy qu'estoit bien avant dans le regne,
Ayant chef rouge proche à la hierarchie,
Aspre[1] et cruel et se fera tant craindre,
Succedera à sacrée[2] monarchie.

CVI,Q57

Interpretation

He who had already had some power earlier, having a red head [ideas] will attain the summit of the hierarchy; intractable and cruel, he will make himself terribly feared and will succeed to the consecrated monarchy.

History

'Maximilian Robespierre, b. 1759 at Arras, son of the advocate to the Council of Artois, himself held this post in 1789. Deputy for Arras in the States-General, he was filled with Rousseauist democratic ideas about the Social Contract, sat on the far left [chef rouge] and on every occasion displayed *his hatred of the monarchy*. In June 1791 he was appointed Public Prosecutor for the Criminal Tribunal of the Seine; he allied himself with the Jacobins and the Commune, and in 1792[3] was elected a member of the Convention. In association with Danton he conducted the trial of Louis XVI; he pleaded vehemently for the death sentence, thwarting Girondin efforts to save the King. After the execution Robespierre set up the Revolutionary Tribunal and established the Reign of Terror throughout France. Sitting almost continuously on the Committee of Public Safety, he authorized the most bloodthirsty measures. He had imposed upon France an extreme and odious tyranny and not spared his colleagues; those who survived, vexed by his arrogance or afraid of his threats, finally united against him.'[4]

[1] Latin *asper*: hard, savage, intractable. DLLB.
[2] Allusion to the coronation.
[3] The French Republic was proclaimed on 21 September 1792. The Convention succeeded the legislative Assembly and lasted from 21 September 1792 to 26 October 1795. It had been convened after the insurrection of 10 August 1792 and the overthrow of the monarchy, in order to form a new constitution. It proclaimed the Republic at its very first sitting. DHB.
[4] DHB.

The Death of Louis XVI, 1793.
Robespierre in Power

Quand le deffaut du Soleil lors sera,
Sur le plein jour le monstre sera veu:
Tout autrement on l'interprétera,
Cherté n'a garde, nul n'y aura pourveu.

CIII,Q34

Interpretation

When the monarchy falls, the monster [Robespierre] will be seen clearly. He will be viewed quite differently. No one will know how to provide against the austerity for none will have foreseen it.

History

'Between the King's execution (21 January 1793) and the Girondins' proscription (2 June) was less than five months. A plan of action prepared by Robespierre between 16 and 19 May revealed the secret of the machinery by which they in their turn would be purged. The Committee of Public Safety, instituted on 5 April 1793, was originally under Danton's control, and after 10 June under Robespierre's. He was called The Incorruptible, but this name soon acquired another meaning! He came to embody Jacobinism, with all its sinister delight in persecution [*monstre*]. Always following the party line, he knew with a *fanatic*'s instinct how to destroy any factions guilty of deviation from it.

The victories of 1793 and 1794 did not slacken the Jacobin dictatorship. On the contrary, the *Terror* grew even worse. There was agitation from a small group led by a former priest, Jacques Roux: taking advantage of poor harvests, it stirred up trouble in the provinces against the Convention, accusing it of reducing the people to *starvation*. After various demonstrations, the Convention formed a policy that brought all essential areas of the economy under the absolute control of the state. Then came the real problem: how to apply these impossible laws. As soon as the maximum rate was announced, the shops were emptied in minutes, with everybody rushing to buy at artifically low prices what *had cost three times as much the day before*; there were *shortages* in every town. Paris no longer had sugar, oil or candles, and the bread was inedible. Black market activities sprang up everywhere.'[1]

[1] HFPG.

Robespierre, the Terror and the Festival of the Supreme Being, June 1794

Des innocents le sang de veufve et vierge,
Tant de maux faicts par moyen ce grand Roge,
Saints simulachres trempez[1] en ardent cierge
De frayeur crainte ne vera nul que boge.

CVIII,Q80

Interpretation

The blood of innocents, widows and virgins will flow; so many misfortunes brought about by this great Red. A false religious cult arranged with blazing candles [bonfires]. Through panic and fear no one will move.

History

'The Vendéans were overwhelmed at Le Mans, where they were surprised at nightfall on 12 December. After a savage battle lasting fourteen hours, they were *massacred*. There were bodies everywhere, *many of them women*: these were naked, for they had been raped by the soldiers before being killed. About 6000 men managed to escape, but they were overtaken, surrounded and shot down at Savenay.'[2]

'Robespierre[3] decreed that *a new religion* of a simple and lay character would be imposed upon everyone. He presided over the first great ceremony, the Festival of the Supreme Being, on 8 June 1794. After this sort of apotheosis he took one of his most ruthless measures, the Law of Prairial (10 June 1794) which gave any accused person practically no chance of escaping the scaffold. During this *Great Terror* there were more than 1000 executions in forty-five days in Paris.

The Revolutionary government: after the violent overthrow of the Girondins, *no opposition to the Convention dared show itself*, and there the Montagnards remained the masters.'[4]

---

[1] For *temprer*, ancient form of *tremper* = to arrange. DAFL.
[2] LRFPG.
[3] From Latin *robeus*, red. DLLB. Robespierre thus means 'red stone'. Cf. CIX,Q20, where Louis XVI is 'the white stone'.
[4] LCH3.

The Montagnards. The White Terror, 1794

L'armée Celtique[1] contre les montaignars
Qui seront sceus et prins à la pipée:[2]
Paysans fresz[2] pulseront tost faugnars[4]
Précipitez tous au fil de l'espée.

CIV,Q63

Interpretation

The army of the Chouans [will rise up] against the Montagnards who, being warned, will trap it; they shall rapidly push back the peasants, forcing them into the marshes, and wiping them all out.

History

'The White Terror claimed many victims. *In Brittany* the Chouans supported a British landing at Quiberon, which was *swiftly surrounded and annihilated* by General Hoche's troops.'[5]

'To confront the victorious advance of the rebel Chouans, the Republic's standing army under Kleber and Marceau had to be mobilized. *Pushed back* before Granville and defeated at Le Mans, the Vendéans suffered a dreadful reverse during their second crossing of the Loire. They continued their resistance in the *marshlands* and the forests until 1795. The armed force of émigrés landed by the British was defeated at Quiberon Bay. The Convention had all the prisoners shot.'[6]

[1] The Chouans in Brittany, a Celtic country.
[2] Snares for catching birds, also 'loaded dice'.
[3] Latin *fressus*, from *frendo*: I crush, wipe out. DLLB.
[4] *faugnars* = *fangeux*, filthy, muddy. DAFL.
[5] LCH3.
[6] HFAM.

The Birth of Napoleon Bonaparte, 15 August 1769

Un Empereur naistra près d'Italie
Qui à l'empire sera vendu bien cher,
Diront[1] avec quels[2] gens il se ralie
Qu'on trouvera moins Prince que boucher.

CI,Q60

Interpretation

An emperor will be born near Italy, who will cost the empire dear. The amount of people with whom he allies himself will be talked about and he will be thought of less as prince than as butcher.

History

When Napoleon was born in 1769, Corsica had been bought by Louis XV only two years previously. It was thus no longer Italian, but it was still not yet French. Hence Nostradamus' phrase '*près d'Italie*'.

'The Congress of Vienna [September 1814–June 1815] claimed to have erased from the map of Europe the changes effected by the French Revolution and the Empire. . . . France, surrounded by buffer-states could no longer hope to attain "natural frontiers".'[3] Thus France had paid dearly in lives, defeats and all manner of disasters.

'Napoleon mobilized the Grand Army: 700,000 men *from every nation*.'[3]

The Battle of Eylau, called 'the *butchery* amid the snow', was one of the bloodiest ever fought by Napoleon.

'By the Treaty of Paris [1815], France lost all her conquests and found herself *even smaller* than she had been before the Revolutionary Wars.'[4]

[1] For '*on dira*' – Latinism.
[2] '*Quels*' in the sense of '*combien*', how many.
[3] LCH3.
[4] DHC.

The Predestined Name of Napoleon

> D'un nom farouche tel proféré sera
> Que des trois seurs[1] aura fato[2] le nom,
> Puis grand peuple par langue et faicts dira[3]
> Plus que nul autre aura bruict et renom.
>
>   CI,Q76

Interpretation

He will come to the fore with such a grim name that this name will be, in predestined fashion, like that of the Three Fates. Then through his speeches and actions he will thin out many people, more than anyone he will be renowned by the noise he will make.

History

The name of Napoleon derives from two Greek words: νεος (new) and ἀπολλύων, present participle of ἀπόλλυμι (exterminating). Taken as a noun, Napoleon thus means 'new exterminator'. The sense of this verse therefore perfectly matches the etymological meaning of the Emperor's name. Think of the slaughter of Eylau (of 'the butchery amid the snow'), the Retreat from Moscow, or the following description of Peninsular War atrocities: 'Whenever our injured, sick, stragglers and orderlies, were taken prisoner anywhere, the luckiest had their throats cut on the spot; many were hurled into vats of boiling water, while others were sawn up between planks or slowly roasted alive.'[4]

'The Spanish War was distinguished by its fanatical ferocity: constant ambushes whittled away [*thin out*] the French Army.'[5]

---

[1] The Three Fates: mythological sisters whose task was to cut the threads of men's destinies; destructive divinities.

[2] Latin, ablative of *fatum*: by or through fate.

[3] Latin *dirare*: to thin out, prune (of trees). DLLB. Beginning with Le Pelletier, commentators have changed this word to *duira* (for *conduira*).

[4] General de Ségur: *Memoirs of an Aide-de-Camp*.

[5] LCH.

The Sardinian Army Surrenders to Napoleon at Cherasco, 29 April 1796. The Austrian Forces Defeated in Three Months. The Battle of Löwen, 18 April 1797

Les sept en trois mois en concorde,
Pour subjuguer les Alpes Apennines,[1]
Mais la tempeste[2] et Ligure[3] couarde,
Les profligent[4] en subites ruyne.

CIII,Q39

Interpretation

The seven [armies] will be allied for three months in order to enslave the Apennines. But the quick action [by Napoleon's forces] and the cowardice of the Sardinian army will cause their defeat and sudden ruin.

History

'During this time the French position in Italy became threatened by Austria's major preparations *to reconquer* this country.

Dejection spread through the armies of the coalition. There was concern in Piedmont; the French were only ten leagues from Turin and the

Austrians could think only of protecting Milan. Thus unsettled, the Sardinian court did not know whose side to take. The King, although warned against the French, did not want to agree to surrender his three main fortresses to his ambitious neighbour, Lombardy. He preferred to *throw himself into the arms of the conqueror* [cowardice] whom he could in any case not fight for very long. The truce was signed on 9 Floréal of Year IV (29 April 1796) at Cherasco. The terms were that the Sardinian king should leave the coalition; Sardinian troops should be sent back to their garrisons; the roads of Piedmont should remain open to the French army; and the fortresses of Ceva, Coni, Tortone or failing that, Alexandria, would at once be surrendered together with all their ammunition and artillery.[5]

The aim of these orders was to reunite on the Rivoli plains early on *14 January 1797* more than 20,000 men, including 1500 cavalry, and 30 cannon. Hoche and Moreau got under way at last and on *18 April 1797* the Austrians signed at Löwen the draft agreement proposed by Napoleon two days earlier. Thus ended this campaign, during which Napoleon *defeated seven armies* and triumphed over four generals sent in succession against him by Vienna.'[6]

'Bonaparte rapidly advanced across the Carinthian mountains, driving back the enemy vanguard. The soldiers of the Rhine, charging with fixed bayonets, flung themselves upon the Austrians with *an impetuousness* that broke their lines.'[7]

---

[1] Apennines: long mountain chain, the backbone of Italy, which separates from the Alps at Cassino, north of Genoa, traces a semicircle around the Gulf of Genoa and ends in Sicily. DHB.

[2] Figurative: impetuous action. DL7V.

[3] Region of ancient Italy that formed the south-west of Cisalpine Gaul. Liguria originally extended from the north coast to the River Po. DHB. Part of the Sardinian states.

[4] Latin *profligo*: I overturn, completely vanquish, ruin. DLLB.

[5] The Sardinian states consisted not only of the island itself but lands in northern Italy, both east and west of the Alps, between Switzerland to the north, France to the west, Lombardy to the east and the Mediterranean to the south.

[6] HFA.

[7] 14 January–18 April = three months, three days. Cf. line 1.

The Italian Campaigns over the Alps, 1796–1800.
The Annexation of Tuscany by Napoleon, 1801.
The Expulsion of Ferdinand III, Grand Duke
of Tuscany

Dela les Alpes grand'armée passera,
Un peu devant naistra monstre vapin:[1]
Prodigieux et subit tournera,[2]
Le grand Toscan à son lieu plus propin.[3]

CV,Q20

Interpretation

The Grand Army will cross the Alps. Shortly before will be born the
monster of Gap, which in an extraordinary and sudden manner will
oblige the Grand Duke of Tuscany to return to a neighbouring place.

History

'The first Italian campaign: *the Army of the Alps*, commanded by Kellermann, holds the heights from Mont Blanc as far as the Largentière Pass,
and the Italian army, commanded by Scherer, extends from the Tende
Pass to the Mediterranean.

Some hold Napoleon's Italian campaign to be "*his undisputed master-
piece*". Napoleon himself seems to have thought as much, because he
stated: "War is a singular art; I assure you that I have fought sixty battles
and have learned nothing more than what I knew from the very first."

Despite serious difficulties, Napoleon's plans succeeded, since 40,000
reserves crossed the St Bernard with their artillery, 5000 men descended
the Little St Bernard Pass, 4000 emerged from Mont Cénis and the
Moncey corps descended through the St Gothard upon Milan [May
1800].'[4]

'Ferdinand III, *Grand Duke of Tuscany*, 1769–1824.[5] During the first
Revolutionary Wars he remained neutral, despite British threats, which
meant that he was not unkindly treated by Napoleon in 1796. But later,
after allowing himself to be drawn into the Second Coalition, he was
driven out of his states by the French [1799], although he was able to re-
enter them a few months later, only to be despoiled yet again after the
Battle of Marengo by the Treaty of Luneville. He withdrew to Vienna
[neighbouring place] while Louis of Parma and Elisa Bonaparte occupied
his throne.'[6]

[1] *Vapincuum*: modern name, Gap. DHB. Allusion to the 100 Days: 'Napoleon had only

passed Sisteron in order to *veer towards Gap* on 5 March, 1815.' NEE. Example of apocope.

[2] To direct or govern (of a person). DL7V.

[3] Latin *propinquus*: near, neighbouring, close. DLLB. Note the similarity of apocope between *vapincuum* and *propinquum*.

[4] NEE.

[5] Nostradamus establishes a relationship between Bonaparte and Ferdinand III, both born in 1769.

[6] DL7V.

Bonaparte's Army Marches from Verona to Venice via Vicenza, 1797. General Lusignan's Defeat near Belluno, 10 March 1797. The Venetian Rulers' Surrender to Bonaparte, 14 May 1797

> Peuple infiny[1] paroistre à Vicence,
> Sans force feu bruler la basilique,[2]
> Près de Lunage[3] deffait grand de Valence,[4]
> Lorsque Vinise par morte prendra pique.
>
> CVIII,QII

Interpretation

The French will appear at Vicenza and without setting it on fire they will destroy the aristocracy. General Lusignan will be defeated near Belluno, when Venice takes up the quarrel to mete out death.

History

'On 20 Ventose of Year V (10 March 1797), the *commander-in-chief* of the Italian Army mobilized his entire line. The intrepid Masséna hurled his troops against the centre, driving it back upon *Belluno*, and advanced into the Ponteba gorges by the Tarwis Pass. During this rapid march he took a thousand prisoners, among whom was *General Lusignan*.

Everything was in turmoil or *on fire* in upper Italy. The Slavonian regiments, landing from the *Lagoons*, advanced towards the rebel villages: meanwhile the peasants ransacked them. They *slaughtered and murdered* any patriots or Frenchmen they could find.

Like all worn-out bodies, the *Venetian* aristocracy had been divided. In addition the principal members of the government could not agree. They all dreaded a siege. The old *oligarchs* were compelled to offer

Napoleon the changes in their constitution that he had demanded some time before. Satisfied at having scared the Venetians, Napoleon thought it better to leave them *to surrender of their own accord rather than overpower them*, and allowed them a few days' grace. He returned to Milan, and the *plenipotentiaries* were quick to follow him.'[5]

'On 25 Floréal, Year V, *the Doge of Venice* was deposed and the French entered the city.'[6]

[1] The expression '*peuple infini*' is always used by Nostradamus for the French, with the dual meaning of their being eternal but also very numerous. Napoleonic France was the most populous country in Europe. Cf. CI,Q98.

[2] Greek Βασιλικός: royal. DFG.

[3] Gallicization of Lunegiano, the region in which Belluno is situated.

[4] Lusignan: from this family sprang the noble houses of Lezé, Eu, La Rochefoucauld, *Valence*, Marais etc. DL7V.

[5] HFA.

[6] HFACAD.

Pius VI's Papacy, 1795–99. The Papal States' Resistance against the Abduction of Pius VI, 1798

Quatre ans le siège[1] quelque peu bien tiendra,
Un surviendra libidineux[2] de vie:
Ravenne et Pyse Veronne soustiendront[3]
Pour eslever[4] la croix de Pape envie.[5]

CVI,Q26

Interpretation

He will keep the Holy Seat well enough for four years. Then a licentious person will intervene. Ravenna, Pisa and Verona will resist the one who wishes to take away the cross [his power] from the Pope.

History

'Pius VI, elected 1775, died at Valence, France, in 1799. The Directorate *invaded papal territory*, and the Pope had to sign the Treaty of Tolentino (1797) with Napoleon: this proved disastrous for the Pope. After the murder in a Rome street of General Duphot, the French government's representative, the Directorate *seized* the Pope and proclaimed the Republic in Rome. Arrested by General Berthier, Pius VI was taken to

Siena, Florence and Turin and finally *taken back* in April 1799 to France. He was moved from Grenoble to Valence where he died.'[6]

'On 8 January 1797 Napoleon, who from Bologna, where he had gone to *threaten* the Pope, had not relaxed his vigilance, learned that *an engagement* had occurred, involving all his advance posts. Immediately he recrossed the Po with 2000 men and went to *Verona* to anticipate Marshal Alvinzi's plans.

The Treaty of Tolentino was drawn up on 19 February 1797. The Pope gave up the legations of Bologna and Ferrara as well as the beautiful province of Romagna.'[7,8] Cf. CI,Q12, CIX,Q5, CVIII,Q33.

[1] Always used by Nostradamus in the sense of the Papal Seat.
[2] Latin *libidinosus*: licentious, debauched. DLLB.
[3] Latin *sustineo*: I resist. DLLB.
[4] Latin *elevo*: I bear off, take off. DLLB.
[5] To wish for oneself. DL7V.
[6] DL7V.
[7] Ancient province of the Papacy, its chief town is *Ravenna*. DHB.
[8] HFA.

The Massacres of Verona and Venice, 1797.
The Annexation of Venetia and the French Revenge.
Napoleon's Capture by Captain Maitland, 15 July 1815

Le grand naistra[1] de Véronne et Vicence,[2]
Qui portera un surnom[3] bien indigne,
Qui à Venise voudra faire vengeance,
Lui-même pris homme du guet[4] et signe.[5]

CVIII,Q33

Interpretation

The greatness of him who bears a name to be despised will result from [the campaigns] of Verona and Venice. He will want to wreak vengeance at Venice and will himself be taken prisoner by a sentinel and a red flag.

History

'On 23 Nivôse, Year V [1797], General Alvinzi attacked Joubert and boxed him in beside Rivoli. The same day Provera pushed forward two advance columns, one aimed at *Verona*, the other at Legnago. Masséna, who was at Verona, made a sortie, overcame this force and took 900 prisoners. *Bonaparte arrived at Verona* just after Masséna had driven back the Austrians.

While there was rejoicing in France, Upper Italy was still in a state of complete turmoil. The *Venetian* towns continued to be at war with the rural population. At *Verona*, particularly, major events seemed to be imminent. On 28 Germinal, Year V, peasant bands entered *Verona* crying "Death to the Jacobins!" Balland retired with his troops into the fortress, but all the French in the streets were butchered and flung into the river. However the *time for vengeance* was not far off. From all sides troops came to the aid of *Verona*. After a bloody fight against the Venetian forces General Chabran surrounded Verona, which surrendered unconditionally. Some of the rebel leaders were shot. This incident, called the *Veronese Easter*, was not the only opportunity the French had *for revenge*. A French lugger which had taken refuge under the batteries of the Lido at *Venice* was bombarded and its crew slaughtered by Slavonian sailors. When Bonaparte learned of the massacres of Verona and the Lido killings he no longer wanted to listen to the two envoys from *Venice*. He issued a long manifesto listing French grievances *against the Venetians* and declared war. The Lion of St Mark was overthrown throughout all the provinces. Everywhere *the abolition of the Venetian Government* was proclaimed. Thus, without compromising himself, Bonaparte overturned the absurd aristocracy which had betrayed him and placed Venice in the same plight as Lombardy, Modena, Bologna and Ferrara. Every day the Revolution made new inroads throughout Italy.'

'The British ship *Bellerophon*, under Captain Maitland, came to reconnoitre the roads. Another British frigate drew closer so as to keep the other frigates' movements *under surveillance*, and afterwards their departure presented some difficulties. . . .

Another warship, the *Northumberland*, received the *great prisoner*.'[6]

[1] *Naître de*: result from. DL7V.

[2] Napoleon set up a Duchy of Vicenza for General Caulaincourt. DL7V.

[3] Allusion to the etymology of 'Napoleon'. Cf. CI,Q76.

[4] Night patrol during a war. DL7V.

[5] Latin *signum*: red flag hoisted when attacking. DLLB. The battle ensign of the Royal Navy was a red cross on a white background. DL7V.

[6] HFA.

Venice Annexed. Napoleon's Occupation of Venice, 1797. Venice and Austria, 1797, 1805 and 1849

La liberté ne sera recouvrée,
L'occupera noir,[1] fier, vilain, inique,
Quand la matière du pont[2] sera ouvrée,
D'Hister,[3] Venise faschée la république.

CV,Q29

Interpretation

The freedom [of Venice] will not be recovered. A proud person [Napoleon] in [a] black [hat] will shamefully and unjustly occupy it when a maritime matter [the fleet] is set under way. Then the Republic of Venice will be troubled by those from the Danube [Austrians].

History

'In 1797 Venice, although apparently neutral, was *occupied* by Napoleon who, under the Treaty of Campoformio, surrendered all his territory in *Austria* (keeping only the south-east islands) in return for the Duchy of Milan and the Rhine border. In 1805, by the Peace of Pressburg, Venice became part of the kingdom of Italy, but it reverted to *Austria* in 1814 and then formed the Lombardo-Venetian Kingdom. Under Austrian domination, Venice declined. In 1848 she heralded the *Republic*, but was *reduced* in 1849 after a long and celebrated siege and her prospects darkened. Venice was subsumed by the kingdom of Italy in 1866.'[4]

'Legislator, arbitrator, counsellor to the peoples of Italy, Napoleon took on still greater responsibilities. He had taken over *the Venetian fleet* and had summoned Admiral Brueys and 4000 French sailors to the Adriatic to seize possession of the Venetian-occupied Greek islands.

Malta was also the object of Napoleon's cupidity. "From these different positions," he wrote to the Directorate, "we shall dominate the Mediterranean." '[5]

---

[1] Allusion to Bonaparte's famous black hat. Cf. CI,Q74
[2] Greek πόντος: sea. DGF.
[3] Old name for the Danube. DHB.
[4] DHB.
[5] HFA.

Charles-Emmanuel II, King of Sardinia, 1798–1802

Dans la Sardaigne un noble Roy viendra,
Qui ne tiendra que trois ans le royaume,
Plusieurs couleurs[1] avec soy conjoindra,
Luy mesme après soin sommeil marrit[2] scome.[3]

CVIII,Q88

Interpretation

Into Sardinia will come a king of noble descent who will keep his kingdom only three years. He will reunite several other states with his kingdom, after taking care of himself [his succession] he will die united with the Society [of Jesus].

History

'Charles-Emmanuel II, associated with the misfortunes of the Bourbons, his allies, was forced to cede *his continental states* to Napoleon and *to retire to Sardinia* in December 1798. *Three years* later, after fruitless attempts to curb rebellious elements, he abdicated in favour *of his brother* Victor-Emmanuel and went to live in Rome, where he died a Jesuit.'[4]

[1] *Couleurs:* flags = states.
[2] Latin *maritus:* united. DLLB.
[3] Anagram of the Latin *comes*, companion.
[4] HFAM.

The End of the First Republic, 6 November 1799. Napoleon and the Civil Code

La république, misérable infélice,
Sera vastée[1] du nouveau Magistrat,
Leur grand amas de l'exil malefice,
Fera Suève[2] ravir leur grand contract.

CI,Q61

Interpretation

The miserable, unfortunate Republic will be devastated by a new magistrate, the great number of exiles causing trouble will make the Germans withdraw their treaty of alliance.

History

'Shortly after the Brumaire coup, Bonaparte presented a new constitution under which he held the *casting vote*. Bonaparte as First Consul had *sole* power of decision, and furthermore held *the right to propose legislation*.

He took the glory for publishing the *Civil Code* (1804), begun by the Constituent Assembly.

The *Grand Empire* dominated Europe at least until 1812. Many states adopted a code of laws and an administration imitating those of France.'[3]

'Prussia was a doubtful ally in 1812, and was Russia's ally in 1813. Austria herself declared against Napoleon, and this example was followed, despite his victory at Dresden, by Bavaria, Würtemburg and Saxony – whose aged King tried vainly to remain within *the French alliance*.'[4]

'The discovery of a new Royalist plot allowed Bonaparte to re-establish the monarchy but to his own advantage: he claimed to believe that they wanted to assassinate him so as to replace him with a royal prince, the young Duke of Enghien. Napoleon had him abducted from *German territory* and shot in the moat of Vincennes Castle in March 1804.'[3]

[1] Latin *vastus*: desert, desolated. DLLB.
[2] Suève: Suevi (Swabians): powerful tribe of ancient Germany. DHCD.
[3] LCH3.
[4] DHCD.

The War Brings about the Fall of the Monarchy, 1792. The Ruin of the Papal States and the Misfortunes of Pius VI. The Coup d'Etat of 18 Brumaire 1799

> Par Mars contraire sera la Monarchie,
> Du grand pescheur[1] en trouble ruyneux;
> Jeune noir[2] rouge prendra la hiérarchie,
> Les proditeurs[3] iront jour bruyneux.

CVI,Q25

Interpretation

The war will be unfavourable for the monarchy. The Revolution will be ruinous for the Pope. A young 'black' will take the hierarchy from the reds and the conspirators will seize power one day of Brumaire.

History

'On 20 April 1792 Dumouriez snatched from the King the declaration of a *war* which would cause terrible bloodshed for ten years, and whose results Europe could not have foreseen. The Assembly were not at all grateful to the King for his co-operation and, even more threatening and demanding, disbanded his bodyguard, sending its commander M. de Brissac to the court of Orleans, so depriving the luckless Louis of any protection from the attacks upon him then being prepared.'[4]

'The French Revolution rolled across the Roman sky like thunder. Rome was apprised of the danger but the revolutionary movement had supporters in Rome itself. It was 1796 before the Romans fully appreciated the danger, when the French army under Napoleon's command entered Italy. The Pope negotiated with the General, and had to pay contributions collected from the Papal States, together with 500 ancient manuscripts and 100 works of art. By the Treaty of Tolentino (19 February 1797) the Pope had to renounce forever all claims to Avignon, also to the Comtat Venaissin, and to pay out 46 million scudi. On 20 February the Pope was made prisoner. Napoleon removed as spoils of war priceless works of art and filled 500 wagons with them.'[5]

'The 18 *Brumaire* [= *jour bruyneux* = drizzly day] was the *day* chosen for the transfer of the Councils, and the nineteenth for the final session. Although the secret of the *conspiracy* had been well kept, everywhere an important event was expected.'[6]

[1] The Fisherman's Ring. When Napoleon forced Pius VII, a prisoner at Savona, to send him St Peter's ring (*pescheur* = fisherman. *Tr.*) the Pope only did so after breaking it. He replaced it with a metal seal depicting St Peter with his Keys. The Fisherman's Ring had been used since the fifteenth century to seal papal documents. DL7V.

[2] Allusion to the black hat worn by Napoleon, but also pejorative adjective. Cf. CV,Q29, CI,Q74, CIII,Q43.

[3] Latin *proditor*: traitor, one who breaks laws. DLLB.

[4] HFA.

[5] DDP.

[6] HFA.

Napoleon against the Revolutionaries, 1799.
The Occupation of Italy, 1797

Aux profligez[1] de paix les ennemis,
Après avoir l'Italie suppérée:[2]
Noir sanguinaire, rouge sera commis[3]
Feu, sang verser, eau de sang colorée.[4]

CVI,Q38

Interpretation

The enemies of peace [revolutionaries] will be conquered [by Napoleon] after he has overcome Italy. This black and bloodthirsty person will compromise the reds. Then through war he will make blood flow, which shall colour the water.

History

'The initiatives taken by the émigrés at foreign courts to influence French affairs had prompted a reaction of French national pride. There were *cries for war* from the Brissots, Vergnauds, Dantons and other firebrands, who had changed their tune and were known by the names of Cordeliers and Girondins ["enemies of peace"].

The elections of Year V proved that the French people were not contented and that they had little confidence in their rulers. Only 5 per cent of the deputies seeking re-election were successful. The citizens elected to the Assemblies not only the hard-line leaders of the regime but very moderate Republicans and even Royalists. The two Presidents of the Assemblies were enemies of the Revolution. While the results of these elections, which proved so disastrous for the Directorate's collective peace of mind, were awaited, the draft text of the Treaty of Löwen reached Paris. What was to be done? Napoleon made clear that he was negotiating, without authorization, in the name of France. The preamble of the treaty was approved. After this, the Directors were forced to let Napoleon do as he pleased and rule at will over Italy.'[5]

---

[1] Latin *profligo*: I conquer totally, annihilate, ruin. DLLB.
[2] Latin *supero*: I conquer, triumph over. DLLB.
[3] Compromise, expose. DL7V.
[4] Allusion to crossing the River Beresina.
[5] HFA.

The Coup of 18 Brumaire, November 1799.
Fourteen Years of Rule: 9 November 1799–6 April 1814

De la cité marine et tributaire,
La teste raze prendra la Satrapie:[1]
Chassez sordide qui puis sera contraire,
Par quatorze ans tiendra la tyranie.

CVII,QI3

Interpretation

From the port which pays him tax [tribute, from war], the 'shaven-headed one' will take [civil] power. He will drive out the squalid men against whom he rebels, and will rule as tyrant for fourteen years.

History

'Immensely energetic and active, Napoleon organized Egypt with a sort of *protectorate*. But he was impatient to return to France, whose political situation was giving him cause for anxiety, and he embarked secretly from Alexandria.'[2]

'Napoleon overthrew the Directorate's regime and made himself Consul. This last coup *put an end to the Revolutionary period*.

Reorganization of the country: Napoleon used the immense powers with which he had been invested to reorganize France. The administration centralized: he created prefects, government representatives in the regions. Finance: a new fixed administration, with new officials – controllers and *preceptors* [Satraps].'[3]

From 19 November 1799 until 6 April 1814, Napoleon held power for 14 years, 3 months, 27 days!

'I passed by on horseback an hour beforehand and my glance rested upon an inscription in huge black letters on the first pillar of the bridge: "*Down with the tyrant!*" I just had time to have it erased.'[4]

---

[1] Satraps were the governors of provinces (prefects) under Persian rule, filling the dual roles of administrators and tax-collectors (preceptors). DL7V.

[2] DHC.

[3] LCH3.

[4] The Emperor's unpopularity in 1814: *Mémoires* of Pasquier. Plon.

The Annexation of Verona, 1805.
The Death of Napoleon, 1821.
The Congress of Verona, 1822

Dans peu dira[1] faulce[2] brute[3] fragile[4]
De bas en hault eslevé promptement:
Puis en istant[5] desloyale et labile[6]
Qui de Veronne aura gouvernement.

CI,QI2

Interpretation

In a short time the scythe [of death] will cut down the mad and vulnerable man, namely he who will have been rapidly raised from low to high.[7] Then, being disloyal, the one with power over Verona will be broken.

History

'In 1796 Napoleon manoeuvred around Verona to reinforce the blockade of Mantua against Austria. But on 17 April 1797, prompted by the Austrians, there was a general massacre of the French in the town. In 1805 the Treaty of Pressburg *gave Verona to the French*, who made it *the chief town* of the Adige district. In 1815 the town fell into Austrian hands again, and in 1822 Austria held the famous Congress there.'[8]

Nostradamus notes here that immediately after Napoleon's death a reunion of the Holy League will take place at Verona!

'The Republic took freedom everywhere, making free men of all those subjected to the petty tyrants it overthrew; the Empire, by contrast, made these free men in turn the subjects of new sovereigns. How greatly had the Revolution and the revolutionaries *degenerated* since the 18 Brumaire coup. The Senate could no longer flatter Napoleon enough, but it was the bishops who were most fulsome in their adulation. No wonder Bonaparte believed himself *the greatest of mortals* and the one chosen by God.'[9]

[1] Latin *dirare*: to thin out. DLLB.
[2] Latin *falcem*: sickle. DAFL.
[3] Latin *brutus*: dull, stupid. DLLB.
[4] Latin *fragilis*: fragile, weak. DLLB.
[5] *Istre*: form of *estre*, i.e. *être* = to be. DAFL.
[6] Latin *caduc*. DLLB. Referring to a broken man. DL7V.
[7] Cf. CVIII,Q57, CV,Q26 and CIX,Q5.
[8] DL7V.
[9] HFA.

The Duke of Brunswick and the Orange Divisions. The Battle of Auerstadt, 1805. His Secret Agreement with Dumouriez, 1792

> Vie fort mort de l'OR[1] vilaine indigne,
> Sera de Saxe non nouveau électeur[2]
> De Brunsvic mandra d'mour[3] signe
> Faux le rendant au peuple séducteur.

CX,Q46

Interpretation

He will lose his life, by violent death, despite the unworthy and treacherous actions of the Orange [divisions]; Brunswick, whose signature Dumouriez will have demanded, will not be the new Elector of Saxony, his false spirit having seduced the people.

History

'By 8 October Prussian troops had entered Saxony, ahead of the Grand Army. But Prussia did not take advantage of the diplomatic initiative she had taken. Her forces were scattered; only 140,000 men under Ruchel, *Brunswick* and Hohenlöhe, bewildered by orders and counter-orders, defended the road to Thuringia.'[4]

'Auerstadt: *Brunswick* had been directing the attack of the *Orange* divisions, and of Wartensleben as well as part of Schmettau's infantry. The French troops were forced to abandon Hassenhausen, which General Morand then succeeded in recapturing. But Prince William of Prussia charged furiously against Morand's division, which was drawn up in squares. The Duke of Brunswick and General Schmettau were mortally wounded ["*vie fort mort*"].'[5]

'Charles William Ferdinand, Duke of Brunswick-Lüneburg and a general in the service of Prussia (who had been known as *hereditary prince*), was chosen in 1792 as commander-in-chief of the Coalition armies against France. After publishing a threatening manifesto he entered Champagne with a sizeable army but was defeated at Valmy and made peace with Dumouriez ["*d'mour signe*"]. After taking up command again in 1805, he was beaten at Jena and *fatally injured* by a bullet near Auerstadt.'[6]

---

[1] For 'orange' by apocope.

[2] Auerstadt, Prussian town ('*Saxe*'). Victory by Davout over the Prussians (14 October 1805). DHB.

[3] Abbreviation of Dumouriez.
[4] NELGI.
[5] LEE.
[6] DHB.

Napoleon's First Marriage, 1796.
His Coronation, 1804. His Divorce and
Second Marriage, 1809

Peu après l'aliance faicte,
Avant solemniser la feste,
L'Empereur le tout troublera,
Et la nouvelle mariée,
Au franc pays par fort liée,
Dans peu de temps après mourra.

Sixain 57

Interpretation

Shortly after being married and before a solemn rite, the Emperor will divorce, and the new bride will be strongly allied with France through this marriage; soon afterwards he will die.

History

'On 8 Ventose (8 March 1796) Bonaparte was nominated general of the Italian army; on the sixteenth he married the beautiful Creole [Joséphine de Beauharnais]. The *coronation* was continually deferred, mainly because of Pope Pius VII who had delayed his journey to France, and did not take place until 2 December 1804. The *previous day* [*"avant"*] Napoleon and Joséphine had celebrated their *religious* wedding ceremony. The coronation took place on 2 December 1804 in Notre-Dame. Before leaving for the Cathedral the Emperor received Talleyrand, who left the following description of the audience: "But for the *solemnity* of the occasion, I would have been hard put to it to preserve my composure."

'In October 1809 he decided to *divorce* and *remarry*. Austria promptly put forward one of her Grand Duchesses, *Marie-Louise*. Napoleon agreed, and on 2 April in the Louvre Chapel, Cardinal Fesch, the Emperor's uncle, solemnized *the marriage* of Napoleon and Marie-Louise. . . .

On the night of 4 May 1821 all the servants stayed in attendance.

Then he stammered out some words of which the following alone could be distinguished: "France . . . my son . . . army . . . head of the army . . . *Joséphine*. . . ."

These were his last words and seemed a synopsis of his life. So died, aged fifty-one, the man who seemed to have lived 200 years.'[1]

[1] NLM.

The Egyptian Campaign, 1799. The Proclamation of the Empire, December 1804

Après séjourné vogueront en Epire[1]
Le grand secours viendra vers Antioche[2],
Le noir poil[3] crespé[4] tendra fort à l'Empire
Barbe d'airain[5] le rostira en broche.

CI,Q74

Interpretation

After a stay [in Egypt] his soldiers will sail towards another continent, they will seek assistance from Antioch or thereabouts, he who wears a black felt hat will aim at the Empire and roast the Republic on a spit.

History

'The Egyptian campaign was planned with great secrecy and began successfully, escaping Nelson's squadrons which were cruising the Mediterranean. But on 1 August 1798 Nelson, he of the black hat, destroyed the French fleet at Aboukir Bay. The French expedition was thwarted as a result. Napoleon repulsed Turkish attacks in *Syria* and Egypt, but was *impatient* to return to France.'[6]

[1] Greek Ἤπειρος: continent, terra firma. DGF.
[2] Latin *Antiochia*: Antioch, capital of Syria. DLLB.
[3] *Noir poil*: felt is made from pressed hair. DL7V.
[4] *Crespe: crêpé, crépu.* DAFL.
[5] Aenobarbus (Latin *Aeneus* = bronze), husband of Agrippina, is shorthand in Nostradamus for the Republic, through a historical parallel. Their child was Nero, who had his mother assassinated, just as Napoleon 'executed' the Republic which raised him to power.
[6] LCH3.

The First Italian Campaign, 1796–97.
The Rise of Napoleon, 1796–1800

Tiers, doigt du pied, au premier semblera
A un nouveau monarque de bas en haut:
Qui Pyse et Luques[1] Tyran[2] occupera,
Du précédent corriger le deffault.

CIX,Q5

Interpretation

The Third Estate, which is no more than a toe of the foot, will come to the fore thanks to a new leader risen from low degree to the summit [of the hierarchy] who will occupy Pisa and Lucca; thus he will compensate for the lack [of power] of the preceding monarch [Louis XVI].

History

'Society at the end of the eighteenth century was officially comprised of three orders: nobility, clergy and the Third Estate.

In the Third Estate the greatest differences were noticeable: the rich bourgeoisie who had made fortunes in shipping, industry or business was most evident. These wealthy merchants bought themselves *titles*.

Although his own tastes were simple, Napoleon thought it expedient to raise his personal prestige by surrounding himself with a sizeable *court* – a sparkling group responsive to a rigorous etiquette imitating that of Versailles.

The war and *the rise* of Napoleon: Napoleon, a general at twenty-seven, was still the "Vendémiaire" General, as he was known after putting down the 1795 uprising.

The war taxes he imposed upon the vanquished allowed Napoleon to maintain his army and send the Directorate indispensable funds. Thus, in the position of victor and overlord, he fixed the terms of the peace signed with Austria at Campo Formio, October 1797: in northern Italy he set up a *Cisalpine Republic*, allied to France.'[3]

The southernmost point of this Republic was formed by Tuscany, including the towns of Pisa and Lucca.

'The French Republic which vowed enmity against *tyrants* also swore fraternity with the people!'[4]

[1] Tuscan towns.
[2] Cf. CVII,Q13: '*Par quatorze ans tiendra sa tyrannie*'.
[3] LCH3.
[4] Napoleon: *Correspondence* (vol.1).

The Plebiscite.
Napoleon's Destructive Megalomania

Par teste rase viendra bien mal eslire
Plus que sa charge ne porte passera
Si grand fureur et rage fera dire,
Qu'à feu et sang tant sexe tranchera.

CV,Q60

Interpretation

'The little shaven-headed one' will unfortunately be elected, he will carry out more things than his power can manage, he will have said of him that he is full of [warlike] fury and rage, and he will put everyone to fire and the sword regardless of sex.

History

'In practice Napoleon *designated* the Assembly's members: all derived from and reverted to him. *The arranged plebiscite* brought him a stunning vote of popular confidence, more than 3 million votes for to 1600 against.'[1]

Letter from a French officer, Moscow, 30 September 1812:

'The occupation of Moscow and *unfortunately* almost total destruction by fire of this rich and marvellous city. . . . We live by *pillage* and marauding. It is claimed that the Russian government set fire to this fine capital so as to deprive us of the resources we could have had. I do not know about that; but I can say that our soldiers added to the blaze: one could see drunken soldiery firing wooden houses with candles, torches and fuses, and this was the spectacle Moscow presented the day after our arrival. *The fire* lasted three days. You never saw a more terrible or heartbreaking sight! In my view, it was *the most dreadful catastrophe* which our century, itself so full of disastrous occurrences, has so far presented.'[2]

[1] LCH3.
[2] 'Textes Historiques', Collection M. Chaulanges.

Wars against Italy, Spain and England. Marriage to Marie-Louise of Austria

Du nom qui oncques ne fut au Roy Gaulois,[1]
Jamais ne fut un fouldre[2] si craintif:
Tremblant l'Itale, l'Espagne et les Anglois
De femme estrange[3] grandement attentif.

CIV,Q54

Interpretation

From a name never borne by a king of France [Napoleon], never would there be seen such a fearful captain [of war]. He shall make Italy, Spain and England tremble, and be very attentive towards a foreign woman.

History

'By the decrees of Berlin and *Milan* (December 1807) Napoleon prohibited trade with *England* from most of the European ports. For the blockade to be effective it had to be enforced everywhere. The *Pope* and the King of Portugal refused to apply the embargo: Napoleon annexed *the Papal States*, imprisoned the Pope and decided to invade Portugal. A French army crossed *Spain* to attack Portugal.'[4]

Nostradamus, like history, links these three countries confronted with the same problem!

Divorced from Joséphine, Napoleon married Marie-Louise of Austria, a foreigner.

---

[1] Announcing the new dynasty.
[2] *Fouldre*, thunderbolt, used in a specialized symbolic sense in this particular phrase to denote an impetuous orator or warrior. DL7V.
[3] *Etrange* is usually taken by Nostradamus to stand for *étranger* (foreigner, alien).
[4] LCH3.

The Battle of Trafalgar,[1] 21 October 1805.
The Sieges of Pamplona. Navarre and Spain

Vaisseaux, gallères avec leur estendar,
S'entrebatteront près du mont Gibraltar
Et lors sera fort faict à Pampelonne,[2]
Qui pour son bien souffrira mille maux,
Par plusieurs fois soustiendra[3] les assaux.
Mais à la fin unie à la Couronne.

Sixain 41

Interpretation

Fleets with their flags will confront each other near Gibraltar, then
reprisals will be taken against Pamplona, which will suffer a thousand
ills for its good. It will resist attacks several times but will finally be
reunited with the crown [Spain].

History

'Trafalgar: *naval battle* won by the English *fleet* under Nelson over the
combined fleets of France and Spain under Admiral Villeneuve. The
French fleet played only an insignificant role in the wars of the First
Empire.'[4]

'The French entered Pamplona in 1808 and 1829. The town often
changed hands during the Spanish Civil Wars of 1831–42.'[5]

'Navarre, province of northern Spain, capital Pamplona. The history
of Spanish Navarre is associated with that of the kingdom of Navarre
until 1512. Since then, Navarre has been distinguished for its attachment
to its ancient rights, its *resistance* (from 1808 to 1814), to the French
troops, and in the nineteenth century by its devotion to Carlism' [united
to the crown].[6]

---

[1] Spanish Cape, near the Straits of Gibraltar. DHB.
[2] Pamplona, town in Navarre.
[3] Latin *sustineo*: I resist. DLLB.
[4] DL7V.
[5] DHB.
[6] DL7V.

The Battle of Trafalgar, 1805.
The Seven 'Three-Deckers' of the English Fleet.
Admiral Gravina's Wounds.
The French Vessels that Survived

Fustes[1] et gallères autour de sept navires,
Sera livrée une mortelle guerre:
Chef de Madric recevra coup de vires,[2]
Deux escchapez et cinq menés à terre.

CVII,Q26

Interpretation

With corvettes and frigates around seven ships, a deadly battle will take place. The Spanish leader will be wounded. Two ships which shall escape will be led back to land by five others.

History

'At 7 a.m. on 21 October, off Cape Trafalgar, the English were seen approaching from the north-west. The Franco-Spanish fleet consisted of 33 warships (18 French and 15 Spanish) and five frigates, 2856 guns in all. Nelson's fleet consisted of only 27 battleships (seven *3-deckers*, however, as opposed to four) and six frigates or corvettes totalling 3214 cannons. The battle ended before 6 p.m., but during that night two violent storms disposed of many disabled hulks: four ships from the Franco-Spanish fleet which had been captured were smashed against the rocky shoreline and the English scuttled or burned four others. But on 22 October Captain Cosmao did succeed in leaving harbour with *five ships* and managed to *recover two* prizes ["*Deux escchapez et cinq menés à terre*"]. Franco-Spanish losses: 14,000 [4408 of these *killed or drowned*]; 2549 wounded and 7000 or more taken prisoner ["*mortelle guerre*"]. Rear-Admiral Magon was killed and Gravina fatally wounded.'[3]

'Gravina: the Spanish admiral was, it was said, the natural son of Charles III. After peace was made with France he *commanded the Spanish fleet* ["*chef de Madrid*"] which joined the French under Admiral Villeneuve at Cadiz in 1805. *He was wounded* ["*recevra coup de vires*"] at Trafalgar and died in 1806, quite soon afterwards, from his injuries.'[4]

---

[1] Long, rather shallow vessel, employing both sails and oars. DL7V.
[2] Crossbow bolt with a sort of screw-thread, which would cause it to revolve. DAFL.
[3] NEE.
[4] DHB.

Würzburg, Starting-point for Napoleonic Conquests, 1806. The Return from Elba. Disembarkation near Antibes

Soulz la pasture d'animaux ruminants,
Par eux conduicts au ventre herbipolique:[1]
Soldats cachez, les armes bruits menants,
Non loing temptez de cité Antipolique.[2]

CX,Q13

Interpretation

After having grazed and ridden his horses as far as Würzburg, [Napoleon] with concealed soldiers which he will lead with martial noise, and will make an attempt [at disembarkation] not far from Antibes.

History

'All the information Napoleon received indicated that war was imminent. On 21 September 1806 he informed Duroc and Caulaincourt that he intended to be at Mainz on the twenty-ninth. The Emperor left Paris on 25 September and arrived at Mainz on the morning of the twenty-eighth. On his arrival at the bank of the Rhine Napoleon could count upon 200,000 fighting men. . . . He arrived that evening at Würzburg where he made for the Grand Duke's Palace. He was welcomed by numerous German princes, whom he engaged in good-humoured conversation. At the same time a Prussian council of war at Erfurt was being attended by the King, the Duke of Brunswick, the Prince of Hohenlohe, Marshal Mollendorf and several ministers and generals. A note was prepared for Napoleon: France was accused of underhand behaviour towards Prussia and her troops were requested to evacuate Germany by 8 October.'[3]

'Würzburg was occupied by the French in 1806 and returned to Bavaria in 1814.'[4]

'On the evening of 26 February 1815 the Emperor boarded the *Inconstant* with his general staff and some of his *1100 men*. The others swarmed aboard six vessels of various types. On the morning of 1 March the flotilla passed the bay of Antibes, and shortly after noon it anchored. They bivouacked in an olive grove between the sea and the road *from Cannes to Antibes*.'[3]

---

[1] Herbipolis: Würzburg, Bavarian town. DHB. The word *'ventre'* (womb or belly) is used by Nostradamus to suggest the importance of this town in the light of subsequent events.

[2] Antipolis: Antibes (DHB).
[3] NEE.
[4] DHB.

The Annexation of Naples and Sicily, 1806. French Troops in Spain, 1807–8

Qui au Royaume Navarrois[1] parviendra
Quand la Sicile et Naples seront joincts,
Bigores[2] et Landes par Foix Loron[3] tiendra,
D'un qui d'Espagne sera par trop conjoinct.

CIII,Q25

Interpretation

He who will come into the kingdom of Navarre, when Naples and Sicily are reunited, will occupy Bigorre and the heathlands near Foix and Oloron, because of a Spanish king too closely allied with him.

History

'In 1805 the Infante Don Carlos, in exchange for Parma and Piacenza, secured from the Emperor *Naples and Sicily*, as well as the Tuscan ports, for himself and his descendants.

In 1806, the *King* of Spain called the Spaniards to arms. Napoleon was in no doubt that this was a provocation directed against France and was probably delighted to have a pretext for attacking the *Spanish Bourbons*, but he had to disguise his fleeting anxiety at having such a timid *ally*. From that moment he vowed the downfall of that monarchy and boasted that he would seize the crown of Spain from the Bourbons in Madrid, just as he had seized that of the two *Sicilies* from the Bourbons of *Naples*.

Napoleon ordered General Junot to head the army of observation from the *Gironde* and march on Lisbon. Junot reached *Bayonne* [across the heathlands] on 5 September and crossed the Pyrenees several days later.

While Junot's force occupied the central areas of Portugal, one new French army was forming near *Bayonne* and another in the *Roussillon* region. Spain put no more difficulties in the way of these troops and soon afterwards French forces invaded Catalonia and Navarre.'[4]

---

[1] The history of Spanish Navarre is associated with that of the kingdom of Navarre

until 1512. Since then, Navarre has been distinguished for its attachment to its ancient rights, and its resistance from 1808 to 1814 to French troops. DL7V.

² In 1284 the marriage of Jeanne de Navarre and Philippe le Bel guaranteed France's acquisition of this county, but it later passed on to the houses of *Foix* and d'Albret, and was finally reunited on Henri IV's accession. DL7V.

³ Town in the Bigorre region.

⁴ HFA.

The Negotiation of the Papal States, 1807. The Retreat from Russia, 1812

Terroir Romain qu'interprétait¹ augure,²
Par gent gauloise par trop sera vexée
Mais nation Celtique craindra l'heure
Boréas,³ classe⁴ trop loin l'avoir poussée.

CII,Q99

Interpretation

The Roman territory negotiated by the Emperor will be too molested by the French, but France will have everything to fear when the hour of the cold strikes, because she will have pushed her army too far.

History

'Following *Augustus*' example, Napoleon wanted to immortalize his memory.'⁵

'The religious difficulties stemmed from Napoleon's having kept the Pope prisoner (at Savona first, then at Fontainebleau, since 1812). The Pope refused to enforce the blockade throughout his territories – so Napoleon occupied them.'⁵

'On 14 September 1812 Napoleon entered Moscow, expecting to establish winter quarters there. In the night a fire destroyed the town and its supplies. Napoleon hoped the Tsar would sue for peace, but there was no question of this as the Russian leader had received reinforcements. Realizing that he had made an error, Napoleon gave the order to retreat. The return march was appalling. The devastated countryside had no resources left and the Cossacks attacked incessantly. Hunger and *an early and severe winter wore out* the soldiers.'⁵

'I asked Napoleon why he thought the expedition had failed. "*Because of the unexpected cold* and the burning of Moscow," he replied. "I was some days in advance; I had studied weather conditions for the past fifty years and the real cold never began until 20 December, three weeks later than in fact happened." [6]

[1] Latin *interpres pacis*: peace negotiator. DLLB.
[2] Latin *augur*, i.e. *augustus*: title of Roman Emperors. DLLB.
[3] Latin *Boreas*: north wind. DLLB.
[4] Latin *classis*: army, fleet. DLLB.
[5] LCH3.
[6] LMSH.

Napoleon's Annexation of the Church

Du grand prophète[1] les lettres seront prinses
Entre les mains du tyran deviendront,
Frauder,[2] son Roy seront les entreprises
Mais ses rapines bien tost le troubleront.

CII,Q36

Interpretation

The bulls will be seized from the Pope and be in the tyrant's hands, he will undertake to despoil and defraud his [spiritual] sovereign, but his rapine will soon trouble him.

History

'No Swedish, English or Russian vessel must enter the Papal States on pain of *confiscation*. I do not intend that the court of Rome should involve itself any longer in politics. I shall protect its states against all comers. It is pointless for the court to show such regard for the enemies of religion. Have *the bulls sent off* to my bishops.'[3]

'If I had not laid hands upon the Papal States,' Napoleon said, 'and thought I could subdue a spiritual power through force, the rest of my misfortunes would not have occurred.'[4] But his 'rapine' was soon to trouble him!

[1] Latin *propheta*: priest. The great priest, i.e. the Pope. DLLB.
[2] Latin *fraudare*: to despoil by fraud, defraud. DLLB.
[3] Letter from Napoleon to his kinsman Cardinal Fesch, 13 October 1806. LCH3.
[4] LMSH.

The Rise of Napoleon. Napoleon and the Church

De soldat simple parviendra en empire,
De robe courte[1] parviendra à la longue
Vaillant aux armes en église ou plus pyre,
Vexer les prêtres comme l'eau faict l'esponge.

CVIII,Q57

Interpretation

From plain soldier he will become emperor, from military man he will
become magistrate, as valiant in war as harmful to the Church, and will
harass the priests much as a sponge absorbs water.

History

'His relationship with the *Church* was apparently good until 1808. But
when his policy led him to occupy the Papal States and imprison the
Pope, who protested and excommunicated him, the *clergy* and Catholics
took the Pontiff's side: thus he lost Catholic support.'[2]

' "You have let yourself be led by the *priests* and nobles who want to
re-establish titles and fiscal laws. I'll deal with them. *I'll* string them
up!" '[2] (Napoleon to the crowds in 1815.)

'The conflict with Spain became daily more pronounced and diverted
the Emperor from his original aim, which was simply to bring the head
of the Roman states to heel. He was already showing that *hostility* to
various types of *priests* which alienated others.'[2]

'Historians were astonished that Pius VII, in order to make the break
final, picked upon what was by and large a political incident. In 1810
Pius VII said to Chabrol: "I have been pushed to the very limit. *The
water had reached my chin* by the time I cried out." '[3]

---

[1] Heraldic tunic: short skirt or kilt worn by heralds in the Middle Ages and which they
retained until the Revolution. DL7V.
[2] LCH3.
[3] NEE.

Napoleon and the Persecution of the Clergy in Italy, 1809. Napoleon's Likeness on the Coinage. His End upon Foreign Soil, 1821

Aux temples saincts[1] seront faits grands scandales,
Comptez seront pour honneur et louanges
D'un que l'on grave d'argent, d'or les medales[2]
La fin sera en tourmens bien estranges.[3]

CVI,Q9

Interpretation

Great scandals will be perpetuated concerning the holy persons of the Catholic Church, among which will be counted honours and flatteries, because of one whose effigy will be engraved upon gold and silver pieces, but who will end tormented by foreigners [the English].

History

'On 10 June 1809 a proclamation signed by Miollis, Salicetti and high-ranking bureaucrats informed the Romans that their city had been annexed like the other domains within the Church's Empire. Opposition, until the *Pope*'s abduction from his palace on 6 July and his transfer to Savona, remained passive. With the Pope a prisoner, *the seven cardinals*, who in December 1809 still remained in Rome, were in their turn evicted. *The monks* then had to be dispersed: disbanded Dominicans, Franciscans, Cordeliers, Augustinians and even three Maronites were expelled from their monasteries. There were more serious problems with the general clergy and bishops, who had to swear an oath of allegiance to the Emperor which Pius VII, from Savona, had secretly forbidden. Canons and other priests resisted, but popular feeling against their evacuation was such that it was decided not to deport clergy over sixty years of age. These men were therefore returned from Piacenza, and were welcomed by the Romans with *veneration*.'[4] [*"honneurs et louanges"*]

---

[1] Priests, bishops, monks. Note Latin construction.
[2] Coinage of the Ancient Greeks and Romans. Under the First Empire, French money bore on one side Napoleon's effigy with the legend '*Napoléon Empéreur*', and on the reverse, '*République Française*'. DL7V.
[3] Cf. CIV,Q35 and CVIII,Q85.
[4] NEE.

The Ravages of the Napoleonic Wars. Napoleon against the Catholic Church. Arrests of Priests, 1809. The Internment of Pius VII at Fontainebleau, 1810

Renfort de sièges manubis[1] et maniples[2]
Changez le sacre[3] et passe sur[4] le prosne,[5]
Prins et captifs n'arreste les preztriples,[6]
Plus par fonds[7] mis eslevé, mis au trosne.

CVII,Q73

Interpretation

There will be still further acts of pillage and armies. The holy laws will be changed and religion no longer practised. Priests will be arrested and imprisoned. Even he who had been placed on the throne [of St Peter, i.e. the Pope] will be kept at Fontaine[bleau].

History

'We have never had *so many* nor such good *troops*,' Napoleon wrote on 7 Fructidor, Year XIII (25 August 1805) to Duroc, Grand Marshal of the Palace. The number of Frenchmen serving under arms between 1802 and 1815 is estimated at 1,600,000.

For material about the priests' arrests, see CVI,Q9.

The application of the *ecclesiastical legislation issued by the Revolution* (changing of the rites etc.) was unacceptable to the Vatican and led to more determined resistance than in the Po Valley or Tuscany. The members of the extraordinary States Council wanted to alter or temper the actual policy, but Napoleon insisted upon the uniformity of *law* within his Empire. Thus the clergy had to be dispersed and secularized.

The imperial annexation of the Church reached its climax with the *Imperial Catechism*, published in 1806.

The Catholic Church, however privileged, had to rely upon herself alone when countering overt or covert hostility, and in order to *lead waverers back into the fold* [*"passe sur le prosne"*]. *Disbelief* increased, nourished by sarcasm and rational objections such as those supplied by Voltaire in particular.

On 6 July 1810 Pius VII was arrested at the Quirinal, and his captivity was to last more than four years, at Savona first, then *Fontainebleau*.'[8]

---

[1] Latin *manubiae*: money from the spoils captured from the enemy. DLLB.
[2] Latin *maniples*, syncope of *manipulus*: troop. DLLB.
[3] Latin *sacer*: sacred. DLLB.

[4] To pass by, have no regard for, pass over. DL7V.
[5] *Prône*: formal homily delivered by priest during service. DL7V.
[6] *Prestrerie*: priesthood, priest's life. DAFL. Example of paragoge for reasons of rhyme.
[7] Latin *fons* (from *fundo*): spring, *fountain*. DLLB.
[8] NEE.

The Siege of Saragossa, 1808–09.
After Italy, the Peninsular War

Pau, Véronne, Vincence, Saragosse,
De glaives[1] loings, terroirs de sang humides:
Peste si grand viendra a[2] la grande gousse,[3]
Proches secours, et bien loin les remèdes.

CIII,Q75

Interpretation

After Verona and Vicenza the Army of the Pyrenees will take the war
further afield, as far as Saragossa, and will fill these territories with
blood. A great calamity will be provoked by a great siege and, despite
help approaching, the remedies will be distant.

History

'In 1808, anticipating the need for a rapid mobilization towards the
Pyrenean frontier or even an incursion into *Spain*, Napoleon ordered the
disposition of troops along the staging road [where Pau is situated]:
cavalry and infantry supported by some guns. Murat, the Emperor's
right-hand man, hurried towards *Bayonne*.'[4]

'Don José de Palafox, Governor of *Saragossa*, organized a stern resistance in this town: after *a siege* of sixty-one days, he forced the French
to withdraw [14 August 1808]. But they returned, and Saragossa had to
undergo a new *siege* ["*grande gousse*"] lasting two months [December
1808–February 1809] and more *vicious* than the first, with each house
and each street fiercely disputed. *Deprived of all means of defence* ["*bien
loin les remèdes*"], he had to surrender.'[5]

'The English Army, which in January 1809 had advanced *deep into
Spain* ["*proche secours*"], ran into difficulties as a result of the Battle of
Tudela. Napoleon had directed that the English should be blocked from
the sea. Moore, worried that his retreat might be cut off, hurried towards
the Galician coast in a series of forced marches. Just then St Cyr had

control of Catalonia and Marshal Launes was occupying Aragon and trying to reduce *Saragossa*."[6]

[1] Symbolic of war and fighting. DL7V.
[2] Latin *a* or *ab*: through, by means of. DLLB.
[3] Husk or pod. DL7V. Image to designate an 'enveloping' siege.
[4] NELGI.
[5] DHB.
[6] HFA.

The Peninsular War, 1808. Wellington Lands, 1808. His March to the Pyrenees, 1813. The Spanish Royal Family in France, 1808

Par mort la France prendra voyage à faire,
Classe par mer, marcher monts Pyrénées,
Espagne en trouble, marcher gent militaire:
De plus grand Dames en France emmenées.

CIV,Q2

Interpretation

France will undertake a deadly voyage; an army that has arrived by sea will march to the Pyrenees. Spain will revolt; armies will march there and the greatest one and his ladies [wife and daughter] will be led back to France.

History

'On 24 March 1808 the new King, Ferdinand VII, entered his capital to the acclamation of the delighted populace. This was the first act in the great drama that would give the Spanish people the chance to escape from the apathy into which they had sunk, and to prove themselves both heroic and cruel in the long and bloody war for independence. This was was *disastrous for France*, who lost the flower of her forces there ["*voyage de mort*"].

The first Portuguese rebellion began at Oporto on 16 June, and spread so rapidly through the northern provinces that the French had to evacuate them. At the same time, at Leiria, *14,000 English* troops under Wellington *landed* ["*classe par mer*"], also 5000 more commanded by General Spencer.

In 1813 Wellington, after seizing San Sebastian, passed through Bidassoa [*"marcher monts Pyrénées"*] and with a sizeable force took up positions upon French territory.[1]

'On 10 April 1808 Ferdinand set off. There was a French detachment at each stage: the beloved ruler of Spain was already virtually *a prisoner*. On 20 April he arrived at Bayonne [*"en France emmenés"*]. Charles IV, his father and Marie-Louise [*"Dame"*] submitted to entering a coach, which, escorted by General Exelmans, *headed for France*. On 30 April at Bayonne they were received with regal honours and Napoleon welcomed them warmly. On 6 May Charles and Marie-Louise were taken to the castle of Compiègne. Ferdinand was given a comfortable prison, the Château of Valençay which belonged to Talleyrand. "I handled that affair very badly," Napoleon declared on St Helena. "It was seen to be altogether too immoral, cynically unjust, and the whole business was a shabby one, once I succumbed to it." [2] [*'voyage de mort'*]

[1] HFA.
[2] NEE.

The Invention of Rockets, 1806.
Napoleon and the Church, 1809.
Massacres in Spain, 1809–10

Seront ouys au Ciel les armes batre:[1]
Celui an mesme les divins ennemis,
Voudront lois sainctes injustement debatre
Par foudre[2] et guerre bien croyants a mort mis.

CIV,Q43

Interpretation

The noise of aerial armaments will be heard; the very year the Church's laws will be overthrown, the Catholics will become enemies [of Napoleon]; the believers will be put to death by Napoleon and the war.

History

'Napoleon seemed scarcely concerned with perfecting armaments. The armourer Pauly, it seems, could have supplied the infantry with a breech-loading gun. In fact it was Prussia who profited by this inventor's researches. Various engineers and French officers suggested *rockets* to the Emperor: they were not encouraged, so it was in England that Congreve's efforts resulted in the creation of the Rocket Corps; these weapons being used at Leipzig and Waterloo by the Allies. Congreve's rockets were used for the first time in 1806 against Boulogne by the Royal Navy.

The quarrel between the two powers [Napoleon and the Papacy of Pius VII] was not primarily due to the complete occupation of the Papal States in 1808, nor to economic factors, but to *religious considerations* [*"lois sainctes"*] on the Pope's side and urgent political and military necessities on the Emperor's. These destroyed the concord between the two rulers in *1809* and *plunged the entire Roman Catholic church into dissension* [*"divine ennemis"*].

The Peninsular War: the Spanish leaders rebelled during 1809 and 1810. Some of them were of the nobility, but they were outnumbered by Churchmen [*"bien croyants"*]. The French resorted to extreme brutality. One sergeant stationed in Navarre related an order received by his unit: "The first village to fire on us *will be burned to the ground and everyone in it killed* [*"a mort mis"*], not excluding babes in arms."[3]

[1] *Battre le fer*: noise or clash of arms. DL7V.
[2] Cf. CIV,Q54.
[3] NEE.

The Zenith of the Empire, 1807.
Embarking for St Helena, 1815

Entre deux mers[1] dressera promontoire[2]
Que puis, mourra par le mors du cheval,
Le sien Neptune[3] pliera voile noire
Par Calpte[4] et classe[5] auprès de Rocheval.[6]

CI,Q77

Interpretation

Between two seas he will reach his peak but will die as a result, champing on the bit; the sea-god will wind him in his shroud [St Helena] after the return of L. Capet and the [English] fleet near Rochefort.

History

'Crowned by the Peace of Tilsit the *"Grand Empire"* appeared *formidable*. All the European powers gravitated around Napoleon, whether as allies or subjected by force [the zenith of his rule].

At that very moment 'Napoleon *annexed the Papal States* and imprisoned the Pope.'[7]

'The Chamber demanded Napoleon's abdication. He wanted to get to the United States, but *the Royal Navy* was blockading the coasts. He finally *gave himself up* to the *English*, who treated him as a prisoner of war and deported him to the small island of St Helena.'[8]

Near *Rochefort* he boarded the Bellerophon which was to take him from the Isle of Aix[9] to St Helena. ' "If I had not laid hands on the Papal States," said Napoleon, "and thought to conquer a spiritual power by force, all my subsequent misfortunes would not have happened." '[10]

[1] The Papal States were situated between the Adriatic and Tyrrhenian Seas.
[2] Latin *promontorium*: culminating point, apex. DLLB.
[3] Albion: name given by the Greeks to England, because of the whiteness of her cliffs or from Albion, son of Neptune. DL7V.
[4] Anagram of Louis Capet: Louis XVIII.
[5] Latin *classis*: fleet, army. DLLB.
[6] *Roche-val*: Latin: fort, fortification. Hence 'rocky fort', 'Rochefort', strong rock.
[7] LCH3.
[8] LCH3.
[9] Aix: fortified islet defending the mouth of the Charente, opposite which are the roads of the Isle of Aix, forming a huge outer habour for Rochefort. DL7V.
[10] LMSH.

The Annexation of the Papal States, 1807.
The Continental Blockade, 1806–7

Le tyran Sienne[1] occupera Savonne,[2]
Le fort gaigné tiendra classe[3] marine,[4]
Les deux armées par la marque d'Ancone,[5]
Par effrayeur le chef s'en examine.

CI,Q75

Interpretation

The tyrant will occupy Siena and Savona, having won [the battles] through being strongest, he will contain the English fleet, and the two armies [beaten], will also occupy the borderland of Ancona. The chief will examine his own conscience concerning this dreadful act.

History

'Without awaiting the arrival of his Russian allies, the King of Prussia began hostilities: that same day his *army* was defeated at Jena by Napoleon and at Auerstadt by Davout [14 October 1806]. They still had to conquer *the Russian army* [the two armies]: the bloody but indecisive Battle of Eylau [February 1807] did not settle the matter, but Friedland [14 June] was a clear victory for Napoleon and led to parleys – the Peace of Tilsit [9 July 1807]. Napoleon then thought of coming to grips with England, which was isolated but still *mistress of the sea*. The continental blockade followed. Napoleon annexed *the Papal States* and imprisoned the Pope at Savona.'[6]

[1] Tuscan town.
[2] Ligurian town.
[3] Latin *classis*: fleet, army. DLLB.
[4] Cf. CI,Q98: '*La marine Grange*'.
[5] In 1532 Ancona was reunited with the Papal States. The French captured it in 1797. In 1809 it became the main town of the Metauro department. DHCD.
[6] LCH3.

Napoleon and the Papal States. The Civil Code. The Struggle against the Royalist Rebels

Par sacrée pompe[1] viendra baisser les aisles,
Par la venüe du grand Législateur:
Humble haussera, vexera les rebelles
Naistra sur terre aucun aemulateur.

CV,Q79

Interpretation

The advent of the great legislator will lay low the power of the Catholic Church. He will raise up the humble and vex the rebels. He will have no equal upon earth.

History

'The Consulate did not limit its legal reforms, but succeeded in unifying the whole range of the law, public and private, through the Civil Code.

In this collective endeavour Napoleon, who presided over 55 out of 107 Council sessions, intervened frequently [*"grand Législateur"*] and often to great effect.'[2]

'Pope Pius VII's refusal to participate in the blockade gave the Emperor an excuse *to confiscate the Papal Border States* and then to occupy Rome. Pope Pius VII, held in the Quirinal, threatened to excommunicate the violators of the Holy City, and just when Napoleon made the serious mistake of arousing the Spaniards' hostility he compounded it by confronting the Pope.'[3]

So that his throne, born of the Revolution, might still be surrounded with the trappings of royalty, the Emperor created an *imperial nobility*, adding to his civil and military collaborators *of humble origins* a great number of former nobles of the *ancien régime* who, though formerly Royalists, had gradually joined his ranks during his seven years in power.

On 11 Vendémiaire [3 October 1795], Parisian electors were illegally convoked *by royalist agitators* [*"rebelles"*] who were at the same time mustering an army. A military operation was mounted against the insurgents, who rallied about 25,000 National Guards. The Convention had only about 5000 regulars with whom to oppose them. Barras was given command. The new leader was decisive and vigorous: he surrounded himself with officers he trusted and who thus began illustrious careers – Brune, Murat and, of course, *Napoleon*.

---

[1] Solemn and sumptuous raiment, the 'pomp' of Catholicism. DL7V.
[2] NEE.
[3] NLM.

Monuments Erected by Napoleon

Gens d'alentour de Tarn, Loth et Garonne
Gardez les monts Appennines passer
Votre tombeau près de Rome et d'Anconne
Le noir poil crespe[1] fera trophée[2] dresser.

CIII,Q43

Interpretation

People of different regions [Tarn, Lot and the Garonne], beware of crossing the Apennine Alps, your tomb shall be near Rome and Ancona, he who wears a black felt hat shall erect a triumphal monument.

History

'Following the example of *Augustus*, Napoleon wanted to immortalize his own memory, by means of monuments, especially in Paris. There he *erected* grandiose memorials [the Arc de Triomphe, the Vendôme Column, the Temple of Glory – which became the Madeleine, the Stock Exchange, etc.] to commemorate his victorious campaigns.'[3]

[1] Cf. CI,Q74: '*Le noir poil crespe*'.
[2] Latin *tropaeum*: trophy, monument of victory. DLLB.
[3] LCH3.

The Directorate's Territorial Acquisitions. The Abductions of Pius VI, 1798, and of Pius VII, 1808. The Annexation of the Papal States, and the Peninsular War, 1808

Les ieux nouveaux en Gaule redressez,
Après victoire de l'Insubre[1] campaigne:
Monts d'esperie, [2] les grands liez, troussez,[3]
De peur trembler la Romaigne[4] et l'Espaigne.

CIV,Q36

Interpretation

New powers will be established in France after the victories of the Italian campaign. Near the Italian mountains the great will be made prisoners and taken away; the states of the Church and of Spain will tremble with fear.

History

'Arriving at Tolentino, from where he planned to march on Rome if necessary, Napoleon stopped to see what effect his swift incursion might have. The Pope dispatched his nephew Duke Braschi and three other envoys to Tolentino to arrange a peace with the conqueror. The Treaty was signed on 1 Ventôse [19 February 1797]. The Pope renounced his claims to Avignon and surrendered the legations of Bologna and Ferrara, also the rich province of *Romagna*.'[5]

'The Directorate ordered the invasion into papal territory, and Pope Pius VI had to sign what was for him the *disastrous* Treaty of Tolentino.

After General Duphot's murder in a Rome street [1798], the Directorate *seized* the Pope and proclaimed the Republic in Rome. *Arrested* by General Berthier [1798], Pius VI was taken to Siena, to a monastery in Florence, and then *taken away* in April 1799 to France – first to Grenoble, then Valence where he died."[6]

'Pius VII refused to enforce the continental blockade. So Napoleon seized Rome [1808] and confiscated the Papal States. Pius VII responded by excommunicating all those who had taken part in desecrating the Holy Seat. General Radet immediately *took him away*, along with Cardinal Pacca, transporting him first to Genoa, then Savona and finally Fontainebleau.'[7]

'Religious fanaticism, which in *Spain* at that time only accentuated nationalistic fervour, found further motivation in *the Pope's abduction*. Pius VII, held in the Quirinal, threatened to excommunicate the violators of the Holy City, and just when Napoleon made the serious mistake of arousing the Spaniards' hostility, he compounded it by confronting the Pope.'[8]

[1] Ancient term for Cisalpine Gaul, roughly corresponding to the present-day Milan region, with its chief town Mediolanum (Milan). DHB.
[2] *Hesperia*: ancient classical name for Italy. DHB.
[3] To pack up in a trunk, take away. DL7V.
[4] Romagna: ancient papal province, capital Ravenna. DHB.
[5] HFA.
[6] DL7V.
[7] DL7V.
[8] NLM.

The Victory over the English at Anvers, 24 December 1809. Napoleon's Divorce, 12 January 1810. The Mediterranean Becomes the Focus of Running the Continental Blockade, 1811. The Death of the Archbishop of Paris and the Arrest of Pius VII

Victor naval à Houche,[1] Anvers divorce,
Né grand,[2] du ciel feu, tremblement haut brule:
Sardaigne bois, Malte, Palerme, Corse,
Prélat mourir, l'un frappe sur la Mule.[3]

Presage 17, June

Interpretation

After a naval victory over the English at Houke, near Anvers, he will divorce. He who is great from birth will unleash thunderbolts from the sky and will be incensed because of provocation from the high-placed one [Napoleon]. Sardinia, Malta, Sicily and Corsica [will resist the blockade], a prelate will die and one [Napoleon] will attack the Pope.

History

'While the envoys of Napoleon and the Emperor Francis were busy working out peace terms, the English, who had been preparing an expedition for some time, mustered at the mouth of the Escaut. Their plan was to capture the town of Anvers and the French fleet moored on the Escaut. The English, masters of Walcheren Island, were simultaneously threatening Belgium and Holland. Anvers was at considerable risk. Marshal Bernadotte left for Anvers and raised more than 12,000 men to defend the town. The squadron moored directly beneath the town walls. On 30 September Lord Chatham's powerful force abandoned its position in order to return to England. On 24 December the English demolished the Flushing arsenals and re-embarked [naval victory]. . . .

The dissolution of the marriage of Napoleon and Joséphine was pronounced on 12 January 1810. . . .

From 1810 English trade with the Continent was gradually blocked and smuggling decreased. In 1811 trade between England and northern and western Europe was drastically limited. By contrast, smuggling in the Mediterranean continued to flourish, from Malta to the Balkans and up to Austria.'[4]

'At the end of 1810 French troops invaded Sicily: the result, for the King of Naples, was huge expense and 1200 men killed on the beaches.'[5]

On 9 June 1808, Cardinal de Belloy ['prélat mourir'], the Archbishop of Paris, died. His successor was to have been Cardinal Fesch, but he refused and Napoleon named Maury archbishop on 5 October 1810.

On 6 July 1810 Pius VII was arrested, the start of over four years' captivity. ['l'un frappe sur la Mule']

---

[1] District of Anvers.
[2] Pius VII, as Count Chiaramonti, was of noble birth. HDP.
[3] Possible allusion to Pius VII's obstinacy of character.
[4] NEE.
[5] HFA.

The Peninsular War and the Fall of the Eagle.
Wellington in the Pyrenees, 1812

Bien contigue des grands monts Pyrénées,
Un contre l'Aigle grand copie[1] addresser:
Ouvertes veines,[2] forces exterminées,
Que jusqu'à Pau[3] le chef viendra chasser.

CIV,Q70

Interpretation

Very near the Pyrenees a [country] will amass many troops against the
Eagle [Napoleon]: after trenches have been opened and forces exterminated, it will pursue him into the lower Pyrenees.

History

'1811 ended indecisively. The French had been *driven out of* Portugal.
Determined to attack Russia, Napoleon realized that communication
between France and Spain needed to be strengthened. He ordered Mar-
mont to attack Salamanca, and then to ensure that the major route from
Madrid to *Bayonne* was protected, which left the field open for the
English *commander-in-chief*, who took advantage of the opportunity to
dispose *the majority of his forces* around Badajoz. Following a fortnight of
open trench warfare, the town was attacked on 6 April. After a heroic
defence the French finally surrendered. *The excesses* of the Anglo-Por-
tuguese soldiery reached a *nadir of brutality* and even upset the taciturn
Wellington. On 21 June 1812 the Battle of Vittoria liberated almost all
of Spain as far as the Basque country and Navarre. The French flooded
back towards the frontier, retaining only Pamplona and San Sebastian in
the region of the Pyrenees. Ever methodical, Wellington wanted *to drive*
the French forces remaining in Spain out of the country altogether. But
the Cabinet insisted on his advance into France. Soult, who arrived in
Bayonne on 13 July, shifted to the offensive. At the end of August his
army began descending the south slopes of *the Pyrenees* towards Pamplona. Wellington pushed him back after a stern struggle. Thus unable
to relieve Pamplona, Soult tried to advance on San Sebastian. The English headed him off and forced him back over the frontier. On 8
September, San Sebastian capitulated and was *ransacked*. On 8 October
Wellington crossed the Bidassoa. Ten days later Napoleon, outnumbered, lost the Battle of the Nations at Leipzig. While the Allies crossed
the Rhine, Soult was forced to abandon the Nivelle line, then the Nive,

and to fall back on the entrenched camp of *Bayonne*. As for Wellington, he made his headquarters at *St-Jean-de-Luz*.'[4]

[1] Latin *copia*: army corps, troops, military forces. DLLB.
[2] Refers here to irrigation and trenches rather than blood-letting.
[3] Principal town of the Lower Pyrenees.
[4] NEE.

Soult at Bayonne. Wellington at St Jean de Luz. Russia Enforces Napoleon's Abdication, 1814. The Death of Napoleon at St Helena, 1821

Entre Bayonne et à Saint Jean de Lux,
Sera posé de Mars le promontoire:[1]
Aux Hanix[2] d'Aquilon[3] Nanar[4] hostera lux,[5]
Puis suffoqué au lict[6] sans adjutoire.[7]

CVIII,Q85

Interpretation

The war will reach its peak between Bayonne and St-Jean-de-Luz. Russia's efforts will take away Napoleon's glory: he will suffocate in his bed without any help.

History

See the preceding quatrain (CIV,Q70) for references to Bayonne and St Jean-de-Luz.

'A few days later Mainz was in sight. A sapper is reported to have said, on seeing the town: "Damn it, we did well, looking for the *Russians* in Moscow, just to bring them back into France!" The garrisons left behind along the Vistula, the Oder and the Elbe were forced one after another to surrender. The disaster was total.'[8]

'*Tsar Alexander*, with no more to fear from Napoleon, immediately demanded Napoleon's abdication, which Caulincort and his companions were directed to obtain.'[9]

'*The sufferings he endured at the end were appalling*: fighting the pain, worn out by quack remedies, harassed by flies and mosquitoes, and weakened by enemas, he struggled against *his annihilation*.'[8]

The end of the Peninsular War and the Battle of Leipzig were certainly the turning-points of the Napoleonic Wars.

[1] Latin *promontorium*: peak. DLLB.
[2] Latin *annixus*: effort. DLLB.
[3] Always denotes Russia, the Northern Empire.
[4] Abbreviation of *N*apoleon B*onaparte*.
[5] Latin: light, glory (symbolic). DLLB.
[6] Die in one's bed, i.e. not unnaturally. DL7V.
[7] Latin *adjutorium*: help, succour. DLLB.
[8] NEE.
[9] NLM.

The Defeat of the Grand Army, 1812–13.
Treachery and the Emperor's Abdication

La grand copie[1] qui sera déchassée
Dans un moment fera besoin au Roy.[2]
La foy promise de loing sera faulsée,
Nud se verra en piteux désarroy.

CIV,Q22

Interpretation

The Grand Army which will be tracked down, at a certain moment will
fail the Emperor. The word given will be broken far away and he will
find himself stripped and in pitiable disarray.

History

'Davout's Army Corps was to become the nub of the new *Grand Army*.
It was a composite army, in fact, for apart from the troops of the 130
departments of the Empire there were contingents from all the allied
European countries.

On 3 June 1812 Napoleon rejoined his headquarters at Thorn on the
Vistula: the core of his army was there, comprising about 400,000 men
in three main groups.

"It was 6 November," Caulincourt wrote, "when the bad news arrived.
The Emperor was already preoccupied with the information he had
received concerning the retreat of his forces along the Dvina at the very
time he most needed their success. He was very concerned when the first
news came in about *the Malet conspiracy*. From that moment on his desire
to return to Paris grew stronger." The Grand Army was now reduced to
24,000 fighting men, followed by another 25,000 stragglers.

On the night of 6 April Caulincourt heard the Tsar thank the Prince of Muscovy for the zeal he had shown in forcing the Emperor to abdicate. While false rumours swept Paris, where *cliques and intrigues* abounded, the Duke of Vicenza defended each clause of the treaty in detail. It is moving to read in his report to the Emperor of 8 April: "The Poles your Majesty exhorted me so firmly to protect will be well looked after." The last faithful allies, they ran through the streets of Fontainebleau with a band of the Old Guard crying: "Long Live the Emperor!" "Death to the traitors!"

Ney remained in Paris, having submitted to the new status quo. The Emperor, who knew him well, told Caulincourt: "He was against me yesterday and would die for me tomorrow." He also declared "Life is *unbearable* to me!" [*"piteux désarroy"*] and on the night of 12 April Napoleon tried unsuccessfully to commit suicide by means of some poison he had carried with him since the retreat from Russia.'[3]

[1] Army corps, troops, military forces. DLLB.

[2] The word *king* is used by Nostradamus *passim* to denote heads of state, whatever their actual titles.

[3] NEE.

The Fall of Napoleon, Waterloo, 1815.
M. de St-Agnan Sent by Napoleon to Frankfurt, 1813.
The Battle of Rheims, 13 March 1814

Le grand du fouldre tombe d'heure diurne,
Mal et prédict par porteur postulaire:[1]
Suivant présage, tombe d'heure nocturne,
Conflict Reims, Londres, Etrusques[2] pestifère.

CI,Q26

Interpretation

The glory of the captain will begin to dwindle by daylight, misfortune being announced by the bearer of a request. Following this presage night will fall; after the combat at Rheims, Etruria, which has brought misery, will be defeated by the English.

History

'On 2 November 1813 the French army, reduced to 70,000 men, crossed the Rhine. There this *bloody* campaign ended. No alternative remained but to try to parley with the Allies or to fight to the bitter end. Peace talks were resumed: M. de St-Agnan was called to Frankfurt by Metternich and on 9 November, in the presence of the ministers from Russia and *England*, the basis for a general peace treaty was laid down. The victors *demanded* that Napoleon abandon Spain, Italy, Germany and Holland. St-Agnan had the task of *conveying* these terms to Napoleon. The Allies stated that if they were met talks would begin in a town by the Rhine, but they also declared that such negotiations would not imply the cessation of hostilities. The French therefore had to prepare for battle.'

'On 13 March 1814 Napoleon reached some hills a mile or so from *Rheims*, which the Russian general St-Priest had just occupied. The Russians were spread out upon these heights just outside *Rheims*. General Krasinsky cut the Rheims road at Berry-au-Bac, and the Allies abandoned the town and withdrew in disorder. The French took 6000 prisoners in this battle. The Imperial Army stayed in the *Rheims* area until 16 March. During this time Napoleon received reports on the general situation of the Empire.'

'On *the morning* of 18 June 1815 Napoleon reconnoitred the entire English line and gave his battle orders to various commanders. Manoeuvring began. Napoleon bore down on Planchenoit to form a second position, making renewed efforts to steady some regiments. But rallying them became impossible *in the night* and this entire fine army was a confused mass amid which one heard cries of "Every man for himself!". *The losses* sustained by the French at Waterloo were *very severe*: 19,000 men lay on the battlefield. The Allies lost even more men, but their victory was decisive, nonetheless.'[3]

[1] Latin *postulo*: I demand, request, claim. DLLB.
[2] The Bonaparte family had two branches: one line became extinct at Treviso in 1447, the other established itself in Florence (capital of Tuscany, i.e. Etruria) and from this were descended the Bonapartes of Sarzane of whom Napoleon I was a member. DL7V.
[3] HFA.

The Return from Elba, 1 March 1815

Le Captif Prince aux Itales[1] vaincu,
Passera Gennes par mer jusqu'à Marseille,
Par grand effort des forens[2] survaincu,[3]
Sauf coup de feu, barril liqueur d'abeille.[4]

CX,Q24

Interpretation

The vanquished prince, prisoner in Italy, will go past the Gulf of Genoa towards Marseille. By making great efforts [of war] the foreign [armies] will conquer him by their superiority. Safe and sound from shots, he will have barrels [of powder] instead of honey.

History

'On the island of Elba, Napoleon was informed that he still had the support of the French people. He *disembarked* at the Gulf of Juan on 1 March. *The Allies* were still gathered at the Congress of Vienna and their armies were encamped near the French frontiers. They declared Napoleon "outlawed from Europe". Obliged to carry on the war, Napoleon marched north with 125,000 men against 100,000 English and 250,000 Prussians ["*survaincu*"]. On the evening of 18 June panic and dismay spread through the French ranks. As for Napoleon, *who had tried to get himself killed* in the battle, ["*sauf coup de feu*"], he gave himself up to the English.'[5]

[1] Latin *Aethalis*: ancient name for the Island of Elba. DLLB.
[2] Foreign, strange. DAFL.
[3] *Sur*: implying superiority over and above.
[4] Honey symbolizing peace, tranquillity, Cf. cx,Q89.
[5] LCH3.

The Return from Elba. Ney Rallies to Napoleon in Burgundy, 17 March 1815. The Declarations of Lyon. The Charter of 1815

Foudre[1] en Bourgogne[2] fera cas portenteux[3]
Que par engin[4] homme ne pourrait faire,
De leur Sénat[5] sacriste[6] fait boiteux
Fera scavoir aux ennemis l'affaire.

CII,Q76

Interpretation

Napoleon in Burgundy will make a deadly prophecy that man cannot triumph by means of his intelligence. Because of unsatisfactory things decreed by the very sacred Senate, he will make his intentions known to his enemies.

History

'Napoleon thought it best to channel rather than confront this renewal of the revolutionary spirit. These tactics were reflected in the series of decrees Napoleon issued from *Lyon*, already couched in magisterial manner. The *Parliaments* were dissolved. The audacity and resolution of Marshal Ney were crucial. He had been given the command of the troops reassembled in the Franche-Comté; decisive action from this quarter could disrupt the advance of Napoleon's army, which was straggling along on the *Lyon–Auxerre* road near *Chalon* and *Autun*. "I'll take care of *Bonaparte*," Ney thundered. "We'll attack the wild beast." Emissaries from Lyon reached him at Lons-le-Saunier on the night of 13 March. They reported on what they had seen and brought a long letter from Bertrand and word from the Emperor himself. "Come and rejoin me at *Chalon*, and I shall receive you as I did the day after the Battle of the Moskva." On the morning of 14 Ney made up his mind, and he joined Napoleon again at *Auxerre* on 17 March.'[7]

'A few days after the signing of this celebrated treaty [20 May 1814] Louis XVIII's government reinstated a number of *senators* to the legislative assembly which Napoleon had dismissed on the preceding 31 December. Both these somewhat fraudulent assemblies ["*fait boiteux*"] were convened at the Palais Bourbon, during which session Louis XVIII gave notice of the treaty and presented the charter he was conferring.

The royal session took place on 16 March. Louis XVIII read a speech that ended thus: "He who would light the torch of civil war among us also brings the scourge of foreign war ['*cas portenteux*']; he comes to destroy this constitutional charter I have given you; this charter which every Frenchman *cherishes* ['*sacriste*'] and which I here swear to uphold." '[8]

---

[1] Cf. CI,Q26 and CIII,QI3, Napoleon '*foudre de guerre*'. DL7V.
[2] Burgundy was divided into various areas, including the Charolais, Macon, Auxerre etc. DL7V.
[3] Latin *portentum*: presage (usually ill-omen). DLLB.
[4] Latin *ingenium*: wit, intelligence. DLLB.
[5] Name given to the Upper or Senior House in certain states with two legislative assemblies, and not at all, or only indirectly, dependent upon popular election.
[6] Latin: superlative of *sacer*, i.e. very or most sacred.
[7] NEE.
[8] HFA.

The Hundred Days. Waterloo, 18 June 1815. St Helena

Au mois troisième[1] se levant du Soleil[2]
Sanglier,[3] liépard[4] au champs Mars[5] pour combattre,
Liépard lassé au ciel[6] estend son oeil,[7]
Un aigle autour du Soleil voit s'esbattre.

CI,Q23

Interpretation

In March, having risen against the monarchy, near the Ardennes, England will fight upon the battlefield. Weary [of Napoleon], England will extend her surveillance upon him, even to a prison cell, after seeing the Emperor disport himself among the monarchists.

History

'Napoleon disembarked on *1 March; avoiding* the Rhône valley, which was *Royalist*-dominated, he took the Alpine route and reached Paris on *20 March*. His progress became a triumphal procession. The troops *sent against him by the King* acclaimed him. . . . *A furious battle* began on the plateau of Mont-St-Jean near Waterloo against the English led by Wellington. . . . Napoleon wanted to get to the United States but the *English* navy controlled the coastline. Finally he surrendered to the *English* who treated him as a prisoner of war and deported him to the small island of St Helena.'[8]

'There he lived for six years under strict *surveillance* in the *prison villa* of Longwood.'[9]

[1] March, third month.
[2] Sun: symbol of the Capets (Louis XIV, '*le roi soleil*').
[3] *Sanglier*: 'the Wild Boar of the Ardennes', name given to Count William de la Marck (1446–85). DL7V.
[4] Leopard: the heraldic leopard is a lion passant rather than rampant. *The Lion of Waterloo*, the victory of the Lion over the Eagle, was a half-symbolic, half-realistic painting by the Belgian artist Wiertz. At Waterloo the Allies erected a 50 ft pyramid topped by a huge cast-iron lion. DL7V.
[5] Mars, god of war.
[6] *Ciel*: Latin *cella*: small cell. DAFL.
[7] *Oeil*: look, and by extension, surveillance. DL7V.
[8] LCH3.
[9] HFAM.

The Battle of Waterloo, 18 June 1815

Prest à combattre fera défection,
Chef adversaire obtiendra la victoire:
L'arrière-garde fera défension,[1]
Les défaillans[2] mort au blanc territoire.

CIV,Q75

Interpretation

[The army], ready to fight, will be found wanting, the enemy leader will gain the victory; the rearguard will defend itself, those who died in the snowy territory will be missed.

History

The army commanded by Grouchy was ordered by Napoleon to pursue Blücher's army. Not only did Grouchy allow Blücher to escape, but his troops were ineffective at Waterloo.

'Napoleon marched north with 125,000 men against 100,000 English and 250,000 Prussians. After a victory at Ligny [16 June], a bitter battle began on the plateau of Mont-St-Jean near Waterloo with the English under Wellington, soon supported by Blücher's Prussians [18 June]. That evening panic and dismay spread through the French ranks: *only the Old Guard* died without asking for quarter.'[3]

Napoleon had lost much of his army during the Russian campaign: 'Napoleon had mobilized the Grand Army: 700,000 men. Hunger and an unexpectedly early and bitter winter wore out the soldiers. The Grand Army, thus reduced to *30,000 men*, painfully crossed the Beresina [*"Mort au blanc térritoire"*].'[3]

[1] Action of defending oneself, defence, DAFL.
[2] *Défaillir: faire défaut*: to be found wanting, or to err. DAFL.
[3] LCH3.

Napoleon on *The Bellerophon*. Fouché against Napoleon. The Second Abdication, 23 June 1815

Par foudre[1] en l'arche[2] or et argent fondu,[3]
De deux captifs l'un l'autre mangera:[4]
De la cité le plus grand estendu,
Quand submergé la classe[5] nagera.

CIII,QI3

Interpretation

Because of the military leader [Napoleon] on a ship, wealth will melt away. One of two prisoners will rise against the other. The greater part of the town [Paris] will be overthrown when the French army is swamped and the [English] fleet forges on.

History

'On 18 June 1815, after the Prussians had been driven back, the Emperor risked the final onslaught with the Old Guard. But at this critical moment a second Prussian corps came into action. The exhausted French army was overcome with panic and began *to flee, pursued and cut down* by the Prussians until almost 2 a.m.'[6]

'The enemy army was larger than ours, but the President of the Provisional Government, Fouché,[7] wanted the junior branch of the Bourbons to accede to the throne, or if that failed, to revert to the older branch of the family. When Napoleon offered to place himself at the head of the forces, Fouché refused and *compelled* the Emperor to leave Malmaison, where he had taken shelter.'[8]

'After his abdication he went to the port of Rochefort, hoping to sail to the United States. But an English cruiser blocked the harbour, so Napoleon decided to ask for asylum from the English government. He boarded the English *ship Bellerophon*, on which he was treated as a *prisoner* of war and transported to St Helena. . . .

England, *mistress of the seas*, kept Malta and the Ionian islands.'[9]

'The second restoration [of Napoleon] *cost France dear*. The Allies had first to be paid 100 million francs, then another indemnity of 700 million, followed by *300 million* special compensation. That was not all: 150,000 foreign soldiers remained for three years on French soil, maintained at French expense. France was *weakened* not only by her own losses, but also as a result of everything her enemies had won.'[10]

[1] Napoleon. Cf. CIV,Q54.

² Reference to Noah's ark, hence to a vessel providing refuge. DL7V.
³ To disappear rapidly: money slipping through one's hands. DL7V.
⁴ To eat someone: i.e. to attack, or fall upon. DL7V.
⁵ Latin *classis*: army, fleet. DLLB. By elision Nostradamus uses the word in both its senses, thus avoiding repetition.
⁶ HFAM.
⁷ Joseph Fouché. Having returned to Paris he was elected president of the Jacobins and quarrelled with Robespierre, whom he helped overthrow. When the tide turned, a warrant was issued for his arrest. DL7V.
⁸ HFVD.
⁹ HFAM.
¹⁰ HFVD.

The Second Abdication, 21 June 1815

La prochain fils de l'aisnier¹ parviendra
Tant élevé jusqu'au règne des fors
Son aspre² gloire un chacun la craindra
Mais ses enfans du règne gettez hors.

CII,QII

Interpretation

The son who succeeds the elder will manage to elevate himself to rule among the most powerful; everyone will fear his savage glory, but those near to him will cast him out of power.

History

'Napoleon reached Lyon and then Paris, from where he counted on organizing once more the defence of the realm. But he was prevented from doing so. At the news of his defeat the deputies had only one thought: the Emperor was going to use even his defeat and the impending invasion in order to dissolve the Assembly and turn dictator on the pretext of the public's good. To forestall this, *it was necessary to make him abdicate*. . . .

He received Davout who immediately advised him to adjourn both chambers, adding that the chamber of representatives, *with its passionate hostility*, would paralyse all public-spiritedness. The deputies were *against him*. Napoleon gave Fouché himself, *whom he now saw through*, the task of conveying to the chamber his abdication.'³

¹ Charles-Marie Bonaparte married in 1767 Laetitia Ramolino, by whom he had five

sons and three daughters: Joseph, *Napoleon*, Marie-Ann-Eliza, Lucien, Louis, Marie Pauline, Marie-Annonciade-Caroline, and Jérôme. DHCD.

² Latin *asper*: of sentient beings, used to mean hard, savage, intractable, tough. DLLB. Cf. CI,Q76.

³ NLM.

Napoleon Betrayed by Women. Napoleon Prisoner of the English. His Agonizing Death, 1821

Le feu estaint, les vierges¹ trahiront,
La plus grand part de la bande nouvelle:
Fouldre² a fer, lance les seuls Roys garderont
Etrusque et Corse, de nuict gorge allumelle.

CIV,Q35

Interpretation

When the war ceases, women will betray [Napoleon] as well as the greater part of the new [monarchist] movement. Napoleon will be a captive, the ministers will want to keep the sword of him who originated from Tuscany and Corsica, then he will have fire in his throat at night.

History

'General Belliard brought Napoleon the news of the capitulation of Paris, signed during the night. After this enemy troops were to occupy the capital. . . . At 6 a.m. he arrived at Fontainebleau where his Guard and the remainder of his army awaited him. Then began the series of salon intrigues which led to the restoration of the Bourbons. Some diplomats and a handful of Royalists and émigrés circulated busily everywhere while *their wives and womenfolk* flourished and waved white handkerchiefs [treason].

The way in which *the ministers* wanted Napoleon treated was somewhat shabby: they had even given orders that his sword be taken from him ["*garderont lance*"].'³

'The next day was appalling. On *the night* of 4 May 1821 all the servants remained in attendance on him. His last struggle began and his *death-rattle* was agonizing and dreadful.'⁴

¹ Latin *virgo*: young woman. DLLB.
² Cf. CIV,Q54, CI,Q26, CII,Q76, CIII,Q13.
³ HFA.
⁴ NLM.

Napoleon at St Helena. Longwood House, 1815–21

Le chef qu'aura conduict peuple infiny
Loing de son Ciel, de meurs et langue estrange,
Cinq mil en Crète,[1] et Tessalie[2] finy,
Le chef fuyant sauvé[3] en la marine grange.

CI,Q98

Interpretation

The leader who will have led the immortal people far from its own sky will end his life in the middle of the sea on a rocky island, with a population of 5000 whose customs and language are different. The leader who will want to escape will be kept in a barn in the middle of the sea.

History

'When Napoleon returned to Paris, the Chamber demanded his abdication. *He wanted to get to the United States*, but the English navy was patrolling the coastline, and he finally gave himself up to the English, who treated him as a prisoner of war and deported him to the small island of St Helena.'[4]

'St Helena is only an African *rock* in the Atlantic, 1900 miles from land. Longwood House where the English installed the Emperor and his devoted retainers had been built to serve as *a barn* for a farm.'[5]

[1] Latin *creta*: rock. DLLB. St Helena, a rocky African island in the Atlantic, population 5000. DHCD.
[2] Greek: Θέσσαλη for Θάλασσα: the sea. DGF.
[3] Latin *salvo*: I keep. DLLB.
[4] LCH3.
[5] NLM.

The Collapse of the Empire

Le divin mal surprendra le Grand Prince,
Un peu devant aura femme espousée
Son appuy et crédit à un coup viendra mince,
Conseil[1] mourra pour la teste rasée.

CI,Q88

Interpretation

The divine curse will surprise the Great Prince, shortly after his marriage, and suddenly his allies and credit will be reduced, the good sense of the man with the cropped head will die out.

History

'As soon as Napoleon married the Archduchess Marie-Louise of Austria, for whom he had divorced Joséphine Beauharnais, Fouché, Bernadotte and various others were more or less alienated from him. Pope Pius VII, whose states he wanted to ransack, excommunicated him, and the violent opposition to Napoleon created new problems for him. In spite of this, he did not hesitate in embarking upon a formidable conflict with Russia.'[2]

[1] Latin *consilium*: good sense. DLLB.
[2] DHCB.

The First Italian Campaign 1796–97.
The Return of the Bourbons. Louis XVIII and Charles X, 1815–30

Tranché le ventre[1] naistra avec deux testes,[2]
Et quatre bras: quelques ans entiers vivra
Jour qui Alquiloye[3] célebrera ses fetes
Fossen, Turin, chef Ferrare suivra.

CI,Q58

Interpretation

When the mother has been decapitated [the monarchy], she will be reborn with two kings and four princes and will live for some years more, [meanwhile] the imperial eagle will celebrate its festivities [in France], then Fossano will follow, Turin, the Pope.

History

In spite of the Queen Mother's execution the Bourbons are to return to the throne with two heads: Louis XVIII's and Charles X's. The four princes who will not reign are Louis Dauphin (Louis XVII), Charles

Ferdinand Duke of Berry, Louis Antoine Duke of Angoulême, Henri-Charles-Ferdinand Duke of Bordeaux and Count of Chambord.

'*Fossano*: fort with an arsenal seized by the French in 1796 (first Italian campaign).'[4]

'Napoleon was thus in control of the *Turin* road. But he did not stop there, savaging the Sardinian army and wiping it out at Mondovi. The Sardinians laid down their arms and had to sign the Armistice of Cherasco, ten leagues from *Turin* [18 April 1796], which was amended on 3 June to a peace treaty giving France Savoy, Nice, etc.

Pius VI signed the Peace of Tolentino with some trepidation; it cost him 30 millions. The Romagna [Ravenna, Rimini] was reunited, along with the legations of *Ferrara* and Bologna, to the Cispadane Republic and Ancona.'[5]

[1] The part here representing the whole: the genetrix. Cf. CX,Q17.
[2] Head: *caput* = *capet*. Cf. CIX,Q20.
[3] Latin *aquila*: eagle. DLLB.
[4] DHCB.
[5] HFVD.

The Second Restoration of Louis XVIII, July 1815.
The Proscriptions

Le blonds au nez forche[1] viendra commettre[2]
Par le duelle[3] et chassera dehors,
Les exilés dedans fera remettre.
Aux lieux marins commettant les plus forts.

CII,Q67

Interpretation

The blond man with the aquiline nose [Louis XVIII] will come to head [the country] because of the mourning [for Louis XVI] and will drive out [the Bonapartists], he will reinstate the exiles [Royalists], sending out the strongest [the generals] beyond the seas.

History

'The government was no sooner assured of the Loire army's adherence than the proscriptions began. Nineteen generals or officers, accused of having abandoned the King prior to 23 March and of having seized power, were immediately placed on reprisals lists and arrested and tried before military tribunals. Thirty-eight other *generals or administrators of the Empire* ["*les plus forts*"] were at the same time *sent far away from their homes*. In this way the minister tried to satisfy *the demands of the ultra-Royalist faction*. When death sentences were requested, there were gasps in the Assembly and Tribunals. *The Royalists* held their ground, seemingly quite confident of forcing the King's hand. Those who wanted severe sentences passed on the regicides had to be placated. The Commission's proposal of *banishment* was adopted. Exile was to be permanent and these declared enemies of France were ordered to leave French soil within a month. They were stripped of civil rights, possessions and titles. France was now *in the hands of the Royalists*. *The most experienced generals* had been purged, and the deputies, *all aristocrats*, did not hesitate to stiffen the tax laws at the very time when commerce was in the greatest difficulties.'[4]

[1] The celebrated profile of the Bourbon.
[2] Put foremost, at the head. DL7V.
[3] *deuil* (mourning), by transposition. DAFL.
[4] HFA.

Charles-Ferdinand of Bourbon, Duke of Berry. His Marriage. Alliance with the Prince of Condé. His Assassination, 1820

Et Ferdinand blonde[1] sera descorte,[2]
Quitter la fleur, suyvre le Macédon:[3]
Au grand besoin[4] défaillira sa routte,
Et marchera contre le Myrmiden.[5]

CIX,Q35

Interpretation

Ferdinand will be in dissent [because of a woman]; he will abandon the monarchy to follow *Ma*[rshal] *Condé*; he will die in the road [causing] great privation and will march against the small man [Napoleon].

History

'In *1789 an émigré*, along with his parents, he served in *the army of Condé*, 1792–97, then in 1801 settled in England, where he married an

Englishwoman, Anna *Brown*. In 1814 Louis XVIII chose him to be commander-in-chief of the army *which was to oppose Napoleon* at the gates of Paris after his return from Elba. *His family, which had not wanted to recognize his first marriage*, made him marry Marie-Caroline-Ferdinande-Louise of Naples in 1816.'[6]

'On 13 February 1829 he was assassinated *at the entrance* of the Opéra, by Louvel, who wanted *to stamp out the Bourbon dynasty*.'[7]

[1] Play of words on Anna *Brown*.
[2] Latin *discors*: what is in dissension, different. DLLB. Nostradamus by a pun here mobilizes both senses of the word, discord and difference.
[3] Macédon: anagram of Ma(rshal) Condé.
[4] Privation. DL7V.
[5] Myrmidon: man of small stature. DL7V.
[6] DL7V.
[7] DHCD.

The Duke of Berry's Assassination by Louvel, 13 February 1820

Par trahison de verges[1] à mort battu,
Puis surmonté sera par son désordre:[2]
Conseil frivole au grand captif sentu,
Nez par fureur quand Berich viendra mordre.[3]

CVI,Q32

Interpretation

Accused of treason he [Louvel] will be executed on the Place de Grèves, having been dominated by his mental disorder. He will be accused of asking for a futile audience with the great captive [Napoleon], when he will sink [his dagger] into the body of the Duke of Berry through hatred of those born [Bourbons].

History

'After more than three months' inquiries and investigation, and despite zealous efforts by the minister and various Royalists to discover in Louvel's crime some traces of *a conspiracy*, M. Bellart, the Public Prosecutor, had to admit in his indictment that he had found no accomplices. The Royalists were disappointed with this conclusion, for they wished to compromise the liberals. But it was only too clear that Louvel had acted quite alone and without any motive but his *own deep hatred* ["*par fureur*"] for the Bourbons. He admitted as much, confessed that the dagger he had used was in fact his [*mordre*] and answered the questions put to him. He had thought about his crime for six years; the Prince had done him no harm, but the Bourbons had greatly harmed France. He had a grudge against the royal family and wanted to kill the King himself, and he had begun with the Prince because he was the hope of the Bourbons. He confessed that he had been troubled by the presence of foreigners in France and had journeyed to Elba in 1814. Yet he had returned *without speaking to Napoleon nor discussing* his plans with anyone. ["*Conseil frivole*" etc. . . .] The court had nominated a celebrated advocate to defend the accused, but M. Bonnet could only present Louvel as the prey of monomania[4] ["*désordre*"]. He was condemned to death and led out the next day to the Place de *Grèves* amid a silent crowd."[5]

[1] Anagram of Grèves.
[2] By analogy, a troubled or disturbed mind.
[3] Penetrate, enter, sink into. DL7V.
[4] Monomania: essentially characterized by partial madness, varying in its object, and manifested in obsessions, compulsions and irresistible fears. DL7V.
[5] HFA.

Bishop Kyprianos at Cyprus, 1810. The Massacre of Clergy and Prominent Greeks, 1821

En ce temps-là sera frustrée Cyprie,[1]
De son secours de ceux de mer Egée:
Vieux trucidez, mais par mesles[2] et Lypres[3]
Seduict leur Roy, Royne plus outragée.

CIII,Q89

Interpretation

At that very moment, Kyprianos will be thwarted at Cyprus in his attempt to help the Greeks: the old [clergy] will be massacred by a dark and wretched trick, their leader being seduced, the mother [Church] will be offended still more.

History

'From 1810 Cyprus was lucky to have as archbishop the young and energetic Kyprianos, who took a lively interest . . . in ecclesiastical affairs.

The Greek War of Independence found the island peaceful. But Kutchuk Mehmed, the governor, feared that the Greek Cypriots would take up arms against Turkey as the Greeks on *the Aegean* islands were doing, and asked Kyprianos for assurances of loyalty which the Archbishop willingly gave. But Kutchuk still had doubts and for security reasons requested 2000 Turkish soldiers to be posted to the island. He ordered all Greeks to be disarmed and as though this were not enough proceeded to arrest *prominent Greeks* and to *execute the Dragoman*. The distribution of several revolutionary tracts made him still more suspicious and he no longer believed the Archbishop's assurances. He wrote to the Sultan demanding the punishment of the rebels and their friends, but the Sultan at first refused to order such measures. Kutchuk Mehmed remained persistent until he received the Sultan's assent. Then, armed with the execution warrant, the governor *invited the priests to his Palace at Nicosia on the pretext* of their signing a "loyalty oath" ["*mesles et Lypres*"]. When, on the morning of 9 July 1821 the archbishop and bishops entered the Palace followed by other *Church dignitaries*, the governor ordered the gates to be closed and the Greeks to be chained. He then read them *their death sentences* and they were immediately executed in the main square of Nicosia. Afterwards Kutchuk ordered *the confiscation of Church property* and *the massacre of prominent Greeks* throughout all the towns of the island. More than 450 people perished; the only ones to escape managed to take refuge inside the French, English or Russian consulates and thence secretly leave the island.'⁴

---

¹ Nostradamus employs the double meanings of Cyprus and Kyprianos.
² Greek μέλας: black, dark. DGF.
³ Greek λυπρός: wretched. DGF.
⁴ HDCAE.

Greek Independence, 1825–33.
The Battle of Navarino, 1827

De l'Ambraxie[1] et du pays de Thrace,[2]
Peuple par mer, mal et secours Gaulois,
Perpétuelle en Provence la trace,
Avec vestiges de leurs coutumes et loix.

CIX,Q75

Interpretation

From Arta to Thrace, the Greek people will be saved from misfortune by France, by means of the sea. In Provence the reminders of this will endure, along with traces of their costumes and laws.

History

'In 1825 Ibrahim Pasha, son of Mohamed Ali, stamped out rebellions on Kassos and Crete, then landed regular troops on the Peloponnese. From 1825 to 1827 he laid waste the region. Through the sack of Missolonghi [1826], the *legendary* exodus from which revived *European Philhellenism*, and the capture of the Acropolis, the Turks became masters of mainland Greece and the rebellion seemed about to peter out.

In July 1827 Russia, England and *France* formed the Triple Alliance, which undertook to mediate between rebel Greece and the Turkish government, on the basis of an autonomous Greece under the overall sovereignty of the Sultan, and which demanded an immediate truce between both sides. The Turks' formal refusal to submit to the authority of the Triple Alliance resulted in the naval *Battle of Navarino* [20 October 1827] in which the Turco-Egyptian fleet was annihilated.'

'Organization of the state: the national and liberal revolution of the Greeks led to the formation of a monarchical state whose organization was controlled by a foreign prince and government. King Otho, still a minor, arrived on 25 January 1833 at Nauplia, provisional capital of the new kingdom, which was composed of the Peloponnese, the Cyclades and mainland Greece from *the demarcation line of* the *Gulf of Arta* to Volos Bay in the north. He was accompanied by a Regency Council under the Presidency of Count Armansperg.'[3]

'Military intervention in the Morea was accomplished without difficulty, agreement being reached with Mohamed Ali in November 1828. Finally, the London Protocols established the borders of Greece. Russia ratified these arrangements by the Treaty of Andrinopolis [a *Thracian*

town] on 14 September 1829. In February 1830, at the London conference, Greece was proclaimed independent.'⁴

---

¹ Ambracia: today Arta, a town in Epirus on the northern coast of a small gulf of the
same name. DHB.
² District of the Ottoman Empire in 1827.
³ HDGM.
⁴ HDT.

The End of the Ottoman Empire (1686–1829).
The Capture of Buda by the Duke of Lorraine, 1686

Près de Sorbin¹ pour assaillir Ongrie.
L'héraut² de Brudes³ les viendra advertir⁴
Chef Bizantin, Sallon⁵ de Sclavonie⁶
A loy d'Arabes les viendra convertir.

CX,Q62

Interpretation

Near Serbia, in order to attack Hungary, the military leader will come
to rage against [the Turks] at Buda; the Turkish chief having converted
to Arab rule [territories] from Salonika to Russia.

History

'The Austro-Hungarian emperors had to deal with successive revolts by
Bethlem-Gabor, Tekely and the Ragotskys. During these upheavals the
Turks had invaded the greater part of the country. They were only finally
driven out ["*advertir*"] in 1699, by the Peace of Carlowitz and the exploits
of Prince Eugène, which led to the Peace of Passarowitz, 1718. The
Hungarians thereafter remained loyal to the House of Austria.

Mohamed II took Constantinople [1453] and through this important
conquest destroyed the Greek Empire [Salonika]. Turkey expanded under Selim I. Suliman II added parts of Europe – some of *Hungary*,
Transylvania, *Slavonia*, Moldavia. The great war of 1682–99, which the
Peace of Carlowitz ended, wrested almost all of Hungary from the Turks.
The *Russians*, with whom they had been fighting since 1672, began to
gain the upper hand. The war of 1790–92 took various Caucasian districts
from the Turks. From 1809 to 1812 there was renewed warfare and the
provinces between the Dnieper and the Danube were lost to *Russia*

through the Peace of Bucharest. In 1819 Turkey lost the Ionian Islands; there followed in 1820–30 the loss of *Greece*, decisively liberated by the Battle of Navarino [1827], and the loss of part of Armenia, ceded to Russia in 1829; and under the Treaty of Andrinopolis [1829], Wallachia, Moldavia and Serbia also became free and under *Russian protection*.

Buda: capital of Hungary, occupied by the Turks from 1530 to 1686. *Recaptured in 1686 by the Duke of Lorraine* [*"héraut de Bude"*], it then remained under Austrian control.

After the Congress of Berlin [1878], a new problem arose in the Balkans. Austria, having become a Balkan power, was increasing her influence upon the Christians in those regions and simultaneously trying to gain Salonika, which led to furtive conflicts with Russia resulting in the First World War.'[7]

[1] Serbs or Sorabs, captive peoples who gave their name to Serbia. DHB.

[2] Public official who had the task of announcing a war, and whose person was sacrosanct.

[3] Epenthesis and apocope: *Brudes* for *Bude* (Buda), the Hungarian capital.

[4] Latin *adverso*: I rage against, punish. DLLB.

[5] Epenthesis and paragoge: for *Salonica*, part of Roumelia (European Turkey at that time). DHB.

[6] Slavonia owes its name to the Sarmatians. European Sarmatia, between the Vistula and the Tanais, is made up of all the countries that today form Poland and Russia. DHB.

[7] DHB.

Middle Eastern Problems, 1821–55.
Greek Independence. The Massacres at Chios.
The Crimean War, 1854–56

Dans les cyclades,[1] en perinthe[2] et larisse,[3]
Dedans Sparte[4] font le Peloponnesse,[5]
Si grand famine, peste par faux coninsse[6]
Neuf mois tiendra et tout le cherronesse.[7]

CV,Q90

Interpretation

In the Cyclades, Greece and the Morea there will be a great famine and a calamity as a result of false alliances, and the Crimea will be occupied for nine months [10 September 1855–June 1856].

History

'In the *Morea*, Germanos, Archbishop of Patras, proclaimed the War of Independence [25 March 1821]; massacres of Greeks followed in Constantinople, and of Turks in Greece. On 12 January 1822 the Assembly of Greek Deputies declared Greek independence also. In April the infamous massacres of *Chios* took place and in May Joannina fell to the Turks. The Greeks waited in vain for help from the Tsar ["*faux coninsse*"], who remained faithful to the principles of the *Holy Alliance*. The Sultan was not slow to act, ordering Mohamed Ali to intervene in the Morea [February 1824], while Egyptian troops had already reconquered Crete [1822]. In 1825 Ibrahim, Mohamed Ali's son, recaptured *the main towns of the Morea*, but his policy of deportations to Egypt alienated French sympathies. The death of Alexander I and his replacement in December 1825 by Nicholas I, who favoured strong, direct methods, worried England. In March 1826 Nicholas gave the Turks an ultimatum, resulting in the Treaty of Akkerman, by which Russia obtained trading rights in all the seas of the Ottoman Empire. It was no longer simply a question of Greece. England, worried by this treaty, stepped in, but the three great powers, England, France and Russia, found their offer of mediation refused by the Sultan. The Allied Fleet attacked and destroyed the Turco-Egyptian navy at Navarino.[8] Finally the Protocols of London [November 1828 and March 1829] fixed the Greek borders. In February 1830, at the London conference, Greece was declared independent. . . .

New negotiations with Russia had broken down that winter, and in March 1854 France, England and Turkey signed an alliance; in June Austria and Turkey signed a treaty designed to get Austrian co-operation in driving the Russians from the Danube principalities. At the end of March 1854 English and French troops landed at Gallipoli [a Thracian town at the entrance of the Sea of Marmora], to proceed towards the Danube. But following the Russian evacuation it was resolved to carry the war into the *Crimea*. Sebastopol fell on 10 September 1855 and was to be evacuated by Anglo-French troops in June 1856 [nine months].'[9]

[1] Aegean archipelago, including Chios. AVL.
[2] Thracian town by the Sea of Marmora. AVL.
[3] Thessalian town. DHB.
[4] Morean town. DHB.
[5] Morea or Peloponnese, southern peninsula of Greece. DHB.
[6] Latin *connexus*: union, alliance. DLLB.
[7] The Chersonese of Tauris, i.e. the Crimea. DHB.
[8] Morean town.
[9] HDT.

Weak Government in Italy and Spain, 1855.
The Trap of Sebastopol, 1854–55

Peuple sans chef d'Espagne d'Italie,
Morts profligez dedans la Cheronese,[1]
Leur dict trahy par légère folie,
De sang nagez partout à la traverse.[2]

CIII,Q68

Interpretation

The Spanish and Italian people will be deprived of a head of state just when Sebastopol is overwhelmed by death. The words [of the French] betray foolishness and blood will run everywhere over the fortifications.

History

'From 1840 to 1875 there seemed to be little else in Spain except generals disputing power. During this time the generals were acting for Queen Isabella II, of whom even the kindest historians say that her natural benevolence was matched by an education so deplorable that one could scarcely wonder that *she completely lacked the capacity to govern*.'[3]

'In 1848 Sicily rose against the King of Naples and proclaimed its independence. Naples, Florence and Turin gave themselves constitutions. Rome called itself a republic. Parma and Modena *drove out their dukes*. The King of Sardinia headed these movements and defeated Austria on several occasions, but soon, weakened by his own supporters' quarrels, he was defeated at Novara [23 March 1849] and decided to *abdicate*.'[4]

'The London press, the cabinet and Prince Albert acclaimed the occupation of the Crimea and the attack on Sebastopol. It was a bold enterprise. Count Benedetti, French *chargé d'affaires* at Constantinople, wrote: "To throw 80,000 men and 200 guns upon an exposed shore, 700 leagues from a formidable fortress, was like stepping into the unknown. Nothing was known about either the terrain or the enemy's strength. Everything was at the whim of *chance* and accident [*légère folie*]."

The old *Chersonese* was only a grassy steppe and towns were few. Only Sebastopol had a large harbour, ill-protected on the land side, but with fortresses ["*traverse*"] on the Black Sea.

The Battle of Inkermann, so fiercely fought, cost the English 3000 men, the French 800, and the Russians more than 10,000 ["*de sang nagez partout*"]. It was a victory, but a hollow one, which proved to the Allies how hazardous the expedition was. On 18 June 1855 the English marched on the Great Redan [fortification] and the French on the Little Redan and the Malakoff. Despite the soldiers' splendid bravery, the attack failed because it had been so badly planned. . . . Pelissier sounded the retreat. There were *so many dead* that a day's truce was called to bury them."[5]

[1] Sebastopol, the military port of the Crimea. Built in 1786 by Empress Catherine II near the ruins of ancient Cherson. DHB.
[2] The fortifications were massive and steep. DL7V.
[3] HEFDP.
[4] DHB.
[5] LSEOA.

The Fall of the Bourbons, 29 July 1830. King Louis-Philippe. The Tricolor

Le Roy Gaulois par la Celtique Dextre[1]
Voyant discorde de la Grand Monarchie
Sur les trois pars fera florir son sceptre,
Contre la cappe[2] de la Grande Hierarchie.

CII,Q69

Interpretation

The King of the French, because of the right wing and seeing the great monarchy in discord, will make his sceptre flourish over the three parts [of the flag] against the Capet hierarchy.

History

'The sovereign would henceforth rule by the will of the nation, the title of King of France being replaced by that of *King of the French*. . . .

Only the bourgeoisie profited from the 1830 Revolution, for they were Louis-Philippe's buttress, caught as he was between the hostility of the masses whose illusions had been shattered and that of the *nobility* who had remained almost completely loyal to the *Bourbon* family. . . .

Until 1835 the government was mainly concerned with fighting the revolutionary, legitimist and republican groups. The legitimists were the supports of the *Bourbons*. They recognized as *legitimate* king the Duke of Bordeaux, in whose favour his grandfather Charles X had abdicated. They organized several absurd conspiracies, which were easily scotched.'[3]

'People of Paris, the deputies of France, presently reassembled in Paris, have asked me to fulfil here the duties of Lieutenant General of the Kingdom. Returning to the town of Paris, *I proudly bore the glorious colours* I have long worn and which you have now taken back. The chamber will sit and discuss the means by which to ensure the rule of law and the maintenance of the rights of the nation.'[4]

'The Prince was received at the Hôtel de Ville by General Dubourg, who thus addressed him: "Prince, the nation fondly sees you *wearing its colours*." '[5]

[1] Latin *dexter*, right. DLLB.

[2] Capet, the surname given to the King of France, is translated into Latin in the ancient chronicles by the word *Capatus*, referring to the regal cloak or cape. In time the surname was applied as a patronymic, and it is worth noting that it was the *ultra-royalist* right-wing authors who resurrected this ancient name. DL7V.

[3] HFAM.

[4] Proclamation by the Duke of Orleans, 1 August 1830. HFA.

[5] HFA.

The Assassination of the Last of the Condés, 26 August 1830. The Second Empire Replaced by the Third Republic. The Château of St-Leu

De nuict dans lict supresme[1] estranglé,
Pour trop avoir seiourné blond esleu,
Par trois l'Empire subroge[2] exancle,[3]
A mort mettra carte, et paquet[4] ne leu.

CI,Q39

Interpretation

By night in his bed the last [Condé] will be strangled for having lived too long with a chosen blonde woman. The exhausted Empire will be replaced by the Third [Republic]. He will be put to death because of his will, with linen, at [St-] Leu.

History

'Louis-Henri-Joseph, Duke of Bourbon, Prince of Condé, the last of the Condés (1756–1830), lived with his small entourage at *St-Leu*, his only occupation being hunting. After the 1830 Revolution he quickly recognized his nephew as "King of the French". This weak, elderly man was completely *dominated by an Englishwoman*, Sophie Dawes, née Clarke, whose past was doubtful, and who had married one of the Prince's household, the Baron de Feuchères. She had cuckolded this loyal soldier for some time, which had been considered a scandal. Under her influence the Prince decided to draft *a will* by which he named the Duke of Aumale his sole beneficiary and which assured Baroness de Feuchères a legacy of 10 million, either in land or in cash. On 26 August 1830 the Prince *retired to bed* as usual at the Château of *St-Leu*. He was found hanged or rather attached to the hasp of the window by *two knotted handkerchiefs*. The circumstances seemed to discount suicide.'[5]

'He was found hanged in his apartment. It was then claimed, but without proof, that he had been *strangled* by his mistress, Mme de Feuchères. The family of Condé died out with him.'[6]

[1] Last: DL7V.
[2] Latin *subrogo:* I substitute. DLLB.
[3] Latin *exantlo:* I wear out, exhaust. DLLB.
[4] Several things strung or wrapped together – can refer to linen or leashes. DL7V.
[5] DL7V.
[6] DHB.

Rebellion in the Rue St-Merri, 5 and 6 June 1832. The Bourbons Ousted by the Duke of Orleans

Par avarice,[1] par force et violence
Viendra vexer[2] les siens chef[3] d'Orléans
Près Sainct-Memire[4] assault et résistance,
Mort dans sa tente[5] diront qu'il dort léans.

CVIII,Q42

Interpretation

Through greed, force and violence the Duke of Orleans will damage his interests. There will be an attack and resistance in the Rue St-Merri; having abandoned his cause [power] it will be said the King sleeps.

History

'The President of the Council followed the same *energetic* internal policy he had determined upon. The legitimists were agitating in western

France, and troops had to crush *insurrection* there. The workers of Lyon were disarmed after an appalling *riot*, and Grenoble too saw *bloodshed*. There were conspiracies in Paris too, but Minister Perier did not waver nor flinch in maintaining order. He dominated the Assembly, his colleagues and even the King himself.'[6]

'Rue *St-Merri* is famous in the history of Parisian revolution because of *the fighting* that took place there after the funeral of General Lamarque. *The resistance* lasted two days behind improvised barricades and claimed many victims.'[7]

'A month after [22 July 1832], the death of Napoleon's son, the Duke of Reichstadt, disposed of another formidable candidate for the *House of Orleans*. Another pretender also failed: the *Duchess of Berry*[8] had started a civil war in western France on behalf of *her son Henri V*. But the area was full of troops, the movement was promptly put down, and the Duchess, caught at Nantes on 7 November, was imprisoned at Blaye.'[9]

[1] Latin *avaritia*: greed, covetousness. DLLB.
[2] Latin *vexare*: stir up, shake, injure. DLLB.
[3] Latin *dux*: leader. DLLB.
[4] Possible typographical error, as the word *'memire'* is unknown.
[5] To retire into one's tent implies withdrawing, abandoning a party or cause. DL7V.
[6] HFVD.
[7] DL7V.
[8] Wife of Charles X, mother of the Duke of Bordeaux.
[9] HFVD.

The Revolutions of 1830 and 1848.
The Abdications of Charles X and Louis-Philippe

Deux révolts faits du malin falcigère[1]
De règne et siècles fait permutation[2]
Le mobil[3] signe[4] à son endroit s'ingère
Aux deux esgaux et d'inclination.[5]

CI,Q54

Interpretation

Two revolutions, inspired by the death-dealing spirit of evil, will completely change power and its secular laws: the red emblem of the flag will install itself on the right and will lead to the weakening of two [kings] in the same way.

History

'The theories of Robert Owen in England and Fourier in France spawned dangerous notions of Utopia which themselves sparked off in 1830 and 1848 terrible *civil strife*. Men who were putting the whole of society and its laws and religion on trial were proposing to *overthrow it utterly*.'[6]

Charles X and the 1830 Revolution: 'On 26 July 1830 decrees were issued suppressing the freedom of the press, annulling the recent elections and creating a new electoral system. This represented a coup d'état against civil liberties, contrary to the conditions of the charter which had returned the Bourbons to the throne *of their ancestors*. Paris replied to the court's provocation by *the three days* [27-29 July] 1830. Charles X had lost. When *he abdicated in favour of his grandson* the Duke of Bordeaux and further revolution threatened it was already too late – 6000 men were *dead* or wounded. By taking back the *flag of 1789*, France also seemed to regain possession of liberties the Revolution had promised but not granted.'[6]

Louis-Philippe and the 1848 Revolution: 'Heated discussion in the Chamber of Deputies concerning the law of assembly. . . . The opposition mounted a vote of censure against the minister, and there was a new *revolution lasting three days. Abdication by the King in favour of his grandson.* The proposal that the Duchess of Orleans be Regent led to stormy scenes in the chamber but did not prevent *the fall of the dynasty* on 24 February. A *bloody battle* in front of the Palais-Royal.'[7]

[1] Latin *falciger*: one who carries a scythe. DLLB. Symbol of death.
[2] Latin *permutatio*: complete change, reversal, revolution. DLLB.
[3] Latin *mobilis*: capable of displacement. DLLB.
[4] Latin *signum*: red flag displayed as signal to attack. DLLB.
[5] Latin *inclino*: I abase, bring low, weaken. DLLB.
[6] HFVD.
[7] CUCD.

The Junior Branch in Power, 1830. The Upheavals of 23 February. The Fall of Louis-Philippe, 24 February 1848

Le deffaillant[1] en habit de bourgeois,
Viendra tenter[2] le Roy de son offense:
Quinze soldats la plupart Ustagois,[3]
Vie dernière et chef de sa chevance.[4]

CIV,Q64

Interpretation

The representative of the younger branch, dressed as a bourgeois, will occupy the kingdom through his offence: fifteen soldiers, the majority of the National Guard, will do what they can so that he will live for the last time as bourgeois leader.

History

'La Fayette declared, presenting the Duke of Orleans to the people at the Hôtel de Ville: "This is the best of Republics." The private virtues of the Prince, his fine family, his previous links with the heads of the liberal party, carefully reawakened memories of Jemmapes and Valmy, *his bourgeois life style*, all gave good cause for encouragement. Louis-Philippe of Orleans, head of *the junior branch* of the Bourbons, was proclaimed king on 9 August. . . . Suppression of the article recognizing Catholicism as the official religion of the state, and of all the peerages created by *Charles X*.'[5]

'A law instituted a National Guard which should "defend the constitutional monarchy". Since the National Guard had *to equip itself at its own expense*, the Guard consisted only of affluent *bourgeois*. This regime favoured *the bourgeoisie* exclusively.'

On the night of 22 February 1848 barricades were erected. On the twenty-third the attitude of the *National Guard*, which prevented the cavalry from charging the demonstrators in the Place des Victoires, alarmed Louis-Philippe who decided to split with Guizot. But that same evening a bloody incident revived the struggle: a group of demonstrators arrived on the Boulevard des Capucines and fired on the troops. The soldiers fired back at point-blank range. *Fifteen* were killed and fifty more injured. On the morning of the twenty-fourth Paris was bristling with barricades, and shouts of "Long Live the Republic!" were heard everywhere.

[1] Lack or end (of a line). The senior branch *lacking*, the junior one would occupy the throne.
[2] Latin *teneo*: I hold, occupy, possess, control. DLLB.
[3] Seigneurial right paid for one's house. DL7V.
[4] Goods, fortune, what one possesses or acquires. DL7V.
[5] HFVD.

The Accidental Death of Louis-Philippe's Eldest Son, 13 July 1842

L'aisné Royal sur coursier[1] voltigeant,
Picquer[2] viendra si rudement courir:
Gueule lipée,[3] pied dans l'estrein pleignant[4]
Trainé tiré, horriblement mourir.

CVII,Q38

Interpretation

The King's eldest son, on a runaway horse, will fall suddenly head-first in its rush, the horse's mouth being injured on the lip, with the rider's foot caught, groaning, dragged and pulled, he will die horribly.

History

'Ferdinand-Philippe-Louis-Charles-Henri-Rose of Orleans was the *eldest* son of Louis-Philippe and Marie-Aurélie of Bourbon-Sicily, and born in Palermo on 3 September 1810. In July 1842 he was about to leave to inspect the troops at St-Omer. He went to Neuilly to say goodbye to his father and *his horses bolted* on the road; he was flung out of the carriage and, *falling backwards on to the ground he broke his skull*.'[5]

[1] Poetic name for horse or thoroughbred. DL7V.
[2] *Piquer (une tête)*: to dive or fall headfirst. DL7V.
[3] *Lippe: lèvre* (lip). DAFL.
[4] To utter groans, cries. DL7V.
[5] DHCD.

The Seven Years' Conquest of Algeria, 1840–47. The February Revolution, 1848

Sept ans sera PHILIP, fortune[1] prospère,
Rabaissera des BARBARES[2] l'effort:
Puis son midy perplex, rebours[3] affaire,
Jeune ogmion[4] abysmera son fort.

CIX,Q89

Interpretation

Fortune will smile on Louis-Philippe for seven years, and he will cut down the Barbarian [Algerian] forces, but will then be in trouble at noon

because of a stubborn horse, and an eloquent young speaker will bring
on his downfall.

History

'The population of Algeria was composed of Algerians and *Berbers*. Since
the sixteenth century the Algerian corsairs had terrorized merchant shipping in the Mediterranean. The fall of Charles X almost cost France
Algeria. Louis-Philippe thought so little of conquest that he recalled all
the French troops from Algeria except for one division of 8000 men. The
idea was to limit France to a partial occupation. It was the native inhabitants who forced the French hand. By their incessant attacks they
turned a partial occupation into a full-scale one and finally, *from 1840
on*, after ten years of hesitation, into a complete conquest. At the end of
1847, tracked down by eight columns and expelled from Morocco where
he had gone a second time for asylum, Abd-el-Kader surrendered [23
December]. His submission ended the war. Charles X had retained the
initiative; the conquest of Algeria remains the main *claim to fame* of the
July monarchy. . . .

The round of banquets surprisingly culminated in the February 1848
Revolution. *Disconcerted* and vacillating, Louis-Philippe decided to recall
the troops. At *noon* the King abdicated. His eldest son the Duke of
Orleans, a very popular prince, had been killed at Neuilly while trying
to jump out of *his carriage*. Louis-Philippe therefore abdicated in favour
of his grandson the Count of Paris, a child of ten. The rebels surrounded
the chamber, shouting for the King's overthrow. Ledru-Rollin and *Lamartine* proposed a provisional government, which was installed by popular acclaim. The democratic Republic succeeded the bourgeois monarchy
of Louis-Philippe. On the steps of the Hôtel de Ville *Lamartine*, seated
on a chair, made the speech in which he *eloquently* opposed the tricolor
which had circled the globe to the red flag which had only gone round
the Champs de Mars.'[5]

[1] Latin *fortuna*: fate, destiny, chance. DLLB
[2] Barbary: North African region including Tripoli, Tunis, *Algiers*, Morocco. DHB.
[3] *cheval rebours*: equestrian term denoting an erratic or obstinate steed apt to *bolt*.
DL7V.
[4] God of *eloquence* and poetry revered by the Gauls. DHB.
[5] HFAM.

Napoleon III's Accession to Power.
The Empire Replaced by the Third Republic

De terre faible et pauvre parentele[1]
Par bout et paix parviendra dans l'Empire
Longtemps regner une jeune femelle[2]
Qu'oncques en regne n'en survint un si pire.

CIII,Q28

Interpretation

Originating from a weak country [Corsica] and poor birth, [the country] at the end of its tether and wanting peace, he will succeed to the Empire. He will then rule a young republic. Such a disastrous person never succeeded to power.

History

'A senate in council proposed the re-establishment of the Empire as personified by Louis-Napoleon Bonaparte, to be *hereditary* in relation to his direct adopted successors. Before his coronation Napoleon III stated: "The Empire means *Peace!*" – a happy formula had it been followed.'[3]

'Just like the bourgeoisie, the peasantry wanted a government which would ensure respect for property and internal peace. The Second Empire was to sweep away such views.

By virtue of the powers vested in him by the plebiscite Louis-Napoleon drafted a constitution on the lines of the *Constitution of Year VIII*. This was promulgated on 14 January 1852.'[4]

'For the first time for four centuries, *France actually shrank*. In 1815 she had at least more or less retained the frontiers established by the old monarchy. By the Treaty of Frankfurt on 10 May 1871 she lost Alsace-Lorraine.'[5]

[1] Parents as a group, parentage. DL7V.
[2] Allusion to Marianne, symbol of the Republic.
[3] HFVD.
[4] HFAM.
[5] HFVD.

The Orsini Affair, 14 January 1858

Un chef Celtique dans les conflict blessé
Auprès de cave[1] voyant siens mort abbattre:
De sang et playes et d'ennemis pressé,
Et secourus par incogneux de quatre.

CV,QIO

Interpretation

A French leader wounded in the conflict, seeing death overcome his people near the theatre, hard pressed by his enemies amid the blood and wounded, will be aided by the crowd [escaping] the four [bombs].

History

'On Thursday 14 January 1858 the Emperor and Empress were due to attend the Opéra. At 8.30 p.m. their landau arrived at the Rue le Pelletier. There were three loud explosions, and cries of terror mingled with agonized screams from soldiers, police and onlookers lying on the ground. Napoleon left his carriage, his hat in tatters and his nose grazed, and the Empress descended, her white dress and cape spattered with *blood*. There were 156 *wounded*, eight of whom died.

Orsini had some mediocre accomplices – Simon Bernard, a neurotic surgeon who provided the explosives; Pieri, an experienced criminal; and two young men of good family, Gomez and Rudio. On 14 January their preparations were complete. Of the *four bombs* they carried, three were thrown.'[2]

[1] Latin *cavea*: part of a theatre or amphitheatre where the spectators sat; by extension, theatre. DLLB.
[2] LSEOA.

The Attempted Assassination of Napoleon III. The Congress of Paris, 25 February 1856.

Le nepveu grand par force prouvera
Le pache[1] fait du coeur pusillanime[2]
Ferrare[3] et Ast[4] le Duc[5] esprouvera,
Par lors qu'au soir sera le pantomime.[6]

CIV,Q73

Interpretation

The great nephew will show off his strength, through a peace too prudently concluded, he who comes from Piedmont and the borderlands will test the sovereign the evening the play is presented.

History

'*Peace* was to be arranged by a congress reunited in Paris. Talks began on 25 February 1856. On 30 March the peace was signed, which, though ending a hazardous enterprise, did not settle the Middle Eastern question so much as shelve it. However, France did derive something from it: *the valour of her soldiers* restored her to a leading place among European powers. Moreover, *Napoleon III's own situation was somewhat relieved.* Summoned to finish a war, *the Congress of Paris paved the way for another one.* It took only three years for this to break out. . . .

On 14 January 1858 the Emperor and Empress were due to attend the Opera. At 8.30 p.m. their landau arrived at the Rue le Pelletier. There were three loud explosions.

Felice Orsini had plotted the liberation of his country since his earliest youth. He stirred up the Italian *border country* against the Austrians, and returned to recruit accomplices with whom to murder Napoleon III. . . . While his trial was going on the Empire was enduring both internal and foreign crises. When on 16 January Napoleon received at the Tuileries numerous politicians who had come to congratulate him on his narrow escape, the pale and grave Emperor had to listen to harangues from some of them. Morny abandoned traditional courtesies and grew indignant: "The people want to know why neighbouring friendly governments are powerless to destroy actual laboratories of assassins." This was directed at Belgium, *Piedmont* and especially England, for offering asylum to all the exiles, leaving them free to conspire at will.'[7]

[1] Latin *pax, pacis*: peace. DLLB.
[2] Prudence or timidity stopping just short of cowardice. DL7V.
[3] Town on the Italian borders.
[4] Asti: town in Piedmont.
[5] Guide, prince, sovereign. DLLB.
[6] Theatrical representation. DL7V.
[7] LSEOA.

Napoleon III near Buffalora, 3 June 1859. The Entry of Napoleon III and Victor Emmanuel into Milan, 6 June 1859. The Peace of Villafranca, 9 June 1859. The Dispersal of the Holy Alliance (Russia, Austria, Prussia, France and England)

Apparoistra auprès de Buffalore,
L'hault[1] et procere[2] entré dedans Milan,
L'Abbé[3] de Foix[4] avec ceux de Sainct Morre,[5]
Ferront la forbe[6] habillez en vilain.[7]

CVIII,QI2

Interpretation

The Emperor will appear near Buffalora, the noble and first personage [King of Italy] will make his entry into Milan, but the owner of Phoebus[8] [Napoleon III] and those of the Holy Alliance will play a shameful trick.

History

'The Holy Alliance: Tsar Alexander, the Emperor of Austria and the King of Prussia signed the pact first, on 26 September 1815. Louis XVIII and the Prince Regent of England followed suit.'[9]

'Napoleon, ensconced in an inn at San Martino, waited before starting the battle to know that MacMahon had reached Magenta. On the stroke of noon he heard the general's cannons in *the Buffalora direction*.'[10]

'The Battle of Magenta had opened up the whole of Lombardy for the Allies, and the French army *entered Milan* to acclamation and rejoicing. The Emperor Napoleon III and King Victor Emmanuel were on *horseback* at the head of the victorious troops.'[9]

'The Austrians continued retreating behind the Adigea and Prussia hastened to mobilize. Tsar Alexander sent word to the Empress to urge her to make peace quickly or be attacked on the Rhine. As for England, her intervention could not be relied upon in the event of conflict with Prussia so the Emperor decided to go directly to his adversary Franz-Josef. He was going *to betray* Cavour. . . . Napoleon III went ahead to Villafranca to meet the *young Emperor*. . . . When Napoleon in his turn passed through *Milan*, the Piedmontese capital gave him a frosty reception. Italy never forgave him for *betraying* her hopes and on his return to France he found public opinion surprised and strained. After the much-vaunted victories, abandoning Venice was like sounding the *retreat*.'[10]

[1] Latin *altus*: noble, elevated. DLLB.
[2] Latin *proceres*: the first citizens (by birth and rank). DLLB.
[3] Latin *abbas*: derived from Syrian *abba*, father. DL7V
[4] Gaston III, Comte de Foix, was nicknamed *Phoebus*. The name was perpetuated by several other members of the family. DL7V.
[5] Latin *mos, moris*: law, rule. *Pacis impossere morem*: to decide upon peace (Virgil). DLLB.
[6] Trickery. DAFL.
[7] Synonym: ugly, shameful, niggardly. DL7V.
[8] 'Napoleon III, mounted on his chestnut, *Phoebus*. . . .' LSEOA.
[9] HFAM.
[10] LSEOA.

The Annexation of the Papal States, 1870.
Victor Emmanuel and Clotilde of Savoy.
The French at Turin and Novara, 1859

L'oeil[1] de Ravenne[2] sera destitué
Quand à ses pieds les aisles failliront:
Les deux de Bresse[3] auront constitué,[4]
Turin, Versel[5] que Gaulois fouleront.

CI,Q6

Interpretation

The Pope's temporal power will be removed when the wings [of the eagle, Napoleon III] fall at his feet, when the two of Savoy [Victor Emmanuel II and his daughter Clotilde of Savoy] give [Italy] a constitution and when the French throng through Turin and Novara.

History

'Victor Emmanuel II energetically defended the rights of the state against the Church, and reinforced his friendship with the Imperial French government by marrying his daughter Clotilde of Savoy to Prince Napoleon, the son of Napoleon III and Empress Eugénie. This friendship was maintained by France during the war against Austria. By this alliance he gained first Lombardy [June 1859], then Tuscany, Parma, Modena and the Romagna. The populations of the kingdom of Naples and *the Papal States* through universal suffrage voted for him by referendum and he became King of Italy [*"auront constitué"*] with his capital at Florence.

In September 1870 he entered Rome, which then became the capital of the kingdom of Italy.'[6]

'The Austrian Field-Marshal Giulay crossed the Ticino and marched upon *Turin* at the rate of 6 km a day. Near the Piedmontese capital he halted to fall back upon Mortara, which presented an admirable opportunity for Napoleon to concentrate his forces and join up with the Piedmontese. On 3 June *the French quartered* on a rather too dispersed triangle between Turbigo, Trecato and *Novara*. They did not know where the Austrians were: only by day was it certain that the latter had bivouacked around Magenta.'[7]

[1] Nostradamus regularly uses *eye* or *eyes* to mean 'power'.

[2] Pepin the Short, son of Charlemagne, had originally made the Pope a gift of these states centred upon the Ravenna area, and this formed the basis of the papal territories which disappeared only in 1870. HFAM.

[3] Bresse was divided into small districts; the main one, Baugé, was subsumed into Savoy in 1292. DHB.

[4] To give a constitution or organization. DL7V.

[5] Verceil: fortress town of Upper Italy, in the ancient Sardinian states (Novara). DHB.

[6] DHB.

[7] LSEOA.

The Tower of Solferino, 24 June 1859.
Savoy Returns to France. The Treaty of Turin, 1860.
The Principle of Nationalities

Mars eslevé à son plus haut beffroy,[1]
Fera retraire[2] les Allobrox[3] de France:
La gent Lombarde fera si grand effroy,
A ceux de l'Aigle compris[4] sous la Balance.[5]

CV,Q42

Interpretation

The war will reach its climax with the Tower [of Solferino] and will force Savoy to return to France. Lombardy will be greatly afraid because of the Emperor's party and will be taken on a pretext of law.

History

'The Lombard capital, where Bonaparte was still remembered by the older folk, was decked out with French and Italian flags. From the clocktower of the Castiglione church, his fieldglasses to his eyes, Napoleon III was intent upon cutting the enemy in two, and he issued orders for a central attack. The *Tower* of Solferino[6] rose square and red atop a rocky crag. The battle went on for hours, *bitterly contested*. At the centre were the steep *heights* of Solferino, which after *furious fighting* were finally captured, along with the cemetery and the Tower itself.

The horrible carnage was *even worse* than that of Montebello and Magenta, when Napoleon III visited the battle area the next day.'[7]

'After numerous vicissitudes, Savoy was ceded to France in 1860 by the King of Sardinia – which was immediately approved by the *universal suffrage* of the inhabitants.'[8]

There appeared in Paris an anonymous pamphlet written by Councillor of State la Guéronnière and supervised by the Emperor himself. The work was entitled *Napoleon III and Italy* and boldly declared his views and intentions. It celebrated the *theory of nationalities* and ended with the hope of a federated Italy from which all foreign influences were excluded.

[1] From Middle High German *becvrit*: defensive tower. Watchtower in which troops are placed for surveillance. DL7V.

[2] Latin *retraho*: I force to come back. DLLB.

[3] Name that reappeared with the Revolution: the Allobrogian *départements* were those of Savoy. DL7V.

[4] Latin *comprehendo*: I take. DLLB.

[5] Political, implying balance or stability of the states in relation to alliances and territory. DL7V.

[6] Solferino: ruins of an old castle with a *tower*. DL7V.

[7] LSEOA.

[8] DHB.

Victor Emmanuel II, King of Italy, 1860. Florence the Capital of Italy

Du vray rameau[1] des fleurs de lys yssu,
Mis et logé héritier d'Hetrurie:[2]
Son sang antique de longue main tyssu[3]
Fera Florence florir en l'armoirie.

CV,Q39

Interpretation

Born from the true line of the fleurs de lis, situated and living in Etruria, his ancient blood long woven will make his coat of arms flourish in Florence.

History

'Victor Emmanuel II, King of Italy [1820–78] was directly descended from Charles Emmanuel II [1634–75], Duke of Savoy and Piedmont, whose mother was Christine of France, daughter of Henri IV, and from her son Thomas-François, who married Marie de *Bourbon*, daughter of Charles, Comte de Soisson.'[4]

'Faced with Austrian intervention, Victor Emmanuel's father, Charles-Albert [1789–1849], was forced to stand down on 21 March 1821. Exiled in *Tuscany*, he was disgraced, but finally succeeded to the throne in 1831 since there was no direct *heir*, and effected some useful reforms. In 1817 he married Marie-Thérèse of Tuscany.'[5]

'Victor Emmanuel II was supported by France in the war against Austria, and through this alliance he gained first Lombardy [June 1859], then *Tuscany*, Parma, Modena and the Romagna. The populations of the kingdom of Naples and the Papal States [other than Rome], voted for him by referendum and he became *King of Italy* with *his capital at Florence*. He enjoyed great popularity during his reign, and adhered to the rules of parliamentary government established in Piedmont under Charles-Albert.'[6]

[1] The Bourbon arms were three fleurs de lis.
[2] Tuscany: Tuscia and Etruria to the ancients. DHB.
[3] Past participle of the verb *tistre* (*tisser*). DL7V.
[4] CUCD.
[5] DHB.
[6] DHB.

Victor Emmanuel II and Cavour.
Italian Unity, 1859–61. Victor Emmanuel II in Florence

Le successeur de la Duché viendra,
Beaucoup plus oultre que la mer de Toscane,
Gauloise branche la Florence tiendra[1]
Dans son giron d'accord nautique Rane.[2]

CV,Q3

Interpretation

The successor to the duchy of Tuscany will occupy much more than the Tuscan coastline. A French branch will install itself at Florence with the consent of him whom England will have had in her lap.

History

'Instead of withdrawing behind his own borders and renouncing all ambition, Victor Emmanuel II, who *succeeded* the defeated Charles-Albert, began preparing for the return of Piedmontese troops to the plain of Lombardy.

Camillo Cavour had been at Victor Emmanuel's side since 1833. He was a Piedmontese who had lived for some time in *London*, Paris and Geneva. After an initial stay in Paris in 1835, he went to London where he conceived considerable admiration for the skill of the English in dealing with the problems of an industrial society, for their good sense and pragmatism.

In two years, from March 1859 to June 1861, a new state emerged in Europe – far beyond the Sea of Tuscany. It covered an area of 259,320 sq km and contained 24,770,000 inhabitants.'[3]

[1] For Victor Emmanuel's French origins and Florence as capital city, cf. CV,Q39.
[2] Latin *rana*: frog. DLLB. Frogs symbolize all the nations in history. DL7V.
[3] HISR.

The Exceptional Pontificate of Pius IX, 1846–78.
The Annexation of Bologna by
Victor Emmanuel II, 1859

Dedans Bologne voudra laver ses fautes
Il ne pourra au temple[1] du Soleil:[2]
Il volera[3] faisant choses si hautes,
En hiérarchie n'en fut onq un pareil.

CVIII,Q53

Interpretation

He will want to make up for his errors in Bologna which he will not be able to retain for the Church because of the Bourbon [Victor Emmanuel II]. He will act alone to achieve such important things that there will never be such a pope in the Catholic hierarchy.

History

'In 1848 there was a nationalistic cry for war against Austria. Sardinia and Piedmont, as well as the occupied provinces of Venice and Lombardy, took up arms. Pius IX refused to wage war on Austria and thus betrayed the popular movement ["*ses fautes*"]. His minister Rossi was assassinated on 15 November 1848, the Quirinal was attacked and the Swiss Guard was disarmed. . . . Between 1857 and 1863 the Pope made journeys through his states including Bologna. Only the presence of the French expeditionary force maintained his temporal sovereignty. In 1860 the conflict with Piedmont began by the occupation of the north of the Papal States [Bologna]. The Pope excommunicated him, and Antonelli protested against the title of King of Italy assumed by Victor Emmanuel ["*le Soleil*"] on 26 February 1861.'[4]

'In 1859 the town and province of Bologna rejected papal authority and recognized the King of Sardinia, Victor Emmanuel. Pius IX *reserved* ["*volera*"] all religious issues for himself and was very active in settling them. *Three great acts* ["*choses si hautes*"] distinguished his papacy: the definition of the Immaculate Conception [December 1854]; the publication of the Encyclical Quanta Cura [December 1864], and its appendix known as the Syllabus. In 1869 the first ecumenical council held since the Council of Trent (1545–63) opened at the Vatican, during which, on 18 July 1870, Papal Infallibility was asserted. He died in 1878, and the news of his death aroused worldwide expressions of respect and veneration.'[5] In fact, a nonpareil.

[1] Poetic usage – the Catholic Church. DL7V.
[2] Reference to Victor-Emmanuel's descent from the Bourbons. Cf. CV,Q39.
[3] Fly with his own wings, act of his own accord. DL7V.
[4] DDP.
[5] DHB.

The Ems Telegram, 13 July 1870
From Bazaine at Metz,
18 August, to the Surrender, 27 October 1870

Le grand conflit qu'on appreste à Nancy,
L'Aémathien[1] dira tout je soubmets:
L'Ile Britanne par vin, sel en solcy,
Hem.[2] mi.[3] deux Phi.[4] longtemps ne tiendra Metz.

                                             CX,Q7

Interpretation

The great war being prepared in Lorraine will say to the King: I surrender all, England will only be concerned for her trade; after the Ems dispatch, Metz will not hold out for long, despite twice 500,000 [soldiers].

History

'King William I was taking the waters at Ems. Thanks to mutual concessions the King had declared himself wholeheartedly in favour of [Leopold of Hohenzollern's] renunciation. Once again peace seemed assured. At the same time Bismarck in Berlin was coolly *preparing* the catastrophe. He received the King's telegram, which told him of the incidents of the day, up to the dispatch of aides-de-camp to Benedetti. The text, doctored by Bismarck, was immediately relayed to Prussian diplomats abroad. Bismarck's calculations were correct; there was a furious German outcry against France. On 19 July the official declaration of war was made in Berlin. . . .

Having first comprised a single army under the sole command of Napoleon III, the 200,000 men were split into two parts, the Alsace army (67,000) and the *Lorraine* army (130,000) under Bazaine. . . .

The defeat of Froeschwiller hastened the loss of Alsace. MacMahon's disorganized army recrossed the Vosges and fell back upon *Nancy*. The same day as the Battle of Froeschwiller, the 1st German Army entered *Lorraine* and defeated General Frossard's force at Forbach. Following this double defeat, Bazaine, the commander-in-chief, led the army back to *Metz*. . . .

Apart from Bazaine's army besieged inside *Metz*, France had 95,000 regular soldiers scattered between Paris and the provinces. On 19 September the Germans succeeding in surrounding Paris. Trochu had more than 500,000 men with which to defend the city. In the provinces Gambetta rallied troops with amazing speed and in several months he had *600,000 men* in the field. These improvised armies, like the Paris militia, were poor. Most of the German troops were static, at Paris and *Metz*. Bazaine's stupid and criminal behaviour destroyed the last chance of French success. On 27 October he surrendered Metz.

On 18 January 1871, in Versailles, German unity came about. The South German princes joined the Federation, which received the title of the German *Empire*.

France lost Alsace, except for Belfort, and north Lorraine including *Metz*.'[5]

'British trade abroad outstripped that of all other countries. In *1872* it exceeded 547 million pounds, more than all French, German and Italian commerce put together.'[6]

[1] Macedonia was divided into numerous provinces or small counties: *Aemathia*, the cradle and centre of the monarchy, often referred to the whole territory. Philip II *reconquered the former provinces*, added new ones, and held all Greece under his sway. Alexander met with success but his Empire was dispersed after his death. DHB. Nostradamus establishes here a parallel between Macedonian and German history.

[2] Hems: ancient name for Ems. DL7V.

[3] Abbreviation of Latin word *missio*: act of dispatching, missive. DLLB.

[4] Twenty-first letter of the Greek alphabet. Numerically *Phi* = 500,000. DGF.

[5] HFAM.

[6] HRU.

Gambetta's Departure by Balloon, 1870.
The Siege of Paris and its Surrender

La république de la grande cité,
A grand rigueur[1] ne voudra consentir:
Roy[2] sortir hors par trompette[3] cité,
L'eschelle au mur, la cité repentir.

CIII,Q50

Interpretation

The republic of Paris will not want to consent to the necessary austerity; the head of government will leave the city in great style, the city will be besieged and rue it.

History

'A government of national defence was constituted, composed of eleven Parisian deputies, among whom was Gambetta. On 19 September 1870 the Germans completed the *investment of Paris*. Paris became the focus of the national defence effort and the next five months saw attempts from the provinces *to raise the siege*. There were hardly 25,000 men left in the provinces, and resistance seemed impossible, but while the government remained inside Paris Gambetta *escaped by balloon* to Tours to organize defence measures. He was the guiding light of the nation's defence.

Paris was doubly threatened, by famine and by revolution. Already on 31 October the national guards at Belleville had tried to topple the government, and there was a further insurrection on 22 January. Bismarck knew of this and when Jules Fabre came to Versailles to plead for an armistice so that Paris might revictual, the former demanded complete *capitulation*, disarmament of the fighting men, occupation of all the forts, and a 200 million franc payment. On 28 January these terms had to be accepted: *the fall of Paris* and the Versailles armistice marked the end of the war.'[4]

[1] Extreme severity, rigour, austerity. DL7V.
[2] Latin *rego*: I govern. (DLLB). One who governs.
[3] Sound the trumpet, do something with verve, style. Reference to Roman triumphs. DL7V.
[4] HFAM.

Garibaldi's Strength and His Wretched End

Le fort Nicene[1] ne sera combattu,
Vaincu sera par rutilant metal:
Son faict sera un long temps débatu,
Aux citadins[2] estrange[3] espouvantal.[4]

CVII,Q19

Interpretation

The powerful Nicean victor will not be defeated in battle but by money. His deeds will for a long time be cause for debate; this foreigner will strike terror among the bourgeoisie.

History

'Revolutionary Europe in the nineteenth century: the field was open for this young man from *Nice* ["*Nicene*"], Garibaldi, who dreamed of adventure, socialism and freedom. Garibaldi would have a hand in European affairs, and intransigently he pursued his policy, formed his army, conducted his campaigns and imposed his presence on the European scene.

The conservative [bourgeois] deputies continued to oppose him. It was a hate composed of a *fear and horror* of revolution, subversion and socialism.

"None of the European powers rose to defend France, which has so often embraced the cause of Europe (cheers from the left). Not a king, nor a state, nobody! Except *one* man. (Wry smiles on the right, cheers from the left.) The powers did not intervene, but one man did intervene and *this man is a power* ['le fort Nicene']. He came and *fought*. I do not wish to wound anyone but I speak only the truth in stating that *he alone*

of all the generals who fought for France, *was never defeated.*" This
tirade from Victor Hugo provoked an indescribable uproar. Leaping
upon their benches, *the deputies of the right* shook their fists at him. . . .

In 1873 Garibaldi published a third novel, *The Thousand*, which met
with only scant success. So he had to resign himself to selling the yacht
his English admirers had given him, receiving a mere 80,000 lire for it.
He entrusted this money to his ex-comrade in arms Antonio Bo, so that
he could bank it in Genoa, but his old friend chose to run off to America
with the *little nest egg* ["*rutilant metal*"]. The Italian newspapers got wind
of his problems and published emotional articles headed: "Garibaldi in
deep distress", and "Italians, help Garibaldi!". One special correspon-
dent painted a picture of the old condottiere: "Every morning, sometimes
using a stick and sometimes on his crutches, painfully pushing a barrow
full of melons for which he might get at most five lire for the lot." "[5]

[1] Nicean: Greek mythology; name given to certain deities regarded as guaranteeing
victory. DL7V. Nostradamus puns on 'victor' and 'born in Nice'.
[2] Strictly speaking, *bourgeois* referred not to all the inhabitants of a 'burgh' or town but
to those involved in the administration and leadership of a *city*. DL7V.
[3] Nice was not French in 1804, Garibaldi's year of birth, and only became so by the
Treaty of Turin in 1860.
[4] Symbolic: object inspiring vain terrors. DL7V.
[5] GP and MR.

Garibaldi and the Thousand. The Conquest
of Sicily and Naples, 1860. The Naples Campaign.
Savoy's Cession to France, 1860

De Languedoc, et Guienne plus de dix
Mille voudront les Alpes repasser:
Grans Allobroges[1] marcher contre Brundis[2]
Aquin[3] et Bresse[4] les viendront recasser.[5]

CVII,Q31

Interpretation

With more than ten, coming from Languedoc and Guyenne, the Thousand would like to return, into Italy. The Duke of Savoy will march
against the inhabitants of southern Italy [Brindisi]. They will come to
recover Savoy and Naples.

History

'Victor Emmanuel II was supported by France in the war against Austria. To this alliance he owed first Lombardy [June 1859], then Tuscany, Parma, Modena and the Romagna, which he annexed, ceding Nice and *Savoy* to France. After Garibaldi's expedition to Sicily and southern Italy [Aquina and Brindisi] in 1860, which he first secretly encouraged and then openly supported, the populations of the kingdom of Naples [Aquina] and the Papal States [except for Rome itself] by universal suffrage declared for him ["*recasser*"] and he became King of Italy.'[6]

'*The Thousand*. Since 1859 the kingdom of *Naples* had been troubled. Liberal ideas gained ground and led to the insurrection which broke out in Palermo on 3 April 1860. It was the opportunity Garibaldi was waiting for. The small army he reunited at Genoa ["*les Alpes*"] on 5 May 1860 was composed of *1085* men. The whole of Italy was represented, and various foreigners also joined; among the *French* were: Ulric de Font-vielle,[7] Cluseret,[8] Maxime du Camp,[9] Lockroy,[10] Henri Fouquier,[11] and de Flotte, commanding a French unit ["*more than ten*"]. He landed at Marsala with *1015* men. After three days of fighting the *Neapolitans* retreated. Garibaldi beat them again at Milazzo. Messina then capitulated. He reached Salerno, then Naples. At that moment the Piedmontese government [Victor Emmanuel, Duke of Savoy], which had secretly helped Garibaldi, intervened and began the military and diplomatic campaign which led to the annexation of Naples.'[12]

[1] Tribe of Transalpine Gaul – the larger area of Savoy. DHB. Victor Amédée II, at first Duke of Savoy, received in 1713 the title of King of Sicily. DHB.

[2] Brindisi: Latin *Brundisium*, Italian town on the Adriatic. DHB.

[3] Village in the kingdom of Naples.

[4] Bresse is divided into small seigniories, the main one, Baugé, being subsumed into the House of *Savoy*, 1292. By the Treaty of Lyon it was ceded to France in 1601. DHB.

[5] Latin *recedo*: I return, recover. DLLB.

[6] DHB.

[7] Toulouse family, Toulouse being capital of *Languedoc*. DL7V.

[8] Fermented revolution in Marseille and was deputy for Toulon. DL7V.

[9] Family from Bordeaux, capital of the *Guyenne* area. DL7V.

[10] Deputy from Bouches-du-Rhône (Aix). DL7V.

[11] Born in Marseille.

[12] DL7V.

Reunion of the Thousand at Genoa, 1859

La cité franche[1] de liberté fait serve[2]
Des profligez[3] et resveurs fait Azyle:
Le Roy changé à eux non si proterve,[4]
De cent seront devenus plus de mille.

CIV,QI6

Interpretation

The city whose freedom has been reduced by slavery, having become free will give asylum to the depraved and the dreamers [i.e. of revolution]. After boldly changing the king, they will go from a hundred to more than a thousand.

History

'Garibaldi established his headquarters in a suburb of *Genoa*, at Quarto, in his old friend Augusto Vecchi's house. Arms were the greatest problem. The Ansaldo factory at *Genoa* was the biggest supplier and secretly assisted their operations. Cavour feared that foreign powers would accuse Piedmont [Genoa] of being too hospitable ["*fait Azyle*"] to the revolutionaries. On 5 May 1860 Garibaldi, standing on the Piedmont bridge, asked "How many of us are there?" "*More than a thousand*, including the sailors." In fact, his "Thousand" were *1049* strong. His men captured the telegraph office at Marsala [Sicily] from which they transmitted false messages to confuse the enemy. Garibaldi proclaimed himself dictator in the name of Victor Emmanuel, "*King of Italy*." '[5]

---

[1] In 1805 Genoa became part of the French Empire ["*de liberté fait serve*"], and in 1814 was given to the King of Sardinia through the Congress of Vienna. DHB.
[2] Latin *servus*: slave. DLLB.
[3] Latin *profligatus*: lost, depraved. DLLB.
[4] Latin *proterve*: boldly, impudently. DLLB.
[5] GP and MR.

Garibaldi at Magnavacca and Ravenna.
Pius IX and Temporal Power. German Unity through
Two Major Wars, 1866 and 1870

Le magna vaqua[1] à Ravenne grand troubles,
Conduicts par quinze[2] enserres à Fornase:[3]
A Rome naistra deux monstres[4] à teste double,
Sang, feu, déluge, les plus grands à l'espase.

CIX,Q3

Interpretation

He [Garibaldi] will experience great upsets at Magnavacca and Ravenna.
Borne by fifteen vessels they will take refuge at the farm of Zanetto
[*FERme de ZANettO*]; will then spawn two prodigies at Rome because
of a double power [the Pope's spiritual and temporal powers], then
blood, war, revolution will affect the great nations, because of space [i.e.
Lebensraum, expansionism].

History

'Garibaldi asked the mayor of Cesenatico for *thirteen* vessels. An hour
later the Austrians entered the village. The thirteen ships made rapid
progress. The next night they skirted *Ravenna*. They were intercepted
in the bay of the Marches of Comacchio by an Austrian warship, whose
captain ordered them to surrender. They refused and were pursued.
Since the Austrians were gaining on them, they decided to head for the
coast. Coming under fire, they rounded the Cape of *Magnavacca*, but
only three got through. Finally no more than thirty of them landed,
among them Garibaldi, and the Austrians and papal police set up a
manhunt to round up the fugitives. It was impossible to get to Venice
since all northern roads were blocked or watched by the Austrians. They
decided to try their luck around *Ravenna*, where the patriots were numerous. He added that Anita should be left behind, for she would not
survive such a journey. He thought of taking her to *Zanetto Farm*.'[5]

'Few Popes have aroused more conflicting comments than Pius IX,
ranging from flattering adulation to open hostility. With hindsight, it
may be said that he lacked the energy to separate *the spiritual and temporal
sides* of the papal sovereignty.'[6]

'In Germany, as in Italy, the question of unity had been posed since
1815. But among the thirty-eight German states two, Austria and Prussia,
were *major* powers. By means of *two full-scale wars* brought about by

Bismarck, the war of 1866 against Austria and that of 1870 against France, German unity was achieved.'[7]

[1] Italian town at the mouth of the Po.
[2] Biographies of Garibaldi mention thirteen ships, while Nostradamus has fifteen.
[3] Anagram and abbreviation of Zanetto Farm where Garibaldi sought shelter.
[4] Latin *monstrum*: divine omen, prodigy. DLLB.
[5] GP and MR.
[6] DDP.
[7] HFAM.

The War of 1870 and the End
of Papal Temporal Power. Anti-clericalism

Mars nous manasse[1] par la force bellique,
Septente fois fera le sang espandre:
Auge[2] et ruyne de l'Ecclesiastique,[3]
Et plus ceux qui d'eux rien voudront entendre.

CI,QI5

Interpretation

War menaces with its bellicose strength and will see bloodshed in [18]70. The Ecclesiastic will be scorned and ruined and all the more so shall be those who do not wish to reach understanding with him.

History

'On 8 December 1869 Pius IX opened the Twentieth Ecumenical Council, during which Papal Infallibility was proclaimed [18 July 1870]. Next day France declared *war* on Prussia. The Pope, as a last hope, tried to mediate between William I and Napoleon III. On 2 September Napoleon surrendered at Sedan, following which Italy informed France of her intention of occupying Rome. Pius IX refused to relinquish the Vatican as requested, and Austria refused to give him the aid he sought against the invaders. Prussia too was on the side of the invaders. General Cadorna *bombarded* ["*ruyne*"] the Porta Pia, and after heroic defence by his troops the Pope had to surrender. The same day his temporal power was annulled at the Capitol. The Papal States had ceased to exist: the Pope was in fact a prisoner. The rulers and governments of the world were indifferent to the annexation of St Peter's estate. The measures directed against the Church continued, and atheistic satires against the Pope himself circulated in Rome.'⁴

¹ *Manasse*: form of '*menace*'. DAFL
² Proverb: 'One might as well carry a pig-trough.' Said with the sense of an expression of scorn for a job or particular work. DL7V.
³ Note capital E to denote the Pope.
⁴ DDP.

Pius IX at the Head of the Church, 16 June 1846. His Alliance with France, 1848–70. His Temporal Power Annulled at the Capitol, 20 September 1870

> Un dubieux¹ ne viendra loin du règne,
> La plus grand part le voudra soustenir:
> Un Capitole ne voudra poinct qu'il règne,
> Sa grande charge ne pourra maintenir.

CVI,QI3

Interpretation

A [pope] who will often be indecisive will come to power. The greater part [French Empire of Napoleon III] will want to support him. At the Capitol, his rule will not be wanted and he will be unable to maintain his great charge [temporal power].

History

'Pius IX seemed to react emotionally to situations demanding reason and forcefulness. Thus the vacillation ["*dubieux*"] between his role of pontiff and that of benevolent despot plunged him into even deeper *confusion*, especially when a nationalistic war against Austria was demanded. By November 1848 he was treated like a prisoner, so he fled to Neapolitan territory. At Rome he was formally deprived of his temporal sovereignty and the Roman republic was proclaimed. When Pius IX asked the main powers to intervene France did so and captured Rome on 2 July 1849. On 12 April 1850 Pius IX re-entered the Holy City *by French invitation* ["*la plus grand part*"]. . . .

On 20 September 1870, the Pope's temporal sovereignty was annulled at the *Capitol*.'²

The Vatican Council, 1870. Napoleon III at Milan, 1859. Bombardment of the Porta Pia at Rome, 20 September 1870

Avant l'assaut l'oraison prononcée,[1]
Milan prins d'Aigle par ambusche[2] déceus,
Muraille antique par canons enforcée,
Par feu et sang à mercy peu receus.

CIII,Q37

Interpretation

Before the assault they will meditate upon doctrine, the eagle [Napoleon III], who had occupied Milan will be tricked by a plot. The old walls [of Rome] will be shattered by cannon. Because of the strife and bloodshed many will need the [papal] blessing.

History

'The Lombard capital was draped in French and Italian flags. Napoleon III and Victor Emmanuel rode in side by side on 8 June 1859. *Milan* welcomed them wildly.'[3]

'The French military presence maintained Pius's temporal sovereignty. In 1860 conflict with Piedmont began: the north of the Papal States was occupied, and the Pope excommunicated Piedmont ["*à mercy peu receus*"]. By virtue of the September 1864 agreement, signed *without the Pope's knowledge* [plot] by which Piedmont undertook not to attack the papal territories, Napoleon withdrew from Rome, which was now left defenceless. Italian legislation grew more anti-clerical. Garibaldi's troops, which were laying waste the Papal States, were beaten at Mentana in 1866 by papal troops and the French who had returned to occupy Rome and protect the Pope.

On 8 December 1869 Pius IX opened the Twentieth Ecumenical Council ["*oraison prononcée*"] at which Papal Infallibility was *proclaimed* [July 1870]. On 2 September 1870 Napoleon surrendered at Sedan, after which Italy informed France that she intended to occupy Rome. General Cadorna *bombarded the Porta Pia* on 20 September 1870, and after heroic

defence by his troops the Pope had to surrender. The same day his
temporal power was annulled at the Capitol.'[4]

[1] *Faire oraison*, i.e. meditate upon Christian doctrine and duties. DL7V.
[2] Plot, machination, ruse, trap. DL7V.
[3] LSEOA.
[4] DDP.

Bazaine's Treason. Metz and Sedan. Garibaldi, 1870

La garde étrange trahira forteresse
Espoir et umbre de plus hault mariage:
Garde déceuë, forte prinse dans la presse
Loire, Saone, Rosne, Gar à mort outrage.

CII,Q25

Interpretation

The guard of the fortress will indulge in strange treachery in the secret
hope of a stronger alliance, the guard will be deceived, the strong town
caught in a vice; the Loire, Saône and Rhône armies, and Garibaldi's,
will be outrageously overcome by death.

History

'Bazaine was reluctant to leave the fortifications of Metz and did not
move for two days. He used the Emperor's authority as an excuse,
without giving any orders, not even destroying the four bridges of the
Moselle over which the enemy had to advance. Moltke sought *to bottle
him in between the Metz fortresses* – thus the Châlons camp was deprived
of all defensive cover and MacMahon was forced to take a decision,
willy-nilly. He gave the order to evacuate the camp and fall back upon
Rheims, hoping to be able *to help out* Bazaine in due course. . . .
Eighty-three thousand prisoners: the Battle of Sedan cost *3000 dead*
and 14,000 injured. German armies reached Paris, and the French could
find no allies. Only *Garibaldi*, the enemy of Imperial France, came to
the aid of Republican France. The improvised *provincial* forces had some
successes. But Bazaine, negotiating secretly with Bismarck – an attempt
at intrigue repulsed by the Empress – *surrendered*, handing over even his
flags.'[1]

[1] LSEOA.

Defeat at Sedan. The Third Republic

L'aigle poussée entour des pavillons,[1]
Par autres oyseaux d'entour sera chassée
Quand bruit des cymbres,[2] tubes[3] et sonnaillons[4]
Rendront le sens de la Dame insensée.

CII,Q44

Interpretation

The Emperor, after advancing right to the battlefield, will be pursued by other [Germanic] eagles nearby, when the noise of trumpets and cavalry bugles from the Germans will turn his mind back to the Republic.

History

'The King of Prussia thought Napoleon had left Sedan. When informed he seemed astonished. *"The Emperor is here!"* he repeated.

It turned into a rout, every man for himself; there was total confusion and different regiments mingled and swarmed back towards the banked fortifications of Sedan. The Prussian infantry harassed them, taking many prisoners. At two o'clock the battle was over, the whole army was overwhelmed and *the Empire lost*.

The Empress, alone in the Tuileries, saw and heard the yelling crowds in the Rue de Rivoli, their flags draped in mourning. Their shouts made the windows rattle: "Down with the Empire! *Long Live the Republic!*" The Republicans took their revenge: they had been waiting *eighteen years* for it. The war and the manner in which it had been conducted were alike unforgivable. The Empire stood condemned by its own acts. Pitilessly the Republicans saw to its downfall.'[5]

[1] Sort of portable, round or square construction formerly used in military encampments. DL7V.
[2] Germanic tribe settled on the right bank of the Elbe. DL7V.
[3] Latin *tuba*: martial trumpet.
[4] *Sonnaille*: in the pl. meaning a group of bells attached to horses' harnesses.
[5] LSEOA.

Napoleon III in the Ardennes. The Third Republic

Le grand Empire sera tost désolé,
Et translaté[1] près d'arduenne[2] silve[3]
Les deux batards[4] par l'aisné décollé,[5]
Et régnera Aenobarb,[6] nez de milve.[7]

CV,Q45

Interpretation

The great Empire will soon be devastated, the Emperor being transported to the area of the Ardennes Forest. The two persons born from two opposed regimes [Empire and Republic] deprived of the monarchy by the elder [the legitimist pretender] will then rule the Republic, Marianne the harpy.

History

'Napoleon seemed to want to trap himself from the very start: witness his bizarre message to Trochu asking whether the Italian troops should be directed towards Belfort or Munich! Trochu wanted to go back. The Emperor, then in *the Ardennes*, asked him to stay where he was. . . .

The consequences of *the catastrophe which engulfed the Second Empire* make it hardly possible for Frenchmen to consider this period dispassionately, even now.'[8]

'*Monarchist* originally, Thiers had reasoned his way towards *the Republic*, and the Assembly showed hostility to him. He resigned and Marshal MacMahon was immediately elected to replace him. Thereupon the monarchists agitated for restoration of the monarchy. The clergy led a vigorous campaign for the Count of Chambord who was already being called Henri V. But negotiations floundered and this idea was considered impossible.'[9]

---

[1] Latin *translatus*: transported. DLLB.

[2] Latin *Arduenna*: the Ardennes. DLLB.

[3] Latin *silva*: forest. DLLB.

[4] Illegitimate, i.e. irregular. DL7V.

[5] Latin *decollo*: I deprive of something. DLLB.

[6] Domitius Aenobarbus: Roman patrician family, its surname 'bronze beard' deriving from the story that the black beard of one of its members turned suddenly *red*. Domitius was Agrippina's husband and their child was Nero. Violent and debauched, Domitius said that Agrippina and himself could only breed a monster. DHCD. Nostradamus here establishes an analogy with the French Republic which added *red* to the national flag. From the 'socialistic' ideas of the eighteenth century which she spread through Europe, she finally spawned the 'monster' of Communism.

[7] Latin *milva*: female kite; harpy in symbolic and abusive sense.
[8] LSEOA.
[9] HFAM.

The Rift between the Orleanists
and the Legitimists, 1871. The Courts Martial
after the Commune

Par detracteur calomnié a puisnay,[1]
Quand istront[2] faicts enormes et martiaux:
La moindre[3] part dubieuse[4] à l'aisné,
Et tost au règne seront faicts partiaux.

CVI,Q95

Interpretation

The representative of the younger branch will be calumniated by a
detractor, when the courts martial for atrocities are done with, the smaller
faction [Orleanists] will have doubts about the elder one; so the parties
will swiftly reach power.

History

'The Republic proclaimed in Paris on 4 September 1870 had difficult
beginnings. It could not prevent *defeat*. The Republicans were still few
and disorganized, but they took advantage of the *rift* between the royalists, divided as they were into legitimists and Orleanists, to organize a
provisional republic presided over by Thiers. The monarchists succeeded
in ousting him from power: they reproached him for his defection to the
Republican ranks. Under MacMahon's presidency they prepared for the
restoration of the monarchy, but could not overcome their differences;
this allowed the Republicans to pass the Constitution Laws of 1875 which
definitively structured the Republic.'[5]

'The courts *martial* were kept incredibly busy in Paris. Since the
morning [28 May 1871] a thick cordon stood around the Châtelet where
a tribunal sat continuously. From time to time groups of fifteen or twenty
would emerge, condemned to death.'[6]

'The first actions of the Republican government were to decide upon
the return of Parliament to Paris. But the Republicans' victory did not
put an end to *party* squabbles.'[7]

[1] *Puiné*: the second-born, younger of a family.DL7V.
[2] *Istre*, form of *issir*: to issue forth. DAFL.
[3] Smallest in quantity or dimension. DL7V.
[4] Latin *dubiosus*: doubtful. DLLB.
[5] DH3.
[6] Aimé Dupuy: *1870–1871, The War, the Commune and the Press*.
[7] HFAM.

The Fall of Napoleon III, 4 September 1870. MacMahon at Versailles, 1871. His Seven-Year Presidency, 1873–79. The Constitution of 1875

En lieu du grand qui sera condamné,[1]
De prison hors, son amy en sa place:
L'espoir Troyen[2] en six mois joint,[3] mort né.
Le Sol à l'urne seront prins fleuves en glace.

CVI,Q52

Interpretation

Instead of the great man [Emperor] who will be rejected once out of prison, his friend will take power in his place: monarchical power will be shackled in six months, stillborn, the monarchy will be abandoned because of a vote, after the rivers have been taken by ice.

History

'The Emperor's surrender at Sedan meant the immediate overthrow of the Empire. . . .

From 5 January 1871 the Germans rained shells on the forts and barracks on the Left Bank of the Seine. Paris was to endure the threats of both famine and revolution. There was neither wood nor coal *through one of the severest winters of the century*, so cold that the wine froze in the barrel.'[4]

'Wounded at the start of the Battle of Sedan, MacMahon was sent off to Germany as a *prisoner of war*. After the Paris treaty he commanded the Versailles army which recaptured Paris from the Commune.'[5]

'On 27 October 1873 negotiations broke down and the Restoration, with the Count of Chambord, was declared impossible. The monarchists still did not renounce the *hope* of re-establishing the royal family. Mac-Mahon took on the presidency for seven years [19 November 1873]. At the end of 1894, after a sort of *plebiscite for or against the Republic*, it could not be doubted that France was largely Republican. Thus at the start of 1875 the Assembly decided to overhaul the laws of the constitution. It voted, in succession, three laws [February–July 1875].[6] These three laws became the basis of the 1875 Constitution which, with slight modification in 1884, is still adhered to in France. The 1875 Constitution *founded parliamentary rule* in France.'[7]

'The senate *elections* gave the monarchists a slim majority, but in the Chamber the Republican majority was 200. MacMahon, to comply with the constitution, took a Republican minister.'[7]

[1] Latin *damno*: I condemn, declare guilty, reject. DLLB.
[2] *The Franciad*: unfinished epic poem by Ronsard, whose central figure, Francus, is a Trojan prince, Hector's son. DL7V. Nostradamus here takes the Trojans as a symbol of the French monarchy.
[3] Latin *junctus*: assembled, linked. DLLB.
[4] HFAM.
[5] DL7V.
[6] Six months.
[7] HFAM.

The Peace of Frankfurt, 10 May 1871.
The Annexation of Alsace and Lorraine.
Rome, Capital of Italy, 26 January 1871

L'élection faicte dans Francfort,
N'aura nul lieu[1], Milan s'opposera:
Le sien plus proche semblera si grand fort,
Qu'outre le Rhin es Marechs[2] chassera.

CVI,Q87

Interpretation

The choice made [France] will not be received at Frankfurt; Milan will be opposed [to Rome]; her neighbour will seem so great and powerful that he will push back the frontiers beyond the Rhine.

History

'The Peace of *Frankfurt*: during the armistice there was an *election* of a National Assembly which decided to negotiate the peace. The preliminaries were signed at *Versailles* on 26 February and ratified on 1 March at *Bordeaux*. France lost Alsace except for Belfort, and north *Lorraine* including Metz. These preliminaries became a definitive peace through the Treaty of Frankfurt, 10 May 1871. From this terrible war Germany thus emerged united, *powerful* and *dominant* in Europe.'[3]

From 25 January 1871 the heir apparent and Princess Marguerite took up residence in Rome. By 94 votes to 39 the Senate voted for the transfer of the capital. After long trials, said the King, Italy had been given back to herself and to Rome. After recognizing the absolute independence of the spiritual authority, he continued, they could be sure that Rome, capital of Italy, would continue to be the peaceful and respected throne of the papacy.

[1] To have no place, not to be received or admitted. DL7V.
[2] *Maresche* or *Maresc*: German, *Marsch*; English, *Marsh*. DAFL. 'Marches' thus often meant the military border of a state. DL7V.
[3] HFAM.

The Annexation of Alsace-Lorraine, 1871.
The Defeats of Chanzy at Le Mans,
of Faidherbe at Cambrai, and of
the Eastern Army on the Swiss Frontier

Des lieux plus bas du pays de Lorraine,
Seront des basses Allemagnes unies:
Par ceux du siège Picard, Normans, du Maisne,[1]
Et aux cantons[2] se seront réunis.

CX,Q51

Interpretation

Territories situated lower than Lorraine [Alsace] will be reunited with Southern Germany because of the combatants [Germans] at the siege [of Paris], in Picardy, Normandy and as far as Maine, and the French troops which will be reassembled in Switzerland.

History

'The final battles: without despairing, Gambetta organized a new initiative. Three armies took the field in December and January: the Northern Army under Faidherbe, the 2nd Loire Army under Chanzy, and the Eastern Army under Bourbaki. Chanzy clung on along the right bank of the Loire, trying to manoeuvre himself into position for a push towards Paris if he were successful. Defeated at *Le Mans*, he tried to reform his army on the Mayenne.

In the north Faidherbe showed the same tenacity. He was victorious at Bapaume on 3 January, but the defeat of St-Quentin [18 January] drove him back upon *Cambrai* [Picardy].

The Eastern Army tried to relieve Belfort. Pushed back upon Besançon, then to the Swiss frontier [*"aux cantons . . . réunis"*], and caught between two German armies, the Eastern Army only escaped surrender by *rushing into Switzerland* where it was disarmed [1 February 1871].

However, to hasten the capitulation of Paris [*"siège"*], the Germans began the bombardment of the town. . . .

The peace preliminaries negotiated by Thiers and Jules Faure were signed on 26 February and ratified on 1 March by the Assembly, reunited at Bordeaux. France lost Alsace except for Belfort [*"lieux plus bas"* etc.], and north Lorraine with Metz.'[3]

[1] Old French province bordered by Normandy in the north, Orleans to the east, Anjou and Touraine to the south and Brittany in the west. Its capital was Le Mans. DHB.
[2] In Switzerland, the term for each state of the Confederation. DL7V.
[3] HFAM.

Bourbaki's Defeat, 1 February 1871. The Peace of Frankfurt, 10 May 1871

Au conclud pache hors de la forteresse
Ne sortira celui en désespoir mis:
Quand ceux d'Arbois[1] de Langres, contre Bresse[2]
Auront monts Dolle,[3] bouscade[4] d'ennemis.

CV,Q82

Interpretation

At the conclusion of the peace outside [Frank]furt, he who will have been reduced to despair will not be able to extricate himself, when those of Arbois, come from Langres against Bresse, will find in the Jura mountains an enemy ambush.

History

'The Eastern Army – 100,000 men concentrated around Bourges – had as their objective the relief of Belfort, which Denfert-Rochereau had held since 3 November. But like the Châlons army it moved so slowly that the Germans had time to organize. Victor of Villersexel [9 January 1871],[5] Bourbaki could not break the lines at *Héricourt* [15–17 January].[6] Pushed back upon Besançon, then to the Swiss frontier, and *caught between two German armies*, the Eastern Army only escaped surrender by rushing into Switzerland, where it was disarmed [1 February 1871].

The peace preliminaries negotiated by Thiers and Jules Faure were signed on 26 February and ratified on 1 March by the Assembly, reunited at *Bordeaux*. These were transformed into a definitive peace by the Treaty of *Frankfurt*, 10 May 1871.[7]

[1] Chief town of the canton of Jura.
[2] Region on the left bank of the Saône, one of whose departments was the *Jura*. DL7V.
[3] Main town of the *Jura* district.
[4] Latin *boscum*: wood, ambush, i.e. place where the enemy can be unexpectedly attacked from a concealed position. DL7V.
[5] Chief town of the Upper Saône canton.
[6] Town in the Upper Saône canton. After the failure at Héricourt, the disastrous retreat of the Eastern Army across the *Jura* began. DL7V.
[7] HFAM.

The Commune and the Civil War, 18 March–28 May 1871

Par arcs[1] feux, poix[2] et par feux repoussés,[3]
Crys, hurlements sur la minuict ouys:
Dedans sont mis par les remparts cassez,[4]
Par canicules les traditeurs[5] fuys.

CII,Q77

Interpretation

Through firing [curved trajectory], pushed back by the blazes caused by oil, cries and shouts shall be heard in the night; they will enter through empty ramparts and the traitors will flee because of the extreme heat.

History

'The murders of Generals Lecomte and Clément Thomas, shot down in the afternoon by rabble and *mutinous soldiers*, exacerbated feuds and made all conciliation impossible. It was the first episode in an atrocious two-month civil war. Thiers did not try to resist in Paris, but withdrew to Versailles and left the field wide open to the *insurgents*, abandoning even *the forts* to them. The Commune organized the fight against the Versailles government. The war was extraordinarily ferocious. When Thiers, together with the prisoners who had returned from Switzerland and Germany, had reconstituted an army of 150,000 men, he began a second siege of Paris, which lasted five weeks. On 21 May, at about 4 p.m., soldiers infiltrated the city by *an abandoned gate* at Auteuil.

The army entered Paris. In desperation the *Federates*, knowing themselves lost, used oil to set fire to the Tuileries, the Palais de Justice, the Gare de Lyon and innumerable houses. The Seine ran between two walls of *fire*. *Incendiary shells* fired from the high ground in the east rained down on the city centre. Hostages were assassinated [24–26 May]. Incensed by these atrocities, the troops gave no quarter. According to official accounts the battle cost 6500 dead in the fighting or executed. There were also 36,000 prisoners who were *prosecuted* by military courts; 13,000 people were condemned to deportation.'[6]

[1] Latin *arcus*: curves. DLLB.
[2] Mineralogy: name often given to bitumens, of which there are four varieties, among them naphtha, petroleum, etc. DL7V.
[3] Latin *repello*: I push back, drive back. DLLB.
[4] Latin *cassus*: empty. DLLB.
[5] Latin *traditor*: traitor.
[6] HFAM.

Bazaine. Metz Abandoned, 1870. The Death of Napoleon III, 1873

Au deserteur de la Grand forteresse,
Après qu'aura son lieu abandonné:
Son adversaire fera grand prouësse
L'empereur tost mort sera condamné.

CIV,Q65

Interpretation

When the deserter of the great fortress has abandoned the place, the enemy will perform feats of great prowess and the Emperor will die soon afterwards.

History

'MacMahon was warned that Bazaine had not moved from Metz, and was inclined to leave him to his fate. On 14 August Napoleon left Metz, followed by his army. Bazaine was to follow on after the retreat. On 19 August the Marshal assured the Emperor that he had only directed a change in the front so as to guard against the enemy swinging round. He had always intended going north to Sedan and even Mézières in order to reach Châlons. He thus deliberately duped his master, and by persuading him that he still intended to rejoin him, led him to disaster. Sedan was actually named in his dispatch. Bazaine, by his *lie*, finally *undid Napoleon*. . . .

Against the advice of Gambetta, who was burning with patriotism and wanted to continue the fight, the government of national defence at last sought a truce and surrendered Paris. *The victorious Germans marched up the Champs Elysées.* Eighteen months later Napoleon III, ready to attempt another 'return from Elba', *succumbed* to his painful disease.'[1]

[1] LSEOA.

The Belle Epoque, 1900. Rheims, Centre of the 1914–18 War

> Après la pluye de laict assez longuette,
> En plusieurs lieux de Reims[1] le ciel touché:[2]
> O quel conflit de sang près d'eux s'appreste,
> Peres et fils Roys n'oseront approché.

CIII,QI8

Interpretation

After a considerable period of easy living, several areas around Rheims will be smitten from the sky: O what a bloody conflict is being prepared near them; fathers and sons, governors, will not dare approach these places.

History

'Almost *forty-four years* to the day after Froeschwiller and St-Privat, the French and German armies clashed again. This war, the biggest and *bloodiest* ever, seemed like a universal cataclysm.'[3]

'The 1914 war, long and atrocious as it was, in hindsight made the turn of the century look like *a golden age*. The easy life of the bourgeoisie alone prompts one to refer to the *belle époque*. But it was the bourgeoisie which gave it its style.'[4]

Preparations, 1913: Germany was arming formidably, allotting huge sums of money to war materials. In 1913 France passed a law increasing military service to three years.

'In Flanders and Picardy Ludendorff's plans had been foiled, but on 27 May 1918, by a surprise offensive, the Germans shattered the French front between Soissons and *Rheims*. The effect on morale was enormous. Ludendorff decided to strike a decisive blow against Foch by attacking on a 90 km front on either side of *the Rheims salient*. For the second time, a victory on the *Marne* settled the outcome of the war.

France had deserved this triumph at the cost of frightful sacrifices. Of all the contenders she had lost most *blood*: more than 1,500,000 killed and nearly 3,000,000 wounded. Huge tracts of her richest land were no more than treeless, depopulated barren *deserts*. Great towns like *Rheims*, Arras, Soissons, Verdun and St-Quentin were little more than piles of rubble.'

---

[1] Chief town of the *Marne* department. Scene of numerous battles, *Rheims*, like the whole of eastern France, suffered greatly in the First World War.

[2] *Touche*: blow, act of striking. DL7V.

[3] LCH3.

[4] HFAM.

The 1914–18 War. Spanish Flu, 1918

L'horrible guerre qu'en Occident s'appreste,
L'an ensuyvant viendra la pestilence[1]
Si fort terrible que jeune, vieil et beste,
Sang, feu, Mercur,[2] Mars, Jupiter,[3] en France.

CIX,Q55

Interpretation

Horrible war brewing in the west; the year after will come an epidemic so terrible that it will strike young, old, animals, when fire, blood, pillage, war, aviation will be in France.

History

'The epidemic of 1918 caused the deaths of almost 15 million people throughout the world.'[4]

'The conflict which began in 1914 was the culmination of the imperialism of the great *European* powers over half a century. The war spread all over the world, by sea, land and air, but the main fronts remained European ["*en Occident*"].[4] The Germans strove to annihilate the enemy, attacking the Verdun sector on 21 February 1916. This was the start of the bloodiest and most violent battle of the war, leaving more than 700,000 dead and wounded.

Flame-throwers and grenades gave the fighting a particularly horrific aspect. But the most feared weapon was poison gas, first used by the Germans in 1915. *Aeroplanes* at first were largely used for surveillance and observation, but soon their function was to gain control of air space.'[5]

[1] Plague, contagious disease in general. DL7V.

[2] Son of Jupiter, messenger of the Gods, and himself god of eloquence, trade and *thieves*. DL7V.

[3] Principal Roman god, sovereign of *the sky* and of the world. DL7V.

[4] EU.

[5] AE.

The German Army, 1914–18. Peace Terms

Le camp[1] plus grand de route mis en fuite,
Guaires[2] plus outre ne sera pourchassé:
Ost[3] recampé et légion[4] réduicte
Puis hors de Gaule le tout sera chassé.

CIV,QI2

Interpretation

The greatest army [German] put to flight and rout will not be pursued far beyond [the Rhine]. Because the troops will bivouac once more [after 1870], the army will be reduced. It will all be chased out of France.

History

'Since the war was vital to their destiny and very existence, the protagonists flung all their resources into it. Almost 14 million Germans and more than 8 million Frenchmen were mobilized between 1914 and 1918.

From the Argonne to the North Sea the offensive continued relent-
lessly. By 1918 the Germans were weakening and were everywhere in
retreat. The November Armistice conditions demanded the evacuation in
a fortnight of occupied territories in France, Belgium and Alsace-
Lorraine; evacuation in one month of the *left bank of the Rhine*, which
would be occupied by the Allies, along with the bridgeheads on *the right
bank* at Mainz, Koblenz and Cologne.

Germany also had to abolish obligatory military service and *reduce its
army* to 100,000 men.

The most important condition from the French point of view was the
return of Alsace-Lorraine to the French nation.'[5]

[1] Terrain where an army lodges, and by extension an army in general. DL7V.
[2] *Guaires, gaires, guères*, i.e. not much. DAFL.
[3] Army, camp, troop. DAFL.
[4] Latin *legio*: legion, troops, army. DLLB.
[5] HFAM.

The 1914–18 War. The Cost in Lives. The Collapse of the Currency

Par guerre longue l'exercite[1] expuiser,
Que pour soldats ne trouveront pecune:[2]
Lieu d'or, d'argent, cuir on viendra cuser,[3]
Gaulois aerain,[4] signe croissant de Lune.

CVII,Q25

Interpretation

Because of a long war the army will be depleted to the point at which
money will not be found to pay the soldiers. They will have to mint
leather instead of gold and silver; French currency will be like a crescent
moon.

History

'The war endlessly demanded *more and more men and munitions*. The
protagonists had thought they would be waging a short and violent
struggle but found themselves in *a prolonged war*. Both sides experienced
from the outset critical shortages of *supplies and equipment*.

As for the financial consequences, they were difficult to estimate, but the respective national debts in 1919 for Britain and France were almost £8 billion and 219 billion francs. *Paper money* issued during the war was no longer *convertible into gold*. Should there be a reduction of the quantity in circulation [deflation]? Or, on the contrary, should inflation be maintained by devaluing the currency? Was there to be a return to *the gold standard*? Many problems had to be faced in the realm of finance.

France's new attitude was explained by the finances of a country whose coffers were empty and *currency* shaky.

The war lasted four years three months. France had 1,393,000 dead and 3 million injured (one casualty per twenty-nine inhabitants).'[5]

¹ Latin *excercitus*: army. DLLB.
² Latin *pecunia*: fortune, goods, riches, money. DLLB.
³ Latin *cudere* argentum: to coin money. DLLB.
⁴ Latin *aes*: bronze, money. DLLB.
⁵ LMC.

Ghent. Town of Alliances and Treaties: 1576, 1678, 1792, 1795 and 1918. The Capture of Anvers and the Floods, 8 October 1914

Au lieu ou LAYE et Scelde¹ se marient
Seront les nopces de longtemps maniées:
Au lieu d'Anvers ou la crappe² charient,
Jeune vieillesse conforte³ intaminées.⁴

CX,Q52

Interpretation

At the junction of the Leie and the Escaut rivers [Ghent] many alliances will be signed. At Anvers the currents will wash away ordure [corpses]. Young and old not yet soiled will sustain [the combat].

History

'The famous Peace of Ghent in 1576 *united* the northern and central provinces of the Low Countries against Spain ["*alliances*"]. Ghent was captured by Louis XIV in 1678, by Lowendahl in 1745, and in 1792 and 1795 by the Republican armies. Under the Empire it became the chief town of the Escaut department ["*Scelde*"]. Louis XVIII retired there

during the Hundred Days [1815]. In 1815 too, Britain and the USA
signed a peace treaty there.'[5]

'On 11 November 1918, at 5 a.m., the Armistice was signed. The
ceasefire sounded at 11 a.m. That morning the front line was near
Ghent.'[6]

'British and French forces managed to help the Belgian army, which
after abandoning *Anvers* [8 October 1914], made a hazardous retreat to
the Yser. In nine days the Germans reduced the fortifications of *Anvers*:
"the loaded pistol at England's heart" fell into dreadful hands. Von
Falkenhayn's men were a motley collection of new recruits and dedicated
soldiers, aged from sixteen to fifty [*"jeune vieillesse"*], who were *eager to
strike the death blows* [*"conforte intaminées"*]. After merciless fighting at
Dixmude on the Yser, a little coastal river, the battle got bogged down
in *the muddy floods* [*"crappe charient"*] and torrential rain.'[7]

'When war was declared young Germans demonstrated their
enthusiasm.'[8]

[1] Escaut, Scaldis (Scelde). Ghent is on the confluence of the Leie and the Escaut. DHB
and AU.
[2] *Crappe*: ordure. DAFL.
[3] *Conforter*: sustain. DAFL.
[4] Latin *intaminatus*: pure, unsullied. DLLB.
[5] DHB.
[6] HFACAD.
[7] *Prologue to Our Century*: Universal History, vol. XI (Larousse 1968).
[8] EU.

The Bolshevik Revolution, 1917.
Foreign Intervention in Russia, 1917–22.
The Proclamation of the USSR, 1922

Courses[1] de LOIN, ne s'apprester conflits,
Triste entreprise, l'air pestilent, hideux:
De toutes parts les Grands seront afflits,
Et dix et sept assaillir vint et deux.

Presage 62

Interpretation

Hostile incursions from far away, people unprepared for conflict because
of a sad enterprise [the Revolution] which will make the air unbreathable

and hideous; from all sides the heads of states will be afflicted and will assail [the Russians] from 1917 to 1922.

History

'The real face of the new regime did not appear in October *1917*. Twenty years of internal strife constituted *a tragic period* ["*triste entreprise*"] in Russian history, the former Empire which in *1922* became the USSR. Following the October Revolution the new government had to struggle against not only internal opposition but also *foreign intervention*. Russia had retired from the war after the Treaty of Brest-Litovsk [3 March 1918] and French, British, American and Japanese forces came to support the Civil War until November 1920, though it continued in the *Far East* until November 1922.'[2]

'The Russian Revolution began without violence but an assassination attempt against Lenin, and the Civil War sparked off the *Terror*. From 1919 to 1920 the victims of executions, famine ["*hideux*"], *epidemics* ["*l'air pestilent*"] numbered almost 7 million. Lenin's words set the tone: Death or Victory.'[3]

[1] Military term: hostile incursions. DL7V.
[2] EU.
[3] LMC.

The October Revolution, 1917. The Mystery of the Romanov Massacre

Voici le mois par maux tant a doubter,[1]
Mors, tous seigner[2] peste, faim, quereller:
Ceux du rebours[3] d'exil viendront noter,[4]
Grands, secrets, morts, non de contreroller.[5]

Presage 89, October

Interpretation

Here is the month [of October] redoubtable for the ills it will bring. All those of the red flag will bring death, sickness, famine and civil war. Opponents will be exiled, and it will not be possible to control the great ones' deaths, which will remain secret.

History

'*In October 1917*, the home situation in Russia was *catastrophic*. Inflation and state debts made bankruptcy inevitable.

The October Rising [25 October–1 November]. While Kerensky left Petrograd to rally the troops he had recalled from the front, soldiers, sailors, workers and *red guards* took over the Winter Palace and arrested the members of the provisional government. The troops advancing on Petrograd did not want to fight and saw their way blocked, as it had been two months earlier; their commanders parleyed with the Bolsheviks; Kerensky escaped arrest. At Petrograd and then at Moscow attempts by young officers to restore the government failed. On a political level the Bolshevik Revolution triumphed on 1 November.'[6]

'While in the hands of the Communists, in July 1918, Tsar Nicholas II, his wife Alexandra and their five children [*"grands"*] disappeared, never to be seen again. Officially they were *killed* by shooting and bayoneting in the house where they were held prisoners. During the next forty-eight hours, however, the *mystery* and contradictions of this affair spread, masking the truth and creating a legend to add to the general confusion of the time. Although the story of the massacre has been questioned, researches into the truth of the Romanovs' fate have not progressed much further [*"non de contreroller"*].'[7]

[1] Example of aphesis.
[2] Latin *signum*: red flag. DLLB. From this, *seigniere*, band of material, sash. DAFL.
[3] Symbolic: opposite, contrary to what is required. DL7V.
[4] Latin *notare*: censure, condemn. DLLB.
[5] Ancient form of '*contrôler*'. DAFL.
[6] EU.
[7] LDR.

The Internationale and Marxism in Russia.
The Spread of Communist Ideas. Prisons

De gent esclave[1] chansons, chants et requestes,
Captifs par Princes et Seigneurs aux prisons:
A l'advenir par idiots sans testes,
Seront receus par divines oraisons.

CI,QI4

Interpretation

The songs and demands of the Russians, whose heads of state will put people in prison, will be accepted as holy writ by the feeble-minded.

History

'There were immense purges: while *arrests* for counter-revolutionary crimes multiplied between 1936 and 1937, the purges extended far beyond the party to include anyone who had any connection with the victims, however slight.

The great *prisons*: three of the five main prisons of Moscow were reserved for political prisoners, although some detainees were ordinary criminals. Work camps were set up almost everywhere. Kargopol camp, in the Archangel district, for instance, contained *almost 30,000 prisoners* in 1940. It had been founded in 1936 by 600 prisoners who had been simply flung off a train passing through the middle of the forest: of necessity, they themselves had to construct their shelter and enclosures.'[2]

[1] Esclavonia: Slavonia, ancient name for Russia, i.e. land of slaves or serfs. DHB.
[2] LGT.

The Soviet Union Builds Itself up through Two World Wars. The Fall of the Tsar. Stalin in Power.

La gent[1] esclave par un heur[2] martial,
Viendra en haut degré tant eslevée:
Changeront prince, naistra un provincial,
Passer la mer, copie[3] aux monts levée.

CV,Q26

Interpretation

Russia will derive such power through the war that she will change her prince for a provincial by birth, then his power will win the sea and will raise troops beyond the mountains.

History

'Russia retired from the war after the Treaty of Brest-Litovsk [3 March 1918] and French, British, American and Japanese forces came to support the Civil War until November 1920, though it continued in the Far East until November 1922. Throwing out the foreign interventionist troops ["*heur martial*"] and the remnants of the White Armies, the Bolshevik government came to grips with its problems. The first three years of the Revolution have well been called the period of "militant communism".

Josef Vissarionovitch Djugashvili was born at Gori in *Georgia* in 1879. [Stalin, the provincial!]

Moving from a defensive to an aggressive position, the USSR entered the Second World War in September 1939 as an ally of Germany, having signed a non-aggression pact, in order to annexe certain areas of Poland inhabited by Byelorussians and Ukrainians. In November 1939 these became part of the USSR. Romania had to yield Bessarabia and northern Bukovina in June 1940, but on 22 June 1941, in the face of German invasion, Russia's war against Germany began. It was to be a turning-point in her history ["*haut degré*" etc.].'[4]

[1] Latin *gens*: race, population. DLLB.
[2] Luck, happy outcome. DL7V.
[3] Latin *copia*: army corps, troops, military forces. DLLB.
[4] EU.

War in the Balkans, 1908–19. Mustapha Kemal, 1920

Les Conseillers du premier monopole,[1]
Les conquérants séduits[2] par la Melite[3]
Rodes, Bisance pour leurs exposant[4] pole,[5]
Terre faudra[6] les poursuivants de fuite.

CII,Q49

Interpretation

The first president's counsellors will be set aside at Malta by the conquerors [the Allies] because of the abandonment of the cities of Rhodes and Constantinople; then these places will be lost to their pursuers who will be put to flight.

History

'In September 1911 Italy, eager to lay hands on Tripolitania, declared war on the Ottoman Empire and disembarked troops at Tripoli. At the same time her fleet conquered Rhodes and the Dodecanese. The fighting in Tripolitania was fierce and these were only the preludes to war in the Balkans which made Turkey *give way*. On 18 October 1912 war was declared by the Balkan states against Turkey. The Greek fleet seized the Aegean islands. . . .

Bulgaria's capitulation [29 September 1918] immediately brought on Turkey's. An armistice was signed on 30 October 1918 at Moudros Bay; its principal clauses were the freedom of the Straits and *occupation of Constantinople*.

On 4 September 1919 the National Congress of Sivas assembled and Mustapha Kemal was elected its first President; his position towards the Allied powers and the Istanbul government was clearly hostile. On 16 March 1920 the British arranged for Allied troops to take control of the War and Navy Ministries, the police and the Post Office, while *deputies* and *influential* people ["*conseillers*"] who were pro-Kemal were arrested and *deported to Malta*. . . .

The Conference of Lausanne, inaugurated on 21 November 1922, led to a peace signed on 24 July 1923. It was a victory for the Turks, who gained territory on the Thracian frontier and recovered the islands of Imbros and Tenedos. The Allies evacuated *Istanbul* six weeks after the ratification of the peace."[7]

[1] Right possessed exclusively by one or a small number of persons. DL7V.
[2] Latin *seductus*: set aside, distanced. DLLB.
[3] Inhabitant of Malta.
[4] Latin *expositus*: abandoned. DLLB.
[5] Greek πόλις: town. DGF.
[6] Future of *faillir*: to lack. DAFL.
[7] HDT.

The Turkish Revolution, 1920.
The Ottoman Empire Loses Egypt. Its Dissolution

La trombe[1] fausse dissimulant folie,
Fera Bisance un changement de loix,
Hystra[2] d'Égypte, qui veut que l'on deslie
Edict changeant monnoye et alloi.[3]

CI,Q40

Interpretation

A false revolution disguising madness will make Turkey change laws. Egypt will leave [the Empire] which will be dismembered. Her edicts will change currencies and exchange rates.

History

'The Congress of Berlin [13 June 1878] was a new and serious stage in the dismemberment ["*deslie*"] of the Ottoman Empire. Though it had lost only *Egypt*, where Britain was increasingly imposing her authority, it possessed few European territories, and these were miserable relics of a dominion gradually being whittled away by the various local nationalist organizations supported by the great powers.

The *revolution* of Mustapha Kemal: by creating a single party and muzzling the opposition, Kemal succeeded in restoring the Turkish nation's confidence in itself [false revolution]. As for internal politics, the main achievements were abolition of polygamy, suppression of religious orders and the banning of the fez [August–November 1925]; new civil, criminal and commercial codes, established on the lines of the Italian, Swiss and German ones; and the enforcement of protective customs tariffs. In 1939 the Central Bank of the Republic was set up which succeeded the Ottoman Bank as the national bank and mint. ["*monnoye*"].'[4]

[1] Latin *tropa*: revolution. DLLB.
[2] Future of *issir*: to leave, go out of. DAFL.
[3] Alloy, general term for gold and silver. DL7V.
[4] HDT.

The Lake of Geneva and the Towns of Geneva and Evian as Centre of International Conferences. The Red Cross

Du Lac Leman les sermons fascheront,
Des jours seront reduicts[1] par des semaines
Puis mois, puis an, puis tous défailleront
Les Magistrats damneront leurs lois vaines.

CI,Q47

Interpretation

The speeches at the Lake of Geneva will cause ferment; days will be followed by weeks, then months and years, then everything will collapse and the legislators curse their vain laws.

History

'The problem of protecting war's victims had taken on an unprecedented urgency by the end of the Second World War. Certain rulings of the *Geneva Conventions* of 1864, revised in 1905 and 1929, were no longer very relevant in the light of the total wars of 1914–18 and, above all, 1939–45. New terms ["*sermons*"] were needed. These were drafted at the International Red Cross Conference in 1948 and submitted to the Geneva Conference of 1949, all countries having agreed that revision was needed. On 12 August 1949 four conventions were signed: the *Geneva Convention* for improving the lot of the sick and injured on the field of battle; the *Geneva Convention* to improve the treatment of the sick, shipwrecked and wounded at sea; the *Geneva Convention* relating to prisoners of war; and the *Geneva Convention* concerning the protection of civilians during wartime. Certain guidelines were common to all four. At all times and in all places the following were forbidden: to take hostages[2] ["*lois vaines*"]; execution without proper trial; torture; and all cruel and dishonourable treatment. Despite some improvements applied to the rules of war, the 1949 Geneva Conventions run into numerous difficulties in the contemporary world. This is the result of the overlapping of concepts, previously clearly defined, about internal and international wars and the implications of revolutionary and guerrilla warfare.'[3]

[1] Latin *reducto*: I lead back. DLLB.
[2] Cf. the American hostages taken by Iran, which took place on the highest level, country v. country (4 November 1979).
[3] EU.

England's Seven Changes of Alliance in 290 Years. The Franco-German Wars Cement Anglo-French Understanding

Sept fois changer verrez gens[1] Britannique
Taints en sang en deux cens nonante ans:
France non point par appui germanique
Ariès[2] doubte son pole[3] Bastarnan.[4]

CIII,Q57

Interpretation

The Britannic nation will be seen to change seven times in 290 blood-stained years, and change towards France which, when no longer supporting Germany, will be suspicious of the latter's guidance, because of German militarism.

History

1628: the siege of La Rochelle.
1. 1657: the alliance of France with Cromwell.
2. 1667: the War of the Spanish Succession. Turenne occupies Flanders.
3. England allies with Sweden and Holland against France in the Triple Alliance. The Peace of Aix-la-Chapelle (1668).
1670: the treaty with England against Holland.
4. 1688: the War of the League of Augsburg. William of Orange, King of England, grouped the League against Louis XIV; Spain, Sweden, Holland, Austria, the Duke of Savoy.
5. The Peace of Ryswick (1697).
6. 1716: the Abbé Dubois goes back to The Hague, his mission to aid the English to persuade the Dutch to resume the alliance against Spain: the Triple Alliance signed on 4 February 1717.
1744: Louis XV declares war on England and Austria.
7. 1914–18: the English fight beside the French against Germany.
1628–1918 = 290 years.

[1] Latin *nation*: a people or country. DLLB.
[2] Astrological sign of the ram: battering ram. DL7V.
[3] Symbolic: that which guides, fixed like the Pole Star. DL.
[4] The Bastarnes: a tribe, extant *circa* the second century AD, who occupied the area between the upper Vistula and the lower Danube. They were of German origin, according to Tacitus. DL7V.

More than 300 Years of English Power, 1600–1945. The Occupation of Portugal by the English, 1703

Le grand empire sera par Angleterre
Le Pempotam[1] des ans plus de trois cens:
Grandes copies[2] passer par mer et terre
Les Lusitains[3] n'en seront pas contens.

CX,Q100

Interpretation

England will be a great empire and be all-powerful for more than 300 years. She will make great armies pass across the earth by land and sea, which will not please the Portuguese.

History

'Elizabeth's cunning government engaged in trade. The chartered companies multiplied, the most prestigious being the East India Company founded in 1600. Comfort and luxury spread among the ruling classes. English *colonialism* in the seventeenth century, far from slowing down, expanded throughout the world. In Europe, by contrast, this century of revolution began a whole period of crises which, when overcome, enabled Great Britain to establish efficient political machinery and acquire *the durability* [300 years] of her moral and physical personality.'[4]

'The war ended in a Europe in which the British and Americans encamped facing the Soviets [1945]. The determination which enabled the British, while overcoming their pre-war troubles and controversies, to stand fast could not disguise the changes which beset *Great Britain's position in world affairs*. Compared with the new giants [USA, USSR and soon Mao's China] she was *weakened* in resources and economy.'[5] 1600–1945 = more than 300 years.

'Since the time of Pedro II, Portugal had favoured England, which in 1703 consolidated its position there through the Treaty of Methven. Soon the English predominated and reduced the Portuguese to a secondary role. Joseph Pombal wanted *to shake off this yoke*, but his efforts were fruitless. During his struggle with England Napoleon forced Portugal to close her ports to the English. Then, having agreed with Spain, in a secret treaty signed at Fontainebleau in 1807, to share Portugal with her, he tried to conquer that country. But England defended it as if it were its *province*. In the general peace of 1815 the Portuguese royal family had to remain in Brazil, and Beresford, the British ambassador, governed the country. In 1820 *a revolution* broke out in Oporto.'[6]

---

[1] Word partly invented from Greek: πας (all) and from Latin *potens*, powerful, i.e. omnipotent.

[2] Latin *copiae*: army corps, troops. DLLB.

[2] Portugal: part of ancient Lusitania. DHB.

[4] HRU.

[5] EU.

[6] DHB.

Franco's Birth in Galicia. His Departure to Morocco and His Assumption of Power, 1936. The Asturian Revolt, October 1934

Du plus profond de l'Espagne enseigne,[1]
Sortant du bout et des fins de l'Europe:[2]
Trouble passant auprès du pont[3] de Laigne,[4]
Sera deffaicte par bande sa grande troppe.

CX,Q48

Interpretation

From furthest Spain [the West][5] will come an officer who will go to the end of the confines of Europe [Gibraltar] at the moment the revolution arrives by the sea of Llanes; and the band of revolutionaries will be defeated by his great army.

History

'Having failed to gain a place at the Naval Academy, at fifteen the *Galician* Francisco Franco entered the Infantry School at Toledo. From 1912 to 1926 he served almost continuously in *Morocco*. At thirty-three he became the youngest *general in Europe*. In October 1934 he *put down* the *revolt* of the left in *the Asturias*. After being chief of the general staff ["*enseigne*"] in 1935, he was sent to the Canaries following the victory of the Popular Front in the February 1936 elections. On 19 July he took command of the African army at Tetuan and immediately asked the Axis for aeroplanes which transported his troops to the urban areas ["*sortant du bout et des fins de l'Europe*"]. After his reverse of November 1936 outside Madrid, he *defeated* the Republican armies and entered Madrid on 1 April 1939.'[6]

[1] Name formerly given to the standard-bearing officer and certain officers of the king's bodyguards. DL7V.
[2] Straits of Gibraltar between the Hispanic peninsula and the kingdom of Morocco. DHB.
[3] Greek: ποντός the sea. DGF. The *Asturian* coastline has many fishing ports, among them is Llanes. AE.
[4] Gallicization of Llanes.
[5] Galicia: Spanish province situated at the north-west *corner* of the peninsula. DHB.
[6] EU.

Franco is Named Head of Government at Burgos, 1 October 1936. Primo de Rivera Allied with Franco in Fascism

De castel[1] Franco sortira l'assemblée,[2]
L'ambassadeur[3] non plaisant fera scisme,
Ceux de Ribière[4] seront en la meslée:
Et au grand goulphre[5] desnieront l'entrée.

CIX,QI6

Interpretation

Franco will emerge from a junta in a strong place in Castile. The representative who has not pleased will make [fa]scism, those with [Primo] de Rivera will be with him; they will refuse to enter into the great gulf of misfortunes [Germany].

History

'A *junta* of generals named him Generalissimo at *Burgos* on 12 September, then head of government on 1 October. After being chief of the general staff he was sent to the Canaries following the Popular Front's victory in the elections of February 1936. . . . Caudillo, chief, concentrating in his person all power and responsible only before God and history [rule of the *caudillaje*, sometimes confused with *fascism*]. . . .

A Fascist despite himself yet an unwitting liberal, at Valladolid on 4 March 1934, Primo de *Rivera* managed to unite the Falange and the National Syndicalists, whose sole leader he became soon afterwards. The assassinations of which the Falangists were victims goaded him to authorize his partisans to carry out reprisals [Falangist terrorism] ["*en la meslée*"].'[6]

'During the Second World War General Franco, in spite of his links with the Axis Powers, remained neutral and *refused to allow the German armies* to cross through Spain.'[7]

[1] Latin *castellum*: stronghold. DLLB. Burgos: Spanish town, main town of old *Castile*, stronghold. DHB. Pun by Nostradamus on Castile/castle.

[2] Junta: council, *assembly* in Spain and Portugal. DL7V.

[3] Diplomatic agent or envoy representing a sovereign or State. DL7V.

[4] Gallicization of Rivera. The *b* and *v* are two interchangeable labials, e.g. Lefèvre and Lefèbre.

[5] Said of misfortune or miseries into which one falls: to fall into a gulf of ills. DL7V.

[6] EU.

[7] AE.

The Axis Powers Aid Franco. The Spanish Civil War, 1936–39. The French Maquis of the South-west against the Germans, June 1944

Les Cimbres[1] joints avec leurs voisins,
Depopuler viendront presque l'Espagne
Gens amassez,[2] Guienne[3] et Limosins
Seront en ligue, et leur feront campagne.[4]

CIII,Q8

Interpretation

The Germans allied with their neighbours [Italians] will come and lay waste the land as far as Spain. People united in Guyenne and Limousin will form a league and take the field against them.

History

'*Italy* sent Franco's *Spain* war materials and expeditionary troops; *Germany* sent technicians and planes [the Condor Legion]. . . . The number of those who died for their political beliefs on either side is difficult to assess, but must have been *very high*. Adding to them the fighting men killed, a rough estimate would be 750,000 dead. The Axis powers [*Germany* and *Italy*] had been great supporters of the Francoists.'[5]

'On 6 June 1944 the Liberation of France began at Normandy. The Germans pushed forward their reserves, among them an armoured SS Division stationed in the Toulouse area. This should have been able to reach the new front in three days at most, but it had not reckoned with the *French Resistance*. Two groups ["*ligue*"], the Hervé and Alsace-Lorraine brigades, waited for it as it crossed the *Dordogne*, the Charente and the *Haute-Vienne*. Fighting took place from 7 June in the *Lot* district, at the Souillac bridge and Cressensac. The SS deployed its infantry to open up a route through this *Dordogne* region which had just held it up for thirty hours. Then it turned east towards *Limoges*. Exasperated, and henceforth in dread of the 'terrorists', the SS became a menace to the local civilian populations, always ready to exact reprisals. On 10 June 1944, *near Limoges*, the massacre of Oradour-sur-Glane was perpetrated.'[6]

[1] Germanic tribe established on the Elbe's right bank. DL7V.

[2] To amass, reassemble, reunite. DL7V.

[3] Guyenne is today composed of seven departments: Gironde, Landes, *Dordogne*, *Lot*, Aveyron, Lot-et-Garonne, Tarn-et-Garonne. DL7V.

[4] The word employed to denote military action in time of war, as opposed to peace – to take the field, go into action. DL7V.

[5] HEFDP.

[6] *Historama*, no. 272.

German positions from March to September 1944.
In each place marked on the map the SS carried out
executions and atrocious crimes. (Coll. Tallendier)
Extract from *Histoire pour tous*, no. 11
(March – April 1979)

The End of the Spanish Republic, 1939.
Massacres of the Clergy. The Capture of Seville, 1936

La vraye flamme engloutira la dame[1]
Que voudra mettre les Innocens[2] à feu,
Près de l'assaut l'exercite[3] s'enflamme,
Quand dans Seville monstre[4] en boeuf[5] sera veu.

CVI,Q19

Interpretation

The real flame [of war] will engulf the Republic, which will want to put
the Innocents to death. The assault forces will be inflamed when they
have seen a disaster in the shape of a person at Seville.

History

'The revolt began on 17 July 1936 at Melilla. Franco left the Canaries by
air and took command of the Moroccan troops. . . . The coup succeeded
quite easily at Saragossa in Old Castile and Galicia, the Republic ["*la
dame*"] retaining the Cantabrian littoral. In Andalusia the military could
only gain control of a few – though important – towns: *Seville* [with
General Queipo de Llano], Cadiz, Cordova and Granada. All the Mediterranean side of Spain remained Republican. On the whole, the army
and the Guardia Civil had favoured the coup, but not the *storm troops*,
who were sent in against the workers' organizations. . . .

On the Republican side the Giral government could not prevent a real
revolution. Except in the Basque country Catholicism was no longer
respected and *thousands of clergy* ["*Innocens*"] perished. . . .

Taking the offensive on the Catalonian front at the end of December
1938, the Nationalists reached the frontier in six weeks. In the Madrid–
Valencia zone, the partisans fought the war to the end, and it ended on
31 March 1939.

The victors of the Civil War built *a new state* around their leader,
Francisco Franco ["*engloutira la dame*"].'[8]

---

[1] Customary use of feminine personage to denote Republic.
[2] Note capital I referring to priests.
[3] Latin *exercitus*: army. DLLB.
[4] Scourge, calamity. DLLB.
[5] Symbolic: coarse or brutal. DL7V.

The Birth of Hitler in Austro-Bavaria, 1889.
His Fight against the Soviet Union.
The Mystery of His Death

Auprès du Rhin des montagnes Noriques[1]
Naistra un grand de gens trop tard venu,
Qui deffendra[2] Saurome[3] et Pannoniques.[4]
Qu'on ne sçaura qu'il sera devenu.

CIII,Q58

Interpretation

Near the Rhine, a great leader of the people will be born in the Noric Alps, come too late; he will defend himself against Russia and Hungary; what becomes of him will be unknown.

History

'Hitler, son of a customs official, born at Braunau-am-Inn, an *Austro-Bavarian* frontier town, in 1889.'[5]

'In this fight against *the USSR*, the Third Reich could count on the support of Romania, *Hungary* and Czechoslovakia. The role of the Regent, Horthy, was more modest, since *Budapest* had no quarrel with Moscow; only a minimal *Hungarian* force of two cavalry and one motorized brigade participated in this first phase of the campaign.'[6]

'At a press conference on 9 June Marshal Zhukov avoided the question uppermost in all our minds: that of Hitler's death. He did refer to it in surprising terms: "The circumstances were very *mysterious*," he said. "We have not identified the body of Hitler. I can say nothing definite about his fate. We found several bodies among which Hitler's might have been, but we cannot confirm that he is dead." On the tenth, the day after the press conference, Zhukov met Eisenhower at Frankfurt, who asked him point blank: "What do the Russians know about Hitler's corpse?" Zhukov replied no less bluntly: "Russian soldiers have found no trace of Hitler's body." '[7]

[1] Noricum, today part of *Bavaria* and Austria. The Noric Alps stretch across Carinthia, the Salzburg area and Austria as far as the Hungarian plains. DHB.

[2] Latin *defendo*: I push back, defend myself against. DLLB.

[3] Fr: Sauromates or Sarmates: those from Sarmathia, a vague name given by the ancients to a vast area west of Scythia, extending from Europe to Asia, between the Baltic and Caspian Seas. European Sarmathia, between the Vistula and the Tanais, including all the countries that today make up *Russia* and Poland. DHB.

[4] Ancient name for Hungary.
[5] DSGM.
[6] LDG.
[7] DSH.

Hitler's Humble Origins, 1889.
His Speeches. His Policies Towards Russia

> Du plus profond de l'Occident d'Europe[1]
> De pauvres gens un jeune enfant naistra,
> Qui par sa langue séduira grande trouppe,
> Son bruit au règne d'Orient plus croistra.

CIII,Q35

Interpretation

In the most easterly region of western Europe a child will be born to poor parents. He will seduce great crowds with his oratory and will make much more noise about the eastern power [USSR].

History

'Son of a customs official, born at Braunau, an Austro-Bavarian frontier town in 1889. After an undistinguished school career, he began his life not as a wastrel or wanderer but as a bourgeois bohemian living off *a meagre inheritance from his parents*.'[2]

'Hitler, according to Alan Bullock, was the greatest *demagogue* in history. It is no accident that these pages of *Mein Kampf* on *the conquest of the masses* ["*séduira grand trouppe*"], winning them over to nationalism, are among the most effective. Putting into practice such an efficient form of *crowd*-rape suggests talents as an *orator* on the grand scale ["*langue*"], with almost a sixth sense of their deepest needs. Hitler possessed these qualities to an extraordinary degree.

The worst trap lay in the myth with which Hitler is finally identified, that of the master race, kept pure at all costs, and which had to look *east* for its expansion. Hence that obstinacy to stake all *upon Russia* and that *fury* ["*bruit*"] with which he turned his murderous ideology into action there.'[3]

¹ Austria is an easterly country of western Europe.
² DSGM.
³ EU.

Austria as a Breeding Ground for Nazi Ideology

Une nouvelle secte de Philosophes,
Méprisant mort, or, honneurs et richesses,
Des monts Germains ne¹ seront limitrophes,²
A les ensuyvre auront appuy et presses.

CIII,Q67

Interpretation

A new sect of philosophers despising death, gold, honours and wealth
will be born on the German borders and those who follow them will have
support and audience.

History

'The influence of *Vienna*: the hardest but most fruitful school of his life,'
Hitler said. He confirmed that he owed to it the foundations of his
general view of society and a method of political analysis. In reality, the
young Adolf had already formed his essential beliefs at Linz, during
history classes run by Dr Poetsch, a pan-Germanist and anti-Semite. But
in the capital of *Austro-Hungary*, daily life brought concrete justification
for his odious theories ["*des monts Germains. . . limitrophes*"].'³

'Goering effectively took over command of the SA in spring 1923. He
vetted each section, checking their loyalty, and made them sign a statement by which they had to be ready to risk their lives for the movement,
to fight for its objectives and obey their superiors and the Führer utterly.
Those who signed were utterly devoted to the cause and formed the hard
core of the Nazi party. They were also the main force behind Hitler's
political power.'⁴

'Hitler noticed Himmler, a twenty-five-year-old SS officer, very
quickly and named him propaganda director in 1926, the year after his
entry into the SS. This post was an excellent stepping-stone for a me-
teoric rise through the Nazi hierarchy ["*appuy et presses*"].'⁵

[1] Certain constructions, uncompleted by another negative, imply affirmative rather than negative. DL7V.

[2] Latin *limes*: limits, frontiers; placed on the limits of. DL7V.

[3] EU.

[4] *Histoire pour tous*, no. 9 (Nov.–Dec. 1978).

[5] *Histoire pour tous*, no. 9 (Nov.–Dec. 1978).

Nazi Factions in Germany

En Germanie naistront diverses sectes,
S'approchant fort de l'heureux paganisme,
Le coeur captif et petites receptes[1]
Feront retour à payer le vray disme.[2]

CIII,Q76

Interpretation

Various sects will spring up in Germany, greatly reminiscent of happy paganism, but their slavish aspects and slender resources will make them be despoiled in return.

History

Factions: the SA, Youth Association of the Nazi party, the SS, the Hitler Youth, Thule Society, etc.

'Religious marriage was replaced by ancient wedding rites. The chief of the SS group presided, and when the couple exchanged rings he would offer bread and salt as a gift. It all diverted the couple away from the Church and towards a new cult, *a sort of Germanic neo-paganism*.

On 30 January, the anniversary of the seizure of power, the aspirant received a provisional SS identity card. On 20 April, Hitler's birthday, he received a full identity card, assumed the famous uniform and swore an oath of loyalty to the Führer: "I swear to you, Adolf Hitler, my leader, fidelity and bravery. I promise you and all those you designate to command me *obedience until death*." '[3]

---

[1] Latin *recepta*: thing received. DLLB.

[2] *Dismer*: despoil, decimate. DAFL.

[3] Initiation rites of the Waffen SS: see *Histoire Pour Tous*, no. 9 (Nov.–Dec. 1978).

Hitler in Power Thanks to the Weimar Republic, 1933. The First Volume of *Mein Kampf*, 1925

Sous ombre saincte d'oster de servitude,
Peuple et cité l'usurpera lui-mesme:
Pire fera par fraux[1] de jeune pute,[2]
Livre au champ[3] lisant le faux proësme.[4]

CV,Q5

Interpretation

Under the saintly appearance of delivering people from servitude he will himself usurp the people's power and the town. He will wreak the worst by trickery with the aid of a new republic, using as text in the struggle the false ideas of the first part of his book.

History

'At Munich, an ill-conceived and executed *putsch* [1923] led to the banning of the National Socialist Party and its Führer, who was condemned to five years' imprisonment [of which he served only thirteen months] in Landsberg Castle. This very comfortable captivity helped him write down his thoughts: *Mein Kampf*, Volume 1 ["*le faux proësme*"] appeared in 1925.

With their battle cadres the Communists in the doomed Weimar Republic ["*jeune pute*"] represented a force which contrived to weaken the regime and actually *assisted* the National Socialists. Hostility to the Treaty of Versailles, to the Weimar Republic, to bourgeois democracy and capitalism all resurfaced along with much else in the National Socialist ideology. At Munich in 1925 the "second founding" of the party took place under the recently freed Hitler's direction. In 1930 107 Nazi deputies were elected. This demonstrated the movement's strength and the success of *propaganda*, which found considerable assistance during the economic crisis and led to the 1933 triumph.'[5]

---

[1] Latin *fraus*: bad faith, trickery, ruse. DLLB.
[2] Latin *puta*: girl. DL7V. Cf. CV,Q12. Nostradamus designates by the term, often derogatory, a Republic.
[3] Said of any sort of struggle and the place where it occurs. DL7V.
[4] Proem: prologue, prelude to a work. DL7V.
[5] EU.

Hitler Seizes Power, 1933. His Thirteen Years of Power, like the Emperor Claudius, 1933–45

Celuy qu'en Sparte Claude ne peut régner,
Il fera tant par voye séductive:
Que du court long, le fera araigner,[1]
Que contre Roy fera sa perspective.

CVI,Q84

Interpretation

He who, like Claudius, does not have what is needed to rule Germany, achieves as much seduction by short speeches as long and will bring about a planned action against the government.

History

Nostradamus establishes a parallel between Hitler and Claudius here, and Nazi Germany and Sparta elsewhere.

'Lycurgus built the Spartan state. He gave the state a military character, maintained by strict discipline, and communal education and meals. He held all executive power in his hands. *The Spartan state was organized upon conquest* and her history was an interminable series of wars. She sucked almost the whole of Greece into her battle with her rival, Athens. . . .

In his infancy the weak, sickly and timid Claudius was *given away to serfs. England* was conquered by Claudius in person. *The Rhine was liberated* and the right bank of the Danube [*Austria*] was conquered. Armenia was recaptured, Thrace [*the Balkans*] was overcome, while in *Africa* the conquest of Mauretania was accomplished. Domestically Claudius had to fight off *republican conspirators, whom he slaughtered.* Like Hitler, Claudius ruled *for thirteen years.*'[2]

'On 30 January 1933 Hitler agreed to form a government. He would become dictator in three stages. First, the Reichstag was dissolved and the new Reichstag voted Hitler, for four years, the full powers he requested. It was the end of the Weimar *Republic.* After a few months he was beset by critics and *opposition.* Hitler, anxious, began *the repression* with the Night of the Long Knives in 1934. Hitler held absolute power . . . he had known poverty, had lodged in doss-houses. . . . Unstable, with hysterical fits of temper and nervous crises, *an orator of extraordinary magnetism,* he carried audiences with him.'[3]

The Peace Declarations, 1938

L'oyseau de proye volant à la fenestre[1]
Avant conflit fait aux Français parure.[2]
L'un bon prendra, l'autre ambigu sinistre,[3]
La partie faible tiendra par bon augure.

CI,Q34

Interpretation

The eagle, doing what he has decided to do, will honour the French before the war. One party will take him in good faith, the other, the left, will be ambivalent towards him. The weaker party will resist, luckily.

History

'Peace overtures by Berlin and Moscow. The Reich and the USSR decided to consult each other upon necessary steps in case their peace proposals were not accepted by France and Britain. They claimed in this way to be establishing a lasting *peace* in central Europe, because they went on to partition Poland.

Communist propaganda: the Communist leaders only know one thing, how to translate Stalin's lies into French. The Bolsheviks must be credited with this – they do know their propaganda. But we who know about the finances of the newspaper industry can easily estimate the cost of such newspapers and magazines, which could explain why *the Communist leaders* find it impossible to sever their links with Moscow. Because it would be to their advantage, on French soil, to declare themselves *independent*.'[4]

---

[1] Come in or go out of the window: to do something no matter what. DL7V.
[2] Symbolic: that which embellishes, honours. DL7V.
[3] Latin *sinister*: left. DLLB.
[4] *L'Intransigeant*, 30 September 1939.

The Munich Agreement, 1938. British Pacifism. The War, 1939

L'honnissement[1] puant abominable,
Apres le faict sera félicité:
Grand excusé,[2] pour n'estre favorable,[3]
Qu'à paix Neptune ne sera incité.

CVI,Q90

Interpretation

Abominable and shameful infamy will follow the act on which they congratulate themselves and which will only be a great pretext without goodwill, to the point where Britain will not be incited to peace.

History

'At the Quai d'Orsay on 6 December 1938 Ribbentrop and Georges Bonnet signed the Franco–German declaration which seemed to end the two nations' traditional hostility. The peace of Europe seemed assured. Without actually declaring it specifically, Hitler seemed to be renouncing forever, through Ribbentrop, any claims to Alsace or Lorraine. Particular *congratulations* were voiced on the French side, in that various international agreements of theirs seemed to have been respected.'[4]

'In the Far East, as in Europe, Britain had long shown herself to be anxious for *peace* and opposed to all direct action. But the most *pacifist* of the heads of state, Neville Chamberlain, totally changed his attitudes from 15 March 1939. The establishment of obligatory military service on 26 April, *in peacetime*, for the first time ever, was readily accepted by public opinion. Though in August 1939 the government increased its efforts to avoid war, it was without the least hesitation that it decided to honour its obligation towards Poland. The British resolution in 1939 was very different from the hesitation of 1914. The war which began for Britain on 3 September 1939 was partly the result of short-sightedness and a *pacifism* which did not know how to organize internationally where the desire for peace was concerned. In 1939 a great dream of pacifism crumbled ["*non incité*"] and Neville Chamberlain admitted this to Parliament.'[5]

---

[1] Shame, infamy. DAFL.
[2] Latin *excuso*: I allege, make pretext for. DLLB.
[3] Latin *favorabilis*: benevolent. DLLB.
[4] LDG.
[5] HRU.

The Death of Pius XI, 1939.
The Pontificate of Pius XII, 1939–58

Par le décès du très vieillard pontife,
Sera esleu Romain de bon aage:
Qu'il sera dict que le Siège debiffe[1]
Et long tiendra et de picquant ouvrage.

CV,Q56

Interpretation

After the very aged Pope's death, a middle-aged Pope will be elected.
He will be accused of harming the Holy See and will last a long time,
doing 'controversial' work.

History

Pius XI, 1857–1939, was indeed elderly. 'Eugenio Pacelli, born in *Rome*
to an aristocratic *Roman* family, succeeded him in 1939 as Pius XII, *aged
sixty-three*. He was unquestionably a forceful personality whose *politics
and opinions have been criticized in various ways*. He had considerable
problems to face and did so vigorously, displaying *immense energy*. His
pontificate was also noteworthy for several acts or statements to which
he tried to lend great doctrinal significance. On some matters, Pius XII
remains a *controversial Pope*.'[2]
He died in 1958 after nineteen years as pontiff.

[1] *Debiffer*: put into a bad state. DL.
[2] EU.

The Death of Pius XI, February 1939.
Five Years of War, 1940–45. The Election of Pius XII

Après le Siège tenu dix et sept ans,
Cinq changeront en tel révolu terme:
Puis sera l'un esleu de même temps
Qui des Romains ne sera trop conforme.

CV,Q92

Interpretation

After a pontificate of seventeen years, five years will see changes that put an end to the revolution. Then at the same time will be elected one [a pope] who will be only too like the Romans.

History

Pius XI was elected Pope on 6 February 1922. He died on 10 February 1939 after a pontificate of seventeen years four days. 'Pius XII, born in *Rome* to an old aristocratic *Roman* family.'[1]

[1] EU.

In this cartoon of Churchill's face
the traditional determination of the British bulldog
is portrayed, symbolizing the spirit of endurance
shown in 1940
Extract from LDG

Churchill Isolated in Politics, 1939.
The German–Soviet Pact, 23 August 1939. War between Germany and Russia, 22 June 1941

Le gros mastin[1] de cité déchassé,
Sera fasché de l'estrange alliance,
Après avoir aux champs le cerf[2] chassé,
Le loup et l'Ours se donront défiance.

CV,Q4

Interpretation

The great British bulldog [Churchill], after being isolated from the City, will be vexed by the strange alliance [the German–Soviet pact]. After chasing Poland from the field [of battle], Germany and Russia will defy each other.

History

'All his life Churchill had a *powerfully* original personality. Everything about him was forceful and exaggerated [the big mastiff]. He was always a fighter who never admitted defeat. On the eve of the Second World War, despite a lively parliamentary and ministerial career, he seemed completely *isolated* from the Conservatives' decision-making bodies.

The Battle for Warsaw began on 9 September 1939 with the Wehrmacht attacking the Polish army. On 17 September, because of the *German–Soviet Pact*, the *Red Army* invaded eastern *Poland*. On 28 September the fifth partition of Poland occurred, this time involving Germany and the USSR ["*Ours*"/bear]. All hopes for her liberation now lay with Britain, who had remained alone in the fight. Hitler did not succeed in conquering her. . . . *Churchill's* resolve was unshakable.

Although the USSR kept to the letter of the economic clauses of the *German–Soviet Alliance*, to Germany's benefit, Hitler decided to drive her out of Europe before dealing with Britain. On 21 June 1941, without formal declaration of war, the Wehrmacht attacked the Red Army.'[3]

'German–Soviet relations, it was agreed, should be clarified before 26 August. The spectacular reconciliation of the Third Reich and Bolshevik Russia was timed to produce in London and Paris the effect of a real earthquake.'[4]

---

[1] The word *dogue* for bulldog appears only rarely in French before the seventeenth century. It was thus considered as a *large mastiff* coming from *England*. DL7V.

[2] Symbolic. In *Christian* legend and on monuments the deer features prominently.
DL7V. Hence the deer used as a symbol for the devoutly Catholic Poland.
[3] EU.
[4] LDG.

The Annexation of Czechoslovakia, 15 March 1939. German Landings in Tripolitania, February 1941

Foibles galeres seront unis ensemble,
Ennemis faux le plus fort en rempart:
Faible assaillies Vratislave[1] tremble,
Lubecq[2] et Mysne[3] tiendront barbare[4] part.

CIX,Q94

Interpretation

When the weak warships are reunited the strongest country [the German Reich] will keep watch against false enemies [the Hungarians]. The weak will be attacked and Bratislava will tremble. Those of Lübeck and Misnen [Germans] will occupy part of North Africa.

History

'*Weakness* of the German navy. Vice-Admiral Kurt Assmann, its historian, wrote: "The situation was the reverse of that of 1914. Then we possessed a powerful fleet but had no strategic position or proper base. Now we had such a strategic base, but not one fleet able to do anything to take any advantage from it."

On 9 March 1939 negotiations between Prague and *Bratislava* on Slovak autonomy reached a dead end, and President Hacha tried to act to unite the state. Shortly afterwards Hitler riposted by giving the Czech government a seven-point *ultimatum*. In this explosive atmosphere, on 14 March, and fearing Hungarian aggression ["*faux ennemis*"] *the Diet of Bratislava* proclaimed Czechoslovakia's independence, while asking the Chancellor–Führer to *guarantee* ["*le plus fort en rempart*"] the existence of the new state and take all necessary measures to *safeguard* its frontiers.

From 1 February to 30 June 1941 no fewer than 81,785 Axis troops disembarked at *Tripoli* with almost 450,000 tonnes of supplies, munitions and fuel. North Africa therefore contained divisions of the Italian army as well as the 5th Light Division which formed the forward unit of the German Afrika Korps ["*ceux de Lübeck*"].'[5]

[1] Bratislava, capital of Slovakia.
[2] Lübeck: German town 15 km from the Baltic.
[3] German town on the North Sea.
[4] Barbary: area of North Africa comprising Tripoli, Tunis, Algiers and Morocco. DHB.
[5] LDG.

The Annexation of Poland, 1939.
The Invasion of France via Holland and Belgium.
The Restitution of Alsace-Lorraine to the
French Republic, 1919

Quand le plus grand emportera le pris[1]
De Nuremberg, d'Ausbourg et ceux de Basle,[2]
Par Agrippine[3] chef[4] Frankfort repris.
Traverseront par Flamant jusqu'en Gale.

CIII,Q53

Interpretation

When the greatest [Hitler] takes the [country] prisoner [Poland] the Germans will cross Flanders [Holland and Belgium] as far as France, after the most important article of [the Treaty of] Frankfurt has been taken back by the Republic [annexation of Alsace-Lorraine by Germany].

History

'Having disposed of *Poland*, Hitler turned his attentions west, and revised his plan of attack on *Belgium* and *Holland*. The main force of German paratroops was scheduled to jump over or into the *Netherlands Redoubt* or *Vesting-Holland*. It was agreed not to transfer the main thrust of the attack to the south of Liège.'[5]

'The Treaty of Versailles was signed on 28 June 1919 in the same Hall of Mirrors which on 18 January 1871 had witnessed the proclamation of the German Empire by Bismarck. The signature of the peace was intended to have the character of a ceremony of expiry. From the territorial point of view, Germany *restored* Alsace-Lorraine to France.'[6]

[1] Used as prisoner, captured.
[2] Towns inhabited by Germanic peoples.
[3] Wife of Domitius Aenobarbus, always taken by Nostradamus as symbol of the Republic.
[4] Figurative: article, division, importance. DL7V.
[5] LDG.
[6] HFAM.

The Maginot Line. The Rhine. Paris Occupied, 14 June 1940

Près du grand fleuve, grand fosse,[1] terre egeste[2]
En quinze pars sera l'eau divisée:
La cité prinse, feu, sang, cris, conflit mettre,
Et la plus part concerne[3] au collisée.[4]

CIV,Q80

Interpretation

Near the great river [Rhine] will be dug a great ditch, the drainage system will be divided into fifteen parts. The town [Paris] will be taken and the conflict will put all to fire and blood; and the majority of the French will be involved in the upheaval.

History

'The original plan of the offensive gave the principal role to the northern forces, Group B, under von Bock. He was to execute a wide sweep across the Netherlands, supported by Group A (von Rundstedt) which was the centre of the German disposition, facing the Ardennes, and by Group C (Leeb) on the left flank in front of the *Maginot Line*. It was a repetition of the 1914 German offensive, therefore unlikely to surprise the Allies; what was more, it meant sending armoured forces into a country criss-crossed by *innumerable canals and little rivers*.

Tanks and armoured vehicles formed a 160 km column extending 80 km beyond the other bank of the Rhine! The plan was an extraordinary success. Hitler wanted to avoid a stalemate such as happened after the Battle of the Marne in 1914. He sought at all costs to deploy his armoured troops in readiness for the second phase of the offensive, the battle for Paris and France. In eleven days it was all over, and on 14 June the Germans *entered Paris*.'[5]

[1] Latin *fossa*: ditch, trench. DLLB.
[2] Latin *egestu* penitus cavare terras: to dig out, throwing up earthworks. DLLB.
[3] Latin *concerno*: I mix. DLLB.
[4] Latin *collisio*: crash, shock. DLLB.
[5] HAB.

The Invasion of the Netherlands and Belgium, 10 May 1940

Par l'apparence de faincte[1] saincteté,
Sera trahy aux ennemis le siège:
Nuict qu'on cuidait[2] dormir en seureté,
Près de Braban[3] marcheront ceux de Liège.

CVI,Q30

Interpretation

Under cover of feigned piety, the country will be besieged by enemies, through treachery, while the people thought they were sleeping safely. The troops who will be in Liège will march across Belgium.

History

'On 6 December 1938 Georges Bonnet, the French Foreign Minister, and his German counterpart, Ribbentrop, signed at the Quai d'Orsay *a joint declaration* which, based on the Munich agreement, *seemed* to put an end to the two countries' traditional hostility. It was thought in Paris that Hitler and Ribbentrop had vetoed any new recourse to aggression or unilateral measures which, three times in less than three years, had almost set Europe alight.'[4]

'The German Army invading *the Netherlands* and France on 10 May 1940 was eighty-nine divisions strong, with forty-seven more held in reserve. The first success was the destruction of the Dutch and Belgian defensive system, made possible because German commanders captured points vital for the offensive and also the famous fort of Eben-Emael on the *Albert Canal* [*Liège*]. The Wehrmacht armour swiftly crossed the Ardennes and the French frontier on 12 May. On 5 June the German Army resumed the offensive by crossing the Somme and advancing southwards. In eleven days it was all over and the Germans entered Paris.'[5]

[1] *Feinte*: sham, pretended. DAFL.
[2] *Croire*: believe. DAFL.
[3] Duchy of three provinces: (1) Noordbraband, comprising the largest province of the kingdom of the Netherlands; (2) Brabant, in Belgium; (3) Anvers, in Belgium. DL7V.
[4] LDG.
[5] HAB.

The Vichy Government. The Occupation, 1940–44.
General de Gaulle in London, 18 June 1940.
The Landing: Rouen and Chartres

Règne[1] Gaulois tu seras bien changé,
En lieu estrange est translaté l'empire:
En autre moeurs et lois seras rangé,[2]
Roan, et Chartres te feront bien du pire.

CIII,Q49

Interpretation

French government, you will be much changed; the empire will be transferred into another country; you will be subjected to other ways and laws. Those who will come through Rouen and Chartres will wreak still further ill upon you.

History

'The fate of the *French Empire* was at stake. There was no one in France to inspire her to resist now that Pétain and a team of defeatists had taken office. If North Africa and the *French Empire* were to be saved it could only be from *London*. . . . I was going to return to England with de Gaulle and help him put his plans into practice. He was right: it was essential that without a moment's delay the call for resistance should come from *England*, as an immediate response to Pétain's demand for an armistice.'[3]

'Then the advance to the Seine, during which the Germans no longer resisted but evacuated as quickly as possible the country they had occupied for four years. Four Allied armies participated in this pursuit: the Canadian 1st Army advanced on *Rouen* and captured it on 27 August. The American 3rd Army thrust towards *Paris*: starting from Alençon and Le Mans, it reached Verneuil, Dreux and Mantes in the north, and *Chartres* and Rambouillet in the south, the final step. After the capture of Paris and the crossing of the Seine the campaign changed decisively.'[4]

---

[1] Latin *regnum*: government. DLLB.
[2] Figurative: to submit to a duty or be obedient.
[3] 'How I took General de Gaulle back to England' by Edward Spears. Dossier: *Historama* no. 23.
[4] HLFRA.

Pétain, Hitler and Stalin.
The Twenty Months of Absolute Occupation

Le vieux frustré du principal espoir,
Il parviendra au chef de son empire
Vingt mois tiendra le règne à grand pouvoir
Tiran cruel en délaissant un pire.

CVIII,Q65

Interpretation

The old [Marshal] frustrated in his principal hope, [Hitler] will reach
the summit of his power and will hold power by force for twenty months,
a cruel tyrant leaving a worse one behind him.

'The progress of the German-Russian collaboration.'
The two tyrants! (LDG)

History

'On 11 November 1942 Free France was occupied by the Germans. . . .
On 6 June 1944, the Allies landed in Normandy.'[1]

From 11 November 1942 to 6 June 1944 = *nineteen months, twenty-five days!*

'From 1951 to 1955 the Russian regime grew more repressive. The
fight against internationalism was distinguished by persecutions of the
Jews in particular.

The assassination of Kirov at Leningrad in 1936 was the signal for a
series of upheavals. The death penalty was the punishment for those out
of step with the regime. It even threatened the highest party officials.
The extent of the repression was only matched by the amazing compla-
cency with which the accused confessed ["*a worse.* . ."!].'[2]

[1] PCHF.
[2] LMC.

Milestones in Hitler's Life:
1889, 1915, 1921, 1939 and 1945

Plusieurs mourront avant que Phoenix[1] meure,
Jusques six cents septante[2] est sa demeure,
Passé quinze ans, vingt et un, trente-neuf,
Le premier est subjet à maladie,
Et le second au fer[3] danger de vie,
Au feu[3] à l'eau[4] est subjet trente-neuf.

Sixain 53

Interpretation

Many will die before the Phoenix [Hitler] dies. After fifty-five years ten
months he will find his [last] home, when the years 1915, 1921 and 1939
have passed. In 1915 he will succumb to illness; in 1921 he will have an
armed force dangerous to his life; 1939 will be subject to a rain of fire.

History

'Adolf Hitler, born in 1889. Corporal, twice *wounded*, 1915.'[5]
'*1921* was a successful one for the party, which now had 6000 or more

supporters, many of whom were in the SA, which the Munich papers dubbed *"Hitler's bodyguard"*.[6]

'While on a recruiting drive through Germany [they had 3000 supporters at the end of *1921*], Captain Roehm, his deputy, mobilized the *paramilitary* wing or assault squads of the SA. Hitler liquidated the right-wing opposition on the Night of the Long Knives [30 June 1934]. Several hundred were massacred, among them Schleicher, who tried to regroup those soldiers who had remained *lukewarm* towards Hitler, and Roehm, the all too powerful and independent leader of the SA.'[7]

'During the last weeks, in *March*–April 1945, the hunted Führer killed himself with a bullet through the mouth.'[5]

'They had news from the outside world of the capture and execution of Mussolini and Clara Petacci. The Duce and his mistress were hung upside-down in Milan. Eva Hitler cried out: "Will they do the same to us?" The Führer assured her that this would not happen and that their bodies would be *consumed* by fire until nothing remained, not even ashes.'[8]

---

[1] The legendary phoenix *lived for several centuries*. It was big as an *eagle*. When its end was approaching it *made itself a nest* of branches oozing sap or resin, exposed it to the sun's rays and was consumed therein. DL7V.

[2] April 1889–March 1945 = 670 months.

[3] Using fire and sword: violent means to attain one's end. Carrying the sword (iron) and flame into a country, meaning to ravage it with murder and war. DL7V.

[4] Biblical sense: deluge, flood. DL7V.

[5] EU.

[6] See *Histoire pour tous*, no. 9 (Nov.–Dec. 1978), about the SA.

[7] AE.

[8] LGESGM.

The Liebensborn.[1] *Mein Kampf*

La voye auxelle[2] l'un sur l'autre fornix[3]
Du muy[4] de fer hor mis brave[5] et genest:[6]
L'escript d'empereur le fenix,
Veu en celuy ce qu'a nul autre n'est.

CVIII,Q27

Interpretation

The means through which sexual relations were facilitated between one and another in the iron movement [SS], except for the wellborn. The book of the emperor phoenix in which one sees what is seen nowhere else.

History

'In the *Liebensborn* or "love camps", where carefully chosen young women were at their disposal, the SS *procreated outside marriage* 6000–7000 children a year of "pure race", who were immediately abandoned to the care of the organization.

Coming as they did out of the Hitler Youth, the SS men had to conform to the Nazis' concept of a Germanic ideal: more than 1.75 m in height, with perfect health and teeth, "Aryan" looks, Nordic origin traceable back to 1750 for the leaders, *bravery* and absolute obedience.'[7]

'*No theoretician had been ready or able* to translate the myth into reality. Hitler the cold auto-didact, prompted by a coarse Darwinism which cheaply invoked "nature" and her cruelty, was ready and clever enough to take this step with implacable logic.'[8]

[1] Love-camps, concentration camps for breeding purposes.
[2] Latin *auxillium*: aid, help. DLLB.
[3] Fornication: sex between unmarried persons who are not tied by any vows. DL7V.
[4] Form of present and perfect of *mouvoir*, to move. DAFL.
[5] Intrepid, *courageous*, great, remarkable. DL7V.
[6] Greek γενέσθαι: aorist infinitive of γίγνομαι to be born. DGF.
[7] DSGM.
[8] EU.

Hitler and the Third Reich.
The Gas Chambers and Massacres. German Prosperity and Disaster

Le tiers premier pis que ne fit Néron,[1]
Vuider vaillant que sang humain répandre:
Rédifier fera le forneron[2]
Siècle d'or mort, nouveau Roy grand esclandre.

CIX,QI7

Interpretation

The first [person] of the Third [Reich] will do worse than Nero. He will be as valiant in draining as in shedding human blood: he will cause ovens to be built; prosperity will be at an end, and this new leader will cause great scandals.

History

'Hitler, *Chancellor* [*"premier"*] of Germany in 1933, properly appointed by President Hindenburg, attained by plebiscite in 1934 absolute power as Chancellor–Führer of the new regime, the Third Reich. He succeeded in curbing the huge unemployment problem [6,200,000 out of work in 1932], in re-establishing *prosperity* [*"siècle d'or"*], and embarking upon housing and other building projects, social benefits schemes etc., which ensured him enormous popular support.'[3]

'Enraged by hatred for the Jews and against Christianity too [Nero!], the Germans also inflicted upon the Russian prisoners of war the worst slavery, by contrast with the *blissful* existence [*"siècle d'or"*] waiting for the German working man.

In 1945 books and films appeared entitled *Germany, Year Zero*, because the country seemed so totally *destroyed* [*"siècle d'or mort"*]. The mass graves and *crematoria* made people understand certain facts about 1945. Germany's unconditional surrender marked the end of *the huge massacre* planned and unleashed by Hitler. The towns were in ruins. *Dead*, prisoners, injured – *millions* of them. Into the chaos created by Hitler's total war millions of Germans were hurled, expelled from central European countries. Occupied Germany was in abject *misery*.'[4]

---

[1] Nero was present at a huge fire which consumed most of Rome. When accused of being its perpetrator, he rejected the Christians' accusation and massacred and tortured them cruelly. DHB. For Nostradamus, the Jews were to be Hitler's scapegoats as the Christians had been for Nero.

[2] Latin *fornus* or *furnus*: oven. DLLB.

[3] DSGM.

[4] EU.

Hitler's Persecutions. The New Nero. The July Plot, 1944

Le Néron[1] jeune dans les trois cheminées,[2]
Fera de paiges[3] vifs pour ardoir[4] jetter,
Heureux qui loin sera de tels menées,
Trois de son sang le feront mort guetter.

CIX,Q53

Interpretation

The new Nero will hurl into three ovens [Auschwitz, Dachau and Birkenau] young people to burn them alive. Happy they who are far from such acts. Three of his blood [Germans] will spy on him to kill him.

History

'The extermination plan's outlines were laid down during a conference near Berlin, on 20 January 1942, under the presidency of Heydrich: "The final solution to the Jewish problem in Europe will be applied to approximately 11 million persons."

Thereafter, under Eichmann's direction, Jews were methodically hunted and rounded up to be sent mostly to Auschwitz for extermination. According to the camp's director, 3 million deportees perished at Auschwitz. In all the camps the victims' bodies were *burned* in ovens ["*cheminées*"]. . . .

Towards the end of the war numerous opposition groups of very varied natures and aims came into existence. The most important of these was one which organized an assassination attempt upon Hitler. It was headed by Karl Goerdeler, ex-burgomeister of Leipzig, and General Beck. Colonel von Stauffenberg ["*trois de son sang*"] placed a bomb (that proved not powerful enough) in Hitler's headquarters on 20 July 1944. The attempt failed: Hitler was only slightly injured.'[5]

[1] Cf. CIX,Q17.
[2] Derived from *caminus*: oven. DL7V.
[3] Young boy. DAFL.
[4] To burn. DAFL.
[5] EU.

Hitler in Power. Stauffenberg's Assassination Attempt on Hitler, 20 July 1944

Avec le noir Rapax et sanguinaire
Issu de peautre[1] de l'inhumain Néron:[2]
Emmy[3] deux fleuves main gauche militaire,
Sera meurtry[4] par joyne chaulveron.[5]

CIX,Q76

Interpretation

With the rapacious [eagle], black and bloody, spawned from the pallet of the inhuman Nero, caught between two rivers[6] because of the armed forces of the left [Russian troops], [Hitler] will be wounded by a young man [Stauffenberg] who will burn him.

> Au grand Empire parviendra tost un autre
> Bonté distant[7] plus de félicité:
> Regi par un yssu non loing du peautre,
> Corruer regnes grande infelicité.

CVI,Q67

Interpretation

In the great German Empire [the Reich] another leader will soon rise to power. But good fortune being distant there will be no more luck. Germany will be ruled by one spawned from the pallet [of Nero] who will hurl himself against countries causing them great miseries.

History

'Stauffenberg had only been gone one or two minutes when at 12.42 a violent blast wrecked the Conference Room, blew in the walls and roof and *set ablaze* the debris which rained upon the occupants. Amid the cries of the wounded and the guards running to the scene, Hitler staggered out from the smoke and confusion, supported by Keitel. The explosion had ripped one of his trouser legs and he was covered in dust and numerous cuts and *bruises* ["*meurtry*"]. His hair was *burned*, his right arm hung limp and stiff, one leg was *burned*: a falling beam had bruised his back and his eardrums had been affected by the explosion.'[8]

---

[1] *Peautre* or *peltre*: pallet, mean bed. DAFL.

[2] Cf. CIX,Q17.

[3] In the middle of. DAFL.

[4] *Meurtrir*: to wound or harm, bruise. DL7V.

[5] From *chalder*: to warm or heat up. DAFL.

[6] Rastenburg, scene of the assassination attempt, is between the Vistula and the Niemen, equidistant from these two rivers.

[7] Latin *distans*: removed, absent, distant. DLLB.

[8] HAB.

Hitler's Power in October 1939

L'autheur des maux commencera régner[1]
En l'an six cens et sept[2] sans espargner
Tous les subjets qui sont à la sangsue,[3]
Et puis après s'en viendra peu à peu,
Au franc pays rallumer son feu,
S'en retournant d'où elle est issue.

Sixain 21

Interpretation

He who will provoke great misfortunes will see the start of his power in October 1939, without sparing the revolutionaries, and little by little will come and make war in France, returning whence he came [Germany].

History

'Having disposed of Poland, Hitler turned his attentions westwards. His arguments were that the likely abandonment by Belgium of her neutrality threatened the Rhineland and thus compelled Germany to *win space*, and that as the British war effort was getting under way it was necessary to prepare methods of launching an offensive. This was to take place between 20 and 25 October, through Holland and Belgium, and would lead to the crushing of the Allied forces, gaining for Germany sufficient territory in northern *France* from which to extend airborne and naval operations. Generals von Brauchitsch and Halder presented, *on 19 October*, a first draft of the invasion plans, entitled the Yellow Plan.'[4]

'Hitler had a horror of Marxism, all the stronger for its being, in his view, a Jewish doctrine, invented by a Marx and spread in Austria by Austerlitzes, Davids and Adlers.'[5]

[1] Latin *regnum*: reign, empire, power. DLLB.
[2] April 1889–October 1939 = 607 months.
[3] Latin *sanguisuga*: bloodsucker. DLLB. Nostradamus uses this word for revolution, the drinker of blood.
[4] LDG.
[5] EU.

Ironies of War, from the Polish Defeat, September 1939, to the Invasion of France, January 1940

Au grand siège encore grands forfaits,
Recommençant plus que jamais
Six cens et cinq[1] sur la verdure,
La prise et reprise sera,
Soldats es[2] champs jusqu'en froidure
Puis après recommencera.

Sixain 14

Interpretation

At the great siege [Warsaw] there will be great forfeits, and beginning again more than ever in September 1939 the army will be in the field ["*verdure*"]. The town will be taken and retaken; the soldiers will no longer be in the field until the cold, then war will begin again.

History

'On 28 September 1939 Warsaw surrendered after two weeks of heroic resistance. The bombing had set fire to its flour mills, and over half its water supply and sewage system was destroyed.

The torrential rains of early autumn 1939 persuaded Hitler to delay till the last moment the offensive due to be launched on 12 November. Up to *16 January 1940* the *weather* caused no fewer than thirteen delays.

On 10 February 1940 the Führer met his generals and staff in his office at the new Chancellery. He informed them of his decision to launch the western offensive on the seventeenth at Aix-la-Chapelle, at dawn, 8.16 a.m. According to him, the meteorological situation prompted this sudden decision. A ridge of high pressure approaching from the east from the twelfth or thirteenth would mean settled, dry weather over Holland, though the temperature would drop *to 10–15° below zero*.'[3]

---

[1] April 1889–September 1939 = 605 months.
[2] Prefix expressing taking away, extraction. DAFL. Hence, literally, out of the field.
[3] LDG.

Hitler on the Champs Elysées

Six cens et six, six cens et neuf,[1]
Un Chancelier gros comme un boeuf,[2]
Vieux comme le Phoenix du monde,
En ce terroir plus ne luyra,
De la nef[3] d'oubly passera,
Aux champs Elisiens faire ronde.

Sixain 25

Interpretation

September 1939, January 1940, a coarse and brutal Chancellor, like the Phoenix in the world, will end by no longer shining in France, his power will pass into oblivion, when he has passed along the Champs Elysées.

History

'*1st September 1939*: the Second World War begins.

Plans of German aggression unveiled. As the invasion on *12 January 1940* was imminent, Hitler addressed a new memorandum to certain factions of his command.'[4]

'On 14 June the first sections of the German 18th Army entered the French capital, declared an open city. At the start of the *Champs Elysées* German officers and an Italian army representative in civilian clothes awaited the arrival of a *column* of troops on to the Place de la Concorde.

The classical image of great politicians – Richelieu, Napoleon and Bismarck, say – is tied up with a certain charm or distinction. Hitler gave this image the lie. His personality was incurably vulgar, *coarse, cruel* [one discovers this from the books about the war period as well as from *Mein Kampf*], and disconcertingly brusque.'[5]

---

[1] From Hitler's birth (April 1889) to September 1939 = 606 months, i.e. fifty years six months; and to January 1940 = 609 months.
[2] Big, brutal. DL7V.
[3] Latin *navis*: ship. *Navis Reipublicae*: the Ship of State (Cicero). DLLB.
[4] LDG.
[5] EU.

The Armistice of Villa Incisa, 22 June 1940.
The Demarcation Line. The Occupation

D'un chef vieillard naistra sens hébété,[1]
Dégénérant[2] par scavoir et par armes,
Le chef de France par sa soeur redoubté,
Champs divisez, concedez aux gens d'armes.

CI,Q78

Interpretation

The good sense of an old leader will be rendered stupid, losing the glory of his wisdom and feats of arms; the chief of France will be suspected by his sister [Latin, i.e. Italy]. Then the land will be divided and abandoned to the soldiers.

History

'Pétain's *senility* explained all. He was not aware of many things and only half understood the rest. The defence counsel was obviously convinced that if he presented his client in this way, he would reinforce his own well-organized defence. While he was speaking, Pétain seemed as angry as the prosecution. "He's pleaded senility!" he said in irritation.'[3]

'The armistice of Villa Incisa: at Bordeaux no one of course knew Mussolini's final conversion to Hitler's point of view about the neutralization of the French fleet. This is why on 22 June, with *Marshal Pétain's approval*, Admiral Darlan sent the other admirals the following telegram: "If a Franco–German armistice is concluded, it must not be effected until one with Italy is also signed, since blackmail is possible. If the Italian conditions are unacceptable, I foresee putting the French fleet into short-term action against military and sensitive areas on the Italian coastline." The Italo–French armistice was signed at Villa Incisa in the countryside near Rome on 22 June at 7.35 p.m.'[4]

---

[1] To render stupid, feeble-minded. DL7V.
[2] Figurative: to lose the brilliance of birth, nobility, merit.
[3] PGB.
[4] LDG.

The Fall of the Third Republic, 22 June 1940

Six cens et quinze, vingt, grand Dame[1] mourra,
Et peu après un fort long temps plouvra[2]
Plusieurs pays, Flandres et l'Angleterre
Seront par feu et par fer affligez,
De leurs voisins longuement assiégés
Contraints seront de leur faire la guerre.

Sixain 54

Interpretation

On the twentieth of the 615th month the Republic will die. Shortly afterwards war will rage for a long time. Several countries and especially Flanders and England will endure a rain of metal and flame; besieged by the Germans, they will have to wage war upon them.

History

Taking our starting-point as 1889, if we add 615 months, we come to 20 June 1940.

'*The collapse of the Third Republic*. By the terms of the 22 June armistice, two-thirds of France was occupied by the Germans and the rest submitted to the authority of the Vichy government. Given full powers by Parliament, Pétain installed the *French state*.

The multiplication of fronts and the first setbacks, June 1940–early 1943: Hitler set out to make *Britain* surrender by means of *intensive bombing*. . . . New powers entered the war. . . .'[3]

The two cities that endured the worst ravages of the V1s and V2s were *London* and *Anvers* (England and Flanders).

[1] Grand Dame: Marianne, symbol of the French Republic.
[2] In the sense of troubled waters, agitation, also.
[3] *Third-Form History* (textbook, Editions Dunod).

The Liberation of Italy by the Americans, British and French 1943-44

Milan, Ferrare, Turin et Aquilleye,[1]
Capue, Brundis[2] vexez par gent Celtique,
Par le Lyon et phalange aquilée,[3]
Quand Rome aura le chef vieux Britannique.

CV,Q99

Interpretation

Milan, Ferrara, Turin, Aquilia, Capua and Brindisi will be harassed by the French, the British lion and the army of the eagle [America], when the old British chief [Montgomery] will hold Rome.

History

'Seeing the risk the *American 5th Army* was running, Alexander called on *Montgomery* ["*le vieux chef Britannique*"] to ask him to ensure that he would surprise the attackers on the bridgehead. Some of the 8th Army had quietly landed in the well-equipped ports of Taranto and *Brindisi*. In spite of the evacuation of Naples on 1 October, they pushed on towards Rome via Cassino and Formia. On 22 November the French expeditionary force ["*gent Celtique*"] began disembarking in Italy.'[4]
On 4 June 1944, Allied Armies entered Rome.

[1] Aquilia: southern Italian town.
[2] Brundisium: Brindisi. DLLB.
[3] Latin *aquila*: eagle. DLLB.
[4] LDG.

The French Expeditionary Force Lands in Italy, Winter 1944. Fierce Fighting at Monte Cassino and the Capture of Rome. Disagreements among Allied Commanders

De vaine emprinse[1] l'honneur indue plainte,
Galliots[2] errans[3] par latins, froid, faim, vagues.
Non loing du Tymbre de sang la terre tainte,
Et sur humains seront diverses plagues.[4]

CV,Q63

Interpretation

A vain and futile enterprise undertaken for reasons of honour will be deplored, [landing] craft will make for the Italian coast, [assault] waves will take place in winter, with starvation; the land will be bloodstained near the Tiber and men will be stricken with different wounds.

History

'General Clark kept us informed of the sad reverses of his landing at Salerno. He had been a hair's breadth away from being driven back into the sea by a German armoured corps. He had only held out thanks to *the support fleet* under Admiral Cunningham which fearlessly moved in nearer shore. . . . Next day, 1 October, we were at Pompeii. One could scarcely take risks in rough *wintry* countryside, yet it still cost us 65,000 men. The December 1943 operations had only gained control of the position we called *"Winter"* which covered the main line of resistance, called "Gustav", from which Marshal Kesselring, our opponent in Italy, hoped to stop all Allied progress towards Rome. In early January 1944 Anzio had allowed the French Expeditionary Force to breach the line for themselves. It was to cost numerous *futile* sacrifices [*"indue"*]. The road down to the Rapido, which had to be used for much of the way, was *quite murderous* [*"de sang la terre tainte"*] during the winter campaign. *Massive slaughter* took place there, only in order to force back the Gustav line to the Belvedere. For later operations and the push north, the French Expeditionary Force resumed its normal position *east of the Tiber* [*"non loin du Tymbre"*], in the mountains. At Carpinetto a French officer and his men, who had preferred to be billeted in a castle where they had been preceded by the Germans, were blown up by a booby-trap mine in the middle of the night and nearly all killed [*"diverses plagues"*].[5]

---

[1] For enterprise, by syncope.
[2] *Galliot*: small craft. DAFL.
[3] To voyage, wander. DAFL.
[4] Latin *plaga*: wound, bruise, contusion. DLLB.
[5] LCI.

The Germans in Paris, 1940.
The Attack on the Soviet Union, 22 June 1941.
Allied Troops in Normandy and the Alps, 1944

En la cité où le loup entrera,
Bien près de là les ennemis seront:
Copie[1] estrange grand pays gastera,
Aux murs[2] et Alpes les amis passeront.

CIII,Q33

Interpretation

In the town which the German enters [Paris], the enemies will be very
close; foreign troops will injure a great country [Russia]. By the cliffs
[of Normandy] and the Alps the Allies shall pass.

History

'The French armistice with Germany was signed on 21 June 1940 at
Rethondes, the one with Italy at Rome on 24 June. They came into force
on 25 June. *Marching into Paris* and singing, the *German* troops crossed
a Place de la Concorde empty of vehicles.

The Atlantic *Wall* was not a fiction, nor was it the seamless system of
fortification described by Goebbels. Boulogne, Le Havre and Cherbourg
were strongly fortified; some large forts were built at the port of Calais,
but the rest was often just a sketch or blueprint.'[3]

'The Wehrmacht was then caught between two theatres; at the end of
April, a month after the landing, there were fifty-two divisions in France,
six in Holland, six in Belgium and twenty-four in *Italy* [*the Alps*] as
opposed to 202 in *Russia* ["*grand pays gâtera*"].'[4]

[1] Latin *copia*: troops. DLLB.
[2] Cliffs – defined as vertical natural walls, mostly limestone. DL7V.
[3] *Historama* no. 271: '*Overlord*' by Raymond Cartier.
[4] HLFRA.

After Sicily, the Landing in Calabria, 3 September 1943

Le nouveau faict conduira l'exercite,[1]
Proche apamé[2] jusqu'auprès du rivage:
Tendant secours de Milannoise eslite
Duc yeux[3] privé à Milan fer de cage.

CIX,Q95

Interpretation

A new feat of arms will lead the army near Apameste [in Calabria] right to the shore, despite an attempt at assistance by the military elite of Milan. Then the Duce, deprived of power, will go to Milan in a cage of iron [a lorry].

History

'On 3 September, taking advantage of the covering fire provided by a naval division commanded by Vice-Admiral Willis, British infantry *landed on the Calabrian coast* north-west of Reggio.

Hitler transferred the 24th Panzer Division and the SS Division Leibstandarte to the eastern front. Kesselring allotted three infantry divisions to the 10th Army, and the remnant of the B armies *stationed in northern Italy* [elite of Milan] was made up into a 14th Army commanded by General von Mackenser.'[4]

'At 6 a.m. Geminazza set off again from Dongo where Audisio had directed the execution of the fifteen Fascists arrested at Rocca di Musso. The bodies of Mussolini and Claretta were put into Geminazza's car which drove off in the rain towards the Azzano road. *The removal van* [*"fer de cage"*] was waiting at the crossroads. The two corpses were thrown on top of the fifteen others. On 29 April 1945, early in the morning, the removal van arrived at *Milan* after passing through several American roadblocks. It stopped in front of the concrete shell of a garage under construction on the Piazzale Loreto.'[5]

[1] Latin *exercitus*: army, corps of troops. DLLB.
[2] Latin *Apamestini*: inhabitant of Apameste in *Calabria*. DLLB.
[3] In the sense of 'power', i.e. 'under his master's *eye*'.
[4] LDG.
[5] MCH.

The Liberation of Corsica, September, 1943.
The Italian Request to the Allies for an Armistice at Lisbon, August 1943. The Collapse of the Italian Republic. The Seventy-two Deaths during the Liberation of Corsica

Arrivera au port de Corsibonne,[1]
Près de Ravenne qui pillera la dame[2]
En mer profonde légat de la Vlisbonne,[3]
Sous roc cachez raviront septante ames.[4]

CIX,Q54

Interpretation

[Germany] will arrive at the port of Bonifacio in Corsica, during which time the [Italian] Republic will be laid waste near Ravenna. The emissary sent to Lisbon will founder. Those who will be hidden in the mountains will kill seventy men.

History

'The question of the Italians was thus settled, but there remained 10,000 Germans on the island, not counting those who when evacuating Sardinia reached *Corsica* through the Straits of *Bonifacio* so as to disembark from Bastia. On the eastern side, the Germans held *Bonifacio* and Porto Vecchio in the south, Ghisonnaccia in the centre, the airfield of Borgo and Bastia in the north. The first elements of the 90th Panzer Division *landed at Bonifacio*, coming from Sardinia. But how were the Allies to attack Bastia? By way of the mountains – during the night, the French advanced painfully across *rocks* and bushes. At dawn, while approaching the summit of the Secco, the French 47th Arab Unit fell into an ambush. In a few minutes it lost twenty-five NCOs and enlisted men. . . . So in twenty-seven days Corsica was liberated by the French. General Henry Martin executed his mission with minimum loss: *seventy-two killed* and 220 wounded. Far from the bloodbath some had claimed!'[5]

'Even when the Germans managed to regroup north of Florence and dig in for the winter on the Gothic Line between Rimini [40 km north of Ravenna] and La Spezia, the violence continued at almost the same level behind the front.'[6]

'On 17 July 1943 Bastiani tried an approach to the Vatican and received a favourable reception from Cardinal Maglione. The two men decided to send *an envoy to Lisbon* to contact the Allies. This man, a banker named

Fummi, granted special authority to speak for the Holy See, had to reach London via *Lisbon*. Unfortunately he waited some days in the Portuguese capital for his British visa, and the events in Rome *rendered his mission pointless [*"en mer profonde"*].*[7]

[1] Word coined by Nostradamus from Corsica and Bonifacio for rhyming purposes.
[2] Consistently used to denote Republic.
[3] Prothesis: letter *v* as prefix to Lisbon.
[4] Nostradamus can be allowed an approximation here: two persons too few dead!
[5] A. Goutard: *The Liberation of Corsica* (Historama).
[6] MCH.
[7] MAB.

The Fight against Germany and Italy.
Their Economic Ruin. The Ruin of the French State
and the Third Reich. The Teheran Conference.
The United Nations

Deux assiegez en ardante[1] fureur,
De soif[2] estaincts[3] pour deux plaines[4] tasses,[5]
Le fort limé,[6] et un vieillard resveur,
Aux genevoix de Nira[7] monstre trasse.

CIV,Q59

Interpretation

Two beleaguered [countries: Germany and Italy] will be drained, because of their violent rage, both will have empty pockets [economic ruin]. The stronger [Germany] will be gnawed, as will the aged dreamer [Pétain]. At Geneva the repercussions [of the Treaty] of Teheran.

History

'On 27 November 1943 the American President, the British Prime Minister and their entourage flew at dawn to *Teheran* where the Eureka Conference was to be held. The Conference's first session opened in a room of the Soviet Embassy on 28 November, at 4.30 p.m. A little earlier Stalin had privately met Roosevelt who told him his views on world reorganization. As regards the alteration of the map and institution of *a new international order*, discussions between Churchill, Stalin and Roosevelt were not so finely balanced for the very simple reason that the

British Prime Minister and the President of the USA ratified every whim of their Soviet ally. At his request, Roosevelt was allowed to set out his ideas about future world organization which, with peace restored, would carry on from *the former League of Nations*. It would be wrong to dissociate Teheran from Yalta and Potsdam.'[8]

'The Yalta Conference [4–11 February 1945] set out the basis for the future United Nations Organization."[9]

[1] Latin *ardeus*: violent. DLLB.
[2] Burning desire. DL7V.
[3] Latin *extinguo*: I drain, exhaust. DLLB.
[4] From *planus*: flat. DAFL.
[5] Pocket. DAFL.
[6] Gnaw, upset. DAFL.
[7] Anagram of IRAN.
[8] LDG.
[9] VCAHU.

The Normandy Landings, 6 June 1944

Quand le poisson terrestre et aquatique[1]
Par force vague au gravier[2] sera mis.
Sa forme[3] estrange suave et horrifique,
Par mer aux murs[4] bien tost les ennemis.

CI,Q29

Interpretation

When the amphibious contrivances, through the number of their waves of attacks, will land on the beach, their composition of strangers will be pleasing [to the French] and terrifying [to the Germans] and will soon strike the enemy, from the sea up to the cliffs.

History

'The defenders saw surging out of the sea, half-immersed, shapeless monsters which seemed to rear up: *amphibious* tanks! Rustling, they advanced across the *sand*. A second *wave* of tanks followed the first.'[5]

'On the beach at Ouistreham a monument commemorates the first landing of *Allied* troops on French soil. It bears the following inscription: On this beach, at dawn on 6 June 1944, Field-Marshal Montgomery's troops and Captain Kieffer's French commandos first set foot on French soil." [6]

'Part of the vanguard of the 5th *American* Army Corps [*estrange*] landed on Omaha Beach with the objective of crossing Grandcamp. The Pointe du Hoc is a salient of *chalky cliffs* that go right up to the sea, about 7 km east of Vierville. These cliffs are 30 m high, and sheer. Below is a shingle *beach* 20 m wide.' [7]

[1] Amphibian: something that lives and grows on both land and water. DL7V.
[2] Beach, shore. DAFL.
[3] Synonym: formation, configuration. DL7V.
[4] Cliffs. Cf. note 2 for CIII,Q33.
[5] *Histoire Pour Tous*, no. 7 (July–August 1978).
[6] HLFRA.
[7] *Histoire Pour Tous*, no. 7 (July–August 1978).

The Landing in Provence, August 1944.
Protests about the War, at Monaco

Au peuple ingrat[1] faictes les remonstrances,
Par lors l'armée se saisira d'Antibe:
Dans l'arc Monech[2] feront les doléances,[3]
Et à Frejus l'un l'autre prendra ribe.[4]

CX,Q23

Interpretation

Remonstrations will be made by the discontented people when the army seizes Antibes. Complaints will be heard at Monaco and at Fréjus one will occupy the shore the other [the German] used to hold.

History

'On the night of 10 August 1944 the concentration of the landing units began. The problem was how to make 2000 ships converge off the Provençal coast – the largest armada the Mediterranean had ever borne. In a speech General de Lattre hid neither the emotion the terrain inspired nor the problems it would pose: "It is a question of France, fighting in France, liberating France. I must *put you on your guard* ["*remonstrances*"] against your own sentiments. Justly proud of your efforts and the sacrifices of too many of your comrades, you might rest on your laurels."

Next day, 16 August, the commanders landed. Admiral Hewitt's account of the first *grounding* is as follows: "When we reached the beach ['*ribe*'], General Patch and myself held back to allow Admiral Lemonnier to take the first step on to his native soil."

On the coast, the French resistance consisted of 3000 men of the Lécuyer group, which fought mainly between Nice and Antibes."[5]

'The concern for humanitarian actions was manifested by Albert I of *Monaco*, who founded the International Peace Institute in 1903. Thereafter Monegasque initiatives were tireless, spurred by the organization of international conferences (for example, that of 1934)."[6]

[1] Latin *ingratus*: discontent. DLLB.
[2] Latin *Monoeci arx*, fortress of the port of Monacus in Liguria, or Monaco.
[3] Piteous cries. DL7V.
[4] Provençal *rivo*, from Latin *riva* (riverside, bank, shoreline). DP.
[5] HLFRA.
[6] EU.

The Retreat of Communism, 1942.
The Abduction of Pétain, 20 August 1944

Es lieux et temps chair au poisson donra lieu[1]
La loi commune sera faite au contraire,[2]
Vieux tiendra fort puis osté du milieu,
Le Pantacoina Philon[3] mis fort en arrière.[4]

CIV,Q32

Interpretation

In these times and places, there will be wavering between two opposed parties, out of weakness; democratic laws will be opposed. The old [Marshal] will hold power, then will be taken away from the place [Vichy], communism being strongly repulsed.

History

'On 20 June 1940 Pétain met the ministers he had summoned to the Council that afternoon: there were two – the others were packing their bags, for the members of the government were due to embark from Port-Vendres. The men who had gone round in circles at Bordeaux *without being able to take a decision* were parliamentarians and there had been over 300 of them at Bordeaux. Not wanting to continue the fight was also to become a vexed issue later. What was to be done?

It was agreed that there should be a plan *different* from Laval's: *suspension of the constitutional powers of 1875*, until the peace was established, full powers to Pétain, more power over the state than Louis XIV. The state was himself and in fact *there was no longer any Parliament* capable of remonstrating against, or ratifying, what he did.'[5]

'On 20 August 1944 Pétain was taken away by the Germans and driven under military escort to Sigmaringen, without any opportunity to attempt an escape.'[6]

'*Soviet resistance routed*: in the north of the Pripet marshes Soviet resistance had been surprised and *overthrown* almost everywhere, as were the reinforcements coming forward to the front. The situation had *rapidly altered* ["*fort en arrière*"] between the Black Sea and the Baltic and not to the defence's advantage. Some days later the Soviet government and central administration left Moscow to establish itself at Kulbychev on the left bank of the Volga.'[7]

---

[1] One does not know whether it's fish or fowl. Said of a vacillator between two opposites. DL7V.

[2] To do the contrary, to oppose. DL7V.

[3] Greek πάντα ἀοίγα φίλων: Everything held in common between friends.

[4] Ablative absolute.

[5] PGB.

[6] HLFRA.

[7] LDG.

Pétain's Treason, 20 August 1944

Le vieux mocqué et privé de sa place
Par l'estranger qui le subornera[1]
Mains[2] de son fils mangées devant sa face
Les frères à Chartres, Orléans, Rouen, trahira.

CIV,Q61

Interpretation

The old [Marshal] will be mocked and relieved of his post by the enemy, who will drive him to a bad action, the power he has created destroyed before his eyes, when the brothers in arms [the Allies] are at Chartres, Orleans and Rouen, he will betray.

History

'The British 2nd Army reached the Seine south of *Rouen*. The American 3rd Army thrust towards Paris: starting from Alençon and Le Mans it reached in the south *Chartres* and Rambouillet, the final stepping-stones. On 15 and 16 August, according to plan, the 3rd Army entered *Orleans and Chartres*.

On 20 August Pétain was *taken away* by the *Germans* and driven under military escort to Sigmaringen, without any opportunity to attempt an escape.

The Marshal's enthusiastic welcome on his final visits to French cities [Paris, 26 April 1944, and St Etienne, 6 June 1944, in particular] showed his personal prestige undiminished despite *the failure of his policies*. But this high percentage of supporters *no longer constituted a political force* in 1944. All Laval's and Pétain's attempts to perpetuate the Vichy government ended in sheer fantasy.'[3]

'On 12 August 1945 the prosecutor, Mornet, made his speech. For four years, he said, to the actual day, France had been the victim of an equivocation which for want of a better word *was known as treason*.'[4]

[1] Latin *subornare*: win over, persuade, or secretly charge to do an evil or wicked action. DLLB.
[2] Latin *manus*: authority, strength, power. DLLB.
[3] HLFRA.
[4] PGB.

The Occupation Zone from Rouen to Bordeaux. The Atlantic Wall. The Liberation. Rouen, 1944

Bordeaux, Rouen et La Rochelle joincts,
Tiendront autour la grand mer Occéane,
Anglois Bretons et les Flaments conjoincts,
Les chasseront jusqu'auprès de Rouane.

CIII,Q9

Interpretation

Bordeaux, Rouen and La Rochelle reunited [in the Occupation] will hold the French ocean coast [the Atlantic Wall], the Anglo-Americans, French and Belgians will push them back as far as Rouen.

The Fall of the French State, 1944.
Pétain's Departure for Sigmaringen.
Pétain at the Ile d'Yeu, 1945

Le vieux monarque déchassé de son règne
Aux Orients son secours ira querre:[1]
Pour peur des croix ployera son enseigne
En Mitylène[2] ira par port[3] et par terre.

CIII,Q47

Interpretation

The old head of state chased from power will go to seek help from the
east [Sigmaringen]: through fear of the [crooked] crosses [i.e. swastikas]
he will fold up his flag and end via port [Joinville] and by land, on the
Island of Mussels [Yeu].

History

'Baron von Neubronn *threatened* that if the Marshal refused to comply,
the *Germans* would bombard Vichy. "I haven't the right to let the women
and children of Vichy be bombed," said Pétain. "I must give in, faced
with such threats."

On 16 November 1945 Pétain was looking obstinately towards the *Ile
d'Yeu*, which was to be his prison. The landing at Port-Joinville was not
going to be easy. Pétain had been transferred from the fort of *Port*alet
on 15 August, immediately after his sentence.'[4]

---

[1] Latin *quaero*: I seek. DLLB. From which comes *quérir*.
[2] Latin *mitylus*: mussel, shellfish. DLLB. The main activity of the island of Yeu is
mussel-gathering.
[3] Nostradamus suggests either Portalet or Port-Joinville for Pétain's landing.
[4] PGB.

Mussolini's Birth between Rimini and Prato, 1883. Left-wing Opposition at Monte Aventino, 1924. The End of Mussolini and Fascism, Piazza Colonna, 1943. The Assassination of Fascists and of their Assassins, 1945

> Du haut de mont Aventin[1] voix ouye,
> Vuidez, vuidez de tous les deux costez:
> Du sang des rouges sera l'ire assomie,[2]
> D'Arimin,[3] Prato,[4] Columna[5] debotez.[6]
>
> CIX,Q2

Interpretation

Those who retreat upon Monte Aventino will make their voices heard; from two sides all will be annihilated; the anger of the reds will be swelled by the blood of the reds. He who originated from Rimini and Prato and those of the Piazza Colonna will be expelled.

History

'Mussolini's autobiography: "I was born on 29 July 1883 at Varnano dei Costa, near the village of Dovia, itself near that of Predappio." '[7]

'On 10 June 1924, the *Socialist* deputy Matteoti was kidnapped in Rome by a Fascist group. His body was recovered on 16 August from some waste land about 20 km from the town. In protest, the *opposition* deputies left the Chamber and *withdrew to Aventino*. . . .

After vainly awaiting a message from Mussolini, Scorza desperately went back to party headquarters on Piazza *Colonna* where he ordered the mobilization of all Fascists in Rome – there were not even fifty Fascists to answer his call. The crowd began invading the homes of the main party militants and burned the offices of various Fascist organizations. A band of demonstrators rushed into the Venetian Palace to lay hands on their country's oppressor for twenty years, but nobody could force the gate and they left waving *red* flags. On the Piazza *Colonna* and elsewhere the crowd sang and danced with joy, crying "Fascism is dead!" '[8]

'On 27 April 1945 the main resistance leaders met in Milan, notably Longo, the fanatical Communist, and Walter Audisio, an ex-volunteer from the International Brigade in Spain. The order for Mussolini's execution had already been given by Togliatti, acting head of the Communist party. Moretti and Cavali were fervent Communists. Less than ten minutes after Bellini's departure Audisio, Lampredi and Moretti hurriedly left Dongo. Their respective fates are interesting. Michele Moretti was supposed to have died, according to some authors. Frangi talked after the death of Mussolini and died under strange circumstances. Luigi Cavali disappeared. His mistress Giuseppina Tuissi resigned herself to his disappearance, and in her turn disappeared. Her friend Anna Bianchi, distressed by this, was found floating in Lake Como: she had been beaten to death. Anna's father swore to find and kill her murderers, but he too was murdered.'[9]

'The first shot fired by Audisio from Moretti's gun killed Claretta. The next hit Mussolini. Six hours later Germi again left Dongo, where Audisio had led the execution of the fifteen Fascists arrested at Rocca di Musso. The removal van was waiting at the crossroads. The two corpses were thrown on top of the fifteen others.'[10]

[1] Retreat or withdrawal to Monte Aventino: vexed by Patrician tyranny, the Plebeians emigrated en masse to the Monte Aventino. This historical episode gave rise to the expression 'withdrawing to Aventino', i.e. severing all relations abruptly until satisfaction is obtained.

[2] Fill up, overload. DAFL.

[3] Latin *Ariminum*: Rimini, town in Umbria. DLLB.

[4] Prato: Tuscan town. Predappio and Prato are quite near one another.

[5] Latin for Italian *colonna*: column. NB capital C.

[6] To expel. DAFL.

[7] MCH.

[8] HISR.

[9] MCH.

[10] HISR.

Mussolini and Cardinal Schuster, 1945. Executions at Piazzale Loreto in Milan

Roy trouvera ce qu'il désiroit tant,
Quand le Prelat sera reprins[1] à tort,
Response au Duc le rendra mal content,
Qui dans Milan mettra plusieurs à mort.

CVI,Q31

Interpretation

The leader will find the one he so wants [arresting Mussolini] when the Cardinal will be wrongly blamed for his answer, with which the Duce will be displeased; and several will be put to death in Milan.

History

'On 13 March 1945 Mussolini's son Vittorio took to *Cardinal* Schuster, Archbishop of *Milan*, a letter requesting certain guarantees for the civilian population in case the Germans evacuated Italy and the Fascist forces took up positions in the Alps. Cardinal Schuster thought this gesture quite futile but transmitted the message to the Allies via the Papal Nuncio at Berne. As soon as it reached general headquarters at Caserta the Allies *answered* it with a dismissal assuming that the Germans had already accepted such a capitulation, but Mussolini refused to take into consideration the Allies' demands.'[2]

'Valerio stopped at Milan in the Piazzale Loreto, the same spot where on 9 August 1944 the Germans had taken reprisals and shot fifteen Italian political prisoners. The dead bodies had been dumped there. At 11 a.m. six corpses were strung up by ropes in the forecourt of a filling station, among them Mussolini and Clara Petacci. Shortly afterwards the former secretary of the party, Achille Starace, was shot in the back there by six partisans and strung up alongside the other dangling corpses.'[3]

[1] To blame. DL7V.
[2] HCH.
[3] MAB.

Massacres at Milan and Florence.
The Duce at Milan, His Capital, 19 April 1945.
The Fall of Fascism in Rome in the Piazza Colonna,
September 1944

> Pleure Milan, pleure Lucques, Florence,
> Que ton grand Duc sur le char[1] montera:
> Changer le Siege pres de Venise s'advance,
> Lorsque Colonne a Rome changera.

> CX,Q64

Interpretation

There will be tears at Milan, Lucca, Florence, because your great Duce will leave by van. The seat of government will change when there is an advance near the Venice [Palace], when there will be a change at the Piazza Colonna.

History

'The *brigate nere* [Fascist blackshirts] did not take reprisals as frequently as the Germans, but they were often no less savage. It was the SS, for instance, who executed almost 700 people at Marzabotto.[2] The Fascist groups contained a criminal element far more dangerous than the least disciplined partisans. Even when the Germans managed to regroup north of *Florence* and winter along the Gothic Line between Rimini and Spezia[3] the atrocities continued at almost the same level behind the front.

On 16 April 1945 he had confided to Mellini: "Now Rome is lost, the Italian Republic can have only *one capital, Milan*." He prepared to leave for Milan on the tenth, escorted by German soldiers. His headquarters was the Monforte Palace, the Milan police department. . . .

Demonstrators rushed into the *Venice* Palace to lay hold of the country's oppressor for twenty years. On the *Piazza Colonna*, the party meeting-place, the crowd sang and danced as if at a carnival: "Fascism is dead!" That night in *Rome*, you would have supported Mussolini only at risk of life and limb. . . .

On 29 April 1945 the removal van reached *Milan* after negotiating several American road blocks. It stopped on the Piazzale Loreto. The bodies were hurled off the truck and a passer-by took the trouble to range them up neatly; he placed Mussolini a little apart. Then two young men appeared who proceeded to kick the body violently in the face. An authoritative voice yelled: "String them up!" '[4]

[1] Four-wheeled vehicle. DL7V.
[2] Village north of Florence.
[3] Line passing through Lucca and Florence.
[4] MCH.

The Fall of the Reich, 1945. The Soviet Counter-offensive. Landings in Sicily, 10 July 1943

> Le neuf empire en desolation
> Sera changé du pôle aquilonnaire[1]
> De la Sicile viendra l'émotion[2]
> Troubler l'emprise[3] à Philip tributaire.

CVIII,Q81

Extract from MAB

Interpretation

The new [German] empire will be in desolation and undergo changes because of the north [USSR]. From Sicily they [Germans] will be chased and Philip's [Pétain's] enterprise of paying tribute will be disturbed.

History

'For the two years following the invasion of *Russia* Hitler was almost entirely absorbed by the progress of the war on the Eastern Front. But in 1943 the loss of North Africa and collapse of *Italy* reminded him that he was at war with a world alliance.

On 30 April 1945 Goebbels and Bormann tried vainly to negotiate with the *Russians*. The answer was: "Unconditional *surrender*." '[4]

'German demands: the victors disposed of millions of prisoners and Vichy France, virtually blackmailed, had already *paid* 631,886 million francs for the occupying forces. . . .

The Allied attack then took shape. In July 1943, Operation Husky gave them *Sicily* and 200,000 prisoners.'[5]

¹ Aquilon: violent and impetuous north wind. DL7V. Symbol of the Russian Empire of the North.
² Latin *emoveo*: I take away, disperse, chase. DLLB.
³ i.e. *entreprise* = enterprise. DL7V.
⁴ HAB.
⁵ LMC.

The Nuremberg Trials, 1945–46.
The Cold War

Des condamnez sera fait un grand nombre,
Quand les monarques seront conciliez:
Mais l'un d'eux viendra si mal encombre¹
Que guerre ensemble ne seront raliez.

CII,Q38

Interpretation

There will be a great number of condemned persons when the heads of state are reconciled. But one of them will make so many difficulties that those who waged war together will not be allies.

History

'On 20 November 1945 the first hearing of the International Military Tribunal at Nuremberg took place, to try German leaders considered to be war criminals. Composed of representatives from the four *Allied* powers [USA, USSR, Great Britain and France], it was to judge twenty-four major political, economic and military leaders of Hitler's Germany and six groups and organizations of the Third Reich. The hearings went on until 1 October 1946. *Numerous* other trials of less notorious war criminals took place in Germany.

The *condemned men* were executed on 16 October 1946 between 1 and 3 a.m.; those sentenced to prison terms were interned at Spandau Prison near Berlin. . . .

On 2 February 1953, in his first speech on the State of the Union, Eisenhower announced that he had settled the neutrality of Formosa; he also envisaged denouncing the Yalta agreement concluded by Roosevelt. The American attitude aroused much anxiety.'²

¹ *Encombrier*: obstacle, embarrassment, damage. DAFL.
² VCAHU.

Franco-German Friendship after the 1870, 1914 and 1939 Wars. Milestones of This Friendship: 1950, 1962, 1963 and 1967

Las quelle fureur! hélas quelle pitié,
Il y aura entre beaucoup de gens:
On ne vit onc une telle amitié,
Qu'auront les loups à courir diligens.[1]

CVIII,Q3a

Interpretation

Alas, what savagery and pity there will be between many people! Never will one see such a friendship as the Germans will make.

History

'Adenauer proposed to France a *Franco-German union* with a single parliament, one economy and a common nationality. . . .
   During 4–12 August 1962 General de Gaulle made an official visit to West Germany. It was a triumph: he won the hearts of a people which despite economic recovery was seared by the guilt complex of 1945. . . .
   The Franco–German treaty, foreseeing periodic summit consultations and cooperation in areas of defence, the economy and the arts, was signed on 22 January 1963. . . .
   On 12 and 13 July 1967 de Gaulle and Kiesinger met at Bonn and decided to set up two joint commissions, one for economic, the other for political, cooperation.'[2]

[1] Latin *diligens*: attached to, liking. DLLB.
[2] VCAHU.

The Return of the Jews to Palestine, 1939–48. The Arab–Israeli Wars

Nouveaux venus lieu basty sans défence,
Occuper la place par lors inhabitable,
Prez, maisons, champs, villes, prendre à plaisance[1]
Faim, peste, guerre, arpen long labourable.

CII,Q19

Interpretation

Newcomers will build towns without defence and occupy hitherto un-inhabitable places. They will take with pleasure fields, houses, land and towns. Then famine, sickness and war will be on this land tilled for a long time [since 1939].

History

'When the Second World War broke out the Jewish population of Israel had risen from 85,000 [11 per cent of the total] to 416,000 [29 per cent], the number of Jewish *settlements* from 79 to 200. *Agriculture* was developing considerably; the area of orange groves had increased from 1000 to 15,000 *hectares*.

Apart from an Arab minority of about 10 per cent, almost all the population was composed of Jewish *immigrants* who had been there less than a century. . . .

Whatever the immediate causes of the June 1967 *war*, it had a profound effect on the psychology of both Arabs and Israelis.'[2]

This quatrain of Nostradamus should be compared to the Book of Ezekiel: 'After many days thou shalt be visited; in the latter years thou shalt come into the land that is brought back from the sword, and is *gathered out of many people*, against the mountains of Israel, which have been always *waste*: but it is brought forth out of the nations, and *they shall dwell safely* all of them. And thou shalt say, I will go up to the land of *unwalled villages* [kibbutzes] I will go to them that are at rest . . . to place thine hand upon the desolate places that are now inhabited.'[3]

[1] Pleasure, joy. DL7V.
[2] EU.
[3] Ezekiel, 38: 8, 11 and 12. AV.

The Hungarian Rising at Budapest, 23 October 1956.
Crushed by Soviet Troops, 4 November 1956

Par vie et mort changé regne d'Ongrie,
La loy sera plus aspre que service:[1]
Leur grand cité d'urlements pleincts et crie,
Castor et polux[2] ennemis dans la lice.[3]

CII,Q90

Interpretation

Power will be changed by life and death in Hungary; the law will be more pitiless than customs. The great town [Budapest] will be filled with screams and cries. Brothers will be enemies in this theatre of struggle [the capital].

History

'In Hungary rebellion broke out in *Budapest* on 23 October 1956 and gathered momentum so fast that even the return of Imre Nagy [Castor] did not calm things down. Under pressure from Nagy, who had formed a coalition government, it was announced on 1 November that Hungary was leaving the Warsaw Pact and requested the UN formally to recognize her neutral status. The very next day Budapest was completely surrounded ["*lice*"] by Soviet tanks, which went into action on the fourth while a puppet government, loyal to Moscow, was formed by Janos Kadar [Pollux]. There was further fighting in Budapest where the rebels, despite fierce resistance, were quickly crushed. The number of deaths throughout the uprising exceeded 25,000. Imre Nagy, who had sought shelter in the Yugoslav embassy, was taken away by police and deported to Romania. More than 15,000 people were deported by the Russians, and another 150,000 managed to get to the West ["*lieu changé*"]. Budapest showed that to seek different versions of socialism only meant, to the Kremlin, a break of the ties ["*loi*"] imposed on eastern European countries since 1945. Continuing agitation obliged the Kadar government to proclaim *martial law* on 8 December; all the revolutionary workers' councils were dissolved.'[4]

[1] Usage, utility, derived from certain things. DL7V.
[2] Two brothers, sons of Jupiter.
[3] Lists: enclosed field for jousting and by extension the scene of some struggle or combat. DL7V.
[4] VCAHU.

The Conquest of North Africa by the Third Republic, 1881–1911. The Fall of the Fourth Republic, 13 May 1958

Barbare empire[1] par le tiers[2] usurpé,[3]
La plus grand part de son sang mettra à mort:
Par mort sénile par luy le quart[4] frappé,
Pour peur que sang par le sang[5] ne soit mort.

CIII,Q59

Interpretation

The Third [Republic] will appropriate the Barbarian Empire and put to death most of its inhabitants. Because of senility the Fourth [Republic] will be beaten to death by it [the Barbarian Empire] for fear that those who have shed their blood might die in vain.

History

'Africa was the main area of French colonial expansion. Since the July monarchy *France* had *possessed Algeria*, but Algeria is only the central part of the Atlas mountains, which continue eastwards through Tunisia and west through Morocco. The *three countries* are so closely bound that one can only be complete master of Algeria by *dominating* the two neighbouring countries. This explains the importance of the Tunisian question, then that of Morocco, in French policy. The incessant *raids* carried out upon Algerian territory by the Tunisian mountain fighters, the Kroumirs, were a pretext for a French army to enter Tunisia in 1881. Tunisia seemed subdued and the troops were recalled. There was an immediate general uprising centred on Kairouan, one of the Moslem holy villages. Repression was swift. . . .

The Act of Algeciras could not definitively settle the Moroccan question. There were new incidents from 1907. The French were massacred by the natives and France *occupied* Casablanca [1907–08]. In 1911 French troops penetrated as far as Fez. . . .

Algeria, Tunisia and Morocco, henceforth closely united, formed a new France in Africa. . . .

The Algerian crisis worsened because Guy Mollet, faced with the hostility of the French in Algeria, renounced on 5 February 1956 the reforms he had promised, and because the President of Council approved a misguided initiative by an irresponsible officer who at Algiers took it upon himself to try to ground the *Moroccan* aircraft carrying the FLN chiefs. This futile act involved the French with the King of *Morocco* and with *Tunisia*. Mollet was defeated on 21 May 1957, but his successor Félix Gaillard did no better, and the French Republic had proved its *ineffectiveness. . . . Instability* and *weakness* led to impotence. . . . General de Gaulle accepted investiture and on 1 June 1958 he obtained full powers. The Fourth Republic lived.'[7]

[1] Barbary: Barbary States, region of North Africa consisting of the states of Tripoli, Tunis, Algiers and Morocco. DHB.
[2] Third in line, succeeding two others. DL7V.
[3] Latin *usurpo*: I pretend to, appropriate for myself. DLLB.
[4] For *'quatrième'*, fourth. DL7V.
[5] *Sanguine barbarorum modico* (Tacitus): the barbarians having lost few men. DLLB.
[6] HFAM.
[7] LMC.

The Six Days' War, 5–10 June 1967.
The Occupation by Israel of Gaza, Transjordan and the Golan Heights

Nouvelle loy terre neuve occuper,
Vers la Syrie, Iudée et Palestine:
Le grand Empire barbare corruer,[1]
Avant que Phebes[2] son siècle détermine.

CIII,Q97

Interpretation

By a new law new territories will be occupied, towards Syria, Jordan and Palestine. Arab power will crumble before the Summer Solstice [21 June].

History

'Arab–Israeli War, 5–10 June 1967: in a campaign directed against Egypt, Jordan and Syria, Israeli armies *occupied* the whole of the Sinai Peninsula[3] as far as the Suez Canal, Transjordan[4] and the Golan Heights.[5]

At dawn on the fifth, Israeli planes attacked Egyptian airports and wiped out most of her aircraft. The Egyptian army was in *disarray* [*"corruer"*] from the first few hours of the fighting; masters of *Gaza* and El-Arich, the Israelis struck across the Sinai Desert, and from the seventh occupied the port of Sharm-el-Sheikh and reached the Suez Canal. On the Jordanian side they encountered more resistance, but the old town of Jerusalem and all the *Transjordanian* part [Judea] of Jordan were *conquered*. *The Arab world* was overwhelmed by the scope and speed of the Israeli successes. The USSR accused Israel of aggression and at her request the General Assembly of the United Nations met on the nineteenth ["*avant que Phebes*"]. The main problem now was that of the occupied Arab territories. On the eleventh General Dayan declared that Israel would keep Gaza, Sharm-el-Sheikh, the Old City of Jerusalem and Transjordan. The Israelis maintained that it was no longer a question of returning to the pre-5 June frontiers, since it was a question not of frontiers but of demarcation lines traced by the 1949 armistices, and never *legally* ["*nouvelle loy*"] recognized by the Arab states. On 27 June the Knesset adopted a "fundamental law" for the protection of the holy places. The government decided to annexe the Old City of Jerusalem."[6]

[1] Latin *corruer*: to fall, collapse. DLLB.
[2] Phoebus: the sun. DLLB.
[3] Including the town of Gaza, in south *Palestine*. EU.
[4] Judea: southern area of *Palestine*, situated between the Dead Sea and the Mediterranean, the greatest part of which today constitutes the southern part of *Transjordan*, the territory Israel seized from Jordan in the Six Days' War of 1967. AE.
[5] Syrian territory.
[6] VCHAU.

The Return of the Jews to Palestine, 1948. Golda Meir and Zionism. The Resignation of Golda Meir, 1974

> La Synagogue[1] stérile sans nul fruit,
> Sera receuë entre les infidèles:[2]
> De Babylon[3] la fille[4] du poursuit,
> Misère et triste, lui tranchera les aisles.

CVIII,Q96

Interpretation

Sterile Zionism,[5] with no fruit, will be received among the Arabs. Come from New York [Babylone] the woman [leader] of the pursued ones [Golda Meir] will lose power through ill-luck and sadness.

History

'Golda Meir: born Kiev (Ukraine), emigrated to the USA with her family in 1906. She made a name for herself as a militant, responsible for the local section of the Zionist Labour Party. In 1924 she rejoined the Histadrut and in 1928 was named secretary of its female organization. In the course of the Second World War she was active alongside Ben Gurion to assure *the return of the Jews* to Zion. In 1946 when Moshe Sharett, head of the political department of the Jewish Agency, was arrested by the British with other activists, she [*"la fille du poursuite"*] replaced him temporarily and fought to get interned activists and immigrant Jews released. Shortly before Ben Gurion proclaimed the creation of the State of Israel she was sent to the UN to make a final plea for the recognition of a *Jewish State of Palestine*. In October 1973 Israel had to face a murderous war with Egyptian and Syrian forces, assisted by various contingents from other Arab states. Golda Meir's government *underwent attack* from the Israeli right wing and criticisms from leading military figures because the country was unprepared. The elections of 31 December were soon to return Golda Meir and her party to power. In March 1974 *the criticisms* of Golda Meir and General Dayan became stronger and the Israeli Prime Minister had to hand in her *resignation* a month later. [*"misère et triste"*].'[6]

NB. Nostradamus establishes a parallel between the first return of the Jews, in captivity in Babylon, and the second, from the modern Babylons: London, Paris and New York.

---

[1] The synagogue seems to have originated with the Jews exiled in Babylon, when far from the Temple and needing to worship together. On their return from exile the first synagogue was built in Jerusalem in the precincts of the Temple. DL7V.

[2] Those not of the true faith. DL7V. The Arabs here as opposed to the Jews.

[3] The great Babylon, the modern Babylon: denotes contemporary big cities such as London, Paris etc. DL7V.

[4] Poetic/symbolic terms: i.e. women of Israel = Daughters of Zion, etc. DL7V.

[5] Politico-religious movement founded by Theodor Herzl at the end of the nineteenth century with the aim of reuniting in Palestine and in their own state Jews dispersed throughout the world. AE.

[6] EU.

The Yom Kippur War, October 1973.
The Surprise Attack by Egypt upon Israel

Celuy qui a les hazards surmonté,
Qui fer, feu, eau, n'a jamais redouté,
Et du pays bien proche du Basacle,[1]
D'un coup de fer tout le monde estouné,
Par Crocodil[2] estrangement donné,
Peuple ravi de voir un tel spectacle.

Sixain 31

Interpretation

The race which has overcome hazards, which has never feared war or revolution, in the country very close to Christianity's point of departure, will be astonished by an act strangely committed by Egypt whose population will rejoice at such a spectacle.

History

'On 6 October 1973 at 1.50 p.m. the Council of Ministers was busy ratifying the decisions taken by Golda Meir, Dayan and Eleazar that morning, when General Lior opened the door to announce that the enemy had just attacked. *The surprise was thus total*: simultaneous attack by the *Egyptians* in the south and Syrians in the north. Five Egyptian divisions, Soviet-trained and -equipped, overcame the forts of the Bar-Lev Line and under missile cover struck 5–10 km deep into Sinai. The Israeli tanks were decimated by the missiles [with their 3 km range], whose extensive use by the Egyptians called into question, at a stroke, the whole art of modern warfare. Were tanks in fact superior to infantry? *1200 Egyptian tanks were used in the attack*.'[3]

'The Rais talked of Egypt, a peaceful society for thousands of years, forced to war, by injustice and occupation. He added: "If we were not good fighters it was because we had never liked fighting. This time was different. We had a humiliation to avenge." '[4]

---

[1] Receptacle used to keep live fish in. DL7V. For the early Christians the fish was their private symbol par excellence. DL7V.

[2] The oldest species known is the Nile variety, which the ancient *Egyptians* worshipped. DL7V.

[3] *L'Express* (13–19 January 1975). *Israel la mort en face:* J. Derogy and J. N. Gurgand (Laffont).

[4] *Le Point*, no. 60 (12 November 1973).

The Yom Kippur War, 6 October 1973.
The Egyptians' Surprise Attack

Dame par mort grandement attristée,
Mère et tutrice au sang qui l'a quittée,
Dame et seigneurs, faicts enfants orphelins,
Par les aspics[1] et par les Crocodiles,
Seront surpris forts, Bourgs, Chasteaux, Villes,
Dieu tout-puissant les garde des malins.

Sixain 35

Interpretation

The lady [Golda Meir] will be greatly saddened by the death [of Israeli soldiers]; the mother and teacher [of the Jewish state] will abandon power because of the bloodshed. With her ministers she will be responsible for the orphans; because of the Egyptians who will attack the fortifications [the Bar-Lev Line] by surprise, also villages and towns. May God Almighty protect them from harm.

History

'On 6 October Israel was in the synagogues for Yom Kippur. At noon, sirens sounded. Israel had been simultaneously attacked north and south by Syria and Egypt. During the first few hours the Golan lines were over-run and Syrian tanks almost reached Galilee, while on the Suez Canal 3000 soldiers had to hold *tens of thousands of Egyptians* [asps and crocodiles]. Far from congratulating themselves, the Israelis wondered: "How was the carelessness of Yom Kippur possible?" Some added with black humour: "We were lucky the Arabs attacked on the Day of Atonement. *God could not refuse us a miracle*" [*"Dieu tout-puissant les garde des malins"*].

The government scornfully rejected repeated warnings from the Pentagon's secret services. A major-general slept behind the *Bar-Lev Line* just as the French in 1939 did behind the Maginot Line [*"forts"*]. At Jerusalem and Tel Aviv 2000 dead were *mourned* [*"attristée"*], a considerable number for a country of only 3 million people, while 3000 wounded lay in hospitals, and on the front more than 150,080 reservists stood guard. On 10 April 1974, in the middle of the Passover, Mrs Meir, saddened and exhausted, handed in her resignation [*"quittée"*] to the President of the State.'[2]

¹ Cleopatra's serpent or asp. DL7V. The allusion to Cleopatra also terms the Egyptians 'crocodiles'.
² *Le Spectacle du Monde*, no. 147, June 1974.

Revolutions, Wars and Famine in Iran, 1979. The Fall of the Shah, 1978–79. Ayatollah Khomeini at Neauphle-le-Château

Pluye,¹ faim, guerre en Perse non cessée,
La foy trop grande² trahira le Monarque:³
Par la finie en Gaule commencée,
Secret⁴ augure⁵ pour à un estre parque.

CI,Q70

Interpretation

Revolution, famine, war will not cease in Iran; religious fanaticism will betray the Shah whose end will begin in France, because of a prophet who will be confined in a withdrawn place [Neauphle-le-Château].

History

'With her *fanatical* demonstrators, brandishing the banners of their *faith* and confronting the weapons of the Shah's soldiers with chests bared, Iran last week furnished the most spectacular example of the astonishing Moslem revival. Meched and Qom in Iran and Al Nadjat and Karbala in Iraq are the sanctuaries of the Shi'ite Moslems. One may add for the present, though it has no mosques or golden minarets or turquoise domes, a third holy city amazed by the turn of events – Neauphle-le-Château. For a *medersa* [Koranic seminary] it has only an ordinary suburban house, but there squats or prays the Ayatollah Khomeini.⁶

On the eve of the Moharran this year, the call from Ayatollah Khomeini inviting the faithful to launch into a sort of *holy rebellion* succeeded in bringing passions to the boil. Do not hesitate to shed your blood to protect Islam and overthrow tyranny, *this exiled prophet* of the Shi'ites requested from his *retreat* at Neauphle-le-Château.'⁷

'Iran is heading for a fanatical *war*, predicted the revolutionary General Hadavi. The religious leader of the Iranian Arabs, Ayatollah Khafani, predicted *bitter tragedies*. General Rahini was indignant: it was shameful to see parts of Iran bathed in fire and blood when the army remained in its barracks.'⁸

¹ As with the words *onde* and *eau*, Nostradamus uses 'rain' to denote revolutionary troubles.
² Religious fanaticism is a blind, irrational faith: *excessive* zeal in support of a religious doctrine. DL7V.
³ Persian *Shah*: king, sovereign. DL7V.
⁴ Latin *secretum*: retired spot, retreat. DLLB.
⁵ Latin *augur*: priest who forecasts the future, *prophet*. DLLB.
⁶ Meaning 'sign of God'.
⁷ *Le Point*, no. 325 (11 December 1978).
⁸ *Le Spectacle du Monde*, no. 209 (August 1978).

The Fall of the Shah of Iran, 16 January 1979. The Military Government, 6 November 1978. Seizure of Power by the Mullahs, 3 February 1979

> Par le despit¹ du Roy soustenant² moindre;
> Sera meurdry³ lui presentant⁴ les bagues:⁵
> Le père au fils voulant noblesse poindre,⁶
> Fait comme a Perse jadis feirent les Magues.⁷
>
>   CX,Q21

Interpretation

Because of his contempt the Shah, in a state of least resistance, will be harmed when showing off his army, the father wanting to display the power of his son. Then will be done in Iran what the holy men did of old [taking power].

History

'On 6 November 1978 General Azhari, commander-in-chief of the army, was named head of government. The army's intervention threw a completely new light on the problem. Only yesterday it had remained a shadowy presence in the background, intervening merely in order to contain the wave of discontent. From now on *the Army* would *take the main role* ["*presentant*"].'⁸

'In 1967, as he was preparing to have himself and Farah crowned Emperor and Empress, Mohammed Reza claimed: "*I shall leave my son a young, developing, proud, completely modern and stable nation, looking ever to the future and to cooperation with the peoples of the entire world.*" In these last years, his father entrusted him with various representative missions which he performed ably. Even in 1971, at the

Persepolis celebrations, the Shah had let it be understood that he would one day hand over *power to his son*.'[9]

'16 January 1979: the Shah's departure for Egypt.

21 January 1979: the resignation of Tehrani, President of the Regency Council.

1 February 1979: the return of Ayatollah Khomeini to Teheran.

3 February 1979: Ayatollah Khomeini announces the creation of a "National Islamic Council."

Iran: 200,000 *mullahs* on the warpath.'[10]

[1] Scorn, contempt. DAFL.
[2] Latin *sustineo*: I resist. DLLB.
[3] Wound, harm, injure. DL7V.
[4] Exhibit, show off. DL7V.
[5] Weapons. DAFL.
[6] Demonstrate. DL7V.
[7] Greek μαγος: mage, priest among the Persians. DGF. In Persia the magi led a hard, austere life. The virtues they possessed or were attributed with gave them limitless authority over the minds of the people and the *nobility*. The king himself boasted of being their pupil and would consult them. DL7V. Nostradamus denotes *the ayatollahs* when using the word in this context.
[8] *Le Spectacle du Monde*, no. 201, 'Revolution of the Ayatollahs' by R. Faucon.
[9] *Le Spectacle du Monde*, no. 203, 'The Common Front against the dynasty.'
[10] Article in *Figaro-Magazine* (19 January 1980).

Ayatollah Khomeini in Iraq, 1963–78. The Islamic Republic, 1979

Il entrera vilain, meschant, infâme,
Tyrannisant la Mésopotamie:[1]
Tous amis faict d'adulterine[2] dame,[3]
Terre horrible noire[4] de phisionomie.

CVIII,Q70

Interpretation

The frightful, wicked and infamous person will enter Iraq in order to impose his tyranny. They will all be friends of a false republic [the Islamic Republic]; the world will be horrified by this hateful physiognomy.

History

'The *mullahs* called the faithful to revolt against the *impious* tyranny. The Shah in person was their target. "Shah, we will kill you!" chanted the fanatical crowds, who had formed processions after hearing speeches in the mosques. Even in 1963, at the time of the first great wave of upheavals in Iran unleashed by Ayatollah Khomeini, since then exiled in Iraq, the rebellion never took on such a widespread fervour.'[5]

'The Islamic Republic, as Ayatollah Khomeini conceived it, demonstrated its inability to rule Iran. Unpopular throughout the country as a whole, the regime only kept going through the fanaticism [*tyrannie*] of the lowest level of the population, which was completely subservient to the power of the "akhonds", the priesthood.'[6]

---

[1] Present-day Iraq: region between the Tigris and Euphrates. DHB.

[2] Latin *adulterinus*: falsified, false. DLLB.

[3] Frequently used word in Nostradamus, signifying the Republic, personified as a woman.

[4] Figurative: atrocious, perverse, odious. DL7V.

[5] *Le Spectacle du Monde*, no. 199, '*Iran, two worlds face to face*'.

[6] DHB.

3
NOSTRADAMUS AS PROPHET

THE PRE-WAR CLIMATE

The Conflicts of the Twentieth Century between East and West: 1914–18, 1939–45, and the Third World War, 1999

Par deux fois hault, par deux fois mis a bas,
L'Orient aussi l'Occident faiblira,
Son adversaire après plusieurs combats,
Par mer chassé au besoing faillira.

CVIII,Q59

Interpretation

Twice raised high to power, twice laid low, the West like the East will be weakened. Its adversary, after several battles, will be chased off by sea and will fall through penury.

The Search for Peace and War. The War in France

La paix s'approche d'un côté et la guerre
Oncques ne fust la poursuite si grande,
Plaindre homme, femme, sang innocent par terre
Et ce sera de France à toute bande.

CIX,Q52

Interpretation

They get ready to sign the peace with one hand and make war with the other. The two were never so much pursued. Then they will mourn men, women; innocent blood will flow upon the earth and particularly in all areas of France.

Peace Negotiations: USA–USSR

> Plusieurs viendront et parleront de paix,
> Entre Monarques et Seigneurs bien puissants;
> Mais ne sera accordé de si près,
> Que ne se rendent plus qu'autres obéissants.

CVIII,Q2a

Interpretation

There will be talk of peace between very powerful heads of states [USA–USSR]; but peace will not be agreed, for the heads of state will be no wiser than any others.

The False Peace Declarations.
The Ignoring of Treaties. The War as far as Barcelona

> On ne tiendra pache[1] aucun arresté,
> Tous recevans iront par tromperie:
> De paix et tresve, terre et mer protesté,
> Par Barcelone classe prins d'industrie.[2]

CVI,Q64

Interpretation

They will take no notice of the decisions of the peace treaties. The men of state will receive each other in trickery. By land and sea peace proclamations will be made. The army will be active as far as Barcelona.

[1] Latin *pax*: peace treaty. DLLB.
[2] Latin *industria*: activity. DLLB.

The Smaller Powers Confronted by the Greater

Beaucoup de gens voudront parlementer,
Aux grands Seigneurs qui leur feront la guerre:
On ne voudra en rien les écouter,
Hélas! si Dieu n'envoye paix en terre!

CVIII,Q4a

Interpretation

Many [little] people will want to engage in [peace] discussions with the great powers which will wage war upon them. But they will not be heard, alas, if God does not send peace upon earth.

Pacifist Myths, Causes of Wars

Les Dieux feront aux humains apparences,
Ce qu'ils seront autheurs de grand conflict,
Avant ciel veu serein, espée et lance,
Que vers main[1] gauche sera plus grand afflict.

CI,Q91

Interpretation

Myths will mislead men because they will cause great wars, before which men will see the sky serene, then land weapons ["*espée*"] and aerial ones ["*lance*"] will be even more distressing towards the forces of the left.

[1] Latin *manus*: force. DLLB.

From the Second to the Third World War.
Great Naval Battles

Un peu après non point long intervalle:
Par terre et mer sera faict grand tumulte:
Beaucoup plus grande sera pugne[1] navalle,
Feux, animaux, qui plus feront l'insulte.

CII,Q40

Interpretation

After a not very long interval a great war will break out on land and sea. The naval combats will be the most important. The ferocity [of men] will be worse than the war itself.

¹ Latin *pugnum*: combat. DLLB.

The Third World War follows the Second.
The Use of Nuclear Missiles

Après grand troche¹ humain plus grand s'appreste,
Le grand moteur² les siècles renouvelle;
Pluye, sang laict, famine fer et peste,
Au ciel vu feu, courant longue étincelle.³

CII,Q46

Interpretation

After a great muster of men [soldiers] another, bigger one is being prepared; God will renew the ages. Revolution and bloodshed will bring famine, war and pestilence; then fire will be seen in the sky and great rockets traversing it.

¹ Batch, bundle, assembly. DAFL.
² By analogy, governor, ruler. 'God is the First Principle and Prime Mover of all creatures' (Bossuet). DL7V.
³ Spark, small particle of matter in combustion which becomes detached from a body. DL7V. Allusion to multiple warhead rockets.

The Revolutionary Climate in Provincial France.
The War in France

Roy contre Roy et le Duc contre Prince,
Haine entre iceux, dissenssion horrible:
Rage et fureur sera toute province,¹
France grand guerre et changement terrible.

CXII,Q56

Interpretation

A head of state will rise up against another ruler. There will be dissension and strife between them. Rage and fury will spread throughout the provinces, then a great war will cause terrible changes in France [one of which is a change of the capital].

[1] Revolutionary movements in Corsica, Brittany and the Basque country.

Shortage of Gold and Silver. Life Becomes Expensive

> Près loing defaut de deux grands luminaires,[1]
> Qui surviendra entre l'Avril et Mars:
> O quel cherté! Mais deux grands débonnaires[2]
> Par terre et mer secourront toutes pars.

CIII,Q5

Interpretation

Shortly after the shortage of the two metals [gold and silver] which will occur between April and March, how expensive life will become! But two heads of state of noble birth will bring help by land and sea.

[1] Latin *lumen*: lustre of a metal. DLLB.
[2] Of good stock, noble. DAFL.

The Economic Crises. The End of the Monetary System

> Les simulachres[1] d'or et d'argent enflez,
> Qu'après le rapt lac[2] au feu furent[3] jettez,
> Au descouvert[4] estaincts[5] tous et troublez,
> Au marbre[6] escripts, perscripts[7] interjettez.

CVIII,Q28

Interpretation

Images produced in gold and silver, victims of inflation, after the theft of prosperity, will be thrown into the fire in anger; exhausted and disturbed by the public debt paper and coin will be pulped.

[1] Latin *simulacrum*: image, representation. DLLB.
[2] Latin *lac, lactis*: milk. DLLB. Symbol of prosperity.
[3] Latin *furens, -entis*: furious. DLLB.
[4] Now known as the balance of payments deficit.
[5] *Estanc*: worn out, exhausted. DAFL.
[6] Mortar, made of *marble* or similar substance in which materials are crushed, pounded or pulped with a pestle.
[7] Latin *perscribo*: I pay by ticket or form. DLLB.

Decadence of Power Due to Inflation. The Corruption of Morals. Paris in Great Confusion

Despit[1] de règne nunismes[2] descriés,[3]
Et seront peuples esmeus contre leur Roy:
Paix, fait nouveau, sainctes loix empirées[4]
RAPIS[5] onc fut en si tresdur arroy.[6]

CVI,Q23

Interpretation

Power will be despised because of the currency devaluation and the people will rebel against the head of state. Peace will be proclaimed; through a new fact, sacred laws will be corrupted. Never was Paris in such dire disarray.

[1] Contempt. DAFL.
[2] Latin *numisma*: small coin (gold or silver). DLLB.
[3] Depreciate. DAFL.
[4] *Empirier* = spoil, corrupt, deteriorate. DAFL.
[5] Anagram of Paris.
[6] For *désarroi* by aphesis.

The Abundance of Money. The Deception of Power

Le grand crédit, d'or d'argent l'abondance
Aveuglera par libide[1] l'honneur:
Cogneu sera l'adultère l'offence,
Qui parviendra à son grand deshoneur.

CVIII,Q14

Interpretation

The importance of credit and the abundance of gold and silver will blind men greedy for honour. The offence of deception will be known by him who attains his own great dishonour.

[1] Latin *libido*: desire, corruption. DLLB.

The Economic Crisis and the Negligence of the Politicians

> La grande poche[1] viendra plaindre pleurer,
> D'avoir esleu: trompez seront en l'aage.[2]
> Guière avec eux ne voudra demeurer,
> Deceu sera par ceux de son langage.

CVII,Q35

Interpretation

They will complain of lost wealth and weep over choosing [responsible politicians] who will make mistakes from time to time. Very few men will want to follow them, deceived as they will be by their speeches.

[1] Empty pockets: to have no money. DL7V.
[2] Latin *in aetate*: from time to time. DLLB.

The End of the Consumer Society. Inflation and Violence. The Prophecies of Nostradamus Fulfilled

> Des Roys et princes dresseront simulachres,[1]
> Augures, creux eslevez aruspices:[2]
> Corne[3] victime dorée, et d'azur,[4] d'acres[5]
> Interpretez[6] seront les exstipices.[7]

CIII,Q26

Interpretation

The heads of states and governments will fabricate imitations [of gold: excess of paper money]; prophets will make forecasts devoid of sense [speeches of politicians and economists]. The horn of plenty [consumer society] will fall victim to them and violence will follow peace. The prophecies will be fulfilled.

[1] Latin *simulacrum*: imitation. DLLB.
[2] Latin *haruspex*: seer, prophet. DLLB.
[3] Abundance, or plenty, an allegorical divinity who had no temple, but symbolized health and prosperity, via her *horn* filled with flowers and fruits, which she is shown holding. DL7V.
[4] Symbolic: innocence, calm, peace, 'sky blue'. DL7V.
[5] Latin *acer*: sharp, hard, violent. DLLB.
[6] Latin *interpretor*: to comment on (an author), translate, explain. DLLB.
[7] Latin *extipex*: soothsayer who examines entrails of sacrifices. DLLB.

Declarations of Peace and War.
The Execution of 300,000 Prisoners

> Sous un la paix partout sera clamée,
> Mais non long temps pille et rebellion,
> Par refus ville,[1] terre et mer entamée,
> Mort et captifs le tiers d'un million.

CI,Q92

Interpretation

Under one [person] peace will be proclaimed everywhere, but shortly afterwards there will be pillage and revolution. Because of the resistance of Paris, land and sea will be invaded and 300,000 prisoners executed.

[1] Nostradamus' use of 'town' with no adjective always refers to Paris, also 'the great city'.

The Revolution in Italy

> Au lieu que HIERON[1] fait sa nef fabriquer,
> Si grand déluge sera et si subite,
> Qu'on n'aura lieu ne terres s'ataquer,
> L'onde monter Fesulan[2] Olympique.

CVIII,Q16

Interpretation

In the place where God has built his Church [Rome] there will be so great and sudden a revolution that no areas or lands will escape attack. The revolution will reach Tuscany [Florence] after the Olympic Games.

[1] Greek ἱερός: holy, sacred, divine. DGF. Allusion to Christ's words to Peter: '. . . on this rock', etc.
[2] Faesula = Fiesole, town in Etruria (Tuscany). DLLB.

Moral Ruin and the Bloody Collapse of Rome. Subversive Literature. Outrages

> O vaste Rome ta ruine s'approche
> Non de tes murs de ton sang et substance:
> L'aspre par lettres fera si horrible coche,
> Fer pointu mis à tous jusqu'au manche.

CX,Q65

Interpretation

O vast Rome your ruin is approaching, not that of your walls but of your lifeblood and substance. Wickedness will work such a horrible attack through writings that all will be persecuted.

Discord among the French. Internal Strife at Marseille

> L'accord et pache sera du tout rompuë:
> Les amitiés polluées par discorde,
> L'haine envieillie, toute foy[1] corrompuë,
> Et l'espérance, Marseille sans concorde.

CXII,Q59

Interpretation

The peace agreement will be completely broken. Alliances will be destroyed by discord. The old hatred will corrupt all confidence and hope. There will not be concord at Marseille.

[1] Latin *fides*: confidence. DLLB.

Common Market Europe and China.
Weakness in International Relations

Predons[1] pillez chaleur, grand seicheresse,
Par trop non estre cas non veu, inoui:
A l'estranger la trop grande caresse,
Neuf pays Roy. L'Orient esblouy.

Presage 41, July

Interpretation

Bandits go on the rampage in a great drought, which will scarcely be an unheard-of event. There will be too much amity towards foreign countries [the East]. The heads of government of 'the Nine' will be seduced by the Orient [China].

[1] Or *préon* (from *préder* or *préer*): bandit, pillager. DAFL.

John-Paul II Flees from the Russian Invasion.
Resistance to the Invaders

Vent[1] Aquilon[2] fera partir le siège,
Par mur jetter cendres, platras chaulx et poussière:
Par pluye après qui leur fera bien piège,
Dernier secours encontre leur frontière.

CIX,Q99

Interpretation

Russian troop movements force the Pope to leave Rome. Plaster, chalk and dust will be reduced to ashes: but the revolution which will follow will be a trap for them, final aid opposed to their border.

[1] Symbolic: impulse, something which sweeps along or produces a general effect. DL7V.
[2] North wind, violent and impetuous; the north. DL7V. Symbol of Russia, the Northern Empire from the Baltic Sea to Vladivostok.

John-Paul II by the Rhône.
The Alliance of the Cock (France) and the Eagle (USA)

> Pol[1] mensolée[2] mourra à trois lieues du Rosne,
> Fuis les deux prochains tarasc détroits:
> Car Mars fera le plus horrible trosne,
> De Coq et d'Aigle[3] de France frères trois.

CVIII,Q46

Interpretation

[John]-Paul II, the travail of the sun, will die near the Rhône, having fled near the passes of Tarascon [and Beaucaire]; for the war will do terrible things to the throne [of St Peter]; then in France there will be three allies of the King of France and the United States.

[1] Nostradamus often invests the word *Pol* with dual significance: John-Paul II's Christian name and the start of the word Poland, denoting his birthplace.

[2] The word appears twice elsewhere (CIX,Q85 and CX,Q29) spelt with an *a*. Invented by Nostradamus from two Latin words: *manus*: man's work, travail, industry, labour, and *sol*: sun. This corresponds with John-Paul's epithet in Malachi's prophecy: '*de labore solis*', the work of the sun.

[3] Cf. CV,Q99: '*Phalange aquilée*'.

The Bombing of Towns in South-West France

> Condom et Aux et autour de Mirande,
> Je vois du ciel feu qui les environne:
> Sol,[1] Mars conjoint au Lyon, puis Marmande,
> Foudre grand gresle, mur tombe dans Garonne.

CVIII,Q2

Interpretation

I see the towns of Condom, Auch and Mirande and the neighbouring area surrounded by fire from heaven, the Pope at Lyon caught up again by the war, then bombing over Marmande and blocks of houses collapsing in the Garonne.

[1] Malachi's prophecy '*de labore solis*'. Cf. CVIII,Q46 above.

The Bombing of the Gers Area. The Earthquake

Tout aupres d'Aux, de Lestore et Mirande,
Grand feu du ciel en trois nuits tombera:
Cause adviendra bien stupende[1] et mirande,[2]
Bien peu après la terre tremblera.

CI,Q46

Interpretation

Quite near Auch, Lectoure and Mirande heavy incendiary bombing will
be carried out for three nights. The cause of it will be astonishing and
amazing and shortly afterwards there will be an earthquake.

[1] Latin *stupendus*: astonishing, marvellous. DLLB
[2] Latin *mirandus*: worthy of and causing astonishment and wonder. Marvellous. DLLB

John-Paul II near Tarascon.
Liberation from Salon to Monaco

Salon, Mansol,[1] Tarascon[2] de SEX,[3] l'arc[4]
Où est debout encore la piramide[5]
Viendront livrer[6] le Prince Dannemarc,
Rachat[7] honny au temple d'Artémide.[8]

CIV,Q27

Interpretation

Near Salon, 'the work of the sun' [John-Paul II] is at Tarascon, since
from Aix-en-Provence to Monaco, where the rock still stands, [the
French] will come to deliver the Prince of Denmark. The saviour will be
honoured in Turkey.

[1] Cf. CVIII,Q46.
[2] Cf. CVIII,Q46.
[3] Cf. CV,Q57.
[4] Arx Monoeci: Monaco. DLLB.
[5] By extension, hill or mountain taking on pyramidal shape. DLLB.
[6] Example of aphesis.
[7] *Rachatere*: redeemer. DAFL.
[8] The goddess Diana (Greek: Artemis), whose most famous temple was undoubtedly
that at Ephesus. MGR. Ephesus was situated in Asia Minor, present-day Turkey. AVL.

The Invasion in the Gironde, in the South-West.
The Conflict Reaches Marseille.
The Vatican Occupied

Passer Guienne, Languedoc et le Rosne,
D'Agen tenans de Marmande et la Roole:[1]
D'ouvrir par foy[2] parroy[3] Phocen tiendra son trosne,
Conflit aupres sainct pol de Manseole.[4]

CIX,Q85

Interpretation

[The invasion] will pass through Guyenne and the Languedoc as far as
the Rhône. From Agen, the occupiers having arrived from Marmande
and La Réole will bring horror to the coast of Marseille, for they will
occupy the throne [of St Peter] and the conflict will get close to the spot
where [John]-Paul II – 'the work of the sun' – is taking refuge.

[1] Town on the Garonne, 67 km south-east of Bordeaux and 18 km from Langon. AVL.
Cf. CI,Q90 and CXII,Q65.
[2] From Celtic *fouy* (for *foui*): term expressing horror at a disgusting thing or event. DP.
[3] Shingle shore or gravel. DAFL.
[4] Cf. CVIII,Q46.

John-Paul's Supporters Arrested and
Imprisoned in Bigorre

De Pol MANSOL[1] dans caverne caprine,[2]
Caché et pris extrait hors par la barbe:[3]
Captif mené comme beste mastine,[4]
Par Begourdans[5] amenée près de Tarbe.

CX,Q29

Interpretation

[The entourage] of [John]-Paul, 'the work of the Sun', sheltering on the
Isle of Capri, will be taken prisoners and led away by the revolutionaries.
They will be taken to prison like animals, across the Bigorre near Tarbes
[Lourdes?]

¹ Cf. CVIII,Q46.
² Capri: island in the Gulf of Naples, noteworthy for its steepness and Blue *Grotto*. DL7V.
³ Abbreviation of Aenobarbus, i.e. representative for Nostradamus of the revolutionary forces of destruction. Cf. Note, CV,Q45.
⁴ Breed of domestic dog. DL7V.
⁵ Inhabitants of the Bigorre; chief town, Tarbes. DL7V.

The Pope at Lyon.
His Journey to Capri and Monaco. His Death

Dans deux logis de nuict le feu prendra
Plusieurs dedans estouffez et rostis:
Près de deux fleuves pour seul il adviendra,
Sol,¹ l'Arq², et Caper,³ tous seront amortis.⁴

CII,Q35

Interpretation

In the night fire will spread through two [ministerial?] blocks where some will be burned and suffocated. The Pope will arrive alone near two rivers [Lyon]; after his journey to Capri and Monaco, all will be put to death.

¹ Allusion to John-Paul's epithet *'de labore solis'*.
² Arx Monoeci: Monaco. DLLB.
³ Capri.
⁴ *Amortir*: to muffle, deaden. DAFL.

The Pope Leaves Rome and Italy.
The End of His Reign

Istra du mont Gaulsier¹, et Aventin,²
Qui par le trou advertira³ l'armée,
Entre deux rocs⁴ sera prins le butin,
De SEXT⁵ mansol⁶ faillir la renommée.

CV,Q57

Interpretation

He will leave Rome and cross the north Italian mountains because of him who will lead his army towards a tunnel [Switzerland]. Between two rocks [Beaucaire and Tarascon] his possessions will be seized. After Aix-en-Provence the renown of 'the sun's work' [John-Paul II] will fail.

[1] Cisalpine Gaul, northern Italy. DHB.
[2] Aventine: one of the Seven Hills of Rome. DL7V.
[3] Latin *adverto*: I turn, direct an object towards. DLLB.
[4] Cf. CVIII,Q46, '*les deux tarasc détroits*'.
[5] Aquae Sextiae: Aix-en-Provence. DLLB.
[6] Cf. CVIII,Q46.

Fighting in the Jura and Alps.
The Death of John-Paul II at Lyon

Après victoire du Lyon[1] au Lyon,
Sus la montagne de JURA secatombe,[2]
Delues[3] et brodes[4] septiesme million,
Lyon, Ulme[5] a Mausol[6] mort et tombe.

CVIII,Q34

Interpretation

After the victory of the violent leader at Lyon, there will be a hecatomb on the Jura Mountains, a seventh of a million soldiers will be annihilated in the Alps. 'The work of the sun' [John-Paul II] will find death and burial at Lyon.

[1] Violent, raging person. DL7V.
[2] Greek ἐχατόμβη: hecatomb. *S* replaces aspirate *h* at the beginning.
[3] Latin *deleo, delui:* annihilate, destroy. DLLB.
[4] Latin Brodiontii, Brodiontes, tribe of the Alps. DLLB.
[5] Anagram of *mule*: Papal white slipper. DL7V.
[6] Cf. CVIII,Q46.

The Death of the Pope at Lyon.
The Left in Power in France

Romain Pontife garde de t'approcher
De la cité que deux fleuves arrose:[1]
Ton sang viendra auprès de là cracher,
Toy et les tiens quand fleurira la Rose.[2]

CII,Q97

Interpretation

Roman Pope, do not approach the town which two rivers water [Lyon].
Your blood and that of your followers will flow near this spot, when the
left gets into power.

[1] Lyon, whose two rivers are the Rhône and Saône.
[2] Emblem of the French Socialist party.

John-Paul's Assassination by Night.
A Good, Gentle, Enterprising and Prudent Pope

Esleu en Pape d'esleu sera mocqué,
Subit soudain esmeu[1] prompt[2] et timide:[3]
Par trop bon doux a mourir provoqué,
Crainte estreinte la nuit de sa mort guide.

CX,Q12

Interpretation

The one elected Pope will be mocked by his electors. This enterprising
and prudent person will suddenly be reduced to silence. They will
instigate his death because of his too great goodness and mildness.
Stricken by fear, they will lead him to his death in the night.

[1] *Esmuir*: to become mute, dumb. DAFL.
[2] Latin *promptus*: (of persons) active, resolute, enterprising. DLLB.
[3] Latin *timidus*: prudent, circumspect. DLLB.

The Death of John-Paul II at Lyon, 13 December. His Journey to Montélimar

Du mont Aymar[1] sera noble[2] obscurcie,
Le mal viendra au joinct de Saone et Rosne,
Dans bois cachez soldats jour de Lucie[3],
Qui ne fut onc un si horrible throsne.

CIX,Q68

Interpretation

From Montélimar the Pope will lose his fame. His misfortune will come at the confluence of the Saône and Rhône [Lyon] because of soldiers hidden in the woods on 13 December. Nothing so horrible will ever have happened to the throne [of St Peter].

[1] Montélimar (by syncope).
[2] The popes, because of their coats of arms, could be considered as nobles. Nostradamus here alludes to nobility of spirit.
[3] St Lucy's Day, i.e.13 December.

The Left in Power. Revolutionary Upheavals.

Sur le milieu du grand monde[1] la rose,[2]
Pour nouveaux faicts sang public espandu:
A dire vray, on aura bouche close:[3]
Lors au besoing tard viendra l'attendu.

CV,Q96

Interpretation

When socialism is in power amid the bourgeoisie, the people's blood will flow because of new acts. To tell the truth, freedom of expression will disappear. Then the awaited [helper] will arrive late because of penury.

[1] *Grand monde*: expression for important, affluent, influential people as a whole or a class. DL7V.
[2] Emblem of Socialist party in France.
[3] To silence someone, i.e. make them keep their mouths shut. DL7V.

The Pope's Flight West. Religious Persecution

Flora,[1] fuis, fuis le plus proche Romain,
Au Fesulan[2] sera conflict donné:
Sang espandu, les plus grands prins à main,
Temple ne sexe ne sera pardonné.

CVII,Q8

Interpretation

You, the nearest Roman [the Pope], flee, flee westwards, the conflict will reach Fiesole: blood will be shed and the greatest will be captured. Neither churches nor sexes will be spared.

[1] Flora, wife of Zephyrus, the west wind.
[2] Latin Faesulae: today Fiesole, Tuscan town. DHB.

The Polish Pope's Flight from Rome

En après cinq troupeau[1] ne mettra hors,
Un fuytif[2] pour Penelon[3] laschera:[4]
Faux murmurer secours venir par lors,
Le chef, le siège lors abandonnera.

CX,Q3

Interpretation

After five [days or months][5] the Church will be expelled; a person will flee, abandoning the Pope: false rumours of help will circulate, the Head [of the Church] will then abandon the Holy See.

[1] Flock, i.e. Christ's: the Church. DL7V.
[2] *fuytif*, i.e. fugitive, often with pejorative sense. DAFL.
[3] *Penelon*, anagram of Polenne – itself an old French word used as collective term denoting the countries which comprised Poland. DHB.
[4] Let go, abandon. DAFL.
[5] Probably five months after the start of the Third World War.

A Comet Visible for Seven Days.
An Appeal for Help from the British Head of State.
The Pope Leaves Rome

La grande estoille par sept jours bruslera
Nuë fera deux soleils apparoir
Le gros mastin[1] toute nuict hurlera
Quand grand Pontife changera de terroir.

CII,Q41

Interpretation

The Comet will blaze for seven days. The sky will display two suns; the British leader will howl all night when the Pope changes countries.

[1] Symbol already used by Nostradamus for an English leader, i.e. Churchill. Cf. cv,Q4

The Capture of the Pope during a Journey.
The Assassination of His Favourite

En navigant captif prins grand pontife;
Grand après faillir les clercs tumultuez;
Second[1] esleu absent son bien debife,[2]
Son favori[3] bastard a mort tué.

CV,Q15

Interpretation

The great pontiff will be taken prisoner in the course of a journey. The Pope will die after that and the clergy will set up a tumult. He who will have been elected second, being absent [from the Vatican], will see his goodness weakened and his favoured friend of humble birth will be killed.

[1] John-Paul II, after John-Paul I.
[2] To weaken, reduce (*debiffer*). DAFL. Cf. cv,Q56.
[3] Perhaps the Secretary of State.

Quarrels between Three Leaders at the Time of the Comet. The Basque Country and Rome in the Grip of Revolution

Durant l'estoille chevelue apparante,
Les trois grands princes seront faits ennemis
Frappez du ciel paix terre trémulent,[1]
Pau, Timbre[2] undans,[3] serpent sur le bort mis.

CII,Q43

Interpretation

While the Comet is seen, the three great leaders will become enemies; they will be hit from the sky and the earth will tremble. The Lower Pyrenees and Tiber will experience upheaval. Satan will install himself on the latter's banks.

[1] Latin *tremo*: I tremble. DLLB.
[2] The Vatican is by the Tiber.
[3] Latin, present participle of *undo*: I am agitated, seethe.

Iraq against the West. The Pope on the Banks of the Rhône. Italy Occupied

Les Citoyens de Mésopotamie[1]
Irez encontre amis de Tarragone:[2]
Jeux, ritz, banquets, toute gent endormie,
Vicaire[3] au Rosne, prins cité, ceux d'Ausone.[4]

CVII,Q22

Interpretation

The Iraqis will march against the allies of Spain while people amuse themselves, laugh, banquet and everyone sleeps; the Pope fleeing beside the Rhône, the Vatican City will be occupied as well as Italy.

[1] Mesopotamia, region between the Tigris and Euphrates, now Iraq. DHB.
[2] Town in Spain (Catalonia). DHB.
[3] Vicar of Christ, i.e. the Pope. DL7V.
[4] Ausonia: ancient region of Italy, by extension all Italy. DLLB.

The Ransack of the Vatican.
The Pope by the Rhône

Lorsqu'on verra expiler[1] le sainct temple,
Plus grand du Rhosne et sacres prophanes:
Par eux naistra pestilence si ample,
Roy faict injuste[2] ne fera condamner.

CVIII,Q62

Interpretation

When the Vatican is seen ransacked, the greatest [the Pope] beside the Rhône, and sacred things profaned [by enemies] who will cause a great calamity, the head of the government can only condemn these cruel acts.

[1] Latin *expilo*: I pillage, steal, sack. DLLB.
[2] Latin *injustus*: hard, wicked. DLLB.

The Death by Poisoning of an
Enemy Head of State. A Rain of Meteorites

L'ennemy grand vieil dueil[1] meurt de poyson,
Les souverains par infinis subjuguez:
Pierres pleuvoir, cachez, soubs la toison,
Par mort articles en vain sont alleguez.

CII,Q47

Interpretation

When the great and old enemy who brings misfortune is poisoned, the sovereigns will be subjugated by innumerable [troops]. The meteorites hidden in the comet's hair will rain down upon the earth, when the articles [Geneva agreements] will be invoked in vain, concerning the rights of war [death].

[1] *Duel*, changed here to *deuil*: sorrow, misfortune, affliction. DAFL.

The Fall of the Invaders. The Comet

Mabus[1] puis tost alors mourra, viendra,
De gens et bestes une horrible défaite,
Puis tout à coup la vengeance on verra,
Cent,[2] main, soif, faim, quand courra la comète.

CII,Q62

Interpretation

The wicked invader will soon die, after provoking a horrible hecatomb
of men and animals. Then suddenly vengeance will come. Because of
endless speeches, force will rule; they will know thirst and hunger, when
the comet crosses the sky.

[1] Some editions have *malus*: wicked, evil, harmful. DLLB.
[2] Latin *cento*: incoherent speech, nonsense. DLLB. Allusion to International Conventions of Geneva.

The Appearance of a Comet near Ursa Minor in June. War in Italy, Greece and the Red Sea. The Pope's Death

Apparoistra vers le Septentrion[1]
Non loing de Cancer[2] l'estoille cheveluë:
Suse,[3] Sienne,[4] Boëce,[5] Eretrion[6],
Moura de Rome grand, la nuit disparuë.

CVI,Q6

Interpretation

The comet will appear towards Ursa Minor around 21 June. Suse and
Tuscany, Greece and the Red Sea will tremble. The Pope of Rome will
die, the night the comet disappears.

[1] Latin *septentrio*: constellation of seven stars, near the Pole Star: Ursa Minor. DLLB.
[2] Sun enters the Sign of Cancer on 21 June. DL7V.
[3] Situated at the junction of the two great Mount Cenis and Mount Geneva approaches, Suse can thus be considered a key to Italy. DHB.
[4] Powerful Tuscan town. DHB.
[5] Boeotia: region of Greece. DLLB.
[6] Erythraeum mare: the Red Sea. DLLB.

The Death of the Pope. The Comet.
Economic Ruin. Italy's Restricted Areas

Un peu devant monarque trucidé,
Castor Pollux[1] en nef, astre crinite,[2]
L'erain[3] public par terre et mer vuidé,
Pise, Ast, Ferrare, Turin,[4] terre interdite.

CII,QI5

Interpretation

A little before the Pope is killed, the Church will have had two brothers
[John-Paul I and II], and the comet will be seen; public money will be
squandered by land and sea, and Pisa, Asti, Ferrara and Turin will be
forbidden areas.

[1] Two brothers, sons of Jupiter.
[2] Latin *crinita stella*: fiery star with tail, comet. DLLB.
[3] Latin *aes, aeris*: silver, money. DLLB.
[4] Tuscany, Piedmont and the Romagna. AVL.

THE FALL OF THE FIFTH REPUBLIC

The Flight of the Head of Government.
Enemies Overwhelmed by Death

Par conflit Roy, règne abandonnera
Le plus grand chef faillira au besoing
Morts profligez, peu en reschappera
Tous destrangez, un en sera tesmoing.

CIV,Q45

Interpretation

Because of the conflict the leader will abandon power. The greatest head
of government [Russia] will succumb through lack of funds and her
people will be overwhelmed by death from which few will escape. They
will all be massacred; one person will bear witness to it.

The Tyrant Executed in a Moslem Country. The War of Revenge against the West. The Fall of the French Republic

> Au port Selin[1] le tyran mis à mort,
> La liberté non pourtant recouvrée:
> Le nouveau Mars par vindicte et remort,
> Dame[2] par force de frayeur honorée.
>
> CI,Q94

Interpretation

The tyrant will be put to death in the Moslem port, but that does not bring back freedom. A new war breaks out, through spite and vengeance; the French Republic will be paid in fear, through force.

[1] Greek Σελήνη: the moon, i.e. Moslem crescent.
[2] Constant reference to French Republic (Marianne).

The Fall of the French Republic. Moslem Troops in Italy. The Occupation Government in Italy

> A[1] Logmyon[2] sera laissé le regne,
> Du Grand Selyn[3] qui plus fera de faict:
> Par les Itales estendra son enseigne
> Sera régi par prudent[4] contrefaict.
>
> CVI,Q42

Interpretation

Power will be abandoned by the French Republic because of Moslem forces which will engage in many actions and extend their power to Italy, which will be ruled by a person who will pretend to be intelligent.

[1] Latin *a* or *ab*: by. DLLB. Often used thus by Nostradamus, hence one of the chief linguistic traps in the Centuries.
[2] Ogmius or Ogmios, Gallic God of Eloquence. DHB. For Nostradamus, denotes the French Republican system.
[3] Greek: Selene. Cf. CI,Q94, note. 1.
[4] Latin *prudens*: clear-sighted, intelligent. DLLB.

The End of the Fifth Republic. The Quarrel Between the Russians and Their Moslem Allies

Quand la lictière du tourbillon[1] versée,
Et seront faces de leurs manteaux couverts[2]
La république par gens nouveaux vexée[3]
Lors blancs et rouges jugeront à l'envers.

CI,Q3

Interpretation

When the bed of revolution is overthrown and [the revolutionaries] resign themselves to their misfortune, the Republic will be injured the moment the whites [the Moslems] and the reds [Eastern Bloc] disagree.

[1] Latin *turbo*: revolution. DLLB.
[2] To envelop oneself in one's cloak, i.e. be resigned, stoically accept the misfortune with which one is threatened. DL7V.
[3] Latin *vexo*: I shake up, damage, injure. DLLB.

THE MIDDLE EAST AND THE THIRD WORLD WAR

Wars in Palestine. Arab–Israeli Conflicts

Les lieux peuplez seront inhabitables,
Pour champs avoir grande division:
Regnes livrez à prudens incapables,
Entre les frères mort et dissention.

CII,Q95

Interpretation

Peopled areas will be made uninhabitable [nuclear fallout?] for very divided territories [Palestine]. The powers will be given over to incapable governments. Death and dissension will reign between brothers [Arab and Jew].

The Eastern Origin of the Third World War

De l'Orient viendra le coeur Punique[1]
Fascher Hadrie et les hoirs[2] Romulides,
Accompagné de la classe Libique,
Tremblez Mellites[3] et proches isles vuides.

CI,Q9

Interpretation

From the East will come the treacherous act which will strike the Adriatic Sea and the heirs of Romulus [Italians], with the Libyan fleet; tremble, inhabitants of Malta and its archipelago.

[1] *Foi punique*: bad faith. DL.
[2] Legal term for an heir. DL7V.
[3] Latin Melita: Malta. DLLB.

Colonel Gaddafy Stirs up the Arab World against the West. The Great King: a Man of Culture against the Arabs

Prince libinique puissant en Occident,
François d'Arabe viendra tant enflammer
Scavant aux lettres sera condescendent,
La langue Arabe en François translater.

CIII,Q27

Interpretation

A Libyan chief of state, powerful in the west, will come to inflame so many Arabs against the French, then comes an educated and well-intentioned man who will translate the Arab language into French.

Moslem Anti-Christian Forces in Iraq and Syria

La grande bande et secte crucigère,[1]
Se dressera en Mésopotamie:[2]
Du proche fleuve compagnie lege,
Que telle loy tiendra pour ennemie.

CIII,Q61

Interpretation

The great band and anti-Christian sect of Moslems will rise up in Iraq and Syria near the Euphrates[3] with a tank force and will hold the [Christian] law to be its enemy.

[1] For *crucifigere*: Latin: to crucify, put on the cross. DLLB. Example of syncope.
[2] I.e. Iraq and northern Syria. AU.
[3] The Euphrates runs through both countries.

Persecution in the Moslem Countries of Asia, Especially in Turkey

Par toute Asie grande proscription,[1]
Mesme en Mysie, Lysie et Pamphylie:[2]
Sang versera par absolution,[3]
D'un jeune noir[4] remply de felonnie.

CIII,Q60

Interpretation

There will be great confiscations [of Christian property] throughout Asia and especially in Turkey where blood will be shed in the name of freedom by a young Moslem leader full of treachery.

[1] Latin *proscriptio*: confiscation, putting outside the law. DLLB.
[2] Regions of Turkey. AVL.
[3] Latin *absolutio*: deliverance. DLLB.
[4] Name given to the Moslem dynasty of the Abassids, because it adopted the colour black for its clothing and flags. DL7V.

The Conference between Arabs and Jews

L'ire insensée du combat furieux
Fera à table par frères le fer luyre,
Les départir mort blessé curieux,
Le fier duelle viendra en France nuyre.

CII,Q34

Interpretation

The mad rage of furious battle will make swords shine even among brothers seated at the same table; in order to decide between them, one of them will have to be fatally injured in a curious way; their proud duel will extend to harming France.

Italy Occupied. Spain in the Conflict. The Libyan Head of State

Saturne et Mars en Leo[1] Espagne captive,
Par chef libyque au conflict attrapé,
Proche de Malte, Heredde[2] prinse vive,
Et Romain sceptre sera par coq[3] frappé.

CV,QI4

Interpretation

At the time the war reaches Léon, captive Spain will be engaged in battle by the Libyan leader, Italy having been suddenly taken. Then the [red] power installed in Rome will be smitten by the French king.

[1] For Léon: one of the fifteen ancient areas of Spain. DHB. Example of apocope.
[2] Latin *heres, -edis*; heir. DLLB. The Italians. Cf. CI,Q9. *'les hoirs Romulides'*: the heirs of Romulus.
[3] Emblem of France, but also of the junior branch, the family of Orleans.

The Russo–Moslem Invasion of the Rhine and Danube. Fighting at Malta and the Gulf of Genoa

En l'an bien proche esloingné de Vénus,
Les deux plus grands de l'Asie et d'Affrique:
Du Ryn et Hister[1] qu'on dira sont Venus,
Cris, pleurs à Malte et costé Lygustique.[2]

CIV,Q68

Interpretation

The year people are ready to abandon treachery, the two greatest powers of Asia [USSR] and Africa [Arab countries] will come as far as the Rhine and the Danube. Then there will be cries and weeping at Malta and the Gulf of Genoa.

[1] Ancient name for the Danube. DHB.
[2] Latin Ligusticus sinus: Gulf of Genoa. DHB.

The Invasion of Italy and the Mediterranean Coast. The Earthquakes

Je pleure Nisse, Mannego, Pize, Gennes,
Savone, Sienne, Capue, Modene, Malte
Le dessus sang et glaive par estrennes,[1]
Feu, trembler terre, eau, malheureuse nolte.[2]

CX,Q60

Interpretation

I bewail Nice, Monaco, Pisa, Genoa, Savona, Siena, Capua, Modena and Malta, which will be covered in blood in the grip of fighting. The war, the earthquakes and the revolution will cause an undesired unhappiness.

[1] Grip, grasp, compression. DAFL.
[2] Latin noltis: archaic for 'non vultis': we do not wish. DLLB.

Peace Breaks Down in the Middle East. France and Portugal Hit by the Conflict

La foy Punique en Orient rompue,
Grand Iud,[1] et Rosne Loire, et Tag changeront
Quand du mulet[2] la faim sera repue,
Classe espargie, sang et corps nageront.

CII,Q60

Interpretation

Moslem duplicity will provoke a split in the Middle East. Because of a great person on the Jewish side, the Rhône, Loire and Tagus will see changes when the greed for gold has died down, the fleet will be engulfed, blood and sailors' bodies will be floating.

[1] Latin Judaei: the Jews. DLLB.
[2] Historical allusion: Philip, King of Macedon, used to say there was no impregnable fortress wherever a mule laden with gold could ascend. An expression of the irresistible power of gold. DL7V.

From Israel the War Extends to Western Europe

Par la tumeur[1] de Heb, Po, Tag Timbre et Rome,
Et par l'estang Leman et Aretin:[2]
Les deux grands chefs et citez de Garonne,
Prins, morts, noyez. Partir humain butin.

CIII,Q12

Interpretation

The troubles of Hebron [Israel] will reach the Po, Tagus, Tiber, Rome, Lake of Geneva and Tuscany. The two leaders in the towns of the Garonne [Bordeaux and Toulouse] will be taken prisoner, put to death and drowned. The human spoils will be shared.

[1] Latin tumor: trouble, agitation. DLLB.
[2] Inhabitant of Arezzo, Tuscany (Italy). DL7V.

Conflict in the Adriatic Sea.
Egypt in the War

Naufrage à classe près d'onde Hadriatique,
La terre tremble, esmuë sus l'air en terre mis,
Egypte tremble augment Mahométique,
L'Héraut[1] soy rendre à crier est commis.

CII,Q86

Interpretation

A fleet will be wrecked near the Adriatic Sea, the earth will tremble when an airborne force is defeated. Egypt, augmented by Moslem troops, will tremble. The commander-in-chief will be asked to give himself up.

[1] Public official, formerly entrusted with the task of proclaiming war, whose person was sacrosanct. DL7V.

MONSIGNOR LEFÈVRE AND THE TRADITIONALIST (TONSURED) PRIESTS

Monsignor Lefève Suspended 'A Divinis'.
The Traditionalist Seminary of Albano

Privés seront Razes[1] de leurs harnois,[2]
Augmentera leur plus grande querelle,
Père Liber[3] deceu fulg.[4] Albonois,
Seront rongés sectes à la moelle.

Presage 54, September

Interpretation

The tonsured ones will be deprived of their vestments, which will increase their quarrelsome spirit even more. He who has become independent from the Pope will be mistaken and those from Albano will be the subject of wrath [from the Vatican]. The sects will be gnawed to the very marrow.

[1] Tonsure: circular space on shaved heads of monks. DL7V.
[2] Vestments. DL7V.

³ Latin *liber a patre*, free from the paternal power. DLLB. Hence, freed from the
Pope's authority.
⁴ Latin *fulgor*: lightning. DLLB.

The Traditionalist Movement.
The Comet and the War

Longue crinite¹ le fer le Gouverneur
Faim, fièvre ardente, feu et de sang fumée:
A tous estats Joviaux² grand honneur,³
Seditions par Razes allumée.

Presage 52

Interpretation

When the great comet is seen the leader of the government will be
stricken by war; famine, plague, smoke of war and blood will be seen in
all western countries with all their external signs, when a rebellion will
be sparked off by the tonsured ones [traditionalists].

¹ Latin *crinitus*: long-haired. DLLB. Cf. CII,Q15, '*astre crinite*'.
² Latin *Jovialis*, pertaining to Jove (Jupiter). The planet Jupiter was regarded by
astrologers as a source of good fortune. DL7V. Nostradamus thus denotes the West and
its wellbeing.
³ Latin *honor*: ornaments, trappings, externals. DLLB.

The Ecône Seminary and Monsignor Lefèvre

Du lieu esleu Razes n'estre contens,
Du Lac Leman¹ conduite non prouvée:
Renouveller on fera le vieil temps,
Espeuillera la trame² tant couvée.³

Presage 50, April

Interpretation

The traditionalists will not be content with the election at the Vatican.
The conduct of those from Lake Geneva will not be approved of because

they will renew the customs of former times,[4] the intrigue so secretly hatched will cause them to be ruined.

[1] The Seminary of Ecône is at Riddes, in Switzerland, on the banks of the Rhône, 30 km from Lake Geneva.
[2] Plot, intrigue.
[3] To develop secretly, hatch.
[4] The traditionalists reject the Second Vatican Council's reforms and will accept only the Mass of Pius V, Pope 1566–72.

The Traditionalists against the Council

En péril monde et Rois féliciter,
Razes esmeu[1] par conseil[2] ce qu'estoit
L'Eglise Rois pour eux peuple irriter[3]
Un montrera après ce qu'il n'estoit.

Presage 99, July

Interpretation

The world will be in danger despite the heads of state, who will congratulate each other.[4] The traditionalists will rebel against what the Council will have decided. The cardinals will excite the people against them. And one of them will then show his true face.

[1] Latin *movere*: to rise up, revolt. DLLB.
[2] Latin *consilium*: deliberating assembly. DLLB.
[3] Latin *irritare*: to excite, provoke, anger. DLLB.
[4] Allusion to the Camp David agreement between Begin, Sadat and Carter.

The Big Mistakes Made by Monsignor Lefèvre. His Supporters Deprived of All Power

De bien en mal le temps se changera
Le pache[1] d'Aust[2] des plus Grands esperance:
Des Grands deul[3] LVIS[4] trop plus trebuchera,
Cognus Razez pouvoir ni cognoissance.

Presage 88, September

Interpretation

The good times will change to ill-fortune, although the peace of the south will give rise to the greatest hopes. The great ones [the cardinals] will deplore Monsignor Lefèvre's acts which will make too many errors. His supporters will no longer have power or understanding.

[1] Latin *pax*: peace. DLLB.
[2] *Auster*: Latin word for south wind. DL7V. Nostradamus here refers to the Camp David agreement signed by two 'southern' countries by contrast with the USSR, the Empire of the North Wind (*Aquila*).
[3] From vb. *doloir*: to suffer, deplore, bewail. DAFL.
[4] Abbreviation of *LefeVre*.

The Deaths of Monsignor Lefèvre and the Pope

> Les deuils laissez, supremes alliances,
> Raze Grand mort refus fait en à l'entrée:
> De retour estre bien fait en oubliance,
> La mort du juste à banquet[1] perpétrée.

Presage 57, December

Interpretation

Sadness abandoned, great alliances having been made, the great tonsured one will die, not having been allowed to return to the fold of the Church. In return, he will end up forgotten; the death of the just man [the Pope] will be commemorated by communion [masses].

[1] The Sacred Banquet: Holy Communion. DL7V.

The End of the Secession of the Traditionalist Movement. An End to Their Ecclesiastical Raiment

> Tout innonder[1] à la Razée perte,
> Vol de mur, mort de tous biens abondance:
> Eschappera[2] par manteau[3] de couverte,
> Des neufs et vieux sera tournée chance.

Presage 101

Interpretation

The revolution will cause the loss of the traditionalist movement when the funds are stolen and the consumer society ends. The traditionalist movement will disappear when deprived of ecclesiastical vestments; the novices' luck, like that of the old, will change.

[1] Water or wave, taken as symbols of revolutionary movements.

[2] To vanish, disappear. DL7V.

[3] Bishop's mantle (*Bischofsmantel*); this vestment, in use in the Middle Ages and which the Germans wore until *c.* 1530, was a cloak of chainmail. DL7V.

The Exodus Brought About by the War.
Vatican Outbursts Against the Traditionalists

Au lieu mis la peste et fuite naistre,
Temps variant vent. La mort des trois Grands:
Du ciel grand foudres estat[1] des Razes paistre.[2]
Vieil[3] près de mort bois peu dedans vergans.[4]

Presage 98

Interpretation

They will begin to flee from the places stricken by war and sickness. The wind of history will change the course of the times and the three great heads of state will die. The great pastor will direct the wrath of heaven against the tonsured ones. The archaic system, near to death, will decline a little more.

[1] Latin *exstare*: to show oneself, be visible. DLLB.

[2] Latin *pastor*. DLLB. Like 'the great prophet' (Cf. CII,Q36), the great pastor signifies the Pope.

[3] Cf. CI,Q7: '*Par le Rousseau sennez les entreprises*'.

[4] Latin *vergo*: I decline, am in decline. DLLB.

Certain Traditionalists Rejoin the Church

Remis seront en leur pleine puissance,
D'un point d'accord conjoints, non accordez:
Tous defiez plus aux Razes fiance,
Plusieurs d'entre eux à bande debordez.

Presage 75, September

Interpretation

The traditionalists will be rehabilitated and rejoin the Church through
an agreement. Those who do not come to terms will be challenged. No
longer will there be any confidence in the Traditionalists, several of
whom will be removed from the confraternity.

The Schism in the Catholic Church.
Prince Charles Murdered in London

Dedans la terre du grand temple Celique,[1]
Neveu[2] à Londres par paix fainte[3] meurtry,
La barque alors deviendra schismatique
Liberté fainte sera au corn[4] et cry.

CVI,Q22

Interpretation

In Vatican territory, when the grandson is murdered in London during
a false peace, the vessel [of St Peter] will become schismatic, and a
feigned freedom will be trumpeted and proclaimed.

[1] Celestial. DAFL. Poetic phrase for 'the Catholic Church'. DL7V.
[2] Formerly meaning 'grandson'. DAFL. Prince Charles of England is the grandson of
the last King of England, George VI.
[3] From *feindre*, to feign or pretend. DAFL.
[4] *Cor*, as in cor anglais. DAFL

Schism during the War

Les forteresses des assiégez serrez,
Par poudre à feu profondes en abysme
Les prod">iteurs[1] seront tous vifs serrez,[2]
Onc aux Sacristes n'advint si piteux scisme.

CIV,Q40

Interpretation

The besieged will be shut inside fortresses which will be engulfed by
incendiary weapons, the traitors will be shut away alive. Never will there
be such a miserable schism in the Church.

[1] Latin *proditor*: traitor, perfidious man. DLLB.
[2] Enclosed spot, but also a bar for closing something up, a lock. DAFL.

The Schism and the Anti-Pope.
The Peace Treaty Signed near Venice

Sept mois sans plus obtiendra prélature[1]
Par son décez grand schisme fera naistre:
Sept mois tiendra un autre la préture,
Près de Venise paix, union renaistre.

CVIII,Q93

Interpretation

He will only obtain the prelature [the throne of St Peter] for seven
months and will cause a great schism by dying. Someone other than the
Pope will occupy the throne of St Peter for seven months, and then
peace will be signed near Venice and the unity of the Church will be
restored.

[1] Body of Roman prelates or officers in the Pope's house. DL7V.

The Schism and the Foreign Pope

Par chapeaux rouges querelles et nouveaux scismes
Quand on aura esleu le Sabinois[1]
On produira contre lui grands sophismes
Et sera Rome lésée par Albannois.

CV,Q46

Interpretation

Because of the cardinals there will be quarrels and a new schism, during which the foreigner will have been elected. Great sophisms will be uttered against him and the Vatican will be harmed by the men from Albano.

[1] The Sabines were 'the foreigners' to the Romans.

The Traditionalists and Spain

Devant le lac où plus cher fut jetté
De sept mois et son ost[1] tout déconfit,
Seront Hispans par Albannois gastez
Par délay perte en donnant le conflit.

CVIII,Q94

Interpretation

Near Lake Geneva, where a more cherished [heresy: i.e. Calvinism] was launched, his supporters will be discomfited at the end of seven months. The Spaniards will be corrupted by the men of Albano [the traditionalists] and the conflict will be the reason for their loss.

[1] Crowd, troop. DAFL.

The Failure of Monsignor Lefèvre's Attempts.
His Death in a Slum House

Pour Razes Chef ne parviendra à bout,
Edicts changez, les serrez mis au large:
Mort Grand trouvé moins de foy, bas dedo[1]
Dissimulé, transi frappé à bauge.[2]

Presage 68, February

Interpretation

The leader of the tonsured ones will not attain his ends; rules having been changed [by the Council], those who were beset [by the Pope] will be given latitude. The leader [of the traditionalists] found dead at the moment when, laid low by circumstances, he will be propped up, hidden, chilled, stricken in a wretched hovel.

[1] For '*debout*', as in some editions.
[2] Miserable dwelling. DL7V.

THE INVASION. MILITARY OPERATIONS

Key definitions

USSR: the Bear, Slavonia, Aquila (the North Wind), the North or Pole Star, the Normans, the Boristhenes, the Reds.

The Warsaw Pact: the Gryphon, the goshawk, the seven countries.

John-Paul II: Memel (the Niemen), Pol Mansol, the Great Pontiff, the noble, Penelon (Polenne), Vicar, the Lamb, Sol.

The Moslem world: the Barbarians, Punic, Hannibal.

The Moslem countries cited: Algeria, Tunisia, Morocco, Libya, Persia (Iran), Mesopotamia (Iraq), Carmania (Afghanistan), Byzantium (Turkey).

The Third World War – Invasion

Map labels:
Russian fleet from Mourmansk
Ghent
Brussels
Rheims
Paris
Sarthe
Eure
Marne
Seine
Loire
Saône
Rhine
Tours
Nantes
Lausanne
Poitiers
Geneva
St Julien
Montluel
Lyon
Chambéry
Vienne
Bordeaux
Dordogne
Lot
Garonne
Montélimar
Langon
Durance
Agen
Condom
Lectoure
Monaco
Nice
Auch
Albi
Orgon
Antibes
Bayonne
Mirande
Toulouse
Castres
Moissac
Pau
Béziers
Agde
Marseille
Iles de Lerins
Tarbes
Carcassonne
Narbonne
la seyne
Foix
Rhone
Perpignan
Barcelona
Russian and Moslem troops

Legend:
■ Towns destroyed or damaged
▸ Invasion routes
• Battles

The Axis of the War. The 45th Parallel.
Bordeaux, Geneva and Baku. The Destruction of Geneva

> Cinq et quarante degrez ciel bruslera,
> Feu approcher de la grand'cité neuve:[1]
> Instant grand flamme esparse[2] sautera,
> Quand on voudra des Normans[3] faire preuve.[4]

CVI,Q97

Interpretation

The fire of war will spread along the 45th Parallel and will approach the great new city [Geneva]. In an instant the great divided flame will leap [above the seas], when they will want to take up the war against the Russians.

[1] Geneva means 'new land' and is situated on the 46th Parallel.

[2] Disseminated, separated, divided. DL7V. Probably an allusion to multiple-warhead missiles.

[3] The men of the north. DHB. The Russians, Empire of Aquilon.

[4] To test: to cause to suffer, to subject to painful tests. DL7V.

The War from the 48th Parallel
to the Tropic of Cancer. Water Pollution

> A quarante huict degré climaterique,[1]
> A fin de Cancer[2] si grand sèeheresse,
> Poisson en mer, fleuve, lac cuit hectique,[3]
> Bearn, Bigorre par feu ciel en détresse.

CV,Q98

Interpretation

From the 48th Parallel to the lines of the Tropic of Cancer, there will be a great drought. The fish will die in the sea, in the rivers, in the lakes scorched by continual heat. The Béarn and Bigorre areas will know distress because of incendiary bombing.

[1] Greek χλιματήρ: rank, degree. DGF. The 48th Parallel marks out the frontier between China and USSR, while Paris and Kiev are also on it.

[2] Tropic of Cancer: crosses what was the Spanish Sahara, Mauretania, Algeria, Libya, Egypt, Saudi Arabia, and the Gulf of Oman where it meets the Persian Gulf.
[3] Continuous. Used of gradual or wasting fever, or degenerative illness.

The Defeat of the West. The Pope's Warnings. The Message of Nostradamus Mocked by the Left and by Germany. The Return of the Monarchy

Le pourvoyeur mettra toute en desroutte
Sangsuë[1] et loup, en mon dire n'escoutte
Quand Mars sera au signe du Mouton[2]
Joint à Saturne, et Saturne à la Lune,
Alors sera ta plus grande infortune,
Le Soleil lors en exaltation.

Sixain 46

Interpretation

The procurer [Russia] will set the West in retreat. Neither the people born of revolution [left-wingers] nor the Germans will listen to my message when the dangers of war are mentioned by the Pope during his pontificate, and under the Republic, then, France, you will know your greatest misfortune. Then the monarchy will return.

[1] Revolution, the drinker of blood, i.e. leech.
[2] Cf. the lamb as symbol in Christian art, as referring to Christ, and hence here to the Good Shepherd, i.e. the Pope. DL7V.

The Defection of Two Warsaw Pact Countries. The Pope, Paris and Provence Attacked despite Poland

Le circuit du grand fait ruyneux,
Au nom septiesme du cinquiesme sera:
D'un tiers[1] plus grand l'estrange belliqueux
Mouton,[2] Lutèce, Aix ne garantira.

CII,Q88

Interpretation

The course of the great war which will bring ruin ensures that what one calls the seven [Warsaw Pact countries] will only be five. The foreign country captured in the war, the largest, and representing one third [of the whole] will not be able to guarantee the safety of the Pope, Paris or Aix-en-Provence.

[1] Respective surface areas of Warsaw Pact countries: GDR 108,178 sq. km; Czechoslovakia 127,876 sq. km; Romania 237,500 sq. km; Bulgaria 110,912 sq.km; Hungary 93,032 sq. km; *Poland 312,677 sq. km.* Total 990,175 sq. km. Hence Poland represents a third of the total land area of the USSR's satellites.

[2] Cf. Sixain 46.

The Use of Chemical Weapons. The Discovery of New Oil Deposits. The Declarations of John-Paul II at St-Denis. The Attack of the Moslem Fleet

Par pestilence et feu fruits d'arbres périront,
Signe[1] d'huile[2] abonder. Père Denys non guères:[3]
Des grands mourir. Mais peu d'éstrangers failliront,
Insult,[4] marin Barbare, et dangers de frontières.

Presage 125, July

Interpretation

By fire and pestilence the fruits of the trees are destroyed, then signs of oil in abundance will be discovered. The [Holy] Father will hardly be heard at [St]-Denis. Heads of state will die,[5] although few strangers will do so. The Moslem fleet will jeopardize frontiers by its attack.

[1] Latin *signum*: indication, trace. DLLB.
[2] Mineral oils – the general term for various hydrocarbon liquids, a group comprising shale oil, naphtha, petroleum etc. DL7V.
[3] At St-Denis Pope John-Paul addressed a large gathering of workers and warned them of the perils of nuclear war. (See *Le Monde*, no. 10,992, 3 June 1980.)
[4] Latin *insulto*: I attack. DLLB.
[5] Tito, Brezhnev, Ayatollah Khomeini and others.

The Preparations and Wiles of the Moslem Forces.
John-Paul II at St-Denis. The West's Lack of Concern

Pleurer le ciel ail[1] cela fait faire,
La mer s'appreste. Annibal[2] fait ses ruses:
Denys[3] mouille[4] classe[5] tarde ne taire,[6]
N'a sceu secret et à quoy tu t'amuses.

Presage 11, September

Interpretation

To see the sky weep prompts a wail of sorrow. The war fleets prepare.
The Moslem leader plans his tricks. [The Pope] swirls up at [St]-Denis.[7]
The army will delay mobilizing because no one will know what is secretly
brewing, and during that time people will be enjoying themselves.

[1] For *aie*: cry of pain, usually repeated. DL7V.
[2] Hannibal: Carthaginian general, son of Hamilcar. In his childhood his father made
him swear unremitting hatred of the Romans. DHB. Nostradamus uses the words Carthaginian, Punic or Hannibal among others to denote the Moslem world. Cf. CIII,Q93.
[3] Nostradamus uses the word Denis three times, always in the sense of St-Denis. Cf.
CIX,Q24.
[4] Reference to John-Paul II's helicopter journeys, also to the wet weather.
[5] Latin *classis*: fleet, army. DLLB.
[6] Not to show or display oneself. DL7V.
[7] 'At St-Denis . . . he met the world of the workers. . . . A huge, patient, orderly
crowd. It was 4.30 p.m. Two hours more to wait, footsore, with every so often hard gusts
of rain *soaking* their faces and making several thousand umbrellas open simultaneously. . . .' (*Le Monde*, no. 10,992, 3 June 1980.)

Two Countries Unite and Quarrel.
Egypt Tried by the War.

Les deux contens[1] seront unis ensemble,
Quand la plupart à Mars seront conjoint:
Le grand d'Affrique en effrayeur et tremble,
Duumvirat[2] par la chasse[3] desioinct.[4]

CV,Q23

Interpretation

The two countries which were quarrelling will unite when most countries
are dragged into war. The great country of Africa [Egypt] will tremble
and this duumvirate will fall out because of their defeat.

[1] Latin *contendere*: to quarrel. DLLB. Iraq and Iran?

[2] Latin *duumviratus*: duumvirs, the name for the two magistrates making up a tribunal. DLLB.

[3] Used ordinarily to signify pursuit, chasing, rushing at. DL7V.

[4] Latin *disjunctus*: disunited, split, separated. DLLB.

Missiles Used against the West and Japan. The Third World War. The Reign of the Reds

Celeste feu du costé d'Occident,
Et du midy, courir jusqu'au Levant,[1]
Vers demy morts sans poinct trouver racine[2]
Troisième aage, à Mars le belliqueux,
Des Escarboucles on verra briller feux,
Aage Escarboucle,[3] et à la fin famine.

Sixain 27

Interpretation

Fire come from the sky [missiles] will strike the West and then the South [the Moslem world] will rush upon Japan. Worms will die of hunger without even finding a root to feed upon. This will be the third world war, which will light the warlike fires of the Reds, who will rule, and at the end there will be famine.

[1] Empire of the Rising Sun (*soleil levant*): Japan.

[2] Image to symbolize (and stigmatize) the scarcity.

[3] The carbuncle or garnet is poppy- or blood-red. DL7V.

Religious Persecution in Poland

Persécutée de Dieu sera l'Eglise,
Et les saincts temples seront expoliez,
L'enfant, la mère mettra nud en chemise,
Seront Arabes aux Polons ralliéz.

CV,Q73

Interpretation

The Catholic Church will be persecuted in Poland and the churches will be expropriated. The mother [Church] will be stripped naked by her children, and the Arabs will ally with the Poles [Warsaw Pact].

The Economic Crisis.
War against the West and the Catholic Church

> Le parc¹ enclin² grande calamité,
> Par l'Hesperie³ et Insubre⁴ fera,
> Le feu en nef, peste et captivité,
> Mercure⁵ en l'Arc⁶ Saturne fenera.⁷
>
> CII,Q65

Interpretation

The economy in decline, there will be a great calamity in the West and Italy, war, disaster, and captivity will affect the Church. The time of pillage will ruin Monaco.

¹ Latin *parcus*: economy. DLLB.
² Latin *inclino*: to lower, decline. DLLB.
³ Greek Ἑσπερις: the West. DGF.
⁴ The Milan region. DHB.
⁵ Son of Jupiter, messenger of the gods, himself the god of eloquence, trade and *thieves*. DL7V.
⁶ Latin Monoeci Arx: Monaco. DLLB.
⁷ Latin *feneror*: to ruin. DLLB.

Debauchery in England.
The Conflict Spreads to the United Kingdom

> Jupiter¹ joinct plus Venus qu'à la Lune,
> Apparoissant de plenitude blanche:
> Venus cachée sous la blancheur Neptune,
> De Mars frappée par la gravée² branche.³
>
> CIV,Q33

Interpretation

The world will be even more in the grip of venomous speech and lust than under the influence of the Republican [i.e. Radical] theories which appear during times of extreme candour. Debauchery will be disguised as frankness in England, which will be hit by the grave spread of the conflict.

[1] God of the sky and of the world. DL7V.
[2] Latin *gravis*: heavy, weighty, grave. DLLB.
[3] Figurative: for 'spread', 'extension'.

The Sapping of English Society. Great Britain Surprised by the War.

Venus, Neptune poursuivra l'entreprise,
Serrez[1] pensifs. troublez les opposans:
Classe en Adrie. citez[2] vers la Tamise,
Le quart bruit[3] blesse de nuict les reposans.

Presage 12, October

Interpretation

Virulent words and debauchery will carry out their purpose in Great Britain. Intellectuals will be imprisoned and opponents tortured. A fleet in the Adriatic will move towards the Thames. The noise [of war] will wake a quarter of the inhabitants from their sleep.

[1] *Serre*: prison. DAFL.
[2] Latin *cito*: I put into motion. DLLB.
[3] Quarrel, dispute. DL7V.

The Attack on England after the Invasion of Germany. War and Revolution

Un peu devant ou après l'Angleterre
Par mort de loup mise aussi bas que terre,
Verra le feu resister[1] contre l'eau,
Le ralumant avec telle force
Du sang humain, dessus l'humaine escorce[2]
Faute de pain, bondance de couteau.[3]

Sixain 50

Interpretation

A little before or after, England will be ruined because of the fall of Germany and will see war put an end to revolution; the war being revived with such force that human blood will be spilt all over the earth, so that food will be lacking and weapons abound.

[1] Latin *resisto*: I stop. DLLB.
[2] The earth's crust.
[3] Poetic: dagger. DL7V.

Revolutionary Movements in Great Britain and Italy

La Grande Bretagne comprise l'Angleterre,
Viendra par eaux[1] si haut inonder,
La ligne neusve d'Ausonne[2] fera guerre,
Que contre eux ils se viendront bander.[3]

CIII,Q70

Interpretation

Great Britain, including England, will be very thoroughly submerged by revolution. The new Italian league will wage war and the Italians will make an effort to resist it.

[1] Symbolizing revolution.
[2] The Ausonii were a tribe in Italy and the name was often extended to mean the whole of Italy. DHB.
[3] To make an effort to resist. DL7V.

The Invasion of Great Britain by the Russians

De l'Aquilon les efforts seront grands,
Sur l'Océan sera la porte ouverte:
Le regne en l'Isle sera réintégrand,
Tremblera Londres par voille descouverte.

CII,Q68

Interpretation

The [war] efforts of Russia will be great; she will have access to the Atlantic Ocean. The government will be re-established in England and London, covered with boats, will tremble.

The British Isles Besieged. Famine

> Ceux dans les Isles de long temps assiegez:
> Prendront vigueur force contre ennemis,
> Ceux par dehors morts de faim profligez
> En plus grand faim que jamais seront mis.

CIII,Q71

Interpretation

The inhabitants of the British Isles will be besieged for a long time; they will strongly resist the enemy. The latter will die of hunger because of those come from outside and they will know greater famine than ever.

The Attack on the British Isles. Combat between the French and the Moslems

> Le grand Neptune du profond de la mer,
> De gent Punique et sang Gaulois meslé:
> Les Isles à sang pour le tardif ramer,[1]
> Plus luy nuira que l'occult mal celé.

CII,Q78

Interpretation

England will be attacked from the bottom of the sea [submarine attack]; French and Moslem blood will mingle. The British Isles will be bloodied because of taking pains too late, this will be far more harmful than hiding the misfortune [from the people].

[1] To take considerable pains, trouble. DL7V.

The Invasion of Aquitaine and England by Moslem Troops

Vers Aquitaine par insuls Britanniques,
De par eux mesmes grandes incursions:
Pluyes, gelées feront terroirs iniques,[1]
Port Selyn[2] fortes fera invasions.

CII,QI

Interpretation

Around Aquitaine and the British Isles there will be great troop landings. Revolutionary movements and a hard winter will render these territories wretched for they will have endured strong invasions from a Moslem port.

[1] Latin *iniquus*: unfortunate, wretched. DLLB.
[2] Greek Σελήνη: the moon. DGF. Denotes the Moslem crescent. The name of the Moslem port involved remains uncertain.

The Siege of London.
The Capture of the British Head of State

La forteresse auprès de la Tamise,
Cherra[1] par lors, le Roy dedans serré,
Auprès du pont[2] sera veu en chemise,
Un devant mort, puis dans le fort barré.[3]

CVIII,Q37

Interpretation

The fortifications near the Thames will collapse then, the leader of the government besieged inside. He will be seen in reduced circumstances by the sea, one having died beforehand, then he will be locked up inside the fort.

[1] Future of *cheoir*: to fall. DAFL.
[2] Greek ποντός: sea. DGF.
[3] To close by means of bars. DL7V.

The War in the Rhône Valley.
The Occupation of England

Sur les rochers sang on verra plouvoir.
Sol Orient, Saturne Occidental:
Pres d'Orgon[1] guerre, à Rome grand mal voir,
Nefs parfondrées et prins le Tridental.[2]

CV,Q62

Interpretation

Blood will be seen raining down upon the mountain ranges when the king comes from the East to re-establish the West. The war will reach Orgon, the Pope will be disgraced in Rome, ships having been sunk and England occupied.

[1] Main town of the canton of Bouches-du-Rhône, on the left bank of the Durance. DHB.
[2] Symbolically, 'Neptune's trident' denotes the empire of the sea. DL7V. Symbol for England.

The Invasion of West Germany and Italy
by the Russians. Yugoslavia Delivered up to Massacre

Laict,[1] sang grenouilles[2] escoudre[3] en Dalmatie,[4]
Conflict donné, peste près de Balennes,[5]
Cry sera grand par toute Esclavonie,[6]
Lors naistra monstre[7] pres et dedans Ravenne.

CII,Q32

Interpretation

After the milk of wellbeing, the blood of the people will flow in Yugoslavia, when war breaks out, as well as a calamity near Ballenstedt. The [war] cry will be loud throughout Russia. Thus, then, a scourge will be born near and in Ravenna.

[1] Milk = biblical symbol. Nostradamus uses it to denote easy living and wellbeing.
[2] Swarms of frogs symbolize all the races of history, and also all people not content with their lot. DL7V.
[3] For *escorre*: flow, rush. DAFL.

⁴ Region of Europe situated between the Adriatic on the west and the Dinaric Alps on the east. Part of the general area of Illyria. DHB.

⁵ Gallicization of Ballenstedt: town of the Duchy of Anhalt, on the Gretel, several kilometres from the border of West Germany and the GDR. DHB.

⁶ Slavonia: under the Romans, made up part of Pannonia (Hungary). Owes its name to the Slavi, Sarmatian tribe which settled there in the seventh century. DHB. Denotes Russia.

⁷ Latin *monstrum*: scourge. DLLB.

The Invasion of Italy and Yugoslavia. Petrol Shortage

Entre Campagne,¹ Sienne,² Flora, Tustie,³
Six mois neuf jours ne pleuvra une goute,
L'estrange langue en terre Dalmatie,
Courira sus, vastant la terre toute.

CII,Q84

Interpretation

Between the provinces of Campania, Siena, Umbria, there will be six months and nine days of total penury [petrol?]. A strange language will be heard in Dalmatia [Russian or Arabic?] which will run through and devastate the whole earth.

¹ Campania: province of Italy, main town Naples; made up of Naples, Salerno, Avellino etc. DL7V.

² Province of Italy (Tuscany). DL7V.

³ Tuscia: comprising Etruria and Umbria. DHB.

Moslem War in the Black Sea and Yugoslavia. Help from Portugal: American Landings?

Conflict Barbar en la Cornere noire,
Sang espandu trembler la Dalmatie
Grand Ismael mettra son promontoire¹
Ranes² trembler, secours Lusitanie.³

CIX,Q60

Interpretation

The Moslems will take the war into the Black Sea and the blood they will shed will make Yugoslavia tremble, where the Moslem leader will reach his zenith. The people will tremble, then help comes from Portugal.

[1] Latin *promontorium*: culminating point. DLLB.
[2] Latin *rana*: frog. DLLB. See CII,Q32, note 2.
[3] Ancient name for Portugal.

The Russian Attack on Yugoslavia and in the Adriatic. The Turkish Head of State. Help Comes from Spain and Her King

Au port de PUOLA[1] et de Saint Nicolas,[2]
Péril Normande[3] au goulfre Phanatique[4]
Cap.[5] de Bisance rues crier hélas.
Secours de Gaddes[6] et du grand Philippique.[7]

CIX,Q30

Interpretation

At Pola, come from Russia [6 December?], the peril of the men of the North [Russians] will reach the Yugoslav coast. The ruler of Turkey will cry for quarter, then help will come from Spain with the descendant of Philip V.

[1] For Pola or Pula, by epenthesis: Yugoslav town on the Adriatic, south of Trieste. Good military *port*. DHB and AU.
[2] Patron saint of Russia, Saint's Day 6 December.
[3] Or North-men, i.e. men of the north. DHB.
[4] Flanatic Gulf, part of the Adriatic between Istria and Illyria, in Yugoslavia, today the Gulf of Kvarner. DHB. Nostradamus drops the *l* by syncope. Pola is situated at the entrance to this gulf.
[5] Latin *caput*: chief, leader. DLLB.
[6] Ancient name for Cadiz, Spain. DHB.
[7] Philip V, head of the Spanish House of Bourbon. DHB. Nostradamus here signifies the King of Spain.

Turkey Ransacked from Yugoslavia

Le plus grand voile[1] hors du port de Zara[2]
Près de Bisance fera son entreprise:
D'ennemi perte et l'amy ne sera,
Le tiers à deux fera grand pille et prise.

CVII,Q83

Interpretation

The greatest airborne force will leave from the port of Zara to make a warlike enterprise in Turkey. It will make a huge slaughter and will not be allied [to the Turks]; it will devastate and ransack two-thirds of the country.

[1] Used by Nostradamus to denote planes (the first planes were partly built of canvas).
[2] Port of Dalmatia, Yugoslavia, on the Adriatic. DHB.

The Moslem Invasion

Le temps purge,[1] pestilence, tempeste,
Barbare insult. Fureur, invasion:
Maux infinis par ce mois nous appreste,
Et les plus Grands, deux moins, d'irrision.[2]

Presage 60, April

Interpretation

The time will be filthy, pestilential and violent because of a furious Moslem attack and invasion. Great calamities are prepared in April and great persons will be ridiculed except for two among them.

[1] Latin *purgamen*: filth, ordure. DLLB.
[2] Latin *irrisio*: mockery. DLLB.

The End of the Good Times.
Devastation Wrought by the Moslems

Triremes pleins tout aage captifs,
Temps bon à mal, le doux pour amertume:
Proye à Barbares trop tost seront bastifs,[1]
Cupide de voir plaindre au vent la plume.[2]

CX,Q97

Interpretation

Ships will lead away prisoners of all ages. Good times will become times of misfortune; bitterness replace sweetness: the Moslems will get hold of the booty all too soon, eager to see [France] and the French complain and float in the wind.

[1] To dispose of, procure for oneself. DAFL.
[2] To be carried by, or float in the wind, as the wind directs. DL7V.

The Battle Fought by German and Spanish Forces
against the Moslems

Guerre, tonnerre, maints champs depopulez,
Frayeur et bruit, assault à la frontière:
Grand Grand failli. pardon aux Exilez,
Germains, Hispans par mer Barba. bannière.

Presage 29

Interpretation

War and bombing will devastate many territories in dread and noise: frontiers will be attacked. The great leader having fallen, exiles having been pardoned. The Germans and Spaniards will attack the Moslem forces by sea.

The Mediterranean Coast Surrendered to Looting

Depuis Monach jusqu'auprès de Sicile,
Toute la plage demourra désolée,
Il n'y aura fauxbourg, cité ne ville,
Que par Barbares pillée soit et volée.

CII,Q4

Interpretation

From Monaco to Sicily, the coastline will be ransacked. Not a town or district will escape the looting of the Moslem troops.

The Invasion of West Germany, the Mediterranean and Atlantic Coasts. Recognition of the Inefficacy of the Geneva Conventions

Par les Sueves[1] et lieux circonvoisins,
Seront en guerre pour cause des nuées:[2]
Camp marins locustes[3] et cousins,[4]
Du Leman fautes seront bien desnuées.[5]

CV,Q85

Interpretation

West Germany and her neighbours [Switzerland, the Netherlands, France and Belgium] will be at war because of the vast hordes [of Russian troops]. The ports of war will be full of planes and ships and the mistakes of Lake Geneva [treaties and conventions of Geneva] will be exposed.

[1] Name given by the Romans to tribes of the German area. The principal seat of the Suevic League, formed in the third century, was south-west Germany, from the Rhine to the Main, the Saale and the Danube. DHB. Today, West German territory.

[2] Innumerable multitude. DL7V.

[3] Latin *locusta*: locust. DHB. Nostradamus refers to aeroplanes by this word. Cf. Revelations: IX.

[4] Genus of Diptera – insects whose origins are aquatic. DL7V. i.e. warships.

[5] Expose, despoil, denude. DAFL.

Bombings in Italy

Planure,[1] Ausonne[2] fertille, spacieuse,
Produira[3] taons si tant de sauterelle,
Clarté solaire deviendra nubileuse,
Ronger[4] le tout, grand peste venir d'elles.

CIV,Q48

Interpretation

So many planes will advance over the fertile and spacious soil of the Po
that the sun will be obscured. These aircraft will bring destruction and
calamity.

[1] Latin *planura*: plain. DLLB.
[2] Latin *Ausonia*: ancient region of Italy, and by extension all Italy. DLLB.
[3] Latin *produco*: I cause to advance, push forward. DLLB.
[4] Attack, then destroy. DL7V.

The Pillage and Ransack of the
Mediterranean Coast

Erins,[1] Antibor, villes autour de Nice
Seront vastées, fort par mer et par terre
Les sauterelles[2] terre et mer vent propice,
Prins, morts, troussez, pillez, sans loy de guerre.

CIII,Q82

Interpretation

The Lerin islands, Antibes and the towns near Nice will be devastated
by sea and land forces, with tanks borne by sea and land, and the wind
[of history] being favourable to them. The inhabitants will be taken
prisoner, massacred, dispatched, ravished, without respecting the rules
of war.

[1] The Lerin islands (example of aphesis), French Mediterranean islands off the coast
of the Var. DHB.
[2] Cf. Revelations: IX, 3 and 7. 'And there came out of the smoke locusts upon the
earth . . . And the shapes of the locusts were like unto horses prepared unto battle' . . .
Cavalry, i.e. tanks.

Moslem Ravages in the Mediterranean, Corsica, Sardinia and Italy

Naples, Palerme, et toute la Cecile,
Par main barbare sera inhabitée,
Corsique, Salerne[1] et de Sardeigne l'Isle,
Faim, peste, guerre, fin des maux intemptée.[2]

CVII,Q6

Interpretation

Naples, Palermo and all Sicily will be laid waste by the Moslem troops, as will Corsica, Sardinia and Salerno, where famine will reign, and sickness and war, then the end of the misfortunes will be reached.

[1] Italian town in ancient Kingdom of Naples.
[2] Latin *intento*: I direct, tend towards. DLLB.

Invasion by Sea at Agde. The Landing of an Army a Million Strong. Western Naval Defeat in the Mediterranean

Au port d'Agde trois fustes[1] entreront,
Portant l'infect[2] non foy et pestilence.
Passant le pont[3] mil milles[4] embleront,[5]
Et le pont rompre à tierce résistance.

CVIII,Q21

Interpretation

Three warships will enter the port of Agde, bringing with them lawless, faithless invasion and pestilence. A million soldiers will assemble to cross the sea and the resistance by sea will thrice be broken.

[1] Low-draught vessel with sails and oars. DAFL.
[2] Latin *inficio*: I mix, impregnate, penetrate. DLLB.
[3] Greek πουτός: sea. DGF.
[4] *Mil fois mille*: i.e. a million.
[5] Aphesis.

The Defeat of a Franco–Spanish Army in the Pyrenees. The War in Switzerland and Germany. The Rhône and Languedoc Hit by the Conflict

Deux grands frères seront chassez d'Espagne
L'aisné vaincu sous les monts Pyrénées,
Rougir mer, Rosne, sang Léman d'Alemagne,
Narbon, Blyterres,[1] d'Agath contaminées.[2]

CIV,Q94

Interpretation

Two great allies will be driven out of Spain. The elder of the two [Juan Carlos I] will be defeated at the foot of the Pyrenees. The sea will be occupied by the red fleet and blood will flow beside the Rhône, on Lake Geneva, and in Germany. Narbonne, Béziers and Agde will be contaminated.

[1] Béziers, conquered c. 120 BC by the Romans, colonized by Julius Caesar, who named it Julia Biterra. DHB. Letter l added by epenthesis.
[2] Latin contamino: I soil, infect. DLLB.

The War in Languedoc. The Defeat of the French Army

Chassez seront sans faire long combat,
Par le pays seront plus fort grevez:[1]
Bourg et cité auront plus grand débat,[2]
Carcas. Narbonne auront coeur esprouvez.

CI,Q5

Interpretation

The French army will be beaten without fighting long. The most powerful will be overwhelmed across the country. Towns and villages will be beset by still greater battles. The centres of the towns of Carcassonne and Narbonne will be hard pressed.

[1] Overwhelm, torment, oppress. DAFL.
[2] Resistance, struggle. DAFL.

The Invasion from Switzerland
to the Paris Area. The Defeat of the Germans,
Swiss and Italians

Du lac Lyman et ceux de Brannonices,[1]
Tous assemblez contre ceux d'Aquitaine,
Germains beaucoup, encore plus Souisses,
Seront defaicts avec ceux d'humaine.[2]

CIV,Q74

Interpretation

From Switzerland to the Eure, troops will gather to march upon south-west France. The [West] Germans and even more of the Swiss will be wiped out with the originators of humanism [the Italians].

[1] Brannovices, a Gallic tribe who inhabited the area between the Sarthe and the Eure. DLLB.
[2] Florence was the first centre of humanism. From Italy humanism (the classics) spread throughout western Europe from the end of the fifteenth century. DL7V.

Power Transferred to Savoy.
The Occupation of Languedoc by
Warsaw Pact Troops

Le monde proche du dernier période,[1]
Saturne encor tard sera de retour:
Translat empire devers[2] nations Brode,[3]
L'oeil[4] arraché à Narbon par Autour.[5]

CIII,Q92

Interpretation

The western world is nearing its end; the epoch of renewal is still slow to come. Power will be transferred to the Savoy area, having been taken from Narbonne by the Warsaw Pact.

[1] The last period, the end. The power of this empire entering its last phase. DL.
[2] Beside, near. DL7V.
[3] 'After the Allobroges, whom the Provençal people by corruption and syncope call Brodes, were conquered by Fabius Maximus near Isère . . .' (César Nostradamus: History of Provence, Lyon 1614). Savoy. DHB.

[4] Power, in sense of surveillance and right of survey.
[5] Genus of predatory bird. DL7V. Has same significance as the gryphon, meaning the Warsaw Pact countries.

The Abandonment of Perpignan by its Inhabitants. The Western Counter-attack in the Mediterranean

La crainte armée de l'ennemy Narbon,
Effroyera si fort les Hespériques:[1]
Parpignan vuidé par l'aveugle darbon,[2]
Lors Barcelon par mer donra les piques.[3]

CVI,Q56

Interpretation

Fear of the enemy army at Narbonne will greatly perturb the westerners [Americans]. Perpignan will be abandoned because of the loss of power at Narbonne; then, near Barcelona, rockets will be launched by sea [nuclear submarines].

[1] Greek Ἐσπερίς: West.
[2] For De Narbo (or Narbonne): anagram. Cf. CIII,Q92.
[3] Allusion to the pointed ends of the missiles.

War in the Pyrenees and Languedoc

Plainctes et pleurs, cris et grands hurlements,
Pres de Narbon à Bayonne et en Foix:
O quels horribles calamitez changemens,
Avant que Mars revolu quelques fois.

CIX,Q63

Interpretation

Laments, tears, cries and loud screams will be heard near Narbonne and the Basses-Pyrénées as far as Ariège. O the changes will be horrible before the time of war has run its course.

The East German Military Leader
in the Pyrenees and Languedoc. The Capet King
in Difficulty

L'Æmathion[1] passer mont Pyrénées,
En Mars Narbon ne fera résistance:
Par mer et terre fera si grand menée,
Cap n'ayant terre seure pour demeurance.

CIX,Q64

Interpretation

The East German leader will pass through the Pyrenees; Narbonne will
not resist during the war. There will be such great actions by land and
sea that the Capetian will not have anywhere to go in safety.

[1] Cf. CX,Q7.

Attack by Portugal as far as
the Pyrenees

Proche del duero[1] par mer Cyrenne[2] close,
Viendra percer les grands monts Pyrénées.
La main plus courte et sa percée gloze,[3]
A Carcassonne conduira ses menées.

CIII,Q62

Interpretation

Near the Douro, by the Libyan coast, which will have been closed, it
will cross the Pyrenees. With inferior forces and by guerrilla action it
will drive on as far as Carcassonne.

[1] For Douro, river of Spain and Portugal, which crosses Portugal from east to west.
DHB.
[2] Cyrenia, capital of Cyrenaica, today Curin or Grennah, town in Libya. DHB and AU.
[3] Gloz, glos, derived from glot and gloton: ruffian, brigand, rabble. DAFL.

The Treason of a Politician. His Death.
Assault in Languedoc

La Cité prise par tromperie et fraude,
Par le moyen d'un beau jeune attrapé,
Assaut donné, Raubine[1] près de l'AUDE,
Luy et tous morts pour avoir bien trompé.

CIII,Q85

Interpretation

Paris will be occupied thanks to a trick and betrayal through a handsome young [politician] who will be caught. The region of the Robines of Narbonne will be attacked; this politician and his supporters will die for their treachery.

[1] Name given in the Midi to small canals, and which now applies to a group of navigation canals: the *Robines* of Narbonne, Vic, and Aigues-Mortes. (Also, *Roubine*.) DL7V.

Moslem Troops in Italy

La faction cruelle à robe longue
Viendra cacher souz les pointus poignards:
Saisir Florence le duc et lieu diphlongue,[1]
Sa descouverte[2] par immeurs[3] et flangnards.[4]

CX,Q33

Interpretation

The cruel sect of Moslems will come, hiding weapons under their long robes. Their leader will seize Florence and burn the place twice, sending in advance cunning men without laws [spies].

[1] From Greek δίς: twice; and φλογόω: set on fire. DGF.
[2] Military term: movement of a reconnaissance patrol. DL7V.
[3] Latin *im* and *mos, moris*: law, hence *lawless*.
[4] From *flasnier*: to trick. DAFL.

The Invasion of Italy by Moslem Troops

Un qui les dieux d'Annibal[1] infernaux,
Fera renaistre, effrayeur des humains:
Oncq'plus d'horreur ne plus dire iournaulx,
Qu'avint viendra par Babel[2] aux Romains.

CII,Q30

Interpretation

A person who will revive the terrifying gods of the Carthaginians will frighten men. The newspapers could never say that more horror had afflicted the Romans, because of their confusion.

[1] Carthaginian general. He recommenced war with the Romans in the middle of a peace, and breaking all treaties, by taking and sacking Saguntum, a town allied with Rome (219 BC). Thinking the Romans could only be defeated at home, he crossed the Alps and invaded Italy. DHB. A parallel between ancient and modern Rome is established here by Nostradamus.

[2] Signifying confusion. DL7V.

The Invasion of Moslem Troops at Port-de-Bouc.
The Arrival of a Western Fleet

La tour de Boucq[1] craindra fuste Barbare,
Un temps, longtemps, après barque hespérique.
Bestail, gens, meubles, tous deux feront grand tare
Taurus[2] et Libra, quelle mortelle picque.

CI,Q28

Interpretation

Port-de-Bouc will fear the Moslem fleet for a while; long afterwards a western fleet will arrive. Animals, men and their possessions will be injured by the two [fleets]. What a deadly blow for fecundity and justice.

[1] Port-de-Bouc, town at the Gulf of Fos. DL7V.

[2] Astrological: second sign of the zodiac, ruled horoscopically by Venus; symbolizing creative forces and fecundity. DL7V.

The Warsaw Pact and the Russians.
The Invasion of France

Comme un gryphon[1] viendra le Roy d'Europe.
Accompagné de ceux de l'Aquilon:
De rouges et blancs[2] conduira grande troppe
Et iront contre le Roy de Babylone.[3]

cx,Q86

Interpretation

The chief of [eastern] Europe will come like a vulture, accompanied by the Russians. He will lead a great force of soldiers from the Communist and Moslem countries which will go against the government of Paris.

[1] Gryphon: from Latin, *gryphus*: vulture. General name for different birds of prey. DL7V. Poland's coat of arms consists of a bird of prey.
[2] Reference to the white burnous worn by Moslems.
[3] Great Babylon, the modern Babylon: ref. to the great centres such as London, Paris. DL7V.

The Turkish Army Lands in Spain.
West Germany Occupied

Le Bizantin faisant oblation,[1]
Après avoir Cordube[2] à foy reprinse:
Son chemin long repos pamplation,[3]
Mer passant proy[4] par Colongna[5] prinse.

CVIII,Q51

Interpretation

The Turkish leader will make a [peace] offer after taking Cordova for the Moslem faith, will halt his expansion after a long journey, when by sea West Germany will be occupied by the Warsaw Pact.

[1] Latin *oblatio*: offer. DLLB.
[2] Latin Corduba: Cordova. DLLB.
[3] Neologism from παν (all) and *ampliatio*, growth, expansion. DLLB.
[4] Reference to griffin, bird of prey denoting Warsaw Pact. Cf. cx,Q86.
[5] Agrippinensis Colonia: colony of Agrippina on the Rhine (Cologne). DLLB. West Germany.

The Russian Invasion of Western Europe

Vers Aquilon grands efforts par hommasse,
Presque l'Europe et l'univers vexer,[1]
Les deux eclypses mettra en telle chasse[2]
Et aux Pannons[3] vie et mort renforcer.

CVIII,QI5

Interpretation

Around Russia great [war] efforts will be made by a mass of men who will come to stir up [western] Europe and almost the whole universe. Between two eclipses, this mass of men will put [the western troops] to such a flight that the Hungarians will receive life and death reinforcements.

[1] Latin *vexo*: I agitate forcibly, stir, shake up. DLLB.
[2] Running away, flight. DL7V.
[3] Pannonia: ancient name for Hungary.

The Leader of Iran's Present to the West. The Attack on France and Italy Launched from Afghanistan

Le grand Satyre[1] et Tigre[2] d'Hircanie,[3]
Don présenté à ceux de l'Occean,
Un chef de classe istra[4] de Carmanie[5]
Qui prendra terre au Tyrren[6] Phocean.[7]

CIII,Q90

Interpretation

The great cynical person from the Tigris and Iran will make a gift to those of the Atlantic Alliance; then a military leader will leave from Afghanistan to land in the Tyrrhenian Sea and Marseille.

[1] Cynical or impudent person. DL7V.
[2] River in Asia, running into the Persian Gulf, in Iran.
[3] Hyrcania: region of ancient Asia extending along the south-east coast of the Caspian Sea, belonging to the Persian Empire. DHB. Today Iranian territory.
[4] *Istre*, form of *issir*: to go out, forth. DAFL.

[5] Province of the old Persian Empire, now part of Afghanistan. DL7V.
[6] Naples, important NATO base.
[7] Nostradamus adds *an* to the word *Phocée*, by paragoge and for the rhyme's sake.

The Russian Invasion of Afghanistan.
Afghan Resistance. Its Extermination

Le sainct empire[1] viendra en Germanie,
Ismaëlites trouveront lieux ouverts:
Anes[2] voudront aussi la Carmanie,
Les soustenans[3] de terre tous couverts.

CX,Q31

Interpretation

The Russians will come into Afghanistan; the Moslems will find these places open. The Afghans would like to keep Afghanistan; but the resistance will be buried.

[1] Russian Empire, the largest state in the world. Orthodox religion dominated Russia and the Tsar was its head since Peter the Great; the *Holy* Synod supported him in the administration of ecclesiastical affairs. DHB. 'Holy Russia' is a well-known expression.
[2] Certain Carmanian tribes, according to Strabo, led donkeys into battle. DL7V. Nostradamus refers to the Afghan resisters of the Soviet invasion.
[3] Latin *sustineo*: I resist. DLLB.

The Use of Nuclear Arms
against Russia

Soleil levant un grand feu on verra,
Bruit et clarté[1] vers Aquilon tendans,[2]
Dedans le rond[3] mort et cris l'on orra,[4]
Par glaive[5] feu, faim, morts les attendans.

CII,Q91

Interpretation

In the East a great fire will be seen, noise and flames [of war] will extend across Russia. There will be deaths within a circle [nuclear bombs] and cries will be heard. By war, fire, famine, men will wait for death.

[1] Light, torch. DL7V.
[2] Latin *tendo*: I hold, extend.
[3] Circle, circular line. DL7V.
[4] Future of *oïr* (*ouir*), to hear. DAFL.
[5] Sword: symbol of war and battle. DL7V.

The Russo–Moslem Alliance

Le fait luysant de neuf vieux eslevé,
Seront si grands par midy Aquilon:
De sa seur[1] propre[2] grandes alles[3] levé
Fuyant meurtry au buisson[4] d'ambellon.[5]

CX,Q69

Interpretation

The remarkable fact of the rise [to power] of a new leader [after the disappearance] of an old one, [efforts] by the Moslems and Russia will be so great that he will muster huge aerial forces [wings] in the neighbouring city [Warsaw Pact] and when hurt will manage, despite weakness, to make shift.

[1] Latin *soror* adj. *soror civitas*: sister city, ally. DLLB.
[2] Latin *proprior*: very close, neighbouring. DLLB.
[3] Latin *ales*: winged, having wings. DLLB.
[4] *Se sauver à travers les buissons* = to shirk the issue, run away from. DL7V.
[5] Latin *imbellis*: weak, unwarlike, defenceless. DLLB.

The Revolution in Paris.
Turkey Agitated by Iran to Revolt
against the West

Par les deux testes, et trois bras[1] séparés,
La grand cité sera par eaux vexée:[2]
Des Grands d'entre eux par exil esgarés,
Par teste Perse Bysance fort pressée.

CX,Q86

Interpretation

Because of two leaders separated from their three executives, Paris will be shaken by revolution. A certain number of its leaders [ministers] will be distanced by exile at the moment when Turkey is spurred [against the West] by the Iranian leader.

[1] As in 'right-hand man'. DL7V.
[2] Latin *vexo*: I stir up, shake. DLLB.

The French Fleet in the Mediterranean. Moslem Troops in the Adriatic: Their Defeat

Si France passe outre mer Lygustique,
Tu te verras en isles et mers enclos:
Mahommet contraire, plus mer Hadriatique,
Chevaux et Asnes[1] tu rongeras les os.[2]

CIII,Q23

Interpretation

If the French fleet goes beyond the Ligurian coast, it will find itself caught between islands [Sardinia, Corsica, Sicily] and the sea. The Moslem troops will oppose it and still more so in the Adriatic. It will finish with the complete ruin of the Moslem forces.

[1] Cf. CX,Q31.
[2] To gnaw something to the bone, i.e. ruin completely and thoroughly, bit by bit. DL7V.

Sounds of War in Russia

Par la discorde effaillir au défaut,
Un tout à coup le remettra au sus:[1]
Vers l'Aquilon seront les bruits si haut,
Lesions,[2] pointes[3] à travers, par dessus.

Presage 26

Interpretation

Through discord [the French] will collapse by default. A [person] will suddenly raise them up. In Russia there will be such great noises [of war] that there will be damage done by rockets across the sky.

[1] Above. DAFL.
[2] Damage, wrong. DAFL.
[3] Thin, tapered end. DL7V. Allusion to the noses of missiles.

The Breaking off of Diplomatic Relations with Iran

Un peu devant l'ouvert commerce,
Ambassadeur viendra de Perse,
Nouvelle au franc pays porter,
Mais non receu, vaine espérance,
A son grand Dieu sera l'offence,
Feignant de le vouloir quitter.

Sixain 8

Interpretation

A little before signing some trade agreements, an ambassador will come from Iran to bring some news to France. But he will not be received and his hope will be vain. He will take it as an offence to his status and will pretend to want to leave the country.

The Hexagon Attacked on Five Sides. Tunisia and Algeria Incited by Iran. The Attack on Spain

France a cinq pars[1] par neglect assaillie,
Tunis, Argal esmeuz[2] par Persiens:
Léon, Seville, Barcelonne faillie,
N'aura la classe[3] par les Vénitiens.

CI,Q73

Interpretation

France will be attacked on five sides because of her negligence. Tunisia and Algeria will be incited against her by the Iranians. León, Seville and Barcelona will succumb and cannot be saved by the Italian army.

[1] Five sides of the hexagon's six, excluding the Pyrenees.
[2] Latin *emovere*: to displace, stir up, move about. DLLB.
[3] Latin *classis*: fleet, army. DLLB.

A Notable Briton and Six
Well-known Germans Captured by the Moslems.
Spain Invaded from Gibraltar. The New
and Redoubtable Iranian Leader

> Le chef d'Escosse, avec six d'Allemagne,
> Par gens de mer Orientaux captif:
> Traverseron le Calpre[1] et Espagne,
> Present en Perse au nouveau Roy craintif.

CIII,Q78

Interpretation

The British leader and the six German notables will be captured at sea by the Orientals who will cross Gibraltar and Spain after giving a present to the new, formidable Iranian.

[1] Latin Calpe: Betic mountain: Gibraltar. DLLB. Example of epenthesis.

The Landing of Moslem Troops at Toulon
and Marseille

> Par la discorde negligence Gauloise,
> Sera passage à Mahomet ouvert:
> De sang trempez la terre et mer Senoise,
> Le port Phocen[1] de voiles et nefs couvert.

CI,Q18

Interpretation

Because of the discord and negligence of the French, the way will be clear for the Moslem troops. The land and sea of the Seine will be bloodsoaked. Marseille will be covered by planes and ships.

¹ Phocée: ancient name for Marseille.

Russian Invasion. Desolation in Italy

Amas s'approche venant d'Esclavonie¹
L'Olestant² vieux cité ruynera:
Fort désolée verra sa Romainie,
Puis la grand flamme estaindre ne sçaura.

CIV,Q82

Interpretation

Massed troops will approach coming from Russia. The destroyer will ruin the old city [Paris]. Italy will be laid waste and no one will know how to extinguish the great fire [of war] which will have been lit.

¹ Cf. CII,Q32, note.
² Greek: Aorist inf. of ἄλλυμι, ἄλεσθαι, to cause to perish. DGF. Nostradamus has coined, partly from the Greek verb, a present participle he uses as a noun.

The Destruction of Tours.
Fighting from Nantes to Rheims.
The End of the War in November

Bien defendu le faict par excellence,
Garde toy Tours de ta prochaine ruine,
Londres et Nantes par Reims fera deffence,
Ne passe outre au temps de la bruyne.

CIV,Q46

Interpretation

The act [of war] will be forbidden on the highest level. Beware, Tours, of your approaching ruin! England and France will defend themselves in the Rheims area, and [the war] will not go on past November.

The Invasion of West Germany and Austria. The European Assembly

Quand les colonnes de bois grande[1] tremblée,
D'Austere[2] conduicte, couverte de rubriche,[3]
Tant vuidera dehors grande assemblée,
Trembler Vienne et le pays d'Autriche.

CI,Q82

Interpretation

When the great forests [of the Warsaw Pact countries] tremble [armoured divisions], the army will be led into West Germany which will be covered by the Red Army; the great [European] assembly will be expelled, Vienna and Austria will be invaded.

[1] The Polish forests are the last primeval forests in Europe.
[2] Latin Austerania: island off coast of Germany. DLLB.
[3] Latin *ruber*: red. DLLB. Cf. *'classe rubre'*, CIV,Q37.

The Red Army on the Rhine. The Invasion of Germany, Austria and Italy

Translatera en la Grand Germanie,[1]
Brabant et Flandres, Gand, Bruges et Bologne;[2]
La trefve feint,[3] le grand Duc d'Arménie[4]
Assaillira Vienne et la Cologne.[5]

CV,Q94

Interpretation

The great Armenian general will cross West Germany, Brabant, Flanders, Ghent, Bruges and Bologna, after feigning peace, and he will attack Austria and the Cologne area.

[1] West Germany is larger than East Germany (248,744 sq. km as opposed to 108,178 sq. km). AU.
[2] Italian town, the most important of the Romagna. DHB.
[3] Ablative absolute.
[4] Probably a Red Army leader of Armenian origin.
[5] West German town on the Rhine.

The Invasion of West Germany, Switzerland and France. The Occupation of Paris

Auprès du Lac Leman sera conduite,
Par garse[1] estrange cité voulant trahir,[2]
Avant son meurtre[3] a Augsbourg la grande fuite,
Et ceux du Rhin la viendront invahir.

CV,QI2

Interpretation

[The Army] will be led near Lake Geneva by a foreign republic [Soviet] wanting to take Paris by force. Before committing this great injury, the inhabitants of Bavaria will flee and those who will have struck at the Rhine [the Russians] will come and invade Paris.

[1] As usual Nostradamus refers to the French Republic in the feminine. Cf. *dame*.
[2] Latin *traho*: I take away by force, steal. DLLB.
[3] Great damage. DL7V.

The Invasion of Marseille, Northern Italy, Yugoslavia and the Persian Gulf. Bases for These Invasions

Voille Symacle[1] port Massiliolique,[2]
Dans Venise port marcher aux Pannons:[3]
Partir du goulfre[4] et Synus Illyrique[5]
Vast à Socille, Lygurs[6] coups de canons.

CIX,Q28

Interpretation

Allied fleets will enter Marseille, the army will enter Venice to leave for Hungary. Troops will leave from the [Persian] Gulf and the Yugoslav coast to devastate Sicily and northern Italy with artillery.

[1] Greek σύμμαχος: ally. DFG.
[2] Latin Massilia: ancient name for Marseille. DHB.
[3] Pannonia: ancient name for Hungary. DHB.
[4] i.e. the Gulf par excellence, the Persian Gulf. DHB.
[5] Illyria: Dalmatia, port of Yugoslavia on the Adriatic Sea. DHB.
[6] Tribe of northern Italy. DHB.

The Destruction of Istanbul by France.
The Deliverance of the Moslems' Prisoners
by Portugal

La grande cité de Tharse[1] par Gaulois
Sera destruite: captifs tous a Turban[2]
Secours par mer du grand Portugalois,
Premier d'esté le jour du sacre Urban.[3]

CVI,Q85

Interpretation

Istanbul will be destroyed by the French: all those captured by the Moslems will be helped by the great Portuguese leader between 25 May and 21 June [summer solstice].

[1] Anagram of *Thrase* [Thrace]. The largest town of Thrace is Istanbul.
[2] Habitual head-dress of many Moslem peoples. DL7V.
[3] St Urban, Pope from AD 222 to 230. Saint's Day 25 May. DL7V.

The War between Greece and Turkey.
Turkey's Defeat

Pendant que Duc,[1] Roy, Royne[2] occupera,
Chef Bizantin captif en Samothrace:[3]
Avant l'assaut l'un l'autre mangera,
Rebours ferre[4] suyvra de sang la trace,

CIV,Q38

Interpretation

While the King, commander-in-chief of the army, occupies the place of the French Republic, the leader of Turkey will be prisoner in Greece, for before the attack one will beat the other and, pushed back, he will be discovered through his trail of blood.

[1] Latin *dux*: leader of an army. DLLB.
[2] *Reine*, queen, like *dame*, is often used by Nostradamus to personify the French Republic.
[3] Aegean island off Thrace. DHB.
[4] Latin *fero*: I bring. DLLB.

Catastrophe in the Black Sea. Shortages in Greece and Italy

Pour la chaleur solaire[1] sus la mer,
De Negrepont[2] les poissons demy cuits,
Les habitans les viendront entamer,[3]
Quand Rhod[4] et Gennes leur faudra le biscuit.

CII,Q3

Interpretation

Because of a heat like the sun's, the fish in the Black Sea will be half cooked, and its inhabitants will come to destroy them, when the Greeks and Italians will need food.

[1] Perhaps an atomic explosion.
[2] Latin *niger*: black; and πουτός: sea.
[3] To destroy. DL7V.
[4] Rhodes: Greek possession since 1947. AE.

The War in the Eastern Mediterranean

A son hault pris plus la lerme[1] sabée[2]
D'humaine chair par mort en cendre mettre,
A l'Isle Pharos[3] par Croisars perturbée,
Alors qu'à Rhodes paroistra dur espectre.[4]

CV,Q16

Interpretation

Because of its very high price [life] will have a taste of tears, because human flesh will be reduced to ash. The Isle of Pharos [Egypt] will be perturbed by the Christians, then in Greece the spectre of war will appear.

[1] Ancient form of *larme*, tear. DAFL.
[2] Latin *sapio*: I taste of. DLLB.
[3] Small island off Egyptian coast, near the port of Alexandria. AVL
[4] Symbolizing dread: the spectre of war. DL7V.

Arabia, Turkey, Greece and Hungary in Conflict

Le grand Arabe marchera bien avant,
Trahy sera par le Bisantinois:
L'antique Rodes lui viendra au devant,
Et plus grand mal par autre Pannonois.

CV,Q47

Interpretation

The great Arab leader will set out well before, and be betrayed by the Turkish leader; ancient Greece will anticipate him and he will sustain greater harm from the Hungarians [Warsaw Pact].

The King of Blois, the Liberator. Alliance with the Pope, Spain and Yugoslavia. The Fall of the Seven Eastern Countries

Par lors qu'un Roy sera contre les siens,
Natif de Blois subjuguera Ligures:[1]
Mammel,[2] Cordube[3] et les Dalmatiens,
Des sept[4] puis l'ombre à Roy estrennes[5] et lémures.[6]

CX,Q44

Interpretation

When the government is divided, the one who comes from Blois will subjugate the inhabitants of northern Italy, with the aid of the Pole [the Pope], Spain and the Yugoslavs, then he will return providentially and put the seven [countries] in the shade.

[1] Liguria: region of ancient Italy, forming the south-western areas of Cisalpine Gaul. DHB.

[2] Memel or Niemen. DHB. The River Niemen, until the eighteenth century, was at the centre of Poland.

[3] Latin *Cordoba*, Spanish town.

[4] The seven countries of the Eastern Bloc: USSR, Romania, Poland, GDR, Bulgaria, Hungary, Czechoslovakia.

[5] Chance, fortune. DAFL.

[6] Latin *lemures*: shadows of the dead, ghosts. DLLB.

The Fall of the Seven Eastern Countries in Turkey. Religious Persecutions Conducted by the Turks

Dieu, le ciel tout le divin verbe à l'onde,
Porté par rouges sept razes[1] à Bisance:
Contre les vingts trois cents de Trebisconde,[2]
Deux loix mettront, et horreur, puis crédence.[3]

CVII,Q36

Interpretation

God, the sacred word, delivered over to revolution and carried by the reds of the seven countries to Turkey, where they will be defeated. Three hundred Turks will issue two laws against the cardinals and make them experience horror, then faith will be re-established.

[1] To demolish, raze to the ground. DL7V.
[2] Trebizond, Turkish port on the Black Sea. DHB.
[3] *Croyance.* DAFL.

The Campaigns of Liberation against the Reds. The Polish Pope

De la partie de Mammer[1] grand Pontife,
Subjuguera les confins du Danube:
Chasser les croix, par fer raffe[2] ne riffe,[3]
Captifs, or, bagues plus de cent mille rubes.[4]

CVI,Q49

Interpretation

Of Polish origin, the great Pope will push back to the limits of the Danube [Black Sea] those who will harass the Christians and who have ransacked and stolen from them in war; he will recover their wealth and take 100,000 Reds prisoner.

[1] For Memel, other name for the Niemen. DHB. Until the eighteenth century the River Niemen was at the centre of Poland.
[2] Ancient form of *rafler.* DAFL.
[3] Ancient form of *rifler*: to pillage, rifle, loot. DAFL.
[4] Latin *rubeus*: red. DLLB.

The USSR Makes the Orient Tremble.
John-Paul II and the Catholic Church.
Battles in Turkey

Quand ceux du pole artic[1] unis ensemble,
En Orient grand effrayeur et crainte:
Esleu nouveau, soustenu le grand temple,[2]
Rodes, Bizance de sang barbare teinte.

CVI,Q21

Interpretation

When the Arctic territories are united [Soviet *Union*] there will be great fear and dread in the Orient. When a new Pope is elected to sustain the Catholic Church, Rhodes and Turkey will be stained with Moslem blood.

[1] Empire of Aquila: USSR and all territories it occupies from the Baltic to Vladivostok.
[2] Poetic: the Roman Catholic Church. DL7V.

The Invasion of Italy at Perugia
and Ravenna

Champ perusin ô l'énorme deffaicte,
Et le conflit tout auprès de Ravenne:
Passage[1] sacre lors qu'on fera la feste,
Vainceur vaincu cheval manger l'avenne.

CVIII,Q72

Interpretation

O enormous defeat in the countryside of Perugia and the war near Ravenna: what is sacred will experience ills when the victor celebrates his victory and his horse eats the hay of the vanquished.

[1] Latin *passare*: to undergo. DLLB.

The Defeat of the French Army in Italy.
The Flight of the People of Rome. French Defeat.
Battles in the Swiss Alps and the Adriatic

> Armée Celtique en Italie vexée,
> De toutes parts conflit et grande perte,
> Romains fuis, ô Gaule repoussée,[1]
> Près de Thesin, Rubicon[2] pugne incerte.

CII,Q72

Interpretation

The French army will be beaten in Italy. The conflict will extend on all
sides and cause great havoc. Flee, Romans; France will be struck when
there is an indecisive battle near Ticino [Switzerland] and in the Adriatic.

[1] Latin *repello*: I smite, strike. DLLB.
[2] Small Italian river flowing into Adriatic. DHB.

The Invasion of Italy by Moslem Troops.

> Pluye, vent, classe Barbare Ister.[1] Tyrrhene,
> Passer holcades[2] Ceres,[3] soldats munies:
> Reduits bien faicts par Flor, franchie Sienne,
> Les deux seront morts, amitiez unies.

Presage 31

Interpretation

Revolution, storm, the Moslem army from the Tyrrhenian Sea to the
Danube will bring well-equipped troops by boat to Ceres. Contentment
will be reduced throughout the West by those who will cross the seas as
far as Siena, when the two leaders allied in friendship have died.

[1] European river, today the Danube. DHB.
[2] Greek ὁλκάς,-άδος: transport vessel, any ship. DGF.
[3] Town in Piedmont, Italy, in the Turin area. DL7V.

Chemical Warfare. The Soviet Government in France. Italy Laid Waste

Soleil ardant dans le gosier coller,
De sang humain arrouser en terre Etrusque:
Chef seille[1] d'eau, mener son fils filer,[2]
Captive dame conduite en terre Turque.

CIV,Q58

Interpretation

Burns stick in the throat. Italy awash with human blood. The leader of the revolutionary sickle [Russia] will prepare to head his regime. The French leaders will be led in captivity to Turkey.

[1] Contraction of *sëeille*, i.e. *faucille* = sickle. DAFL.
[2] To prepare (with reference to future). DL7V.

Invasion from Marseille as far as Lyon. Invasion through the Gironde and Aquitaine.

Du tout Marseille les habitans changéz,
Course et poursuite aupres de Lyon,
Narbon, Toloze, par Bourdeaux outragée,
Tuez captifs presque d'un million.

CI,Q72

Interpretation

Throughout Marseille the inhabitants will be changed, they will be pursued almost to Lyon. Narbonne and Toulouse will be damaged by the invasion coming from Bordeaux. Nearly a million prisoners will be executed.

The Invasion of Marseille by Sea

Pieds et cheval à la seconde veille,[1]
Feront entrée vastant tout par la mer.
Dedans le port entrera de Marseille,
Pleurs, crys, et sang, onc nul temps si amer.

CX,Q88

Interpretation

Infantry and tanks [cavalry] will enter Marseille between 9 p.m. and
midnight, laying all waste, by sea. There will be such tears, cries and
blood, such a bitter time was never seen.

[1] Latin *vigilie*: one of the four watches of the night. First watch 6–9 p.m. Second watch
9 p.m.–midnight. DLLB.

The Invasion of the Mediterranean Coast from Barcelona to Marseille. The Occupation of the Islands

De Barcelonne par mer si grande armée,
Tout Marseille de frayeur tremblera,
Isles saisies, de mer ayde fermée,
Ton traditeur[1] en terre nagera.[2]

CIII,Q88

Interpretation

From Barcelona to Marseille there will be seen a great armada at sea
which will fill all with dread. The islands [Balearic, Corsica, Sardinia,
Sicily] will be occupied. A possibility of help coming by sea will be
blocked [Gibraltar]. He who has betrayed you will be buried.

[1] Latin *traditor*: traitor. DLLB.
[2] Fate of those guilty of treason.

Three Allied Countries Start a War

Les bien aisez subit seront desmis[1],
Le monde mis par les trois frères en trouble.
Cité marine saisiront ennemis,
Faim, feu, sang, peste, et de tous maux le double.

CVIII,Q17

Interpretation

The rich will be easily brought low. The world will be plunged into revolution by three allies. Enemies will seize Marseille, which will know great famine, arson, killing and plague.

[1] Latin *demissus*: sunk, lowered, brought low. DLLB.

The Invasion of Western France and Provence

Bourdeaux, Poitiers au son de la campagne,[1]
A grande classe[2] ira jusqu'à l'Angon,[3]
Contre Gaulois sera leur tramontane,[4]
Quand monstre[5] hideux naistra[6] près de Orgon.

CI,Q90

Interpretation

The tocsin will be heard at Bordeaux and Poitiers; the great army will go as far as Langon; the Empire of Aquila will march against the French, when a frightful thing happens near Orgon.

[1] Latin *campana*: bell. DLLB.
[2] Latin *classis*: fleet, army. DLLB.
[3] Port on the Garonne, formerly Alingo. DHB.
[4] From Italian *tramontana*: north, then the North Wind; called this in the Mediterranean because for Italy the north lies beyond the Alps. DL7V.
[5] Latin *monstrum*: divine omen, strange thing, scourge. DLLB.
[6] Latin *nascor*: to be born, begin, start. DLLB.

Invasion in the South-West

A tenir fort par fureur contraindra,
Tout coeur trembler. Langon advent[1] terrible:
Le coup de pied mille pieds se rendra;[2]
Guirond, Guaron, ne furent plus horribles.

CXII,Q65

Interpretation

Its fury compels one to resist and makes all hearts anxious. At Langon
a terrible invasion takes place which covers a lot of ground. There were
never such horrible events in the Gironde and Garonne areas.

[1] Latin *adventus*: arrival, presence; *adventus gallicus* = the invasion of the Gauls. DLLB.
[2] To make haste, pick one's feet up. DL7V.

The Invasion of South-West France
from Italy through Toulouse and Bayonne

Par arnani[1] Tholoser Ville Franque,
Bande infinie par le mont Adrian,[2]
Passe riviere, Hutin[3] par pont[4] la planque,[5]
Bayonne entrer tous Bichoro criant.

CVIII,Q86

Interpretation

From Umbria up to Toulouse and Villefranche, a huge army will pass
through the mountains bordering the Adriatic and will cross rivers after
fighting at sea, so as to enter Bayonne, with all the inhabitants of the
Bigorre crying out with fear.

[1] Anagram of Narnia, Umbrian town on the Nar. DLLB. Today, Narni.
[2] The mountains of Yugoslavia and Italy.
[3] For *hustin*: dispute, struggle. DAFL.
[4] Greek ποντός: the sea. DGF.
[5] Place, spot, house. DL7V.

The War in Burgundy in August.
Massacres and Executions, March–June

De la sixieme claire splendeur celeste,[1]
Viendra tonnerre si fort en la Bourgongne,
Puis naistra monstre de tres hideuse beste
Mars, Avril, Mai, Juin grand charpin[2] et rongne.[3]

CI,Q80

Interpretation

Towards the end of August the thunder of war will be intense in Burgundy, then an appalling thing will happen because of a horrible and brutal person who will instigate a great massacre and executions.

[1] Virgo: the sixth zodiac sign, which the sun, leaving Leo, enters on 22 August. Followed by Libra, it is known as the Sign of Virgo. DL7V.
[2] From *charpir: écharper* = to hack to pieces. DAFL.
[3] To cut off a head. DAFL.

Great Naval Battles in the Atlantic

Après combat et bataille navalle,
Le grand Neptune[1] à son plus haut befroy[2]
Rouge adversaire de peur deviendra pasle
Mettant le Grand Occean en effroy.

CIII,QI

Interpretation

After a naval combat, England will know her greatest alarm. Then the Soviet adversary will pale with fear, having sown terror in the Atlantic [or the Atlantic Alliance].

[1] God of the sea. Always symbolizes England.
[2] Belfry: tower with a bell for sounding the alarm. DL.

France Allied with England. The Invasion of Provence and Languedoc

Classe Gauloise par appuy de grande garde,
Du grand Neptune et ses tridens soldats,
Rongée Provence pour soustenir grande bande,
Plus Mars Narbon par javelots et dards.

CII,Q59

Interpretation

The French army with the help of the English Guards and soldiers will see Provence wrecked defending itself against a large force, and the war will be still fiercer at Narbonne, hit by rockets and shells.

The Occupation of Paris by the Russians

Poeur, glas grand pille passer mer, croistre eregne,[1]
Sectes, sacrez outre mer plus polis:
Peste, chant,[2] feu, Roy d'Aquilon l'enseigne,
Dresser trophée[3] cité d'HENRIPOLIS.[4]

Presage 34, 1559

Interpretation

Fear, alarms when [the enemy] comes by sea to wreak great destruction; the 'throneless one' will begin to grow stronger and despite factions will be crowned overseas by more civilized people: epidemics, wails of lamentation, fire, the Russian leader will rejoice at his victory over the town of Henri IV [Paris].

[1] *Esregner*: to dethrone, deprive of a throne. DAFL.
[2] Songs of grief, victory, joy etc. DL7V.
[3] Victory, success. DL7V.
[4] Neologism by Nostradamus: *Henri* and the Greek πόλις: town. Henri IV's famous phrase was: 'Paris is worth a mass'.

The Attack on Paris and its Siege.
Communism Brings the Fall of the French Republic

Siège à Cité et de nuict assaillie,
Peu eschappez, non loin de mer conflit,
Femme de joie retour fils deffaillie,
Poison es lettres caché dedans le plic.

CI,Q41

Interpretation

Paris will be besieged and attacked by night and few will be able to
escape. Not far from there, there will be a naval engagement. On the
return of her son [Communism] the Republic will collapse because of
dangerously compromising documents which had been hidden.

The Attack on Paris and the Occupation of Rome.
Great Naval Battles

Tout à l'entour de la grande Cité,
Seront soldats logez par champs et ville,
Donner l'assaut Paris, Rome incité[1]
Sur le pont[2] lors sera faict grand pille.

CV,Q30

Interpretation

All around Paris soldiers will be lodged in the town and countryside,
and inside the town when Paris is besieged and Rome invaded, there will
then be great havoc caused at sea.

[1] Latin *incito*: I throw myself upon. DLLB.
[2] Greek ποντός: sea. DGF.

The French Army of Liberation Fights
the Red Army in Italy

Gaulois par sauts monts viendra penetrer,
Occupera le grand lieu de l'Insubre,[1]
Au plus profond de son ost[2] fera entrer,
Gennes, Monech pousseront classe rubre.[3]

CIV,Q37

Interpretation

The French cross the mountains in quick stages and occupy the Milan area. They will invade in depth and from Genoa and Monaco will drive back the Red Army.

[1] The Milanese. DHB.
[2] Army, camp. DAFL.
[3] Latin *ruber*: red. DLLB.

The Flight from France of a Leading Cleric.
The Turco–Tunisian Alliance

Le grand Prelat Celtique à Roy suspect,
De nuict par cours sortira hors du regne:
Par Duc fertile à son grand Roy Bretagne,
Bisance à Cypres et Tunes insuspect.[1]

CVI,Q53

Interpretation

The great French prelate will be suspected by the head of state and will leave the country by night. Prosperity will be restored to Brittany by the great soldier king. Turkey will not be suspected by Cyprus and Tunisia.

[1] Latin *insuspecte*: without suspicion. DLLB.

Algeria's Important Role in the Conflict. The Russian Landing. Invasion of Switzerland through the Grisons

Amoura legre[1] non loin pose le siege,
Au saint barbare[2] seront les garnisons:
Ursins Hadrie pour Gaulois feront plaige,
Pour peur rendus de l'armée aux Grisons.[3]

CX,Q38

Interpretation

The headquarters will be established not far from Amoura and Algiers, where the garrisons of Mohammed's soldiers will be. Then the young Russian soldiers will land in France from the Adriatic, when they will go into Switzerland, via the Grisons, to terrorize the army.

[1] Nostradamus here juxtaposes Amoura, a town in southern Algeria in the Ouled-Nail range, and the town of Algiers. AVL.
[2] The prophet Mohammed.
[3] One of the Swiss cantons, containing five great valleys: upper and lower Rhine, the Engadine, Albula and Prettigau. DHB.

The Attack by Air on Marseille and Geneva. The Invasion of Greece by Iran

Flambeau ardant au ciel soir sera veu,
Pres de la fin et principe[1] du Rosne,
Famine, glaive, tard le secours pourveu,
La Perse tourne envahi Macedoine.[2]

CII,Q96

Interpretation

A missile will be seen in the evening sky near the mouth and source of the Rhône. Famine, war, will reign and help will be too late, when Iran mobilizes to invade Macedonia.

[1] The Rhône begins in the Valais, Switzerland, near Mont St Gothard, running westwards to Lake Geneva which it joins and from where it flows to Geneva. DHB.
[2] Kingdom of ancient Greece. DHB.

The Invasion of Switzerland
through Tunnels

Jardin[1] du monde auprès de cité neuve,[2]
Dans le chemin des montagnes cavées,[3]
Sera saisi et plongé dans le cuve,
Beuvant par force eaux soulphre envenimées.

CX,Q49

Interpretation

The richest country of the West, near Neufchâtel will be seized and
overwhelmed by means of the mountain tunnels, and its population will
be forced to drink polluted water.

[1] Figurative, for 'fertile': DL. 'Garden of the world' in that it constitutes the strongbox
of the West.
[2] Neufchâtel, Neuenburg (German), Novisburgum (Latin) = new city. Swiss town at
the foot of the Jura. DHB.
[3] Latin *cavo*: I hollow out or pierce. DLLB.

Invasion through Northern Italy
and Switzerland. Famine and Shortages

Les deux copies aux murs ne pourront joindre,
Dans cet instant trembler Milan, Ticin:[1]
Faim, soif, doutance si fort les viendra poindre
Chair, pain, ne vivres n'auront un seul boucin.[2]

CIV,Q90

Interpretation

The two Western armies could not join up as far as the defences. At that
moment Milan will be in dread and in Ticino famine, thirst and anxiety
will afflict the inhabitants who will have neither meat, bread nor even
scraps to eat.

[1] Latin Ticinus. DLLB.
[2] Provençal *boucoun*: scrap, morsel. DP.

The Invasion of France via Switzerland

Pres du Tesin les habitans de Loyre
Garonne et Saone, Seine, Tain et Gironde
Outre les monts dresseront promontoire,
Conflict donné, Pau granci,[1] submergé onde.

CVI,Q79

Interpretation

Near Ticino [Switzerland] the enemies will cross the mountains where they will set up strategic bases so as to attack the inhabitants of the Loire, the Saône, the Seine, the Tain and the Gironde. War will break out, the town of Pau will be protected, revolution will submerge all.

[1] *Garance*: protection, guarantee. DAFL. Example of syncope.

Invasion from Switzerland to the Basses-Pyrénées

Pour la faveur que la cité fera,
Au grand qui tost perdra camp de bataille
Puis le rang[1] Pau Thesin versera,[2]
De sang, feux mors[3] noyez[4] de coups de taille.[5]

CII,Q26

Interpretation

Because of the favour Paris will do the great country [USA] which will leave the field of battle at the start of the war, the [Russian] army from Ticino will drive towards the Basses-Pyrénées where blood will flow and the inhabitants will undergo the bite of fire and be killed by weapons.

[1] Military formation, *rank*. DL7V.
[2] Latin *verto*: I go towards, take a direction. DL7V.
[3] *Morsure*. DAFL.
[4] Latin *necare*: to kill. DL7V.
[5] Cutting edge or blade of a weapon. DL7V.

The Invasion and Sack of Switzerland

Le chef du camp au milieu de la presse,
D'un coup de flesche sera blessé aux cuisses,[1]
Lors que Genève en larmes et en detresse
Sera trahy[2] par Lozan et par Soysses.

CIV,Q9

Interpretation

The head of the besieged army will be wounded through his protection, while the inhabitants of Geneva will be in distress and will weep and be ravaged by an invasion across Switzerland and through Lausanne.

[1] *Cuissel*: armour covering the thigh. DAFL.
[2] Take by force, ravish, steal. Latin *Trahere pagos* = to pillage the villages. DLLB.

Property Ransacked in France and Switzerland

Geneve et Langres par ceux de Chartres et Dole[1]
Et par Grenoble captif au Montlimard,
Seysset,[2] Losanne, par frauduleuse dole,[3]
Les trahiront[4] par or soixante marc.

CIV,Q42

Interpretation

Geneva and Langres, attacked by those who will occupy Chartres and the Swiss Jura and who, arriving from Grenoble, will take Montélimar as well as Seyssel and Lausanne, will be despoiled of their gold by a piece of trickery.

[1] Mountain of the Swiss Jura in the canton of Vaud on the French border. DL7V.
[2] Seyssel: principal town of the canton of Ain, but also another town in the canton of Haute-Savoie. DHB.
[3] *Dol*: fraudulent manoeuvre, trickery. DL7V. Deception or fraud. DAFL.
[4] Cf. CIV,Q9.

The War in Lyon and Roussillon

Clarté fulgure[1] à Lyon apparante,
Luysant,[2] print Malte, subit sera estainte,
Sardon,[3] Mauris[4] traitera décevante,[5]
Genève à Londes[6] a Coq trahison fainte.

CVIII,Q6

Interpretation

The light of the blaze to be seen at Lyon, after Malta has been quickly captured, will suddenly be extinguished. A deceptive treaty will be signed in Roussillon with the Moslems, because of treachery against the [French] King by Switzerland and England.

[1] Latin *fulgur*: lightning flash. DLLB.
[2] Figurative: to appear brilliantly, swiftly. DL7V.
[3] Sardones: tribe of the Narbonne area. Their country once formed Roussillon and is today the department of Pyrénées-Orientales. DHB.
[4] Latin *maurus*: Moor. DLLB.
[5] Latin *decipere*: to trick, deceive. DLLB.
[6] Lond[r]es: London. DHB.

The War Conducted in Switzerland, England and Italy, the Countries Most Affected

Pleurs, cris et plaincts, hurlements, effrayeurs,
Coeur inhumain, cruel noir,[1] et transy:[2]
Léman, les Isles, de Gennes les majeurs,
Sang espancher, frofaim,[3] à nul mercy.

CVI,Q81

Interpretation

Because of an inhuman person – cruel, odious and terrifying – weeping, cries, complaints and screams of fear will be heard in Switzerland and the British Isles, and from the Italian leaders. Blood will flow there. Cold and hunger will reign: there will be no mercy for anyone.

[1] Symbolic: perverse, evil, hateful. DL7V.
[2] *Transir*: to make one shudder with fear. DL7V.
[3] *Miséricorde*, i.e. mercy. DAFL.

Fear in Switzerland

Près du Leman la frayeur sera grande,
Par le conseil, cela ne peut faillir:
Le nouveau Roy fait apprester sa bande,
Le jeune meurt faim, poeur fera faillir.

Presage 4, February

Interpretation

Fear will be great near Lake Geneva, because of a [United Nations] resolution, and this is inevitable. The new leader prepares his army, and when the young leader dies of hunger, people will give way to fear.

The Flight of the Inhabitants of Switzerland and Savoy

EIOVAS proche esloigner, lac Léman,
Fort grands apprest, retour, confusion:
Loin les nepveux,[1] de feu grand Supelman,[2]
Tous de leur fuyte.

CXII,Q69

Interpretation

It will be necessary to escape from the environs of Savoy and Lake Geneva. Great preparations [for war] will be made, which will bring back confusion. One must keep away from the Germans and from the great war upon Geneva, whence all the inhabitants will flee.

[1] Title given by German Emperors to the Secular Electors of the Empire. DL7V.
[2] For super Leman: on Lake Geneva. (Fr. Lac Léman.)

The People of Geneva and Their Leader
Put to Death

Devant le pere l'enfant sera tué,
Le pere apres entre cordes de jonc:
Genevois peuple sera esvertué,[1]
Gisant le chef au milieu comme un tronc.[2]

CX,Q92

Interpretation

The child will be killed in front of its father, who will be imprisoned thereafter. The inhabitants of Geneva will be destroyed, their leader to die by decapitation.

[1] Latin *everto*: I destroy, ruin, overthrow. DLLB.
[2] Latin *truncus*: mutilated body, headless trunk. DLLB.

The Destruction of Geneva.
Switzerland and Iran

Migrés, migrés de Genève trestous,
Saturne[1] d'or en fer se changera:
Le contre RAYPOZ[2] exterminera tous
Avant l'advent le ciel signes fera.

CIX,Q44

Interpretation

All you inhabitants of Geneva, leave your town! Your golden age will change into an age of war. He who will rise up against the Iranian leader will exterminate you all. Before this event there will be signs in the sky.

[1] God of time.
[2] Anagram of Zopyra: one of the seven Persian nobles who assassinated the pseudo-Smerdis and made Darius I king. DL7V.

The Destruction of Paris and Geneva.
The Exodus of their Populations

Auprès des portes et dedans deux citez
Seront deux fléaux onc n'aperceu un tel,
Faim, dedans peste, de fer hors gens boutez,
Crier secours au Grand Dieu immortel.

CII,Q6

Interpretation

In the suburbs and within two cities [Paris and Geneva] there will be two scourges the like of which have never been seen. Hunger and plague shall reign in these cities, people will be driven out of them, beseeching Almighty God for aid.

The Destruction of Geneva.
The Defeat of the Moslem Troops

Seicher de faim, de soif, gent Genevoise,
Espoir prochain viendra au defaillir,
Sur point tremblant sera loy Gebenoise,[1]
Classe au grand port ne se peut accueillir.

CII,Q64

Interpretation

The inhabitants of Geneva will die of hunger and thirst, [Switzerland] will succumb with no hope near. At this point in the war the Moslem law will be shaken. Marseille will not be able to welcome the army.

[1] Latin Gebanitae: Gebanites, tribe of ancient Arabia. DLLB.

Catastrophe at Lausanne

Puanteur grande sortira de Lausanne
Qu'on ne sçaura l'origine du faict,
L'on mettra hors toute la gent lointaine
Feu veu au ciel, peuple estranger deffaict.

CVIII,QIO

Interpretation

From Lausanne there will issue a foul stench whose origin will be unknown. The population will be evacuated, when fire will be seen in the sky [missiles] and a foreign country [Germany or Italy] will be defeated.

The Invasion from Switzerland to Paris.
The Fall of the Head of State

Verseil, Milan donra intelligence,
Dedans Tycin sera faicte la playe:[1]
Courir par Seine, eau, sang, feu par Florence,
Unique cheoir d'hault en bas faisant maye.[2]

CVIII,Q7

Interpretation

There will be secret agreements with the enemy in northern Italy. The army breakthrough will occur in Ticino and continue on to the Seine, where revolution will reign, blood and war having struck Florence. The head of state will fall while celebrating.

[1] Poetic, for 'breech' or 'gap'. DL7V.
[2] Maye: Maya, mother of Mercury, whose festival is celebrated in early May. DP. May also represents rejoicing, fine weather. DAFL.

Battles near Orgon and the Albion Plateau.
The Defeat of Iraq in France

Aux champs herbeux d'Alein[1] et du Varneigue.[2]
Du mont Lebron[3] proche de la Durance,
Camp des deux parts conflit sera si aigre,
Mesopotamie[4] defaillira[5] en la France.

CIII,Q99

Interpretation

On the plain of Alleins and Vernègues and the Albion plateau, near the Durance, the battle will be very fierce for both sides and Iraq will lose her forces in France.

[1] Alleins, near Orgon, small town in Bouches-du-Rhône. DL7V.
[2] Vernègues, small town off N7, in Bouches-du-Rhône.
[3] Lubéron or Léberon: mountain in southern France (Basses-Alpes et Vaucluse), above the valley of the Durance. DL7V. The Albion plateau is part of the Lubéron range.
[4] Region between the Tigris and Euphrates, today Iraq. DHB.
[5] To lose one's strength. DL7V.

The Transportation of Gold
along the Rhône

Par la fureur d'un qui attendra[1] l'eau,
Par la grand rage tout l'exercite esmeu:
Chargé des nobles[2] à dix-sept bateaux
Au long du Rosne, tard messager venu.

CV,Q71

Interpretation

Through the zeal of one person the revolution will spread. With great fury the whole army will be mobilized. A fleet of seventeen ships laden with gold will go up the Rhône, the messenger arriving too late.

[1] Latin *attendo*: I tend, drive towards. DLLB.
[2] Numismatic term. In 1344 Edward III of England coined gold 'nobles' whose weight was later modified. One pound of gold went into forty-five nobles. DL7V.

The Invasion of Lyon Distinguished by Satellite

Le ciel (de Plencus[1] la cité) nous présage
Par clers[2] insignes et par estoilles fixes,[3]
Que de son change subit s'approche l'aage,
Ne pour son bien ne pour les malefices.

CIII,Q46

Interpretation

The sky announces to us by luminous signals and satellites that the moment of a change experienced at Lyon is approaching, neither for the town's good nor for its ill.

[1] Munatius Plancus, orator and Roman general. He founded, or at least discovered, Lugdunum (Lyon) while proconsul in Gaul. DHB.
[2] Early form of *clair*, clear. DAFL.
[3] Stars thus termed have their own fixed, or apparently fixed, positions in space. DL7V.

THE DESTRUCTION OF PARIS

The Occupation of Paris by the Red Army. Its Destruction: Great Loss of Life

Grand Cité à soldats abandonnée,
Onc n'y eust mortel tumult si proche,
O qu'elle hideuse mortalité s'approche,
Fors une offense ny sera pardonnée.

CVI,Q96

Interpretation

Paris will be abandoned to the [enemy] soldiers. Such a conflict so close to the town was never seen. What a fearful mortality there will be. An offence will not be forgiven.

Paris Burned

Sera laissé le feu vif, mort caché,
Dedans les globes[1] horrible espovantable,
De nuict a classe cité en poudre[2] lasché,
La cité à feu, l'ennemy favorable.

CV,Q8

Interpretation

He who hides will be burned alive in horrible and dreadful whirlwinds
of flame. The town will be reduced to dust by night, by the [aerial] fleet.
The town in flames will be favourable to the enemy.

[1] Latin *globus*: mass, heap. *Globi flammarum* (Virgil) = whirlwinds of flames. DLLB.
[2] Latin *pulvis*: dust. DLLB.

Paris saved in 1945.
Paris Destroyed in the Third World War

La ville sens dessus dessous
Et renversée de mille coups
De canon: et fort dessous terre:
Cinq ans tiendra: le tout remis,
Et laschée à ses ennemis,
L'eau leur fera après la guerre.

Sixain 3

Interpretation

The town turned upside down by a thousand cannon blasts, and strong
below the ground [the métro]. It will resist for five years [1940–45],
everything will be restored to its place, then the town will be abandoned
to its enemies, against whom the revolution will wage war.

A Missile against Paris.
Revolutionary Troubles in the City

De feu volant la machination,[1]
Viendra troubler au grand chef assiegez;
Dedans sera telle sedition,
Qu'en desespoir seront les profligez.

CVI,Q34

Interpretation

An incendiary, flying war machine will come to trouble the leader of those who are besieged. Within, there will be such sedition that the unfortunate people will be desperate.

[1] Latin *machinatio*: mechanical apparatus, machine. DLLB.

The Destruction of Paris

Le Celtique fleuve changera de rivage,
Plus ne tiendra la cité d'Aggrippine[1]
Tout transmué, hormis le vieil langage,
Saturn, Leo, Mars, Cancer en rapine.[2]

CVI,Q4

Interpretation

The banks of the French river [the Seine] will change their appearance. Paris will no longer last. All will be transformed except the French language, for it will be a time of totalitarianism, war and misery caused by looting.

[1] Nostradamus calls Paris by this name, comparing the Revolutionary French Republic of 1789 to Agrippina, and Communism, the Revolution's child, to Nero. And as Agrippina was killed by her son Nero, so the Republic will be put to death by her child: Communism will burn Paris just as Nero burned Rome.

[2] Theft, accompanied by violence, committed by a band of armed men.

The Destruction of Paris

La grand Cité sera bien désolée,
Des habitants un seul n'y demourra,
Mur sexe, temple et vierge violée,
Par fer, feu, peste, canon peuple mourra.

CIII,Q84

Interpretation

Paris will be badly devastated. Not a single one of its inhabitants will remain there. Buildings, churches will be destroyed, women and young girls raped. By the sword of war, fire, sickness and artillery the people of Paris will die.

The Paris Region Made Uninhabitable. The Invasion of England

Long temps sera sans estre habitée,
Où Seine et Marne[1] autour vient arrouser,
De la Tamise et martiaux temptée,[2]
De ceux les guardes en cuidant repousser.

CVI,Q43

Interpretation

The confluence of the Seine and Marne will remain for a long time uninhabited when the warriors attacking England will think about driving back her defences.

[1] Paris is at the confluence of the Seine and Marne.
[2] Latin *tempto*: I attack. DLLB.

The King against the Occupier of Paris.
A Missile Will Burn Paris. The Hated Military
Governor of the Occupation

Prince sera de beauté tant venuste,[1]
Au chef menée, le second faict trahy:
La cité au glaive de poudre face[2] aduste,[3]
Par trop grand meurtre le chef du Roy haï.

CVI,Q92

Interpretation

The prince will be handsome and charming and intrigue against the leader of the government; also the second [government] will be betrayed. The city [Paris] given over to massacre will burn because of an incendiary rocket. The [red] head of government will be hated for his too blatant murders.

[1] Latin venustus: charming, agreeable. DLLB.
[2] Latin fax: firebrand. DLLB.
[3] Latin adustus: burnt. DLLB.

THE CONSPIRACY

The Moslem Attack

Soldat Barbare le grand Roy frappera,
Injustement non esloigné de mort,
L'avare[1] mère du faict cause sera
Conjurateur et regne en grand remort.

CVIII,Q73

Interpretation

The Moslem troops will smite the great Leader, whose death, unjustly, will not be far off; the avarice of the mother [the French Republic] will be the cause of this event. Conspirator and seat of power alike will be greatly stricken.

[1] Latin avarus: greedy, miserly. DLLB.

The Three Years and Seventy Days
of the Red Regime. The Conspiracy

La déchassée[1] au regne tournera,
Ses ennemis trouvez des conjurés:
Plus que jamais son temps triomphera
Trois et septante à mort trop asseurés.

CVI,Q74

Interpretation

The left will be in power. It will be discovered that its enemies have
been plotting. More than ever, its time will triumph, but it is certain to
die after three years and seventy days.

[1] Dance step towards the *left*, as opposed to the chassé, in the other direction. DL7V.

The End of the Republican System
by means of a Conspiracy. The Senility
of Rousseau's Ideas

Tard arrivé l'exécution faite,
Le vent contraire, lettres au chemin prises:
Les conjurez XIIII d'une secte,
Par le Rousseau senez les entreprises.

CI,Q7

Interpretation

[The saviour] having arrived late, the execution [of the regime] will be
accomplished, the wind [of history] having changed and documents being
seized. Fourteen conspirators of one party will render the enterprises
begun by Jean-Jacques Rousseau outdated.

The End of the Red Leader.
The Conspirators

De nuict passant le Roy près d'une Androne,[1]
Celui de Cypres[2] et principal guette,
Le Roy failly, la main fuit long du Rosne,
Les conjurez l'iront à la mort mettre.

CV,Q17

Interpretation

Passing through straits [the Bosphorus?] by night which are watched by the Cypriot leader, the [enemy] leader will be ruined when his forces flee along the Rhine; the plotters will then go and put him to death.

[1] Provençal *androuno*: narrow passage, alleyway. DP.
[2] Old French for Chypres, i.e. Cyprus.

THE VICTORY OF THE WEST

The Fifth Republic: Just over Twenty Years.
The Return of the Monarchy until 1999. The End and Fulfilment of the Prophecy of Nostradamus, 1999

Vingt ans du règne de la Lune passéz,[1]
Sept mille ans autre tiendra sa Monarchie
Quand le soleil prendra ses jours lasséz,[2]
Lors accomplir et mine[3] ma prophétie.

CI,Q48

Interpretation

After twenty years of republican power, another will establish the monarchy until the seventh millennium [1999]. When the Bourbon knows misfortune then shall my prophecy be accomplished and terminated.

[1] Beginning of the Fifth Republic: September 1959; end: September 1984 at latest.
[2] Latin *lassae res*: ill fortune. DLLB.
[3] For *terminer*: to end. Aphesis.

Portugal, Departure Base for the Liberation of France. Fighting in the South-West and Languedoc

Albi et Castres feront nouvelle ligue,
Neur[1] Arriens[2] Libon et Portugues:
Carcas. Tholose consumeront leur brique,
Quand chef neuf monstre[3] de Lauragues.[4]

CX,Q5

Interpretation

A new party will be set up in the Tarn, then a new Arrian, from Lisbon in Portugal, will destroy its manoeuvres as far as Carcassonne and Toulouse, when the new leader will bring about a calamity in the Lauragues.

[1] For *neuf*, new. DAFL.
[2] Arrian, Greek historian, statesman and soldier. He was made consul in return for his military services. DHB. Nostradamus establishes a parallel between Arrian and the French leader who will drive back the East German army of occupation. DHB.
[3] Latin *monstrum*: scourge, calamity. DLLB.
[4] Region including the departments of Haute-Garonne and the Aude. DHB.

The Collapse of the Russo–Moslem Bloc

La loy Moricque[1] on verre déffaillir,
Après une autre beaucoup plus séductive:
Boristhènes[2] premier viendra faillir,
Par dons et langue une plus attractive.

CIII,Q95

Interpretation

The Moslem law will be seen to collapse, following another far more seductive law [Communist]. Russia will collapse first and be drawn by the benefits and language [of the French].

[1] Mores or Maures: Moors, i.e. Moslems.
[2] Ancient name of the Dnieper, river of European Russia. DHB.

The Naval Defeat of the Russo–Moslem Troops. The Defence of the Great Pope

Par mer, le rouge sera prins de pyrates,
La paix sera par son moyen troublée:
L'ire et l'avare[1] commettra[2] par sainct acte,
Au Grand Pontife sera l'armée doublée.

CV,Q44

Interpretation

At sea the Soviet forces will be caught with the Moslems who will have troubled the peace. Anger and greed will unite against the Church's actions. Measures by the army for the great Pope's protection will be doubled.

[1] Latin *avaritia*: greed. DLLB.
[2] Latin *committo*: I assemble, join, reunite. DLLB.

Great Battles in the Black Sea. Iranian Troops in Turkey. Arab Naval Defeat in the Adriatic

Par feu et armes non loin de la marnegro,[1]
Viendra de Perse occuper Trebisonde:[2]
Trembler Phato,[3] Methelin,[4] sol alegro,
De sang Arabe d'Adrie couvert onde.

CV,Q27

Interpretation

By fire and weapons of war not far from the Black Sea, Iranian troops will come to occupy Trebizond. The mouth of the Nile, and Greece, will tremble because of the skill of the Bourbon, who will cover the Adriatic with Arab blood.

[1] Latin *mar[e]*: sea, plus *negro* (from *niger*), black. DLLB.
[2] Turkish town on the Black Sea. DHB.
[3] Phatnitique: an ancient tributary of the Nile, today the Damietta. DHB.
[4] Mytilene, ancient capital of the island of Lesbos; one of the main Greek towns of Asia. DHB.

Fighting between England and East Germany.
The War in France. The Occupation of Marseille.
The Victory of the West

Au temps du deuil que le félin monarque[1]
Guerroyera le jeune Aemathien[2]
Gaule bransler pérecliter la barque.
Tenter[3] Phossens[4] au Ponant[5] entretien,[6]

CX,Q58

Interpretation

The moment the English leader wages war on the young German commander, France will be shaken, the Church will be in jeopardy. Marseille will be occupied, then the West will endure [suffering].

[1] Allusion to the leopard on the English coat-of-arms.
[2] Symbolizes the German spirit of conquest and war. Cf. CX,Q7.
[3] Latin *teneo*: I hold, occupy. DLLB.
[4] Phocéens: the inhabitants of Marseille.
[5] Word once used in the Mediterranean to denote the Ocean or the West, as opposed to the Levant. DL7V.
[6] To keep in a good state, render durable. DL7V.

The Victory of the West

Loin près de l'Urne[1] le malin[2] tourne arrière,
Qu'au grand Mars feu donra empeschement:
Vers l'Aquilon au midy le grand fiersl,[3]
FLORA[4] tiendra la porte en pensement.[5]

Presage 8, June

Interpretation

At the approach of the Aquarian Age, the devil will turn back, and he will be given obstacles where the fire of the great war is concerned. From Russia to the Moslem countries the great proud one will rule, and the West will maintain freedom of thought.

[1] Latin Urna: attribute of Aquarius. DLLB.
[2] Devil or demon. DL7V.

¹ Proud, haughty. DL7V.
⁴ Zephyr, the west wind, celebrated by the classical poets for the freshness it brought
to the hot lands they inhabited. Its mild yet powerful breath brought life to nature. The
Greeks gave it a 'wife', Chloris, the Roman goddess Flora. MGR.
⁵ Action of thinking. DL7V.

The Decadence of the West. The War

Venus¹ la belle entrera dedans FLORE,
Les exilez secrets² lairront³ la place:
Vesves beaucoup, mort de Grand on déplore,
Oster du regne, le Grand Grand ne menace.

Presage 32, November

Interpretation

When sexual licence enters the West, exiled ones will leave the place
seeking retreats. There will be many widows and the death will be
deplored of a great person who has given up power; the greatness of this
person threatened none.

¹ Sexual desire personified by Venus, goddess of love. DL7V.
² Latin *secretum*: retreat, quiet or secluded spot. DLLB.
³ Future of *laier* = to leave. DAFL.

The Liberation of France via Nantes.
The Great Navy Sunk in the Red Sea. A Scourge in
Germany Provoked by Russia and Turkey

De nuict par Nantes Lyris apparoistra,
Des arts marins susciteront la pluye:
Arabiq goulfre¹ grand classe parfondra,
Un monstre en Saxe naistra d'ours et de truye.²

CVI,Q44

Interpretation

Peace will be glimpsed by night, starting from Nantes when [the French]
will start naval bombardments. A great fleet will be sunk in the Red Sea,
when a scourge is born, because of Russia and Turkey, in Germany.

[1] Red Sea, or Arabian Gulf.
[2] Latin Troja, Troy. DL7V. Nostradamus refers here to Turkey, for Troy is in Asia Minor.

The Franco–Belgian Armies against the Moslem Troops. The Death of the Moslem Leader in the Red Sea

Satur[1] au boeuf[2] iove[3] en l'eau, Mars en fleiche,
Six de Fevrier mortalité donra:
Ceux de Tardaigne[4] à Bruge[5] si grand breche,[6]
Qu'à Ponterose[7] chef Barbarin mourra.

CVIII,Q49

Interpretation

When the time comes for violence and the atmosphere is of revolution, the war will spread. On 6 February there will be fatality. The French and Belgians will make such a breach in the enemy troops that the Moslem commander will die in the Red Sea.

[1] Saturn, in Greek Kronos: time.
[2] Poetic: brutal. DL7V.
[3] Jupiter, Jovis: air, sky, atmosphere. DLLB.
[4] Tardenois: ancient minor region of France, in the Soissons area, today subsumed under the Aisne department. DHB.
[5] Belgian town, the main town of west Flanders. DHB.
[6] By analogy, hole made in a group of men. DL7V.
[7] Neologism from πουτός sea, and rose (pink, red).

The Victory of the West. Battles against the Moslem Troops

Les Rhodiens[1] demanderont secours,
Par le neglet de ses hoyrs delaissée,
L'Empire Arabe ravalera[2] son cours[3]
Par Hespéries[4] la cause redressée.

CIV,Q39

Interpretation

The Greeks will ask for help because of the negligence of their heirs, who will have abandoned them. The expansion of the Arab Empire will be halted and the West will redress the situation.

[1] Rhodes: Aegean Island returned to Greece in 1947.
[2] To lower, beat down, check. DL7V.
[3] March, progression, expansion. DL7V.
[4] Greek Έσπερις: West. DGF.

The Victory of the West.
The Fall of the Seven Eastern Bloc Countries

> Libra verra regner les Hesperies,
> Du ciel et terre tenir la Monarchie,
> D'Asie forces nul ne verra peries
> Que sept ne tiennent par rang la hiérarchie.[1]

CIV,Q50

Interpretation

Justice will see the Westerners reign, the Monarchy will maintain heaven and earth, but the forces of Asia will not be destroyed as long as seven countries are grouped together.

[1] The seven Warsaw Pact countries: USSR, GDR, Poland, Romania, Hungary, Czechoslovakia and Bulgaria.

Revolution in the Eastern Bloc.
A Rain of Meteorites on Land and Sea.
The Fall of the Seven Warsaw Pact Countries

> Nouvelle pluye[1] subite, impétueuse,
> Empeschera subit deux exercites:
> Pierres, ciel, feux faire la mer pierreuse,
> La mort de sept terre et marins subite.

CII,Q18

Interpretation

A new, sudden and violent revolution will swiftly hinder [in their advance] two armies. Blazing meteorites falling from the sky will bombard the sea and provoke the sudden fall of the seven countries [Warsaw Pact] by land and sea.

[1] Constant symbol in Nostradamus of the revolution.

The Burning of Paris. The Invasion of Sardinia by the Moslems. The Victory of the West

Par le feu du ciel la cité presque aduste,[1]
L'urne[2] menace encore Ceucalion,[3]
Vexée Sardaigne par la Punique fuste,[4]
Après le Libra[5] lairra[6] son Phaëton.[7]

CII,Q81

Interpretation

By the fire fallen from heaven the city burns almost totally; revolution and death still threaten the upright man. Sardinia will be ravaged by a Moslem fleet, after which war will give way to justice.

[1] Latin *adustus*: burnt. DLLB.
[2] Vase for water carrying, collecting votes, or containing the ashes of the dead in ancient times. DL7V. Taken here by Nostradamus to symbolize revolution (water) and death.
[3] Typographical error for Deucalion (cf. CX,Q6 and Presage 90). Son of Prometheus, in whose reign the famous flood was sent by Jupiter, who, seeing men's wickedness increase, determined to drown the human race. The surface of the earth was submerged except for one mountain on which the boat carrying Deucalion, the most upright of men, ran aground. MGR.
[4] Italian *fusta*: long shallow-draught boat which had both sails and oars. DL7V.
[5] Latin *libra*: scales, the zodiacal sign. DLLB. Also symbol of justice.
[6] Future of *laier, laisser* = to leave. DAFL.
[7] Greek name for the planet Jupiter. The Cyclops gave Jupiter thunder and lightning, Pluto a helmet, and Neptune a trident. With these weapons the three brothers conquered Saturn. MGR. Used as symbol for war. [Phaethon: son of Helios, the sun god and Clymene, was killed by Jupiter (Zeus) while driving the chariot of the sun. Tr]

The King of Spain against the Moslems

Dans les Espagnes viendra Roy très puissant
Par mer et terre subjugant le midy:
Ce mal fera, rabaissant le croissant,
Baisser les aesles à ceux du vendredy.[1]

CX,Q95

Interpretation

A very powerful King will come to Spain, subjugating the countries of
the south [North Africa] by sea and land; this he will do to reduce the
power of the crescent [Arabs] and make the worshippers of Friday lower
their wings.

[1] Holy day for the Moslems.

The Defeat of the Moslems

Logmion[1] grande Bisance approchera,
Chassée sera la barbarique ligue:[2]
Des deux loix l'une l'estinique[3] lachera,
Barbare et franche en perpétuelle brigue.[4]

CV,Q80

Interpretation

The eloquent person will approach great Turkey, the Moslem alliance
will be beaten: of the two Moslem laws one [Shi'ite] will be abandoned;
there will be continual upheavals between Moslems and French.

[1] Ogmios or Ogmius, the Gauls' god of eloquence and poetry depicted as an old man,
armed with bow and club, attracting to himself a variety of people by means of nets of
amber and gold coming out of his mouth. DHB.
[2] Alliance, confederation of several states: offensive and defensive league. DL7V. Cf.
'And the barbaric sect will be greatly afflicted and driven out by all the Nations.' (Letter
to Henri, Second King of France).
[3] Latin ethnicus: pagan. DLLB. The Sunnites, a Moslem sect derived from the Arab
word sunnah (tradition), because its adherents claimed to be preserving the true tradition.
The Shi'ites, a Moslem sect opposed to the Sunnites, derived their name (meaning
heretics, schismatics) from the Sunnites who called themselves the only orthodox believers.
(The two Moslem laws). DHB.
[4] Tumult, brawl. DAFL.

The King of France in Italy.
Fighting in the Alps

L'an que les frères du lys seront en l'aage,
L'un d'eux tiendra la Grande Romanie,
Trembler les monts, ouvert latin passage,[1]
Pache marcher[2] contre fort d'Arménie.

CV,Q50

Interpretation

The year the Bourbon brothers [kings of France and Spain] arrive, one
of them [the King of France] will occupy Italy, the mountains [Alps]
will shake, the passage into Italy will be open. Peace will be delayed
because of armies in Armenia.

[1] Col of Mont-Cenis, Tende or Mont Blanc.
[2] Latin *marcens pax*: sluggish peace. DLLB.

The Movements of Large Forces in Iran and
Armenia. The Defeat of the Moslem Troops

Aux chands de Mede,[1] d'Arabe et d'Arménie,
Deux grands copies[2] trois fois s'assembleront:
Près du rivage d'Araxes[3] la mesgnie[4]
Du grand Soliman en terre tomberont.

CIII,Q31

Interpretation

In the territories of Iran, Arabia and Armenia, two great armies will
reassemble; they will be concentrated on the Iran–Armenia border, then
the soldiers of the great Moslem commander will fall.

[1] Medea: part of Asia Minor. The plain, well irrigated at the foot of some mountains,
becomes infertile towards the east and south-east, and ends by forming, at the centre of
the Iranian plateau, what is called the great Medean Desert. DL7V.
[2] Latin *copiae*: army, troops. DLLB.
[3] River border between Russian Armenia and Iran, which flows out into the Caspian
Sea.
[4] Or *maisnie*: troop, force. DAFL.

The Duration of the Third World War:
Three Years and Seven Months. The Revolt of Two
Socialist Republics. Victory in Armenia

> Le règne a deux laissé bien peu tiendront,
> Trois ans sept mois passés[1] feront la guerre:
> Les deux vestales[2] contre rebelleront
> Victor[3] puisnay[4] en Armonique terre.

CIV,Q95

Interpretation

The two persons to whom power has been abandoned will keep it only
a short time. The war will last a little more than three years and seven
months. Two of the Warsaw Pact Republics will rebel against [the
USSR], and the younger [the King of France in relation to the King of
Spain] will be victor in Armenia.

[1] Cf. *Revelations*: 13: 'And I stood upon the sand of the sea, and saw a beast rise up out
of the sea, having seven heads and ten horns . . . [seven Warsaw Pact countries] . . . the
beast which I saw was like unto a leopard, and his feet were as the feet of a bear [USSR]
and his mouth as the mouth of a lion . . . and power was given unto him to continue *forty
and two months* . . . .'
[2] Name given to priestesses of Vesta. Their clothing consisted of a tunic of grey and
white linen, covered by a big *purple* cloak. DL7V. Nostradamus always personifies
republics as feminine.
[3] Latin *victor*: conqueror. DLLB.
[4] *Puîné*: person born after another (i.e. younger of two children). DL7V.

The Two Years of Soviet Occupation.
The End of the Soviet Empire

> Le grand empire chacun an devait estre,
> Un sur les autres le viendra obtenir:
> Mais peu de temps sera son regne et estre
> Deux ans aux naves[1] se pourra soustenir.

CX,Q32

Interpretation

The great [Soviet] empire, which seems set to survive, will gradually obtain countries one after the other, but its power and existence will not be very prolonged. It will be able to keep going only two years thanks to its navy.

[1] Latin *navis*: vessel, ship. DLLB.

Great Changes in International Relations. The Liberation of Marseille

L'ordre fatal[1] sempiternel par chaine,
Viendra tourner par ordre conséquent:
Du port Phocen[2] sera rompuë la chaine[3]
La cité prinse, l'ennemy quant et quant.[4]

CIII,Q79

Interpretation

The universal order obtaining everywhere will be changed by the order succeeding it. The occupation of Marseille will be thrown off, after the city has been occupied by so many enemies.

[1] Universal order: according to Malebranche, the law governing all God's decisions, as it must also rule ours. DL7V.
[2] Phocéen: Marseillais. Phocea was the ancient Greek name for Marseille.
[3] Dependence, servitude. DL7V.
[4] Latin *quantum*: a great quantity. DLLB.

The Anglo–American Landing at Bordeaux. The Liberation of South-west France. The Proclamation of an Occitanian Republic

Par la Guyenne infinité d'Anglois,
Occuperont par nom d'Anglaquitaine:
Du Languedoc I. palme[1] Bourdelois,
Qu'ils nommeront après Barboxitaine.[2]

CIX,Q6

Interpretation

A huge number of Anglo-Saxons and Americans will land at Guyenne, which they will occupy, calling it Anglo-American Aquitania. After winning victory from the Languedoc to the Bordeaux area, they will name this region the 'Republic of Occitania'.

[1] Symbolic: sign of victory. DL7V.
[2] Word made up of *Barbe* (Aenobarbe, i.e. Domitius Aeonobarbus, husband of Agrippina, symbolizing 'Republic'), and *Occitan*.

The Landing on the Coast of Guyenne. The Battles of Poitiers, Lyon, Montluel and Vienne

Le grand secours venu de la Guyenne
S'arrestera tout auprès de Poitiers:
Lyon rendu par Mont Luel[1] et Vienne,[2]
Et saccagez par tous gens des mestiers.[3]

CXII,Q24

Interpretation

The great aid coming from Guyenne will stop close to Poitiers. The liberation army will go back to Lyon via Montluel and Vienne, which will be ransacked by the soldiers.

[1] Montluel: main town of the canton of Ain. DHB.
[2] Main town of the district of the Isère, at the confluence of the Gère and the Rhône. DHB.
[3] The *métier* of arms, i.e. the profession of war, soldiering.

The Occupation of Toulouse. The Desecration of Its Cathedral

Les cinq estranges entrez dedans le Temple,
Leur sang viendra la terre prophaner,
Aux Thoulousains sera bien dur exemple,
D'un qui viendra ses lois exterminer.

CIII,Q45

Interpretation

The five foreign leaders will enter the cathedral where their blood will profane the soil; this will be a fearful example to the inhabitants of Toulouse because of him who will come to annihilate their laws.

Revolutionary Movements in the South-west of France. The Republic of Occitania

Bazar,[1] Lestore, Condon, Auch, Agine,
Esmeus par loix, querelle et monopole:
Car Bourd, Tholose Bay mettra en ruyne,
Renouveler voulant leur tauropole.[2]

CI,Q79

Interpretation

Bazas, Lectoure, Condom, Auch and Agen will rebel against the laws and political quarrels of Paris, for the war will ruin Bordeaux, Toulouse and Bayonne which will want to reconstitute a republic.

[1] For Bazas, main town of the Gironde district.
[2] Greek ταυροπόλος: worshipped or adored in Tauris, i.e. Diana or Hecate. DGF. The moon, symbol of the Republic.

Communist Forces Crushed at Toulouse

Vuydez, fuyez de Tholose les rouges,
Du sacrifice faire expiation:
Le chef du mal dessous l'ombre[1] des courges[2]
Mort estrangler carne[3] omination.[4]

CIX,Q46

Interpretation

Abandon and flee from Toulouse, Communists! You will pay for your extortions. The leader who has brought misfortune under the appearance of foolishness will be put to death according to a human prophecy.

[1] *Sous ombre de*: i.e. under the pretext or appearance of. DL7V.
[2] Provençal *coucoureou*: imbecile, fool. DP.
[3] Latin *carnea lex*: law of human origin. DLLB.
[4] Latin *ominatio*: prophecy, presage. DLLB.

The Crushing of the Revolutionary Forces at Nîmes and Toulouse

Quand lampe[1] ardente[2] de feu inextinguible,
Sera trouvée au temple des Vestales:[3]
Enfant[4] trouvé, feu, eau[5] passant par crible,[6]
Nismes eau périr, Tholose cheoir les hales.[7]

CIX,Q9

Interpretation

When an incendiary missile which provokes an inextinguishable fire will be found in Rome, something considered abominable, the war will be at its height, the revolutionaries will be overwhelmed and perish at Nîmes; the churches of Toulouse will crumble.

[1] Latin *lampas*: meteor, light in the sky. DLLB.
[2] Latin *ardens*: flaming, blazing. DLLB.
[3] At Rome the house of the Vestals was between the Forum and the Palatine, near the small temple of Vesta. DL7V.
[4] Latin *infans*: abominable. DLLB.
[5] Symbol of revolution, along with words like wave, rain and whirlwind.
[6] To overwhelm. DL7V.
[7] From Anglo-Saxon *halla*: palace, temple. DL7V.

Destruction in the Aude by Missiles or Meteors. Internecine Struggles among Perpignan and Toulouse Revolutionaries. The Death of the Revolutionary Leader

Gorsan,[1] Narbonne, par le sel[2] advertir,[3]
Tucham,[4] la grâce Parpignan trahie,[5]
La ville rouge n'y voudra consentir,
Par haulte[6] voldrap[7] gris[8] vie faillie.

CVIII,Q22

Interpretation

Coursan and Narbonne will be damaged by a missile, because of revolutionaries, Perpignan will want to claim the honour [of the revolutionary movement] but Toulouse will oppose this, and the bloody one will be put to death by him who will bear a noble standard [the King of France, the liberator].

[1] Coursan: town in the Aude, 7 km from Narbonne on the N113.

[2] Greek σέλας: sort of meteor, blaze, light. DGF.

[3] Latin *adverto*: I rage against, punish. DLLB.

[4] The Revolt of the Tuchins: a peasant rebellion, 1382–84, in southern France (including *Toulouse*), during which chateaux were destroyed and many nobles and priests were massacred. DL7V. Nostradamus establishes parallel between the Tuchins and the revolutionary movements of south-west France.

[5] Latin *rei sibi gratiam trahere*: to take the honour or credit for something. DLLB.

[6] Latin *altus*: noble. DLLB.

[7] Neologism from *volt*: image, idol, and *drapeau*, flag. DAFL.

[8] Allusion to Robespierre's donkey: Robespierre's donkey, it was said, was the guillotine, drunk with the blood it had swallowed. DL7V.

The Revolutionary Movements in South-west France. Their Pillage and Extortion. Revolt against Them

Encore seront les saincts temples pollus[1]
Et expillez par Senat Tholosain:
Saturne deux trois[2] siècles revollus;[3]
Dans Avril, May, gens de nouveau levain.

CIX,Q72

Interpretation

The churches will be desecrated and ransacked again by the members of a Toulouse group. The era [of pillage] will return six centuries later [1982], then in April and May new people will rise up [to resist].

[1] Latin *polluo*: I profane. DLLB.

[2] For twice three, i.e. six.

[3] Tuchin Revolt, 1382 + six centuries = 1982. Cf. CVIII,Q22.

Organized Groups against the Communists

Contre les rouges sectes se banderont[1]
Feu, eau, fer, corde[2] par paix se minera[3]
Au point mourir ceux qui machineront,
Fors un que monde sur tout ruynera.

CIX,Q51

Interpretation

Various groups will resist the Communist forces during the war and the revolution; the spirit of peace will weaken. The traitors will die except for one of them, who will bring ruin to the world.

[1] Make an effort to resist. DL7V.
[2] Latin *cor, cordis*: intelligence, wit, good sense. DLLB.
[3] To consume, deteriorate, progressively weaken. DL7V.

The Revolution and the Sack of Toulouse

Pont et molins[1] en Decembre versez,
En si hault lieu montera la Garonne:[2]
Murs, édifices, Tholose renversez,
Qu'on ne saura son lieu autant matronne.

CIX,Q37

Interpretation

The bridges and mills of Toulouse will be destroyed in December; the revolution will be so strong on the banks of the Garonne that the houses and public buildings will be destroyed so that even mothers of families will not recognize their homes.

[1] Ancient form of *moulins*, mills. DAFL.
[2] Flood, rain, water, waves, always symbolizing revolution.

The Occupation of Carcassonne by the Russians

Aux lieux sacrez animaux veu à trixe,[1]
Avec celui qui n'osera le jour:
A Carcassonne pour disgrace propice,
Sera posé pour plus ample séjour.

CIX,Q71

Interpretation

The Russians will be seen in the churches with the person who will not be bold enough to show himself in broad daylight. After a propitious disgrace he will establish himself for a greater period of time at Carcassonne.

[1] Greek θρίς, τρίχος: hair, fleece, pelt. DGF. Bears are heavy, large animals covered with *thick fur*. DL7V.

The Alliance of Romania, England, Poland and East Germany. Their Struggle with the Moslems in the Mediterranean

La gent de Dace,[1] d'Angleterre, et Polonne,
Et de Boësme[2] feront nouvelle ligue:
Pour passer outre d'Hercules la colonne,[3]
Barcins,[4] Tyrrans dresser cruelle brigue.[5]

CV,Q51

Interpretation

Romania, England, Poland and East Germany will form a new alliance, in order to go beyond Gibraltar [into the Mediterranean] and against the Moslems who will have instigated a cruel tumult so as to impose their tyranny.

[1] Dacia: ancient name for Romania. DHB.
[2] Bohemia: today part of Czechoslovakia. AVL.
[3] Pillars of Hercules: Gibraltar. DHB.
[4] Barcinus: powerful Carthaginian family whose leader was Hamilcar Barca, and other

members of which were Hannibal and Hasdrubal. Always sworn enemies of Rome. DHB.
As with the words 'Hannibal' and 'Punic', Nostradamus here refers to the Moslems.
[5] Tumult. DAFL.

The End of the War. Misery in Italy.
Moslem Troops Arrive from the Danube and Malta.
Their Setback in the Drôme Region

L'indigne[1] orné[2] craindra la grande fornaise,
L'esleu premier, des captifs n'en retourne:
Grand bas du monde, l'Itale non alaise[3]
Barb. Ister,[4] Malte. Et le Buy[5] ne retourne.

Presage 15, January

Interpretation

The notorious military leader will fear the great furnace. The first choice
will not be among the returning prisoners. The great power [USSR] will
be low in world status, Italy will undergo misfortune because of the
Moslems who come via the Danube and Malta. They will retreat in the
Drôme area.

[1] Latin indignus: infamous. DLLB.
[2] Latin orno: I equip, arm. DLLB.
[3] Greek αἴσιος: happy. DGF.
[4] Hister: ancient name for the Danube. DHB.
[5] Le Buis: main town of the canton of the Drôme.

The USSR and the War in Europe.
The USSR and Turkey

Des régions subjectes à la Balance[1]
Feront troubler les monts par grande guerre,
Captif tout sexe deu[2] et tout Bisance,
Qu'on criera à l'aube terre à terre.

CV,Q70

Interpretation

The regions subject to the USSR will come to trouble the mountains
[the Alps] with a major war and will take prisoners of both sexes through-

out Turkey, so that at dawn there will be cries from one country to another.

[1] Seventh sign of the Zodiac: the Egyptians consecrated Libra and Scorpio to the god of evil, Typhon (or Set) who, not content with this astronomical homage, also required the sacrifice of red-haired men. DL7V. There is thus a triple allusion to the seven Eastern Bloc countries; to the revolution (Typhon/Typhoon); and to the Reds.

[2] Contraction of *de le*. DAFL.

Negotiations for the Entry of England into the Common Market, July 1970

La soeur aisnée de l'Isle Britannique,
Quinze ans[1] devant le frère aura naissance,
Par son promis moyennant verrifique,
Succedera au regne de balance.[2]

CIV,Q96

Interpretation

The elder sister of Britain [USA] will succeed to Soviet power. Fifteen years earlier, the British brother will be born [in Europe] on condition of verifiable promises.

[1] 1–12 December 1969: the European Summit of the 'Six' at The Hague. The principle of British entry into the Common Market established, negotiations began in July 1970. On his return to Paris President Pompidou stated that this reunion had contributed to dispel *unjustified distrust* ('*promis verrifique*'). VCAHU. 1969 + 15 years = 1984, which is thus the turning point in the war and fall of the USSR.

[2] Cf. CV,Q70 and CV,Q61

The War between the King of France and the USSR

L'enfant du Grand n'estant à sa naissance
Subjuguera les hauts monts Appenis,[1]
Fera trembler tous ceux de la balance,[2]
Et des monts feux jusques à Mont-Senis.

CV,Q61

Interpretation

The heir of the great [monarchical power], being only at the beginning of his rule, will subjugate Italy, make all those in the USSR tremble, and will take the war as far as Mont-Cenis.

[1] Nostradamus by syncope removes one letter from '*Appenins*' (the Apennines) to make a rhyme with Mont-Cenis.
[2] Cf. CV,Q70 and CV,Q46.

The Russian Army Beaten at Chambéry and in the Maurienne Area

Grande assemblée près du lac du Borget,[1]
Se raillieront près de Montmelian:[2]
Passant plus oultre pensifs feront projet,
Chambry, Moriane[3] combat Saint-Julian.[4]

CX,Q37

Interpretation

Great armies will assemble near Lake Bourget and will regroup near Montmélian. Not being able to go further, the baffled military leaders will make plans and be beaten at Chambéry and St-Julien-de-Maurienne.

[1] Lake in Savoie, not far from Chambéry and Aix-les-Bains. DL7V.
[2] Town in Savoie, 15 km from Chambéry. DHB.
[3] Valley of the Maurienne: commands access to Italy by the Mont-Cenis pass.
[4] Village near St-Jean-de-Maurienne.

Reconquest from Barcelona to Venice. The Defeat of the Moslem Troops. Their Retreat to Tunisia

De Barcelonne, de Gennes et Venise,
De la Secille peste Monet[1] unis:
Contre Barbare classe prendront la vise,[2]
Barbar poulsé bien loing jusqu'à Thunis.

CIX,Q42

Interpretation

From Barcelona and Genoa to Venice, from Sicily to Monaco, the pestilence will reign, and will reconnoitre the Moslem army and push it back as far as Tunisia.

[1] Monoeci Arx: Monaco. DLLB.
[2] *Visere copias hostium*: to reconnoitre the enemy army. DLLB.

The Defeat of the Western Navy by the Russians. The Persecution of Clergy. The Victory of the West, in November

Navalle pugne[1] nuict[2] sera supérée,[3]
Le feu, aux naves à l'Occident ruine:
Rubriche[4] neusve, la grand nef,[5] colorée,
Ire a vaincu, et victoire, en bruine.[6]

CIX,QIOO

Interpretation

A naval battle will occur at night and the war will ruin the Western [US] Navy. A new Red Army will cause bloodshed at the Vatican, the vanquished will be overwhelmed, but will end by gaining victory in November.

[1] Latin *pugna*: fight between two armies, battle. DLLB.
[2] This quatrain has been attributed by commentators to the Battle of Trafalgar, which lasted from 11 a.m. to 5 p.m.! DL7V.
[3] Latin *supero*: I have the advantage (in war), I conquer. DLLB.
[4] Latin *ruber*: red. DLLB. Cf. CI,Q82 and CIV,Q37.
[5] Refers to the ship of the Catholic Church.
[6] Cf. CVI,Q25, the coup d'état of 18 Brumaire.

THE LAST AND GREATEST OF THE KINGS OF FRANCE, 1983/6–1999

Nostradamus gives this king several names, titles or attributes which all suggest the idea of legitimacy:

1. *CHIREN*, anagram of *HENRIC*, from Latin Henricus, for Henri.
2. *The King of Blois*: Counts of Blois were descended from the family of Hugues Capet.[1]
3. *Le Coq*: the first medal upon which a rooster appears was minted in 1601, the year of Louis XIII's birth.[2]
4. *Hercule*: frequently Hercules is an exemplar of strength and courage.[3]

[1] DHB.
[2] L. A. de Gremilly: *The Cock*, Flammarion, 1958.
[3] DL7V.

The King of France Enters Rome.
The Alliance between the Pope and the King of France.

Le Grand Celtique entra dedans Rome
Menant amas d'exilez et bannis:
Le grand pasteur mettra à port[1] tout homme
Qui pour le Coq estoyent aux Alpes unis.

CVI,Q28

Interpretation

The great Frenchman will enter Rome leading many exiles and banished persons. The great Pope will shelter every man who helped the King of France in the Alps.

[1] Latin *portes*: shelter, retreat. *In portu esse*: to be out of danger. DLLB.

The War of the King of France against Libya.
The Latter Driven out from Hungary to Gibraltar

Par grand fureur le Roy Romain Belgique
Vexer voudra par phalange barbare:
Fureur grinssant[1] chassera gent Libyque,
Depuis Pannons[2] jusques Hercules[3] la hare.[4]

CV,Q13

Interpretation

Driven by great wrath, the King arrived from Rome will enter Belgium harassed by Moslem troops. In fury and anger he will pursue the Libyans and track them down from Hungary as far as Gibraltar.

[1] Figurative: to be angry. DL7V.
[2] Pannonia: ancient name for Hungary.
[3] The Pillars of Hercules: name given by the Ancients to the African and European sides of the Straits of Gibraltar.
[4] *Harer*: to track down, harass. DAFL.

The King against the Revolutionaries.
His Arrival in Provence

Ce qu'en vivant le père n'avait sceu,
Il acquerra ou par guerre ou par feu,
Et combattra la sangsue[1] irritée,[2]
Ou jouyra de son bien paternel
Et favory du grand Dieu Eternel,
Aura bien tost sa Province héritée.

Sixain 40

Interpretation

What his father never knew in his lifetime, war and fire will enable him to acquire, and he will combat sterile revolution. He will benefit from his father's property and, favourite of the Almighty, will soon inherit Provence.

[1] Revolution: the leech or bloodsucker.
[2] Latin *irritus*: useless, vain, sterile. DLLB.

War in Norway, Romania and England.
The French Leader's Role in Italy

Norneigre[1] et Dace,[2] et l'isle Britannique,
Par les unis frères seront vexées:[3]
Le chef Romain issu du sang Gallique,
Et les copies[4] aux forêts repoussées.

CVI,Q7

Interpretation

Norway, Romania and Great Britain will be damaged by the united allies [Soviet Union and the Warsaw Pact].[5] Then the Roman commander of French origin will drive back their troops through the forests.

[1] Anagram of NERIGON, to which Nostradamus adds *re* (by paragoge) – ancient name for Norway. DHB.

[2] Traces of Roman domination are still to be found there: the Wallachians and Moldavians call themselves Romanians. DHB. Romania.

[3] Latin *vexo*: I trouble, ill-treat. DLLB.

[4] Latin *copiae*: troops, army. DLLB.

[5] 'On 14 May 1955, the treaty of friendship, cooperation and mutual assistance, the Warsaw Pact, was concluded between the USSR, Albania, Hungary, Bulgaria, Poland, the GDR, Romania and Czechoslovakia. A *single* military command was instituted.' VCAHU. Note that Albania withdrew from the pact and that Romania is the most controversial of these.

The Role of the Saudi 'TAG' Society in France's Liberation

Jamais par le découvrement[1] du jour,[2]
Ne parviendra au signe sceptrifère,
Que tous ses sièges ne soient en séjour,
Portant au Coq don du TAG[3] armifère.

CVIII,Q61

Interpretation

He will never attain monarchical power through the exposure [of his origins] as long as all the cities are not liberated when the TAG will offer its armaments to the King.

[1] Action of uncovering, exposure. DL.

[2] Figurative: what enlightens, serves to make one understand. DL7V.

[3] The Society of the Saudi Akkram Ojjeh, a good friend to France, is called the TAG and has its headquarters at Geneva.

The King of France against the Russians.
The Sack of the Balearics

Par le grand Prince limitrophe du Mans,[1]
Preux et vaillant chef de grand exercite:[2]
Par mer et terre de Gallois et Normans,[3]
Caspre[4] passer Barcelonne pillé Isle.

CVII,Q10

Interpretation

The great prince originating from Blois, who will be the valiant and
courageous leader of a great army, [will lead the war] by land and sea
between French and Russians, who since Barcelona will have reached
the Balearics in order to ransack them.

[1] The Loir-et-Cher, where Blois is situated, borders the Sarthe.
[2] Latin *exercitus*: army. DLLB.
[3] Or Northmen, men of the North. DHB. Nostradamus refers to the Russians, inhabiting the country of Aquila, the North Wind.
[4] Capraria: Cabrera, one of the Balearics, south of Majorca.

Henri V Established at Avignon

Le Roy de Blois[1] en Avignon régner,
Une autre fois le peuple en monopole,
Dedans le Rosne par murs fera baigner
Jusques à cinq[2] le dernier près de Nole.[3]

CVIII,Q38

Interpretation

The King of Blois will govern in Avignon, which will serve as the French
people's capital; the Rhône will bathe the walls of his dwelling place.
He will be the last of five [Henri V] and will go almost as far as Nole.

[1] The Counts of Blois were descended from the family of *Hugues Capet*. DHB. Nostradamus thus stresses the Capetian connection of this king.
[2] Cf. '*Le Lorrain V*', Presage 76.
[3] Town in Italy, 37 km south-east of Capua. DHB.

The Occupation of West Germany by the Warsaw Pact. Invasion via the Loire Valley

Le Roy de Bloys dans Avignon regner,
D'Amboise et seme[1] viendra le long de Lyndre:
Ongle à Poitiers, sainctes aisles ruyner,
Devant Boni.[2]

CVIII,Q52

Interpretation

The King of Blois will rule in Avignon. The seven countries will come along the Indre as far as Amboise: [the Russian bear] will show his claws at Poitiers and will ruin the West's airforce, but before that he will have occupied Bonn.

[1] Sedme: from Latin *septimum*: seventh. DAFL. Russia and the six other Warsaw Pact countries.
[2] Latin *Bonna*: Bonn. DLLB. Capital of West Germany.

Avignon, Capital of France

Le grand empire sera tost translaté
En lieu petit qui bientost viendra croistre
Lieu bien infime d'exiguë comté[1]
Où au milieu viendra poser son sceptre.

CI,Q32

Interpretation

The great empire [French] will be transferred to a small place which will soon grow. A place as small as a *comté* where [the King] will come and establish his power.

[1] Comtat Venaissin. This area is sometimes (wrongly) called the *comtat* of Avignon. DHB.

NOSTRADAMUS

Avignon, Capital of France

Dans Avignon tout le chef de l'Empire
Fera arrest pour Paris désolé:
Tricast[1] tiendra l'Annibalique[2] ire,
Lyon par change sera mal consolé.

CIII,Q93

Interpretation

The capital will be moved to Avignon because Paris will be destroyed.
The Tricastin will be the cause of Moslem anger. Lyon will be very
upset by the change of capital.

[1] Tricastin: in the Bas-Dauphiné area, redivided between the departments of the
Drôme (cantons of St Paul-Trois Châteaux, Grignan and Pierrelatte) and the Vaucluse
(canton of Bollène). DL7V. This is where the uranium plant, financed by Iran, is
situated.

[2] Hannibal, Carthaginian general, son of Hamilcar. His father made him swear undying
enmity to Rome from his childhood days. DHB. Nostradamus uses Carthaginian, Hannibal or Punic to denote the Moslem world.

Great Change in France.
The Capital in Provence

Le changement sera fort difficile,
Cité, province au change gain sera:
Coeur haut, prudent mis, chassé luy habile,
Mer, terre, peuple son estat changera.

CIV,Q21

Interpretation

Change will be very painful. The province [or Provence] will gain by the
change of capital. The [King] with noble and wise heart will attain power
after driving off [the enemy] through his skill; he will change the condition of people upon land and sea.

The Installation of the King in Avignon. Offers from Other Cities Declined

En lieu libere[1] tendra son pavillon[2]
Et ne voudra en citez prendre place:
Aix, Carpen, l'Isle[3] volce,[4] mont Cavaillon,
Par tout ces lieux abolira sa trasse.

CV,Q76

Interpretation

In a liberated place he will establish residence and will not wish to install himself in the following towns: Aix, Carpentras, L'Isle-sur-Sorgue, Cavaillon, nor to be any longer in the Languedoc, where he will suppress all traces of his passing.

[1] Avignon remained a possession of the Holy See until 1791 when it was reunited with France at the same time as the Comtat Venaissin. This reunion was confirmed by the Treaty of Tolentino, 1797. DHB.
[2] Portable tentlike dwelling, round or square, once used by campaigning troops. DL7V.
[3] L'Isle-sur-Sorgue: main town of the canton of Vaucluse, 22 km east of Avignon. DHB.
[4] Volces: Gallic tribe from the Narbonne area, which used to occupy the greater part of the Languedoc. DHB.

Henri V Brings Victory and Reigns over France and Italy

Premier en Gaule, premier en Romanie,
Par mer et terre aux Anglais et Paris
Merveilleux faits par celle grand mesnie[1]
Violant,[2] terax[3] perdra le NORLARIS

CVIII,Q60

Interpretation

[Henri V] will be the first person in France and Italy. By land and sea, for the English and Parisians, exceptional deeds will be accomplished by this great house [the Bourbons] and the man from Lorraine will dispose of the monster [the Russian bear] by attacking it.

[1] From *mansionem: maison* (house). The group inhabiting the house, family. DAFL.

[2] Latin *violo*: I do violence to, attack someone. DLLB.

[3] Greek τέρας: prodigy, monster. DGF.

Henri V, Descendant of the Capets and Guises. His Military Exploits on the Black Sea

L'ensevely sortira du tombeau,
Fera de chaînes lier le fort du pont,[1]
Empoisonné avec oeufs du Barbeau,[2]
Grand de Lorraine par le Marquis[3] du Pont.[4]

CVII,Q24

Interpretation

The descendant of the buried Capet [Louis XVI] will come out of the shadow and put an end to the maritime power [of the Russians] which will be poisoned by this descendant of the Guises. The great Lorrainian will be the guarantor of the borders of the Black Sea.

[1] Greek ποντός: sea. DGF.

[2] Bar-le-Duc, the Duke of Guise's home ground. The town's coat of arms consisted of two barbels (mullet). DL7V.

[3] Nobleman entrusted to guard the marches or frontier areas, originally a form of warlord.

[4] Kingdom of Pontus: in southern part of Asia Minor, on the edge of the Euxine (Black Sea). DL7V. Now Armenia.

The Lorrainian V Puts an End to Dissensions

Par le legat[1] du terrestre et marin,
La grande Cape a tout s'accomoder:[2]
Estre à l'escoute tacite LORVARIN,[3]
Qu'à son advis ne voudra accorder.

Presage 76, October

Interpretation

Because of the ambassador of the land and sea power, the great Capetian will be reconciled with everyone: he will know how to listen to them without saying anything, the Lorrainian, so that they will be only too ready to agree with his view.

[1] Latin *legatus*: envoy, deputy, ambassador. DLLB.
[2] To come to agreement, reconcile. DL7V.
[3] Duchy of Lorraine: the first Duke was Frederick of Alsace, related to Hugues Capet. DHB. Nostradamus calls Henri V by this epithet to stress his Capetian antecedents. LORVARIN = anagram of LORRAIN V.

The Liberation of the Vatican by Henri V

Par le[1] cinquiesme et un grand Herculès,
Viendront le temple[2] ouvrir de main bellique:
Un Clément, Jule[3] et Ascans[4] reculés,
Lespe,[5] clef[6] aigle, n'eurent onc si grand picque.

CX,Q27

Interpretation

Through the fifth [Henri] who will also be a great and strong person, the Vatican will be opened again by military means. A pope named Clement will be elected, the two Germanys having retreated. Spain and the papacy will never have had so great an attack by a military force [eagle].

[1] Some editions have *Carle* instead of *Par le*.
[2] Poetic term for the Catholic Church. DL7V.
[3] Jülich: town now in West Germany.
[4] One of the oldest German families, branch of the Anhalts, who provided Brandenburg and Saxe with rulers. DHB. Now part of East Germany.
[5] Some editions give *L'Espagne* instead of Lespe.
[6] Keys: attributes of the papacy, and gifts bestowed by popes upon other sovereigns on certain ceremonial or festive occasions.

The King of France, Italy and Denmark. The Liberation of Italy and the Adriatic

Hercules[1] Roy de Rome et d'Annemarc,
De Gaule trois le Guion[2] surnommé:
Trembler l'Itale et l'unde de Sainct Marc.[3]
Premier sur tous Monarque renommé.

CIX,Q33

Interpretation

Hercules [the King of France] will be King of Rome and Denmark. He will be given the name 'Leader of France' by three rulers [military or party]. Italy and the Adriatic Sea will tremble. First among all heads of state, he will be a renowned monarch.

[1] Nostradamus dubs the last King Hercules to signify his strength and the 'labours' he must accomplish.

[2] Guide, leader. DAFL.

[3] Lion of St Mark: winged lion, symbol of the Venetian Republic, whose patron is St Mark. DHB.

The Reconquest of France.
The Defeat of a Warsaw Pact Leader.
The Role of the Tank Divisions

Les ennemis du fort bien esloignez,
Par chariots conduict le bastion:
Par sur les murs de Bourges esgrongnez[1]
Quand Hercules battra l'Haemathion.[2]

CIX,Q93

Interpretation

Enemies will be driven back and the defence assured because of tanks; they will be cut to pieces at Bourges when the King of France defeats the [East] German commander.

[1] *Esgruignier*: to reduce to pieces, cut apart. DAFL.

[2] Word which always denotes a German leader. Cf. cx,Q7.

The King of France Acknowledged.
His Victory over the German Leader.
The Submission of the Moslem World

Roy salué Victeur, Imperateur,[1]
La foy faussée le Royal faict cognu:
Sang Mathien. Roy faict superateur[2]
De gent superbe[3] humble par pleurs venu.

Presage 38, April

Interpretation

The king will be hailed as conqueror and leader, after a piece of treachery his royal origin will be known. He will be victor through the blood of a German leader. The Moslems will become humble because of their misfortunes.

[1] Latin *imperator:* commander, chief. DLLB.
[2] Latin *superator:* victor. DLLB.
[3] Latin *superbes:* violent, tyrannical, proud. DLLB. Cf. CII,Q79: '*La gent cruelle et fière.*'

The War in Greece. The Burning of Istanbul by the King of France

La legion[1] dans la marine classe
Calcine,[2] Magne,[3] souphre et poix[4] bruslera,
Le long repos de l'asseurée place,
Port Selin,[5] Hercle feu les consumera.

CIV,Q23

Interpretation

A seaborne army will set fire to Thrace and the Morea, after long peace in these areas, Hercule [the King of France] will set the Moslem port [Istanbul] ablaze.

[1] Latin *legio:* troops, army. DLLB.
[2] Chalcedon: town in Bithynia, on the Thracian Bosphorus facing Byzantium (Istanbul). DHB.
[3] Magnia: area of the Morea, Greece. DHB.
[4] Mineralogy: bitumens etc. DL7V. Probably reference to napalm.
[5] Greek Σελήνη:the moon. DGF. The Moslem crescent.

The Restoration of a Bourbon.
The End of the Revolutionary System

D'un rond,[1] d'un lis[2] naistra un si grand Prince,
Bien tost, et tard venu dans sa Province,[3]
Saturne en Libra en exaltation:[4]
Maison de Venus en decroissante force,
Dame en apres masculin soubs l'escorce,[5]
Pour maintenir, l'heureux sang de Bourbon.

Sixain 4

Interpretation

From a Capet, from a lily [of the Bourbons] a very great Prince will be born, coming early and late into his Provence, the time of justice having risen again: the established rule of lies and lust seeing its strength decrease after the reign of the Republic under its masculine exterior, in order to maintain the fortunate blood of the Bourbon.

[1] Latin *rota*: the chariot of the sun. DLLB. Symbol of the Capets.
[2] The royal emblem. DL7V.
[3] The Roman province: Provence. DLLB.
[4] Latin *exalto*: I raise up again, exalt. DLLB.
[5] Appearance, exterior. DL7V.

The Death of the Head of State.
His Replacement by a Young Prince

La mort subite du premier personnage
Aura changé et mis un autre au règne:
Tost, tard venu à si haut et bas aage,
Que terre et mer faudra qu'on le craingne.

CIV,QI4

Interpretation

The sudden death of the chief of state will cause a change and put another in power, one who has come both early and late, so young despite his ancient descent that he must be feared by land and sea.

Henri V – a World Leader

Un chef du monde le grand CHIREN[1] sera:
PLUS OULTRE apres aymé craint redoubté:
Son bruit et los les cieux surpassera,
Et du seul titre Victeur fort contenté.

CVI,Q70

Interpretation

The great Henri will be a world leader. More and more he will be loved, feared and dreaded. His renown and praise will reach the skies and he will be well content with the single title of Victor.

[1] Anagram of HENRIC, from Latin Henricus: Henri.

Henri V, King of France

Le grand CHYREN soy saisir d'Avignon,[1]
De Rome lettres en miel plein d'amertume
Lettre ambassade partir de Chanignon,[2]
Carpentras pris par duc noir rouge plume.

CIX,Q41

Interpretation

Great Henri will seize Avignon when he receives bitter letters from Rome; a diplomatic mission will leave from Canino, when Carpentras is taken by a black general of the red persuasion.

[1] Cf. *'En Avignon tout le chef de l'Empire.'*
[2] Gallicization of the Italian town of Canino.

The Defeat of the Red Army in Italy.
The Enemy Leader a Prisoner of King Henri

Le grand mené captif d'estrange terre,
D'or enchaîné au Roy CHYREN offert:
Qui dans Ausone[1] Milan perdra la guerre,
Et tout son ost[2] mis a feu et a fer.

CIV,Q34

Interpretation

The great head of a foreign country [Russia?] will be taken prisoner and
presented with his gold to King Henri. In Italy, at Milan, this man will
lose the war and all his army will be surrendered to war's fire and iron.

[1] Latin Ausonia: ancient district of Italy, by extension Italy. DLLB.
[2] Army, camp. DAFL.

The Invasion of Austria, Germany and France.
The Defeat of the Russo–Moslem Troops in the Alps

Dans le Dannube et du Rhin viendra boire,
Le grand Chameau[1] ne s'en repentira:
Trembler du Rosne, et plus fort ceux de Loire,
Et pres des Alpes Coq le ruinera.

CV,Q68

Interpretation

The great Russo–Moslem commander will come to drink from the Danube and Rhine. Those who dwell beside the Rhône will tremble and
those by the Loire still more so. Then, near the Alps, the French King
will ruin him.

[1] Camels seem to have originated in central Asia. The most useful transport animal of
central Asia (*Turkestan, Afghanistan*, Mongolia, southern *Siberia*, northern *Persia*). DL7V.
Nostradamus indicates here a Russo–Moslem commander. Cf. CX,Q37.

The End of the Revolution.
The King Received at Aix and Crowned at Rheims

L'an que Saturne en eau sera conjoinct,
Avecques Sol, le Roy fort et puissant,
A Reims et Aix sera receu et oingt,
Après conquestes meurtrira innocens.

CIV,Q86

Interpretation

The year the Revolution and the monarchy are joined, the strong and powerful King will be received at Aix and anointed at Rheims, after rendering his enemies inoffensive by killing them.

The King of France Ends the War.
He Liberates the South-west

Le grand puisnay fera fin de la guerre,
Aux dieux assemble les excusez:[1]
Cahors, Moissac iront loin de la serre[2]
Refus[3] Lectore, les Agenois razez.

CVII,Q12

Interpretation

The younger [Henri V born after Juan Carlos I] will end the war and by God's grace reassemble those who had been exiled. These latter will liberate Cahors and Moissac. The occupiers of Lectoure will be driven back and Agen will be razed.

[1] Latin *excussus*: banished, exiled, rejected. DLLB.
[2] Action of grasping, submitting to pressure. DL7V.
[3] Latin *refusus*: pushing or driving back. DLLB.

The Great King Raises a Liberation Army.
Fighting in the Languedoc

Le Grand Monarque que fera compagnie
Avec deux Roys unis par amitié:
O quel souspir fera la grand mesgnie[1]
Enfans Narbon à l'entour, quelle pitié!

CI,Q99

Interpretation

The great King will raise an army. The two Kings [France and Spain] will be united by friendship. O what a sigh [of relief] the great army will utter. Pity the children in the Narbonne area!

[1] Troop. DAFL.

The King of France's Headquarters
in the Ariège

Moyne moynesse d'enfant[1] mort exposé,
Mourir par ourse et ravy par verrier[2]
Par Fois et Pamyes le camp sera posé,
Contre Tholose Carcass dresser forrier.[3]

CIX,Q10

Interpretation

A monk and a nun will see a child threatened with death. It will be put to death by the Russians after being captured by an Italian leader. The liberation army's camp will be set up in the Ariège and an officer sent by the King will rise up against [occupied] Toulouse and Carcassonne.

[1] Only events will reveal the identity of the child in question.
[2] The great glassworks flourished first under the Romans, then in medieval Italy. EU.
[3] Officer who preceded a travelling ruler; his duties involved arranging lodging for the retinue. DL7V.

The King of France Arrives in the Pyrenees.
The Monarchy and the End of Universal Suffrage

Dans Fois[1] entrez Roy cerulée[2] Turban,
Et régnera moins evolu[3] Saturne:
Roy Turban blanc Bisance coeur ban,[4]
Sol, Mars, Mercure[5] près la hurne.[6]

CIX,Q73

Interpretation

The King of France, with the blue emblem, will reign a short time. The Turkish leader in the white turban will be banished from his heart; the monarchy will rule after the war and the disappearance of universal suffrage.

[1] Principal town of Navarre.
[2] Azure, blue. DAFL. Colour of the dukes of France. DL7V.
[3] Latin *evolutus*: elapsed, passed. DLLB.
[4] Noun from bannir, to banish, ban. DL7V.
[5] God of thieves. DL7V.
[6] The urn, symbol of universal suffrage.

Liberation from the Pyrenees to Rome

Autour des Monts Pyrénées grand amas,
De gent estrange secourir Roy nouveau:
Près de Garonne du grand temple du Mas[1]
Un Romain chef le craindra dedans l'eau.

CVI,QI

Interpretation

Large numbers of foreign [American] troops will be massed around the Pyrenees and will come to the new King's aid, near Mas-d'Agenais in the Garonne, which a leader in Rome ought to fear during the revolution.

[1] Mas-d'Agenais: main town of the canton of Lot-et-Garonne, on the Garonne. In this neighbourhood the Gallo-Roman temple of Vernemet is thought to lie. DL7V.

The Reconquest from Spain to Italy

Dessus Jonchère[1] du dangereux passage,
Fera passer le posthume[2] sa bande,[3]
Les monts Pyrens passer hors son bagage,[4]
De parpignan courira[5] Duc[6] à Tende.[7]

CX,QII

Interpretation

Over the dangerous pass of Junquera, the last [of the Bourbons] will lead his troops and will cross the Pyrenees with his armaments and pursue the [enemy] general as far as the Tende Pass.

[1] Gallicization of Junquera: town in Spain (Catalonia) at the southern foot of the Alberas. DL7V.
[2] Latin *posthumus*: the last, born after his father's death. DLLB.
[3] Army organized to fight under a single flag. DL7V.
[4] For *bague* (ring, weapon). DAFL.
[5] To pursue, try to catch up with and seize.
[6] Latin *dux*: commander of an army, general. DLLB.
[7] One of the passes in the Alpes-Maritimes, between Nice and Coni. DHB.

The Young Prince Restores Peace.
His Coronation

Le jeune prince accusé faussement,
Mettra en trouble le camp[1] et en querelles:
Meurtry le chef pour le soustenement[2]
Sceptre appaiser: puis guerir escrouëlles.[3]

CIV,QIO

Interpretation

The young prince will be wrongly accused, and will bring controversy and dismay upon the territory. He will kill the [enemy] commander courageously, will bring back peace through his power, and will then heal the scrofula [he will be crowned.]

[1] Latin *campus*: territory. DLLB.
[2] Latin, *sustinentia*: patience, courage. DLLB.
[3] Kings of France (and England) were supposed to be able to heal scrofula ('the King's

evil'). In France the king, after the coronation ceremony, would for the first time touch sufferers from scrofula. Laying hands upon them he would say: 'The King touches you, may God cure you.' This custom continued until Louis XIV, who touched almost 2000 sufferers. DL7V.

The King Crowned by the Pope.
His Struggle against the Left-wing Forces in Italy

Au Roy l'Augur[1] sur le chef la main mettre,
Viendra prier pour la paix Italique:
A la main gauche viendra changer de sceptre,[2]
De Roy viendra Empereur pacifique.

CV,Q6

Interpretation

The Pope will come to lay his hand on the King's head [to crown him] and to beg him to restore peace in Italy. He will change the power in the hands of the left and this King will become a peaceful sovereign.

[1] Latin for prophet. DLLB. Note capital A. Used by Nostradamus to denote the Pope. Cf. CII,Q36. '*Du grand prophète* . . .'
[2] Absolute authority. DL7V.

The Death of the French Republic in the War.
The End of the Great Republics: the USSR

Au menu peuple par débats et querelles,
Et par les femmes et défunts grande guerre:
Mort d'une Grande. Celebrer escrouëlles.
Plus grandes Dames expulsées de la terre.

Presage 10, May

Interpretation

The little people [proletariat] will be agitated by debates and quarrels because of the womenfolk and the deaths in the great war. The Republic ['*une grande*' = Marianne, French Republican symbol] will die. The coronation will be celebrated and the greatest Republics [e.g. the USSR] will be driven from the earth.

The End of the Bolshevik Revolution

De FLORE[1] issuë de sa mort sera cause,
Un temps devant par jeusne et vieille bueyre[2]
Car les trois Lys luy feront telle pause,
Par son fruit sauve comme chair cruë mueyre.[3]

CVIII,QI8

Interpretation

Its Western origin will cause its [the Revolution's] death, due just previously to a renewed yet old confusion, for the three lilies [of the Bourbons] will halt it so that its rescued child [Louis XVII] will be transmuted into living flesh.

[1] Wife of Zephyrus, the West Wind.
[2] Provençal: mixture, confusion. DP.
[3] *Muer:* to change. DAFL.

The Capetian Origin of the King.
The King Drives out the Moslems. The King Returns the Church to its Original State

De sang Troyen naistra coeur Germanique,
Qui deviendra en si haute puissance:
Hors chassera gent estrange Arabique,
Tournant l'Eglise en pristine prééminence.

CV,Q74

Interpretation

Of Capetian blood, the king will be born with pro-German sentiments and will become so powerful that he will chase the Moslems from France and restore the Catholic Church to its former eminence.

The Liberation of the Arabs' Christian Prisoners by Henri V

La barbe crespe et noire par engin[1]
Subjuguera la gent cruelle et fière:
Un grand Chyren ostera du longin[2]
Tous les captifs par Seline bannière.

CII,Q79

Interpretation

He will subdue by his intelligence the proud and cruel race with the curly black beards. The great Henri will free from afar all the prisoners of the Crescent banner.

[1] Latin *ingenium*: intelligence, wit. DLLB.
[2] Latin *longinque*: from far off. DLLB.

The King of Monaco. The Fall of the Warsaw Pact

Dedans Monech[1] le Coq sera receu,
Le Cardinal de France apparoistra:
Par Logarion[2] Romain sera deceu?
Foiblesse à l'Aigle, et force au Coq naistra.

CVIII,Q4

Interpretation

The king will be received at Monaco; a French cardinal will appear. The Roman leader [the Pope] will be disappointed by the speeches of the British leader, the Eagle [Warsaw Pact] will weaken and the king's power begin to show itself.

[1] Monaco. DHB.
[2] Neologism from two Greek words λογος: speech, word, and Αριων: Arion, the name of the horse Neptune with his trident caused to leap from the earth. DL7V. Nostradamus always refers to England via Neptune and his trident.

The King's Landing at Monaco.
He Installs His Chief of Staff at Antibes,
and he Drives off the Moslem Troops

Grand roy viendra prendre port près de Nisse
Le grand empire de la mort si en fera
Aux Antipolles[1] posera son genisse[2]
Par mer la Pille[3] tout esvanouyra.

CX,Q87

Interpretation

The great king will disembark near Nice [Monaco] and will act against
the great [Soviet] empire, he will reveal his spirit at Antibes and drive
out the ravagers of the sea.

[1] Antipolis: Antibes. DHB.
[2] For *génie*, by paragoge, for the rhyme.
[3] Cf. CII,Q4.

The Reconquest as far as Israel

Dans peu de temps Medecin du grand mal,
Et la Sangsuë[1] d'ordre et rang inégal,
Mettront le feu à la branche d'Olive,[2]
Poste[3] courir,[4] d'un et d'autre costé,
Et par tel feu leur Empire accosté
Se ralumant du franc finy salive.[5]

Sixain 30

Interpretation

In a short time he will bring the remedy for the great catastrophe [the
Third World War], and the countries of the Revolution [Eastern Bloc],
unequal in nature and rank, will carry the war into Israel; then he will
pursue them from their positions on all sides and the [Soviet] Empire
will be hit by the fire of war, which when lit will end the regime of
political speeches in France.

[1] Leech, drinker of blood.
[2] Mount of Olives, i.e. Jerusalem, and Israel by extension. DL7V.

³ Position. DAFL.
⁴ To pursue, chase out. DL7V.
⁵ Allusion to electoral campaign speeches.

Great Henri and the Moslems.
A Spanish Army Aids Israel

Soubs la couleur du traicté mariage,
Fait magnanime par grand Chyren¹ selin:²
Quintin, Arras recouvrez au voyage,
D'Espagnols faict second banc³ macelin.⁴

CVIII,Q54

Interpretation

Under the pretext of an alliance treaty, great Henri will take a magnan-
imous attitude towards the Moslems. St-Quentin and Arras will be liberated in the course of his journeying. And a second exploit of war will
be accomplished by the Spanish in Israel.

¹ Anagram of HENRICUS, Henri.
² Greek Σελήνη: the moon. DGF. The Moslem crescent.
³ Latin *bancus*: fish of uncertain species. DLLB.
⁴ Latin *macellum*: market (where one sells *fish* etc.) DLLB. Allusion to the Holy City,
Christianity's starting point. Cf. Le Basacle, Sixain 31.

Rivalry between the Kings of France and Spain.
The Fall of the Moslem Forces. The Liberation
of England and Italy

Entre les deux monarques eslongnez,
Lorsque le Sol par Selin¹ clair perdue:
Simulte² grande entre deux indignez,
Qu'aux Isles et Sienne la liberté, rendue.

CVI,Q58

Interpretation

Between the two kings [France and Spain] who will be far away from
each other, when the Bourbon makes the Crescent's forces lose their

lustre [power], there will be a great rivalry, unworthy of them, when the British Isles and Italy will be liberated.

[1] Greek Σελήνη: moon, moonlight. DGF.
[2] Latin *simultas*: rivalry. DLLB.

The Liberation of Italy by the King of France. His Fight against the Moslem Forces

SELIN[1] Monarque l'Italie pacifique,
Regnes unis, Roy Chrestien du monde:
Mourant voudra coucher en terre blésique,[2]
Après pyrates avoir chassé de l'onde.

CIV,Q77

Interpretation

The King of France will bring back peace to Italy by defeating the Moslems; the countries will unite. He will be a Christian world ruler, and ask to be buried at Blois, after chasing the Moslem fleets from the seas.

[1] Greek Σελήνη: the moon. DGF. Denotes Moslem crescent.
[2] For Blaisois or Blésois: small region with Blois as its capital. DHB.

Secession in Italy. The King of France's Assistance

Crier victoire du grand Selin[1] Croissant,
Par les Romains sera l'Aigle clamé,
Ticcin, Milan, et Gennes ny consent,
Puis par eux mesmes Basil[2] grand réclamé.

CVI,Q78

Interpretation

Victory over the Moslems will be announced with jubilation. The Romans will call the Eagle [Americans] to their aid. Ticino and northern

Italy will refuse this assistance, then they will call back the great king [of France].

[1] Greek Σελήνη: the moon. DGF. Denotes Moslem crescent.
[2] Greek βασιλεύς: king. DGF.

John-Paul II's Successor.
The Alliance between the Pope and the King of France

> Nouveau esleu patron du grand vaisseau,[1]
> Verra long temps briller le cler flambeau
> Qui sert de lampe[2] à ce grand territoire,
> Et auquel temps armez sous son nom,
> Joinctes à celles de l'heureux de Bourbon
> Levant, Ponant, et Couchant sa mémoire.
>
> Sixain 15

Interpretation

When a new commander of the great vessel of the Church is elected, this bright torch which will serve as symbol of life on earth will be seen shining for a long time. At this period armies will be reunited under his name and allied to those of the King of France, whose memory will remain in the Eastern countries, the Arab and African countries and in America.

[1] St Peter's boat.
[2] Metaphorical, source of light or of life. DL7V.

The Quarrel between the Three Great Ones
(USA, USSR and China). The End of the Reign
of the King of France

> Icy dedans se parachevera
> Les trois Grands hors[1] le BON BOURG sera loing:
> Encontre d'eux l'un d'eux conspirera,
> Au bout du mois on verra le besoin.[2]
>
> Presage 44, October

Interpretation

Here [in France] his reign will end. The three great powers [USA, USSR and China] will hatch plots and the Bourbon will be far away. One of the three [China] will conspire against the two others and, at the end of October, her work will be seen.

[1] For *horde*: machination, ruse. DAFL.
[2] *Besogne* (fem. form of *besoin*) = work, labour. DL7V.

The End of Protestantism in Europe.
The Death of the Great King

Apparoistra temple[1] luisant orné[2]
La lampe et cierge[3] à Borne[4] et Breteuil:[5]
Pour la Lucerne[6] le canton destorné,[7]
Quand on verra le grand Coq au cercueil.

CVIII,Q5

Interpretation

The Catholic Church will be seen shining and honoured; masses will be said in Holland and Picardy. In Switzerland religion will change when the great king dies.

[1] Poetic term for the Catholic Church. DL7V.
[2] Latin *ornatus*: distinguished, honoured. DLLB.
[3] Allusion to the lamp and candles lit on the altar during mass.
[4] Village in the Netherlands. DL7V. A country with a Protestant majority.
[5] Main town of the Oise canton, near the source of the *Noye*. DL7V. In Picardy.
[6] Swiss town 94 km south-east of *Basle*. DHB.
[7] To change direction. DL7V. Nostradamus here describes the end of the Protestant 'heresy', by mentioning the precise geographical areas connected directly with the life of Calvin. 'John Calvin, founder of Protestantism in France, was born at *Noyon* in Picardy in 1509 and died at Geneva in 1564. In 1534 he retired to Strasbourg, then to *Basle*. In this town he finished his book in 1535. At the same time he occupied himself with propagating his doctrine; he corresponded with France, the *Netherlands*, Scotland, England, Poland.' DL7V.

The King of France Welcomed in Cairo

Les vieux chemins seront tous embellis.
L'on passera à Memphis[1] somentrées:[2]
Le Grand Mercure[2] d'Hercules fleur de lys,
Faisant trembler terre, mer et contrées.

CX,Q79

Interpretation

The old roads will be decorated for the journey to Cairo[4] whose population will have been told about the powerful king of the fleur de lis, who will make several countries tremble by land and sea.

[1] Town of ancient Egypt, on left bank of the Nile, south of the famous Gizeh pyramids. When all of Egypt was reunited into a single kingdom, it was for a while the capital. DHB.
[2] *Somondre* or *semondre*: to warn. DAFL.
[3] Represented as a handsome young man. DHB.
[4] Cf. CV,Q81.

The King of France in Egypt.
The Fall of the Berlin Wall. The Russians in Paris in Seven Days

L'oyseau Royal sur la cité solaire[1]
Sept mois devant fera nocturne augure:
Mur d'Orient cherra tonnerre esclaire,
Sept jours aux portes les ennemis à l'heure.

CV,Q81

Interpretation

The king, in Cairo, will give a gloomy warning, seven months before [the end of the war]. The wall of East [Berlin] will fall under the thunder and fire of war, as will the enemies who had reached Paris in seven days.

[1] Latin Solis Urbs: Heliopolis. DLLB. Heliopolis, i.e. town of the sun, is 11 km north-east of Cairo. DHB.

THE IMPORTANT ROLE OF SOUTH AFRICA
IN THE THIRD WORLD WAR

The USSR and the Warsaw Pact against South Africa.
Fighting in Palestine

Tost l'Éléphant[1] de toutes parts verra
Quand pourvoyeur au Griffon[2] se joindra,
Sa ruine proche, et Mars qui toujours gronde:
Fera grands faits auprès de terre saincte,
Grands estendars[3] sur la terre et sur l'onde,
Si[4] la nef a esté de deux frères enceinte.

Sixain 56

Interpretation

South Africa will see [things happen] on all sides when the supplier [Russia] joins up with the Warsaw Pact. Her ruin approaches and the war which always rumbles will cause great upheavals near the Holy Land [Israel]. By land and sea there will be great military forces when the Church has given birth to two brothers. [John-Paul I and John-Paul II.]

---

[1] Olifant (from Latin *elephantus*: elephant]. Name given to several mountains and rivers in southern Africa, after the elephants the first Europeans encountered there. The Olifant mountains are in the western part of Cape Colony, near a little river, the Olifant, which flows into the Atlantic. DL7V.
[2] Cf. CX,Q86 '*Comme un gryphon viendra le Roi d'Europe*'.
[3] Battle flag. DL7V.
[4] Latin: when, at such time as. DLLB.

Eastern Europe and the South African Army

Le Griffon[1] se peut apprester
Pour à l'ennemy resister,
Et renforcer bien son armée,
Autrement l'Elephant[2] viendra
Qui d'un abord le surprendra,
Six cens et huict, mer enflammée.

Sixain 29

Interpretation

Eastern Europe [Warsaw Pact] can prepare itself to resist the enemy and reinforce its army well, for the troops from South Africa will come and surprise it.

[1] Cf. cx,Q86 and Sixain 56.
[2] Cf. Sixain 56.

The Defeat of the Eastern Bloc

Le pourvoyeur du monstre sans pareil,
Se fera voir ainsi que le Soleil,
Montant le long la ligne Méridienne,
En poursuivant l'Éléphant et le loup,[1]
Nul Empereur ne fit jamais tel coup,
Et rien plus pis à ce Prince n'advienne.

Sixain 39

Interpretation

The supplier [Russia] of a scourge without equal will come to the fore at the same time as the Bourbon, following along the meridian, pursuing South Africa and Germany. No Emperor [e.g. Hitler] ever succeeded in such a coup, but nothing worse could happen to this leader.

[1] South Africa (the Cape) and Germany are on the same meridian.

THE END OF WESTERN CIVILIZATION AND THE WARS OF THE ANTICHRIST

The Holy See Moves

Par la puissance des trois Roys temporels,
En autre lieu sera mis le saint-siège:
Où la substance de l'esprit corporel,[1]
Sera remis et reçu pour vray siège.

CVIII,Q99

Interpretation

Because of the power of three leaders, the Holy See will be installed in another place [than the Vatican] and mass will be celebrated once again there.

[1] *Corporal*: piece of sacred linen the priest lays upon the altar and on which the chalice and host are placed during mass. Originally represented Christ's shroud, and thus was far larger than today's version. DL7V.

John-Paul's Successor Is Installed and Dies on Monte Aventino

Le penultième du surnom de prophète,[1]
Prendra Diane[2] pour son jour et repos:
Loing vaguera[3] par frenetique teste,[4]
En delivrant un grand peuple d'impos.

CII,Q28

Interpretation

The penultimate pope will establish himself upon Monte Aventino and die there, the throne of St Peter will be vacant because of a mad leader come from afar, who will have delivered a great people [the Chinese] from taxation.

[1] Latin *propheta*: priest who predicts the future. DLLB. The Pope is a priest too. Cf. CII,Q36.
[2] The Temple of Diana in Rome is situated on Monte Aventino. DL7V.
[3] *Vaguer*: old form of *vaquer*. DAFL. To be vacant, idle. DL7V.
[4] Stricken by wild madness. DL7V.

The Antichrist, Son of a Buddhist Monk. The Antichrist a Twin

Devant moustier[1] trouvé enfant besson,[2]
D'héroicq[3] sang de moyne vetustique,[4]
Son bruit par secte, langue et puissance son,
Qu'on dira soit eslevé le vopisque.[5]

CI,Q95

Interpretation

A twin will be found in front of a monastery, the child of the noble blood of an aged monk. Through his party, his language and the power of his voice, his noise will be such that they will demand the surviving twin to be elevated to power.

[1] Popular form for *monastère*, monastery. DENF.
[2] Twin. DAFL.
[3] Noble, elevated, epic. DL7V.
[4] Latin *vetustico*: I age, grow old. DLLB.
[5] Latin *vopiscus*: surviving twin. DLLB.

The Birth of the Antichrist in Asia His Invasion as Far as France

Naistra du gouphre et cité immesurée.
Nay de parents obscurs et ténébreux:[1]
Quand la puissance du grand Roy revérée,
Voudra destruire par Rouen et Evreux.

CV,Q84

Interpretation

He will be born in misfortune, in an immeasurable city [Chinese or Japanese] and of obscure and secretive parentage: when the great king of France's power has been honoured, he will want to destroy [the West] right up to Rouen and Evreux.

[1] Secret, perfidious. DL7V.

The Invasion from Asia into Italy and France

L'Oriental sortira de son siège
Passer les monts Apennins voir la Gaule:
Transpercera le ciel les eaux les neiges
Et un chacun frappera de sa gaule.[1]

CII,Q29

Interpretation

The Asiatic leader will leave his country to cross the Apennines and enter France. He will cross the sky [airborne invasion], the rivers and the mountains, and strike each country with his tax.

[1] Levy, toll or tax. DL7V.

Aerial Attack on the King of France's Base. Seven Months of Fierce Fighting. Invasion at Rouen and Evreux, and the Fall of the King

Du feu celeste au Royal édifice
Quand la lumière de Mars deffaillera:
Sept mois grand guerre, mort gent de maléfice,
Rouën, Evreux au Roy ne faillira.

CIV,Q100

Interpretation

The king's palace will be destroyed by a rocket when the flashing lights of war die down. The war will be large-scale for seven months, and its calamities will be responsible for loss of life. The invasion at Rouen and Evreux will bring the king's downfall.

The Birth of the Antichrist. Famine on Earth

L'enfant naistra à deux dents en la gorge,
Pierre en Tuscie[1] par pluy tomberont,
Peu d'ans après ne sera bled ni orge,
Pour saouler ceux qui de faim failliront.

CIII,Q42

Interpretation

The child will be born with two teeth in his throat [sic], there will be a rain of stones [bombs?] in Italy [Tuscany]. Some years later there will be neither corn nor barley to satisfy men, who will die of hunger.

[1] One of the seventeen diocesan provinces of Italy in the fourth century, comprised of Etruria and Umbria, with Florence as its principal town. DHB.

The Antichrist: the Greatest Enemy of the Human Race

Tasche de murdre[1] enormes adultères,[2]
Grand ennemy de tout le genre humain:
Que sera pire qu'ayeuls, oncles ne pères,[3]
En fer, feu, eau, sanguin et inhumain.

CX,QIO

Interpretation

Soiled by murders and abominable crimes, the great enemy of the human race will be worse than all his predecessors. By the sword and flame of war he will shed blood in inhuman fashion.

[1] Early form of *meurtre*, murder. DAFL.
[2] Latin *adulterium*: criminal activity. DLLB.
[3] Hitler included!

The Birth of the Antichrist.
The Use of Defoliants. Starvation. Deportations in Asia (Cambodia, Vietnam)

Entre plusieurs aux isles desportez,
L'un estre nay a deux dents en la gorge:
Mourront de faim les arbres esbrotez,[1]
Pour eux neuf Roy, nouvel edict leur forge.

CII,Q7

Interpretation

Several men having been deported on to islands, one of them will be born with two teeth in his throat. Men will die because of defoliants. A new leader will impose new laws upon them.

[1] Provençal *esbroutar* = *ébourgeonner*, i.e. to disband, trim (of trees).

The Election of the Antichrist.
He Conquers the Greatest States

Esleu sera Renard[1] ne sonnant mot,[2]
Faisant le sainct public vivant pain d'orge,[3]
Tyrannizer apres tant a un cop?
Mettant à pied des plus grands sur la gorge.[4]

CVIII,Q41

Interpretation

A wily man will be elected without saying anything; he will play the
saint, living in simple fashion. Then he will suddenly exercise his
tyranny, putting the greatest countries in a state of utter coercion.

[1] Figurative: cunning or wily (as a fox). DL7V.
[2] *Ne sonner mot = ne dire mot*: to say nothing, be silent. DL7V.
[3] *Grossier comme du pain d'orge*: to be very coarse, rustic. DL7V.
[4] To put one's foot on an enemy's throat, i.e. hold him absolutely at one's mercy.
DL7V.

The Antichrist. The Asian Communist Countries
Dragged into the War, 1999

Le chef de Londres par regne l'Americh,
L'isle d'Escosse t'empiera par gelée:[1]
Roy Reb[2] auront un si faux Antechrist,
Que les mettra trestous dans la meslée.

CX,Q66

Interpretation

The head of the British government will be supported by the power of
the United States, when the cold will make Scotland hard as stone: the
red leaders will have at their head an Antichrist so false that he will drag
them all into war.

[1] Allusion to a particularly severe winter.
[2] Latin *robeus*: red. DLLB.

The Twenty-seven Years of the War of the Antichrist, 1999–2026

L'antechrist trois bien tost annichilez,
Vingt et sept ans sang durera sa guerre:
Les heretiques[1] morts, captifs exilez,
Sang corps humain eau rougie greler terre.

CVIII,Q77

Interpretation

The Antichrist will soon annihilate three countries. The war he will wage will last twenty-seven years. Opponents will be put to death and prisoners deported. Blood from bodies will redden the water, the land will be riddled with blows [missiles, bombardments].

[1] By extension, whoever professes opinions contrary to those generally held. DL7V.

The Alliance between the Moslems and the Yellow Races. The Invasion of Europe. The Persecution of the Christians

De Fez le regne parviendra à ceux d'Europe,
Feu leur cité, et lame tranchera:
Le grand d'Asie terre et mer à grand troupe,
Que bleux,[1] pers,[2] croix à mort déchassera.

CVI,Q80

Interpretation

The power of Morocco will reach into Europe, set its towns on fire and massacre its inhabitants. The great Asiatic leader will launch new armies by land and sea; the Yellow People, of cadaverous or livid hue, will hunt down the Christians to kill them.

[1] No particular or clearly defined colour; wan, pallid, from Latin *flavus*: yellow. DAFL.
[2] Cadaverous, wild. DAFL.

Great Changes with the End
of the French Republic. Airborne Invasion

Vous verrez tard et tost faire grand change,
Horreurs extrêmes et vindications.
Que si la Lune conduicte par son ange,
Le ciel[1] s'approche des inclinations.[2]

CI,Q56

Interpretation

You will see, sooner or later, great changes, appalling horrors and acts
of revenge, until the Republic is dead, and from the sky these changes
will approach.

[1] Allusion to CX,Q72: '*Du ciel viendra un grand roi d'effrayeur*'.
[2] Latin *inclinatio*: change, variation, vicissitude. DLLB.

The Yellow Invasion across Russia
and Turkey

Du pont Euxine,[1] et la grand Tartarie,[2]
Un Roy sera qui viendra voir la Gaule,
Transpercera Alane[3] et l'Arménie,
Et dans Bizance lairra[4] sanglante Gaule.[5]

CV,Q54

Interpretation

From the Black Sea and China, a leader will come as far as France, after
crossing Russia and Armenia and leaving his bloody standard in Turkey.

[1] Euxinus: ancient name for the Black Sea.
[2] Asiatic Tartary was divided into Chinese Tartary (Mongolia, Manchuria, etc.) in the
east, and independent Tartary (or Turkestan) in the west. DHB.
[3] Latin Alani, tribe of Sarmatia (ancient name for Russia). DLLB.
[4] Future of *laier, laisser* = to leave. DAFL.
[5] Marine term for a flagstaff or flagpole. DL7V.

The End of the King of France.
The Asiatic Leader's Power

Tant attendu ne reviendra jamais,
Dedans l'Europe, en Asie apparoistra:
Un de la ligue yssu du grand Hermes[1]
Et sur tous Roys des Orients croistra.

CX,Q75

Interpretation

[The Bourbon King] so long awaited will never come back to Europe. In Asia someone appears who will thieve and loot and hold power over all the Asian countries.

[1] In Latin Mercury, the god of thieves. Ambassador of the gods, he was present at the signing of treaties, alliances, and declarations of war between cities and nations. MGR.

The Antichrist against Henri V. The Recession of Communist Power. New Moslem Terror

MENDOSUS[1] tost viendra a son haut regne,
Mettant arrière un peu le Norlaris:
Le Rouge blesme[2] le masle à l'interegne[3]
La jeune crainte et frayeur Barbaris.

CIX,Q50

Interpretation

The deceiver will soon reach the height of his power, giving the Lorrainian a setback. Communist power is weakened between the two conflicts, and once again it will be the Moslems who should be dreaded and feared.

[1] Latin *mendosus*: one who has defects or faults, vicious, false. DLLB.
[2] To weaken. DL7V.
[3] Third World War and Wars of the Antichrist, 1999.

The End of the Bourbon.
Israel's Economic Ruin

Princes et Seigneurs tous se feront la guerre,
Cousin germain le frère avec le frère,
Finy l'Arby[1] de l'heureux de Bourbon,
De Hierusalem les Princes tant aymables,
Du fait commis enorme et execrable
Se ressentiront sur la bourse sans fond.

Sixain 34

Interpretation

All the heads of states and governments will be warring, there will be fighting between brothers and cousins. The supreme arbitration of the fortunate Prince of Bourbon will be ended. The friendly rulers of Israel, because of a monstrous and execrable act, will experience economic ruin.

[1] Latin *arbiter*: master, supreme arbiter. DLLB.

The Conquest of Spain by Moslem Troops

De la Felice[1] Arabie contrade,[2]
Naistra puissant de la Loy Mahométique,
Vexer l'Espagne conquester la Grenade,
Et plus par mer à la gent Ligustique.

CV,Q55

Interpretation

From the territory of rich Arabia will be born a powerful Moslem ruler who will harass Spain by the conquest of Granada, and Italy still more, by sea.

[1] Latin *felix*: fecund, rich, opulent. DLLB. Oil.
[2] Early form for *contrée*, country or region. DAFL.

The Last War of the Twentieth Century, 1999

Chefs d'Aries,[1] Jupiter[2] et Saturne,[3]
Dieu éternel quelles mutations,
Puis par long siècle son maling temps retourne
Gaule et Italie, quelles émotions.

CI,Q51

Interpretation

What changes will be provoked by the military leaders before the return to light and the Golden Age; then after a long century [twentieth] the time of the evil one [destruction] will return. What troubles in France and Italy.

[1] Latin name for the constellation of the ram: itself a machine of war used by the ancients to batter down walls. DL7V.
[2] Jupiter was worshipped by all the Latins, for whom he personified light and celestial phenomena. DL7V.
[3] Or Cronos: symbol of time. In mythology, the time of Saturn and Rhea, the Golden age, will last as long as Saturn governs the universe.

Asiatic Communism against Europe and Black Africa

Un peu de temps les temples des couleurs,
De blanc et noir des deux entremeslée:
Rouges et Jaunes leur embleront les leurs
Sang, terre, peste, faim, feu d'eau affollée.

CVI,Q10

Interpretation

For a short while the Churches will recover their influence. The Whites and Blacks will unite with each other. The Reds and Chinese will ally and the earth will be maddened by blood, plague, starvation, war and revolution.

The Invasion of Europe by China

De maison sept par mort mortelle suite,
Gresle, tempeste, pestilent mal, fureurs:
Roy d'Orient d'Occident tous en fuite,
Subjuguera ses jadis conquereurs.[1]

Presage 40, June

Interpretation

For having sown death, the seven Eastern European countries will know
a fatal consequence. They will be overwhelmed by bombing, tempest,
epidemic and their enemies' savagery. The leader of Asia will put all the
Westerners to flight and will subjugate his former conquerors.

[1] 'In 1839, China having seized cases of Indian opium, *England* embarked upon the
"Opium Wars". The Treaty of Nanking gave England Hong Kong and opened five
Chinese ports for her trade. These ports, by the Treaty of Whampoa (1884), were open
to trade with the *United States, France,* then other *Western Countries.* Under Hien-Foung
(1851–62), the murders of Christian missionaries led to *Anglo–French* intervention, the
capture of Canton (1857) and Tientsin (1858). The treaty was annulled, *Peking occupied*
(1860) and China forced to sign the second Treaty of Tientsin. In the north, China had
to give up territory to Russia. In 1871 Russia occupied Kouldja and the Illi Valley. From
1882 to 1885 China was at war with France over Tonkin, but had to renounce her claims
and make trade agreements with France. China was finally eroded not only by Japan but
by *Russia, Germany, England* and *France.'* DL7V. ('*ses jadis conquereurs*'!)

The Airborne Invasion of France
in July 1999

L'an mil neuf cent nonante neuf sept mois,
Du ciel[1] viendra un grand Roy d'effrayeur
Ressusciter le grand Roy d'Angoulmois,[2]
Avant apres Mars regner par bonheur.

CX,Q72

Interpretation

In July 1999 a great, terrifying leader will come through the skies to
revive [the memory of] the great conqueror of Angoulême. Before and
after war will rule luckily.

The End of Henri V's Reign.
The End of the Catholic Church

Par l'univers sera fait un Monarque,
Qu'en paix et vie ne sera longuement.
Lors se perdra la piscature barque,[1]
Sera régie en plus grand détriment.[2]

CI,Q4

Interpretation

A monarch will be revered by the world but he will not live for long in peace. Thus the Church will collapse, ruled in the greatest disaster.

¹ Barque of St Peter, or ship of the Church, symbols adopted by the early church. DL7V. Allusion to Christ referring to Peter as a 'fisher of men'.
² Disaster. DL7V.

The Invasion from Asia Reaches Turkey
and Egypt. The End of the Catholic Church

Le prince Arabe, Mars, Sol, Venus, Lyon,[1]
Regne d'Eglise par mer succombera:
Devers la Perse bien près d'un million,
Bizance, Egypte, ver. serp.[2] invadera.[3]

CV,Q25

Interpretation

The Arab leader will launch war and subversion against monarchical power, and the Church's power will succumb through a naval invasion. Almost a million soldiers will be in Iran and Satan will invade Turkey and Egypt.

¹ Emblem of sovereignty. DL7V.

[2] Latin *versus serpens*: serpent coiled back upon itself. Allusion to Revelations XII, v.9: 'And the great dragon was cast out, that old serpent called the Devil, and Satan, which deceiveth the whole world: he was cast out into the earth, and his angels were cast out with him.'

[3] Latin: to attack, cross, invade. DLLB.

The Fall of the Western European Countries

La fin le loup, le lyon, boeuf[1] et l'asne,[2]
Timide dama[3] seront avec mastins[4]
Plus ne cherra[5] à eux la douce manne,
Plus vigilance et custode[6] aux mastins.

CX,Q99

Interpretation

When the ends of Germany, England, South Africa and the Moslem troops are to be seen, timid Poland will be allied with England. They will no longer have an easy life and the English will no longer be under surveillance and guard.

[1] Lucanian ox, the name given to the elephant by the Romans. DL7V. The elephant represents South Africa (cf. Sixains 26, 39 and 56).

[2] Cf. CIII,Q23 and CX,Q31.

[3] Latin *dama*, French *daim*: deer. DLLB. Cf. CV,Q4.

[4] Cf. CV,Q4. Nostradamus certainly does not reunite the deer (Poland) and the bulldog (England) yet again in a quatrain by accident.

[5] From *cheoir*: to fall. DAFL.

[6] Latin *custos*: guard, sentry. DLLB.

The Persecution of the Clergy.
Life Grows Expensive

En bref seront de retour sacrifices,
Contrevenans seront mis à martyre,
Plus ne seront moines, abbés, novices,
Le miel sera beaucoup plus cher que cire.

CI,Q44

Interpretation

Sacrifices of believers recommence; those who oppose authority will be martyred. There will no longer be monks, priests, or novices, and there will be a rise in the cost of living.

The Burning of Rome. A Cardinal Expelled by the Pope. Scandals Perpetrated by the Clergy

> Mont Aventin[1] brusler nuict sera veu,
> Le ciel obscur tout à un coup en Flandres,
> Quand le Monarque chassera son neveu,[2]
> Leurs gens d'Eglise commettront les esclandres.
>
> CIII,QI7

Interpretation

Rome will be seen burning at night. The sky will darken abruptly in Belgium when the Pope will drive out a cardinal, and the clergy will commit scandals.

[1] One of the hills of Rome. DL7V.
[2] *Cardinal neveu*: a cardinal is the 'nephew' of the current pope. DL7V.

The Pope's Assassination. The Death of the Capetian. The Landing on the Var Coast

> Dix envoyez, chef de nef mettre à mort,
> D'un adverty,[1] en classe guerre ouverte:
> Confusion chef. l'un se picque et mord,[2]
> Leryn,[3] Stecades[4] nefs, cap[5] dedans la nerte.[6]
>
> CVII,Q37

Interpretation

Ten men will be sent to murder the Pope but one of them will be opposed to it; war will be started by the army. In the confusion the leader [of the group] will commit suicide and die, ships will disembark on the Var coastline, the Capetian will then be buried.

[1] Latin *adversor*: I am opposed to, go against. DLLB.
[2] From *mordrir*: to murder, kill.
[3] French islands in the Mediterranean, off the coast of the Var *département*, facing the gulf of La Napoule. DHB.
[4] Staechades: the Iles D'Hyères, the four islands off the Var coast – Porquerolles, Port-Cros, Bagneaux and the Isle of Levant. DHB.
[5] The Capetian: cf. Louis XVI and Varennes, CIX,Q20.
[6] Or Hertha, the Earth, German goddess. DLLB.

The Ruin of Rome and the Vatican

La grand montagne ronde de sept stades,[1]
Après paix, guerre, faim, inondation,
Roulera loing, abismant grand contrades,[2]
Mesmes antiques, et grand fondation.

CI,Q69

Interpretation

The great town with the seven hills, after a period of peace, will know war, famine and revolution which will be widespread, ruining great countries and even ancient ruins and the great foundation [the Vatican].

[1] Step. DL7V. 'No town in the world offers so many *ancient* and modern monuments accumulated in so small a space. At first built upon *seven* hills, it gradually appropriated several others and ended by including in its environs twelve *mountains*.' DHB.
[2] *Contrede*: early form of *contrée*, country, region. DAFL.

The Ruin of Rome and the Vatican.
The Capture of the Pope

Bien pres du Tymbre presse la Lybitine,[1]
Un peu devant grande inondation:
Le chef du nef prins, mis à la sentine,[2]
Chasteau,[3] palais en conflagration.

CII,Q93

Interpretation

Very near the Tiber death threatens. There will have been a great revolution shortly before. The head of the church will be taken prisoner and rejected. The castle [Sant'Angelo] and the Palace [of the Vatican] will be in flames.

[1] Latin *Libitina*: goddess presiding at funerals, and by extension death. DLLB.
[2] Latin *sentina*: dregs, reject. DLLB.
[3] The Castle faces the Vatican. DL7V.

The End of the Monarchy and the Ruin
of the Catholic Church

Les mal'heureuses nopces celebreront,
En grande joye mais la fin mal'heureuse:
Mary et mere nore[1] desdaigneront,
Le Phybe[2] mort, et nore plus piteuse.

CX,Q55

Interpretation

Men will congratulate themselves upon unfortunate alliances which will please them, but in the long run will bring unhappiness. They will scorn the Virgin Mary and the Church. The monarchy will end and the Church will be in an even more pitiful state.

[1] *Nora* for *nurus*. DAFL. Daughter-in-law, wife of the son. DLLB. Bride of Christ, the Church of Christ. DL7V.
[2] Phoebus, Apollo, the Sun God. DL7V. As usual, Nostradamus here refers to the monarchy.

EPILOGUE

'Man is a reed, the weakest in
nature, but he is a thinking reed.'

Pascal

If we consider the breadth of knowledge necessary for complete com-
prehension of a work like that of Nostradamus, we must conclude that
no human could be capable of such understanding. Faced with such
monumental learning, we can only feel humble. The more I continued
with my work and the more the quatrains accumulated in meaning, the
more certain I became of the authenticity and seriousness of the Centuries. Increasingly it seemed to me that I held the key to the riddle, and
yet I felt even more ignorant and inadequately equipped to grasp the
amazing intelligence demonstrated throughout Nostradamus' work.

If, from the letter he wrote on 1 March 1555 to his son and translator,
I dare apply a particular passage to myself, it would undoubtedly be this
one: '. . . and I do not want to talk here of the years which have not yet
transpired, but of your months of struggle during which you will not be
capable in your deficient understanding of comprehending what I shall
be constrained, after my death, to leave you.' I do not claim, unlike
certain others, to have definitively decoded Nostradamus' message. I feel
I have made only a modest contribution, undertaken with the utmost
sincerity and an intellectual honesty which I hope will not be doubted.
Despite the twenty years I have spent on this book, preparing and
accumulating documentation, reading numerous historical works, and
committing to memory the vocabulary of Nostradamus and a great many
quatrains and sixains, I feel a sense of imperfection. I am only too aware
of the risk of errors and subjective comment or digression. It is quite
possible, for instance, that I have attributed certain quatrains to the
Third World War when they actually refer to the War of the Antichrist
beginning in 1999. This kind of mistake is easy to make since the

Moslems appear to be the allies of the Russians in the Third World War, and the Chinese during the War of the Apocalypse. For this reason quatrains referring to the Moslem world are difficult to date – precisely, at any rate.

This book includes about half of the 1160 quatrains and sixains Nostradamus wrote: the remaining verses will be the subject of a second book. The texts translated here are generally the most specific ones and give some idea of the overall design, from the linguistic point of view as much as the philosophical one. I selected quatrains and sixains precise enough to convey a good grasp of past and future events as prophesied by Nostradamus.

After translating and matching up against historical facts over two hundred quatrains dealing with past events, I wondered for some time why Nostradamus had included details that are unverifiable at first glance. There are probably three reasons. First, Nostradamus wanted to impose considerable work on his translator to show that there are no short cuts to learning. Secondly, he was obliged to make his message obscure because of the religious background of the sixteenth century, and historical details had little chance of being understood or recognized; this guaranteed for four hundred years the necessary obscurity, so that his message might reach the twentieth-century reader. Finally – and this is probably the main reason – the abundance of astonishingly precise information found in the quatrains brings almost irrefutable proof of the authenticity, value and correctness of his prophecies. Examples such as the French army with MacMahon at Buffalora; Garibaldi landing at Magnavacca; the flight to Varennes; the number of Nelson's great three-deckers at Trafalgar; and the exact length of Hitler's life all make the Centuries difficult to gainsay.

Nostradamus' opponents are mostly people who do not really know the work but contest it because the little they do know of it upsets their personal convictions or beliefs. There are other sceptics (and they are more excusable), who have read translations that are as inaccurate as the original text (once the indispensable philological and historical research is done) is accurate. When I recall my work in supplying half the text, with all the imperfections of which I am aware, I wonder how so many people can allow themselves to discuss, criticize and challenge the prophecy of Nostradamus. The widespread twentieth-century tendency in the West, where whatever one does is criticized and disputed even before its value is assessed, acts as a curb on the creative spirit. Two principal defects are responsible for man's destructive instincts: pride and jealousy. If the individual did not always think himself superior to his neighbour, on whatever pretext – class, education, breeding, race etc. – he would open the gates of knowledge. In fact, through his pretension, he closes his mind.

The message revealed here will certainly not be to everyone's taste, for man's history appears in Nostradamus independent of political, philosophical, ideological or religious commitment. In 1938 my father wrote about the Franco-German war, Germany's loss of that war and Hitler's miserable end. He was subsequently accused of Germanophobia, which led to the seizure and destruction of his book. Similarly today I risk accusations of Russophobia or entrenched anti-Communism, whereas Sovietism is only a relatively brief episode in the history of Russia compared to the ten consecutive centuries of tsarist rule. The French Republican system, to take another example, adds up to only about 115 years compared to the thirteen centuries of the monarchy.

I should like the reader, whatever his race, religion or politics, to try to wipe the slate clean of everything formerly considered as the truth, which is only ever a subjective view, and to open his mind to a transcendental vision of history which perhaps prophecy alone can help him acquire. To attain an awareness uncluttered by prejudice, one should reflect on the analysis made about 441 BC by the Greek historian Thucydides, writing about the Peloponnesian War:

> Thucydides showed what war was, why it happened, what it did and must continue doing, at least until men learn better conduct. Athenians and Spartans fought for only one reason . . . because they were powerful and through this fact were obliged (in Thucydides' own words) to seek to increase their power. The two adversaries fought not because they were different – Athens a democracy, Sparta an oligarchy – but because they were alike. The war had nothing to do with divergences of opinion or conceptions of good and evil. Is democracy good and oligarchy bad? To ask this question would have been, for Thucydides, to move away from the problem. There was no power representing the good. *Power*, whoever exercised it, was the demon, the corruptor of men . . . Thucydides was probably the first to grasp (and in any case to express in words) this new doctrine which would become that of the entire world.[1]

Don't we talk today of the two superpowers, the USA and USSR, as Sparta and Athens were in their day? And since Thucydides examples of the rivalry of powers have multiplied: antagonisms hidden for most of the time behind differences of religion or ideology.

To come down on the side of one of the two great powers or the other would be to come down on the side of war. Letting oneself be hoaxed

---

[1] Edith Hamilton: *The Great Age of Greek Literature*, New York, 1942.

by the political or ideological aspect of the problem allows the heads of states – consumed by ambition and the desire for power – to mass their armies in order to satisfy their supremacist lunacy. Ordinary people kill each other, when their deepest aspirations are in all probability exclusively peaceable.

When will the French stop glorifying victories like Austerlitz, Jena and Eylau which for their enemies were defeats, just as the English victories at Trafalgar and Waterloo were defeats for the French? Both sides, after all, inflicted or suffered rape, massacre and all the other nauseating fruits of war. When will we stop erecting monuments to the dead? The Arc de Triomphe commemorates Napoleon's victories, but is something obtained through thousands of deaths and indescribable suffering really a triumph? When will we decide to glorify life with all the potential it embodies for man's happiness?

The philosopher Montesquieu wrote in his *Persian Letters*: 'You say you fear that someone will invent a method of destruction crueller than the existing one. No. If a deadly invention came to be discovered, it would soon be prohibited by the law of man.' This is the archetypal anti-prophecy which Cartesianism made the eighteenth-century thinkers proclaim – at their head Jean-Jacques Rousseau, the man largely responsible, according to Nostradamus, for the dramas of the twentieth century. His Utopias were taken up again by the nineteenth- and twentieth-century philosophers such as Proudhon, St-Simon and Karl Marx, 'refurbished' by ambitious politicians and used ruthlessly as weapons with which to achieve their ambitions. In Germany Adolf Hitler created a National *Socialist* regime. Socialism? What crimes have been committed and go on being committed in that name!

My concern is for the ordinary people, basically good, and believers in a kind of socialism not far removed from Christ's teaching, which was intended to overthrow the powerful men of society and to make them face the responsibilities they bear for the misery of nations. Is it mere chance that whatever party politicians belong to, their speeches tend to show not the slightest sincerity? Power and love of one's neighbour cannot co-exist. Hence, perhaps, the profound meaning of Christ's words: 'Render unto Caesar that which is Caesar's, and unto God that which is God's.' Caesar is power, God is love.

In 1937 my father, deep in decoding the quatrains, wrote:

For sixty years more man will recklessly strive over the whole surface of the wretched speck of dust we inhabit within the infinite circle of the sky, to accumulate and perfect engines of destruction and death, to a rhythm here and now begun, and the massacres will be such that the earth will be depopulated, corroborating not only the Old Testament prophets' words but those of Nostradamus too, who tells us here that 'of the three parts of the world, more than two will be lacking'.[1]

The atomic bomb did not then exist, but soon the destruction of Hiroshima started the fulfilment of this 'prophetic vision'. The research, development and testing of nuclear, chemical and bacteriological weapons continued to accelerate, even though the countries possessing these weapons had all signed the 1925 Geneva Convention prohibiting them.

On 14 July 1790 the goddess Reason was consecrated on the altar of atheism, and by exporting the ideas of the French Revolution would inspire many countries who were gradually to regroup in the League of Nations and then in the United Nations Organization. However, all the countries fighting each other since the Second World War – the USA against North Korea, the USA against Vietnam, Turkey against Cyprus, the USSR and Cuba against Angola and Ethiopia – are members of this organization.

Hitler began his expansionist war by rushing to the aid of the German minorities in Europe. Whether wars are waged by monarchies, dictatorships or republics, they all have the same aim, power, and the same result, the people's misfortune. One might wonder why the Nostradamus prophecy centres mainly on man-made catastrophes. Indeed, the number of quatrains and sixains attributed to any event is proportional to its destructive and terrifying aspect. Louis XIV's France, much smaller than the present-day country, and with a mere 20 million inhabitants and a 300,000-strong army, interested Nostradamus less than twentieth-century France. In 1914 France had a population of 41 million: on the battlefields of the Marne she left 1,400,000 dead. Germany, with a population of 58 million, lost 2 million. Total losses in the 1914–18 War were 8,700,000; the Second World War claimed 36 million. To these figures should be added millions of 'survivors', mutilated, crippled, handicapped, gassed, burned, driven mad and unable to adapt to a normal life. And what can one say about the massive destruction of civilian populations: Hiroshima – 160,000 dead; Dresden – 300,000; and death camps saw the extermination of millions of Jews, gipsies, Armenians, Vietnamese, Cambodians and so on.

On the threshold of the twenty-first century the race towards ever larger scales of destruction still does not cease to burden humanity with the threat of annihilation. The twentieth century has seen so much of mankind coerced into power struggles even harsher and more dangerous than in preceding ages. Doubtless this explains why the vision of Nos-

[1] Letter to 'Henry, Roy de France Second', Adyar, 1937.

tradamus is so preoccupied with much based upon this period, when leaders, along with their fearful and apocalyptic weapons, have confronted each other with a destructive fury hitherto unparalleled. From the crossbow to the neutron bomb there is a terrible constant, representing an acceleration towards the perfection of death-dealing instruments.

The fundamental question is whether man, after millennia of scientific progress, has made any progress in the human sphere. It seems unlikely. If man, in his materialism, is left to his own devices, he rushes towards destruction.

However, we must not despair. If we had only the analyses of politicians, doomwatchers, demographers, sociologists and economists to go by, man's horizon would be completely blocked. Absolute and irreversible pessimism would be the rule. The only remaining hope is the prophetic message brought to man. Whether the prophets are those of the Old or the New Testaments, Christ or Nostradamus, they all announce the realization of the 'Kingdom' when universal peace shall at last reign among men.

For then shall be great tribulation, such as was not since the beginning of the world to this time, no, nor ever shall be.

And except those days should be shortened, there should no flesh be saved: but for the elect's sake those days shall be shortened. . . .

For there shall arise false Christs, and false prophets, and shall shew great signs and wonders; insomuch that, if it were possible, they shall *deceive the very elect*. . . .

For as the lightning cometh out of the east, and shineth even unto the west; so shall also the coming of the Son of man be.[1]

The Prophet Malachi[2] confirms this, attributing to the last Pope the following Latin commentary:

In persecutione extrema sacrae Romanae Ecclesiae, sedebit Petrus Romanus qui pascet oves in multis tribulationibus; quibus transactis, civitas septicollis diruetur, et Judex tremendus judicabit populum. (In the final persecution of the Holy Roman Church, Peter the Roman will occupy the See, who will guide his flock through numerous tribulations. These tribulations past, the town of seven hills [Rome] will be destroyed and the terrible Judge shall judge the people).[3]

In other words, Christ will come at the appointed time as prophesied, to chastise the arms vendors as He did the moneylenders in the Temple.

Nostradamus' prophecies centre upon the history of Israel, bearer of the Old Testament, and that of the Catholic Church, bearer of the New.

---

[1] Matthew XXIV, vv. 21, 22, 24, 27. AV.
[2] Author of the famous prophecy on the popes.
[3] Abbé Joseph Maître: *Les Papes et la Papauté*, Paris, 1902.

The emblem of Israel is a six-pointed star, and modern France is referred to as a hexagon (in which the six-pointed star can be drawn). Israel's flag is blue and white; the national flag of France before 1790 was a blue escutcheon with three fleurs de lis on a white ground.

At the end of the twentieth century the planetary significance of these two countries, around which the most important international problems revolve, is disproportionate compared to their material and economic power. Three cities receive more attention than any others: Jerusalem, with its Holy Places; Rome, with its Pope; and Paris, whoever governed France. These three towns constitute the three pillars of western Judeo–Christian civilization, whose first six millennia have elapsed. In fifty years the seventh millennium will begin, the Age of Aquarius, which will bring man universal peace and spiritual as well as material prosperity.

The importance of the message for man is this positive aspect, which Nostradamus noted in his Letter to César: 'For according to the signs in the sky[1], the Golden Age will return, after a revolutionary period which will turn all upside down, and which from the present moment of writing will begin in 177 years 3 months 11 days, bringing in its wake corruption of ideas and morals, wars and a long famine. . . .' The period of time indicated by the prophet, from March 1555 when he wrote the letter, corresponds with the arrival of Rousseau in Paris in 1732.

We are living through the end of *a* world, not the end of *the* world, as some exploiters of the morbid are claiming. This death of one civilization among so many others will herald the birth of a new civilization freed from the aberrations of its predecessor. This is what Henry Miller sensed, when he wrote in 1945:

A new world is being born, a new kind of man is springing up today. The great mass of mankind, destined in our time to suffer more cruelly than ever before, ends by being paralysed with fear, becoming introspective, shaken to the very core, and does not hear, see or feel anything more than everyday physical needs. It is thus that worlds die. First and foremost, the flesh dies. But although few clearly recognize it, the flesh would not have died if the spirit had not been killed already.

Every civilization thinks itself immortal: I am certain that the Romans of AD 200–250 could not imagine, according to their own prophets, that a few centuries later the ruins of their once immense and brilliant empire would be visited by tourists.

In conclusion, the prophecies of Nostradamus, like those of the great Old Testament prophets, Christ or the Revelation of St John are therefore not morbid speculation on uninterrupted catastrophes, nor imprecations

[1] The sun passing from Pisces into Aquarius, represented by a horn of plenty, fish living in water, symbol of revolution.

directed against man, but a message of hope. What would man's future be without this divine message? Man without God, but worshipper of the goddess Reason, should, we were promised, establish the rule of the Rights of Man upon earth. After two centuries of this so-called new world order it would require considerable disingenuousness to claim that man, his reason, and above all his pride, had bettered the lot of nations.

I learned history at school from mediocre textbooks, which mainly proved to be effective soporifics. When I left, only a little of what I had been taught remained with me; what was more serious was that these were false ideas, for the historians of right and left had distorted historic facts in order to accommodate them within their ideologies. I hope that this book will give younger readers a passion for history comparable to that which the prophecy of Nostradamus has instilled in me.

Despite the tribulations predicted by the prophets, I want to believe in man and his perfectibility, particularly at the time of writing (1980) when the clouds seem to be gathering before the storm. Let me end by quoting some words Shakespeare makes Hamlet speak:

What a piece of work is a man! How noble in reason! how infinite in faculty! in form, in moving, how express and admirable! in action how like an angel! in apprehension . . . how like a god! the beauty of the world! . . .

> What is a man,
> If his chief good and market of his time
> Be but to sleep and feed? A beast, no more.
> Sure he that made us with such large discourse,
> Looking before and after, gave us not
> That capability and godlike reason
> To fust in us unus'd.

BIBLIOGRAPHY

Abbreviations

BN: Bibliothèque Nationale
BMA: Bibl. Municipale Aix-en-Provence
BML: Bibl. Municipale Lyon

Allaines, Henri d' : *Actualité de l'Apocalypse,* La Colombe, Paris, 1963.
Alleau, René : 'Nostradamus le plus grand prophète de l'histoire', *Sallonensa* Salon, 1957.
Alliaume, Maurice: *Magnus Rex de Nostradamus et son drapeau,* publ. at author's expense at Chartres, 1948.
  Predictions vraies de Nostradamus et Mandragore, publ. at author's expense at Chartres, 1949.
Amadou, Robert : 'Le Devin et son Art', *Le Crapouillot,* no. 18, 1952.
Amiaux : *Nostradamus,* Sorlot, Paris.
Anon. : *La Première Invective du Seigneur Hercules, Le François, contre Nostradamus,* Michel Jove, Lyon, 1558.
  Huictain contre Nostradamus, Roux, Lyon, 1557.
  Déclaration des abus, ignorances, séditions de Michel Nostradamus, Pierre Roux et Jean Tremblay, Avignon, 1558.
Anquetil, Georges : *L'Anti-Nostradamus,* Ed. de la Maison des Ecrivains, Paris, 1940.
Artigny, Abbé d' : *Nouveaux mémoires d'histoire, de critique et de littérature,* 1794.
Astruc, Jean : *Mémoires pour servir à l'histoire de la faculté de Montpellier,* 1767.
Auclair, Raoul : *Les Centuries de Nostradamus,* Deux Rives, Paris, 1958.
  Le Crépuscule des Nations, La Colombe, Paris.
  Les Centuries de Nostradamus ou le dixième livre sibyllin, Nouvelles Editions Latines, 1957.
Barbarin, Georges : *Les Derniers Temps du Monde, de l'Antéchrist au Jugement dernier,* 'History & Tradition' series, Ed. Dervy, Paris, 1951.
Bareste, Eugène : Editions des Centuries, Maillet, Paris, 1840–42. (BMA)
Bartoshek, Norbert : *Nostradamus und Seine berühmte Prophezeiungen,* 1946.

Belland, Dr : *Napoléon, premier empereur des français, prédit par Nostradamus*, Paris, 1806.

Beltikhine, G. : 'Un document chiffré : Le Secret des Centuries', *Inconnues*, no. 12, Lausanne, 1956.

Bertrand, Michel : 'Histoire secréte de la Provence', *Histoire secrète des provinces françaises*, Albin Michel, Paris, 1978.

Bjorndahl-Veggerby, Paul : *Nostradamus et les ruines gallo-romaines à Martres-Tolosane*, Ed. Leisner, Copenhagen, 1976.

Blanchard and Reynaud-Plense : *La Vie et l'Œuvre de Michel Nostradamus*, Imp. Léon Guillaumichon, Salon, 1933. (BMA)
Histoire de Salon, Salon, 1935.

Boniface, A. : *Buonaparte prédit par des prophètes et peint par des historiens, des orateurs et des poètes ou morceaux en prose et en vers sur les circonstances actuelles, recueillis par A. Boniface*, d'Hautel, Paris, 1814.

Bonnelier, Hippolyte : *Nostradamus, roman historico-cabalistique*, A. Ledoux, Paris, 1833, 2 vol.

Bonnet, Jean : *Résumé des prophéties de Nostradamus. Les événements et les symboles*, followed by : *Commentaires de la Bible par Nostradamus et de détermination des dates dans Nostradamus*, Jean Bonnet, Paris, 1973.

Bonnot Jean de : *Les Oracles de Michel de Nostredame dit Nostradamus*, annotated by Anatole le Pelletier and Serge Hutin, Paris, 1976, 2 vol.

Boroch, Erick Karl : *Der Prophet Nostradamus*, 1912.

Boswell, Rolfe : *Nostradamus speaks*, 1941.

Bouche, Honoré : *La Chorographie et l'Histoire de Provence*, Charles David, Aix-en-Provence, 1664.

Bouchet, Marguerite : *Les Oracles de Michel de Nostredame*, Les Livres Nouveaux, Paris, 1939.

Boulenger, Jacques : *Nostradamus*, Excelsior, Paris, 1933.

Bousquet, Raoul : *Nostradamus, sa famille et son secret*, Fournier-Valdes, Paris, 1950.
'La Maladie et la Mort de Nostradamus', *Aesculape*, November 1950.

Boutin, André : *Michel de Nostre-Dame, astrologue et médecin*, MD thesis, Librarie Le François, Paris, 1941.

Bouys, Théodore : *Nouvelles considérations sur les Oracles et particulièrement sur Nostradamus*, Paris, 1806, Desenne, Debray.

Boyer, Jean : 'Deux peintres oubliés du XVIIᵉ siècle, Etienne Martellange et César Nostradamus', *Bulletin de la Société de l'histoire de l'Art Français*, 1971, pp. 13–20.

Bricaud, Joanny : *La Guerre et les Prophéties célèbres*, Paris, 1916.

Buget, P. F. : 'Etude sur Nostradamus', *Bulletin du bibliophile*, Librairie Techner, Paris, 1860.

Buset, Claude : *Nostradamus et autres prophètes du Père et de l'Esprit*, La Pensée Universelle, Paris, 1974.

Cadres, Geoffroy : *L'Etrange docteur Nostradamus*, La Pensée Universelle, Paris, 1978.

Candolle, comte de : *Armorial de César de Nostredame*, Arles, 1899. (BMA)

Cavanagh, John : *Michel de Nostradamus*, 1923.

Cave, Térence C. : 'Peinture et émotion dans la poésie religieuse de César de Nostredame', *Gazette des Beaux-Arts*, vol. LXXV, Jan. 1970. (BMA)

Centurio, N. : *Nostradamus, der Prophet der Welgeschichte*, Richar Schikowski, Berlin, 1955.

Chabauty, abbé E. A. : *Lettres sur les Prophéties modernes et concordance de toutes les prédictions jusqu'au règne de Henry V*, Ed. Henri Houdin, Poitiers, 1872.

Chavigny, A. de : *Les Pléiades du Sieur de Chavigny, Beaunois, divisées en VII livres, prises et tirées des anciennes prophéties et conférées avec les oracles du tant célèbre et renommé Michel de Nostredame, jadis conseiller et médecins de trois Rois très chrestiens. Où est traité du renouvellement des siècles, changement de l'Empire et advancement du nom Chrestien*, Lyon, Pierre Rigaud, 1604.

Chavigny, J. A. de : *Commentaires du Sieur de Chavigny sur les Centuries et Prognostications de feu Michel de Nostredame du Breuil*, Paris, 1596.

La première Face du Janus français extraite et colligée des Centuries de Michel Nostradamus, par les héritiers de Pierre Roussin, Lyon, 1594. (BML)

Vie et testament de Michel Nostradamus, Paris, 1789.

'Bref discours sur la Vie de Michel de Nostredame', *Revue de l'Agenois*, 1876.

Cheetham, Erika : *The Prophecies of Nostradamus*, Capricorn Books, Putnam's, New York, 1973.

Chollier, Antoine : *Les Prophecies de maistre Michel Nostradamus*, Imp. Allier, Grenoble, 1940.

Chomorat, Michel : *Nostradamus entre Rhône et Saône*, Ed. Ger, Lyon, 1971.

Supplément à la bibliographie Lyonnaise des Nostradamus. Centre culturel de Buenc, Lyon, 1976. 100 numbered copies.

'New research on the prophecies of M. N.', *Revue française d'histoire du livre*, no.22, spring 1979.

Bibliographie lyonnaise de Nostradamus, followed by a checklist of MSS relating to the Nostradamus family, Centre Culturel de Buenc, Lyon, 1973.

Colin de Larmor : *La Guerre de 1914–1918 vue en 1555 par Nostradamus*, La Roche-sur-Yon, 1922.

Merveilleux Quatrains de Nostradamus, Nantes, 1925. (BMA)

Colin-Simard : 'Rois et Reines au rendez-vous des astrologues', *Historia*, no. 157, 1959.

Corvaja, Mireille : *Les Prophéties de Nostradamus*, Vecchi, Paris, 1975.

Couillard, Antoine : *Les Contredits aux prophéties de Nostradamus*, Charles l'Angelier, Paris, 1560.

Crescimbeni, Giovanni-Mario : *Istoria della volgar poesia-TII : Le vite de'piu celebri poeti provenzali, seritte in lingua francese da G.M. Crescimbeni*. B.U. Montepellier (see Jean de Nostredame).

Cristiani, Chanoine : *Nostradamus, Malachie et Cie*, Le Centurion, 1955.

'Un Curieux Homme : Nostradamus', *Ecclesia*, no. 73, 1955.

Crouzet, François : 'Nostradamus, Poète français', *Idée Fixe*, Julliard, Paris, 1973.

Daudet, L. : 'Nostradamus', *Revue universelle*, 1925, vol. I. (BMA)

David-Marescot, Yves and Yvonne : *Prédictions et Prophéties*, Ed. Idégraf et Vernoy, Geneva, 1979.

D. D. : *The Prophecies of Nostradamus concerning the kings and queens of Great Britain*, London, 1715.

Delcourt, Marie : *L'Oracle de Delphes*, 1954.

Demar-Latour : *Nostradamus et les Evénements de 1914–1916*, Paris, 1916. (BN)

Deperlas, Félix : *L'Avenir ou les Grands Personnages et les Grands Evénements de ce temps*, Paris, 1885.

Révélations de la Providence, Paris, 1885.

Dupont-Fournieux, Y. : *Les Derniers Jours des Derniers Temps* (Preface by Dr Fontbrune), La Colombe, Paris, 1959.

Edouard, P. : *Texte originál et complet des Prophéties de Michel Nostradamus*, Les Belles Editions, Paris, 1939.

Edouard and Mezerette : *Texte original des Prophéties de Nostradamus de 1600 à 1948 et de 1948 à l'an 2000*, Les Belles Editions, Paris, 1947.

Erlanger, Ph. : 'La Reine du Massacre', Historia, no. 340, March 1975.

Fervan, Jean : *La Fin des temps*, Ed. La Bourdonnais, Paris, 1937.

Fontbrune, Dr de : *Les Prophéties de Nostradamus dévoilées. Lettres à Henry Second*, Adyar, 1937.

Les prophéties de Maistre Michel Nostradamus expliquées et commentées, Ed. Michelet, Sarlat, 1938, 1939, 1940, 1946, 1958 & 1975, J.-Ch. de Fontbrune, Aix-en-Provence, distributed by le Groupe des Presses de la Cité.

Fontbrune, Dr Max de : *Ce que Nostradamus a vraiment dit*, Preface by Henry Miller, Ed. Stock, 1976.

Fontbrune, Dr de : *La Prédiction mystérieuse de Prémol*, Michelet, Sarlat, 1939, o.p.

La divine Tragédie de Louis XVII, Michelet, Sarlat, 1949, available from J.-Ch. de Fontbrune, 3, cours Gambetta, Aix-en-Provence.

Fontbrune, Dr de : *L'Etrange XXᵉ siècle vu par Nostradamus*, Michelet, Sarlat, 1950, o.p.

'Pourquoi je crois en Nostradamus', *Ecclesia*, no. 82, 1956.

'Le docteur Nostradamus vous parle,' *Les Cahiers de Marottes et Violons d'Ingres*, no. 10, Paris, 1953.

'Nostradamus', *Synthèses*, no. 3, August 1955.

Foretich, Rodolphe : *La Prophétie des Papes, analysée à la lumière des prédictions de Nostradamus*, Salvador, 1961. (BN)

Forman, Henry-James : *Les Prophéties à travers les siècles*, Payot, 1938.

Frontenac, Roger : *La Clé secrète de Nostradamus*, Denoël, Paris, 1950.

Fulke : *Contra inutiles Astrologorum praedictiones*, Nostradamus, Cunningham, 1560. (British Museum)

Garçon, Maurice : 'Il y a 450 ans Nostradamus naissait', *Historia*, no. 85, 1953.

Garencieres, Theophilus : *The True Prophecies of Prognostications of Michael Nostradamus*, London, 1672.

Gauquelin, Michel : 'Les Astres ont-ils changé le cours de l'histoire?', *Historia*, no. 203, 1963.

Gay-Rosset, Claude : 'Michel de Nostredame, une rencontre du quatrième type,' *Midi-Mutualité*, no. 12, Jan.-Feb. 1979. (Marseille)

Gimon, Louis : *Chroniques de la ville de Salon depuis son origine jusqu'en 1792*, Aix-en-Provence, 1882.

Girard, Samuel : *Histoire généalogique de la Maison de Savoie*, 1660.

Gravelaine, Joëlle de : *Prédictions et Prophéties*, Hachette, Paris, 1965.

Guérin, Pierre : *Le Véritable secret de Nostradamus*, Payot, Paris, 1971.

Guichardan, S. : *La Chasse aux prophéties*, Bonne Presse, Limoges, 1941.

Guichenou, Joseph : *Catalogue de tableaux au musée Calvet*, Avignon, 1909.

Guynaud, Balthazard : *Concordance des prophéties depuis Henri II jusqu'à Louis le Grand*, Jacques Morel, Paris, 1693.

Hades : *Que sera demain?*, La Table Ronde, Paris, 1966.

Haitze, Pierre Joseph de : *La Vie de Nostradamus*, Aix-en-Provence, David, 1712.
Vie et Testament de Nostradamus, 1789.

Haitze, Pierre Joseph de : *La Vie de Nostradamus*, Aix-en-Provence, 1911.

Harold, R. A. : *Les Prophètes et les Prophéties de l'Apocalypse à nos jours*, Ed. La Caravelle, Brussels; l'Avenir, Paris, 1948.

Hildebrand, Jakob : *Nostradamus sueddeutsche monatshefte*, 1932.

Holtzauer, Jean-Louis : *Nostradamus, un praticien sous la Renaissance*, Laboratoires S.O.B.I.O., Ed. Labo, 92 – Levallois, 1975.

Hutin, Serge : *Les Prophéties de Nostradamus avec présages et sixains*, Pierre Bellefond, Paris, 1962, 1972, 1978, Poche-Club, Paris, 1966; Hachette, Paris, 1975.
Les Prophéties de Nostradamus, Club Géant Historique, Les éditions de la Renaissance, Paris, 1966.

Iacchia, U. : *La Tunisie vue par Nostradamus*, Imp. d'Art, Tunis.

IAF : *Le Substrat mathématique de l'Œuvre de Nostradamus*, Ed. de Psyché, Paris, 1949.

I.M. : *Le vrayes centuries de Me Michel Nostradamus expliquées sur les affaires de ce temps*, I. Boucher, 1652.

Ionescu, Vlaicu : *Le Message de Nostradamus sur l'Ere Prolétaire*, publ. at author's expense, distributed by Dervy Books, Paris, 1976.
'Nostradamus et la gnose', *Atlantis*, no. 301, Jan.-Feb. 1979, 30, rue de la Marseillaise 94300 – Vincennes.

Jacquemin, Suzanne : *Les Prophéties des Derniers Temps*, La Colombe, Paris, 1958.

Jant, chevalier de : *Prédictions tirées des Centuries de Nostradamus qui, vraisemblablement peuvent s'expliquer à la guerre entre la France et l'Angleterre contre les provinces unies*, 1673.
Prophéties de Nostradamus sur la longueur des jours et la félicité du règne de Louis XIV, 1673.

Jaubert, Etienne : *Eclaircissement des véritables quatrains de Nostradamus et Vie de M. Nostradamus*, Amsterdam, 1656.

Kerdeland, Jean de : *De Nostradamus à Cagliostro*, Ed. Self, Paris, 1945.

Klinckowstroem, G. C. Von : *Die ältesten Ausgaben des Prophéties des Nostradamus*, March 1913.

Kniepf, Albert : *Die Weisagungen des alt Französischen Sehers Michel Nostradamus und der Weltkrieg*, Hamburg, 1915.

Krafft, Karl E. : *Nostradamus prezice vütorul Européi*, Bucharest, 1941.

Labadie, Jean : *Peut-on dire l'avenir?* Aubanel, Avignon, 1941.

Lamont, André : *Nostradamus sees all*, 1942.

Lamotte, Pierre : *De Gaulle révélé par Nostradamus il y a quatre siècles*, Le Scorpion, Paris, 1961. (BN)

Langlois, Charles : *Les Contradictions de Nostradamus*, 1560.

Laurent : *Prédictions jusqu'à l'an 2000. Prophéties du Christ, de Nostradamus, des Papes St Malachie*, Laurent, 91 Brunoy.

Laver, James : *Nostradamus*, Penguin Books, 1942.

Nostradamus, the future foretold, George Mann, Maidstone, 1973.

Legrand, Jean René : 'Pronostics pour l'an 1959', *Initiation et science*, no. 47, Jan.-March 1959, Omnium littéraire, Paris.

Leoni, Edgar : *Nostradamus, life and literature*, 1961.

Le Pelletier, Anatole : *Les Oracles de Nostradamus, astrologue, médecin et conseiller ordinaire des rois Henry II, François II et Charles IX*, Le Pelletier, 40, rue d'Aboukir, Paris, 1867, 2 vol.

Le Roux, Jean : *La Clé de Nostradamus, Isagoge ou Introduction au véritable sens des Prophéties de ce fameux auteur*, Pierre Giffard, rue Saint-Jacques-près-les-Maturins, Paris, 1710. (Musée d'Arbaud, Aix-en-Provence)

Leroy, Dr Edgar : 'Les origines de Nostradamus', *Mémoires de l'Institut historique de Provence*, vol. 18, Marseille, 1941.

Sur un quatrain de Nostradamus.

'Jaume de Nostredame et la Tour de Canillac', *Mémoires de l'Institut historique de Provence*, vol. 19, Marseille, 1942.

'Pierre de Nostredame de Carpentras', communication à l'Institut historique de Provence, 1948.

'Nostradamus et le curé d'Argœuvres', *Cahier de Pratique Médiocochirurgicale*, Avignon, 1939, no. 5.

Saint-Paul de Mausole à Saint-Rémy de Provence, Imp. générale du Sud-Ouest, Bergerac, 1948.

Nostradamus, ses origines, sa vie, son œuvre, Imp. Trillaud, Bergerac, 1972.

Romanin, les cours d'amour de Jehan de Nostredame, Avignon, 1933. (BMA)

Saint-Rémy de Reims, Marseille, 1937. (BMA)

Nostradamus, détective avant la lettre, Avignon, 1949. (BN)

Le Latin du tabellion provençal Jaume de Nostredame, notaire à Saint-Rémy-de-Provence dans les actes de 1501 à 1513, Avignon, 1961.

'Saint-Paul-Tricastin et Saint-Paul-de-Mausole, Contribution à l'histoire d'une légende', *Bull. Philologique et Historique*, 1959.

Ligeoix-de-la-Combe : *La Troisième Guerre Mondiale d'après les prédictions de Nostradamus*, Bordeaux, 1961.

Loog, C. L. : *Die Weisagungen des Nostradamus*, 1921.

Loriot, Louis : 'Entretien de Rabelais et de Nostradamus', Nogent-Le-Rotrou, 1960 & Paris, 1907, *Revue des Etudes rabelaisiennes*, vol. 5, pp. 176–84.

Mabille, Pierre : 'Nostradamus, ses prophéties, son temps', *Inconnues*, Lausanne, 1955.

Maby, Pascale : 'Le Dossier des Prophètes, voyants et astrologues', *Les Chemins de l'Impossible*, Albin Michel, Paris, 1977.

MacCann, Lee, *Nostradamus, the man who saw through time*, 1941.

MacNeice, Louis : *L'Astrologie*, Tallandier, Paris, 1966.

Madeleine, Georges : *La Prochaine Guerre Mondiale vue par Nostradamus*, Toulon, 1952, Ed. Proventia.

Maidy, Léon-Germain de : *Sur une inscription liminaire attribuée à Nostradamus*, Nancy, 1917.

Marques da Cruz : *Profecias de Nostradamus*, Ed. Cultrix, Sao Paulo.

Marteau, Pierre : *Entretiens de Rabelais et de Nostradamus*, 1690.

Menestrier, François : *La Philosophie des images énigmatiques*, Lyon, 1694.

Mericourt, M. J. : *Gesta Dei per Francos*, Paris, 1937.

Nostradamus et la crise actuelle, Paris, 1937.

Mondovi, Pierre : 'Un Provençal hors du commun : Nostradamus', *Racines*, no. 4, May 1979, Aix-en-Provence.

Monnier : *Résurrection merveilleuse en 1877 de Michel de Nostredame*, various pamphlets from 1889 to 1896.

Monterey, Jean : *Nostradamus, prophète du XXᵉ siècle*, La Nef, Paris, 1963.

Motret : *Essai d'explication de deux quatrains de Nostradamus*, Nevers, 1806.

Mouan, L. : 'Aperçus littéraires sur César Nostradamus et ses lettres inédites à Peiresc', Mémoires de l'Académie, vol. 10, Aix, 1873. (BMA)

Moult, Thomas-Joseph : *Prophéties perpétuelles, très anciennes et très certaines*, seventeenth-century almanac.

Prophéties perpétuelles, Ed. des Cahiers astrologiques, Nice, 1941.

Moura, Jean, and Louvet, Paul : *La vie de Nostradamus*, Gallimard, Paris, 1930.

Muraise, Eric: *Du Roy perdu à Louis XVII*, Julliard, Paris.

Saint-Rémy de Provence et les secrets de Nostradamus, Julliard, Paris, 1969.

Histoire et Légende du grand Monarque, 'Les Chemins de l'Impossible', Albin Michel, Paris, 1975.

Necroman, Don : *Comment lire les Prophéties de Nostradamus*, Ed. Maurice d'Hartoy, Paris, 1933.

Neyral, Georges : *La Vraie Vie de Michel de Nostredame*, Thesis, Toulouse, 1951.

Nicoullaud, Charles : *Nostradamus, ses prophéties*, Perrin et Cⁱᵉ, Paris, 1914.

Nostradamus, César : *Poésies*, Colomiez, Toulouse, 1606–8.

L'Entrée de la reine Marie de Médicis en sa ville de Salon, Jean Tholosan, Aix-en-Provence, 1602.

Histoire et Chroniques de Provence, Simon Rigaud, Lyon, 1614.

Nostradamus, Michel : *Les Prophéties de M. Michel Nostradamus :* Principal Editions :

    Macé Bonhomme, Lyon, 1555;

    Antoine du Rosne, Lyon, 1557–58;

    Barbe Régnault, Paris, 1560;

    Pierre Rigaud, Lyon, 1566;

    Benoist Rigaud, Lyon, 1568; in *8. B.U. Montepellier*, no. 48340.

Charles Roger, Paris, 1569;

Pierre Meunier, Paris, 1589;

Jean Poyet, Lyon, 1600 (BN);

Benoist Rigaud, Lyon, 1605;

Pierre Rigaud, Lyon, 1605 (BN);

Pierre Rigaud, Lyon, 1610 (BN), 1649;

Claude La Rivière, Lyon, 1611;

Vincent Sève, Beaucaire, 1610;

Pierre Chevillot, Troyes, 1611;

Simon Rigaud, Lyon, 1644;

Pierre de Ruau, Troyes, 1649 (BN);

Winckermans, Amsterdam, 1657;

Jean Balam, Lyon, 1665;

Jean Ribon, vis-à-vis la Sainte Chapelle à l'image saint Louis, Paris, 1669;

Jean Huguetan, Lyon (17th century);

Jean Ianson, Amsterdam, 1668;

Jean Besongne, Rouen, 1681;

Besson, Lyon, 1691;

Jean Viret, Lyon, 1697 (BML);

Lambert-Gentot, *Nouvelles et Curieuses prédictions de M. Nostradamus, pour sept ans depuis l'année 1818 jusqu'à l'année 1824*, Lyon, 1818.

Landriot, Riom, no date (19th century);

Facsimiles of the 1611 Chevillot edition by Delarue, Paris, and of the 1668 Amsterdam edition by Ed. Adyar, Paris 1936.

Prognostication nouvelle et prédiction portenteuse pour l'an 1555 composées par Maistre M. Nostradamus, Jean Brotot, Lyon.

Démonstration d'une comette, Jean Marcorelle, Lyon, 1571 (BN)

Prognostication et prédiction des quatre temps pour 1572, Melchior Arnoullet, Lyon, 1572. (BN)

Prophéties par l'Astrologue du Très Chrétien Roy de France et de Madame la Duchesse de Savoye, F. Arnoullet, Lyon, 1572. (BN)

Nostradamus, Michel : *Lettre de Maistre Michel Nostradamus de Salon-de-Craux-en-Provence à la Royne, mère du Roy*, Benoist Rigaud, Lyon, 1566

Almanach pour l'an 1573 avec les présages, Pierre Roux, Avignon, 1562.

Prophétie ou Révolution merveilleuse des 4 saisons de l'an, Michel Jove, Lyon, 1567.

Traité de fardements et confitures, Antoine Volant, Lyon, 1555.

Paraphrase de C. Galen, trans. by Nostradamus, Antoine du Rosne, Lyon, 1557.

Excellent et très utile opuscule de plusieurs exquises receptes, Benoist Rigaud, Lyon, 1572.

Almanach pour l'an 1567, Benoist Odo, Lyon.

La Grant Pronostication nouvelle avec la déclaration ample de 1559, Jean Brotot, Lyon, 1558.

Prophéties sur Lyon, La France et le monde entier dans les premières années du XXe siècle, 5 booklets, Lyon, P. Bousset & M. Paquet, 1907, 1909.

Almanach des prophéties, P. N. Jausserand, Lyon, 1871–72.

Les Merveilleuses Centuries et Prophéties de Nostradamus, colour illustrations by Jean Gradassi, Ed. André Virel, Ed. Artisanales SEFER, 880 copies, Nice, 1961.

Les Prophéties de Nostradamus (complete), Club des Champs Elysées, Ed. Baudelaire, Paris, 1967.

Prophéties nouvelles de Michel Nostradamus trouvées dans sa tombe au moment de l'ouverture dans l'église des Cordeliers de Salon pour 1820, 1821, 1822, 1823, 1824, 1825 et 1826, A Toulon de l'Imprimerie de Calmen, imprimeur du Roi, 11, rue d'Angoulême.

Les Prophéties de Nostradamus (complete), Les Cent un chefs d'œuvre du Génie Humain, Prodifu, 5, rue du Cog Héron, 75001 – Paris.

Les Prophéties de Nostradamus, pub. by the author, Marc Billerey, Mallefougasse (Alpes de Provence), 1973.

Undated edns (16th and 17th centuries) : Antoine Baudraud et Pierre André, Lyon.

Nostredame, Jean de : *Les Vies des plus célèbres et anciens poètes provençaux qui ont fleuri du temps des comtes de Provence*, Basile Bouquet, Lyon, 1575.

Novaye, Baron de : *Aujourd'hui et demain*, Paris, 1905.

Pagliani, Coraddo : 'Di Nostradamus e idi sue una poco nota iscrizione Liminare torinen', *Della Rassegna mensile Muncipale*, no. 1, Turin, 1934.

Parisot, F. : *Le Grand Avènement précédé d'un grand prodige*, typographie des Célestins, Bar-le-Duc, 1873.

Parker, Eugène : *La Légende de Nostradamus et sa vie réelle*, Paris, 1923.

Patrian, Carlo : *Nostradamus, le Profezie*, Edizioni Méditerranée, Via Flaminia, Rome, 1978.

Pelaprat, Jean Marie : 'Varennes et 1792, sauvent Nostradamus', *Historia*, no. 397(2), *Voyance et Prophéties*, Ed. Tallendier, Paris.

Pichon, Jean-Charles : *Nostradamus et le Secret des temps*, les productions de Paris, 1959.

Nostradamus en clair, R. Laffont, Paris, 1970.

Le Royaume et les Prophètes, R. Laffont, 1963.

Piobb, P. V. : Facsimile of Amsterdam edn, Adyar, Paris, 1936.

Le Sort de l'Europe d'après la célèbre Prophétie des papes de Saint-Malachie, accompagnée de la Prophétie d'Orval et de toutes dernières indications de Nostradamus, Dangles, Paris, 1939.

Privat, Maurice : *1938, année de relèvement*.

1938, année d'échéance.

1939, année de reprise, Editions Médicis, Paris, 1938.

Demain, la guerre.

1940, prédictions mondiales, année de grandeur française, Editions Médicis, Paris.

Putzien, Rudolf : *Friede unter volkern? Die Weisagungen des M. Nostradamus und ihre Bedeutung fur Atomzeitaler*, Drei eichen Verlag, H. Kissener, München, 1958.

Reed, Clarence : *Great Prophecies about the war*, Faber & Faber, London, 1941.

Reynaud, Jean-Lucien : *Nostradamus n'a pas menti*, lecture, ville d'Avray, 1948. *Nostradamus délié*, ville d'Avray, 1949.

Reynaud-Plense : *Les Vraies Prophéties de Nostradamus*, Salon, 1939.

Robb, Steward : *Nostradamus on Napoleon*, Oracle Press, New York, 1961. *Nostradamus on Napoleon, Hitler and the present crisis*, Scribner's, New York, 1941.
Prophecies on world events by Nostradamus, New York, 1961.

Robert, Henry : *The Complete Prophecies of Nostradamus*, Ed. H. Robert, Great Neck, New York, 1971. Japanese trans. by Kasuko Daijyo with Hidéo Uchida, Ed. Tama, Tokyo, 1975.

Rochetaille, P. : *Prophéties de Nostradamus. The key to the 'Centuries', with special reference to the history of Third Republic*, Adyar, 1939.

Roisin, Michel de : 'Ulrich de Mayence, maître de Nostradamus', *Aesculape*, no. 5, 1969, 52nd year.
'Plus forte que Nostradamus : Ulrich de Mayence', *Constellation*, no. 199, November 1964.

Rollet, Pierre : *Interprétation des Hiéroglyphes de Horapollo*, Ramoun Bérenguié, Aix-en-Provence, 1968.

Roudene, Alex : *Les Prophéties, vérité ou mensonge*, 'Mondes Magiques series', Ed. de l'Athanor, Paris, 1976.

Rouellond de la Rouellondière de Chollet : *La Prophétie de Rouellond, Manuscrit du XVIe siècle*, Victor Pipeau, Beauvais, 1861.

Rouvier, Camille : *Nostradamus*, Marseille, La Savoisienne, 1964.

Ruir, Emile : *Le Grand Carnage d'après les prophéties de Nostradamus de 1938 à 1947*, Ed. Médicis, Paris, 1938.
L'Ecroulement de l'Europe, d'après les prophéties de Nostradamus, Paris. 1939.

Ruir, Emile : *Nostradamus, ses Prophéties, 1948–2023*, Paris, 1948.
Nostradamus. Les Proches et Derniers Evénements, Ed. Médicis, Paris, 1953.

Ruzo, Daniel : *Les Derniers Jours de l'Apocalypse*, Payot, 1973.
Los ultimos dias del apocalipsis, Michel Shultz, Mexico.

Sede, Gérard de : *Les Secrets de Nostradamus*, Julliard, Paris, 1969.

Spica-Capella : *La Clef des prédictions nostradamiques*, Ed. des soirées astrologiques, 1941.

Tamizey de Larroque : *Les Correspondants de Pieresc, César Nostradamus*, unpublished letters from Salon to Peiresc, 1628–29, Typographie Marius Olive, Marseille, 1880.

Tarade, Guy : 'La Clef des centuries de Nostradamus', *Pégase*, no. 3, 1974.
Les Dernières Prophéties pour l'Occident, 'Les Enigmes de l'Univers' series, Robert Laffont, Paris, 1979.

Torne-Chavigny, H. : Reissue of the *Prophecies of Nostradamus*, 1862 edition, enlarged in 1872.
Prospectus : interprétation de 30 quatrains, 1860.
L'Histoire prédite et jugée par Nostradamus, 3 vol., Bordeaux, 1860.
Affiches : tableau de l'histoire prédite et jugée, 1862.
Prospectus des lettres du grande prophète : interprétation de 20 quatrains.
Les lettres du grand prophète.

Henri V à Anvers.
Nostradamus et l'astrologie.
Les Blancs et les rouges.
La Salette et Lourdes.
La mort de Napoléon III.
MacMahon et Napoléon IV.
Le roy blanc et la fusion.
Portraits prophétiques d'après Nostradamus.
Prophéties dites d'Olivarius et d'Orval.
L'Apocalypse interprétée par Nostradamus, 1872.
Almanach du grand prophète Nostradamus pour 1873.
Nostradamus éclairci ou Nostradamus devant monseigneur Dupanloup, Saint-Denis-du-Pin, 1874.
Ce qui sera d'après le grand prophète Nostradamus, followed by *Almanach pour 1878.*
Influence de Nostradamus dans le gouvernement de la France, 1878.
Concordance de Nostradamus avec l'Apocalypse, Veuve Dupuy, Bordeaux, 1861.
Touchard, Michel : *Nostradamus,* Grasset, 1972
'Histoire des personnages mystérieux et des sociétés secrètes' series, Ed. Celt, Paris, 1972.
Touchard, Michel : 'Les Prophéties de Michel Nostradamus. Le rêve fou', *Historia,* no. 34, 1974.
Tronc de Condoulet : *Abrégé de la vie de Nostradamus,* followed by *Nouvelle découverte de ses quatrains,* J. Adibert, Aix-en-Provence. (BMA)
Van Gerdinge, René : 'Le Nez de Cléopâtre', *Messidor,* no. 29, Montfavet, Vaucluse.
Verdier, du : *Les Vertus de notre maistre Nostradamus,* Geneva, 1562.
Viaud, Jean : '1999, Un tournant dans l'histoire des hommes', *Constellation,* no. 166, Feb. 1962.
Vidél, Laurent : *Déclaration des abus, ignorances et séditions de Michel Nostradamus,* Avignon, 1558.
Vignois, Élisée du : *Notre Histoire racontée à l'avance par Nostradamus,* Paris, 1910.
L'Apocalypse, interprète de la Révolution, d'après Nostradamus, Noyon, 1911.
Vogel, Cyrille : *Saint Césaire d'Arles,* 1937.
Voldben, A. : *After Nostradamus,* Neville Spearman, London, 1973.
Ward, Charles A. : *Oracles of Nostradamus,* London, 1891.
Willoquet, Gaston : *La Vérité sur Nostradamus,* Ed. Traditionnelles, Paris, 1967.
Winckermans : *Editions des Centuries,* Amsterdam, 1657.
Woolf, H. I. : *Nostradamus,* London, 1944.
Yram : *Prophéties connues et prédictions inédites,* Preface by Papus, l'Edition d'Art, Paris.
Zevaco, Michel : *Nostradamus* (novel), Fayard, 1909, Livre de Poche, no. 3306.

NOSTRADAMUS
INTO THE TWENTY-FIRST CENTURY

To my brother François Gurbert, artist.
To my wife Laura.
To my children Béatrice, Guillaume, Sophie and Isabelle.
To my nieces Isabelle, Véronique and Axelle.
To my nephews Alexandre, Jérôme, François Junior,
Arnaud and François-Xavier.

Letter from Henry Miller

In 1953, when I was eighteen, I had the pleasure of meeting Henry Miller, who had come to the Périgord to visit my father. I took Miller on a trip round the Lascaux caves and the Roman remains at Périgueux. These outings with one of the giants of American literature helped me to discover both the splendours of antiquity and the living heritage of the classics.

I wrote to him in 1975, letting him know I was in the process of thoroughly re-examining Nostradamus' writings. He replied on 6 June 1975 (my father had died on 6 June 1959), as follows:

Dear Jean-Charles de Fontbrune –
My reply must be brief unfortunately. About a year ago I lost the sight in my right eye. As a consequence I read and write very little. (I can only glance through the new edition you sent me.)

As for the letters, no, I do not have any of your father's letters here. Perhaps I gave them to the Library of UCLA – 405 Hillgard Ave. LA (24). Write to the Head of the Dept of Special Collections there.

I am glad to see that you are vitally interested in Nostradamus. No doubt you are an 'auteur'.

Yes, you have my permission to publish my letters to your father. Only I think you should let me look them over before printing them. I am afraid the market is glutted with books of H. M. correspondence avec [?] les un tel, [illegible] etc. etc. So pay attention!

All the best to you and to your mother if she is still alive.
Henry Miller

PS Was this book ever translated into English[1]

[1] The first volume, *Nostradamus: Countdown to Apocalypse*, by Jean-Charles de Fontbrune was published in Britain on 6 June 1983.

Dear ~~Jean~~ Charles de ~~Fontbrune~~ —
My reply must be brief unfortunately. About a year ago I lost
the sight in my right eye. As a
consequence I read and write very
little. (I can only glance thru the
new edition you sent me.)
As for the letters, no, I do not
have any of your father's letters
here. Perhaps I gave them to
the Library of U.C.L.A. – 405
~~N~~ Hilgard Ave. L.A. (24). Write

to the Head of the ~~Dept~~ of
Special Collections there.
I am glad to ~~see~~ that
you are vitally inter-
rested in Nostradamus. No
~~doubt~~ you are an "auteur".
₁ Yes, you have my per-
mission to publish my
letters to your father.
Only I think you should
let me look them over
before printing them.
I am afraid the market
is glutted with books of
H. M. Correspondence a rec
~~La int Jel, in~~, etc. So
pay ~~attention~~!
All the best to you
and to your mother if
she is still alive.
Henry Miller
P.S. Was this book ever translated into English?

I
NOSTRADAMUS:
Countdown to Apocalypse (Vol. 1)
A Review of Its Readers and Critics

'In France, arsonists are left in peace,
and those who sound the alarm are persecuted.'

Chamfort (1741–94)
Thoughts and Maxims

When in 1961 I was called up for military service in Algeria, I left the cosy comfort of Western consumer society and was plunged into a new, often traumatic and also completely unknown world. It was like landing on another planet altogether.

After the Second World War, during my adolescence in fact, I often heard my father mention a future Moslem revolt in North Africa. This was one of the main predictions he had derived from the Centuries of Nostradamus. So I remembered his comments in 1961, the year of General de Gaulle's 'Algeria for the Algerians', and became aware that this was the start of a Moslem rebellion against the Christian West. By 1963, after military service, I could no longer contain the curiosity that impelled me to check the predictions made in my father's book.

I was sorely disappointed, however. I found it dreadfully obscure: Nostradamus's text as translated by my father remained, as far as I was concerned, completely inaccessible.

So in my own researches I decided to start from scratch, checking the original text and working very systematically, asking my programmer friends to run the prophet's entire vocabulary through their computers. I took into account both the successes and mistakes of my father's predecessors – Bareste, Le Pelletier, Colin de Larmor, Elisée du Vignois, the Abbé Torné-Chavigny, and the rest. I soon realized that no one had ever really studied the minutiae of the text, which seemed to me to be 'encoded'. First of all I had to classify the key words: proper nouns, historical and geographical names and any recurring, invented or unusual terms. I classified all these names alphabetically, in every instance noting in which quatrain and Century they occurred.

Some years later, when I mentioned my system to a computer expert, he suggested extending such lists to cover Nostradamus' entire vocabulary, also involving a word count and an even more detailed placing and comparison of every word used. This was of invaluable assistance but could never be a substitute for an author's memory and analytical mind. To quote only one example from my filing system: I chose the word *autour*, used ten times by Nostradamus. On nine occasions the meaning was the usual one, *around* (the preposition), but once it was used in its rarer sense, as a noun meaning *goshawk*. Only when checking all ten quatrains incorporating the word *autour*, and then restoring it in context, would one be aware of the philological trap.

At last, by the end of 1979, I had arrived at an overall view of Nostradamus' 'message', along with an insight into the precision of his language and the details of his coding methods. I tried to interest several publishers without success, encountering the usual protest: 'Not *another* book on Nostradamus!' But I returned to Paris in April 1980 and saw the Business Manager of Presses de la Cité, Jean-Paul Bertrand. He was enthusiastic about my rather different, methodical approach to Nostradamus, and arranged for publication by Editions du Rocher, one of the publishing group's smaller subsidiaries.

My background is in the pharmaceutical industry and I am not a professional writer, so I was even more overjoyed. The first printing in France of *Nostradamus: Countdown to Apocalypse* was a modest run of 6,000 copies, which went on sale in the first week of November 1980. Largely through word of mouth, sales were brisk, and by late November a reprint was called for. By 10 May 1981 – the date of the French Presidential Elections – it had sold 15,000 copies. During this time the book was scarcely reviewed or even mentioned in the French press.

This silence may be explained partly by the fact that Nostradamus foretold the rise to power of the current French Socialist government, which must have disturbed some political pundits. Then as predicted, François Mitterrand swept to power on what the media dubbed 'the Socialist landslide'.

Three days later, another equally astonishing event occurred. A young Turkish fanatic tried to assassinate Pope John Paul II in St Peter's Square, Rome. In one of Nostradamus' quatrains (CII,Q97) I had discovered that the Pope's life would be in danger at such time as the Rose (Nostradamus' symbol for Socialism, and also that of the French Socialist Party) flourished in France.

These two events stimulated sudden and enormous media attention for the book, which by the end of that August had sold no fewer than

300,000 copies in France alone. Since then it has been translated and reprinted all over the world, arousing controversy wherever it has appeared.

DETRACTORS AND SUPPORTERS

'When I stop getting indignant, my
old age will have begun.'

André Gide (1869–1951)

If the various petty campaigns against my book were intended to discourage or silence me, they certainly failed. Everything I experienced in the way of journalistic hostility had all too often been encountered by more illustrious men of letters in the past, and I shall confine myself here to quoting their own words, which express far better than I could do the rational responses to unreasonable judgements and biased reviews.

Nostradamus should, appropriately, be quoted first. He himself had warned his son (see the Letter to his son César, in Vol. 1) that his prophecies would encounter hostility and derision in the years to come, and this in itself was prophetic enough. While in the important Letter to Henri, Second King of France (included here for the first time in English) he addressed this future monarch thus: 'I could have, had I wished, put a date to each quatrain; but this would not have been to everyone's liking and my interpretations would have pleased them no better, unless I had been granted enough protection to do so and had given slanderers no pretext for attacking me.'

Let us see what some thinkers and writers who came after Nostradamus have written.

'Journalists say a thing that they know isn't true,
in the hope that if they keep on saying it long
enough it *will* be true.'

Arnold Bennett (1867–1931)

'I count it one of the blessings of life that I
do not write for the newspapers. This affects my
income – but my conscience benefits from it.'

Gustave Flaubert (1821–80) *Correspondence*

'The difference between journalism and literature is that journalism is unreadable and literature is not read.'

Oscar Wilde (1854–1900)

'A libel in the newspapers is as the grass in a
meadow. It springs up of its own accord. Newspapers are an especially bright green.'

Victor Hugo (1802–85) *Stone Cairns*

'Writing allows one to forget the rabble.'

Charles de Gaulle (1890–1970) *Fallen Oaks*

Now I would like to sympathize with those journalists who came to
interview me after reading my book for themselves, only to find their
editors censoring their copy because they had taken an independent
(though not necessarily favourable) line. I remember after my lecture at
the Olympia, the famous Paris theatre, on 15 February 1982, a celebrated
left-wing journalist from a big daily called to see me. He had heard me
talk to an audience of 1,200 people ('a few Fontbrune supporters', as
another reporter claimed on the radio on the following day), and had
formed his own objective, on-the-spot opinion. He certainly did not
consider my statements mere sensation-seeking. The journalist I spoke to
concluded our interview quite cordially, referring me to his forthcoming
article. The article was definitely written but never appeared. Yes,
censorship *does* exist, as all journalists well know. Here then is some
food for thought for the censors:

'*Dat veniam corvis, vexat censura columbas.*'
(Censorship absolves the ravens, harasses the
doves.)

Juvenal (60–140)

'Censorship of whatever sort seems monstrous
to me; a thing worse than murder. An offence
against thought is an attempt to assassinate the
soul. The death of Socrates still weighs heavily
upon the human race.'

Gustave Flaubert (1821–80) *Correspondence*

'In France every writer is on trial.'

Henri Rochefort (1830–1913) *The Lantern*

'Assassination is the extreme form of censorship.'

George Bernard Shaw (1856–1950)
The Shewing-Up of Blanco Posnet

All sorts of political labels have been unsuccessfully attributed to me. The proof of this is that I have been attacked from every political angle and by the Church too. To be predicting, in May 1980, against all the odds, the advent of Socialism (the Rose) in France, drew the wrath of the Right, while Leftists were also incensed that my book predicted the end of such a regime – then not even established. Yet right-wing indignation did nothing to prevent the change of government on 10 May 1981: history and circumstances make a mockery of the partisan views of men.

Various priests and theologians have also attacked me, usually *ad hominem*, hence (and this is actually more serious for them) many people imagine that such attacks are motivated by some anti-religious bias in my book. I must assure them that this is not the case. They could not, anyhow, speak for their Church as a whole. And when they launched their personal and ill-informed attacks they appeared to have quite forgotten such precepts as Matthew 7:1–5:

Judge not, that ye be not judged. For with what judgment ye judge, ye shall be judged: and with what measure ye mete, it shall be measured to you again. And why beholdest thou the mote that is in thy brother's eye, but considerest not the beam that is in thine own eye? Or how wilt thou say to thy brother, Let me pull out the mote out of thine eye; and, behold, a beam is in thine own eye? Thou hypocrite, first cast out the beam out of thine own eye; and then shalt thou see clearly to cast out the mote out of thy brother's eye.

The rather terrifying aspect of Nostradamus' prophecy is what seems to have stung them. But St Thomas Aquinas, recounting a vision of St Catherine of Siena's, wrote: 'The Prophecies which come from Me [Christ] at first inspire terror, and are fulfilled in a sense of security.'

That I have been attacked by so many different people has in some respects reassured me, especially on rereading Luke 6:26: 'Woe unto you, when all men shall speak well of you! for so did their fathers to the false prophets.'

In the sixteenth century the words 'astronomer' and 'astrologer' meant roughly the same thing. They embraced the science of astronomy and of the planetary influences described by Ptolemy, who had carried on the work of his predecessor, Hipparchus. Today the terms have very different meanings, and the confusion between them generally infuriates only the astronomers.

Some contemporary astrologers are knowledgeable scientists, well aware of the laws of celestial mechanics. They are all too rare, however, and for the most part shun publicity. One or two of them have written me interesting letters, passing on valuable information. I am grateful to them.

Superficiality, amateurishness, vanity, jealousy, stupidity and inaccuracy are just some of the constant failings displayed by the unfortunately far more numerous and vocal group of fake astrologers who were roused to anger by my first book. They should have felt far more concerned by Nostradamus' own condemnation of themselves: 'Omnesque Astrologi, Blenni, Barbari procul sunto.' (Let all astrologers, fools and barbarians keep off.)

Instead, they lay claim to understanding Nostradamus better than anyone else through some fantastic 'system' or other! They call themselves experts in the Centuries, and consider that no one but themselves has the ability or the right to approach the subject. Which doubtless explains why they see in Nostradamus a means of making a living rather than any genuine intellectual interest. It also, of course, explains their hostility towards me, which will only increase upon reading this. Let them consider the following comments by Chrysale, from Molière's *Les Femmes Savantes:* 'Do not strive to find out what goes on upon the moon, but concern yourselves a little with your own affairs, where we see everything going topsy-turvy.'

'Few men can without some stirrings of envy
pay homage to the success of a friend.'

Aeschylus (525–456 BC)

'A prophet is not without honour, save in his
own country, and in his own house.'

Matthew 13:57

The publication of *Nostradamus: Countdown to Apocalypse* taught me that in France, at least, the achieving of bestseller status is far from restful. This is especially true if such fame is unforeseen, and one has been abruptly hauled out of provincial obscurity and deposited on to the front pages.

Success is usually frowned upon. Critics of every sort impute to authors a host of Machiavellian intrigues in order to explain away what is, mostly, simply the fruit of their own labours. I was welcomed in other countries, such as Britain, Belgium, Spain, Switzerland and Germany. None of the many readers of my book whom I met could understand the hostility I had encountered in France. Here I except the French Canadians, to whom I am grateful for their unfailing courtesy and open-mindedness.

The book has been translated into a dozen languages and translations are in progress in scores of others. It has created work, generated revenue and brought in foreign currency. I can thank my own country for such recognition . . . but I have also begun to understand why successful Frenchmen have gone off to more receptive, less hostile countries than their native land.

Within months of the success of my book, no fewer than ten other works on the same subject were published in France, several by firms which had originally rejected my own manuscript. These attempts to climb aboard the bestseller bandwagon ranged from insult to plagiarism, by way of imitation, piracy and the reissue of old editions, with new or carefully revamped covers. Here is a list, in order of appearance, of the bandwagon climbers.

France

The Prophecies of Nostradamus by Serge Hutin (Belfond,1972). Reprinted in 1981 with new cover and corrections, the latter the result of plundering my book.

Nostradamus Betrayed by Elisabeth Bellecour, Introduction by Albert Slosman (Laffont, 1981). Ninety-nine of its 284 pages are taken up with misrepresenting and indeed insulting my father and myself. The cover itself incorporates a prime lie. It boasts: 'Complete and original text of the ten Centuries, from the 1605 edition.' I myself have worked from this 1605 Lyon edition of Benoit Rigaud's: it comprises twelve Centuries, plus sixains, presages, the Letter to César and the Letter to Henri, Second King of France. Yet these two individuals called me an impostor!

The Real Centuries and Prophecies (Nice, 1981). Reprint of the 1611 Troyes edition of Pierre Chevillot. At least it is complete and decently printed.

The Prophecies of Nostradamus by J. Q. Laroche-Valmont (S.I.P.E., 1981). A piracy of my own book and duly withdrawn by law. This work appeared in September 1981 with a cover which boasted: 'The book which predicted Mitterrand's victory!' What was more, it also quoted some appreciative comments lifted from reviews of my own book.

A Guide to Nostradamus by Jean-Paul Clébert (Lattès, 1981). A very incomplete dictionary of Nostradamus' vocabulary, compiled mainly from Le Pelletier, Colin de Larmor, Reynaud-Plense and the definitions established in my book. Nostradamus' text, as I have pointed out, is liberally misprinted in many of the old editions. The above author is blithely unaware of most of them, and, even more hilariously, cannot distinguish between the letters *s* and *f*, which in sixteenth-century typography were interchangeable. His compilation accordingly reads like a nonsensical riddle.

Nostradamus' Reply to Jean-Charles de Fontbrune by Jean Robin (Editions de la Maisnie, 1981). A lightweight concoction with many references to occultists and alchemists, such as Paracelsus and Nicholas Flamel. The author repeats the Slosman-Bellecour slanders (q.v.), in particular the curse levelled against me by those two 'authors'. Robin conveniently avoids mentioning what happened on 25 October 1981. On that date Albert Slosman, appearing on television, again threatened me with the so-called curse of Nostradamus which was, in fact, his own invention.

Before he could leave the studios, however, Slosman suffered a coronary; he died three days later – ironically, my birthday.

Nostradamus, Prophecies from Today until AD 2000 (Florian, 1982). An insipid 93-page mini-compilation, consisting of various interpretations drawn from commentators and incorporating further attacks against myself.

Darkness: The Prophecies. An anonymous booklet which repeats the mockeries of Slosman and Bellecour.

Nostradamus' Jam Recipes, selected and adapted by F. Guérin. (Orban, 1981).

Handbook of the Magical Formulae of Nostradamus and Other Contemporary Sages (S.E.I.T.E.C., 1981). Adapted and translated from the Italian.

The Testament of Nostradamus by Daniel Ruzo (Editions du Rocher, 1982). Reprint of a 1975 book. I can scarcely reproach my own publishers for getting on the bandwagon when rivals were doing so with such gusto.

Germany

Nostradamus, Weissagungen über den Atomkrieg by Rudolph Putzien (1981). Reprint of a 1958 book.

Nostradamus, prophetische Weltgeschichte by Alexander Centurio. Reprint of a 1977 book.

Die grossen Weissagungen über die Zukumft der Menschheit by A. Voldben. Reprint of 1975 edition.

Nostradamus, Prophezeiungen bis zum Jahr 2000 by Andrée Wollher (1981). A piracy, withdrawn by law.

Die grossen Prophezeiungen des Nostradamus in moderner Deutung by Kurt Allgeier (1982).

Italy

Centurie e Presagi by Renuccio Boscolo. Reprint of 1972 edition.
Nostradamus, le Profezie by Carlo Patrian. Reprint of 1978 edition.
Italian version of *Handbook of Magical Formulae* (see under French bibliography).

Belgium

1981–2000: Twenty Years Which Will Transform the World by P. L. B Emir (Bolen). A 115-page booklet, some of whose interpretations are fairly obviously derived from mine.

Numerous other books in a variety of languages including Japanese have appeared. The Nostradamus 'industry' has also resulted in an (unsuccessful) pop record in France, and in Chrysler of Quebec using a bust and a quatrain of Nostradamus in order to promote a new model of car. Indeed it should be emphasized that it is the aberrations of our consumer society which are to blame for the world recession!

THE THIRD WORLD WAR

One of the most frequent accusations levelled against me is that I have profited by 'doom-mongering'. Yet scarcely a day passes without my reading newspaper headlines like: 'Western Fears of War', 'Europe at the centre of WW3', 'War: the French Army's Role', 'Three Scenarios of Apocalypse', 'Will Europe Burn?' etc. So who does in fact indulge in doom-mongering?

Public opinion is being gradually prepared for the notion that a Third World War is inevitable, as though (and this is certainly true for the arms dealers and manufacturers) it were the only way to resolve the world recession and reduce increasing unemployment. Nostradamus certainly never promoted such views, nor do I. I have always held to the belief that the only solution is in total multilateral disarmament, conventional as well as nuclear weaponry included.

At the time of writing (June 1982) and since the first volume of my book appeared in France, the planetary situation seems to have taken a distinct turn for the worse. We have seen President Sadat's assassination; an attempt on the Pope's life (13 May 1981); the Iran-Iraq War; the military coup in Poland (13 December 1981); the Falklands War; and, most disturbing of all in the light of Nostradamus' prophecy, the new Palestinian-Israeli wars. During the latter conflicts, Beirut the city of Hashem (cf. Letter to Henri, Second King of France) has been besieged and attacked by numerous armies (Israeli, Lebanese, Palestinian, Syrian, Falangist Christians, etc.) and largely destroyed. All these dramatic events are like warning lights on the dashboard of history in motion.

What then have the United Nations done to intervene during this period? They have uttered pious platitudes termed 'resolutions', which have never yet resolved any important question. In wars the principle of 'might is right' has always obtained and the creation in the twentieth century of international organizations such as the UN has not altered it.

Every day war gains a little more ground from peace. The main reason for this is because the planet is over-armed. It is surely absurd for the industrialized countries, which have vested interests in producing weapons of destruction, to sell huge quantities of armaments to what are called 'developing' countries. The latter's economies, the most severely hit by the world recession, are unable to ensure such development; in fact most of them are markedly impoverished, underdeveloped – with all that that implies in terms of starvation and misery.

Mao Tse Tung once wrote: 'War can be abolished only by war. It is necessary to take up the rifle so as to ensure that rifles are no longer required.' This statement is as false and malicious as the Romans': 'If you want peace, prepare for war.' Perhaps if the majority of mankind stopped accepting war as an inherent factor in man's nature we could escape from the age-old vicious circle.

Such deeply entrenched attitudes do not leave us much room for hope that wars will end on this beleaguered planet. But we can turn to and take heed of the prophetic messages of Nostradamus and the biblical prophets (despite the numerous tribulations announced by them, especially for our present century, with its two world wars to date).

Nostradamus clearly predicts (in his Letter to Henri, Second King of France) a universal peace, that celebrated Golden Age which, according to an astrologer I met in Montreal, should start in March 2023. In the same text Nostradamus writes: 'And at this juncture such a great pestilence begins that more than two-thirds of mankind shall perish.' Man is thus warned against the follies he can continue to perpetrate. He saw that modern warfare with its appalling methods of destruction – whether nuclear, bacteriological, chemical or conventional – can lead to catastrophes imperilling the entire human race.

So I hope that political leaders and heads of state will at once try to prove Nostradamus and his translator wrong. Let the warmongers, arms dealers and manufacturers be outlawed. To end war, the means of waging it must be extirpated. For a start, all governments, through their intermediary (the so-called United Nations), should organize a worldwide referendum, which would surely have the approval of ordinary people everywhere, asking the simple question: 'Should there be world disarmament?'

The fact that murders of and assassination attempts against men of peace and goodwill continue is a clear sign of the impending Apocalypse prophesied in Revelations. Men like Gandhi, Martin Luther King, Sadat and Pope John Paul II are apostles of peace over and above their particular religious beliefs. In a climate of violence and war they herald the universal peace predicted by Nostradamus and this is why they are the targets of the warmongers.

During the last few years various books have been published which promise or forecast a Third World War. Some of these are truly alarmist and all the more credible since their authors are high-ranking officers and experts on warfare. Those so-called rationalists, who invariably deride or attack Nostradamus because they cannot explain away the phenomenon of prophecy, might well inveigh against these purportedly 'reasonable' books which actually scare the public infinitely more. I list here just a few of these works, in chronological order:

The Third World War by General Sir John Hackett (Collins, 1979).

1984: The Apocalypse? by Pierre Jean Moatti (Lefeuvre, 1980).

The Apocalypse Has Already Begun by Claude Duvernoy (Editions du Guetteur, Switzerland, 1980).

How We May Lose the Third World War by General Robert Close (Belfond, 1981).

Who's Afraid of the Eighties? by Nicholas Mélot (Le Rocher, 1981).

Before the War by Cornelius Castoriadis (Fayard, 1981).

War Tomorrow by Patrick Schmoll (C.L.E.P.S., 1981).

War Today? by Jacques Depret, Preface by General Close (Le Rocher, 1982).

1982–1984: Three Years To Disrupt The World by Pierre Jean Moatti (Schrotter, 1982).

My own first book also tried to warn man, but through the medium of prophecies, to curb his aggressive propensities. I must sadly acknowledge its ineffectiveness, to date, in this respect. Special mention must be made here of the US bestseller *Freeze* by Senator Edward Kennedy. One 1982 reviewer maintained that it was partly due to this book and to the subsequent pressure of American public opinion that President

Reagan did a virtual U-turn in policy and began talking arms reduction to the Russians. It is true that Kennedy's book effectively exploits fear and terror, but I do not begrudge him its success: his book proved effective on the political front, where mine, alas, did not!

'Every reader collaborates in every book.'

Maurice Barrès (1862–1923)

After the first volume of this book appeared I received thousands of letters from readers. Many asked me a wide variety of questions which I was quite unable to answer individually. I trust that they will accept my apologies and my thanks for their support. Out of thousands of letters, only three were abusive; each of these was anonymous. This second volume thus gives me an opportunity to reply generally to most of the questions the letters posed.

1. Where should one settle or move to in order to escape war?

This was one of the most frequent questions, and during the twentieth century scarcely anyone has been able to give a satisfactory answer. This century war has spread so cancerously that it has affected countries, regions and communities which had previously lived in tranquillity far from aggressive Europe, the initiator of both world wars. It is a terrible regression where mankind is concerned, and yet there were theologians who believed that Apocalypse had arrived with the Battle of Verdun in 1916. For centuries supposedly Christian Europe had crusades, wars, the Inquisition, religious strife and bloody revolutions of all kinds, and managed to export quite a few to other continents.

If the phenomenon of war has become both endemic and epidemic, where can one take refuge? Nowhere, of course. We have to put our faith in divine providence. The media widely reported the following cautionary anecdote: two Canadians, quite convinced of the imminence and inevitability of a Third World War which Canada could not escape, decided to emigrate to a place that would be safe because it was isolated, poor, virtually unpopulated and had an uninviting climate. They researched various possibilities before discovering their haven of peace far from all artillery and bombs. The couple then duly departed – to the Falklands.

Let us imagine that in 1940, in order to escape the bombs raining on the capital, a Londoner decided to take refuge in Commonwealth territory, somewhere far-flung and safe from the European theatre of conflict.

He might conceivably have chosen a promising tropical paradise in the Solomon Islands – Guadalcanal. That, of course, was the scene of the most bloody fighting between the Americans and Japanese between August 1942 and February 1943.

My answer, then, is not an evasion – I have merely concluded that our entire planet now lives in a state of insecurity.

2.   Queries on Nostradamus' letter to Henri II

Many readers have asked for an interpretation of the Letter to Henri, Second King of France, and this text, included for the first time (see pp. 59–80), is of prime importance. It reinforced much of what I had translated previously and also helped me to be more precise on certain points. Thus Babylon, as mentioned by Nostradamus in the Letter to Henri and in three quatrains (cviii, q96 and cx, q86 in Vol. 1, and ci, q55), was translated in Vol. 1 according to the dictionary definition as 'large centre, such as Paris or London', whereas Nostradamus was making parallels between the history of the three German Reichs and that of Babylonian persecution (under three kings) of the Jews. In both cases the persecution lasted approximately three years.

3.   Did Nostradamus prophesy through divine inspiration?

Throughout his book of prophecies Nostradamus, within the confines of his code, is specific and concise. This in itself constitutes one of the main problems as regards understanding his work. The only time Nostradamus departs from his particular conciseness is when mentioning the origins of his vision into and across four and a half centuries of history. Like a *leitmotiv* the divine source of his inspiration is stressed on numerous occasions, especially in the Letter to César (see Vol. 1). And in the very first quatrain of the first Century, Nostradamus states once again: 'a small flame comes out of the solitude and brings things to pass which should not be thought vain'. Here he is alluding to the Holy Spirit, symbolized by the tongues of flame descending on the Apostles' heads at Pentecost. We should remember that in the Middle Ages the descent of the Holy Spirit was re-enacted by symbolic actions, one of which was the dropping of lighted tow from the eaves and galleries of churches and houses.

The second quatrain of the first Century affirms: 'divine splendour, divinity itself, sits beside him' (in order to dictate its message). Those who insist that Nostradamus must have used occult means, or that he drew his prophecies solely from planetary configurations, are contradicting Nostradamus' numerous affirmations of his divine inspiration.

Nostradamus specifically said in the Letter to César that 'understanding created by the intelligence cannot be acquired in occult fashion'. The language of Nostradamus is therefore the language of faith.

In 1981, after a brutal military coup had flung many thousands of Polish workers in jail, there remained only their own indestructible faith with which to celebrate a Christmas, barely a fortnight later, of utter penury and hardship. There were pious noises of regret from the West, which carried on revelling and carousing, while the Poles were on their own – a people martyred yet again.

And while Beirut, the peaceful capital of the 'Switzerland of the Middle East', was turned into a hell, Westerners calmly watched World Cup soccer from their armchairs. The Lebanese have only their faith left, be it Moslem, Christian or any other. And it is not true to say that this is all Israel's doing, for the Russians and Americans have surely had a hand in the affair too.

The Iran-Iraq War, the Lebanese situation, the Falklands War, Afghanistan etc. all keep the munitions factories busy for as long as they continue. And the spectre of unemployment haunts us. . . .

4. Is there a scientific explanation of prophecy?

No, given the current state of scientific research and knowledge. Here I would like to suggest a possible line of research in order to try to understand the prophetic phenomenon.

Paul Langevin, who publicized Einstein's Theory of Relativity in France, formulated in 1913 a theory known as the 'paradox of the twins'. To summarize: a pair of twins, A and B, will diverge at a precise point in time and space (such and such a spot at such and such a second). Twin A describes a straight line, twin B a curve of space-time and their respective trajectories will intersect at a second point. Their travelling speeds remain less than the speed of light (300,000 km/sec).

Twin B, subjected to acceleration, has aged less rapidly in transit between the two points than twin A. It is as if the first twin has remained stationary on earth while the second has travelled in a spacecraft. In other words, twin B has regained in time the greater amount of space covered in relation to twin A.

This paradox, not really paradoxical at all, has been observed using particle accelerators: an unstable particle, when projected at a speed close to that of light, has a shorter life than when at rest.

In 1971 the Americans verified this paradox convincingly. They placed an atomic clock in a Boeing and another on the ground, both synchronized. An atomic clock is accurate to 10^{-14} second. The airborne clock, moving eastwards as a second airborne clock moved west, 'gained' 59 ± 10

nanoseconds while the one moving westward lost 273 ± 7 nanoseconds (10^{-9} second).

The paradox allows us to suggest the proposition of a spacecraft projected at the speed of light whose crew cover in a given period T (for terrestrial time) space equivalent to several light years. At the end of one cosmic 'year', twin B, the traveller in space, would find on his return to earth not just that his twin had died, but he would also probably be confronted with another civilization altogether.

As regards the prophetic phenomenon, let us imagine that Nostradamus is twin B and Henri II, the king during whose reign Nostradamus prophesied, is twin A. Nostradamus will 'travel' in a few days or months through 450 years of history, yet without this section of man's history being predetermined, since he would have been 'living' it before his own contemporaries and hence before twin A. This would explain his comments on man's free will in the Letter to César, his son, also the question of man's full responsibility for the catastrophes he had seen during his 'voyage'. Doesn't this extract from the Letter to César link Nostradamus with Einstein four hundred years later?:

Eschewing any fantastic imaginings, you may through good judgement have insight into the future if you keep to the specific names of places that accord with planetary configurations, and with inspiration places and aspects yield up hidden properties, namely that power in whose presence the three times (past, present, and future) are understood as Eternity whose unfolding contains them all. . . .

5. Was Nostradamus influenced by the Cabala?

I did try to trace any such influences in Nostradamus' writings, but found none.

I participated in a 1982 Nostradamus symposium during which Dr Isidore Simon, an authority on the history of the Jews in Provence, lectured interestingly on the Marranos (Jews compelled to convert to Christianity), who nonetheless continued secretly to observe various Judaic rituals and traditions. Dr Simon correctly stressed that Nostradamus was neither a Marrano nor even descended from one, because his great-great-grandfather willingly became a Catholic convert. It should be remembered that the Jewish community in a sixteenth-century town had its own quarter: contacts between Jews and Catholics were as rare as those between Catholics and Protestants. Under the historical circumstances, it is surely inappropriate for so many occultists and esoteric devotees to claim that Jewish 'initiates' could have conveyed their secrets to a devout Catholic – one, moreover, received at the French royal court.

6. Are extra-terrestrials mentioned in the Centuries?

Not unless particular quatrains are wilfully distorted. Thus some interpreters have chosen to identify the 'great and terrifying leader' who will
come 'from the heavens' [*ciel* = heaven or sky. *Tr.*] during the seventh
month of 1999 (cf. CX, Q72, Vol. 1). They forget that aviation has
progressed so rapidly during the last few decades that thousands of troops
can be transported tens of thousands of miles in a few hours. What
technical advances, then, might there be between now and the year 2000?
Designers already have on their drawing boards plans for planes capable
of transporting several thousand men per flight. Nostradamus, too, had
quite enough to concern him upon earth without his looking further
afield, to the moon or elsewhere.

7. What about Nostradamus and chronology?

Everybody would like to read the future, arranged in chronological order
as in the history books. In this, too, looking to Nostradamus' prophecies
would prove futile. He states himself in his Letter to Henri, Second
King of France that had he wished he could have dated each quatrain,
but that this would not have pleased one and all. For this reason his text
is comprised of mere scraps of time – temporal hints and dates are
codified.

History, as taught in schools, unfortunately tends to turn into a dreary
succession of events juxtaposed willy-nilly, without proper explanation
of those causal links which would allow us to understand such events.
Besides the judgements he passes on statesmen or political regimes,
Nostradamus the historian establishes links of cause and effect between
different events, sometimes even when these are greatly separated in
time. Thus in one quatrain he connects French 'usurpation' (a value
judgement indeed) of the Maghreb (North-west Africa) by the Third
Republic with the fall of the Fourth Republic in 1958 (cf. CIII, Q59,
Vol. 1). How should such a quatrain be classed – under the history of
the Third or of the Fourth Republic? The interpreter has, then, to make
an arbitrary choice when (as here) both hypotheses can be equally well
sustained.

8. What use have you made of computers?

In 1981 I took part in a German television programme on Nostradamus.
When I saw the German interviewer at my home, he showed me various
articles from the French press in which my use of a computer was
discussed. He pointed out that critics had been dismissive of this idea.

On a previous occasion I had mentioned to him that none of these hostile critics had come to visit me and that I wondered how they could have written as they did without even bothering to see for themselves. Eventually I took him into my office and showed him my *two* computer files. He remained nonplussed and asked why I had not shown these to my detractors. I would happily have done so, had any of them wanted to see them!

I showed him an article in the specialist magazine *Telesoft*, written by Patrick Coston, with whom I had spent a couple of hours, and who had questioned me at length not only about my use of computers but also on the whole subject. Patrick Coston's opinion was as follows:

De Fontbrune is certainly no charlatan. He is a remarkably erudite historian and linguist, who knows Latin, Greek and the ancient sixteenth-century French Nostradamus used. If the logic of his procedure were not so rigorous his interpretations would certainly not be so impressively convincing. What is more, some curious coincidences have backed up his revelations. . . .

So, far from denying the whole phenomenon of prophecy as so many sceptics do, Coston kept an open mind – the constructive attitude which has enabled man to cure major diseases and to progress from discovering the wheel to landing on the moon.

As to programming and how I use my systems, that will remain my own secret for the time being. I have been criticized for not revealing the names of the programmers who have worked for me. They themselves wished to remain anonymous, but here in this second volume I thank them all for their invaluable assistance.

9. *What is the point of revealing numerous prophecies of disasters?*

What if the purpose of such prophecies of disaster were to avoid or alleviate certain catastrophes? Revelations, Matthew, Chapter 24, and the Books of Ezekiel, Jeremiah, Isaiah and Daniel are all, if anything, gloomier than Nostradamus. And what about the notorious Third Secret of Fatima, still jealously kept by the Roman Catholic Church itself? Would that message be worse than my interpretations of Nostradamus' prophecies?

The use of a prophecy predicting disasters for man is, once revealed, to lead each individual to reflect on the dangers inherent in the world in which he or she lives and also on the responsibility of those in power everywhere, especially those motivated by corruptive power alone. The second stage of the prophetic message is only evident if, unhappily, the predicted catastrophe actually occurs. The prophecy then becomes a source of comfort, a refuge for all those ordinary folk who have been sucked unwillingly into the whirlpool of conflicts over which they have virtually no control. Prophecy fulfilled is, finally, the only circumstantial evidence – or at least a strong defence case – for the existence of God, the Supreme Being. Throughout history, one of man's most enduring characteristics has been to acknowledge the existence of some force greater than himself. Cartesianism has been unable to explain away that particular phenomenon. One can but observe it. Curiously enough, civilizations decline when they abandon their gods – that is, the metaphysical or spiritual principle. This change in thinking leads to a materialism whereby men seek only to satisfy physical needs, needs almost always artificially created. And the decadent civilizations then brand as 'barbarians' those who fall upon them in order to seize their possessions.

10. Nostradamus and 'Grand Chiren' or 'Grand Henric'

The prediction concerning a future King of France was probably one of the main (if unadmitted) reasons for French hostility towards my book. On this one issue there was unanimous opposition to my interpretation from the entire bourgeois French intelligentsia, Left and Right alike. The reason is quite clear.

French politicians adhere more rigidly to a political system than to that liberty which their system should respect. When in Spain for the launch of Vol. 1's Spanish edition, I met numerous journalists who asked me about the Bourbon leader mentioned by Nostradamus. This prediction particularly interested them since a Bourbon descendant of Louis XIV is currently on the throne of Spain. In 1975, when Juan Carlos succeeded General Franco, the French media were indulging in gloomy forecasts of what might happen to this 'Fascist stooge'. The Spanish people were expected to rebel against him, expelling him as swiftly and dramatically as possible. Actually – and this bears out my comments on French political behaviour – the French were the prey of wishful thinking, for their predictions never came true.

In 1981 Lieutenant Colonel Tejero planned his abortive military coup against the Spanish Parliament: Juan Carlos I was seen to risk his own life by barring the rebel advance. The next day Carillo, leader of the Spanish Communist Party, while emphasizing that he was no monarchist, paid special homage to the King for saving democracy in Spain. This was a fine example of the democratic spirit.

As for the 'Grand Chiren', some critics have even disputed this anagram of Henric (abbreviation of the Latin Henricus). But Nostradamus had foreseen this very controversy, since he seems to have given his friend Jean-Aimé de Chavigny the key to the word. Chavigny, who came from Beaune in Burgundy, stayed several times with Nostradamus at the

latter's house in Salon, Provence. In 1594 he produced a bilingual
(French and Latin) book, printed on Pierre Roussin's press at Lyon,
called *The French Janus*, which is the first attempt to interpret the
Centuries. This is what he wrote about the word Chiren:

> It was the last age, a royal Dame,
> Carrying in one hand an imperial crown,
> In the other a globe upon which read
> (Great mystery) Chiren, forming when turned
> The sacred name Henric; set at the world's head
> He must one day command that round machine.

Certain commentators maintain that Nostradamus' own quatrains about
this Chiren refer to Henri IV, but Jean-Aimé de Chavigny is specific: he
maintains 'the last age' signifies the last period of Nostradamus'
prophecy, the twentieth century.

Readers have asked me who this future king would be, and for details
about his origins, astrological background, etc. Such questions are impossible to answer. On 17 June 1940 (to make just one comparison), no one
could have guessed that as from the next day a certain Brigadier Charles
de Gaulle would begin playing a major role in the history of France.

11. Is the predicted comet Halley's?

Many of my readers believed that the extraordinary comet described by
Nostradamus (CII, Q41, Vol. 1) was Halley's. Nothing of the sort. It
must be emphasized that many thousands of comets travel through the
solar system. Astronomers discover on average two or three of them
every year. Since these are invisible to the naked eye, there is little
publicity and only scientists know about and study them. When with
the aid of a telescope a comet is discovered, it takes three or four months
from that moment to the perihelion, the comet's passage round the sun.
Almost as much time elapses before it disappears from sight. Not having
any light of its own, it borrows its light from the sun, as does the moon.

In 1973 the Czech astronomer Kohoutek discovered a comet which
was named after him. Scientists indulged in calculations that proved
false: these were the errors which led to its being dubbed 'the comet of
the century', and therefore more significant than Halley's Comet. In the
circumstances, few could see it without a telescope. One important and
far-reaching event (for it precipitated the world economic crisis) did
'coincide' with Kohoutek's perihelion: the Yom Kippur War.

Bearing in mind the characteristics of comets, let us return to the one
announced by Nostradamus. Several readers have pointed out to me that
a comet which appears on 21 June and which is visible to the naked eye

for seven days cannot possibly disappear on 13 December, since seven months rather than seven days separate these dates. To answer this objection I should point out that it *is* possible, since the comet can be discovered (hence known about) on 21 June, can enter the perihelion at the end of September and be visible to the naked eye for seven days, disappearing in December. Readers must accept my apologies for not supplying these explanations in Vol. 1.

So the predicted comet is therefore still unknown, and if Nostradamus is to be believed, it will be far more important than that of Halley. Indeed, if two 'suns' are to be seen in the sky (i.e. the comet will be visible by day), it will be very unusual and implies an exceedingly large comet.

12. It has been claimed that Nostradamus never in fact foretold the destruction of Paris. Is this a de Fontbrune prophecy?

First of all, I am neither a prophet nor a clairvoyant of any kind. Some critics have challenged my interpretations of cvi, Q4 (Vol. 1):

> Le Celtique fleuve changera de rivage,
> Plus ne tiendra la cité d'Aggrippine
> Tout transmué, hormis le vieil langage,
> Saturn. Leo, Mars, Cancer en rapine.

Interpretation

The banks of the French river [the Seine] will change their appearance. Paris will no longer last. All will be transformed except the French language, for it will be a time of totalitarianism, war and misery caused by looting.

My detractors claim that this actually refers to the American destruction of Cologne in 1945, since the ancient name of this town is Colonia Agrippina. I was well aware of this interpretation, borrowed (unattributed) from Serge Hutin by the critics.

Common sense refutes this hypothesis. Is Cologne, Agrippina's city, *really* situated on the banks of a French river on French (*Celtique*) territory? This typically 'Nostradamic' trap has fooled most people, because the Cologne theory is an attractive solution – but for the simple fact that the city is not on a French river. . . .That is why I opted for Paris: the Seine is the 'French river' *par excellence,* and as such waters the capital.

Nostradamus' phrase 'the great city' always refers to Paris. This expression recurs in Sixain 52 and cIV, Q8 (both dealing with the

Mons.r Le Ch.r Daubigné ayant donné a Fontbrune
Lieut. en second de la charge de Lieutenant — en la Comp.e
de grenadiers de ... campdante mon reg.t de ... Mrr
que vous commandés, vacante par la mort de
Cambe ... , je vous écris cette lettre pour vous
dire que vous ayés a le recevoir a faire reconnoitre en lad.e charge
de tous ceux, a qui il apartiendra, en la présente n'estant
pour autre fin, je prie Dieu qu'il vous ayt Mons.r Le Ch.r
Daubigné en sa S.te garde, écrit au Camp de la
Commanderie du Vieux Jonc le sept Juillet 1747.

Louis

De Voyer D'Argenson

Jean-Louis de Fontbrune's orders, dated 7 July 1747, and signed by Louis XV

Massacre of St Bartholomew's Eve, Paris, 1572), and again in CIII, Q50 (the Siege of Paris, 1870). In CV, Q30, as well as the 'great city' reference, Paris is actually named.

Unfortunately, however, there are even more unequivocal quatrains. I shall quote two of them, to make it quite obvious that I am not inventing this disastrous prophecy. First, CVI, Q43:

> Long temps sera sans estre habitée,
> Où Seine et Marne autour vient arrouser,
> De la Tamise et martiaux tentée,
> Deceus les gardes en cuidant repousser.

Interpretation

The confluence of the Seine and Marne will remain for a long time uninhabited when the warriors attacking England will think about driving back her defenders.

Since 1555 such an event has been unimaginable, which is why I have 'placed' it in the future (see Vol. 1).

CIII, Q93 is even clearer, and specifies that Avignon will become the French capital – another prophecy I have been accused of inventing:

> Dans Avignon tout le chef de l'Empire
> Fera arrest pour Paris désolé:
> Tricast tiendra l'Annibalique ire,
> Lyon par change sera mal consolé.

Interpretation

The capital will be moved to Avignon because Paris will be destroyed. The Tricastin will be the cause of Moslem anger. Lyon will be very upset by the change of capital.

The front page of *Le Monde* (10 January 1975) ran the following story: 'Financing the Tricastin nuclear plant: Iran lends a billion dollars to the French Atomic Energy Commission in return for a 10% share in Eurodif.' Thus the Tricastin complex was part financed by the late Shah. In 1555 who would have connected Tricastin, a rural district of the small Drôme department of France, with the Arab world? Who if not Nostradamus? *Le Figaro* (4 December 1979) began an article: 'Franco-Iranian Problems: Iran's holding in Eurodif, the uranium refinery of Tricastin, has been frozen by the Paris Chamber of Commerce. This measure involves repayments of almost a billion dollars agreed upon by Teheran in 1975. . . .'

13. *Why were you accused of scare-mongering?*

A widely syndicated interview with Marie-Thérèse de Brosses (*Paris-Match*, 17 July 1981), engendered considerable publicity for my book both in France and abroad. In this lengthy interview one important passage was ignored by the media, almost without exception. A great many magazines dwelt only upon the disasters Nostradamus had predicted since 1555. Well, weren't the two world wars appalling disasters? And was Nostradamus wrong to warn the generations to come? Surely not, I maintain, for thanks to the prophecies man is more than ever responsible for his follies, since he commits them knowingly.

I reproduce here the relevant passage from the *Paris-Match* interview:

J.-C.de F.: 'The Greek word 'apocalypse' means revelation and *not* appalling catastrophe or destruction, as it has come to mean currently. This revelation will be vouchsafed to man after 1999.'
M.-T.de B.: 'What was Nostradamus' purpose in publishing the Centuries?'
J.-C.de F.: '*To bring man a message of hope.*'
M.-T.de B.: 'I fail to see the hope in all the calamities he predicts for us!'
J.-C.de F.: 'He proclaims that the Apocalypse is going to bring man an era of extraordinary prosperity: the Age of Aquarius, the Golden Age. The Golden Age will return, he says so in his Letter to César, but meanwhile mankind will undergo the direst tribulations. . . .'

Two world wars, Hiroshima and Nagasaki, the French wars in Indo-China, the Korean War, the Algerian War, the Vietnam War, Cambodia and, more recently, Afghanistan, El Salvador, Nicaragua, Ethiopia, Angola, Iraq and Iran, the Falklands, the Middle East, Lebanon – aren't all these wars and revolutions actual catastrophes far more frightening than a book of prophecies?

In a 1981 review of a Morris West novel the journalist Jacques Cabau wrote 'One of a horde of imitations in the wake of current interest in Nostradamus. Approaching the year 2000, Apocalypse is in the air, and Morris West is its prophet.' Cabau concludes: 'West is no Graham Greene, but he exploits men's great millennial fears and his novel ends by pulling out all the stops, on a note of suspenseful ambiguity where fiction gets dangerously close to an uncertain reality.' But West did not have to put up with the sort of insults and lies which I came in for.

A 1982 article in *Le Monde* contained an account of the death of Michel Fazilleau, who killed himself using a method described in *How to Commit Suicide*, a book by Claude Guillon and Yves Le Bonniec. The journalist commented: 'This is the first accredited case directly linking any death with this book's publication. Its publisher is not surprised. He was expecting something of the sort.'

My book is not known to have caused any suicides, and those who were scared by it were those who went to see films like *Jaws, Towering Inferno*, and *Earthquake*. Will disaster movies now be banned?

14. How do you arrive at the equation 3797=1999?

In his Letter to César, Nostradamus wrote: 'I have composed books of prophecies, each containing one hundred astronomical quatrains, which I wanted to condense somewhat obscurely. The work is comprised of prophecies from today to the year 3797. This may perturb some, when they see such a long time span. . . .'

Most commentators have taken the date 3797 quite literally. I was not content to do so because one must always bear in mind that Nostradamus 'condensed', deliberately obscured or codified his texts – by his own admission. Nostradamus dropped a sly, even humorous, hint when he stated that some people might be put off by such a distant date, i.e. 3797. Why should he have written that, had not this figure concealed some sort of trap for the interpreter?

But there is an even more obvious clue here. There was no need to give this 'date' and then add 'from today to', for it is surely self-evident that since his letter is dated 1 March 1555, and as he is talking of prophecy, his quatrains cannot refer to any earlier date. This tautology is untypical, for Nostradamus' style is concise.

The phrase 'from today to the year 3797' must therefore be looked at carefully, as though it were strictly mathematical: when in mathematics one says 'from point A to point B', it indicates a straight line, and Nostradamus is indicating between point 1555 and point 3797 a precise segment of time. The value of this segment of time is calculated by subtracting the former from the latter, and the result is 2,242 years.

This should be carried over to the biblical chronology given in the Letter to Henri, Second King of France, i.e. 4,757 years from Adam to Christ. If one adds to these 4,757 years 2,000 years AD, the result is 6,757 – which does not make up the full seven millennia. I believe this is the reason why Nostradamus 'fabricated' this extra segment of time – in order to cover the 242 years required to reach the year 7000 according to global chronology (6,999-6,757=242). By adding this segment of 2,242 years to the biblical reckoning one obtains 4,757 + 2,242=6,999 (i.e. 1999 AD, a date clearly specified in CX, Q72.

Two quatrains corroborate this calculation. The first, included in Vol. I, is CI, Q48:

> Vingt ans du règne de la Lune passés,
> Sept mille ans autre tiendra sa monarchie
> Quand le soleil prendra ses jours lassés,
> Lors accomplir et mine ma prophétie.

Interpretation

After twenty years of republican power, another will establish the monarchy until the seventh millennium [1999]. When this monarchy knows misfortune [Latin *lassae res:* ill fortune] then shall my prophecy be accomplished and terminated.

The second quatrain, CX, Q74, is from this second volume and concerns the first resurrection announced in Revelations 20:

> Au revole du grand nombre septième,
> Apparaîtra eu temps jeux d'Hécatombe:
> Non éloigné du grand âge millième,
> Que les entrés sortiront de leur tombe.

Interpretation

When the seventh millennium is reached, there will then take place a veritable hecatomb which will happen near the millennium. Then those who have entered the tomb will emerge from it.

All this confirms what I have always maintained – that Revelations, like Nostradamus' prophecies, is a message of hope. This knowledge may be a comfort during one of the darkest and most painful moments in the history of mankind.

As regards the end of the world, this does not concern us, our children or our grandchildren, since both Revelations and Nostradamus see this happening around 3000 AD, when the forces of destruction and misfortune are unleashed anew, following the thousand-year period of universal peace.

Abbreviations

AE	*ALPHA Encyclopédie,* 17 vols.
AVL	*Atlas Vidal-Lablache.*
AU	*Atlas Universalis.*
CUCD	*Chronologie Universelle,* Ch. Dreyss, Hachette, 1873.
DAFL	*Dictionnaire d'Ancien Français Larousse.*
DDP	*Dictionnaire des Papes,* Hans Kuhner, Buchet-Chastel, 1958.
DENF	*Dictionnaire étymologique des noms de famille,* Albert Dauzat, Librairie Larousse, 1951.
DGF	*Dictionnaire Grec-Français,* A. Chassang.
DH3	*Documents d'Histoire,* 3, Cours Chaulanges.
DH4	*Documents d'Histoire,* 4, Cours Chaulanges.
DHB	*Dictionnaire d'Histoire,* N. M. Bouillet, Hachette, 1880.
DHCD	*Dictionnaire d'Histoire,* Ch. Dezobry, 2 vols.

DL   *Dictionnaire Littré*, 4 vols.

DLLB   *Dictionnaire Latin*, Le Bègue.

DL7V   *Dictionnaire Larousse*, 7 vols.

DP   *Dictionnaire de la Provence et du Comté Venaissin*, Jean Mossy, Marseille, 1785.

DSGM   *Dictionnaire de la Seconde Guerre mondiale*, Jean Dumont, Historama, 1971.

DSH   *Dossiers secrets de l'Histoire*, A. Decaux, Librairie académique Perrin, 1966.

EU   *Encyclopaedia Universalis*, 20 vols.

GP & MR   *Garibaldi*, Paolo et Monika Romani, Les géants de l'Histoire, Fayolle, 1978.

HAB   *Hitler*, Alan Bullock, Marabout University, 1963.

HC4   *Histoire classe de 4*, Fernand Nathan.

HDA   *Histoire de l'Allemagne*, André Maurois, Hachette, 1965.

HDCAE   'Histoire de Chypre', Achille Emilianides, *Que sais-je?* no. 1009.

HDGM   'Histoire de la Grèce moderne', Nicolas Svoronos. *Que sais-je?* no. 578.

HDMJG   'Histoire de Malte', Jacques Grodechot, *Que sais-je?* no. 509.

HDVFT   'Histoire de Venise', Freddy Thiriet, *Que sais-je?* no. 522.

HEFDP   *Histoire d'Espagne*, Fernando Diaz Plaja, France-Loisirs.

HFA   *Histoire de France*, Anquetil, Paris. 1829.

HFACAD   *Histoire de France et des Français*, André Castelot et Alain Decaux, 13 vols, Plon et Librairie académique Perrin, 1972.

HFAM   *Histoire de France*, Albert Malet.

HFJB   *Histoire de France*, Jacques Bainville.

HFPG   *Histoire des Français*, Pierre Gaxotte.

HFVD   *Histoire de France*, Victor Duruy.

HRU   *Histoire du Royaume-Uni*, Coll. Armand Colin, 1967.

HISR   *Histoire de l'Italie, du Risorgimento à nos jours*, Sergio Romano, Coll. Point, Le Seuil, 1977.

HLFRA   *Histoire de la Libération de la France*, R. Aron, Fayard.

HSF   *Histoire de la Société Française*, L. Alphan et R. Doucet.

LCH3 et 4   *La Classe d'Histoire, 3, 4*.

LCI   *La campagne d'Italie*, Maréchal Juin, Ed. Guy Victor, 1962.

LDG   *La Dernière Guerre*, Ed. Alphée, Monaco.

LDR   *Le Dossier Romanov*, Anthony Summers, Tom Mangold, Albin Michel, 1980.

LFL XIV   *La France de Louis XIV*, Culture, Art, Loisirs.

LEGESGM   *Les Grandes Enigmes de la Seconde Guerre mondiale*, Ed. St-Clair, Paris.

LGR   *Les Guerres de Religion*, Pierre Miquel, Fayard, 1980.

LGT   *La Grande Terreur*, Robert Conquest, Stock, 1970.

LMC   *Le Monde Contemporain*, Hatier.

LMSH   *Le Mémorial de Saint-Hélène*, Las Cases.

LRFPG   *La Révolution française*, Pierre Gaxotte, Fayard.

LSEOA   *Le Second Empire*, Octave Aubry, Fayard.
LTR   *Le Temps des Révolutions*, Louis Girard.
LXIVJR   *Louis XIV*, Jacques Roujon, Ed. du Livre Moderne, 1943.
MAB   *Mussolini, le Fascisme*, A. Brissaud, Cercle Européen du Livre, Robert Langeac, 1976.
MCH   *Mussolini*, Christopher Hibbert, R. Laffont, 1963.
MGR   *Mythologie grècque et romaine*, Classiques Garnier.
NEE   *Napoléon et l'Empire*, Hachette, 1968.
NELGI   *Napoléon et la Garde Impériale*, Commandant Henry Lachouque, Ed. Bloud et Gay.
NLM   *Napoléon*, Louis Madelin, Hachette.
PCHF   *Précis chronologique d'Histoire de France*, G. Dujarric, Albin Michel, 1977.
PGB   *Pétain*, Georges Blond, Presses de la Cité, 1966.
VCAHU   *Vingt-cinq ans d'Histoire Universelle*, Michel Mourre, Ed. Universitaires, 1971.

2

THE EVIDENCE

What better way is there to reply to the sceptics than by pointing out the 'coincidences' between a number of events and various quatrains and sixains I translated up to and before May 1980 – when the manuscript of Vol. 1 went to press.

I am thus including in this chapter various texts from Vol. 1. To distinguish them from material newly translated for this volume, an asterisk precedes the title of all such texts. The cover of the 7 January 1982 issue of the magazine *L'Express*, bearing the headline '1981: SHOCK YEAR' provides perhaps both a good introduction and a good illustration. It features a long article looking back over the main events of 1981, with this introductory paragraph:

Another year ended – one which will leave its mark on twentieth-century history. Was the 1981 vintage good or bad? Let's not reply hypocritically: 'That depends.' It's almost impossible to list all the major events of the last twelve months – they're still happening. *For the French, it was the Year of the Rose, emblem of the new socialist government. . . .Abroad, coups, assassination attempts, wars. Poland, the Middle East, Iran, Afghanistan,* Africa, Indo-China, Latin America, Ireland, Spain: we live in ever more callous times, dominated by violence and threatened with a future none dare confront. *Pacificism itself could become dangerous.* . . . [My italics stress the particularly 'Nostradamic' comments.]

The article – to say the least – seems more catastrophic than pessimistic. No one was offended by it as they were by my book. Indeed, the article promises us sacrifices, violence and warfare. As regards the violence and warfare, *L'Express* was unfortunately all too accurate: riots in Paris, bloodshed in the Falklands, Iran, Afghanistan, the Lebanon. . . .

In 1980 no one had foreseen this shocking year – except for Nostradamus. I certainly did not – and I say this advisedly, after reading such a large number of articles that gave the impression that *I* rather than Nostradamus was the prophet! My sole aim was, and still is, to try to shed light upon what has been considered by too many people, for far too long, as meaningless nonsense.

MALTA AND LIBYA

* The Middle Eastern Origin of the Third World War

De l'Orient viendra le coeur Punique[1]
Fascher Hadrie et les hoirs[2] Romulides
Accompagné de la classe Libique,
Tremblez Mellites[3] et proches isles vuides.

CI,Q9

Interpretation

From the East will come the treacherous act which will strike the Adriatic Sea and the heirs of Romulus [Italians], with the Libyan fleet; tremble, inhabitants of Malta and its archipelago.

[1] *Foi punique:* bad faith. DL.
[2] Legal term for an heir. DL7V.
[3] Latin Melita: Malta DLLB.
See page 287 of *Nostradamus: Countdown to Apocalypse.*

History and commentary:

'*Malta: Base for Gaddafy?* At Malta a Libyan mission is turning the former British military airstrip at Hal Far into a helicopter base. There is concern in NATO circles that Col. Gaddafy, who maintains excellent relations with Maltese Prime Minister Dom Mintoff, is seeking to replace the British presence there, which ends on 31 March when the UK finally abandons her Maltese bases.' (*L'Express*, 20 January 1979)

This is exactly what did happen.

In its 9 February 1980 issue, *L'Express* wrote: '*Mediterranean Alert.* There are signs of covert Libyan involvement in Chad, the Sahara, Bangui and Gafsa . . .', while the ransacking of the French Embassy in Tripoli exposed Gaddafy's real schemes.

That leads me to the quatrains which directly followed the one above:

* Colonel Gaddafy Stirs up the Arab World against the West. The Great King: A Man of Culture against the Arabs

Prince libinique puissant en Occident,
François d'Arabe viendra tant enflammer
Scavant aux lettres sera condescendent,
La langue Arabe en François translater.

CIII,Q27

Interpretation

A Libyan chief of state, powerful in the West, will come to inflame so many Arabs against the French, then comes an educated and well-intentioned man who translates the Arab language into French.

See page 287 of *Nostradamus: Countdown to Apocalypse*.

History and commentary

Indeed, reporting the wrecking of the French Embassy at Tripoli, Christian d'Epenoux wrote: 'Since 28 January, the day after the attack on Gafsa by Libyan-trained commandos, Gaddafy's radio began a rabid hate campaign. Frustration is evident beneath all the triumphant communiqués and the interminable fantasizing speeches: this time *they had to rouse the Libyan masses against the French "aggressors" and direct their 'rightful anger' against them.* Matters came to a head on 4 February, when a crowd of 'spontaneous' demonstrators invaded the French Embassy, scaling the walls to ransack and burn the place. Vociferous young Libyans lowered the French flag and replaced it with the colours of the "Jamahirya". . . . That afternoon, *the same popular indignation was directed against the French consulate at Benghazi,* the country's second most important city, *and it too was destroyed. . . .*'

THE BOLOGNA STATION MASSACRE
2 AUGUST 1980

* The Revolution in Italy

Au lieu que HIERON[1] fait sa nef fabriquer,
Si grand déluge sera et si subite,
Qu'on n'aura lieu ne terres s'ataquer,
L'onde monter Fesulan[2] Olympique.

CVIII,QI6

Interpretation

In the place where God has built his Church [Rome] there will be so great and sudden a revolution that no areas or lands will escape attack. The revolution will reach Tuscany [Florence] after the Olympic Games.

[1] Greek ἱερός: holy, sacred, divine. DGF. Allusion to Christ's words to Peter: ' . . . on this rock', etc.
[2] Faesula = Fiesole, town in Etruria (Tuscany). DLLB.
See pages 269–70 of *Nostradamus: Countdown to Apocalypse.*

History and commentary

This quatrain typifies the difficulties that face the translator of Nostradamus. I had translated *Fesulan* as Fiesole, whose Roman name was Faesula. But Nostradamus had added an *n* on the end of the word, and this could not be for reasons of paragoge, for such an addition was not in order to aid the metre.

Bologna was in fact the town indicated, for its Latin name was Felsina – from which Nostradamus makes an anagram here, substituting *u* for *i*, which was then quite usual, these letters being typographically interchangeable at the time, as were *s* and *z*.

The Opening Ceremony of the 22nd Olympic Games, held in Moscow, took place on 19 July 1980. On 2 August following, a powerful bomb exploded inside Bologna railway station, killing 86 and injuring 200 more.

Rome had been the first major city affected by the revolutionary movements in Italy, whether Left or Right. Aldo Moro's assassination was the most spectacular exploit of the Red Brigades, which deeply influenced public opinion in Rome.

Nostradamus makes it clear that few countries will escape terrorist action of some sort: France, West Germany, Great Britain, Spain,

Ireland, Austria and Belgium are just some of the European countries involved. . . .

My error shows just how important it is to track down verbal minutiae in such a text.

AFGHAN RESISTANCE FIGHTERS BURIED SEPTEMBER 1980

* The Russian Invasion of Afghanistan. Afghan Resistance. Its Extermination

Le sainct empire[1] viendra en Germanie,
Ismaëlites trouveront lieux ouverts:
Anes[2] voudront aussie la Carmanie,
Les soustenans[3] de terre tous couverts.

CX,Q31

Interpretation

The Russians will come into Afghanistan; the Moslems will find these places open. The Afghans would like to keep Afghanistan; but the resistance will be buried.

[1] Russian Empire, the largest state in the world. Orthodox religion dominated Russia and the Tsar was its head since Peter the Great; the *Holy* Synod supported him in the administration of ecclesiastical affairs. DHB. 'Holy Russia' is a well-known expression.
[2] Certain Carmanian tribes, according to Strabo, led donkeys into battle. DL7V. Nostradamus refers to the Afghan resisters of the Soviet invasion.
[3] Latin *sustineo:* I resist. DLLB.
See page 328 of *Nostradamus: Countdown to Apocalypse.*

History and commentary

L'Express of 6 September 1980 ran an article on Afghanistan whose headline ran: '*The Buried Hospital:* Afghan Resistance Fighters Die Daily in Antiseptic Wilderness'. Patrick Laburthe's article described how two doctors from the International Medical Organization had helped construct an *underground* hospital from which wounded Afghan guerrillas unfortunately had only a slim chance of emerging, since it lacked even the most rudimentary antiseptics.

France-Soir reported a few days after this: 'Inhabitants of some Afghan villages relate that every evening after dark the noise of heavy bulldozers can be heard. Their sordid so-called *'excavation work'* is horrifying. Prisoners, teachers, intellectuals thought to be hostile to the regime, women and children too, were being *buried alive*, crushed and torn apart in the process.'

And Nostradamus in 1555 wrote 'the resisters will be covered by earth'. He also predicts that resistance to the invasion will continue.

THE ARMIES OF AFGHANISTAN AND IRAN. THE WAR BETWEEN IRAQ AND IRAN, 1981–82

* The Leader of Iran's Present to the West. The Attack on France and Italy Launched from Afghanistan

> Le grand Satyre[1] et Tigre[2] d'Hircanie,[3]
> Don présenté à ceux de l'Occean,
> Un chef de classe istra[4] de Carmanie[5]
> Qui prendra terre au Tyrren[6] Phocean.[7]

CIII,Q90

Interpretation

The great cynical person from the Tigris and Iran will make a gift to those of the Atlantic Alliance; then a military leader will leave from Afghanistan to land in the Tyrrhenian Sea and Marseille.

[1] Cynical or impudent person. DL7V.
[2] River in Asia, running into the Persian Gulf, in Iran.
[3] Hyrcania: region of ancient Asia extending along the south-east coast of the Caspian Sea, belonging to the Persian Empire. DHB. Today Iranian territory.
[4] *Istre*, form of *issir:* to go out, forth. DAFL.
[5] Province of the old Persian Empire, now part of Afghanistan. DL7V.
[6] Naples, important NATO base.
[7] Nostradamus adds *an* to the word *Phocée*, by paragoge and for the rhyme's sake. See pages 327–28 of *Nostradamus: Countdown to Apocalypse.*

History and commentary

In this quatrain Nostradamus mentions the Tigris and Iran. The main fighting in the war between Iraq and Iran has taken place, and continues, in and around the main towns of Bassorah and Abadan, both situated on the Tigris. It seems that Iraq may end up losing this war, and that a sort of northern front, involving Syria also, is under formation.

As for the Afghan army, *Le Soir* (28 April 1980) headlined: '5000 Russian tanks deployed along the *Afghan-Iranian* border' and the same article asked the question: 'Is so much armour and an undisclosed amount of missiles necessary just to "pacify" one country? *Doesn't this hide a far more important plan? What if this army moved into Iran tomorrow?*'

L'Express (21 May 1982) echoed *Le Soir*'s fears: 'Afghanistan: Soviet troops are now backed up by Mig 23 fighters and equipped with SA8 Gecko ground-to-air missiles capable of hitting their target at 6000 metres. American intelligence is said to be uneasy at the presence of this sophisticated weaponry, unnecessary for use against the Afghan resistance.'

Both papers, in articles two years apart, were asking Nostradamic questions without realizing it.

THE BALANCE OF POWER, THE USSR AND THE TYPHOON
9 FEBRUARY 1981

* The USSR and the War in Europe.
The USSR and Turkey

Des régions subjectes à la Balance[1]
Feront troubler les monts par grande guerre,
Captif tout sexe deu[2] et tout Bisance,
Qu'on criera à l'aube terre à terre.

CV,Q70

Interpretation

The regions subject to the USSR will come to trouble the mountains [the Alps] with a major war and will take prisoners of both sexes throughout Turkey, so that at dawn there will be cries from one country to another.

---

[1] Seventh sign of the Zodiac: the Egyptians consecrated Libra and Scorpio to the god of evil, Typhon (or Set) who, not content with this astronomical homage, also required the sacrifice of red-haired men. DL7V. There is thus a triple allusion to the seven Eastern Bloc countries; to the revolution (Typhon/Typhoon); and to the Reds.

[2] Contraction of *de le*. DAFL.

See pages 385–86 of *Nostradamus: Countdown to Apocalypse*.

History and commentary

Interpreters of this quatrain have all hitherto taken the word *Balance* to refer to the USA, because of the symbolic scales of justice.

I did not share this view for two reasons. First, I noticed that Nostradamus had written 'Balance' with a capital B, and the word was printed thus in all the old editions, even though it is a common noun. Secondly, it seemed odd to envisage the USA coming to initiate a full-scale war in the Alps, which Nostradamus simply called 'the mountains', referring to the most important mountain range in Europe.

So I came to the conclusion that the zodiacal sign Libra was intended, i.e. the USSR in symbolic terms. This mythological method of concealing the meaning through riddles is common in the Centuries.

The magazine *Le Point* (9 February 1981) ran an article on the USSR's new submarine, called the Typhoon, and I quote: 'The Typhoon is simply a nuclear submarine armed with nuclear missiles . . . but it is one and a half times larger than any of its Western counterparts. We can assume, then, that it is also capable of launching far more nuclear missiles with multiple warheads.'

As if this were not enough to confirm my interpretation, one reads elsewhere in the same issue: 'SALT: Row Over Typhoon. By coding information received from their new Typhoon missile, the Soviets are thwarting US surveillance attempts. It is proving impossible to confirm whether the new missile, still in the testing stage, has more than the fourteen nuclear warheads authorized by the SALT 2 agreement. The latter has not yet been ratified by the Americans, but its violation by the Russians could prompt the Reagan administration to follow suit.' It is not the USA but the USSR, then, which has named both a new type of submarine and a new missile Typhoon.

10 MAY 1981

* The Left in Power. Revolutionary Upheavals

Sur le milieu du grand monde[1] la rose,[2]
Pour nouveaux faicts sang public espandu:
A dire vray, on aura bouche close:[3]
Lors au besoing tard viendra l'attendu.

CV,Q96

Interpretation

When socialism is in power amid the bourgeoisie, the people's blood will
flow because of new acts. To tell the truth, freedom of expression will
disappear. Then the awaited helper will arrive late because of penury.

[1] *Grand monde:* expression for important, affluent, influential people as a whole or a class. DL7V.
[2] Emblem of Socialist party in France.
[3] To silence someone, i.e. make them keep their mouths shut. DL7V.
See page 278 of *Nostradamus: Countdown to Apocalypse.*

History and commentary

François Mitterrand was elected President of the Republic on 10 May
1981. The following month this victory was confirmed by a sweeping
left-wing majority in the National Assembly. The first opinion polls in
M. Mitterrand's favour appeared only a month before 10 May, six
months after publication of the first volume of this book. The rose had
indeed 'blossomed' in France (cf. the next quatrain). *Le Point* (27 April
1981) wrote: 'Mitterrand: Rosy Prospects. For the first time the Socialists
top 25% according to opinion polls. On 22 May, the new President will
be returned to office holding a rose.'

Nostradamus predicted in this quatrain that after the rose had arrived,
civilian blood would be shed. One must not therefore expect assassination
attempts against specific individuals, but blind terrorism directed against
innocent passers by.

On 29 March 1982, less than a year after the change of government,
a bomb exploded in Toulouse, killing 5 people and injuring 27 more.
On 22 April 1982 a booby-trapped car exploded in Rue Marbeuf, Paris,
leaving one dead and 63 injured. This incident prompted one French
magazine to declare on its cover: 'Terrorism: War Declared on France'.
On 21 July 1982 another bomb exploded – on the Place St-Michel, Paris

– wounding 11 people, 3 of them seriously. Since then the bloodshed has steadily increased and in the following months there were various incidents which 'made the people's blood flow'.

Le Point (16 August 1982) wrote: 'A year ago, in their prophecies about France, the most hardened pessimists might have put their money on an economic decline like England's or a breakdown of law and order like Italy's. Unfortunately their wager must remain open.'

* The Death of the Pope at Lyon.
The Left in Power in France

Romain Pontife garde de t'approcher
De la cité que deux fleuves arrose:[1]
Ton sang viendra auprès de là cracher,
Toy et les tiens quand fleurira la Rose.[2]

CII,Q97

Interpretation

Roman Pope, do not approach the town which two rivers water [Lyon]. Your blood and that of your followers will flow near this spot, when the left gets into power.

[1] Lyon, whose two rivers are the Rhône and Saône.
[2] Emblem of the French Socialist party.
See page 277 of *Nostradamus: Countdown to Apocalypse.*

---

* Extract from *Prophecies of Maistre Michel Nostradamus, explained and annotated,* by Dr M. de Fontbrune (Cahors, 1958, 11th edition):

Sur le milieu du grand monde la Rose[1]
Par nouveaux faicts sang public espandu:
A dire vray on aura bouche close
Lors au besoing tard viendra l'attendu.

CV,Q96

Interpretation

Among people of importance, England, as the result of a new state of things, will see the blood of her people shed. . . .In fact, people will be forced to keep silent, but then, if required, the expected saviour will come in due course.

¹ Rose: symbol here for the Houses of York and Lancaster.

History and commentary

On 13 May 1981, three days after the election of Mitterrand, there was an assassination attempt against Pope John-Paul II, committed by a young Turkish Moslem fanatic in St Peter's Square, in the very heart of the Vatican.

These two quatrains (CII,Q97 and CV,Q96) were largely responsible for the publicity my book received, but the one about the Pope, in particular, was pressed into service by fantasizing interpreters who wanted to link Nostradamus' text to this specific incident at all costs. But the quatrain mentions a city on two rivers: the Vatican *City* itself stands on none. The misrepresentation experts then discovered two Roman rivers not in the Vatican City – the greater and lesser Tiber, which anyhow are only one river! I would advise all such fashionable disprovers of my reading of this quatrain that in Vol. 1 there are several more quatrains that make it clear that Lyon is being referred to, namely: CVII,Q22; CVIII,Q46; CVIII,Q62; and CIX,Q68.

As regards the word 'rose', I have been accused of misrepresenting Nostradamus' text by substituting a capital *R* for a lower-case one. There again my critics omit to mention that CV,Q96 in Vol. 1 is included with a lower case *r*, and that in both instances, capital letter or otherwise, I translated the word 'rose' as socialism! Had they wanted to research the matter properly, they would have seen that it is in my father's book that rose is written with a capital *R*. I merely forgot to correct one of the two. I would also add that I have found no edition, ancient or recent, giving the word 'rose' with a capital *R*. (I reproduce here verbatim the relevant passage from my father's 1958 book, in which 'Rose' is written with an initial capital and translated as England.)

Being familiar with this quatrain, I knew that the Pope's life would be in danger whenever (and not because) socialism gained power in France. The question that must be asked today is this: was the May 1981 assassination attempt a warning or a precursor of an eventual assassination – on 13 December at Lyon – of Pope John-Paul II?

An additional proof that this quatrain cannot apply to the 13 May attempt is that Nostradamus wrote: '*toi et les tiens*' (you and your entourage) – and no member of the Papal escort was wounded.

Without wishing to draw any conclusion from them, I shall now list various strange 'coincidences' that have struck me between the famous prophecy of Fatima in Portugal and the attempt on John-Paul's life in St Peter's Square on 13 May 1981.

The first 'vision' at Fatima occurred on 13 May 1917, announcing not only the approaching end of the First World War, but also the installation in Russia of an anticlerical and atheist power with all its attendant executions and imprisonments.

The other appearances took place on the thirteenth day of the following months until 13 October 1917, and the Bolshevik Revolution! On 13 May 1981, the shot which hit the Pope was fired at exactly 17.19, as reported by numerous papers. Reversed, these paired numbers make 19 and 17, i.e. 1917. Over twenty-four hours, the number of combinations possible between the minutes and hours is so great that the likelihood of the assassination attempt occurring either at 19.17 or 17.19 is extremely slight.

In addition, the would-be assassin was a young Moslem fanatic. And it is curious indeed that the town of Fatima, which bears the name of Mohammed's daughter, was the site of these incidents.

Finally, in CIX,Q68, I 'interpreted' St Lucy's Day (and Lucia is the name of the last survivor among the three children from Fatima) as being 13 December – the date of the *eventual* assassination of the Pope.

THE ASSASSINATION ATTEMPT AGAINST JOHN-PAUL II AT FATIMA
12 MAY 1982

* The Traditionalists and Spain

Devant le lac où plus cher fut jetté
De sept mois et son ost¹ tout déconfit,
Seront Hispans par Albannois gastez
Par délay perte en donnant le conflit.

CVIII,Q94

Interpretation

Near Lake Geneva, where a more cherished [heresy: i.e. Calvinism] was launched, his supporters will be discomfited at the end of seven months. The Spaniards will be corrupted by the men of Albano [the traditionalists] and the conflict will be the reason for their loss.

[1] Crowd, troop. DAFL.
See page 299 of *Nostradamus: Countdown to Apocalypse*.

* The Schism and the Foreign Pope

Par chapeaux rouges querelles et nouveaux scismes
Quand on aura esleu le Sabinois[1]
On produira contre lui grands sophismes
Et sera Rome lésée par Albannois.

CV,Q46

Interpretation

Because of the cardinals there will be quarrels and a new schism, during which the Foreigner will have been elected. Great sophisms will be uttered against him and the Vatican will be harmed by the men from Albano.

[1] The Sabines were 'the foreigners' to the Romans.
See page 299 of *Nostradamus: Countdown to Apocalypse*.

History and commentary

On 12 May 1982, at Fatima, the Pope was the victim of an attack which the magazine *Spectacle du Monde* (no. 243, June 1982) described thus: 'Just as the Holy Father was leaving the Chapel a priest rushed towards him shouting "Down with the Pope!", "Death to the Council!" and "Death to Communism!" When arrested by the police, Father Juan Fernandez Krohn, *a Spaniard,* was found to be carrying a bayonet from a 1917 model Mauser rifle, as still used by the Portuguese Republican Guard. He confessed: "Yes, I wanted to kill the Pope." '

SOUTH AFRICA: A BASE FOR THE WEST? THE IMPORTANT ROLE OF SOUTH AFRICA IN THE THIRD WORLD WAR

* The USSR and the Warsaw Pact against South Africa. Fighting in Palestine

Tost l'Éléphant[1] de toutes parts verra,
Quand pourvoyeur au Griffon[2] se joindra,
Sa ruine proche, et Mars qui toujours gronde:
Fera grands faits auprès de terre saincte,
Grands estendars[3] sur la terre et sur l'onde,
Si[4] la nef a esté de deux frères enceinte.

Sixain 56

Interpretation

South Africa will see [things happen] on all sides when the supplier [Russia] joins up with the Warsaw Pact. Her ruin approaches and the war which always rumbles will cause great upheavals near the Holy Land [Israel]. By land and sea there will be great military forces when the Church has given birth to two brothers [John-Paul I and John-Paul II].

[1] Olifant (from Latin *elephantus:* elephant). Name given to several mountains and rivers in southern Africa, after the elephants the first Europeans encountered there. The Olifant mountains are in the western part of Cape Colony, near a little river, the Olifant, which flows into the Atlantic. DL7V.
[2] Cf. CX,Q86 '*Comme un gryphon viendra le Roi d'Europe*'.
[3] Battle flag. DL7V.
[4] Latin: when, at such time as. DLLB.
See page 416 of *Nostradamus: Countdown to Apocalypse.*

History and commentary

After Ronald Reagan's election, Bernard Ullmann of *L'Express* wrote on 17 January 1981: 'The first spectacular initiative announced by Haig, and directly after the failure of the Geneva Conference on Namibia, is a tour of southern Africa which (excluding countries like Angola, under Cuban or Soviet control) will very probably take in South Africa. Such a visit would have been out of the question for a Democrat President.'

'Out of the question', perhaps, for politicians indulging in speculations and theories, but not for Nostradamus in 1555!

The sudden importance of South Africa in American eyes was confirmed by a report in *Le Monde* (12 June 1981), which began: 'South Africa: Visit by Haig's chief aide. Washington will now be pledging firm support for the Pretoria regime.'

PACIFISM – JULY 1981

* Pacifist Myths, Causes of Wars

Les Dieux feront aux humains apparences,
Ce qu'ils seront autheurs de grand conflict,
Avant ciel veu serein, espée et lance,
Que vers main[1] gauche sera plus grand afflict.

CI,Q91

Interpretation

Myths will mislead men because they will cause great wars, before which men will see the sky serene, then land weapons [*espée*] and aerial ones [*lance*] will be even more distressing towards the forces of the left.

[1] Latin *manus:* force. DLLB.
See page 264 of *Nostradamus: Countdown to Apocalypse.*

History and commentary

The Peace Movement's first great demonstrations began in July 1981, originating in West Germany and spreading throughout Western Europe.

L'Express (31 July 1981) wrote: 'The Pacifist Pandemic: Peace Movement gaining ground throughout Europe, with the exception of France.'

The same weekly (1 January 1982) wrote: 'Even pacifism could become dangerous', and 'What if pacifist theories led to a war of annihilation?' These questions were almost verbatim the same ones I had posed in analyzing CI,Q91 in Vol. 1, back in 1980. The language of *L'Express* was more explicitly 'apocalyptic' than mine, but the point is that in October 1980 the Peace Movement as such had not greatly flourished.

SADAT'S ASSASSINATION
6 OCTOBER 1981

* The Conference between Arabs and Jews

L'ire insensée du combat furieux
Fera à table par frères le fer luyre,
Les départir mort blessé curieux,
Le fier duelle viendra en France nuyre.

CII,Q34

Interpretation

The mad rage of furious battle will make swords shine even among brothers seated at the same table; in order to decide between them, one of them will have to be fatally injured in a curious way; their proud duel will extend to harming France.

See page 289 of *Nostradamus: Countdown to Apocalypse*.

History and commentary

When identifying this quatrain with the Camp David Agreement, it was impossible to tell which of the two signatories would be assassinated, since Nostradamus had not been specific on that point. But in fact the assassination of neither Sadat nor Begin (had the latter happened) would have done anything other than destabilize the precarious balance of the peace in that sensitive part of the world. The proof of this is the way Egyptian policy towards Israel has changed since Sadat's assassination. Definitely one of President Mubarak's most publicized actions was the immediate release from prison of the Moslem Brothers jailed by his predecessor.

On 6 October 1981 the road to Heliopolis ('the solar city' as Nostradamus calls it) was packed. Egyptians had turned out in vast numbers to the festivities celebrating the anniversary of the crossing of the Suez Canal by their troops eight years previously. The Raïs was on the stand along with his Vice-President, Mubarak, various ministers and other religious, political and diplomatic VIPs. It was one o'clock when an army lorry from the procession halted in front of the grandstand. The driver and six other men leaped from it and opened fire on the stand. The Raïs fell, fatally *injured*, and died shortly afterwards. The media everywhere stressed the extraordinary nature of this political murder, labelling it 'unprecedented' and *unusual*.

As for the 'proud duel', one can perhaps, without distorting facts, point to international terrorism spreading.

The first country to welcome the assassination of the 1978 Nobel Peace Prizewinner was Libya, followed almost immediately by Algeria. (See CIII,Q27 and CX,Q38, Vol. 1.)

We should remember, finally, that at Camp David Sadat and Begin had declared themselves to be blood *brothers,* in that one was a descendant of Isaac, the other of Ishmael.

MILITARY RULE IN POLAND
13 DECEMBER 1981

* Religious Persecution in Poland

Persécutée de Dieu sera l'Eglise,
Et les saincts temples seront expoliez,
L'enfant, la mère mettra nud en chemise,
Seront Arabes aux Polons ralliéz.

CV,Q73

Interpretation

The Catholic Church will be persecuted in Poland and the churches will be expropriated. The mother [Church] will be stripped naked by her children, and the Arabs will ally with the Poles [Warsaw Pact].

See pages 306–307 of *Nostradamus: Countdown to Apocalypse.*

History and commentary

Before 13 December 1981 my understanding and interpretation of the above quatrain were fiercely disputed by critics, who quoted it as an example of my so-called fantasizing.

Since the Catholic Church supported Solidarity, the persecution by the military authorities of Lech Walesa and the worker-members of his union was thus also a direct attack upon the Church. That alone would have upheld my interpretation, but there are further supporting facts. In April 1982 the magazine *Le Méridional* said: 'Poland: two priests face a military court. For the first time since the Stalin Era, two priests are to be charged – one with sedition, the other with receiving and concealing weapons. This puts the Polish Church, hitherto perhaps too influential, into a tricky situation within a country virtually under siege.'

As for the alliance between Arabs and Poles (to which I added as personal commentary 'Warsaw Pact'), the mass circulation Italian daily *Corriere della Sera* headlined an August 1981 article: ('Libya Warns: We Should Join the Warsaw Pact'). This in fact took place in September, aboard a Russian vessel of the Soviet Mediterranean Fleet in the Gulf of Sirte off the Libyan coast. An account in *L'Express* (5 February 1982) further verifies the interpretation of this particular quatrain: '*Poland: Exchanges With Tripoli.* More than 200 Libyan army cadets have just arrived in Warsaw to undergo special arms training. A member of the Polish military council recently met Gaddafy in Tripoli.'

As regards Poland persecuted 'by her own children', this was how *Le Méridional* (14 April 1982) reported a broadcast on Radio Solidarity: 'The female announcer criticized the authorities for "declaring war *on their own people*".'

THE FALKLANDS: WARNING SIGNS?

* From the Second to the Third World War. Great Naval Battles

Un peu après non point long intervalle:
Par terre et mer sera faict grand tumulte:
Beaucoup plus grande sera pugne[1] navalle,
Feux, animaux, qui plus feront d'insulte.

CII,Q40

Interpretation

After a not very long interval a great war will break out on land and sea. The naval combats will be the most important. The ferocity [of men] will be worse than the war itself.

[1] Latin *pugnum:* combat. DLLB.
See pages 264–65 of *Nostradamus: Countdown to Apocalypse.*

History and commentary

Philippe Bernert, in an article in *VSD* (17 June 1982), wrote: 'According to London, on this occasion informed by American intelligence, the Soviets would have used the Falklands War to good effect, by testing their methods of electronic surveillance . . . Admiral Woodward's adjutant explained to us that it was as if the Russians were intending to rehearse for a naval war they would one day wage. . . .

'In the end, Soviet assistance delayed the British victory by only one week. Yet it was also a victory for Moscow, this time a technological one. Soviet spy satellites can now observe any area of the globe.'

The correspondence between the quatrain and this journalist's 'vision' is striking.

THE FALKLANDS WAR
2 APRIL – 14 JUNE 1982

* Great Naval Battles in the Atlantic

Après combat et bataille navalle,
Le grand Neptune[1] à son plus haut befroy[2]
Rouge adversaire de peur deviendra pasle
Mettant le Grand Occean en effroy.

CIII,QI

Interpretation

After a naval combat, England will know her greatest alarm. Then the Soviet adversary will pale with fear, having sown terror in the Atlantic [or the Atlantic Alliance].

[1] God of the sea. Always symbolizes England.
[2] Belfry: tower with a bell for sounding the alarm. DL.
See page 347 of *Nostradamus: Countdown to Apocalypse*.

History and commentary

On 2 April the Argentine army invaded the Falkland Islands. Who could have foreseen, in 1980, that the UK would have been involved in a major sea battle in the Atlantic? Nostradamus did!

The media all noted that not since the Second World War had there been a naval battle on such a scale, during which a dozen ships, both Argentine and British, were sunk.

In my interpretation of this text, the Soviet Union was involved in the war, which was principally a naval conflict.

Philippe Bernert wrote: '. . . As a rule the Argentines were not in a position to pick up and decode such communications. They had no reconnaissance vessel or aircraft in the immediate vicinity of the Falklands. Yet they were informed in very great detail. Wave after wave of Skyhawks and Mirages carried out rocket attacks on the two large troop carriers, *Sir Tristram* and *Sir Galahad*. It was something of a massacre. . . .

' "The Americans refused to lend us their AWACS, which would have averted the loss of several ships," sighed one of Admiral Woodward's adjutants. "But the Russians *did not hesitate to pitch in against us. . . .*"

'From first indications, the Russians appear to have been apprised of Argentine intentions since March. . . .Indeed, the vast Soviet electronic surveillance system over the South Atlantic was operative well before the Argentine attack. . . .'

This journalist goes on to explain that the Russians had launched two spy satellites on 31 March, followed by a third on 2 April, the very day of the Argentine landings on the Falklands. As though this already sophisticated system were not enough, four other satellites, with varying yet precise objectives, were launched on 16, 21, 23 and 29 April.

'Black Tuesday' had caused England her *greatest alarm* since 1945.

EVENTS AT MARSEILLE, 1982

* Discord Among the French.
Internal Strife at Marseille

L'accord et pache sera du tout rompuë:
Les amitiés polluées par discorde,
L'haine envieillie, toute foy[1] corrompuë,
Et l'espérance, Marseille sans concorde.

CXII,Q59

Interpretation

The peace agreement will be completely broken. Alliances will be destroyed by discord. The old hatred will corrupt all confidence and hope. There will not be concord at Marseille.

[1] Latin *fides:* confidence. DLLB.
See page 270 of *Nostradamus: Countdown to Apocalypse.*

History and commentary

The Auriol and Lucet affairs, a judge's murder, the siege on 23 June of a Moroccan district of the town by taxidrivers, and, above all, a 'fake invoice' racket, directly implicating the council of France's second city, form proof enough of discord in the Phocean city.

The magazine *Le Point* (5 July 1982), carried the headline 'Marseille: The Big Swindle' and continued: 'Smell of Scandal at Marseille. Twenty-one people questioned, including eleven council employees. An unhappy affair.'

It concluded: 'Since the news broke, the authorities have suspended the council employees concerned. Gaston Defferre has stated he will take legal action. This course of action will not be sufficient to dispel *the poisonous atmosphere that has been created.* For this sort of racket could only have come about thanks to a whole network of complicity, nepotism and double-dealing which the police are gradually uncovering. *At Marseille, people are awaiting the next episode.* And the ones after that.'

THE FIFTH ARAB-ISRAELI WAR.
THE FALL IN GOLD PRICES

* Peace Breaks Down in the Middle East. France and Portugal Hit by the Conflict

La foy Punique en Orient rompue,
Grand Iud,[1] et Rosne Loire, et Tag changeront
Quand du mulet[2] la faim sera repue,
Classe espargie, sang et corps nageront.

CII,Q60

Interpretation

Moslem duplicity will provoke a split in the Middle East. Because of a great person on the Jewish side, the Rhône, Loire and Tagus will see changes when the greed for gold has died down, the fleet will be engulfed, blood and sailors' bodies will be floating.

¹ Latin *Judaei:* the Jews. DLLB.
² Historical allusion: Philip, King of Macedon, used to say there was no impregnable fortress wherever a mule laden with gold could ascend. An expression of the irresistible power of gold. DL7V.
See page 291 of *Nostradamus: Countdown to Apocalypse.*

History and commentary

The magazine *VSD* (8 July 1982) reported that the Israelis had discovered a gigantic military complex being built underground in the vicinity of Sidon. This was going on while Yasser Arafat travelled on diplomatic public relations trips to Western capitals. It was undoubtedly the main reason for the Israeli invasion of Lebanon, since it enabled Israel to demolish not only the Sidon installations but also the Russian SAM missile bases on the Bekaa plain. This operation was initiated by a Jewish head of state, Begin, just when gold prices had been falling for several months (when hunger for the proverbial mule will be satisfied!)

As regards the engulfed fleet, this probably refers to the dozen or so Argentine and British ships sunk during the Falklands War in the South Atlantic. Nine hundred Argentine sailors swam or floated until rescued, apart from 350 more who drowned.

The possible sequence of events implied by this quatrain is hardly reassuring.

3

LETTER TO HENRI, SECOND KING OF FRANCE
Original text, interpretation and notes

This letter, with that to César reproduced in *Nostradamus: Countdown to Apocalypse*, page xx, is the second prose text of Michel de Notredame's prophetic work. In all the old editions (prior to 1610) it is placed between the seventh and eighth Centuries. In most of the post-1610 editions the letter has been printed at the start of the work, immediately after the Letter to César. This reorganizing of the texts might seem unimportant if the texts themselves did not vary. However, when I began working on the Centuries, twenty years ago, I followed the hypothesis that the position in the text of the Letter to Henri, Second King of France should provide the translator with a clue: namely, that it could not be properly 'decoded' until just over half the quatrains had been translated. That is why this letter does not appear in Vol. 1 of *Nostradamus: Countdown to Apocalypse*.

My own comments and interpolations are printed in italic; Nostradamus' own words are in roman type.

To the invincible, all-powerful and most Christian Henri, Fortunate King of France,[1] Michel Nostradamus his very humble and obedient servant and subject wishes victory and happiness. *[Most editions subsequent to those of Chevillot, Troyes, 1611[2] displace the word 'second' in this dedication address, so that 'Henry, Roi de France second' becomes 'Henry Second [or Henri II], King of France'].*

Because of the royal attention you have granted me, O truly Christian

---

[1] *Second*, from Latin *secundus*: fortunate, favoured, happy, auspicious. D.LAT. The adjective agrees with *Henry*, not *France*, and in this context the specialized Latinate usage rather than the more normal numerical connotation is always to be understood. *[Tr.]*

[2] Cf. Bibliography.

and victorious king, my face having been so long obscured,[1] I here
present myself before the deity of your boundless Majesty, and since I
was continually dazzled thereby, do not cease[2] to honour and justly to
revere that day when I presented myself before it for the first time, as
one does before such an extraordinary[3] and humane Majesty. Now, in
searching for an occasion to manifest to you my warm regard and frankness with determination I would strive to make fuller knowledge available
for your most serene Majesty. To this end, it was not possible for me
personally to make these things known to you, despite my particular
desire to bring to your acquaintance the sudden illuminations which have
brought me from the darkness and shadows before the face of your
sovereign power[4] and of the first Monarch of the Universe. So long was
I in doubt as to whom I should dedicate these three final Centuries of
my prophecies which make up the thousand [quatrains], and I decided,
after long and due deliberation upon my rash audacity, to address them
to your Majesty, as one not astonished (as that gravest of authors Plut-
arch, in his life of Lycurgus, relates) by the sight of offerings and gifts
made as sacrifices within the temples of the immortal Gods of that age,
lest any be astonished that no gold or currency dare be presented.
Nonetheless, seeing that your Royal splendour is also linked to an incom-
parable kindness, I address myself to you not as one did to those Kings
of Persia with whom one could not seek audience, still less approach,
but as to a very sage and prudent Prince. Thus I have dedicated my
nocturnal and prophetic prognostications, composed thanks to a natural
instinct, with the aid of poetic transports, according to the rules of
poetry, and for the most part in accordance with the calculations of
Astronomy corresponding to the years, months and weeks, and to the
regions, countries and most of the towns and cities of all Europe,
including Africa and part of Asia that shall know frontier changes, and
which draw near in all these climes – the whole being composed as by
a natural technique. Those who would do better to mind their own
business will retort that while the rhythm is easy enough, to understand
the ideas is difficult. And yet, O most humane of Kings, the greater part
of the quatrains are so improper that one would not know how to make
sense of them, still less interpret them. I was hoping, however, to leave
behind in written form events which will pertain to years, towns, cities
and regions, even for the years 1585 to 1606, starting from today, 14
March 1557. And going well beyond these dates until the coming of the

[1] Latin *obnubilare* = *assombrir* = obscure. D.LAT.
[2] Latin *desistere* = *cesser* = cease. D.LAT.
[3] Latin *singularius:* rare or extraordinary. D.LAT.
[4] Latin *oculus:* eye or power. D.LAT.

beginning of the seventh millennium, through careful consideration, as far as my astronomical computation and other knowledge has allowed me to range: the epoch [*start of the seventh millennium*] in which the adversaries of Jesus Christ and His Church shall begin to multiply; the whole has thus been composed and calculated by selected and well-arranged hours and days, as correctly as possible. And I have made my prognostications concerning events in times to come with a free spirit and out of reach; using the past and understanding the present, for thus shall one know the future by the course of time through all regions; and as I here specify I have put in nothing superfluous, so much so that it may be said: rigorous exactitude about the future is not entirely determined. It is indeed true, Sire, that thanks to my natural instinct passed on to me by my ancestors[1] I could only believe I would be prophesying; I have therefore admitted and joined this natural gift to my lengthy calculation, while emptying my mind, heart and soul of all care, concern and worry in order to ensure calm and tranquillity of spirit. All was achieved and presaged and this in part thanks to the tripod.[2] As many people attribute to me what credit is mine as what is not; only eternal God, who alone truly knows the pious or brave works of men, is the judge, whose defence I solicit against the calumny of the wicked who would furthermore inquire to know how your own ancestors, Kings of France, cured scrofula or those of other nations healed the bites of serpents, or yet others had divinatory powers, and many other cases it would take too long here to recount. And so despite the malignity of the spirit of evil which will manifest itself in the course of time, after my death my writing will be better known than during my lifetime; and even were I to be mistaken in my calculation of epochs, none could do anything about that. May it please your more than Imperial Majesty to pardon me, protesting before God and His Saints, since I affirm that I have written nothing in the present letter contrary to the true Catholic faith, conveying the astronomical calculations in accordance with my knowledge: for the spaces of time, since the first men who preceded us, are such, and I start from the correctness of the most reputable judgement, that Adam, the first man, preceded Noah by 1,242 years, not calculating the times by Gentile reckoning as Varro has described them, but going solely by the Holy Scriptures and by my own weak intellect aided by my astronomical computations. After Noah, his day, and the universal flood, came

---

[1] Latin *avitus:* concerning one's ancestors. D.LAT.

[2] Greek Τρίπους: aloft, from a tripod, like the Sibyl. DG. Sibyls were the legendary priestesses of Apollo, endowed with the gift of prophecy. Erythrea was the most revered of these, as acknowledged by the author of the *Dies Irae* ('*Teste David cum Sibylla*'). David announced the end of the world, or day of wrath, as did the Sibyl. DL7V.

Abraham 1,080 years later, who was a remarkable Astrologer by all accounts, inventing the Chaldean alphabet. After him came Moses, 515 or 516 years later, and from Moses to David's time 570 years elapsed. Thereafter, from David to the time of Our Saviour and Redeemer Jesus Christ, born of the unique Virgin, 1,350 years passed: some might object that this reckoning is not accurate since it differs from that of Eusebius. And since the era of man's Redemption up to the detestable seduction of the Saracens, 621 years went by; from which one can readily calculate years past, although my reckoning is not good and valid for all nations because the whole has been calculated by the heavenly courses, along with intuitions in some subsecive hours and by the spirit of my distant ancestors: but the injustice[1] of our epoch, O Most Serene King, requires that these most secret events be manifest only by enigmatic phrases having but one sense and one meaning alone, without any ambiguity therein or doubtful calculation; but rather I profoundly obscured all by natural intuition, drawing closer to the language of the one thousand and two prophets acknowledged since the Creation of the world, according to the reckoning and to the Phoenician[2] Chronicle of Joel.[3] 'I will pour out my spirit upon all flesh; and your sons and your daughters shall prophesy'.[4] But such a prophecy proceeded from the mouth of the Holy Spirit, which was the sovereign eternal power, so that certain of these prophets, with the aid of the celestial movements, predicted great and marvellous happenings. But I do not here ascribe such a title for myself. Certainly[5] if it please God, I confess that all comes from Him and therein I render Him thanks, honour and immortal praise, without my having used divinatory methods derived from[6] fate, but thanks to God and my natural intuition, the whole in accord with the movement of heavenly bodies, so that I saw as in a burning mirror, as if by an obscured vision, the great, sad and prodigious incidents and calamities which affect most inhabitants.[7] First, God's Churches, secondly those purely material forces, will enter into such a decadence, with thousands of further calamitous events, and in due course of time the future will be known.

★ ★ ★

[1] Latin *injuria*: injustice. D.LAT.

[2] The Carthaginians, or Punic peoples (*Poeni*) were of Phoenician origin. DCEM. The Phoenicians were Semitic.

[3] Old Testament prophet, whose prediction of the Last Judgement in the Valley of Jehosaphat ends his book. Part of the Jewish canon, his book has always been regarded by the Church as inspired. DL7V.

[4] Joel 2:28 (AV). *Tr.*

[5] *Ia*: certainly, indeed. DAFL.

[6] Latin *provenire*: to grow, develop, derive from. D.LAT.

[7] Latin *cultor*: inhabitant or dweller. Virgil. D.LAT.

Nostradamus' general account of his prophecy ends here. Besides describing the divine origin of his nocturnal visions; his work methods and arrangement of the quatrains; the way he used 'coincidences' between planetary positions – by astronomy, and his chronology of man's history, this first section also gives a significant pointer both to the purpose and to the geographical boundaries of his vision.

This is of prime importance to the interpreter who, seeking to decode a great number of geographical names, should therefore look for cities, mountain ranges, rivers, villages etc. within the areas specifically mentioned.

To confuse the unperceptive, Nostradamus wrote that his quatrains are so 'improper [*i.e. unpolished*] that one would not know how to make sense of them, still less interpret them'. *Further on he stresses that his enigmatic phrases have one meaning and one only, and ends this first section with* 'the future will be known'. *This bears out a phrase in his Letter to César:* 'these things will be universally understood upon earth'. *The occultists and esoteric commentators who try (drawing on CI,QI, which refers to the bronze tripod) to prove that Nostradamus used divinatory methods (i.e. astrology, geomancy, necromancy, chiromancy etc.) cannot have read this important passage:* 'without my having used divinatory methods derived from fate, but thanks to God and my natural intuition'. *This statement carries additional weight, for it contradicts those who advocate that man's history is predestined – an unacceptable attitude which relieves man of responsibility for his acts and thus for his history. God would thus become a sort of sadist, amusing Himself by playing out a huge cosmic war game with men's lives. One can understand why Nostradamus, writing to César, therefore talks of man's free will.*

This is also why Nostradamus warns modern astrologers bound by Ptolemaic theories. Such inflexibility allows man only the despair of a life over which he would have neither responsibility nor control.

The conclusion (and this is borne out by the Old and New Testaments), is that prophecy is a warning to man. This explains why prophecies are generally of disasters, since their aim is to inform man of the misfortunes towards which he is heading through acts for which he is entirely responsible. St Thomas Aquinas, relating one of St Catherine of Siena's visions, wrote: 'The prophecies which come from Me [God] strike terror at first, but are fulfilled in a sensation of security.'[1]

At this point the prophetic section of the Letter to Henri begins. Nostradamus is to move back and forth through time, giving the impression (as in the

---

[1] *Introduction to the Theology of St. Thomas Aquinas*, R. Sineux (Paris, 1975).

quatrains), that he has set down sentences and phrases without any particular or precise order.

For God will watch the long sterility of the Great Lady, who shortly afterwards shall conceive two principal children. . . .

The phrase 'Great Lady', as used by Nostradamus, refers to the Queen (cf. Sixain 55, Vol. 1) whose descendants will not reign, hence the word 'sterility' as applied here to denote the end of the elder line of the Bourbons. Marie Antoinette, married in 1770, did not give birth to her first child until 1778. This was Marie-Thérèse Charlotte, Duchess of Angoulême. Her second child, Louis-Joseph, was born three years later, in 1781, dying in 1789. The third and last child, Louis XVII, was born on 27 March 1785. After Louis-Joseph's death, then, Marie Antoinette was left with two principal (surviving) children who would be imprisoned with her.

But [*the Queen*] being in peril, she will find herself in the fray[1] because of the audacity of the era of death [*the Terror*] endangering [*the monarchy*] in the eighteenth century, and it will not go beyond the thirty-sixth [*king*] and there shall remain three men and one woman.

Here Nostradamus places the end of the monarchy as the end of the eighteenth century, later giving the precise date, 1792. The main Bourbon line is to die out with the demise of Charles X, brother of Louis XVI. From Hugues Capet to Charles X there are thirty-six kings of France. The Capets comprise Hugues Capet, Robert II, Henri I, Philip I, Louis VI, Louis VII, Philip II, Louis VIII, Louis IX, Philip III, Philip IV, Louis X, John I, Philip V, Charles IV – a total of fifteen kings in the direct Capet line. Then come the Valois rulers: Philip VI, John II, Charles V, Charles VI, Charles VII, Louis XI, Charles VIII – a total of seven kings, followed by one Valois-Orléans, Louis XII, and the Valois-Angoulême line: François I, Henri II, Francis II, Charles IX and Henri III (five kings). These are succeeded by the elder branch of the Bourbons: Henry IV, Louis XIII, Louis XIV, Louis XV, Louis XVI, Louis XVII (six kings) and finally by Louis XVI's two brothers, Louis XVIII and Charles X.

After the disappearance of Louis XVII, there will thus remain three men who become king: Louis XVIII, Charles X and Louis-Philippe I, and one woman, Madame Royale, Marie-Antoinette's daughter.

Then there will be two emperors: [*Napoleon I and Napoleon III*] who will not have had the same father, besides the three brothers [*Louis XVI, Louis XVIII and Charles X*], who will be very different, then finally united and in accord, and three-quarters of Europe shall tremble.

Louis XVIII was at first with the opposition, whether in the Assembly of

---

[1] *Ajostée:* mêlée, engagement. DAFL.

Notables or in the States General, but after the first excesses, he declared
himself for the counter-revolution.

The future Charles X, who entered Paris in April 1814, managed to
conciliate most people with his friendly demeanour, but the goodwill
towards him was soon dissipated when he signed, with a haste which
even cast a slur on Louis XVIII himself, a treaty depriving France of
her conquests since 1792.[1]

By going as far as Moscow, Napoleon I had indeed made three-quarters
of Europe tremble. But allusion is also made here to wars waged by Napoleon
III: the Crimea, Italy and the Franco-Prussian War.

During a shorter period [*in comparison with the thirteen centuries of*
continuous monarchical rule from 496 to 1792], the Christian monarchy will
be upheld and increased, the parties [*those of the French Revolution, i.e.*
Jacobins, Montagnards, Girondists etc.] having suddenly risen to power
but being just as quickly abased.

The Arabs will decline [*the conquest of Algeria began in 1830*], after
Kingdoms have been created [*Napoleon I's creation of Kingdoms in Europe*
for his brothers] and new laws having been promulgated [*the Civil Code*].

With other children [*Napoleon Bonaparte's brothers*], the first [*Napoleon*
I] will occupy kingdoms comprising a Lion, which will be enraged
because held in check by his relatives [*brothers*] thanks to the intrepidity
of his armies.

The following kingdoms included a lion in their coats-of-arms or on their
flags, and were occupied by Napoleon: Spain, Italy with the Lion of Venice,
Belgium and the Netherlands. The same is true of a great many German
provinces – Baden-Württemberg, Berlin, Rhineland, Bavaria, Hesse and
Schleswig-Holstein.

The successor [*Napoleon III*] will invade so far into Italy that for the
second time [*after Napoleon I*] the fury of war shall strike Rome.[2] He
shall fall because of Spain. [*The candidature to the throne of Spain of Prince*
Hohenzollern, cousin of the King of Prussia, was contested by the French
government. This opposition precipitated the Franco-Prussian War, the defeat
at Sedan, and the fall of the Emperor.] He will not be replaced by the
ancient monarchy [*but by the Third Republic*]. And thus will come about
the third inundation of human blood [*after the fall of the Ancien Régime.*
The first blood-letting was the Napoleonic Wars, the second the Franco-
Prussian War and the third the 1914–18 War].

And for a long time war will not be idle [*reference is made here to the*
wars of the twentieth century].

[1] DHB.
[2] Jovis – for Jupiter. On the Palatine Hill in Rome are the Temples of Jupiter Stator
and Victor, with another temple of Jupiter on the Capitol.

And the Republic[1] will be installed, which will cause the dominator [*the Tsar*] to fall with the help of a new pagan party [*Russian Communist Party*]. She will spawn two clans, one which will be faithful to her [Communist Party], the other which will remain unfaithful because of the encouragement of the Catholic Church.

Nostradamus refers here to the struggle which would develop after 1917 between the Communist party and the Catholic Church, especially in the Baltic States.

Then will be born another party [*Nazi*] which would like to ruin the former [*Communist*]; then there will be three regions which will create very different alliances, namely Italy, Germany and Spain, which will breed different parties by means of military coups.[2]

Nostradamus is predicting the creation of military dictatorships in Italy, Germany and Spain in their correct chronological order. Mussolini seized power in 1922 through his 'blackmail march' on Rome. In 1933 Hindenberg called Hitler to the Chancellery, and in 1936 General Franco came to prominence in Spain.

Leaving aside the fiftieth and fifty-second parallels. [*The fiftieth parallel crosses Cornwall, the fifty-second South Wales. Situated between the two, on the fifty-first parallel and thirty minutes, is London. Great Britain was to escape invasion during World War II.*]

And these countries will pay homage to the ancient religions[3] in the regions of Northern Europe [*Germany*]; beginning with the one on the fortieth parallel, which will tremble because of a useless fear; then shall tremble the most westerly, the most southerly and the most easterly. Their power will be such that they will form alliances and invincible unions through their warlike conquests.

The Nazi sects (the SS, SA etc.) would adopt the symbols and emblems of the Roman Empire, along with banners and huge, impressive military parades. This is why Nostradamus compares Hitler to Nero.[4] Madrid is situated on the fortieth parallel. The Spanish Civil War began in 1936, a prelude to the world war which followed. Then Hitler hurled his divisions westwards against Belgium and France. The Axis powers moved south, landing in Libya on 1 February 1941, and finally, on 22 June 1941, the Wehrmacht attacked the Soviet Union from the Baltic to the Black Sea. Moreover, in December 1941 the United States and Japan were at war also.

---

[1] Nostradamus frequently uses *fille* or *dame* to signify the French Republic (popularly symbolized as Marianne).

[2] Latin *manus*: force. D.LAT.

[3] Cf. CIII,Q76, Vol. I.

[4] Cf. CIX,Q17; CIX,Q53;CIX,Q76; and CVI,Q67, all Vol. I.

Here again Nostradamus lists the main theatres of World War II in their correct chronological order. The alliances formed by Nazi Germany constitute the historical term 'Axis powers'.

These military powers will be equal [*military regimes*] but very different in beliefs. [*Indeed there were considerable differences between Hitler, Mussolini and Franco, especially as regards their Asiatic ally, Japan.*]

Then a democracy still more powerful than the second [*France of 1789, after England*] will be received by two peoples [*USSR and China*], whose origin will be in the first democracy that has had power over all the world [*England and her power in the nineteenth century*] and then also in the second [*France*] and the third [*USSR*] extending its forces beyond Eastern Europe [*Asia*] as far as Hungary[1] which will have been conquered and occupied.

Nostradamus notes that the Soviet empire will extend both east and west after the fall of the Western European military dictatorships.

Then thanks to its navy the USSR will disembark[2] in Sicily[3] and the Adriatic after going through Greece[4] and [*West*] Germany, which will have succumbed, and the Arab forces after passing through Italy will be pursued and afflicted. Then the great empire of the Antichrist will begin in the Altai[5] Mountains and at Sevrej[6] whence he shall descend with innumerable troops, so that the coming of the Holy Spirit that advances along 48° longitude shall change place, pursued by the abomination of the Antichrist waging war against the great king [*Henri V*] who will be the great Vicar of Jesus Christ at the right and proper time; this event will precede the obscurest and darkest eclipse of the sun seen since the creation of the world, from the passion and death of Jesus Christ until then; then in the month of October there will be a great translatory movement, so much so that it will be thought the earth has lost its natural motion and is plunged into perpetual darkness. Before this there shall have been signs of the spring equinox[7] [*20 March 1999*].

In this passage Nostradamus puns upon Attila (whose epithet was The

---

[1] Pannonia: ancient Roman name for Hungary. DHB.

[2] Latin *exponere:* to disembark. D.LAT.

[3] Trinacria: name given to Sicily, because of the three capes in which the island ends. DHB.

[4] Myrmidons: name of ancient tribe in Thessaly (Greece). DL.

[5] Attila (Atila in French; *Tr.*) is an anagram of Altai: large mountain range in Central Asia, forming the northern edge of the great central plateau of Asia. It is divided into the Lower Altai, 47°55′ north by 80°155′ west, and the Higher Altai, south of Lower Altai, and north of Mongolia, on 48° latitude north. DHB.

[6] Zerfes: anagram of Sevrej, small town in the Lower Altai. AU. Note the equivalence of the interchangeable *f* and *v*.

[7] '*Point vernal*' – synonym for spring equinox. DL.

Scourge of God) and the Altai Mountains, to signify that, like Attila, the Antichrist will be born in Mongolia. As for the town of Sevrej, which Nostradamus writes 'Zerfes', it seems to have been transcribed phonetically, as if the name but not the spelling of the place had been dictated to him.

Nostradamus tells us that the Holy Spirit will be chased from the forty-eighth parallel. Not only does Paris lie on this, but also Ulan Bator, capital of Mongolia.

As in CII,Q72, Nostradamus precisely indicates that this invasion from Asia is to be launched before the eclipse of 11 August 1999, which will be visible in the Northern Hemisphere, along 48° longitude, and which will be total. He states that this invasion is to start in July 1999. In October of that same year there will be a natural phenomenon on a vast, global scale.

So as to be even more specific about this year, 1999, Nostradamus gives a point of reference (20 March) which allows us to situate the invasion threat.

And this will succeed extreme changes of power and revolutions,[1] with tremblings of the earth [*allusion to the tanks which are going to appear in the World War II theatres of operations*], with multitudes of the new Babylon,[2] unhappy daughter whose abomination will be increased by the first holocaust; and she will last only seventy-three years and seven months.

Nostradamus establishes a parallel between Nebuchadnezzar, who persecuted the Jews and led them captive into Babylon (now Iraq), and Nazi Germany's persecution of the Jews – to which history has now given that very same epithet 'The Holocaust'! As regards the duration of this new Babylon, German unity was born with the Treaty of Frankfurt, 10 May 1871, one of whose most important conditions was the annexation of Alsace-Lorraine.[3]

Between 4 and 12 December 1944, Alsace and the Saar were progressively liberated. From 10 May 1871 to 10 December 1944 there are precisely seventy-three years and seven months.

Then [*a branch*] will spring from the trunk that has long remained barren, and will come from the fifth rank[4] to renew the whole Christian church. And a great peace, union and agreement will be made between people[5] separated and lost because of the various powers. And there will be such a peace that the one who has originated and set in motion the

---

[1] Latin *permutatio:* revolution. D.LAT.

[2] Babylon: The Jews were held in captivity in this town for seventy years (605–536 BC). DHB.

[3] Cf. CVI,Q87, Vol. I.

[4] Of nobility. Each generation counted since the first member of the particular family in question was ennobled. DL7V.

[5] *Front:* brow; in poetic terms, the actual person. DL.

warring faction against the diverse religions [*the Soviet atheistic and anti-religious system*] shall be cast into the depths of a prison[1] and the Country of the Violent[2] [*USSR*] shall be united, having played the sage.

Countries, towns, cities, powers and regions which will have abandoned the first paths they took [*Marxism*] in order to free themselves, shall be deprived of their liberty [*Hungary, Czechoslovakia, Angola, Afghanistan, Poland*], sinking into a deep captivity, and religion will be completely persecuted. They will begin by attacking the left [*Communist Party revisionists*] only to attack the right in turn, ruining[3] godliness for a long time with their own holy writ [*or Bible*]. After this great dog will appear the even greater hound [*the Antichrist*] who shall destroy all, even what had been destroyed[4] before him, after the churches are restored to their first state and the clergy functioning once again, then he shall spread debauchery and lust[5] and shall commit a thousand crimes.

This will come to pass shortly after another desolation [*World War II*], which will culminate in the military powers [*the Axis*] losing in two wars[6] [*the two world wars*] and they shall keep only[7] their flags [*allusion to the partition of Germany*].

These military powers will drag their nations into a swing towards the right [*fascist regimes*], when they will not want to accept putting out the cutting hand [*reference to the fascist salute*] and will affect the entire world [*world war*] until the birth of an offspring from that branch for so long sterile [*the Bourbons*].

This suggests that the Bourbon child will be born in 1945 or 1946, which would make his age today about thirty-eight.

He shall deliver the people of the world from this well-meaning[8] and voluntary servitude [*the countries opting for Marxist regimes*], being himself under the protection of Mars [*war*] which will have despoiled God[9] [*religion*] of honour and dignity, in order to liberate the town built and situated in another very small Mesopotamia [*Lyon, between the Saône and the Rhône*].[10]

---

[1] Latin *barathrum:* deep pit, after a ravine west of Athens, into which criminals were thrown, whose sides were planted with knives to cut the malefactors in their fall. DL7V.

[2] Latin *rabiosus:* fierce, violent. D.LAT.

[3] Latin *profligare:* to annihilate, ruin. D.LAT.

[4] Latin *perpetrare:* to achieve, execute, carry out thoroughly. D.LAT.

[5] Latin *mertricius:* trade of courtesan, prostitution. D.LAT.

[6] Sword – symbol of war and battle. DL7V.

[7] *Oter:* to take away, deprive of. DL7V.

[8] Latin *benignus:* generous, benevolent. D.LAT.

[9] Jupiter: father of heaven, ruling principle or God.

[10] Cf. CIII,Q46; CII,Q35; CIX,Q68; and CVIII,Q62, all Vol. 1.

The head of the government [*Pflimlin in 1958*] will be expelled from power and swept away like a feather, unaware of the conspirators' plot: they will have at their head the second Thrasibulus [*General de Gaulle*], who for a long time will have organized all this affair.

Parallels drawn between the first Thrasibulus, the Athenian general during the Peloponnesian War (431 BC) and the second, General de Gaulle, are referred to in Vol. 1.

Then enormities and abominations shall shamefully come to the fore [*debauchery of the consumer society which will come into being after World War II*] and be manifest in the shadows darkening the spirit, and that will happen[1] towards the end of the change in his power [*allusion to May 1968, followed by the departure of General de Gaulle in 1969*]; and the heads of the Church will show themselves remiss when it comes to the love of God [*disputes in the Church*][2] and some among them will abandon the true faith, and of the three factions [*left, centre and right*] that of the middle [*or centre*] will be somewhat in decline.[3] The first [*the left*] shall win all Europe [*West Germany, France, Greece, Portugal, Spain etc.*] and most of Africa through the destruction of the third [*the right*], with the aid of the poor in spirit, who, thanks to demented people, shall establish corruption and debauchery. The people will rise up to resist[4] and attack those who would promulgate new laws; also it seems that the countries weakened by the Orientals [*USSR, Poland, Romania, Czechoslovakia, Hungary, East Germany and Bulgaria*] may be victims of Satan freed by the creator of infernal prisons, in order to bring to birth great Gog and Magog[5] who shall wreak so much abominable destruction upon the Churches that the reds [*Communists*] and the whites [*Moslems*] shall thereby lose their judgement, power and strength. And their power shall be taken from them. And then there shall be more persecutions of the Churches than ever before. And at this juncture such a great pestilence[6] shall begin that more than two-thirds of mankind shall perish. So much so that one will no longer know the owners of the fields and houses, and the grass shall grow above knee height in the streets of the towns. And the clergy shall endure a total desolation and the warmakers [*USSR*]

---

[1] Latin *cedere:* to walk, go, come. D.LAT.

[2] On 29 July 1968 Pope Paul VI published the encyclical *Humanae Vitae*, on birth control. It pronounced against the findings of the commission of experts convened by the Pope himself in 1963, and led to much debate and controversy within the Church. VCAHU.

[3] The elections of 23–30 June 1968 saw the Gaullists triumph. They ended up with 358 out of 458 seats in the Assembly.

[4] Latin *sustinere:* to resist. D.LAT.

[5] Many editions have 'Gog and Magoh' for 'Dog and Doham'.

[6] Germ warfare?

shall use[1] the events at Cairo[2] in order to go from Malta as far as the Var coastline[3] and the great straits of the Bosphorus[4] shall be opened [*by the Russian fleet*].

Then there will take place a landing on the beaches to deliver Spain[5] from the Moslem occupation. And none of these attacks will be negligible and the place where Abraham lived [*Sichem*][6] will be attacked by the venerators of the West[7] [*to liberate it*]. And the city of Hashem[8] [*Beirut*] shall be surrounded and attacked in great strength from all sides by armies. But their [*Soviet*] fleet will be weakened by the Westerners, and this country [*USSR*] will know a great desolation; her greatest cities shall be depopulated and those who enter therein shall serve the vengeance of the wrath of God.

This section from the Letter to Henri should be compared with Ezekiel 38:

Son of man, set thy face against Gog, the land of Magog, the chief prince of Meshech [*Moscow*] and Tubal [*Tobolsk*] and prophesy against him. . . . And I will turn thee back, and put hooks into thy jaws, and I will bring thee forth, and all thine army, horses and horsemen, all of them clothed with all sorts of armour [*tank divisions*]. . . . Persia [*Iran*], Ethiopia, and Libya with them; all of them with shield and helmet [*Russian armaments*] . . . Gomer [*Turkey*], and all his bands; the house of Togarmah . . . and many people with thee . . . in the latter years [*before 1999*] thou shalt come into the land that is brought back from the sword, and is gathered out of many people [*the State of Israel in 1948*], against the mountains of Israel, which have been always waste . . .[9] And thou shalt say, I will go up to the land of unwalled villages [*the kibbutz*]; I will go to them that are at rest. . . . So that the fishes of the sea, and the fowls of the heaven, and the beasts of the field, and all creeping things that creep upon the earth, and all the men that are upon the face of

---

[1] Latin *usurpare*: to make use of, lay claim to. D.LAT.

[2] Greek Ἡλιούπολις: Heliopolis, i.e. City of the Sun, a town in Lower Egypt, was situated 11 km north-east of Cairo. DHB. Cf. CV,Q81, Vol. 1. Reference to President Sadat's assassination?

[3] Staechades: the four islands known by this name lie off the coast of the Var department of France. DHB. Cf. CVII,Q37, Vol. 1.

[4] Bosphorus, from a Greek word signifying passage or cattle track. DHB.

[5] Cf. CI,Q31; CI,Q93; and CVIII,Q48.

[6] Abraham left Haran with all his family, and, aged seventy-five, came to live in Sichem. DHB. Today Tell Balatah, town in Transjordan, occupied territory since 1967.

[7] Jovialis: pertaining to Jove/Jupiter. D.LAT. The planet Jupiter was regarded as fortunate by astrologers. DL7V. Nostradamus thus denotes the West, its allies and its good fortune. Cf. Presage 32; Presage 129; and CX,Q73, all Vol. 1.

[8] Hashem, tenth incarnation of Albar, supreme god of the Druze. DL7V. The Druze live on and around Mt Lebanon. Nostradamus thus indicates Lebanon here.

[9] Cf. CII,Q19, Vol. 1.

the earth, shall shake at my presence, and the mountains shall be thrown down, and the steep places shall fall, and every wall shall fall to the ground.

Chapter 39 continues:

Therefore, thou son of man, prophesy against Gog, and say, Thus saith the Lord God; Behold, I am against thee, O Gog, the chief prince of Meshech [*Moscow*] and Tubal [*Tobolsk*]. And I will turn thee back, and leave but the sixth part of thee [*the six Soviet satellite states*], and will cause thee to come up from the north parts [*Russia*], and will bring thee upon the mountains of Israel. . . . Thou shalt fall upon the mountains of Israel, thou and all thy bands, and the people that is with thee. . . . And I will send a fire on Magog. . . . And they that dwell in the cities of Israel shall go forth, and shall set on fire and burn the weapons, both the shields and the bucklers, the bows and the arrows, and the handstaves, and the spears [*missiles*] and they shall burn them with fire seven years . . . [*disarmament?*]

There is a remarkable parallel between Nostradamus and these two chapters of Ezekiel, the vision of the former being centred upon France and Europe and that of the latter upon Israel and the Middle East. Ezekiel's vision is even darker than Nostradamus'. Nostradamus goes on:

And the Holy Sepulchre[1] shall long remain venerated, at evening,[2] under the universal contemplation of the sky, the sun and the moon; then the Holy Places [*Jerusalem*] shall be exchanged [*annexation by Israel*] and shall shelter a small herd [*numerically: the Israelis*] and a large [*in terms of its importance to the West*] and they will be adapted to profane ideas [*Christian and Moslem alongside Jew*].

O what calamitous affliction shall the pregnant women then know, and the main Oriental chief [*China*] will be moved by the USSR[3] which will have conquered the West, put to death and imprisoned its children and women; and thus shall be accomplished the prophecy of the royal prophet:[4] please heaven that the cries of the prisoners[5] be heard and that their sons be delivered from massacre.[6]

---

[1] The gospels recount how Joseph of Arimathea buried Jesus' body in a new tomb hollowed from rock and situated in a garden near the site of the crucifixion. In AD 70 the suburbs of Jerusalem were destroyed during the Roman army's building of fortifications. In the fourth century St Helena, the Emperor Constantine's mother, had the ground dug up, exposing the sepulchre. Eusebius relates how a vast construction site appeared on Calvary. . . . The Holy Sepulchre became a place of pilgrimage for Christians. DL7V. From the fourth century until 1999 – '*longtemps*'.

[2] *Serain*: evening, nightfall. DAFL.

[3] Septentrion: the north, used, along with the word 'Aquilon', to denote the USSR, 'The Empire of the North'.

[4] David, second King of the Israelites. Poet and prophet, he left the Psalms as his enduring literary bequest. DL7V.

[5] Latin *compeditus*: one whose feet are shackled. D.LAT.

[6] Latin *interemptus*: killed; *interemptio*: murder. D.LAT.

The Psalms of David constitute a promise of deliverance to the people of Israel. To quote some particularly interesting and relevant passages: Psalm 22: 6–7:

But I am a worm, and no man; a reproach of men, and despised of all the people. All they that see me laugh me to scorn; they shoot out the lip, they shake the head. . . . [*verse 12*] Many bulls have compassed me: strong bulls of Bashan[1] have beset me round.

After this reference to antisemitism, the royal prophet speaks of the danger the Golan represents for Israel: this explains the outright annexation effected in 1981.

Psalm 46:

God is our refuge and strength, a very present help in trouble. Therefore will we not fear, though the earth be removed, and though the mountains be carried into the midst of the sea. . . . There is a river, the streams whereof shall make glad the city of God [*Jerusalem*], the holy place of the tabernacles of the most High. God is in the midst of her; she shall not be moved. . . .The heathen raged, the kingdoms were moved: he uttered his voice, the earth melted. . . . Come, behold the works of the Lord, what desolations he hath made in the earth. He maketh wars to cease unto the end of the earth.

This passage guarantees that Jerusalem will endure, untouched by war. Like Nostradamus, David announces an important depopulation of the earth and the coming of a universal peace.

Psalm 83:

For, lo, thine enemies make a tumult: and they that hate thee have lifted up the head. . . . They have said, Come, and let us cut them off from being a nation: that the name of Israel may be no more in remembrance. For they have consulted together with one consent: they are confederate [*the Arab League*] against thee. The tabernacles of Edom [*Jordan*], and the Ishmaelites [*Saudi Arabia*]; of Moab [*Jordan*], and the Hagarenes [*Saudi Arabia*]; Gebal [*tribes of Arabia Felix*], and Ammon [*Jordan*], and Amalek [*Egyptians of Sinai*]; the Philistines [*Palestinians from Gaza*], with the inhabitants of Tyre [*Palestinians from Lebanon*]; Assur [*Iraq*] also is joined with them: they have holpen the children of Lot [*head of the Moabites and Ammonites*]. Do unto them as unto the Midianites[2]. . . . Who said, Let us take to ourselves the houses of God in possession [*claims on Jerusalem*].

Nostradamus continues:

What great oppression will be wrought then upon heads of government and states, even those of Japan [*maritime and Oriental*], and their languages will be mixed in a great society [*UNO*], the Latin and Arab tongues,

---

[1] Today the Golan Heights.
[2] The Midianites, an Arab race who lived south of the Moabites, were defeated by Gideon. DHB.

through Carthaginian [*Libyan*] communication,[1] and all the heads of state of Asia shall be hunted, persecuted or exterminated, not by means of USSR forces, but in the century which is to come [*the twentieth, the aim of the prophecy*] because of three countries which have made a secret alliance and which lament[2] death and set traps for each other,[3] and this triumvirate[4] will renew itself for seventy years[5] and the renown of this party shall extend throughout the planet, and in spite of it, the sacrifice of the Sacred and Immaculate Host shall be carried on [*Poland, Lithuania etc.*] and two heads of the Soviet Union shall be victors over the Orientals [*Japan*] and there will be made among them such a noise and warlike tumult that all the Orient [*China*] will tremble with fright because of their brothers [*Japanese*], no brothers to the USSR. This is why, Sire, in this discourse, I include these predictions almost confusedly, and in order to know when each event will happen by counting the time which follows – is not necessary knowledge, or at least little in accordance with heaven. These predictions made with the aid of astronomy and other methods, and even by the Holy Scriptures, cannot not happen. Had I wished I could have put a calculation of time into each quatrain; but that would not have pleased everyone, and my interpretations still less, unless your Majesty granted me enough protection to do this, so as not to give slanderers pretext for attacking me.

Here Nostradamus takes up a theme he had already sounded in his Letter to his son César, repeating that his prophetic message will not be to most people's liking. (Indeed, criticisms of Nostradamus: Countdown to Apocalypse, *illustrate his point admirably!)*

However, I calculated that the years from the creation of the world to the birth of Noah came to 1,506 years, and from Noah's birth until the Ark was finished, that is up to the time of the flood, 600 years passed (it had better be established if the years were solar or lunar, or whether they took account of the mixture of ten [*days*][6] [*Gregorian calendar*]; Holy Scripture indicates that they were solar. And at the end of these 600 years, Noah entered the Ark and was saved from the flood. This universal deluge then lasted one year and two months. From the end of the flood to Abraham's birth there were 295 years. From Abraham's birth to

---

[1] Cf. CIII,Q27; CI,Q9; CV,Q14; and CIII,Q60 – pages 287, 288 and 289 respectively in Vol. 1.

[2] Latin *queri calamitatem:* to lament one's misfortune. Caesar. D.LAT.

[3] Latin *insidiari:* to set traps or ambushes. D.LAT.

[4] Reference to the Troika of the Soviet system?

[5] Nostradamus has 'cut down' this time span in order to keep the 7 of 1917 and that of 70 – the length of time Communism will have to spread over the world, i.e. until 1987.

[6] In 1582 Pope Gregory XIII, aided by a Calabrian expert called Lilio, deleted ten days from the calendar to bring the equinox to 21 March.

Isaac's birth 100 years elapsed. From Isaac to Jacob, sixty years passed. From Jacob's entry into Egypt until his departure was 130 years. And from Jacob's entry into Egypt until his departure 430 years elapsed. And from the departure out of Egypt up to the building of Solomon's Temple, in the fourth year of his reign, 480 years passed. Finally, from the building of the Temple to Jesus Christ, according to the calculations of the Gospel writers, 490 years elapsed. And thus, by this reckoning derived from Holy Writ, I calculate 4,073 years eight months, more or less. Now from Jesus Christ until the era of the differing sects [*twentieth century*] I shall add nothing, for I have reckoned and calculated my present prophecies according to the rules of astronomic links, and by my natural instinct, and when, some time later, Saturn makes his revolution from 7 April to 25 August, Jupiter from 14 June to 7 October, Mars from 17 April to 22 May, Mercury from 3 to 24 February and from 25 September to 16 October, Saturn in Capricorn, Jupiter in Aquarius, Mars in Scorpio, Venus in Pisces, Mercury for a month in Capricorn, Aquarius, and Pisces, the Moon in Aquarius, the head of the Dragon [*Draco*] in Libra: its tail in its opposing sign following a Jupiter-Mercury conjunction, with a quadrant giving an aspect from Mars to Mercury, and the head of the Dragon will be with a Sun-Jupiter conjunction; the year will be peaceful and without eclipse, and then not so at all, for it will mark the beginning of a persecution of the Christian Church more widespread than anything that has been done in Africa; and that will correspond to the end of [*the monarchy*] which will last until the year 1792 [*21 September 1792: abolition of the French monarchy and proclamation of the Republic*], which will be thought to be a new era; after which the Roman people will start to rise up and chase some obscure shadows in order to find again their original verve [*Italian unity and the Risorgimento*], not without great divisions and continual changes [*of governments*].

Venice in great strength shall raise the wings of power so high that she shall not be too far removed from the power of Ancient Rome. And in that time a great Turkish fleet shall be allied with the Italians[1] [*in the partition of Greece*], with the help of the Russian power, which will prevent the two Greeces[2] [*Royalist and Venizelist*] from having the same objectives. The country where the ancient triumphal arches were built [*Italy*] shall be allied with England.

There will be a great disorder in the Adriatic [*the Balkan question which would trigger off the First World War, following the assassination at Sarajevo, Bosnia*]. There will then be great disorder in the Adriatic [*Northern Epirus, Italy, Albania, Bosnia*], when what was united is

---

[1] *Ligusticus sinus:* Gulf of Genoa. DHB.
[2] *Cretenses:* inhabitants of Crete, hence Greeks.

reduced to barely a single house [*burning of Smyrna by the Turks*], and the superpower[1] Germany[2] will be involved in the conflict around the 45th parallel [*Austro-Hungarian Empire, which would disappear during the First World War*] as well as the 41st, 42nd and 37th parallels.

After Italian unity, Rome will adopt a policy of conquest. Nostradamus focuses upon the Balkans question which led to the First World War. To do this, he will give the latitudes of the towns, areas and countries surrounding the Balkans, and which are to be the scene of bitter and bloody fighting. Thus the 37th parallel crosses the Cyclades, the Morea and Cilicia. The 41st crosses Macedonia and Thrace, via Istanbul, Salonica, Monastir, Evros and Stroumitza. The 42nd takes in Macedonia, Albania, Italy and Bulgaria, via Rome, Andrinopolis and Skopje. The 45th goes through Serbia, Bosnia and Italy, also Belgrade, Bucharest and Venice. Readers who wish to understand more of the geographical, historical and constitutional factors involved in the events leading to World War I, including the relevant Greek background, should turn to Professor Nicholas Svoronos' book, which excellently describes the Balkan crisis which preceded it.

After geographically situating the starting point of World War I, Nostradamus goes on to describe Hitler as the second Antichrist (after Nero).[3] Hitler is thus designated as much for his persecution of the Jews as for his persecution of Christians. After service during World War I as a corporal in the Austrian Army, from 1919 Hitler was a member of the German Socialist party.

And in this same time and in this region [*the Mesopotamia of Europe*] the infernal power [*Nazism*] will attack the Church of Jesus Christ, giving all power to the adversaries of Christian law; it shall be led by a second Antichrist [*Hitler*] who persecutes this Church and the Pope, with the help of goverments[4] which shall fall[5] and be seduced by speeches [*of Hitler*], through their ignorance, and who shall do worse than a madman armed with a sword [*persecution of the Jews*]. The power of this Antichrist will last only until the end of him who is born near the end of the age [*the twentieth century, principal aim of the prophecy; Hitler being born in 1889*] and until [*the liberation of*] Lyon,[6] allied with the chosen one of Modena [*Mussolini. The Modena region, with Ferrara and Bologna, were the key starting points of Fascism*], who will support him[7] [*his power once*

---

[1] Cf. CX,Q100, Vol. I.
[2] The Mesopotamia of Europe: Germanic tribes between the Rhine and the Danube.
[3] Cf. CIX,Q17; CIX,Q53; CIX,Q76; CVI,Q67, all in Vol. I (pages 222, 223, 224 and 225 respectively).
[4] The Axis powers.
[5] Temporal, what passes with time, as opposed to eternal. DL.
[6] Cf. CIII,Q46, Vol. I.
[7] Latin *fulcire*: to support, sustain. D.LAT.

begun], through Ferrara, and he will keep himself in power from Liguria to the Adriatic, a little while after [*the invasion of*] Sicily.[1]

In 1921, prior to Mussolini's march on Rome, three towns in particular were important bastions of Fascism. On 3 April an extraordinarily well-attended demonstration took place at Bologna: 'The Festival of the Fascist Party'. A few days later, on 15 May, parliamentary elections were held. The Fascists scored a resounding victory: 35 candidates were elected, one of them being Benito Mussolini, who gained 172,491 votes at Bologna.[2] One of the main Fascist leaders was Italo Balbo of Ferrara.[1]

A year later, on 12 May 1922, Balbo flung his 40,000 troops into the conquest of Ferrara, then Rovigo and Bologna. The Fascist forces were also in action in Liguria.

At the start of September 1944, Lyon was liberated. One might ask why Nostradamus chose Lyon as the temporal reference point to mark the link between this town's liberation and the German Army's retreat in Italy behind the Gothic Line between Rimini and La Spezia, i.e. between Liguria and the Adriatic. There are two reasons. First, to indicate time: Lyon's liberation and the investment of the Gothic Line took place simultaneously. Secondly, because of the importance of Lyon in the history of the French Resistance. Robert Aron[3] wrote: 'On 28 August, the pincer movement began to operate from both sides. Paris, which had been liberated two days previously, was crossed by Allied divisions, some driving on deep into north-eastern France and Belgium, while others pushed towards Dijon. . . .The first objective was to be the link-up of the Allied forces in Provence with those in Normandy. To achieve this, they had to march on Lyon.

'Lyon, which with Dijon was to provide the mouse-trap in which the Wehrmacht could be caught, had since June 1940 played a vital role in France. As the centre of the Resistance, it also consequently became the capital of repression, terror and sometimes of discord. . . .' As for the persecution directed against the Catholic Church and its Pope by Hitler and Nazism, Hans Kuhner[4] wrote: 'The Concordat signed with Germany in 1933 was to the Nazi terror regime only a piece of paper and had been violated since its signature; shortly after it, a bloody persecution of Catholics began which lasted until the end of World War II. When Hitler came to Rome in 1938, the Pope refused to see the murderer of thousands of innocent people. He had the Vatican closed and left Rome conspicuously.'

★ ★ ★

[1] Trinacria, Sicily.
[2] The new Emilia was made up of the ancient provinces of Bologna, *Ferrara*, Forlì, Massa and Carrara, Modena, Parma, Piacenza, Ravenna and Reggio.
[3] HLFRA.
[4] DDP.

After reaching this point in his Letter to Henri, Nostradamus goes on to elaborate upon the Third World War and the Wars of the Antichrist (1999) waged by the Marxist regimes of the Soviet and Asiatic empires, allied with the Moslem countries.

Then Rome shall disappear.[1] The French Communist leader will be accompanied by a large number of people coming from the distant Soviet Empire which will impose the great law [*Communist*], and thus for some time the blood of the innocent shall be shed by the harmful[2] who will have risen up [*from their headquarters*]; then because of great revolutions[3] the things which keep memory [*books*] shall experience great losses, as will literature; and that shall be from the Russian side through divine will, and shall take place when once Satan is bound. Thus there will be a universal peace among men and the Church of Jesus Christ be delivered from all tribulation, after the inhabitants of Gaza[4] will have wished to mingle gall with honey by their infamous seduction, and that shall be close to the seventh millennium [*the year 2000*], so that Jesus Christ's sanctuary [*Jerusalem*] will no longer be trampled[5] by the feet of the unfaithful ones coming from Russia, the world approaching a great conflagration, although my calculations in my prophecies do not cover the whole course of time, which goes far further.

Nostradamus once again insists that his prophecy has a temporal limit – the seventh millennium.

In the letter I wrote some years ago, addressed to my son César, I quite clearly stated various points other than these presages. [*A summary of the method and thought behind the prophecies, as well as the origin of the latter and some cautions to the reader.*]

But here, Sire, I have included diverse great and marvellous events which our successors will see. And it is during this astrological calculation according to Holy Scripture that the persecution of the clergy shall begin, through the power of the Soviet Union united with the Orientals [*China?*]. And this persecution shall last just under eleven years and thus shall collapse the main leader of the Soviet Union [*Russia*]. When these eleven years have ended, its Southern ally [*the Moslem countries of the south: Iran, Syria, Iraq, Afghanistan, the Palestinians etc.*] will come to the fore to persecute the clergy even more violently, for three years, through a seductive apostasy, and via a person who shall derive absolute

---

[1] *Passer*: to die, disappear. DL7V.

[2] Latin *nocere*: to harm, be malevolent. D.LAT.

[3] Deluge, water, flood, whirlpool and typhoon are often used by Nostradamus to signify political upheavals or revolutionary movements.

[4] Azotos, in Greek, for Ashdod, one of the five Philistine towns. GAB. Nostradamus here denotes the Palestinians.

[5] Latin *conculcare:* to trample underfoot. D.LAT.

power from the militant Church [*Moslem fundamentalists?*], and the holy people of God who observe His Law and all religious orders shall be greatly persecuted and afflicted, so much so that the blood of the true ecclesiastics shall flow everywhere and one of these horrible temporal Rulers [*Iran?*] will receive such praise from his adherents that he shall spill more human blood of innocent churchmen than there is wine. And this leader shall commit unbelievable crimes against the Church, so that human blood runs in the streets and churches like heavy rain; and the rivers near us shall turn red with blood and the sea too will redden from a great naval war, so that it may be said of the relations between one head of state and another: naval battles have turned the sea's surface red. Then in this same year and during the following ones, there shall be the most horrible pestilence which will add to the preceding famine and such great tribulations will not have been known since the foundation of Christ's Church, and that will be throughout all regions of Italy. And it shall also leave its mark on all areas of Spain. Thus then the third leader of the Soviet Union, listening to the complaint of the people, and his main claim, will equip a very large army and cross the straits [*Bosphorus, Straits of Ormuz, Gulf of Aden*] which had been coveted by his forefathers and great-grandfathers [*cf. the Will of Peter the Great*], to reclaim it for his state, then the great Capetian shall be restored to his original state; but in the end, his reign shall be desolated and all abandoned, so that the destruction of the Saints of Saints [*Rome*] shall occur through paganism. The Old and New Testaments shall be forbidden and burned, after which the Antichrist shall be the infernal prince; and for the last time all the Christian countries shall tremble and also because of the unfaithful ones[1] [*the Moslems*], for twenty-five years,[2] there shall be wars and battles still more ruinous, and towns, villages, castles and other buildings shall be burned, laid waste or destroyed, with a great flood of the blood of young girls, married women, violated widows, suckling infants thrown against the walls of towns, dashed[3] thus and bruised; and so many misfortunes will be provoked by Satan, Prince of Darkness, that almost all the planet will be in chaos and laid waste. After this time, which men shall find long, the peace of the earth shall be renewed through the coming of the Golden Age. God the Creator, hearing the affliction of His people, shall order Satan to be bound and cast into the abyss of Hell,[4] into the deepest pit: thus shall commence a universal peace between God and men, and Satan shall remain bound for about a

---

[1] Cf. CVIII,Q96, Vol. I, and CIX,Q83.
[2] Cf. CVIII,Q77, Vol. I.
[3] Latin *allidere:* to hit. D.LAT.
[4] Latin *barathrum:* Hell. D.LAT.

thousand years, which will bring a greater strength to the power of the Church; and then he will once again be released.

All these outlines are in accord with the Holy Scriptures and things visible in the sky [*astronomy*], namely Saturn, Jupiter and Mars and other planets in conjunction, as one can see in more detail in certain quatrains. I could have made more detailed calculations and matched some against others, but considering, O Most Serene King, that censorship might bring certain difficulties, I have therefore withdrawn my pen from the paper during the calm of my nights. Indeed, O Most Powerful Ruler of all things, many happenings to come are clearly expressed with good sense and conciseness, but I neither wished nor was able to assemble them all in this letter to you; for in order to understand certain events, it is necessary for a little of destiny to be accomplished; and so that your dignity and humanity may be great throughout the earth, as well as your piety towards God, show yourself worthy of being the only one to bear the name of very powerful and most Christian King which the authority of all religion shall grant you.

But what I wish most fervently, O most clement King, is that through your unequalled and wise humanity you reflect upon my heartfelt desire and complete intention of obeying your serenest Majesty, since my vision has made me see your solar splendour [*reference to Bourbon origins*], a greatness to which my work, for all its importance, does not aspire.

Salon, this 27 June 1558.

NOSTRADAMUS AS HISTORIAN

SUBJECTS OF THE QUATRAINS AND SIXAINS

Moorish Revolt in Granada, 1567 – Their Expulsion from Spain, 1610

The Thirty Years War, 1618–48 – Gaston of Orleans in Lorraine, 1630

The Secret Marriage of Gaston of Orleans to Marguerite of Lorraine

Wallenstein and the Thirty Years' War, 1618–34 – His Treachery and Execution with His Accomplices, 1634

Marie de Medici's Exile to the Spanish Low Countries – Her Death, 1642

Charles I of England Driven from Power, 1649 – Cromwell Becomes Protector, 1653

William III against Louis XIV's France, 1672–1702 – The War of the League of Augsburg, 1688–97

The Duke of Anjou as King of Spain, 1700 – The War of the Spanish Succession, 1701–14

The Farnese Succession in Italy, 1732–33 – Don Carlos, Son of Philip V, King of Spain

The French Revolution, Cause of Napoleon's Accession – The Oath of the Tennis Court, 20 June 1789 – The National Assembly, 17 June 1789 – The Royal Family Imprisoned, 10 August 1792

War between France, Germany and Spain, 1795 – The Fall of the Republican System

The First Italian Campaign, 1796–97 – Napoleon at Villanova, Cremona and Mantua

The Egyptian Campaign, 1798 – Bonaparte's Administration of the Country

Masséna in Genoa, May 1800 – The Defeat of the Imperial Army – The Besieged Eat Oat Bread

Seven Years of War for the Milanese, 1792–1800 – Napoleon in Milan, 2 June 1800

18 Brumaire – Bonaparte and His Two Brothers – The French Army on the Var

Napoleon Emperor Thanks to His Victories – Louis XVII Welcomed by the Vatican – Coalitions against Napoleon

Louis XVI, Madame Elizabeth, Louis XVII and His Sister in the Temple – The False Dauphins and the Bourbon Characteristics

Napoleon's Military Coup against the Quirinal, 6 July 1809 - Rebellion in Rome and the Campagna – Failure of Conscription

The Beresina, November 1812 – The Grand Army between the Dniepr and the Dwina

Preparation for the Return from Elba, 1815 – Napoleon and His Old Comrades-in-Arms

Napoleon and the Return from Elba, 1 March 1815 – The Treachery of Marie-Louise, September 1814

The Battle of Navarino, October 1827 – Greek Independence, February 1830

The War of Greek Independence, 1821–28 – Chios, Tripolis, Navarino, Trebizond

War in Piedmont – Mortara, March 1849 – Defeat of Mortara before that of Novara

Garibaldi from Sicily and Naples to Rome, 1860–67 – The Agreement between Garibaldi and the British – The Shortcomings of Francis II, King of the Two Sicilies

End of the Pope's Temporal Power, 1870 – Role of the Secret Societies – Internal Struggles

Garibaldi in Brazil, 1835 – The Hohenzollern Candidacy to the Spanish Throne – The Duke of Aosta as King of Spain, 1870 – Garibaldi's Landing at Marseille, 1870 – The Advent of the Third Republic

The Succession to the Spanish Throne a Cause of the Franco-Prussian War of 1870 – French Troops Surrounded at Metz – The Eastern Army at Villersexel – 1830–70: Forty Years of War – 1871–1914: Forty Years of Peace

The Russian Revolution Leads to Famine and Disaster, 1917 – Human Rights Ignored – Battles of the Somme, 1916–18

The First World War Follows the Belle Epoque – Progress in Travel by Land, Sea and Air – Twentieth-century Wars

The Russo-German Pact, 23 August 1939 – The German Wheat Shortage, 1939

Mussolini and Clara Petacci Taken by Lorry to Milan – The Seven Corpses at Piazzale Loreto in Milan, 29 April 1945

Hesitation over the Provence Landing, August–December 1943 – The German Occupation as Far as Monaco – Imprisonment of Mussolini – Mussolini Hanged in Milan, 29 April 1945

The Link-up between the French, American, British and Russian Armies on the Danube, April–May 1945 – Mussolini in a Van and the Fall of Hitler, 29 April 1945

Socialism and François Mitterrand – The First Steps in the Rise to Power

Nostradamus' Prophecy Carried Worldwide by the Media, 1981

The Prophecy of Nostradamus Attacked by the Clergy, 1981

Moorish Revolt in Granada, 1567. Their Expulsion from Spain, 1610

Par les contrées du grand fleuve Bétique,[1]
Loin d'Ibère[2] au royaume de Grenade[3]
Croix repoussées par gens Mahométiques,
Un de Cordube[4] trahira[5] la fin contrade.[6]

CIII, Q20

Interpretation

Across the regions bordering on the Guadalquivir, from as far as the Ebro to the Kingdom of Granada, the Mohammedans will drive back [conversion to] the Cross. Finally they shall be driven out of Cordoba and the country.

History

'Already masters of all the Eastern Mediterranean, the Turkish vessels indulged in piracy between France and Italy. . . . *The Moors of Granada*, supported by Constantinople, whence they received subsidies and arms, revolted in 1567 and were only crushed by a bloody war, part guerrilla combat, part pitched battles, won by Don John of Austria, Philip II's half-brother, to whom he had entrusted the command. In order to avoid further insurrections and to reduce the vulnerability of the coastline to Turkish attacks, Philip II ordered the transportation of Granada's Moors to central Spain. Resettled in *Estremadura* [Cordova], La Mancha, Old Castile and Galicia, they returned as labourers to those provinces their ancestors had occupied as conquerors seven centuries earlier.

From Oran, their furthest eastern stronghold, the turbanned corsairs harassed solitary Spanish ships and ransacked coastal villages. . . .Local help and contacts were not lacking, and this support was particularly strong in Spain *between Algeciras*[7] *and the mouth of the Ebro* [*D'Ibère au royaume de Grenade*].

An internal political decision, the most important of his reign, was to add to the stagnation. This was *the expulsion of the Moors*. . . .*The considerable efforts made* since Philip II *to convert them had failed.* [*Croix repoussées par gens Mahométiques*]. . . .In 1609 and 1610 royal edicts forbade their *leaving their allotted territory* [*trahira contrade*].' [8]

[1] Guadalquivir (from the Arab Oued-al-Kebir, *the great river*), the *Boetis* of the ancients, runs through Adujar and Cordova. DHB. This river flows north of the Betic Cordillera.

[2] Iberus, now the Ebro: Spanish river. DHB.

[3] Founded by the Moors in the tenth century. Originally part of the Kingdom of *Cordova*. DHB.

[4] Cordoue, Corduba, i.e. Cordova, town in Spain on right bank of the Guadalquivir. DHB.

[5] Latin *trahere:* to take by force. D.LAT.

[6] Or *contrede*, early form of *contrée* (region/area). DAFL.

[7] Town 1km from Gibraltar, south-west of Granada. AVL.

[8] HDEJP.

The Thirty Years' War, 1618–48.
Gaston of Orleans in Lorraine, 1630

Dedans Hongrie par Boheme, Navarre,[1]
Et par Bannieres fainctes[2] seditions:
Par fleurs de lys pays portant la barre,[3]
Contre Orléans fera esmotions.

CV, Q89

Interpretation

In Hungary, because of Bohemia, and also in Navarre, there will be deceptive seditions which will occupy [the King of France] and Navarre, who will revolt in Lorraine against Gaston of Orleans.

History

'It was the *Bohemian* revolt which led to the Thirty Years' War. It began spontaneously on 23 May 1618 with the famous defenestration of Prague. . . .

A French intervention helped the imperial cause far more than was Louis XIII's ministers' intention. At the start of the winter, Ferdinand had sent the Prince of Fürstenberg to Paris as his ambassador, to ask the devoutly Christian king for his aid in conquering the heretics. He emphasized the danger which would threaten the Church were the Protestants to triumph in *Bohemia*. The pious Louis XIII was swayed by this. He too had to combat rebellious subjects, the Calvinists of the *Béarn* region, ever since he had undertaken to re-establish Catholicism in their territory. It was natural that he should make the connection between *Béarnais resistance* to the royal edict and *the Bohemian revolt*. . . .

The two main armies met near Prague. The King of Bohemia's army was comprised of a very few Czechs, but numerous Germans from all regions, Austrians, *Hungarians,* and even Englishmen. . . .

In 1629, on the occasion of a disagreement over the Bishopric of Metz, the Emperor had installed garrisons in two dependent towns, Vic and Moyenvic, while in 1630 the King of France had affirmed his sovereignty by extending over the Three Bishoprics the powers of a judicial intendant. . . . It was far easier for Richelieu to find a pretext to intervene in Lorraine, since Duke Charles IV had taken a distinctly hostile line towards Louis XIII. When, after the Day of Dupes and Marie de Medici's flight to Brussels,[4] Gaston of Orleans in his turn left the kingdom, it was to Nancy, close to the Duke of *Lorraine,* that he withdrew, and the rumour quickly circulated that *the Duke supported the betrothal of Monsieur to Marguerite of Lorraine,* his sister. The King of France could hardly allow the imperial troops to be installed permanently at Vic and Moyenvic, so near to Metz. In December 1631 a French army besieged Moyenvic and seized the town. Charles IV thus had to accept an agreement which became the Treaty of Vic, signed on 6 January 1632. He ceded the fortress of Marsal, north-east of Nancy, to the King of France; allowed the French troops unrestricted movement through his duchy; and undertook to abstain henceforth from all *intelligences, leagues, associations, and frequentation* that he had or might have with any Prince or State prejudicial to the King's cause, States, and territory under his allegiance or protection [*fainctes seditions*].'[5]

---

[1] Province forming part of the Béarn-et-Navarre district. DHB.

[2] Banners or standards being raised implied open hostility: the nobility was often 'up in arms', flags flying, against Richelieu. DL7V.

[3] Barrois, ancient area of France within Lorraine. DL7V. The arms of Lorraine were composed of a bar.

[4] Cf. CIX,Q78.

[5] LGDTA.

The Secret Marriage of Gaston of Orleans to Marguerite of Lorraine

Dame à l'absence de son grand capitaine,
Sera priée[1] d'amour du Viceroy:[2]
Faincte promesse et malheureuse estreine,[3]
Entre les mains du grand Prince Barroys.

                                        CVII,Q9

Interpretation

The Lady [Marie de Medici] in the absence of her great captain [Gaston of Orleans, Lieutenant of the Realm] will be invited to share the tender overtures engineered by the viceroy [Charles IV, Duke of Lorraine] which are to be made through a secret promise and because of an unfortunate fate; this having been arranged by the great Lorrainian Prince [Charles IV].

History

Cf. The historical texts quoted after the preceding quatrain.

'But in order to take the necessary precautions on the Rhine, the French troops' route from Champagne through Lorraine into Alsace had first to be opened. The situation of Lorraine, between the Kingdom of France and the Empire, thus became greatly confused, for the term Lorraine was itself only a geographical one. To the west, the region of Bar-le-Duc, called the "*Barrois* Mouvant" was in the domain of the King of France: i.e. its Duke was *vassal to the King*. . . .'[4]

Wallenstein and the Thirty Years War, 1618–34. His Treachery and Execution with his Accomplices, 1634

Un capitaine[1] de la grand Germanie,[2]
Se viendra rendre par simulé secours:
Au Roy des Roys ayde de Pannonie,[3]
Que sa révolte fera de sang grand cours.

CIX,Q90

Interpretation

An army commander from great Germany will falsely bring support to the Emperor-King aided by Hungary. And his revolt will cause much blood to flow.

History

'Albert of Wallenstein *entered the service* of Ferdinand[4] during the Duke of Styria's war against Venice. In 1618, at the beginning of the Thirty Years War, he was thirty-five. He had formed and was *commanding* a regiment in Moravia [*un capitaine*]. *He took the King's side* when Moravia declared support for the rebels.

Maximilian thought Wallenstein was in agreement with the King of Spain in wanting to give the House of Hapsburg "universal Monarchy" [*Roy des Roys*].

Disagreements between Wallenstein and the Archduke Ferdinand became more pronounced.

Richelieu was redoubling diplomatic activity in Germany, seizing every opportunity that chance might present him with. One such occasion was Wallenstein's treason. . . . The initial overtures made by Wallenstein to the Emperor's enemies reached France very early on.

Wallenstein summoned the senior officers of his army on 11 January 1634 at Pilsen for a council of war. The Emperor had knowledge of this meeting and was in no doubt as to Wallenstein's intentions: what was being planned could only be an attempt by the *commander in chief* [*capi-*

taine] to organize an officers' *plot* against the Emperor and to persuade the entire army to throw in its lot with him. . . . The drama unfolded on the evening of 24 February, in two distinct acts. The first was a banquet to which were invited Wallenstein's closest henchmen: Trcka, Kinsky and two senior officers, Ilow and Niemann. The banquet had scarcely ended before the officers in charge of the executions admitted the dragoons, who at once slaughtered Kinsky and Ilow. Trcka managed to escape from the room but was killed by musket shots in the courtyard. Niemann met a similar fate and the *massacre* was complete. The second act was even grimmer. Wallenstein had remained on his sickbed, unaware of what had happened. After a brief deliberation the officers decided to kill him too, although he was in no fit state to defend himself.'[5]

[1] General term for head of an army, senior commander: Alexander, Hannibal, Caesar, Napoleon I etc. are some of the greatest 'captains' in history. DL7V.

[2] See any map of the (Holy Roman – in effect German) Empire during the seventeenth century.

[3] Pannonia: European region between Norica and Dacia (Hungary). D.LAT.

[4] Ferdinand II was crowned King of Bohemia in 1617, *King of Hungary* in 1618, and Emperor in 1619. This monarch's generals were Maximilian of Bavaria, Tilly and Wallenstein. DHB.

[5] LGDTA.

Marie de Medici's Exile to the Spanish Low Countries. Her Death, 1642

La dame Grecque de beauté laydique,[1]
Heureuse faicte de proces[2] inumérable:
Hors translatée au règne Hispanique,
Captive, prinse mourir mort misérable.

CIX,Q78

Interpretation

The lady who is as beautiful as the Greek courtesan Laïs [Marie de Medici] will be happy until she indulges in numerous quarrels. She shall leave [France] in order to surrender to the kingdom of Spain [the Spanish Low Countries]. Imprisoned, arrested, she will die wretchedly.

History

'Marie de Medici,[3] daughter of Francis I, Grand Duke of Tuscany, was *a remarkable beauty.* . . . Named Regent after Henri IV's death in 1610, she was only interested in destroying what that great king had achieved. . . .When she had succeeded in giving Richelieu administrative power (1624) she started *perpetual intrigues* against him. She accused him of ingratitude because he would not sacrifice the interests of France for her.

She tried, but failed, to have Richelieu disgraced [The Day of Dupes, 12 November 1630]. *Arrested,* she managed to escape and reached the *Low Countries,* where she died destitute.'[4]

[1] Greek: Λαΐς, -ΐδος, Lais.DG. Greek courtesan celebrated for her wit and beauty, born at Hycara in *Sicily.* DHB. Nostradamus here alludes to the Greeks populating Italy.

[2] Figurative: quarrel. DL7V.

[3] Ancient Guelph family of Florence. When she attained supreme power, there was much talk of her *distant and brilliant origins.*DL7V.

[4] DHB.

Charles I of England Driven from Power, 1649. Cromwell Becomes Protector, 1653

Pour ne vouloir consentir au divorce,
Qui puis après sera connu indigne:
Le Roy des Isles sera chassé par force,
Mis à son lieu qui de Roy n'aura signe.

CX,Q22

Interpretation

Because of his refusal to divorce, the King of the [British] Isles shall be declared unworthy [of governing] and driven out of power by force [execution]; a person who will not have the title of king shall be set in his place.

History

'Charles I, whose family life was blameless, lacked intuition and was reputedly influenced by *his wife*[1] and his favourites of the moment. This explained the growing opposition to absolute monarchy. . . .'[2]

'The Protestants rebelled and drew up the famous Covenant, whereby they undertook to defend their faith to the death [1638]. Charles, unable to silence them, was obliged to summon a new Parliament in 1640. But this Parliament set itself up *in judgement over his behaviour* [*connu indigne*], condemned his chief minister, Strafford, to death, and formed an army to oppose him, led by Essex and Cromwell. The royal troops were *beaten* in various encounters [*par force*]. . . . Charles I, who had taken refuge in Scotland, was handed over to the rebels by the Scots [1647]. Brought before Parliament, he was condemned to death as a tyrant and executed in 1649.

Oliver Cromwell proclaimed a Republic. Four years later he was recognized as Head of State under the title of *Protector* [*de Roy n'aura signe*]. From that time on, Cromwell ruled as *absolute sovereign*.'[3]

[1] The king had married Henrietta of France, daughter of Henri IV and sister of Louis XIII.
[2] HRU.
[3] DHB.

William III against Louis XIV's France, 1672–1702. The War of the League of Augsburg, 1688–97

> L'aisné vaillant de la fille du Roy,[1]
> Repoussera si profond les Celtiques,
> Qu'il mettra foudres,[2] combien en tel arroy[3]
> Peu et loing, puis profond es Hesperiques.[4]

CIV,Q99

Interpretation

The courageous elder son [William III] of the daughter of the king [Charles I] will drive back the French so far that he will put them in great disarray through his forceful actions, not numerous but far-reaching, then deep into Spain.

History

'William was elected Stathouder of Holland in 1672, with the title of Prince of Orange, and led the Republic's troops in the war against Louis XIV. Although often defeated in this war, he fought the enemy on every front and more than proved his *courage*, prudence and skill, concluding with France the honourable Peace of Nijmegen, which assured the independence of the United Provinces in 1678.'[5]

'The Treaties of Ryswick which ended the War of the League of Augsburg were signed on 20 September and 30 October 1697. Louis XIV recognized William III as King of England, gave back Catalonia to *Spain*, and in the Low Countries surrendered Mons, Courtrai and Charleroi. He returned to the Duke of Lorraine territories occupied since his reign began; to the Emperor, Philipsburg, Brisach, Freiburg and Trier; and to Sweden, the Principality of Deux-Ponts. This eleven-year war drained the country, and finances were shaky. While it left Louis XIV's prestige undimmed, it increased British power dangerously. The House of Commons, indeed, was to thank William III "for the honour he had given back to England of holding the balance of Europe".

On 16 September 1701, King James II of England died at St Germain. Louis XIV immediately recognized as James's successor his son, under the title of "James III". The instant consequence of this was to give William III a pretext for declaring war. In fact, on 7 September William III had signed with Holland and the Empire *the Grand Alliance against France*. In 1703, the war was to become general.

On 19 March 1702, William of Orange, King of England and *Louis XIV's implacable enemy*, died from injuries received after falling from his horse. . . . The Grand Alliance was not affected by his death. "It was so well established," said St-Simon, "that William's spirit continued to animate it." '[6]

---

[1] William III, born in 1650 at The Hague, was the son of William II of Nassau, Prince of Orange, and of Henrietta Maria Stuart, *daughter of Charles I, King of England*. DHB

[2] Powerful effect, having a violent quality to its energy. DL7V.

[3] For *désarroy*, by aphesis.

[4] Hesperia, the name originally given by the Greeks to Italy, was then used to refer to Spain, when Greek geographical knowledge extended further west. DHB.

[5] DHB.

[6] L.XIV.JR.

The Duke of Anjou as King of Spain, 1700. The War of the Spanish Succession, 1701–14

Nul de l'Espagne, mais de l'antique France,
Ne sera esleu pour le tremblant nacelle[1]
A l'ennemy sera faicte fiance,
Qui dans son regne sera peste cruelle.

CV,Q49

Interpretation

A king of ancient France and not of Spain shall be chosen by a tottering power. There will be trust in yesterday's enemy [France]. And under his reign there will be a cruel calamity.

History

'Charles II: *the agony of Spain.* As if he wished to symbolize in his own person *a dying Spain,* Charles II was sickly and melancholy. . . . It was this *diminished* Spain which had to confront a France at the summit of her power. . . . Exhausted and dispirited, King Charles II bequeathed his crown to the claimant who, since he was the strongest, had the best chance of keeping his enormous inheritance united. This was Philip of Anjou, grandson of Louis XIV [*de l'antique France*].'[2]

'The War of the Spanish Succession was to last thirteen years. It was *the longest and most terrible of* Louis XIV's reign. It was waged simultaneously in *Spain,* Italy, Germany, the Low Countries, and eastern and northern France. . . . The Peace of Utrecht was signed in 1713. Philip V was to keep Spain and her colonies, formally renouncing all his claims to the French throne. . . . The War of the Spanish Succession had been futile and *ruinous* [*peste cruelle*]: France had not profited in any way from this enterprise, and had also forfeited her dominance in Europe; *she had been drained of blood and money.*'[3]

---

[1] Latin *navicella*, diminutive of *navis*, vessel. Symbolically speaking, the craft on which one is supposed to travel through the vicissitudes of life (depicted as a 'sea'). DL7V. Appropriate image denoting Spain, surrounded as she is by sea from Irun past Gibraltar to Barcelona.

[2] HEFDP.

[3] HFAM.

The Farnese Succession in Italy, 1732–33. Don Carlos, Son of Philip V, King of Spain

Par[1] car[2] Nersaf,[3] à ruine grande discorde,
Ne l'un ne l'autre n'aura election:
Nersaf du peuple aura amour et concorde,
Ferrare[4] Collonne[5] grande protection.

CVIII,Q67

Interpretation

There will be a great, ruinous discord between the Duke of Parma on the one side and Don Carlos and Elizabeth Farnese on the other. Neither the one [Duke of Parma] nor the other [Elizabeth Farnese] will be chosen. Don Carlos [the Farnese heir] shall have love and concord and be protected in the Papal States.

History

'The Spanish Succession in Italy had scarcely been settled before the issue of the Duchy of Parma and Piacenza provoked dissension and intrigue. Francis,[6] *Duke of Parma,* had as heirs one brother, Antonio, aged forty-five and grotesquely obese, who was not expected to live long, and one daughter, Elizabeth, who was married to King Philip V of Spain. It was obvious that the Duchy would revert to Elizabeth, and the Emperor of Germany was prepared to recognize the claims of *Don Carlos,* one of Philip's sons. . . . The old rivalry between the Houses of Hapsburg and Bourbon was thus reawakened in Italy. . . . The Emperor ordered the Governor of Milan to enter the Duchy and assert his rights of suzerainty. For his part the King of Spain sent six thousand troops commanded by his son Don Carlos into Tuscany. . . . At the start of 1733, in the north, Villars and Charles Emmanuel I, King of Sardinia, invaded the Milan region and promptly took possession of it. In the south, Don Carlos first drove the Duke of Modena from his territories and advanced *across the Papal States* to attack the Kingdom of Naples. The Imperial Viceroy, Visconti, left without assistance, had to give in, and *Don Carlos' march was a triumph.* The Neapolitans, happy to have a king of their own, ran enthusiastically ahead of Don Carlos, opened their towns to him one after the other, and ceremonially proclaimed him King of the Two Sicilies on 10 May. Capua and Gaeta, which the Viceroy wanted to defend, each capitulated swiftly. The following year Don Carlos, at the head of a considerable fleet, sailed from Naples towards

Palermo, where he was crowned with *the same speed and rejoicing [amour et concorde]*.' [7]

[1] For Parma, by apocope.
[2] For Carlos, by apocope.
[3] Anagram of Farnes(e). Most commentators have read this word as an anagram of France.
[4] Town south-east of Parma. AVL. Papal State.
[5] Town east of Rome. AVL. Papal State.
[6] Francis Farnese, Duke of Parma (1694–1727). DHB.
[7] HIIZ.

The French Revolution, Cause of Napoleon's Accession. The Oath of the Tennis Court, 20 June 1789. The National Assembly, 17 June 1789. The Royal Family Imprisoned, 10 August 1792

> Enfans sans mains[1] jamais veu si grand foudre,[2]
> L'enfant Royal au jeu doesteuf[3] blessé,[4]
> Au puy[5] brises[6] fulgures[7] allant mouldre,
> Trois sous les chaines par le milieu troussées.[8]

CI,Q65

Interpretation

One will never have seen a child, without parental authority, become so great a war leader, when the royal child [Louis XVII] is affected by the Oath of the Tennis Court, [the king], through having wished to suppress the Assembly, will unleash thunderbolts [from the people] by going [to play] baker; three years later he will be taken away from the centre [power] and imprisoned.

History

'Napoleon was ten. . . . It was not enough to be a good pupil to obtain subsidy: your parents had to prove they lacked *sufficient resources*. Marboeuf attested to their poverty, declaring that the Bonapartes, with three children, had no money.

On 17 June 1789, the States-General became known as the National *Assembly*. This change of name was vitally significant.

On 23 June the King made his declaration to the States-General. . . .
The monarch began by *quashing and annulling* as illegal and unconstitut-
ional the resolution of the seventeenth, the one whereby the States-
General would henceforth be called the National Assembly.

The women who preceded the royal coach as it entered Paris were
displaying various *flours* to the multitude, and pointing towards the king
and his family, shouting: "Don't worry, friends, we won't be short of
bread any longer. We're bringing you the baker, the baker's wife and
the little baker's boy" [*allant mouldre*].' [9]

From 17 June 1789 to 10 August 1792, the date of the Royal Family's
incarceration in the Temple Prison, is a period of three years.

[1] Latin *manus:* authority, power; paternal authority in particular. DL.
[2] 'Napoleon was a great military leader.' DL7V. Cf.CII,Q76; CIII,Q13; CIV,Q43; and
CIV,Q54 all Vol. I.
[3] *Esteuf:* term for the ball used for tennis. DAFL.
[4] *Atteindre:* to hit, wound. DL7V.
[5] Certain assemblies in ancient times were held on *puys* or hillocks. DAFL.
[6] *Briser:* to destroy, suppress. DL7/FV.
[7] Latin *fulger:* thunderbolt. DL.
[8] To carry off, take away. DAFL.
[9] HFA.

War between France, Germany and Spain, 1795.
The Fall of the Republican System

> Un an devant le conflict Italique,
> Germains, Gaulois, Espagnols pour le fort,
> Cherra l'escolle maison de république,
> Où hors mis peu, seront suffoquez mors.

CII,Q39

Interpretation

A year before the Italian campaign, Germans, Frenchmen and Spaniards
will try their strength, then the republican teaching will collapse, except
for some who will be killed and suffocated.

History

'Treaties of Basle and The Hague. The French victories and Polish
affairs led in 1795 to an initial disruption of the coalition. *The King of*

Prussia was anxious not to let Russia and Austria proceed separately towards a third partition of Poland, and the *King of Spain*, threatened with *a French invasion*, signed the Peace of Basle [April 1795]. Prussia recognized the occupation by French forces of the territories on the left bank of the Rhine, and in Belgium and the other Imperial domains. The King of Spain surrendered Spanish San Domingo in the Antilles.'

'The Italian campaign lasted one year, from April 1796 to April 1797.' [April 1795–April 1796 – one year before the Italian campaign.]

Conspiracies. Bonaparte's dictatorship had created numerous malcontents among both the republican generals and the disappointed royalists. Several plots were hatched against the usurper. . . . In August 1803, a former *Chouan* leader, Georges Cadoudal, at the head of a band of determined followers, had schemed to attack and kill the First Consul and his escort. . . . The conspiracy was unmasked in January 1804. . . . The Duke of Enghien, a suspected conspirator, was taken to Vincennes, brought before a military tribunal, sentenced and shot. Shortly afterwards Cadoudal was guillotined, and Pichegru strangled [*suffoqué*] in his house. Moreau was exiled.

Cadoudal's conspiracy hastened the transformation of the Consulate into an hereditary monarchy. On 18 May 1804, a *senatus-consultum* established that *the government of the Republic* was entrusted to the Emperor Napoleon.[1]

[1] HFAM.

The First Italian Campaign, 1796–97. Napoleon at Villanova, Cremona and Mantua

A cité neuve[1] pensif pour condamner,
L'oisel de proye[2] au Ciel[3] se vient offrir:
Après victoire à captifs pardonner,
Crémone et Mantoue grand maux aura souffert.

                              CI,Q24

Interpretation

At Villanova no one will think further of condemning Bonaparte who will make offers to the Church. After his victory he will give proof of his clemency towards the prisoners. The towns of Cremona and Mantua will have suffered much.

History

'The next morning Bonaparte took up the pursuit again, making for Vicenza. Once he had reached the Brenta–Verona road, by way of *Villanova*, he entrusted the cavalry alone with the task of pursuing the enemy, and considered returning to Verona by the *Villanova* and Caldiero road, in order to come to Vaubois' aid. . . . When the inhabitants of Verona saw this handful of men who had previously left as fugitives through the Milan gate now return through the Venice gate as victors, they were astonished. *Neither friends nor enemies could contain their admiration.* From that time on, no one ever feared that the French might be driven out of Italy.'

'Bonaparte now faced the River Adda, which could not, like the Ticino, be skirted, because he would only have had to cross the Po at *Cremona.* . . . Serrurier's and Laharpe's divisions had been left at Pizzighettone, Lodi, *Cremona* and Cassano, to guard the Adda.'

'Bonaparte had scarcely signed the capitulation of *Mantua*, when he departed without waiting for Marshal Würmser to parade before him, and arrived at Bologna *to lay down the law to the Pope.*

Bonaparte assembled *the prisoners* taken that day along the banks of the Senio, and spoke to them in Italian. These unfortunates imagined that their throats were going to be cut. Bonaparte reassured them, announcing to their great astonishment that he *was setting them free* provided they would then enlighten their compatriots as to *the intentions of the French, who had not come to destroy religion or the Holy See,* but wished only to dismiss the bad counsellors surrounding the Pope.' [4]

¹ Villanova: i.e. *cité neuve*, new city.
² The Napoleonic eagle.
³ Used with capital letter to denote the Catholic Church.
⁴ HDRAT, Vol. 2.

The Egyptian Campaign, 1798. Bonaparte's Administration of the Country

Combien de fois prinse Cité solaire¹,
Seras changeant les loix barbares et vaines:²
Ton mal s'approche. Plus seras tributaire,
Le Grand Hadrie recouvrira tes veines.³

CI,Q8

Interpretation

How many times shall the town of Cairo be taken, where the worthless
Moslem laws shall be changed. Your misfortune approaches. You shall
pay yet another tribute. Starting from the Adriatic the great personage
[i.e. Bonaparte] will seize your wealth.

History

'*Cairo* was *taken* by the Turks in 1517, by the French in 1798, and by
the English in 1801, when it was immediately returned to the Porte
[Turkey].'⁴

'It was in Italy, while thinking about the Levant, that he first conceived
the idea of the famous expedition launched the following year. "It is in
Egypt," he wrote, "that England must be attacked." [Letter of 16 August
1797]. To attain his ends, he had summoned Admiral Brueys in the
Adriatic, with six warships, several frigates and a few corvettes. . . .

The army had succeeded in landing; it was now necessary to create at
Alexandria an administration in line with the customs of the country,
and to halt an invasion plan to seize Egypt. . . .

Bonaparte made arrangements to establish French authority in Alexandria, then to leave the Delta and seize *Cairo*, capital of Egypt. . . .
Bonaparte established a divan at Cairo as he had done at Alexandria. This
divan, or municipal council, was to help him win over the Egyptians. It
was agreed that similar ones were to be set up in all the provinces, and
that these special divans would send deputies to the Cairo divan, which
would thus be a great national divan [*changeant les lois barbares*].'⁵

'On 21 October 1798, Cairo rebelled: a terrible outbreak, which cost
some 250 French lives, including that of the Governor of Cairo, General
Dupuy. *The reprisals were as dreadful* as they were discreet [*ton mal
s'approche*]. The work of pacification and *organization* was more remarkable: all the necessary resources [*tributaire*] for the army had to be
collected, and this in a wretchedly poor country.'⁶

¹ Heliopolis, i.e. City of the Sun, 11 km north-east of Cairo. On 20 March 1800
Kléber won a resounding victory there over the Turks.DHB.
² Latin *vanus:* worthless. DLLB.
³ Symbolic: wealth, resources to be used. DL7V.
⁴ DHB.
⁵ HDRAT.
⁶ NEE.

Masséna in Genoa, May 1800. The Defeat of the Imperial Army. The Besieged Eat Oat Bread

Le conducteur de l'armée françoise,
Cuidant perdre le principal phalange:
Par sus pavé de l'avaigne[1] et d'ardoise,[2]
Soy parfondra[3] par Gennes gent estrange.

CVII,Q39

Interpretation

The leader of the French army [Napoleon], thinking his principal army [Masséna] lost, when on the street bread made from oats and slates will be eaten, shall in Genoa trouble the strangers [Austrians].

History

'If Napoleon could have emerged into Italy, he would already have seized the *Austrian* general [*gent estrange*] and snatched him away from the walls of Genoa. Others were claiming that Bonaparte *the general had deemed the Ligurian army a necessary sacrifice* [*cuidant perdre le principal phalange*] in a major operation. The Genoese and our own soldiers themselves considered that they had been sacrificed to the glory of France.

Masséna's fortitude held out to the very end. Before surrendering, the soldiers were saying, he would have them eat their very boots; a dismal sort of bread, made with *oats* and beans, had been devoured also. . . . *The streets* [*sus pavé*] were littered with unhappy wretches dying of starvation.

Thus ended the memorable siege, during which *a French army* had distinguished itself by great devotion and heroism. It had taken more prisoners and killed more enemy soldiers than it numbered in its own ranks. With 15,000 men, it had captured or disposed of 18,000 *Austrians* [*gent estrange*]. Above all, it had destroyed the morale [*parfondra*] of the [Austrian Imperial] army by compelling it to make constant and extraordinary efforts. But at what price had this brave garrison of *Genoa* achieved such things? . . . Soult, the second in command, remained in enemy hands. . . .'[4]

[1] Latin *avena:* oats. D.LAT.
[2] They made bread from chopped-up straw, writes D'Aubigné in *Histoire Universelle.*
[3] Latin *perfundere:* to distress, disturb. D.LAT.
[4] HDEAT.

Seven Years of War for the Milanese, 1792–1800. Napoleon in Milan, 2 June 1800

Devant cité de l'Insubre[1] contrée,
Sept ans sera le siège devant mis:
Le très grand Roy y fera son entrée,
Cité puis libre hors de ses ennemis.

CVII,QI5

Interpretation

Milan and the Milanese will be besieged for seven years. Then the very great leader [Napoleon] will make his entry there. The city will then be freed from its enemies.

History

'The republics of both Venice and Genoa, where the patriciate was closely identified with the State, but where too the resistance towards Austria [the enemy, for the Italians] and the King of Sardinia was considerable, seemed, despite their neutrality, to incline towards France.

Such were the dispositions of the Peninsula when the Emperor Francis declared war *in 1792* upon the French Revolution, thus throwing Italy into the struggle. . . . As soon as the war began, the rulers of Italy might well have concluded that they did not have only the French to contend with. The Emperor Francis had fresh troops go down through the Alps into the Po Valley to contain *the Milanese* and support Victor-Amadeus II. . . .

In May *1800*, Mélas got ready to cross the Var to invade Provence; there was no hope left for Masséna, besieged with the last French troops in Genoa. Suddenly Bonaparte descended through the Great St Bernard Pass, came under fire – guns, baggage and all – from the stronghold of Bard, and occupied part of Piedmont. After a long and heroic resistance Masséna had surrendered the city of Genoa to the Austrians on 4 June. But *the First Consul had already been in Milan* for two days, and there he proclaimed the Republic anew, amid joy bordering on delirium. Mélas led his troops back to the Po as fast as he could, hoping that such boldness would prove justified. But Bonaparte again assumed command of his army and on the plains of Marengo that 10 June completed what his crossing of the St Bernard had begun so well. The French re-entered Genoa; *the Emperor Francis*, quite stunned, *asked for an armistice so that peace could be discussed: and France once again became the arbiter of Italian destiny [Cité puis libre hors de ses ennemis].*'[2]

¹ Insubres: tribe of Cisalpine Gaul, who inhabited the northern Po region between the Adda, the Ticino and the Alps. Their main town was Mediolanum (Milan).DHB.
² HIJZ.

---

18 Brumaire. Bonaparte and His Two Brothers. The French Army on the Var

Aux fins¹ du Var changer le Pompotans,²
Près du rivage les trois beaux enfans³ naistre:
Ruyne au peuple par aage competans⁴
Regne au pays changer plus voir croistre.

CVIII,Q97

Interpretation

It is on the borders of the Var that the all-powerful aspects of England shall be changed. The career of three persons, as yet speechless, is to be born. After the ruin of the people which the [revolutionary] era had allowed, power shall know changes and grow still more.

History

'Fame and credit are due to Masséna, who had just executed one of the most perfect operations in the history of war, and who had saved us at a moment more dangerous than those of Valmy and Fleurus. . . . Zurich was the finest feather in Masséna's cap. . . .

While such fortunate events were going on in Switzerland, victory was ours once again in Holland. Brune had been only weakly pressed by the enemy and had time to concentrate his forces. *After defeating the British and the Russians* at Kastrikum, he had cornered them at the Zip and *forced them to surrender*. . . .

France was saved, but that was all; she had in no sense recovered her former standing, and still had dangers to contend with on the *Var*.

In the meanwhile Napoleon was quite calmly sailing the seas, which were *full of English ships*. Fearing after the recent events that the south of France might be invaded, he made not for *the coast of Provence but for that of the Languedoc*. He wanted to land at Collioure or Port-Vendres. Strong winds drove him towards Corsica. After that he sailed towards Toulon. Just as he was arriving, at dusk, thirty enemy ships were sighted to port, in the rays of the setting sun. It was suggested that a small boat should be lowered so they could land unobserved. Bonaparte, always a believer in destiny, said they would have to wait. Indeed, the enemy disappeared and on 17 Vendemiaire, Year VIII [8 October 1799], at daybreak, the frigates *Muiron* and *Carrère* and the xebecs *Revanche* and *Fortune* lay at anchor in the bay of Fréjus [*Près du rivage*]. . . .

His two brothers Lucien and Joseph [*trois beaux enfans*], along with his own deputies, *each day scored new victories* in the councils.

Such was the 18 Brumaire revolution, which was judged so differently: seen by some as the coup which destroyed our liberty, by others as a bold but necessary step *that ended anarchy* [*Ruyne au peuple*].'[5]

¹ For *confins*, borders, by aphesis.
² Used to denote England. Cf. CX,Q100, Vol. I.
³ *Infans*: one who does not talk, deprived of speech. D.LAT.
⁴ *Si ejus competeret aetas:* if his age allowed him. Suetonius. D. LAT.
⁵ HDEAT.

Napoleon Emperor Thanks to His Victories. Louis XVII Welcomed by the Vatican. Coalitions against Napoleon

Dresser copies[1] pour monter à l'Empire
Du Vatican le sang Royal tiendra:[2]
Flamens, Anglois, Espagne avec Aspire[3]
Contre l'Italie et France contendra.[4]

CVI,Q12

Interpretation

He [Bonaparte] will raise troops to ascend to the Empire. Royal blood will remain at the Vatican. The Flemish, the English, the Spanish united with the Germans will fight against Italy and France.

History

'The Directorate, driven by necessity, wanted an all-out simultaneous offensive. War must nurture war. *Italy* had to be conquered so as to be exploited. . . . On Bonaparte's arrival, the Italian Army was 35,000 strong. . . . The Directorate decided to dispatch 40,000 more men as reinforcements. . . .'

'Waterloo: England, Prussia, Austria and Russia each strove to keep

50,000 men in the field. An army made up of *Englishmen, Dutch* and *Germans* was united under Wellington in *Belgium.*'

'Although eleven months of effort and success had seen him almost back at his starting point, the year 1812 was not a fruitless one for Wellington. . . . The British general returned to Cadiz and had himself named C-in-C of *the Spanish troops.* The French evacuated Valladolid, then Burgos, and withdrew beyond the Ebro. Under a merciless sun the Spanish, Portuguese and British troops pursued them. . . .'

'By the peace treaty of 30 May 1814, France had abandoned all the conquests of the Revolution and the Empire; *Italy,* to which Napoleonic domination had at least bestowed an appearance of unity in its northern half, together with a government and national flag, was once again partitioned into ancient kingdoms and fell under the unwelcome hegemony of Austria. . . .'[5]

[1] Latin *copiae:* army corps, troops, military forces. D.LAT.

[2] Louis XVII would have been protected by the Vatican after his escape from the Temple Prison. Cf. CVI,Q51; CII,Q58; CIX,Q24 all Vol. 1.

[3] For French Spire (by prothesis); English Speyer. Town in the Rhineland on a minor river of the same name. DHB.

[4] Latin *contendere:* to fight, struggle against. D.LAT.

[5] NEE.

Louis XVI, Madame Elizabeth, Louis XVII and His Sister in the Temple. The False Dauphins and the Bourbon Characteristics

Frères et soeurs en divers lieux captifs,
Se trouveront passer près du monarque:
Les contempler ses rameaux ententifs,[1]
Displaisant voir menton, front, nez, les marques.

CII,Q20

Interpretation

Brothers and sisters will be imprisoned in various areas [of the Temple]. They will be seen passing close to the king. People wishing to be descendants will be observed. Signs will be seen on the chin, forehead and nose of a disagreeable person [Naundorff].

History

'When they arrived at the Temple the illustrious captives were at first held in the part of the building called the Palace. . . . *Louis XVI slept on the second floor*. The Queen and *Madame Royale occupied a room on the first floor; the Dauphin*, his governess Madame de Tourzel, and the prince's chambermaid *were all lodged in one room adjoining;* the Princess de Lamballe was installed in a kind of antechamber. *Facing the King's room was another* which would serve as kitchen, and where the utensils were kept: *this was the accommodation for Madame Elizabeth* and Mlle de Tourzel [*En divers lieux*].'²

Brothers and sisters: on the one hand Louis XVI and his sister Madame Elizabeth, on the other, Louis XVII and his sister Madame Royale.

'What was more, according to expert opinion, Naundorff was nothing like the Bourbon type. Thus Louis Journot, invited by Senator Delahaye to compare portraits of Louis XVII and those of Naundorff [*contempler*], unhesitatingly remarked upon the two different types.'³ In all the portraits Louis XVII has a straight *brow and nose*, while Naundorff has a bulging *forehead*, his *nose* prominently hooked. 'Once again then, Dr Galippe declared that none of the *descendants* [*rameaux*] showed the typical Hapsburg profile, that hereditary perculiarity which, even though absent in Naundorff, should have manifested itself among them.'³

¹ *Attentif:* intent, intention, end for which one aims. DAFI.
² *Historical Memoirs on Louis XVII*, M. Eckard, Paris, 1817.
³ *Louis XVII, Critical Studies*, J.de Lathuy, Gembloux, 1976.

Napoleon's Military Coup against the Quirinal, 6 July 1809. Rebellion in Rome and the Campagna. Failure of Conscription

Dans temple¹ clos le foudre² y entrera,
Des Sitadins dedans leur fort³ grevez⁴
Cheveaux, boeufs, hommes, londe,⁵ mur⁶ touchera,
Par faim soif, soubs les plus foibles armez.

CIII,Q6

Interpretation

Napoleon's army will enter the palace of the Catholic Church which had been closed. The town's inhabitants will be oppressed and in anguish. The men who deal with horses and cattle [peasants] will revolt as far as Rome, where hunger and thirst will be experienced, with very few conscripts.

History

'The Pope had Cardinal Pacca installed in his own apartment and put the Quirinal in a state of defensive readiness; thereafter entry was only to be effected *by breaking the doors in.* . . . General Miollis had to put the town *under martial law [grevés]* so as to prevent serious disorder. . . . The Pope was abducted on 6 July 1809 from his palace, whose doors were staved in by the leader of the Guard, Radet. . . .

A more general and perhaps more regrettable *opposition* came from the poor who had been *reduced to abject misery* by the banning of pilgrimages and the dispersion of the clergy – whose alms had kept these paupers idle while they rescued them from *starvation.* The population of *beggars,* 30,000 strong in Rome in 1812, numbered over 12,000 by the end of 1810, and begged even in front of the prefect's door. Rome in those days had a population of less than 140,000. . . .

The atmosphere changed completely when the Imperial administration sought to apply conscription to the towns and *countryside* surrounding the Papal State. . . . The percentage of conscripts reporting for call-up, out of all those actually conscripted, was *very low:* only 24 out of 300 showed up at Marino! In Umbria, the prefect of Trasimene was proud of having raised 140, but between Perugia and Florence they nearly all deserted. . . . Mass executions took place in Rome as well as in the Campagna.'[7]

1 Poetic, for the Catholic Church. DLV.
2 Cf. CI,Q65; CIII,Q44; and in Vol. 1 CII,Q76; CIII,Q13; CIV,Q43; CIV,Q54.
3 Beset, in an anxious state. DAFL.
4 To overwhelm, torment, oppress, tyrannize. DAFL.
5 Nostradamus uses this word *passim* to denote revolt or rebellion.
6 Cf. CIII,Q37, Vol. 1.
7 NEE.

The Beresina, November 1812. The Grand Army between the Dniepr and the Dwina

Entre deux fleuves se verra enserré,
Tonneaux et caques[1] unis à passer outre:
Huict pont rompus chef à tant enferré,[2]
Enfans parfaicts[3] sont jugulez[4] en coultre.[5]

CVIII,Q55

Interpretation

He [Napoleon] will see himself squeezed between two rivers [Dniepr and Dwina]. Barrels and casks of powder will have been bound together in order to cross to the other side; eight bridges will have been cut; the leader [Napoleon] will have fallen into a trap; children, having grown up, will be massacred.

History

'Among these stubborn marauders were many conscription-evaders and very few veterans. . . . Generally they were the *youngest*, the least unruly, the latter *taken from their families* by conscription [*enfans parfaicts*]. . . . The Young Guard, decimated by fighting and fatigue, still contained two thousand men.

Wittgenstein had taken up positions behind the Oula, which forms *the junction of the Dwina and Dniepr rivers*, beside the Lepel Canal and the Beresina. . . . In order to march on Moscow, Napoleon had gone through the open area *between* the Dniepr and the Dwina. Setting off, he had the Dwina on his left, the Dniepr on his right; on his return, the opposite was the case [*entre deux fleuves*].

It was not only *the bridges* over the racing waters which they found *cut*, but the bridges over the marshes, which were far longer and more difficult to cross. In contrast, by going along the Beresina towards its junction with the Oula, they discovered places where the river bed was shallow and sandy, and there they crossed with the waterline up to their belts [*enferré*].

The enemy, also exhausted, ceased firing round about midnight, sure of capturing every one of that handful of brave men who were stubbornly trying to get their *throats cut* [*jugulez en coultre*].[6]

[1] Barrel or cask for gunpowder or saltpetre. DL7V.
[2] To tie up, ensnare one's adversary, entrap him. DL7V.
[3] Latin *perfecta aetas:* legal age of majority, no longer a child. D.LAT.

[4] Latin *jugulare:* to cut a throat, massacre, slaughter. D.LAT.
[5] Latin *culter:* knife, either sacrificial or for butchery or hunting. D.LAT.
[6] HDEAT.

Preparation for the Return from Elba, 1815. Napoleon and His Old Comrades-in-Arms

Les Exilez par ire, haine intestine,
Feront au Roy grand conjuration:
Secret mettront ennemis par la mine,[1]
Et ses vieux siens contre eux sédition.[2]

CI,QI3

Interpretation

The exiles, because of [the people's] anger and internecine hatred, will make a great conspiracy against the King. By secret machination they will mobilize against their enemies; and his former companions [Murat, Ney, etc.] will openly resist the King's authority.

History

'All the faults of Louis XVIII's administration were not lost upon the man *exiled* on the rocky Isle of Elba. . . . Bonaparte also watched with delight as papal anathema was directed against those who requisitioned national resources. From that moment he sought the next opportunity to overthrow the Bourbon dynasty [*Secret mettront ennemis par la mine*]. . . . All these acts – likely to alarm lovers of freedom – quickly bore fruit: the eastern departments showed themselves *hostile* to the government, while those in the Midi experienced outbursts of the most deplorable *feuds*. . . . Generals, officers and soldiers [*vieux siens*] all missed their tricolour cockades, their eagles, victories and, ultimately, their leader. . . .

Joachim Murat, learning that France was insisting that the crown of the Two Sicilies be restored to the lawful king of that country, declared his intention of crossing Italy in order to attack France. However absurd the idea of attacking France with 30,000 Neapolitans might have seemed, to Bourbon rule it was alarming, all the same. Napoleon counted on *his former comrades-in-arms* and on the irresistible power of public opinion. He did not toy with hatching a *conspiracy* – the first rumours of which would inevitably have resulted in his being kept under the most embarrassing surveillance – but confiding his *secret* to none, he prepared to carry out the boldest plan. Surrounded by eight or nine hundred soldiers of his *Old Guard* and a few friends like Generals Bertrand, Drouot and Cambrone, Napoleon anticipated the possibility of ending his *exile*, crossing the Mediterranean and presenting himself to his *former* companions in glory, with whom he hoped to overthrow the Bourbon dynasty. . . . The very evening the Elba battalion was due to embark, a carnival was held at Porto Ferrajo, and inhabitants as well as visitors attended without suspecting its purpose as cover for the departure of their celebrated host.'[3]

[1] *Mine secrète:* a secretive look, implying that one is hatching some kind of shady plot. DL7V.
[2] Attack on or open resistance against established authority. DL7V.
[3] HFA.

Napoleon and the Return from Elba, 1 March 1815. The Treachery of Marie-Louise, September 1814

> Quand l'animal[1] à l'homme domestique,[2]
> Après grands peines et sauts[3] viendra parler,
> De foudre[4] à vierge[5] sera si maléfique,
> De terre prinse[6] et suspendue en l'air.[7]

CI I I,Q44

Interpretation

When the animal [Napoleon] comes to address the officers of his guard, after great difficulties and leaps forward, the young woman [Marie-Louise] will be very wicked towards the lightning [Napoleon], after he has disembarked [from Elba], ready to set out.

History

'Napoleon was eager to give himself all the trappings of power. Ministers . . . a court . . . above all, an army and a navy. To the 400 men of the *Old Guard* were added 200 volunteers. . . . Since January 1815, suggestions casually mooted showed that the idea [of returning] exercised his mind [*suspendue en l'air*].

The audacity and resolution of Marshal Ney were being counted upon most of all. . . . "I'll deal with Bonaparte," Ney bellowed. "We'll attack that *beast!*"

Marie-Louise's treachery: instead of going to Italy, Marie-Louise returned to Vienna, where precautions had been taken to keep her son. . . . Since 8 September she had written that she would never go to Elba and would place in Metternich's hands all letters she might receive from Napoleon. Meanwhile, the *unfortunate* betrayed husband still deluded himself, and had apartments for his wife prepared. But her silence, along with bits of information garnered here and there, gradually enlightened him. His bitterness welled up in moving complaints: "My wife no longer writes to me. My son has been taken from me, as children of the vanquished once were, in order to deck the victors' triumph. In modern times one cannot think of such a *barbarity! [maléfique]*." [8]

[1] Beast is the term for an animal entirely devoid of intelligence. Animal, however, only applies *to creatures of a certain magnitude.* DL7V.

[2] Historical term, which after the fourth or fifth century AD referred to a body of soldiers of the *imperial guard,* and from the sixth applied specifically to officers. DL7V.

[3] Latin *saltus:* jump or rush forward. D.LAT.

[4] Cf. CI,Q65; CIII, Q6; and in Vol. I CII, Q76; CIII, Q13; CIV, Q43; CIV, Q54.

[5] Latin *virgo:* young woman. D.LAT. Marie-Louise, born 1791, was twenty-three in 1814.

[6] To land, disembark, reach land. DL7V.

[7] To be always in the air, i.e. ready to leave, run, jump. DL7V.

[8] NEE.

The Battle of Navarino, October 1827. Greek Independence, February 1830

Nautique rame invitera[1] les umbres,[2]
Du grand Empire[3] lors viendra conciter:[4]
La mer Aegée des lignes[5] desencombres,
Empeschant l'onde Thirrene[6] defflotez.

CV,Q95

Interpretation

A maritime power [nineteenth-century England] will challenge those who are no more than the shadows of their former selves [the Ottoman Empire in decline]. The great [British] Empire will mobilize its fleet to free the

Aegean Sea of [Turkish] battleships which were preventing navigation on the sea that bathes Thyrea [the Aegean].

History

'The death of Alexander I and his replacement by Nicholas I [December 1825], a believer in the strong approach, caused concern in *England*. In March 1826 Nicholas issued the Porte with an ultimatum whose consequence was the Treaty of Akerman: by it Russia secured the right to trade on all Ottoman Empire waters; *Greece* was not involved. *England*, unhappy with this Treaty, therefore *intervened*, and the London agreements anticipated the mediation of the three major powers [England, France and Russia] between Turkey and Greece. The Sultan rejected the offer of mediation and the Allies threatened him with armed intervention; *their fleet engaged* the Turkish and Egyptian fleets at Navarino where the latter were destroyed [October 1827]. . . . Finally the London Protocols [November 1828 and March 1829] established Greek borders, but it was the Russian Army which was entrusted with getting the new State recognized. . . . In February 1830, at the *London Conference*, Greece's independence was proclaimed. . . . Russian subjects were granted freedom of trade throughout all territories of the Ottoman Empire; at last the Bosphorus and Dardanelles Straits were *open to all merchant shipping* [*desencombres*].[7]

[1] Latin *invitare:* to provoke, challenge, engage. D.LAT.
[2] Symbolic, for person or thing whose brightness is diminished. DL7V.
[3] England. Cf. CX, Q100, Vol. I.
[4] Latin *naves concitare:* to set sail. D.LAT.
[5] Nautical term for battle formation or ships at anchor. DL7V.
[6] Thyrea: town in Morea, in the Peloponnese, on the borders of Argolis and Laconia, near the Aegean coast. DHB. Example of paragoge.
[7] HDTRM.

The War of Greek Independence, 1821–28. Chios, Tripolis, Navarino, Trebizond

Au Chalmé[1] Duc, en arrachant[2] l'esponce,[3]
Voile Arabesque voir, subit descouverte:[4]
Tripolis[5] Chio,[6] et ceux de Trapesonce,[7]
Duc prins: Marnegro[8] et la cité déserte.

CVI, Q55

Interpretation

Because of General Maison's refusal to abandon [the Greeks] the Ottoman fleet will be spotted and exposed to enemy fire [Navarino]. After the massacres of Tripolis and Chios, with the aid of those [who will march on] Trebizond [the Russians], the commander-in-chief [Ibrahim] having surrendered, the Black Sea shall be liberated, the town [Tripolis] laid waste.

History

'The Morea expedition had just been decided upon. General *Maison* won the command from all his rivals. He was entrusted with the dubious honour of pursuing Ibrahim and stopping that ferocious *Arab's* depredations in Greece.'[9]

'In 1824 Ibrahim assumed command of the Egyptian Army sent to fight the Greeks. Attacked at sea by Admiral Miaoulis, he lost half his force but landed at Modos [February 1825] and took Navarino, Tripolitza, Argos and Missolonghi. Blockaded after the sea battle of Navarino, Ibrahim Pasha, on his father's orders, signed an honourable *surrender*. [*Duc prins*].'[10]

'In the Morea, Germanos, Archbishop of Patras, declared a War of Liberation [25 March 1821]. . . . In April the notorious massacres at *Chios* took place and in May Joannina fell to the Turks. . . . On 20 December 1827 the Sultan proclaimed a Holy War, which gave the Russians a pretext to declare war on him in April 1828. . . . French military intervention in the Morea was effected without difficulty, an agreement being signed with Mehmet Ali (November 1828). Finally the London Protocols (November 1828 and March 1829) fixed the borders of Greece, but the Russian Army took on the task of enforcing recognition of the new State: attacking in the east, it seized Erzerum and advanced upon Trebizond. . . . Freedom of trade was granted to Russian subjects throughout the entire Ottoman Empire, and at last the Bosphorus and Dardanelles Straits [*Marnegro*] were open to all merchant shipping.'[11]

'*Tripolitza*, prosperous capital of the *Morea* under the Turks, was captured and recaptured during the War of Independence, notably by Mehmet Ali (1825), and almost *razed* [*et la cité déserte*].'[12]

[1] From *chalme* or *chaume*. DAFL. Hence *chaumière*, small thatched *house* or cottage. DL7V. An astonishing codification of General Maison's name.
[2] Figurative: to banish or deprive of. DL7V.
[3] *Esponce:* archaic word meaning scattering or abandonment. DL7V.
[4] To expose oneself to an enemy's or opponent's blows. DL7V.
[5] Tripolitza, *Tripolis*. Greek town, almost in the centre of the *Morea*. DHB.
[6] Greek island near the Turkish coast: Chios is its chief town. DHB.
[7] Trebizond, Trapezus, town and port in Asia Minor on the *Black Sea*. DHB. The -us ending has been changed for the sake of the rhyme with *esponce*.
[8] Neologism from two Latin words, *mare* and *niger*, the Black Sea.
[9] HFA.
[10] DL7V.
[11] HDTRM.
[12] DHB.

War in Piedmont. Mortara, March 1849. Defeat of Mortara before that of Novara.

Le tremblement de terre à Mortara,[1]
Cassich[2] sainct George[3] a demy perfondrez:[4]
Paix assoupie, la guerre esveillera.
Dans temple[5] à Pasques abysmes[6] enfondrez.[7]

CIX,Q31

Interpretation

War will shake the earth at Mortara. Because of a trap, half the Italian Army will be overthrown. Peace being weary, war shall break out again. In the Catholic Church, at Easter, there will be disaster.

History

'On 5 March, after the Turin Parliament and the Council of Lombard refugees *had formally called for war*, the King accepted Gioberti's resignation, and took on a new government comprised of *the pro-war majority*, with Ratazzi as President. On the twelfth, and this despite French and English representations, the King denounced the armistice to General Radetzky. . . . Hostilities began on the twentieth. The same day, rioting broke out at Brescia. Crzanowski's intention was to force the Austrians back on the Naviglio Grande so he could press on to Milan; Ramorino, on the right flank, and sent to *Mortara*, had the job of keeping watch on the enemy at Pavia and of aiding La Marmora. But during the night of the nineteenth Radetzky had withdrawn his troops to Pavia, and for his part had thrown a bridge across the Lower Ticino, over which two of his brigades had crossed to the right bank, encountering no resistance from Ramorino, who remained inactive. This grave error proved decisive. On the twenty-first the Piedmontese Army recrossed the Ticino to confront the Austrians, who were continuing to emerge from Pavia. Durando was sent in the vanguard to reinforce *Mortara*. Crzanowski led the rest to Sforzesca and Vigevano in order to support him. But delay in the arrival of supplies halted several brigades. The Piedmontese resisted brilliantly at Sforzesca on the twenty-first, without being able to check the Austrian advance, and Durando, almost cut off at *Mortara*, allowed this village to be captured in a night attack *at a cost of two thousand men killed or taken prisoner* . . . The defeat at Novara led to the fall of Brescia. . . .

Mazzini, who had been in Rome since 6 March, became a member of the Triumvirate on the twenty-ninth, the day on which news of the defeat at Novara reached Rome. A new Rienzi, who combined a tribune's passion with a mystic's fervour, he believed he could save the situation by invoking, in that eternal city, God and the people, *on the ruins* of the government and *of the Church*.'[8]

[1] Town in Italy (Piedmont), 23 km south-south-east of Novara. DHB.
[2] Traps, ambushes. D.LAT.
[3] Company of St George, regiment of *condottieri*. 'He had taken on to his payroll the Company of St George, a wholly Italian group. . . .' HIJZ.
[4] Latin *perfundere:* to disrupt, disturb. D.LAT.
[5] Poetic allusion to Roman Catholic Church. DL7V.
[6] Fig.: dangers or perils. DL7V.
[7] Latin *infundere:* to penetrate, introduce into. D.LAT.
[8] HIJZ.

Garibaldi from Sicily and Naples to Rome, 1860–67. The Agreement between Garibaldi and the British. The Shortcomings of Francis II, King of the Two Sicilies

Le mouvement des sens, coeur, pieds et mains,
Seront d'accord Naples, Lyon, Sicille.[1]
Glaives,[2] feux, eaux puis aux nobles Romains,
Plongez, tuez, morts par cerveau debile.

CI,QII

Interpretation

Through the progress of ideas, by a common feeling, feet and hands united, they shall be in accord with the British Lion for the expedition against Naples and Sicily. The battles, fires and revolutionary upheavals will win over the noble Romans [clergy]; the revolutionaries having been killed and put to death by one of feeble mind [Francis 11].

History

'Francis II, aged twenty-three, a dreary and simple character [*cerveau débile*] had succeeded Ferdinand upon the latter's death in 1859. . . . Dominated by a gerontocracy, the royal family of *Naples* was also wracked by sinister intrigues which weakened it day by day. Crispi reported to Garibaldi that *the revolution* had been *bloodily suppressed* [*plongez, tuez, morts*] at Palermo [Sicily], but that it continued nonetheless to *spread* [*mouvement des sens*] in the country areas. . . . After the Palermo setback the Bourbon troops in Sicily were augmented to about five thousand soldiers, based at Messina. The rest of the island came under the control of the new dictatorial government. The London *Times* hailed Garibaldi's triumph in the headline: "He Succeeds!" . . . At that time Garibaldi was the only foreigner to arouse such enthusiasm in *England* [*Lyon*], with his Sicilian expedition [*accord . . . Lyon, Sicille*]. . . . After the seizure of Palermo it became necessary to extend the war to the mainland, with Naples as objective. . . . The expedition against *Rome*, in autumn 1867, was one of the saddest episodes in Garibaldi's life. There he experienced one of the rare military defeats of his career, all the more bitter because it was inflicted by the French and the Pope. . . . Garibaldi succeeded in scoring an initial success by routing the papal forces and occupying Monterotondo. . . . The battle took place at Mentana. The enemy was numerically superior, with nine thousand papal troops [*nobles Romains*] and two thousand Frenchmen against five thousand on Garibaldi's side. . . .'[3]

¹ The Kingdom of the Two Sicilies consisted of two distinct parts: the Kingdom of Naples, and Sicily itself. . . . Francis II was expelled from Naples in 1860. His departure saw the end of the Kingdom of the Two Sicilies, which was annexed in 1861 and became part of the Kingdom of Italy. DHB.
² Symbol of war and battles. DL7V.
³ GP and MR.

End of the Pope's Temporal Power, 1870. Role of the Secret Societies. Internal Struggles

> Romain pouvoir sera du tout à bas,
> Son grand voisin imiter les vestiges:¹
> Occultes haines civiles et debats,
> Retarderont aux boufons leur folies.

CIII,Q63

Interpretation

[The Pope's temporal] Power shall be laid low in Rome, following in the footsteps of his great neighbour [France]. The hatred of the secret societies, in civil wars and disputes, will delay the follies of these clowns.

History

'There remained to Pius IX Rome, Civitavecchia and a few small fortresses manned by French garrisons. An attack by Garibaldi in 1867 was repulsed at Mentana by papal troops supported by French forces. But after the disasters of 1870 the French left *Rome* and the King of Italy's army entered the city after a brief skirmish on 20 September, the day *the Pope's temporal power*, constituted by Pepin the Short and by Charlemagne, *came to an end*. Rome became the capital of the Kingdom of Italy.'²

'The vote on the civil constitution of the clergy in July 1790 had graver consequences. This constitution had been drawn up by the Gallican Catholics who were *opposed to Papal supremacy*. The Pope did not even officiate at the spiritual investiture: he was merely informed of the election.'³

'In Italy, the pioneers of the revolution called themselves "Carbonari". The Carbonari were *a secret society* [*occultes haines*] which preached assassination as a political weapon and whose ultimate aim was the destruction of authoritarian regimes and the creation of egalitarian republics. One of its leaders was Filippa Buonaroti, an Italian aristocrat and naturalized Frenchman, *a friend of Robespierre* and precursor of revolutionary socialism. . . . A first insurrection fermented by Sardinian and Neapolitan officers *affiliated to* the Carbonari erupted simultaneously at Turin and Naples in 1821. . . . Nine years later, the *French Revolution of July 1830 had repercussions in Italy*. Modena and Bologna were the centres of rebellions which Metternich brutally suppressed. . . . In 1833, *Garibaldi made an important discovery as regards his political thinking: he became familiar with St-Simon's form of socialism.* Count St-Simon, an aristocrat who had miraculously escaped the guillotine during the Terror, wrote works in which he outlined a plan for the equal distribution of wealth and common ownership of property.'[4]

¹ Latin *vestigium:* trace. D.LAT.
² DHB.
³ HFAM.
⁴ GP and MR.

Garibaldi in Brazil, 1835. The Hohenzollern Candidacy to the Spanish Throne. The Duke of Aosta as King of Spain, 1870. Garibaldi's Landing at Marseille, 1870. The Advent of the Third Republic

Siècle nouveau,[1] alliance nouvelle,
Un Marquisat[2] mis dedans la nacelle,[3]
A qui plus fort des deux l'emportera;
D'un Duc[4] d'un Roy, gallere de Florence,[5]
Port à Marseille, Pucelle dans la France,
De Catherine fort chef on rasera.

Sixain 1

Interpretation

In a century of revival [the nineteenth], new alliances will take place. The head of a marquisate will be chosen for Spain. Will the Duke [of Aosta] or the King [William] be successful? A ship shall take [to Spain] [the heir] of Florence. [Garibaldi] shall land at Marseille to assist the return of the Republic to France; he who will have been present at the devastation of [Santa] Catarina.

History

'In September 1835, the eight thousand kilometres separating *Marseille* from Rio were travelled in eighty days. This richly adventurous period established him as a legendary fighter for freedom and national liberation. . . .'

The inhabitants of Santa Catarina soon lost their illusions after welcoming Gonzalves and his men as liberators. When several towns rebelled against the tyranny of the gauchos, Gonzalves decided to punish them for their disobedience and ordered Garibaldi to administer a stern lesson to one of their number, Imahury. The *repression was viciously cruel* and its memory was to haunt Garibaldi to the end of his days. The republicans were let loose to wreak savage havoc, *sacking and burning* houses and shops, massacring children and old people and raping women.'[6]

'On 15 July 1870, Benedetti met *King* William in the Park at Ems. He asked the latter for permission to announce that he would forbid Prince Hohenzollern to renew his candidature [for the Spanish throne].'[7]

'*Who would be king? Spain* entrusted her ambassadors with interviewing all the available princes of Europe. There were numerous refusals, but some acceptances, among them that of Leopold of Hohenzollern. Discussions between France, opposed to the rule of a Prussian in Spain, and Bismarck, led to the famous Ems Telegram which started the Franco-Prussian War of 1870. Finally, Amedeo of Savoy, Duke of Aosta, son of Victor Emmanuel II, declared his willingness to assume the throne of Spain. . . . The new sovereign arrived in Madrid on 2 January 1871.'[8]

'The Italian government was hardly concerned at seeing the dangerous agitator [Garibaldi] leave to work miracles in France. The war with the Prussians represented a good way of getting rid of him, and many of Victor Emmanuel II's entourage must have hoped he would not return. At Bonifacio Garibaldi found a yacht – the *Ville de Paris* – lent by a wealthy Marseille businessman of republican and progressive views. At *Marseille* he received a triumphant welcome. Delighted and moved at his reception by the people of Marseille, Garibaldi wrote to a friend: "To my dying day I shall be proud *to serve the sacred cause of the Republic.*" '

---

[1] The nineteenth century saw changes not only of rule but also of institutions and laws (*Code Civil* in France). All the alliances of the Ancien Régime would be revised.

[2] The Marches were called *marchiones*, later Margraves or *Marquises*. In Charlemagne's time the marches were composed of the Saxon March and the Friulian March in Italy . . . DL7V. Thus the use of the word marquisate for the Val d'Aosta.

[3] Denotes Spain. Cf. cv,Q49.

4 Amedeo I abdicated on 10 February 1873. He returned to Italy, took up his previous title of Duke of Aosta, and received his former emolument. DL7V.

5 Amedeo I was the son of Victor Emmanuel II, King of Italy, whose capital was *Florence*. Cf. CV,Q39, Vol. 1.

6 GP and MR.

7 LSEOA.

8 HDEJP.

The Succession to the Spanish Throne a Cause of the Franco-Prussian War of 1870. French Troops Surrounded at Metz. The Eastern Army at Villersexel.

Tous ceux de Illerde[1] seront dans la Moselle,
Mettant à mort tous ceux de Loire et Seine,
Le cours[2] marin viendra près d'Hautevelle,[3]
Quand Espagnols ouvrira toute veine.

CI,Q89

Interpretation

Germans and Austrians will enter the Moselle area, decimating the armies of the Loire and Paris. He who will have come by sea shall approach Hautevelle. When the Spaniards leave open the succession to the throne [good fortune for the Hohenzollerns].

History

'Owing to a revolution, *the Spanish throne had been vacant* since 1868. *The Spaniards were seeking a king.* Suddenly, on 2 July 1870, Prince Leopold of Hohenzollern, cousin of the King of Prussia, announced his candidacy. Public opinion in France fell into the trap and all common sense was instantly abandoned. It seemed obvious to everyone that a Prussian Prince ruling Spain meant that France would be caught between two fires, and there was talk of the return of the Empire of Charles V. . . .'

'Following the agreements of 1866, men from Baden and *Württemberg*, as well as *Bavarians*, marched alongside the Prussians. . . . There were three French armies in the field that December and January: the Northern Army under Faidherbe, the 2nd *Loire* Army under Chanzy, and the Eastern Army under Bourbaki.'[4]

'According to Moltke's plan, the Germans regrouped into three armies. The first, on the right flank, marched along *the Moselle*. . . . Facing the Crown Prince was MacMahon, who had *hastened from Algeria* [*cours marin*] and now had to defend Alsace. . . .'[5]

'Victor of *Villersexel* [9 January 1871], Bourbaki could not break the lines at Héricourt. Pushed back upon Besançon, then to the Swiss frontier, and caught between two German armies, the Eastern Army only escaped surrender by rushing into Switzerland, where it was disarmed.'

'However, to hasten the capitulation of Paris [*Seine*] the Germans began the bombardment of the town. . . . A sortie was attempted by ninety thousand men on 19 January, pushing towards Buzenval and Montretout on the plateaux overlooking the Seine, west of Paris. This proved a new and *bloody* failure.'[6]

[1] The Iller, German river, whose source is in the north-west Tyrol, separates *Bavaria from Württemberg*, and meets the Danube 2 km above Ulm. DHB. Nostradamus denotes, by naming this river, both Germans and Austrians. Example of paragoge.
[2] Fig.: march, progress. DL7V.
[3] Commune of the Haute-Saône, 15 km from Villersexel.
[4] HFAM.
[5] LSEOA.
[6] HFAM.

1830–70: Forty Years of War.
1871–1914: Forty Years of Peace

Par quarante ans l'Iris[1] n'apparoistra,
Par quarante ans tous les jours sera veu:
La terre aride[2] en siccité[3] croistra,
En grand déluges[4] quand sera aperceu.

CI,QI7

Interpretation

For forty years peace will not be known, then for forty years there will be peace every day. The minds of men will become arid and dry when great revolutions are seen [1917].

History

1830: Departure from Toulon of the French fleet, sent to Algiers.

1831: French expedition in Portugal.

1832: Occupation of Ancona by the French. Siege of Anvers and capture of that town.

1833: Naval battle at Cape St Vincent.

1834: The French repel six thousand Kabyles invading from Bejaia in Algeria.

1835: Expedition against Mascara.

1836: Tlemcen and Constantine expeditions.

1837: Constantine captured.

1838: French intervention at La Plata: capture by the French of Martin-Garcia Island (Argentina). French intervention in Mexico.

1839: French actions at Portes-de-Fer, Algeria.

1840: Heroic defence by the garrison of Fort Mazagran. Occupation of Cherchell, Medeah, Milianah. Bombardment of Beirut and fall of Sidon, Lebanon.

1841: Seizure by the French of the Nossi-Bé and Nossi-Komba islands in the Indian Ocean.

1842: Occupation of Mayotte and the islands of Tahiti and the Marquesas.

1843: Duke of Aumale captures the Smala of Abd-el-Kader. Occupation of Assinia, Grand-Bassam, and Gabon.

1844: Capture of Oujda. Bombardment of Tangier and Mogador. Campaign against the Kabyles.

1845: Anglo-French expedition against Tamatava. Kabyle uprising. Anglo-French fleet goes into battle against the dictator Rosas, at Obligado, in support of Uruguayan independence.

1846: Abd-el-Kader leaves the desert, swoops upon the Titteri territory and appears among the Kabyles of the Dellys circle; the Emir is pursued into Moroccan territory by General Cavaignac.

187: In Algeria, the surrender of the agitator Boumaza. Cochin China expedition. Failure of Anglo-French operations against the Hovas on Madagascar. Surrender of Abd-el-Kader.

1848: Revolution and fierce fighting in Paris. State of siege declared.

1849: French expeditionary force sent to Italy to aid the King of Piedmont. Siege and occupation of Rome (2 and 3 July). In Algeria, rebellions against the French are suppressed.

1850: Riots in Algeria. Arrests at Lyon and Avignon over a conspiracy involving several departments in the Midi.

1851: Bombardment of Rabat and Sale by Rear-Admiral Dubourdieu.

1852: Surrender by ninety-two delegates from seventeen different branches of the Zaouaouas, in Greater Kabylia. The Sherif of Ourgla is forced into Laghonat, which falls to General Pelissier.

1853: Occupation of New Caledonia. Generals Bousquet and MacMahon defeat the Kabyles of the Babor Mountains between Setif, Bejaia and Djidjelli.

1854: Landings in the Crimea. Victory of the Alma. Siege of Sebastopol.

1855: Military advances as far as the oases of Ouargla and Metlili. Operations in the Djurjura – capture of Touggourt. Capture of Sebastopol in the Crimea.

1856: Expeditions by the Renault and Yusuf divisions against the Kabyles.

1857: Generals Renault and Yusuf force the Kabyle surrender. War with the Moors on the left bank of the Senegal River.

1858: After three years of war, treaty with the King of the Trarzas in Senegal.

1859: War in Italy – battles of Magenta and Solferino.

1860: French expedition into Syria against the Druzes. China expedition. Capture of Peking.

1861–62: War in Cochin China. Treaty of Hué. The French from Rome occupy Terracina.

1863: Mexico: expeditionary force sets out from Orizaba against Puebla – occupation of Queretaro. War in Cochin China against Tu-Duc.

1864: Riots in various Algerian towns. Struggle of the Franco-Chinese army against the Taipings.

1865: An uprising of the Babor tribes in Algeria is suppressed. Pinet campaign. Laprade in Gambia. Mexican War.

1866: Mexican War. Insurrections at Sidon and Géryville. Expedition in Cochin China against the Cambodians. Fighting against the cannibals in New Caledonia.

1867: End of war in Mexico. In Senegal, struggle against Maba partisans. Fighting in Cochin China. Intervention against Garibaldi in Italy.

1868: Rebellion in western Algeria after the death of Si-Hamza. Demonstration of St Denis, Réunion Island, bloodily suppressed. French outpost surprised by force of Annamites.

1869: Rebellion of the Ouled-Sidi-Sheik in Algeria. In Senegal, expedition against a fanatical chieftain, Ahmadou Sekhou, and against Lat-Dior.

1870: Franco-Prussian War.

Forty years of war on an extraordinary variety of different fronts!

1871–1913: Forty-two years of peace centred round the Belle Epoque.

[1] Iris, personification of the rainbow, regarded as the messenger of the gods. DCBM. Rainbow: symbolizes all that is pleasant, alluding to the biblical meteor by which God showed Noah that he would never again lose the earth by *flood*. DL7V.

[2] 'There came a time of *dryness* and lassitude, when *arid* speculations were indulged in.' St-Evremont. DL.

[3] Dryness (*sécheresse*).

[4] By analogy, a considerable cataclysm with the earth its theatre. DL7V. Here implying, as do the words *water* and *flood*, revolution.

The Russian Revolution Leads to Famine and Disaster, 1917. Human Rights Ignored. Battles of the Somme 1916–18

Si grand famine par unde[1] pestifère
Par pluye[2] longue le long du polle artique:
Samarobryn[3] cent lieux de l'hemisphere
Vivront sans loy exempt de pollitique.[4]

CVI,Q5

Interpretation

A disastrous revolution will lead to a great famine. This revolution will affect a hundred places in the Northern Hemisphere during the battles. Men shall live without law in aid of the citizens.

History

'Revolution in Russia. In Switzerland in January 1917 Lenin said that his generation would not live long enough to see the triumph of the Revolution in Russia, and, in a single week, from 8 to 15 March, the Romanov Empire was finished.'[5]

'Ludendorff's offensives. Picardy, 21 March–5 April. The *Michel* operation was intended to drive the British back to the sea and surrounding the French left flank . . . The sequence of battle began with the destruction of Gough's army south of the Somme, followed by a rapid push for *Amiens*, whose outskirts were reached on the thirtieth. . . .'[5]

'The Great Purge, by which he [Stalin] set himself up as undisputed dictator, consisted of three basic elements: above all, the scale of the operation created *millions of victims*, while each member of the population felt threatened; then there were the methods adopted, in particular the extraordinary ordeal of confession, during which the dictator's main opponents publicly accused themselves of treason; finally, there was the air of mystery surrounding it: the only exception to this was a number of show trials held in public and various announcements of executions. Otherwise, nothing of the Purge was officially admitted [*sans loy exempt de pollitique*].'[6]

'The economic revival was halted in 1922 by *the great famine* which ravaged the entire agricultural region of the Ukraine, and those of the Volga and Western Siberia.'[7]

[1] Latin *unda:* movement of a crowd, agitation, trouble. D.LAT.
[2] Rain, used in the same sense as above.
[3] Samarobriva, town in Gaul, capital of the Ambii. D.LAT. Now Amiens.
[4] Greek: Πολιτικός, relative or proper to citizens, civil, civic. DG.
[5] PANS.
[6] LGT.
[7] USDH.

The First World War Follows the Belle Epoque. Progress in Travel by Land, Sea and Air. Twentieth-century Wars

Les fleurs[1] passez, diminue le monde,[2]
Long temps la paix, terres inhabitées,
Sur marchera par ciel, terre, mer et onde,
Puis de nouveau les guerres suscitées.

CI,Q63

Interpretation

After the Belle Epoque, there shall be fewer people; after a long period of peace [1871–1914], lands shall no longer be inhabited. Men will know how to travel in the sky, by land, sea and under water. Then new wars will break out.

History

The First World War brought France brutally out of the Belle Epoque and plunged her into a nightmare. The battle zones, littered with shells and mines, were to remain uninhabited for some years afterwards.

The 1871–1914 period would see engineering developments and improvements change the face of man's travel: trains, motor cars, aeroplanes, steamships and submarines [onde].

Anarchist Movements in Spain, 1897–1939. Exile of Alfonso XIII, 1931. Franco and the Civil War Bloodbath, 1936–39

> Lorsque serpens[1] viendront circuire[2] l'are,[3]
> Le sang Troyen[4] vexé par les Espagnes:
> Par eux grand nombre en sera faict tare,[5]
> Chef fruict,[6] caché[7] au mares dans les saignes.

CI,QI9

Interpretation

When the Anarchists come and show themselves in the [Spanish] land, Bourbon blood will be troubled in the regions of Spain. A great number of deaths will be caused by these Anarchists. A leader [Franco] will benefit from this and drive them into pools of blood.

History

'Anarchism. The Spanish workers' demands are much the same as those of other European proletarian movements. What distinguishes Spain however is the *Anarchist* element, far more influential in the Iberian peninsula, where it became guerrilla ideology. Its ideal was direct action, *assassination*. . . .

Between 1897 and 1923 Anarchism had to its credit the assassinations of three heads of government, Canovas, Canalejas and Dato, not counting several unsuccessful attempts upon the life of the King of Spain. The Anarchists declared war on the Church, the Army and society. As regards the former, various churches in Barcelona had been burned down since the 'Tragic Week' of 1909, and this happened again at the start of the Civil War in 1936. As for the bourgeoisie, a bomb was thrown into the stalls of the Lyceum Theatre in Barcelona, and during a religious procession in the same town.'[8]

The Republic was proclaimed in 1931, when Alfonso XIII was forced into exile.

'In the Republican zone, persecution of the Church had begun in 1936 at the start [of the war]; numerous religious buildings were burned and sacked, and many priests shot or imprisoned. . . . In the Nationalist zone, anyone suspected of contacts with left-wing organizations became the target for persecution. Various executions were carried out also by unaffiliated groups. But the majority of the death sentences were pronounced by the military tribunals which functioned continuously throughout the conflict. . . . The number of those on both sides who died because of their political beliefs was very high. A rough estimate was 750,000 dead [pools of blood]. . . .'[8]

1 Nostradamus here denotes revolutionary anarchists. Cf. C I I , Q43 , Vol. I.
2 To go the rounds of. DAFL.
3 The entire surface. Used here to denote the whole country.
4 Cf. CVI, Q52, Vol. I.
5 *Tarer:* to spoil, corrupt. DL.
6 Fig.: profit, advantage, useful result. DL7V.
7 Latin *cogere:* to push in front of one, chase, force, drive violently. D.LAT.
8 HEFDP.

The Russo-German Pact, 23 August 1939. The German Wheat Shortage, 1939

La Sangsue[1] au loup[2] se joindra,
Lorsqu'en mer le blé défaudra,
Mais le grand Prince sans envie,
Par ambassade luy donra
De son blé pour lui donner vie,
Pour un besoin s'en pourvoira.

Sixain 7

Interpretation

The USSR will ally with Germany when the supplies of wheat by sea are lacking. But the great leader [Stalin] will gladly bring his aid through an embassy and will supply the wheat to alleviate want.

History

'The USSR is neutral should there be a German-Polish War. Even more curious and important is the recent approach by the Soviet *ambassador* in Warsaw, Mr Charonov, who was eager to convince Colonel Beck that the Soviet government had nothing but friendly intentions towards Poland.'

'In Germany at this very time the civilian population has been enlisting. . . . Starting today, *bread ration cards* are being introduced. To quote Dr Schacht: "One cannot end a war with bread rationing, nor can one begin a war with bread rationing." Does Herr Hitler distrust the warning given by the man who in the Third Reich has the reputation of being the most realistic of politicians?'[3]

[1] The leech, or blood-drinker, i.e. the revolutionary USSR. Cf. Sixains 21, 30, 40, and 46, Vol. I.
[2] Cf. CV,Q4, Vol. I.
[3] Extracts from an article by Jean Thouvenin in *L'Intransigeant*, 29 August 1939.

Mussolini and Clara Petacci Taken by Lorry to Milan. The Seven Corpses at Piazzale Loreto in Milan, 29 April 1945

Serpens[1] transmis[2] en la cage de fer,
Où les enfans[3] septains[4] du Roy sont prins:
Les vieux et pères sortiront bas de l'enfer,
Ains mourir voir de fruict mort et cris.

CI,QIO

Interpretation

The wicked one will be transported in a lorry to the place where the seven abominable persons of the [Fascist] Regime are guarded. The elderly and the relatives will leave their homes [in order to indulge in] mean acts. They will want to see the dead, amid cries and fruits [refuse].

History

'It was 8 p.m. when a large yellow *van* from Dongo reached Mezzagra with its macabre load. Clara was thrown on top of the heap first, followed by Mussolini. At 8.15 the van moved on towards Como and Milan.'

'Around 7 a.m. in the cold Sunday dawn of 29 April 1945, the first passers-by approached. The crowd swelled rapidly. The news spread that Mussolini's corpse was there! At 9 a.m. there was complete hysteria.

A woman came and fired five revolver shots into the Duce's body, *screaming* [*cris*] that she was thus avenging her five sons killed during the war. . . . It triggered off a chain reaction. The crowd soon became uncontrollable. Assorted scraps of *vegetables* were thrown at the bodies. People spat on them. . . . Anyone who wanted to do so "heroically" kicked Mussolini's body and Clara Petacci's too. One termagant urinated on the Duce's face. . . . A man stuck a stick into Mussolini's hand for a sceptre and a crown of *cabbage* leaves round his head [*bas de l'enfer*].

At 11 a.m. the corpses were strung up by ropes on the forecourt of a filling station: Mussolini, Clara, Pavolini, Zerbino, Barracu and Porta. The crowd *shrieked* with joy and insulted the *idol* [*serpent*] it had worshipped. Shortly afterwards, at 11.10 a.m., the former general secretary of the party, Achille Starace, was led there and six partisans shot him in the back. His body also was strung up alongside those hanging there [6+1=7]. The crowd was delirous until almost one o'clock, its collective *hysteria* indescribable.'[5]

¹ Symbolic of a perfidious, evil person. DL7V.
² Latin *transmitto:* I transport. D.LAT.
³ Latin *infans:* abominable, frightful. D.LAT.
⁴ Septain – group of seven similar things. DAFL.
⁵ MAB.

Hesitation over the Provence Landing, August–December 1943. The German Occupation as far as Monaco. Imprisonment of Mussolini. Mussolini Hanged in Milan, 29 April 1945

De sang et faim plus grand calamité,
Sept fois¹ s'appreste à la marine plage:
Monech de faim, lieu pris, captivité,
Le grand mené croc² enferrée³ cage.⁴

CIII,QIO

Interpretation

Through blood and famine the calamity will be still greater. Several times preparations will be made to land on the coast [of Provence]. Hunger will reach Monaco, this place having been occupied. After his captivity the great [Mussolini] shall be driven in a van and displayed from an iron hook.

History

'The operation codenamed Anvil had been called Dragoon since 1 August in order to throw German intelligence off the scent, and *this operation*, which ought to have liberated the whole of the South of France in record time, *had run into difficulties from the first*. Within Allied Command itself, as well as in its relationship with the French, different arguments had *cast doubt* upon the success and even the very *existence of the operation*.

First, the whole principle of the landing had been criticized, on political as well as military grounds.

While the Quebec Conference of August 1943, convened to decide on the creation of the second front, had suggested a southern landing to liaise with the Normandy one, and the December 1943 Teheran Conference had confirmed the plan, *the appropriateness of Operation Anvil was constantly being questioned* [*sept fois s'appreste*] as the date set for it drew ever nearer. . . .'[5]

'German Defences. The 19th Army had the task of defending the 650 km of coastline between *Menton* and Cerbère, and on *the day of the landing* six infantry divisions were regrouped along either bank of the Rhône.'[6]

'Between 1940 and 1944, *the principality was occupied* first by the Italians, then by the Germans, for military purposes.'[7]

'Mussolini's imprisonment at the de Marias': "As a temporary *prison*, it was ideal. . . . At 11 a.m. six of the corpses were strung up by ropes on *the forecourt* of the filling station: Mussolini, Clara, Pavolini, Zerbino, Barracu and Porta. . . ." '[8]

---

[1] In the Bible, the number 7 is often used to denote a considerable amount, as we might say 'hundreds'. DL7V.

[2] Another name for the hooks used to hang meat from. DL7V.

h5[3] Latin *inferre:* to present, display. D.LAT.

[4] Cf. CI,Q10; CII,Q24, in Vol. I, and CIX,Q95.

[5] HLFRA.

[6] LDG.

[7] From *History of Monaco* by J. B. Robert. PUF: *Que Sais-je*, No. 497.

[8] MAB.

The Link-up between the French, American, British and Russian Armies on the Danube, April–May 1945. Mussolini in a Van and the Fall of Hitler, 29 April 1945

Bestes farouches de faim fleuves tranner,[1]
Pluspart du champ encotre Hister[2] sera,
En cage de fer[3] le grand fera traisner,
Quand rien enfant[4] de Germain observera.

CII,Q24

Interpretation

They shall cross the rivers like wild and ravenous beasts. The larger part of the field [of battle] will be on the Danube. The great one [Mussolini] will be hauled in a van, when nothing more of the abominable German [Hitler] can be seen.[5]

History

'The Rhine-*Danube* Campaign. The fifth and final act of the "Rhine and *Danube*" campaign consisted of a pincer action by Monsabert and Béthouart, whose objective was Ulm [Ulm is on the Danube]; the former, with his 5th Armoured Division and 2nd Infantry Division (General de Linarès) north of the *Danube*, the latter thrusting his 1st Armoured Division (General Sudre) at the main Donaueschingen-Biberach road, *south of the river. . . .*'

'Liberation of *Vienna*. But already by 2 April, advancing between Lake Neusiedl and the *Danube*, Malinowski had forced the Mur at Bruck, while Tolbukin, in possession of the important industrial centre of Wiener Neustadt, pushed forward one column on to the Semmering road towards Graz and another on to Mödling and the Austrian capital. . . . Marshal Tolbukin, who was revelling in the capture of 130,000 prisoners, 1,350 tanks and 2,250 guns, *went back along the Danube's* right bank, but did not take his armour beyond the small town of Amstetten, 125 km west of Vienna. On 4 May his patrols on the outskirts of Linz [on the Danube] met up with the American 3rd Army's. On the Graz road, that same day, they came into contact with British 8th Army reconnaissance parties.'[6]

'*The removals van* [*cage de fer!*] was waiting at the crossroads. *The two corpses were thrown* on top of the other fifteen. Early in the morning of 29 April 1945 the furniture removals van reached Milan, after passing through several American roadblocks. It stopped in front of an unfinished concrete garage on the Piazzale Loreto.'[7]

'The night of 30 April 1945, Goebbels and Bormann tried vainly to negotiate with the Russians. The answer was: "Unconditional Surrender".'[8]

[1] Latin *tranare* or *transnare:* to journey over, cross. *Tranare flumina curru* (Statius), to cross a river on a chariot or float. D.LAT.

[2] Ancient name for the Danube. Most commentators persist in reading the word as 'Hitler'.

[3] Cf. CIX,Q95, Vol. I.

[4] Latin *infans:* abominable, dreadful. D.LAT.

[5] Typical example of concomitance between two events.

[6] LDG.

[7] MCH.

[8] MAB.

Socialism and François Mitterrand. The First Steps in the Rise to Power

La belle rose[1] en la France admirée,
D'un très grand Prince[2] à la fin désirée,
Six cens et dix, lors naistront ses amours
Cinq ans après, sera d'un grand blessée,[3]
Du trait d'Amour,[4] elle sera enlassée,[5]
Si à quinze du Ciel reçoit secours.

Sixain 44

Interpretation

The fine rose [of Socialism] will be admired in France and its great leader [Mitterrand] shall be sought after at last. At the end of just over fifty years his passion [for the State] will be born. Five years later Socialism will be impressed by a great man [Mitterrand] and will not be harmed by the critics [political attacks], since after fifteen years he will receive Heaven's aid [Jews and Catholics].

History

1916: François Mitterrand born; 610 months = 50 years; 1916 + 50 = 1966. 'On 5 May 1966, François Mitterrand announced the formation of an alternative government similar to the British Shadow Cabinet.'[6]

1966 + 5 = 1971. On 16 June 1971, the new French Socialist Party under Mitterrand's leadership was formed.

Interpretation

The USSR shall crumble and that will be good for France's new growth. Alliances will be made. Two great countries will unite under the influence of France.

Communism Abandoned in Seven Countries. Homage Paid to the King of France and Navarre

> Le procrée naturel dogmion[1]
> De sept à neuf du chemin destourner,
> A roy de longue[2] et amy au my[3] hom.
> Doit à Navarre fort de Pau[4] prosterner.
>
> CVIII,Q44

Interpretation

The natural heir to the system based upon political discourses [the Communism stemming from the parliamentary system born in 1789 with the Oath of the Tennis Court] will cease in seven countries out of nine, because of him who will become king after a long while, and for whom there will be friendship among men, who should bow down before the powerful person from Pau, King of France and of Navarre.

[1] Several editions have '*d'ogmion*' or '*d'Ogmion*'. Cf. Presage 39; and in Vol. I CV,Q80 and CIX,Q89.
[2] Feminine ending, for '*longue durée*', i.e. of time. DL7V.
[3] *A my* or *a mi*, meaning amid. DAFL.
[4] Henri V, successor of Henri IV whose birthplace was Pau.

World Wars. Return of the Monarchy

> Tant d'ans en Gaule les guerres dureront,
> Outre la course de Castulon[1] monarque:
> Victoire incerte trois grands couronneront,
> Aigle,[2] coq,[3] Lune,[4] Lyon,[5] Soleil en marque.
>
> CI,Q31

Interpretation

Wars will last in France for many years, after the reign of the King of Spain. Three heads of states [USA, France and England] will celebrate an indecisive victory. The USA, the King of France, the Republic, England will see the sign of the monarchy.

[1] Castulon, town in Tarragona, today Carbona. DLLB. Tarragona was one of the three great provinces of ancient Spain, and consisted approximately of the modern provinces of Catalonia, Aragon, Navarre, Biscay, Asturias, Galicia, Minho and Douro, Tras-os-Montes, Leon, Old (and some of New) Castile, and Valencia. DHB. Nostradamus, as he often does, denotes the King of Spain by referring to a small town within the chief province of that country. Cf. CV, Q99, Vol. I, and CVIII,Q9.
[2] The American Eagle. Cf. CV,Q99, Vol. I, and CVIII,Q9.
[3] Cf. pp. 388–89, Vol. I.
[4] Taken as symbol of the Republic, as opposed to the Sun, symbol of the Monarchy.
[5] The British Lion.

Peace Returns. Union of France and Spain

Croix paix, soubs un accomply divin verbe,
Espagne et Gaules seront unis ensemble:
Grand clade[1] proche, et combat tres acerbe,
Coeur si hardy ne sera qui ne tremble.

CIV,Q5

Interpretation

The Christians [Catholics and Protestants] will be at peace; God's word [the prophecy] will be fulfilled. Spain and France shall be united, after a major defeat and a very bitter war affects them, so much so that even the most courageous will tremble.

[1] Latin *clades:* loss, calamity, disaster – especially of a military reverse or defeat. D.LAT.

SUBJECTS OF THE QUATRAINS AND SIXAINS

The Yellow Invasion – 1999

The Yellow Invasion Preceded by the Russian Revolution

The End of the 'Western Era' – Quarrels among the Theologians

The End of Communism in Russia – The USSR Besieged by the Eastern Bloc (China, Japan) – The Golden Age

Disastrous Harvests – Appalling Climatic Conditions – Asia (Japan and China) Arms – France Besieged

The Vatican Ravaged by the Asiatic States (China and Japan)

Scotland, then England, Attacked by the Yellow Peril

The Fall of the Asiatic Empire – Danger at Salon in Provence

The End of Wars – The First Resurrection

Universal Peace for a Thousand Years – The First Resurrection, 2026–3000

The Yellow Invasion Preceded by the Russian Revolution

Beaucoup avant telles menées,[1]
Ceux d'Orient par la vertu Lunaire:
L'an mil sept cents seront grand emmenées,[2]
Subjugant presque le coing Aquilonnaire.

CI,Q49

Interpretation

Well before such great attacks coming from Asia by a Republican system [People's Republic of China], in the year 1917 the great ones [Tsar and his family] will be carried off [by the Revolution] which will put Russia under its yoke.

[1] Charge, attack, pursuit. DAFL.
[2] Cf. Presages 62 and 89, Vol. 1.

The End of the 'Western Era'. Quarrels among the Theologians

> Le temps présent avecques le passé,
> Sera jugé par le grand Jovialiste:[1]
> Le monde tard par luy sera lassé,
> Et desloyal par le clergé juriste.
>
> CX,Q73

Interpretation

The great leader of the West shall judge the present and the past. He will abandon the [western] world towards its end [1999], the theologians then showing their disloyalty.

[1] Cf. Letter to Henri and Presage 129. Does this refer to the King of France and his end, c. 1999?

The Chinese Flood through the West. Subversion in Africa. The Golden Age Comes from Asia

> Mer par solaires[1] seure[2] passera,
> Ceux de Venus[3] tiendront toute l'Afrique:
> Leur Regne plus Saturne[4] n'occupera,
> Et changera la part Asiatique.
>
> CV,QII

Interpretation

The sister of the Japanese [China] will cross the sea. The subversives will be everywhere in Africa. Their power will not last until the Golden Age, since change will come from part of Asia.

[1] The word *solaires* in the plural is only used by Nostradamus in this particular quatrain. He seems here to be referring to the Japanese.
[2] The sister of Japan, China.
[3] Cf. CIV,Q28, Vol. I.
[4] The time of Saturn and Rhea: Golden Age which is to last while Saturn governs the universe. DL7V.

The End of Communism in Russia. The USSR Besieged by the Eastern Bloc (China, Japan). The Golden Age

Froid, grand déluge[1] de regne dechassé,
Niez, discord. Trion[2] crient mine:
Poison, mis siege, de la Cité chassé,
Retour felice, neuve secte en ruine.

Presage 21, October

Interpretation

During the winter the great [October] revolution will be driven out of power because it will have been led by fools who will disagree. The States of Asia will threaten the USSR with chemical warfare; the latter will be besieged. [The Russians] will be driven from Moscow. Then happiness shall return, when the new party [Communist] is in ruins.

[1] Words such as water, wave, whirlpool, flood, typhoon etc. are always used as symbols of revolution.

[2] Trion: astronomical term; Septentrion is the name given to the seven stars forming the constellations of Ursa Major and Minor. DL7V. Allusion to Russia in Europe and Russia in Asia, as well as to the seven Warsaw Pact countries. USSR is called the bear (Latin *ursa*) elsewhere.

Disastrous Harvests. Appalling Climatic Conditions. Asia (Japan and China) Arms. France Besieged

Les bleds trop n'abonder, de toutes autres fruits,
L'esté, printemps humide, hiver long, neige, force,[1] glace:
En armes l'Orient, la France se renforce,
Mort de bestail prou miel, aux assiegez la place.

Presage 124, June

Interpretation

Wheat will be in short supply. Among all the other fruits of the earth, violence will predominate. After a rainy spring and summer there will be a long, snowy, glacial winter. The Orient will arm itself, France reinforce herself. The death of cattle will put an end to prosperity for those besieged in their own land [France].

The Vatican Ravaged by the Asiatic States (China and Japan)

En débats Princes et Chrestienté esmeuë,
Gentils¹ estranges, siege à Christ molesté:
Venu tres mal, prou² bien, mortelle veue.
Mort Orient peste, faim, mal³ traité.

Presage 83, April

Interpretation

When there are discussions between heads of state and Christianity is agitated, the seat of Christianity [the Vatican] will be tormented by brave foreigners. This will be very untimely, under cover of benevolence, and will turn out to be fatal. The Orient will bring death, calamity and famine, because of a bad treaty.

¹ Valiant, generous. DAFL.
² *Pour*, for. DAFL.
³ Bad, wicked. DAFL.

Scotland, then England, attacked by the Yellow Peril

Soubs le terroir du rond globe lunaire,¹
Lors que sera dominateur Mercure,²
L'Isle d'Écosse³ sera un luminaire,⁴
Qui les Anglois mettra à déconfiture.

CV,Q93

Interpretation

Under the jurisdiction of the great Yellow Empire run by a rogue, Scotland will be in flames and after that the English will be discomfited.

[1] Allusion to sallow hue of the Asiatics. Cf. CVI,Q80, Vol. I.

[2] God of thieves. Ambassador plenipotentiary to the gods, he presided over alliances and treaties, sanctioning and ratifying them, and was no stranger to declarations of war between cities and nations. MGR. Cf. CX,Q75, Vol. I.

[3] Cf. CX,Q66, Vol. I.

[4] Symbolic. For *flambeau*, torch. DL7V.

The Fall of the Asiatic Empire. Danger at Salon in Provence

Quand seront proches le défaut des lunaires,[1]
De l'un à l'autre ne distant grandement,
Froid, siccité, dangers sur les frontières,
Mesme où l'oracle a pris commancement.

CIII,Q4

Interpretation

When the fall of the Asiatic armies is near, it will not be long between their peak and their fall.[2] There will be cold, drought and various dangers on the frontiers, even where the prophecy began [at Salon in Provence].

[1] Cf. CV,Q93.
[2] Cf. CVIII,Q77, Vol. I.

The End of Wars. The First Resurrection

Les os des pieds et des mains enserrez,[1]
Par bruit maison longtemps inhabitée,
Seront par songes[2] concavant[3] deterrez,
Maison salubre et sans bruit habitée.

CVII,Q41

Interpretation

Those whose skeletons were enclosed and who had left their houses a long time uninhabited because of the noise [of war] shall leave their tombs in their sleep and shall inhabit a healthy house without noise [of war].

---

[1] To lock away, enclose, shut in. DAFL.

[2] In dream, during sleep. DL7V.

[3] Latin *concavare:* to make hollow, hollow out, empty. D. LAT. The present participle is used here as a noun.

Universal Peace for a Thousand Years. The First Resurrection, 2026–3000

> Au revole[1] du grande nombre septiesme,[2]
> Apparoistra au temps jeux d'Hécatombe:[3]
> Non esloigné du grand eage milliesme,[4]
> Que les entrez sortiront de leur tombe.

CX,Q74

Interpretation

When the seventh millennium is reached [7000=2000] there shall then be a veritable hecatomb which will happen close to the millennium [1999]. Then those who entered the tomb shall leave it.

Comparison with Revelations 20: 1–5

And I saw an angel come down from heaven, having the key of the bottomless pit and a great chain in his hand.

And he laid hold on the dragon, that old serpent, which is the Devil, and Satan, and bound him *a thousand years.*[5]

And cast him into the bottomless pit, and shut him up, and set a seal upon him, that he should deceive the nations no more, till the thousand years should be fulfilled [the year 3000]: and after that he must be loosed a little season.

And I saw thrones, and they sat upon them, and judgement was given unto them: and I saw the souls of them that were beheaded for the witness of Jesus, and for the word of God,[6] and which had not worshipped the beast, neither his image, neither had received his mark upon their foreheads, or in their hands; and *they lived*[5] and reigned with Christ *a thousand years.*[5]

But the rest of the dead lived not again until the thousand years were finished. This is the first resurrection.

[1] Latin *revolutus:* having made its revolution, passed.
[2] Cf. CI,Q48, Vol. I.
[3] Great public sacrifice, the number and type of victims unspecified. DL7V.
[4] According to Nostradamus, this thousand-year period begins in 2026, not 2000.
[5] Author's italics.
[6] For Nostradamus, the Word of God is prophecy. Cf. CII, Q27 and CIII,Q2.

BIBLIOGRAPHY

Abbreviations

BN: Bibliothèque Nationale
BMA: Bibl. Municipale Aix-en-Provence
BML: Bibl. Municipale Lyon

Allaines, Henri d': *Actualité de l'Apocalypse*, La Colombe, Paris, 1963.
Alleau, René: 'Nostradamus le plus grand prophète de l'histoire', *Sallonensa*, Salon, 1957.
Alliaume, Maurice: *Magnus Rex de Nostradamus et son drapeau*, publ. at author's expense at Chartres, 1948.
   Prédictions vraies de Nostradamus et Mandragore, publ. at author's expense at Chartres, 1949.
Amadou, Robert: 'Le Devin et son Art', *Le Crapouillot*, no. 18. 1952.
Amiaux: *Nostradamus*, Sorlot, Paris.
Anon: *La Première Invective du Seigneur Hercules, Le François, contre Nostradamus*, Michel Jove, Lyon, 1558.
   Huictain contre Nostradamus, Roux, Lyon, 1557.
   Déclaration des abus, ignorances, séditions de Michel Nostradamus, Pierre Roux et Jean Tremblay, Avignon, 1558.
Anquetil, Georges: *L'Anti-Nostradamus*, Ed. de la Maison des Ecrivains, Paris, 1940.
Artigny, Abbé d': *Nouveaux mémoires d'histoire, de critique et de littérature*, 1794.
Astruc, Jean: *Mémoires pour servir à l'histoire de la faculté de Montpellier*, 1767.
Auclair, Raoul: *Les Centuries de Nostradamus*, Deux Rives, Paris, 1958.
   Le Crépuscule des Nations, La Colombe, Paris.
   Les Centuries de Nostradamus ou le dixième livre sibyllin, Nouvelles Editions Latines, 1957.
Barbarin, Georges: *Les Derniers Temps du Monde, de l'Antéchrist au Jugement dernier*, 'History & Tradition' series, Ed. Dervy, Paris, 1951.
Bareste, Eugène: Editions des Centuries, Maillet, Paris, 1840–42. (BMA)
Bartoshek, Norbert: *Nostradamus und seine berühmte Prophezeiungen*, 1946.
Belland, Dr: *Napoléon, premier empereur des français, prédit par Nostradamus*, Paris, 1806.

Beltikhine, G.: 'Un document chiffré: Le Secret des Centuries', *Inconnues*, no. 12, Lausanne, 1956.

Bertrand, Michel: 'Histoire secréte de la Provence', *Histoire secrète des provinces françaises*, Albin Michel, Paris, 1978.

Bjorndahl-Veggerby, Paul: *Nostradamus et les ruines gallo-romaines à Martres-Tolosane*, Ed. Leisner, Copenhagen, 1976.

Blanchard and Reynaud-Plense: *La Vie et l'Oeuvre de Michel Nostradamus*, Imp. Léon Guillaumichon, Salon, 1933. (BMA)
Histoire de Salon, Salon, 1935.

Boniface, A: *Buonaparte prédit par des prophètes et peint par des historiens, des orateurs et des poètes ou morceaux en prose et en vers sur les circonstances actuelles, receuillis par A. Boniface*, d'Hautel, Paris, 1814.

Bonnelier, Hippolyte: *Nostradamus, roman historico-cabalistique*, A. Ledoux, Paris, 1833, 2 vol.

Bonnet, Jean: *Résumé des Prophéties de Nostradamus. Les événements et les symboles*, followed by: *Commentaires de la Bible par Nostradamus et de détermination des dates dans Nostradamus*, Jean Bonnet, Paris, 1973.

Bonnot, Jean de: *Les Oracles de Michel de Nostredame dit Nostradamus*, annotated by Anatole le Pelletier and Serge Hutin, 1976, 2 vol.

Boroch, Erich Karl: *Der Prophet Nostradamus*, 1912.

Boswell, Rolfe: *Nostradamus speaks*, 1941.

Bouche, Honoré: *La Chorographie et l'Histoire de Provence*, Charles David, Aix-en-Provence, 1664.

Bouchet, Marguerite: *Les Oracles de Michel de Nostredame*, Les Livres Nouveaux, Paris, 1939.

Boulenger, Jacques: *Nostradamus*, Excelsior, Paris, 1933.

Bousquet, Raoul: *Nostradamus, sa famille et son secret*, Fournier-Valdes, Paris, 1950.
'La Maladie et la Mort de Nostradamus', *Aesculape*, November 1950.

Boutin, André: *Michel de Nostre-Dame, astrologue et médecin*, MD thesis, Librairie Le François, Paris, 1941.

Bouys, Théodore: *Nouvelles considérations sur les Oracles et particulièrement sur Nostradamus*, Paris, 1806, Desenne, Debray.

Boyer, Jean: 'Deux peintres oubliés du XVIIe siècle, Etienne Martellange et César Nostradamus', *Bulletin de la Société de l'histoire de l'Art Français, 1971*, pp. 13–20.

Bricaud, Joanny: *La Guerre et les Prophéties célèbres*, Paris, 1916.

Buget, P. F.: 'Etude sur Nostradamus', *Bulletin du bibliophile*, Librairie Techner, Paris, 1860.

Buset, Claude: *Nostradamus et autres prophètes du Père et de l'Esprit*, La Pensée Universelle, Paris, 1974.

Cadres, Geoffroy: *L'Etrange docteur Nostradamus*, La Pensée Universelle, Paris, 1978.

Candolle, Comte de: *Armorial de César de Nostredame*, Arles, 1899. (BMA)

Cavanagh, John: *Michel de Nostradamus*, 1923.

Cave, Térence C.: 'Peinture et émotion dans la poésie religieuse de César de Nostredame', *Gazette des Beaux-Arts*, vol. LXXV, Jan. 1970. (BMA)

Centurio, N.: *Nostradamus, der Prophet der Weltgeschichte*, Richar Schikowski, Berlin, 1955.

Chabauty, Abbé E. A.: *Lettres sur les Prophéties modernes et concordance de toutes les prédictions jusqu'au règne de Henry V*, Ed. Henri Houdin, Poitiers, 1872.

Chavigny, A. de: *Les Pléiades du Sieur de Chavigny, Beaunois, divisées en VII livres, prises et tirées des anciennes prophéties et conférées avec les oracles du tant célèbre et renommé Michel de Nostradame, jadis conseiller et médecin de trois Rois très chrestiens. Où est traté du renouvellement des siècles, changement de l'Empire et advancement du nom Chrestien*, Lyon, Pierre Rigaud, 1604.

Chavigny, J. A. de: *Commentaires du Sieur de Chavigny sur les Centuries et Prognostications de feu Michel de Nostredame du Breui*, Paris, 1596.
La première Face du Janus français extraite et colligée des Centuries de Michel Nostradamus, par les héritiers de Pierre Roussin, Lyon, 1594. (BMA)
Vie et testament de Michel Nostradamus, Paris, 1789.
'Bref discours sur la Vie de Michel de Nostredame', *Revue de l'Agenois*, 1876.

Cheetham, Erika: *The Prophecies of Nostradamus*, Capricorn Books, Putnam's, New York, 1973.

Chollier, Antoine: *Les Prophéties de maistre Michel Nostradamus*, Imp. Allier, Grenoble, 1940.

Chomorat, Michel: *Nostradamus entre Rhône et Saône*, Ed. Ger, Lyon, 1971.
Supplément à la bibliographie Lyonnaise des Nostradamus. Central culturel de Buenc, Lyon, 1976. 100 numbered copies.
'New research on the prophecies of M. N.', *Revue française d'histoire du livre*, no. 22, spring 1979.
Bibliographie lyonnaise de Nostradamus, followed by a checklist of MSS relating to the Nostradamus family, Centre Culturel de Buenc, Lyon, 1973.

Colin de Larmor: *La Guerre de 1914–1918 vue en 1555 par Nostradamus*, La Roche-sur-Yon, 1922.
Merveilleux Quatrains de Nostradamus, Nantes, 1925. (BMA)

Colin-Simard: 'Rois et Reines au rendez-vous des astrologues', *Historia*, no. 157, 1959.

Corvaja, Mireille: *Les Prophéties de Nostradamus*, Vecchi, Paris, 1975.

Couillard, Antoine: *Les Contredits aux prophéties de Nostradamus*, Charles l'Angelier, Paris, 1560.

Crescimbeni, Giovanni-Mario: *Istoria della volgar poesia-TII: Le vite de'piu celebri poeti provenzali, scritte in lingua francese da G. M. Crescimbeni*. B. U. Montpellier (see Jean de Nostredame).

Cristiani Chanoine: *Nostradamus, Malachie et Cie*, Le Centurion, 1955.
'Un Curieux Homme: Nostradamus', *Ecclesia*, no. 73, 1955.

Crouzet, François: 'Nostradamus, Poète français', *Idée Fixe*, Julliard, Paris, 1973.

Da Cruz Marques: *Profecias de Nostradamus*, Ed. Cultrix, Sao Paolo.

Daudet, L.: 'Nostradamus', *Revue universelle*, 1925, vol. I. (BMA)

David-Marescot, Yves and Yvonne: *Prédictions et Prophéties*, Ed, Idégraf et Vernoy, Geneva, 1979.

D. D.: *The Prophecies of Nostradamus concerning the kings and queens of Great Britain*, London, 1715.

Delcourt, Marie: *L'Oracle de Delphes*, 1954.

Demar-Latour: *Nostradamus et les Evénements de 1914–1916*, Paris, 1916. (BN)

Deperlas, Félix: *L'Avenir ou les Grands Personnages et les Grands Evénements de ce temps*, Paris, 1885.

Révélations de la Providence, Paris, 1885.

Dupont-Fournieux, Y.: *Les Derniers Jours des Derniers Temps* (Preface by Dr Fontbrune), La Colombe, Paris 1959.

Edouard, P.: *Texte original et complet des Prophéties de Michel Nostradamus*, Les Belles Editions, Paris, 1939.

Edouard and Mezerette: *Texte original des Prophéties de Nostradamus de 1600 à 1948 et de 1948 à l'an 2000*, Les Belles Editions, Paris, 1947.

Erlanger, Ph.: 'La Reine du Massacre', *Historia*, no. 340, March 1975.

Fervan, Jean: *La Fin des temps*, Ed. La Bourdonnais, Paris, 1937.

Fontbrune, Dr Max de: *Les Prophéties de Nostradamus dévoilées. Lettres à Henry Second*, Adyar, 1937.

Les prophéties de Maistre Michel Nostradamus expliquées et commentées, Ed. Michelet, Sarlat, 1938, 1939, 1940, 1946, 1958 & 1975, J. -Ch. de Fontbrune, Aix-en-Provence, distributed by le Groupe des Presses de la Cité.

Fontbrune, Dr Max de: *Ce que Nostradamus a vraiment dit*, Preface by Henry Miller, Ed. Stock, 1976.

Fontbrune, Dr Max de: *La Prédiction mystérieuse de Prémol*, Michelet, Sarlat, 1939, o.p.

La divine Tragédie de Louis XVII, Michelet, Sarlat, 1949, available from J.-Ch. de Fontbrune, 3, cours Gambetta, Aix-en-Provence.

Fontbrune, Dr Max de: *L'Etrange XXe siècle vu par Nostradamus*, Michelet, Sarlat, 1950, o.p.

'Pourquoi je crois en Nostradamus', *Ecclesia*, no. 82, 1956.

'Le docteur Nostradamus vous parle', *Les Cahiers de Marottes et Violons d'Ingres*, no. 10, Paris, 1953.

'Nostradamus', *Synthèses*, no. 3, August 1955.

Foretich, Rodolphe: *La Prophétie des Papes, analysée à la lumière des prédictions de Nostradamus*, Salvador, 1961. (BN)

Forman, Henry-James: *Les Prophéties à travers les siècles*, Payot, 1938.

Frontenac, Roger: *Le Clé secrète de Nostradamus*, Denoël, Paris, 1950.

Fulke: *Contra inutiles Astrologorum praedictiones, Nostradamus*, Cunningham, 1560. (British Museum)

Garçon, Maurice: 'Il y a 450 ans Nostradamus naissait', *Historia*, no. 85, 1953.

Garencieres, Theophilus: *The True Prophecies of Prognostications of Michael Nostradamus*, London, 1672.

Gauquelin, Michel: 'Les Astres ont-ils changé le cours de l'histoire?', *Historia*, no. 203, 1963.

Gay-Rosset, Claude: 'Michel de Nostredame, une rencontre du quatrième type,' *Midi-Mutualité*, no. 12, Marseille, Jan.-Feb. 1979.

Gimon, Louis: *Chroniques de la ville de Salon depuis son origine jusqu'en 1792*, Aix-en-Provence, 1882.

Girard, Samuel: *Histoire généalogique de la Maison de Savoie*, 1660.

Gravelaine, Joëlle de: *Prédictions at Prophéties*, Hachette, Paris, 1965.

Guérin, Pierre: *Le Véritable secret de Nostradamus*, Payot, Paris, 1971.

Guichardan, S.: *La Chasse aux prophéties*, Bonne Presse, Limoges, 1941.

Guichenou, Joseph: *Catalogue de tableaux au musée Calvet*, Avignon, 1909.

Guynaud, Balthazard: *Concordance des prophéties depuis Henri II jusqu'à Louis le Grand*, Jacques Morel, Paris, 1693.

Hades: *Que sera demain?*, La Table Ronde, Paris, 1966.

Haitze, Pierre Joseph de: *La Vie de Nostradamus*, David, Aix-en-Provence, 1712.
Vie et Testament de Nostradamus, 1789.
La Vie de Nostradamus, Aix-en-Provence, 1911.

Harold, R. A.: *Les Prophétes et les Prophéties de l'Apocalypse à nos jours*, Ed. La Caravelle, Brussels; l'Avenir, Paris, 1948.

Hildebrand, Jakob: *Nostradamus Sueddeutsche Monatshefte*, 1932.

Holtzauer, Jean-Louis: *Nostradamus, un praticien sous la Renaissance*, Laboratoires S.O.B.I.O., Ed. Labo, 92-Levallois, 1975.

Hutin, Serge: *Les Prophéties de Nostradamus avec présages et sixains*, Pierre Bellefond, Paris, 1962, 1972, 1978, Poche-Club, Paris, 1966; Hachette, Paris, 1975.
Les Prophéties de Nostradamus, Club Géant Historique, Les éditions de la Renaissance, Paris, 1966.

Iacchia, U.: *La Tunisie vue par Nostradamus*, Imp. d'Art, Tunis.

IAF: *Le Substrat mathématique de l'Oeuvre de Nostradamus*, Ed. de Psyché, Paris, 1949.

I.M.: *Le vrayes centuries de Me Michel Nostradamus expliquées sur les affaires de ce temps*, I. Boucher, 1652.

Ionescu, Vlaicu: *Le Message de Nostradamus sur l'Ere Prolétaire*, publ. at author's expense, distributed by Dervy Books, Paris, 1976.
'Nostradamus et la gnose', *Atlantis*, no. 301, Jan.–Feb. 1979, 30 rue de la Marseillaise, 94300 Vincennes.

Jacquemin, Suzanne: *Les Prophéties des Derniers Temps*, La Colombe, Paris, 1958.

Jant, Chevalier de: *Prédictions tirées des Centuries de Nostradamus qui vraisemblablement peuvent s'expliquer à la guerre entre la France et l'Angleterre contre les provinces unies*, 1673.
Prophéties de Nostradamus sur la longueur des jours et la félicité du règne de Louis XIV, 1673.

Jaubert, Etienne: *Eclaircissement des véritables quatrains de Nostradamus et Vie de M. Nostradamus*, Amsterdam, 1656.

Kerdeland, Jean de: *De Nostradamus à Cagliostro*, Ed. Self, Paris, 1945.

Klinckowstroem, G. C. Von: *Die ältesten Ausgaben des Prophéties des Nostradamus*, March 1913.

Kniepf, Albert: *Die Weissagungen des altfranzösischen Sehers Michel Nostradamus und der Weltkreig*, Hamburg, 1915.

Krafft, Karl E.: *Nostradamus prezice vütorul Européi*, Bucharest, 1941.

Labadie, Jean: *Peut-on dire l'avenir?*, Aubanel, Avignon, 1941.

Lamont, André: *Nostradamus sees all*, 1942.

Lamotte, Pierre: *De Gaulle révélé par Nostradamus il y a quatre siècles*, Le Scorpion, Paris, 1961. (BN)

Langlois, Charles: *Les Contradictions de Nostradamus*, 1560.

Laurent: *Prédictions jusqu'à l'an 2000. Prophéties du Christ, de Nostradamus, des Papes St Malachie*, Laurent, 91 Brunoy.

Laver, James: *Nostradamus*, Penguin Books, 1942.
Nostradamus, the future foretold, George Mann, Maidstone, 1973.

Legrand, Jean René: 'Pronostics pour l'an 1959', *Initiation et science*, no. 47, Jan.–March 1959, Omnium littéraire, Paris.

Leoni, Edgar: *Nostradamus, life and literature*, 1961.

Le Pelletier, Anatole: *Les Oracles de Nostradamus, astrologue, médecin et conseiller ordinaire des rois Henry II, François II et Charles IX*, Le Pelletier, 40, rue d'Aboukir, Paris, 1867, 2 vol.

Le Roux, Jean: *La Clé de Nostradamus, Isagoge ou Introduction au véritable sens des Prophéties de ce fameux auteur*, Pierre Giffard, rue Saint-Jacques-près-les-Maturins, Paris, 1710. (Musée d'Arbaud, Aix-en-Provence)

Leroy, Dr Edgar: 'Les origines de Nostradamus', *Mémoires de l'Institut historique de Provence*, vol. 18, Marseille, 1941.
Sur un quatrain de Nostradamus.
'Jaume de Nostredame et la Tour de Canillac', *Mémoires de l'Institut historique de Provence*, vol. 19, Marseille, 1942.
'Pierre de Nostredame de Carpentras', communication à l'Institut historique de Provence, 1948.
'Nostradamus et le curé d'Argoeuvres', *Cahier de Pratique Médiocochirurgicale*, Avignon, 1939, no. 5.
Saint-Paul de Mausole à Saint-Rémy de Provence, Imp. générale du Sud-Ouest, Bergerac, 1948.
Nostradamus, ses origines, sa vie, son oeuvre, Imp. Trillaud, Bergerac, 1972.
Romanin, les cours d'amour de Jehan de Nostredame, Avignon, 1933. (BMA)
Saint-Rémy de Reims, Marseille, 1937. (BMA)
Nostradamus, détective avant la lettre, Avignon, 1949. (BN)
Le Latin du tabellion provençal Jaume de Nostredame, notaire à Saint-Rémy-de-Provence dans les actes de 1501 à 1513, Avignon, 1961.
'Saint-Paul-Tricastin et Saint-Paul-de-Mausole, Contribution à l'histoire d'une légende', *Bull. Philologique et Historique*, 1959.

Ligeoix-de-la-Combe: *La Troisième Guerre Mondiale d'après les prédictions de Nostradamus*, Bordeaux, 1961.

Loog, C. L.: *Die Weissagungen des Nostradamus*, 1921.

Loroit, Louis: 'Entretien de Rabelais et de Nostradamus', Nogent-Le-Rotrou, 1960 & Paris, 1907, *Revue des Etudes rabelaisiennes*, vol. 5, pp. 176–84.

Mabille, Pierre: 'Nostradamus, ses prophéties, son temps', *Inconnues*, Lausanne, 1955.

Maby, Pascale: 'Le Dossier des Prophétes, voyants et astrologues', *Les Chemins de l'Impossible*, Albin Michel, Paris, 1977.

MacCann, Lee, *Nostradamus, the man who saw through time*, 1941.

MacNeice, Louis: *L'Astrologie*, Tallandier, Paris, 1966.

Madeleine, Georges: *La Prochaine Guerre Mondiale vue par Nostradamus*, Toulon, 1952, Ed. Proventia.

Maidy, Léon-Germain de: *Sur une inscription liminaire attribuée à Nostradamus*, Nancy, 1917.

Marteau, Pierre: *Entretiens de Rabelais et de Nostradamus*, 1690.

Menestrier, François: *La Philosophie des images énigmatiques*, Lyon, 1694.

Mericourt, M. J.: *Gesta Dei per Francos*, Paris, 1937.
Nostradamus et la crise actuelle, Paris, 1937.

Mondovi, Pierre: 'Un Provençal hors du commun: Nostradamus', *Racines*, no. 4, May 1979, Aix-en-Provence.

Monnier: *Résurrection merveilleuse en 1877 de Michel de Nostredame*, various pamphlets from 1889 to 1896.

Monterey, Jean: *Nostradamus, prophète du XXe siècle*, La Nef, Paris, 1963.

Motret: *Essai d'explication de deux quatrains de Nostradamus*, Nevers, 1806.

Mouan, L: 'Aperçus littéraires sur César Nostradamus et ses lettres inédites à Peiresc', Mémoires de l'Académie, vol. 10, Aix, 1873. (BMA)

Moult, Thomas-Joseph: *Prophéties perpétuelles, très anciennes et très certaines*, seventeenth-century almanac.
Prophéties perpétuelles, Ed. des Cahiers astrologiques, Nice, 1941.

Moura, Jean, and Louvet, Paul: *La vie de Nostradamus*, Gallimard, Paris, 1930.

Muraise, Eric: *Du Roy perdu à Louis XVII*, Julliard, Paris.
Saint-Rémy de Provence et les secrets de Nostradamus, Julliard, Paris, 1969.
Histoire et Légende du grand Monarque, 'Les Chemins de l'Impossible', Albin Michel, Paris, 1975.

Necroman, Don: *Comment lire les Prophéties de Nostradamus*, Ed. Maurice d'Hartoy, Paris, 1933.

Neyral, Georges: *La Vraie Vie de Michel de Nostredame*, Thesis, Toulouse, 1951.

Nicoullaud, Charles: *Nostradamus, ses prophéties*, Perrin et Cie, Paris, 1914.

Nostradamus, César: *Poésies*, Colomiez, Toulouse, 1606–8.
L'Entrée de la reine Marie de Médicis en sa ville de Salon, Jean Tholoson, Aix-en-Provence, 1602.
Histoire et Chroniques de Provence, Simon Rigaud, Lyon, 1614.

Nostradamus, Michel: *Les Prophéties de M. Michel Nostradamus:* Principal Editions:
   Macé Bonhomme, Lyon, 1555;
   Antoine du Rosne, Lyon, 1557–58;
   Barbe Régnault, Paris, 1560;
   Pierre Rigaud, Lyon, 1566;
   Benoist Rigaud, Lyon, 1568; in *8. B.U. Montepellier*, no. 48340.
   Charles Roger, Paris, 1569;
   Pierre Meunier, Paris, 1589;
   Jean Poyet, Lyon, 1600 (BN);
   Benoist Rigaud, Lyon, 1605;
   Pierre Rigaud, Lyon, 1605 (BN);
   Pierre Rigaud, Lyon, 1610 (BN), 1649;
   Claude La Rivière, Lyon, 1611;
   Vincent Sève, Beaucaire, 1610;
   Pierre Chevillot, Troyes, 1611;
   Simon Rigaud, Lyon, 1644;

Pierre de Ruau, Troyes, 1649 (BN);

Winckermans, Amsterdam, 1657;

Jean Balam, Lyons, 1665;

Jean Ribon, vis-à-vis la Sainte Chapelle à l'image Saint Louis, Paris, 1669;

Jean Huguetan, Lyon (17th century);

Jean Ianson, Amsterdam, 1668;

Jean Besongne, Rouen, 1681;

Besson, Lyon, 1691;

Jean Viret, Lyon, 1697 (BML);

Lambert-Gentot, *Nouvelles et Curieuses prédictions de M. Nostradamus, pour sept ans depuis l'année 1818 jusqu'à l'année 1824*, Lyon, 1818.

Landriot, Riom, no date (19th century);

Facsimiles of the 1611 Chevillot edition by Delarue, Paris, and of the 1668 Amsterdam edition by Ed. Adyar, Paris 1936.

Prognostication nouvelle et prédiction portenteuse pour l'an 1555 composées par Maistre M. Nostradamus, Jean Brotot, Lyon.

Démonstration d'une comette, Jean Marcorelle, Lyon, 1571 (BN)

Prognostication et prédiction des quatre temps pour 1572, Melchior Arnoullet, Lyon, 1572. (BN)

Prophéties par l'Astrologue du Très Chrétien Roy de France et de Madame la Duchesse de Savoye, F. Arnoullet, Lyon, 1572. (BN)

Nostradamus, Michel: *Lettre de Maistre Michel Nostradamus de Salon-de-Craux-en-Provence à la Royne, mère du Roy*, Benoist Rigaud, Lyon, 1566.

Almanach pour l'an 1573 avec les présages, Pierre Roux, Avignon, 1562.

Prophétie ou Révolution merveilleuse des 4 saisons de l'an, Michel Jove, Lyon, 1567.

Traité de fardements et confitures, Antoine Volant, Lyon, 1555.

Paraphrase de C. Galen, trans. by Nostradamus, Antoine du Rosne, *Excellent et très utile opuscule de plusieurs exquises receptes*, Benoist Rigaud, Lyon, 1572. Lyon, 1557.

Almanach pour l'an 1567, Benoist Odo, Lyon.

La Grant Pronostication nouvelle avec la déclaration ample de 1559, Jean Brotot, Lyon, 1558.

Prophéties sur Lyon, La France et le monde entier dans les premieres années du XXe siècle, 5 booklets, Lyon, P. Bousset & M. Paquet, 1907, 1909.

Almanach des prophéties, P. N. Jausserand, Lyon, 1871–72.

Les Merveilleuses Centuries et Prophéties de Nostradamus, colour illustrations by Jean Gradassi, Ed. André Virel, Ed. Artisanales SEFER, 880 copies, Nice, 1961.

Les Prophéties de Nostradamus (complete), Club des Champs Elysées, Ed. Baudelaire, Paris, 1967.

Prophéties nouvelles de Michel Nostradamus trouvées dans sa tombe au moment de l'ouverture dans l'église des Cordeliers de salon pour 1820, 1821, 1822, 1823, 1824, 1825 et 1826, A Toulon de l'Imprimerie de Calmen, imprimeur du Roi, 11, rue d'Angoulême.

Les Prophéties de Nostradamus (complete), Les Cent un chefs d'oeuvre du Génie Humain, Prodifu, 5, rue du Coq Héron, 75001 Paris.

Les Prophéties de Nostradamus, pub. by the author, Marc Billerey, Mallefougasse (Alpes de Provence), 1973.

Undated edns (16th and 17th centuries): Antoine Baudraud et Pierre André, Lyon.

Nostredame, Jean de: *Les Vies des plus célèbres et anciens poètes provençaux qui ont fleuri du temps des comtes de Provence*, Basile Bouquet, Lyon, 1575.

Novaye, Baron de: *Aujourd'hui et demain*, Paris, 1905.

Pagliani, Coraddo: 'Di Nostradamus e idi sue una poco nota iscrizione Liminare torinen', in *Della Rassegna mensile Muncipale*, no. 1, Turin, 1934.

Parisot, F.: *Le Grand Avènement précédé d'un grand prodige*, typographie des Célestins, Bar-le-Duc, 1873.

Parker, Eugène: *La Légende de Nostradamus et sa vie réelle*, Paris, 1923.

Patrian, Carlo: *Nostradamus, le Profezie*, Edizioni Méditerranée, Via Flaminia, Rome, 1978.

Pelaprat, Jean Marie: 'Varennes et 1792, sauvent Nostradamus', *Historia*, no. 397(2), *Voyance et Prophéties*, Ed. Tallendier, Paris.

Pichon, Jean-Charles: *Nostradamus et le Secret des temps*, Les Productions de Paris, 1959.
Nostradamus en clair, R. Laffont, Paris, 1970.
Le Royaume et les Prophètes, R. Laffont, 1963.

Piobb, P. V.: Facsimile of Amsterdam edn, Adyar, Paris, 1936.
Le Sort de l'Europe d'après la célèbre Prophétie des papes de Saint-Malachie, accompagnée de la Prophétie d'Orval et de toutes dernières indications de Nostradamus, Dangles, Paris, 1939.

Privat, Maurice: *1938, année de relèvement*.
1938, année d'échéance.
1939, année de reprise, Editions Médicis, Paris, 1938.
Demain, la guerre.
1940, prédictions mondiales, année de grandeur française, Editions Médicis, Paris.

Putzien, Rudolf: *Friede unter Völkern? Die Weissagungen des M. Nostradamus und ihre Bedeutung für Atomzeitaler*, Drei Eichen Verlag, H. Kissener, Munich, 1958.

Reed, Clarence: *Great Prophecies about the war*, Faber & Faber, London, 1941.

Reynaud, Jean-Lucien: *Nostradamus n'a pas menti*, lecture, Ville d'Avray, 1948.
Nostradamus délié, Ville d'Avray, 1949.

Reynaud-Plense: *Les Vraies Prophéties de Nostradamus*, Salon, 1939.

Robb, Steward: *Nostradamus on Napoleon*, Oracle Press, New York, 1961.
Nostradamus on Napoleon, Hitler and the present crisis, Scribner's, New York, 1941.
Prophecies on world events by Nostradamus, New York, 1961.

Robert, Henry: *The Complete Prophecies of Nostradamus*, Ed. H. Robert, Great Neck, New York, 1971. Japanese trans. by Kasuko Daijyo with Hidéo Uchida, Ed. Tama, Tokyo, 1975.

Rochetaille, P.: *Prophéties de Nostradamus. The key to the 'Centuries', with special reference to the history of the Third Republic*, Adyar, 1939.

Roisin, Michel de: 'Ulrich de Mayence, maître de Nostradamus', *Aesculape*, no. 5, 1969, 52nd year.

'Plus forte que Nostradamus: Ulrich de Mayence', *Constellation*, no. 199, November 1964.

Rollet, Pierre: *Interprétation des Hiéroglyphes de Horapollo*, Ramoun Bérenguié, Aix-en-Provence, 1968.

Roudene, Alex: *Les Prophéties, vérité ou mensonge*, Mondes Magiques series, Ed. de l'Athanor, Paris, 1976.

Rouellond de la Rouellondière de Chollet: *La Prophétie de Rouellond, Manuscrit du XVIe siècle*, Victor Pipeau, Beauvais, 1861.

Rouvier, Camille: *Nostradamus*, Marseille, La Savoisienne, 1861.

Ruir, Emile: *Le Grand Carnage d'après les prophéties de Nostradamus de 1938 à 1947*, Ed. Médicis, Paris, 1938.

L'Ecroulement de l'Europe, d'après les prophéties de Nostradamus, Paris. 1939.

Ruir, Emile: *Nostradamus, ses Prophéties, 1948–2023*, Paris, 1948.

Nostradamus. Les Proches et Derniers Evénements, Ed. Médicis, Paris, 1953.

Ruzo, Daniel: *Les Derniers Jours de l'Apocalypse*, Payot, 1973.

Los ultimos dias del apocalipsis, Michel Shultz, Mexico.

Sede, Gérard de: *Les Secrets de Nostradamus*, Julliard, Paris, 1969.

Spica-Capella: *La Clef des prédictions nostradamiques*, Ed. des soirées astrologiques, 1941.

Tamizey de Larroque: *Les Correspondants de Pieresc, César Nostradamus*, unpublished letters from Salon to Peiresc, 1628–29, Typographie Marius Olive, Marseille, 1880.

Tarade, Guy: 'La Clef des centuries de Nostradamus', *Pégase*, no. 3, 1974.

Les Dernières Prophéties pour l'Occident, 'Les Enigmes de l'Univers' series, Robert Laffont, Paris, 1979.

Torne-Chavigny, H.: Reissue of the *Prophecies of Nostradamus*, 1862 edition, enlarged in 1872.

Prospectus: interprétation de 30 quatrains, 1860.

L'Histoire prédite et jugée par Nostradamus, 3 vol., Bordeaux, 1860.

Affiches: tableau de l'histoire prédite et jugée, 1862.

Prospectus des lettres du grande prophète: interprétation de 20 quatrains.

Les lettres du grand prophète.

Henri V à Anvers.

Nostradamus et l'astrologie.

Les Blancs et les rouges.

La Salette et Lourdes.

La mort de Napoléon III.

MacMahon et Napoléon IV.

Le roy blanc et la fusion.

Portraits prophétiques d'après Nostradamus.

Prophéties dites d'Olivarius et d'Orval.

L'Apocalypse interprétée par Nostradamus, 1872.

Almanach du grand prophète Nostradamus pour 1873.

Nostradamus éclairci ou Nostradamus devant monseigneur Dupanloup, Saint-Denis-du-Pin, 1874.

Ce qui sera d'après le grand prophète Nostradamus, followed by *Almanach pour 1878*.

Influence de Nostradamus dans le gouvernement de la France, 1878.

Concordance de Nostradamus avec l'Apocalypse, Veuve Dupuy, Bordeaux, 1861.

Touchard, Michel: *Nostradamus*, Grasset, 1972
'Histoire des personnages mystérieux et des sociétiés secrètes' series, Ed. Celt, Paris, 1972.

Touchard, Michel: 'Les Prophéties de Michel Nostradamus. Le rêve fou', *Historia*, no. 34, 1974.

Tronc de Condoulet: *Abrégé de la vie de Nostradamus* followed by *Nouvelle découverte de ses quatrains*, J. Adibert, Aix-en-Provence. (BMA)

Van Gerdinge, René: 'Le Nez de Cléopâtre', *Messidor*, no. 29, Montfavet, Vaucluse.

Verdier, du: *Les Vertus de notre maistre Nostradamus*, Geneva, 1562.

Viaud, Jean: '1999, Un tournant dans l'histoire des hommes', *Constellation*, no. 166, Feb. 1962.

Vidél, Laurent: *Déclaration des abus, ignorances et séditions de Michel Nostradamus*, Avignon, 1558.

Vignois, Elisée du: *Notre Histoire racontée à l'avance par Nostradamus*, Paris, 1910.

L'Apocalypse, interprète de la Révolution, d'après Nostradamus, Noyon, 1911.

Vogel, Cyrille: *Saint Césaire d'Arles*, 1937.

Voldben, A.: *After Nostradamus*, Neville Spearman, London, 1973.

Ward, Charles A.: *Oracles of Nostradamus*, London, 1891.

Willoquet, Gaston: *La Vérité sur Nostradamus*, Ed. Traditionelles, Paris, 1967.

Winckermans: *Editions des Centuries*, Amsterdam, 1657.

Woolf, H. I.: *Nostradamus*, London, 1944.

Yram: *Prophéties connues et prédictions inédites*, Preface by Papus, l'Edition d'Art, Paris.

Zevaco, Michel: *Nostradamus* (novel), Fayard, 1909, Livre de Poche, no. 3306.

Table of Quatrains, Sextains and Prophecies

In the following pages the reader will find cross-references to all the quatrains, sextains and prophecies which appear in Volumes 1 and 2. Page numbers which refer to the latter are in italics.

The centuries run chronologically – in roman figures – along the top row, the years in the first column, and the page references to the quatrains, sextains and prophecies appear at the appropriate point in the grid itself.

	I	II	III	IV	V	VI	VII	VIII	IX	X	XI	XII	S	P
1	1	311	*347/55*			405							*116*	
2	2	52	*131*	112				272	243					43
3	286	337	*142*		160				169	279			362	
4	429		*153*		213	*363/29*	142	409					400	356
5	320		266	*148*	207	*122*		414	99	368				
6	157	358	*104*		407	283	319	355	378				30	
7	366	421				390		359		162			*125*	
8	*97*		200	16	362								331	370
9	*287/38*		241	354		109	*86*	*145*	381				56	
10	*126*		127	406	154	427	392	359	404	421				407
11	*114*	131		71	*150*	18		85	62	406				305
12	95	*139*	291	185	335	*102*	403	156		277				308
13	*107*		130	389		171	94 (xxvii)			104				
14	190			400	289			267					227	
15	170	284	44		280		*100*	327					413	385
16				168	337			269/40	199					
17	*119*		431		367			345	222	63				119
18	332	373	183	28				408	35	22				
19	*124*	249				202	165	76						
20		*103*	*83*		84				60					
21				394		341		319	73	259			226	*151*
22		*135*		123		297	281	381		*89*				
23	128		330	399	305	267	58	58		238				
24	*96*	129			*144*		396		66	125		379		
25		173	105			429	91	186					228	
26		353	269			191	86	103	37	31				330
27		*132*	*287/39*	273	369	*137*		221		397			306	

	P
101	295
102	
103	
104	
105	
106	
107	
108	
109	
110	
111	
112	
113	
114	
115	
116	
117	
118	
119	
120	
121	
122	
123	
124	*151*
125	304
126	
127	*139*

	I	II	III	IV	V	VI	VII	VIII	IX	X	XI	XII	S	P
28	325	418	153	46		389		266	335					
29	237	419			89		3		29	274			416	316
30		325	17		349	217			314				410	*138*
31	*147*		376			244	166		*112*	328/41			256	342
32	393	312		239		137				377				371
33			233	307	72			87	397	324				
34	209	289/52	77	402		363		276	55				426	348
35	5 (xxix)	275	204	132			268		136				257	
36		107		118		340					11			
37			172	350			431	311	383	387				
38		248		336		93	151	392		351				398
39	146	*95*	82	372	159		*99*						417	*136*
40	193	264/54		298						75			390	428
41	349	280					*153*	422	401				102	271
42			420	354	158	285		147	387					
43		281	117	113	364/31					48			34	
44	430	174	*108*	284	369	371		*147*	357	338			*130*	413
45			379	333	175					25			*134*	
46	273	265	361		299/49			272	380	96		265	303	
47	194	282	242		338									
48	367/33			318				*140*		198				
49	*149*	192	218	62	*92*	340		372	40	352				
50	*143*		164	373	376				425				308	293
51	427		19		384	64		326	383	179				
52		*143*				177		393	262	187		7	15	293
53		45	215			350		161	223				220	
54	148		*144*	101	425			411	235				230	292

	P
128	
129	*146*
130	
131	
132	
133	
134	
135	
136	
137	
138	
139	
140	
141	9

	I	II	III	IV	V	VI	VII	VIII	IX	X	XI	XII	S	P
55			20		427	*111*		*106*	184	433			67	
56	424				211	322						265	*416/50*	
57	61	50	195		275	76		108					97	295
58	134	65	203	343		411			57	370			*146*	
59		348	252	236				262				*270/56*		
60	80	*291/57*	288	21	100	33		395	313	290				315
61	90		288	240	386			391	10					
62	47	283	323	6	312	27		282		141				188
63	*123*		115	79	231	53			322					
64		358	13	149		263			323	245				
65	*94*	307		182				219		270		346		
66			70							422				
67		135	205			225		*93*						
68		309	144	290	402				278					300
69	432	145								329		356		
70	258		309	121	*385/43*	401		260						
71	*141*		310		360			28	384					
72	343	342		*135*				341	382	428				
73	331			154	*306/53*		110	365	405	*150*				
74	98	*140*		321	408	366			*154/34*					
75	115		111	129		14			140	425				297
76	81	126	206		395				224					396
77	114	181		412				423						
78	229	310	332			412			*88*					
79	380	409	378		116	353				415				
80	347			216	375	423		78						
81		374			415	355		246						

	I	II	III	IV	V	VI	VII	VIII	IX	X	XI	XII	S	P
82	334		318	333	180									
83							315		*136*					*152*
84		313	364		419	208								
85			324		317	336		122	274					
86	68	292		403				346	24	326				
87			38			178				410				
88	133	303	344	8				20		344				294
89	*118*		138	42	*84*				151	39				189
90	345	250	327/42	352	142	210			*87*					
91	264/60	328												
92	269		321		211	365				357				
93	*138*	432	394/31		*152*			298	398					
94	285	317		320	334			299/48	214					
95	415	286	368	377	*109*	176			234	375				
96		351		386	278/45	361		254						
97		277/46	253			302		*101*		316				
98	133	69	18		302	49	279							296
99	404	106	360	*90*	231			417	271	430				294
100				420					388	196				